male fantasies

Theory and History of Literature
Edited by Wlad Godzich and Jochen Schulte-Sasse

male fantasies

volume 1:
women
floods
bodies
history

klaus theweleit

translated by stephen conway
in collaboration with
erica carter and chris turner

foreword by barbara ehrenreich

university of minnesota press
minneapolis

Originally published as *Männerphantasien*, Volume 1. *Frauen, Fluten, Körper, Geschichte* by Klaus Theweleit, copyright © 1977 by Verlag Roter Stern.

Published by the University of Minnesota Press,
2037 University Avenue Southeast, Minneapolis MN 55414

Printed in the United States of America

Library of Congress Cataloging-in-Publication Data

Theweleit, Klaus.
    Male fantasies.

    (Theory and history of literature; v. 22)
    Translation of : Männerphantasien.
    Bibliography: p.
    Includes index.
    Contents: v. 1. Women, floods, bodies, history.
    1. Germany. Heer. Freikorps. 2. Soldiers—Germany—Sexual behavior.
3. Fascism and sex. 4. Fascism and women. 5. Psychoanalysis and
culture—Germany. 6. Fantasy. I. Title. II. Series.
UA717.T47 1985   355.3'5   86-25052
ISBN 0-8166-1448-2 (v. 1)
ISBN 0-8166-1449-0 (pbk.: v. 1)

Text designed by Gale Houdek.
Cover designed by Craig Carnahan.
Cover illustration: "Santo Domingo" by Mary Griep, courtesy of the
    MC Gallery, Minneapolis, Minnesota

Contents

Foreword
Barbara Ehrenreich

The fantasies with which this book is concerned belong to a particular group of men: members of the Freikorps, the volunteer armies that fought, and to a large extent, triumphed over, the revolutionary German working class in the years immediately after World War I. The Freikorps were organized by officers returning from the war, in which many of their leaders had commanded "shock troops," trained to penetrate the lines of trench warfare with sudden, daring assaults. Most of the men who organized the Freikorps and were recruited to them belonged to a class that has no precise analogue in American history: a kind of rural "petty bourgeoisie" with semifeudal traditions. Hired by the socialist Chancellor Ebert to bring order to revolutionary Germany in 1918 (he did not trust the regular army, with its working class rank and file), the Freikorps became roaming, largely autonomous armies each commanded by its own charismatic leader. Between 1918 and 1923, they fought Polish communists and nationalists, the Russian Red Army and Latvian and Estonian nationalists in the Baltic region, and the German working class throughout Germany.

The Freikorpsmen fought, first of all, because they were paid to, and, by the standards of postwar Germany, were paid generously. They fought also for revenge, believing that the German army had been betrayed in World War I—"stabbed in the back," as it was so often said—by the communists, with their internationalist ideology, as well as by the vacillating socialists and other, insufficiently resolute, civilian forces. But they fought, most of all, because that was what they did. Robert Waite, in his classical history of the Freikorps, quotes a member of the famous Ehrhardt Brigade, a man who had started his military career in World War I at the age of sixteen:

> People told us that the War was over. That made us laugh. We ourselves are the War. Its flame burns strongly in us. It envelops our whole being and fascinates us with the enticing urge to destroy. We obeyed . . . and marched onto the battlefields of the postwar world just as we had gone into battle on the Western Front: singing, reckless and filled with the joy of adventure as we marched to the attack; silent, deadly, remorseless in battle.[1]

For the American reader, the most important thing about the Friekorpsmen is that they managed to survive the relatively warless years between 1923 and 1933, becoming the core of Hitler's SA and, in several cases, going on to become key functionaries in the Third Reich. The author of the above quote, for example, became the supreme SA-leader for Western Germany; another Freikorps leader, Rudolf Höss, later commanded the death camp at Auschwitz. There is still some debate over how critical the Freikorps were to the rise of Nazism, but a recent and impressively exhaustive study by Richard Hamilton suggests we ought to focus less on the mass social-psychological appeal of fascism, and give more credit to the organizational strength and armed might of the Freikorps.[2] Certainly the Nazis themselves were proud to claim the ruthless Freikorpsmen as their comrades and progenitors.

So these are the men we are dealing with—men who were first soldiers in the regular army, then irregulars serving the cause of domestic repression, and finally Nazis. They are men for whom the period between 1914 and 1945 was continuous, almost uninterrupted war, in no small part because they made it so. I should add that there may have been as many as 400,000 of them, or according to another estimate, no more than 50,000.

Hold on to this information—it may provide you with an illusion of security in what follows. We set out to read about fascism in a hardheaded, instrumental frame of mind. After all, we know the last chapter, which is the Holocaust, which is "unthinkable," so we command ourselves to think as hard as possible, to ask the right questions, to run through a checklist of morbid possibilities. Confronted with a group of fascist, or in this case, soon-to-be fascist personnel, like the Freikorpsmen, we want to know, above all: what *kind* of men they were. And we want to know for the sound, pragmatic reason that we would like to be able to detect any similar men in our contemporary political world, and do our best to expose and isolate them. That is, we approach the subject of fascist men with the mind-set of a public health official: We want to get near (to the toxin or the protofascists) in order to get as far away as possible. And that, unfortunately for the composure of the reader, is exactly what Klaus Theweleit will not let us do. He looks too close and consequently draws us in *too far*. So you will want to look up from these pages from time to time and try to reassure yourself that you are reading about a certain group of men, of a certain class and nationality, who lived at a certain time now two generations behind us.

There are other, far less disconcerting, ways to approach the study of fascism. There are liberal sociological theories of totalitarianism; there are Marxist theories of fascism as the inevitable outcome, given certain "conjunctures," of the course of capital accumulation. The problem is that these theories have very little to tell us about what we ultimately need most to understand, and that is murder. In the sociological or Marxist worldview, fascist murder appears either as an instrumentality—the terrorist spectacle required to maintain absolute authority—or as an intrusion of the "irrational," which, for most social scientists, is also the unknowable. Then there are the psychoanalytic theories of fascism, which at least have the merit of addressing the "irrational" as a subject of inquiry. The problem here is that, too often, fascism tends to become representational, symbolic. In the commonplace attenuated version of psychoanalytic theory that most of us have unthinkingly accepted, fascism is "really" about something else—for example, repressed homosexuality. Fascist murder becomes a misdirected way of getting at that "something else"—a symbolic act, if not a variety of performance art. Such an account goes almost as far as the stock Marxist theories in obliterating the human agency in fascism: We "know" what the fascist really wants (but is too deluded or psychotic to go after), just as we "know" what the masses really need (but are, once again, too confused or foolish to fight for). We know, and are therefore human; they, fumbling in darkness after what-they-do-not-know, can only be objects of our knowing, hence not fully human. Reassuringly, the "unthinkable" becomes also the "inhuman."

As a theory of fascism, *Male Fantasies* sets forth the jarring—and ultimately horrifying—proposition that the fascist is not doing "something else," but doing what he wants to do. When he throws a grenade at a working-class couple who are making love on the grass, he is not taking a symbolic stand against the institution of heterosexuality. When he penetrates a female adversary with a bullet or bayonet, he is not dreaming of rape. What he wants is what he gets, and that is what the Freikorpsmen describe over and over as a "bloody mass": heads with their faces blown off, bodies soaked red in their own blood, rivers clogged with bodies. The reader's impulse is to engage in a kind of mental flight—that is, to "read" the murders as a story about something else, for example, sex . . . or the Oedipal triangle . . . or anything to help the mind drift off. But Theweleit insists that we see and not "read" the violence. The "bloody mass" that recurs in these men's lives and fantasies is not a referent to an unattainable "something else," and the murders that comprise their professional activity are not mere gestures. What is far worse, Theweleit forces us to acknowledge, these acts of fascist terror spring from irreducible human desire. Then the question we have to ask about fascism becomes: How does human desire—or the ceaseless motion of "desiring production," as the radical psychoanalytic theorists Deleuze and Guattari call it—lend itself to the production of death?

You will see at once that this question applies to much more than twentieth-century German fascism—as if that were not enough. The Freikorpsmen were not the first men in history to make war—or death production—into a way of life. For my generation of historians (in which I claim membership only as an amateur), the history of war and warriors has taken second place to social history—the attempt to reconstruct how ordinary people have gone about their business, producing what they need and reproducing themselves. Reinforced by Marxism and later feminism, we have rejected the conventional history of "kings and battles" for the "hidden history" of everyday life, almost to the point of forgetting how much of everyday life has, century after century, been shaped by battles and dominated by kings or warrior elites. It has not been stylish to pay attention to those warrior castes who neither planted nor herded, but devoted their lives to pillage and forgotten causes: the illiterate Greek chieftains on their decade-long excursion to the plains of Asia Minor; the tribal bands of Northern Europeans who raided Rome and then its Christian outposts; the Asiatic "hordes" who swept through medieval Europe; the Crusaders who looted the Arab world; the elite officership of European imperialism; and so on. These were men—not counting their conscripts and captives—who lived only parasitically in relation to the production of useful things, who lived for perpetual war, the production of death.

Then in our own time—and I write in a time of "peace," meaning that the wars are so far "local" and endured only by peripheral, or third world, people—what do we make of the warrior caste that rules the United States and, in combination with its counterpart in the Soviet Union, rules the world? These men wear civilian clothes or well-pressed uniforms; they go home at night to wives and children. Yet are they not also men who refuse, at all costs, to disarm? Men who have opted for perpetual war—the "cold war" of nuclear terror? In fact, their relationship to production is not only parasitical: they have succeeded in enlisting the human and mechanical energy of production for the cause of death. The mounted warriors of remote history looted farms in order to continue their conquests (and further looting); our executive warriors pave over the farm and build a munitions factory. In my country, as more and more human and material resources are appropriated by the warrior caste, it becomes harder and harder to draw the line between production, as an innately purposeful human activity, and the production of death.

Perhaps because we have not spent enough time studying the warriors of the past, we do not have a psychology with which to comprehend our own warrior caste. We are watching them now in a time of little murders— Vietnam, El Salvador, Lebanon—just as Theweleit watches the Freikorps- men engaged in what are comparatively minor skirmishes. In both cases, we know the last chapter: the Holocaust, Armageddon. So do our warrior leaders. Are they "evil"—which is a way of saying that their motives lie out- side "normal" human drives and desires, that they themselves are inhuman? Or are they only absentminded, lacking the imagination or powers of con- centration to broach the "unthinkable?" Or is it just possible, Theweleit forces us to ask, that they are human beings (i.e., not totally unlike ourselves) doing, more or less consciously, exactly what they want to do?

So the question posed by the Freikorpsmen's lives—the question of how "desiring production" becomes death production—is of more than historic interest, more than a matter for specialists. You will have some premonition of the answer from the subject Theweleit takes up at the beginning: not how the Freikorpsmen thought about fighting, or about the fatherland, or how they felt about Jews or workers, but how they felt about women. Here I can- not give you a shortcut to Theweleit's conclusions (in fact, there are no "conclusions," only more and more paths to follow). But I will say that, for the feminist reader, some of these paths will begin to look familiar, and you will find yourself following them with a sense of foreboding: The Freikorps- men hate women, specifically women's bodies and sexuality. It would not be going too far to say that their perpetual war was undertaken to escape women; even the motherly battlefront nurse is a threatening intrusion in the unisexual world of war. This hatred—or dread—of women cannot be ex- plained with Freud's all-purpose Oedipal triangulation (fear that heterosex- ual desire will lead to punishment by the father, homosexual yearnings for the father, or some such permutation of the dramatic possibilities). The dread arises in the pre-Oedipal struggle of the fledgling self, before there is even an ego to sort out the objects of desire and the odds of getting them: It is a dread, ultimately, of dissolution—of being swallowed, engulfed, annihilated. Women's bodies are the holes, swamps, pits of muck that can engulf.

In the Freikorpsman's life, there are three kinds of women: those who are absent, such as the wives and fiancées left behind, and generally un- named and unnoted in the Freikorpsmen's most intimate diaries; the women who appear in the imagination and on the literal battlefront as "white nurses," chaste, upper-class German women; and, finally, those who are his class enemies—the "Red women" whom he faces in angry mobs and sometimes even in single combat. The best category is, of course, absent women. But then, women of the white-nurse variety are never entirely present; they are indistinct, nameless, disembodied. In fantasy, the good woman, the white nurse, has no body at all; there is only a smooth white plain. In fantasy, she is already dead.

The Red woman is a more obstinate case. She is vividly, aggressively sexual; in fantasy, always a whore. Her mouth is enormous, spewing out insults at our Freikorpsmen as they attempt to ride, straight-backed, through the city streets. The Red women is, in addition, armed, or is so at least in fantasy: she might have a gun under her skirt, or she might lead the Freikorpsmen through a dark passageway to an ambush. In other words, there is no distinguishing her sexuality from the mortal danger she presents. So when the Freikorpsman kills her (as he will do over and over in these pages), he kills her in what appears to him to be *self-defense*. In the brief moment of penetration—with bullet or knife—he comes close, thrillingly close, to her and the horror of dissolution. But once it is over, he will still be intact, erect (and we must imagine, quite clean and dry), and she will be—a "bloody mass." With her absent, the world becomes "safe" and male again.

Feminist readers will recognize, in Theweleit's men, the witch-hunter, for whom female sexuality and power is evil incarnate . . . or the rapist who mimics (and often accompanies) murder with sexual intercourse . . . or the garden-variety sadist, who finds relief in images of women battered and humiliated . . . or . . . But let us come back to the issue of what *kind* of man we are talking about. We are, remember, dealing with the Freikorps, the vanguard of Nazism, and we know that what they are about is not a witch-hunt. In the 1920s, the time of these "fantasies," they are at war with the communists, and beyond them, the entire politicized German working class. And what they will finally undertake is not "sexocide," as some feminists have termed the witch-hunts of sixteenth-century Europe, but genocide. What is the connection?

Here Theweleit takes us beyond any ground so far explored by feminist theory: from the dread of women to the hatred of communism and the rebellious working class. I will not retrace his path, because my job is not to convince you, but only to prepare you. Always bear in mind that primal fear of dissolution. Communism—and this is not the communism of Lenin or Stalin, but the communism of Rosa Luxemburg, the most potent and horrifying of the "Red women," and even, briefly, of Wilhelm Reich— represents a promiscuous mingling, a breaking down of old barriers, something wild and disorderly. ("Represents" is too weak a word. This is what communism *promises* the oppressed and, we must imagine, usually hungry, working class of postwar Germany.) The Freikorpsmen recount with icy horror a working-class seizure of a castle, where the occupiers proceed to glut themselves, fornicate indiscriminately (this is the Freikorpsmen's account, anyway), and find a hundred ways to desecrate this tower of feudal, nationalist pride. To the Freikorpsmen, the Reds, like individual women, are a nameless force that seeks to engulf—described over and over as a "flood," a "tide," a threat that comes in "waves." A man must hold himself firm and upright, or be "sucked in" by this impure sea . . . All that is rich and various must be smoothed over (to become like the blank facades of fascist architecture); all that is wet and luscious must be dammed up and contained; all that is "exotic" (dark, Jewish) must be eliminated.

Now, having come so close to the "last chapter," we can no longer postpone the question of *which* men we are talking about and *whose* fantasies these are. For if the fascist fantasy—which was of course no fantasy for the millions of victims—springs from a dread that (perhaps) lies in the hearts of all men, a dread of engulfment by the "other," which is the mother, the sea or even the moist embrace of love . . . if so, then we are in deep trouble. But even as I say that, I am reminded that we who are women are *already* in deep trouble. As Theweleit says, the point of understanding fascism is not only "because it might 'return again'," but because it is already implicit in the daily relationships of men and women. Theweleit refuses to draw a line between the fantasies of the Freikorpsmen and the psychic ramblings of the "normal" man: and I think here of the man who feels a "normal" level of violence toward women (as in, "I'd like to fuck her to death") . . . the man who has a "normal" distaste for sticky, unseen "feminine functions" . . . the man who loves women, as "normal" men do, but sees a castrating horror in every expression of female anger . . . or that entirely normal, middle-class citizen who simply prefers that women be *absent* from the public life of work, decisions, war. Here Theweleit does not push, but he certainly leaves open the path from the "inhuman impulse" of fascism to the most banal sexism.

I think it should be said though—especially since Theweleit himself does not say it—that the equation does not work both ways. It would be a perverse reading of *Male Fantasies*, and a most slovenly syllogism, which leaps to conclude that "all men are fascists" or that fascism and misogyny are somehow the "same thing." The fascist enterprise was not, after all, a modern witch-hunt, and the Jewish (and communist) men who fell victim to it were not substitute women, symbolic whores, or anything of the kind, but real men whose crime was their Jewishness, or their politics. Neither feminism nor antifascism will be well served by confounding fascist genocide with the daily injuries inflicted by men on women—and I urge the feminist reader to resist the temptation to do so. The problem is not that any comparison "trivializes" the Holocaust (we need comparisons if we are to inch our way up to some comprehension of the "unthinkable"), but that we need to preserve the singularity of the horrors we seek to understand. One example: the Freikorpsmen do not rape the "Red women" they capture; they beat them or kill them. We may say that rape is *like* murder, but it is not the same as murder. And the Freikorpsman's predilection for murder, over rape turns out to be a clue.

There is a further bit of historical specificity to keep in mind: These Freikorpsmen do not emerge on the plain of history fresh from the pre-Oedipal nursery of primal emotions, but from the First World War. That war was a devastating experience not only for the men who lost, like these, but for those who "won." It was the first modern technological war, the first war to produce its own specific psychosis—"shell shock." Obviously very few of the survivors—and only an elite minority of the Germans—went on to create fascist movements. But in considering the so-far unending history made by men of the warrior caste, it may be helpful to recall that it is not only that men make wars, but that wars make men. For the warrior caste, war is not only death production, but a means of *reproduction*; each war deforms the human spirit and guarantees that the survivors—or some among them—will remain warriors. I do not offer this as an "excuse" (there are none) but as a thought that may have practical value: If we cannot, certainly not in one generation, uproot the murderous fantasies, we can at least try to stop the war.

The fantasies are another problem. If I may extrapolate from the work of the American feminist theorists Dorothy Dinnerstein and Nancy Chodorow, it seems to me that as long as women care what we are in this world—at best, "social inferiors," and at worst, a form of filth—then the male ego will be formed by, and bounded by, hideous dread. For that which they loved first—woman and mother—is that which they must learn to despise in others and suppress within themselves. Under these conditions, which are all we know, so far, as the human condition, men will continue to see the world divided into "them" and "us," male and female, hard and soft, solid and liquid—and they will, in every way possible, fight and flee the threat of submersion. They will build dykes against the "streaming" of their own desire. They will level the forests and pave the earth. They will turn viciously against every revolution from below—and every revolution starts with a disorderly bubbling over of passion and need. They will make their bodies into hard instruments. They will confuse, in some mad revery, love and death, sex and murder. They may finally produce the perfect uniformity, the smooth, hard certainty that transcends anything that fascism aspired to: a dead planet.

There is another fantasy that is a male fantasy and also a human fantasy. Theweleit expresses it not only in what he sometimes says, but in the way he says it all. Attend to how your mind moves as you read: how you dart, curiously, from one thing to another; how you will be sometimes made aware of your*self* reading—you (Theweleit will remind you), with a body and pulse that races with the narrative; and, then, how you will sometimes *lose* yourself, as the story, which will take you far beyond the Freikorpsmen, releases in you some forgotten sense of the possible. Read as skeptically and cautiously as you can, and, I promise, you will still be engulfed.

It is Theweleit's brilliance that he lets us, now and then, glimpse this other fantasy, which is the inversion of the fascists' dread: Here, the dams break. Curiosity swims upstream and turns around, surprising itself. Desire streams forth through the channels of imagination. Barriers—between women and men, the "high" and the "low"—crumble in the face of this new energy. This is what the fascist held himself in horror of, and what he saw in communism, in female sexuality—a joyous commingling, as disorderly as life. In this fantasy, the body expands, in its senses, its imaginative reach—to fill the earth. And we are at last able to rejoice in the softness and the permeability of the world around us, rather than holding ourselves back in lonely dread. This is the fantasy that makes us, both men and women, human—and makes us, sometimes, revolutionaries in the cause of life.

Preface

Let's hope that power trips everyone's alarm some day.

Vlado Kristl, *Sekundenfilme*

Along the Hindenburg Dam, which isn't visible in the frontispiece, the trains travel back and forth between the island of Sylt and the *terra firma* of Schleswig-Holstein.

I found that picture postcard of the train on the dam at high tide while looking through my mother's photo albums this spring. She was already unconscious from a stroke and on that journey that is no journey. When people die, we look at their photo albums and hear the voices that belonged to the images.

Käte, née Minuth, eleventh child of a tailor from Cranz, where people from Königsberg went to enjoy the Baltic waters, 1900-1977, would have liked to have lived to see this work (and the attendant doctorate) completed and to fulfill her dream of reaching a hundred—a dream she mentioned less and less in recent years.

The picture postcard was loosely inserted in the album, among the pictures of the immediate family. A photo of Hindenburg, one of my earliest heroes, hung above the desk of my father, the railroad man, with a facsimile signature I long considered genuine. Paul von Hindenburg, field marshal, had signed a picture for my father: the thought pleased me. Alongside of Hindenburg (himself a dam—a soldier dam connecting one Reich with another across the Red floods of the Weimar "Republic") hung Bismarck and Frederick the Great (where the Führer's portrait must have hung at one time).

In 1954 my father proudly showed the Hindenburg Dam to my sister Helga and me. Not as if it were his property, but as if *he himself* were the RAILWAY in whose train we were sitting and under which the dam belonged. I was twelve, and this is the only time I remember being at the seashore with my father. He never went into the water on Sylt. It was too rough for him, and besides, he was "no great fan of it."

The illegitimate son of an East Prussian estate-holder, my father was raised by an aunt. As a father himself, he was therefore all in favor of having a *proper* family. But he was primarily a railroad man (body and soul, as he put it), and only secondarily a man. He was a good man, too, and a pretty good fascist. The blows he brutally lavished as a matter of course, and for my own good, were the first lessons I would one day come to recognize as lessons in fascism. The instances of ambivalence in my mother—she considered the beatings necessary but tempered them—were the second.

Honest public servant that he was, he didn't even cheat at cards (skat and *Doppelkopf*) the way she did (often in my favor, so I put up with it). A disappointed public servant in the end (not even his last boss cared about a lifetime of *service*), he succumbed to alcohol and to German history. Bruno, 1901-1966.

None of his sons wanted to be a railroad man. The youngest of my three older brothers became one anyway. The trade he'd learned, dairy management, had become a career "with no future," that is, with no present. He is not a body-and-soul railroad man.

My older siblings were born for the coming Reich that somehow never came. *Reinhold—Siegfried—Brunhilde—Günter*: Nibelungen, 1929-1935. The two *latecomers* were given the names of defeat. Klaus and Helga, 1942 and 1944: children of Stalingrad. Out of Staningrad came Elvis, the movies, and the rest of America, from screens and loudspeakers across the big ocean.

Along the dam that isn't visible in the picture, Monika Kubale also crossed over to the mainland, drawn from *the island* she'd lived on for eighteen years to the same city whose university had attracted me: Kiel, like the thing ships have underneath.

*　*　*

For *Spellbound*, Hitchcock secured the collaboration of
Dalí, who was to do the dream sequences for him. Hard,
pointed, jagged, they were to penetrate the surface of the everyday world. Just like the mountains the train glides past in this
film: rooted. One dynamic space moving through another. The
railroad and film must have common roots. Unfortunately,
Freud wrote only about the railroad. And about how the unconscious stores its painstakingly gathered representations of the

self. Iris Henderson has her monogram sewn onto her pockets, scarves, and handkerchiefs, as if these things could help her to safeguard her identity. . . .

If verisimilitude dares to raise its ugly head, if you reject my view of this film as mere fantasizing, *then of course I am defenseless*. (Frieda Grafe on *The Lady Vanishes*, in *Filmkritik* 12, 1971.)

Jimi: After you've gone thru all of the hell of dying, you've got to find out—and face—the facts to start a nationwide rebirth. But I'm not a politician, you see. All I can say is what I've been seeing: common sense.
Interviewer: But the masses are saying just the opposite.
Jimi: You know who is REALLY living in fantasy land? It's the damned masses. The masses. The point is, WHO is wrong and WHO is right? That's what the point is—not how many people . . . . What I'm trying to say is that somebody has got to make a move. The others are just waiting around until you run to jelly. Then, they tick you off. (Jimi Hendrix, in an interview in *Circus*, March 1969.)

*   *   *

When I hear Monika talking about her clinical experience, it is not only academic theories of fascism that begin to appear inane: the very idea of producing a critique of them seems equally trivial. In fact, the whole effort would be superfluous if we had a convention for understanding and behaving, a way of listening that sensed the significance of all this for the theoretical pronouncements we deliver form on high: children committed to psychiatric care, who articulate in the language of the "deviant" or the dumb a whole system of disabilities that make up this life and who carry that system about with them in their own helplessly rebellious bodies, expressing it in images that compel any viewer to perceive their sickness as a superior form of innocent wholeness, though their bodies are said to have "broken down." When she tells me of contact, true contact with lightning and rolling thunder, of the production of an intimacy through the feeling and exploration of distances—an intimacy that is not consuming, distance that is not far away—a place where caution is a beautiful word, related to foresight and to a feeling for the reality of a suffering that wishes for change but is caught in impasse and double bind, I think then of the studied or hectic nonchalance of all those (myself included) who are striving to combat fascism here and now, but are blind to the experience of the nonfascist . . . at this point, the sentence seems to want to continue, "I begin to despair" (but this is the reality of a frozen semantics, not, in the end, of any feeling I might have).

Monika consistently confronted me with her different reading of the manuscript. Whether I handed her quotes, half-finished sections, reworked pages, or finished copy, she seldom reacted as I had hoped and expected. The things I bypassed were often the ones that said most to her; unperturbed, she pronounced "ambivalent" the very passages in which I aimed to reveal self-evident truth, passages where I had developed brilliant formulations that I was now forced to abandon. (I now have a very ambivalent attitude toward the word "ambivalence".)

Monika and Margret Berger, veterans of clinical work with children,* were also the ones who gave me most support whenever I, a person with no clinical experience, ventured to reformulate accepted psychoanalytic views on the fascistic type. I was working with nothing but patients' reports— soldier males wrote their memoirs in that form without realizing it—and with the terror enacted by these men. I am especially indebted to Margret Berger for her generally positive reaction to my thought on the ego-structure of the not-yet-fully-born (volume 2), as well as for her references to the psychoanalytic literature.

* * *

From time to time, I would find a manila envelope in my mailbox. The envelope held one, sometimes two, steno pads in which Erhard Lucas had relayed his reactions—concise and friendly, or sharp when he found something he didn't like—to portions of the manuscript I had shipped off to him in Oldenburg. This book began as a chapter on "White terror" for Lucas's *Märzrevolution 1920*. When it grew beyond that, he followed its progress in the way that I, given a choice, would have wanted a ready-critic-colleague to follow it. This book is dedicated to Erhard Lucas, without whom it would never have been written.

---

*The conditions of some of those children have a lot in common with the predicament of adult fascists, as we will see.

male fantasies

Chapter 1
Men and Women

SEVEN MARRIAGES

> I got married when I was a young naval lieutenant. Because I
> belonged to the North Sea Fleet, I felt confident I'd be stationed
> mainly in Wilhelmshaven. Naturally, I was very happy when my
> father-in-law from Hamburg had a little cottage built for me out
> in Rüstringen.[1]

"For *me*, the man says, not "for us." That is now Lieutenant
Ehrhardt, leader of the Ehrhardt Naval Brigade—most infamous of all the
Freikorps in the early years of the Weimar Republic—introduces the reader
to the event of his marriage and to its first consequence, the gift of a little
cottage. Not one word about his wife, not even her name. The father-in-law
appears to have money. The relationship to Wilhelmshaven seems more
important than the relationship with the nameless wife.

The next paragraph of Ehrhardt's commentary records his comrades'
reactions—to the "villa," not the marriage. Contrary to his expectations,
the lieutenant is transferred to Kiel, where the work is hard:

> When I came home in the evening, I opened up my stuffed
> briefcase and sat down to work until midnight or one in the
> morning. My wife often complained about this. She used to say,
> "The only part of my husband I'm familiar with is his back."[2]

So much for the first years of the marriage.

> In spite of all that, life in the beautiful city of Kiel was brighter, freer, and happier for my wife and children than in eternally mist-shrouded Wilhelmshaven, the premier German naval town.[3]

That is the first and only extended reference to wife and children, all on a single page of the book. Beyond the benefits of the weather in Kiel, they have no claims whatsoever. Kiel, the beautiful city, and Wilhelmshaven, eternally mist-shrouded yet quintessentially German, captivate the lieutenant more powerfully than his wife and children, even in the only paragraph devoted to the latter. While Lieutenant Ehrhardt doesn't conceal the fact that his wife, and even his children, have impinged on his military existence from time to time, they nevertheless remain nameless.

There is one other woman in the book, princess Hohenlohe. He says it was chance that led him to find refuge with her in Munich when he was being pursued as an instigator of the Kapp Putsch. She spent half a year in prison for that. He praises her "princely sense of loyalty toward her ward,"[4] but offers no hint that she will later become his second wife.[5] Nor does he mention how the first wife passed out of his life.

* * *

First Lieutenant Gerhard Rossbach, commander of a Freikorps, ascribes his survival to his wife's aversion to wallpapered doors. Because she had placed a wall-hanging over one such door, the gestapo failed to locate the study in which Rossbach kept his correspondence with SA-leader Ernst Röhm. Rossbach would not have survived that discovery. Thanks to his wife, Rossbach was not among the prominent Nazi party members who were murdered when the SA was deprived of its power in June/July 1934. (The leadership of the Reichswehr was primarily responsible for this action, which is still inaccurately called the "Röhm Putsch.")[6] In any case, this fortunate turn of events induces Rossbach to mention his wife. Inevitably, Rossbach has to spend a bit of time in jail.

> When I came home, I found my wife suffering from a severe nervous disorder. She died soon afterward.[7]

Her name is never given, nor is she mentioned again. Two pages further on he writes:

> The honeymoon with my second wife, an actress with Heinrich George's Schiller Theater, gave me the opportunity I needed.

He means the opportunity to travel outside the country. Rossbach introduces his second wife as a casual contributor to that main goal. She has no name either. The name that dominates the sentence is that of a man, Heinrich George, through whom the obscure wife gains a certain importance. The shadow of the wife appears just once more in the narrative of Rossbach's eventful life. Child in arms, she is attempting to enter the American internment camp where Rossbach is being held in 1945, and where he is considering how to make the Americans understand that he has opposed Hitler since 1923—despite the fact that he participated in Hitler's abortive coup attempt in Munich on November 9 of that year. Rossbach succeeds in convincing his captors that he belonged to the anti-Hitler faction in the behind-the-scenes struggle for control of the "People's (*Völkisch*) Movement." His wife is not admitted, however; he sees her only from a distance.[8]

* * *

At the start of 1919, naval lieutenant Martin Niemöller belonged to a circle of officers in Kiel. The central figure of that circle, a person much admired by Niemöller, was a man named von Loewenfeld, who would later become a Freikorps commander. Niemöller refused to report to his assigned naval brigade, simply because he could not bring himself to violate his loyalty to the kaiser by swearing allegiance to the revolutionary Ebert-Scheidemann government.[9]

Niemöller describes the events that led to his early marriage:

> The eldest sister of my friend and schoolmate Hermann Bremer was studying in Berlin at that time. Especially because neither of us had many acquaintances in Berlin, we fell very naturally into the habit of meeting before or after duty on Sundays to sail on the Wannsee and the Havel. The early summer of 1917 was full of sun and warmth! Out of this renewal of our childhood acquaintance came first a lively correspondence, then in the next year an engagement.[10]

"The eldest sister of my friend and schoolmate Hermann Bremer" is adequate designation for his future bride. In addition, things happened "very naturally," though to an extent through force of circumstance, since neither of the two friends "had many acquaintances in Berlin." Then again, this was the "renewal of a childhood acquaintance." Niemöller offers a litany of excuses to justify his marriage. The exclamation point after "sun and warmth" indicates that some bodily feelings were in play, but those are ascribed to the weather; the "warmth" does not emanate from the "sister."

In the following year, the war allows him to take a break:

> And so I did something I should have done long before. On July 18, I traveled to Vienna and from there to Berlin, not to renew old ties with the admiralty, but to obtain the consent of my bride and offer her my own.[11]

"It's no great secret that the sun and moon are having marriage problems." From Grandville's *Un autre monde* (1844).

Vienna, Berlin, but not to visit the admiralty. A heavy buildup, which results in the most impersonal formulation imaginable, describing an exchange of consents. Still no name, either, though a precise date is given (July 18, 1918) to show that this is no mere dream.

> After twenty-four hours in Berlin, we went on to celebrate our engagement with our parents and parents-in-law in Elberfeld, knowing that the future was absolutely uncertain and might well be dismal. Yet something we had both learned in wartime now came back to me with vivid clarity: life is not something we can predict and know; it is something we must risk and have faith in![12]

The description of the future as "uncertain and dismal" certainly refers to the consequences of Germany's defeat, already familiar to Niemöller when he wrote his book. Yet unconsciously he may also be referring to the marriage, since this is the first time such language appears in his autobiography. The marriage supplies him with words like "risk" and "have faith in." With the arrival of the wife, life seems to lose much of its predictability. It is no longer a matter of "knowing," because what, after all, can you "know" about women?

"Today there'll be a great celebration in the heavens."
From *Un autre monde*.

Niemöller never enters the Freikorps. He leaves the navy to study agriculture, living apart from his wife. They see each other only on Sundays:

> Those Sundays had a stamp all their own: In the morning we
> would attend service in the church in Kappeln, where my mother
> had been baptized, confirmed, and married; or we would take an
> hour's hike across the hills to my father's old village, where
> Aunt Johanna, his eldest sister, did her farming on the Schaberg
> estate. We would visit the little church where my grandfather
> had played the organ until his untimely death. In the afternoon
> we stayed at home, reading, or playing music. As a rule, eve-
> nings were spent with relatives and friends. Our conversations
> often turned then to the future of the family lands, that is, when
> our great concern about political developments did not dominate
> the conversation, as was only natural in the early summer of
> 1919.[13]

Only he and his own family exist in these sentences, which seem to be written under the watchful eye of some internal censor. Is he trying to prove to someone that there were few opportunities for sexual relations? Even the nights were abbreviated, with Niemöller leaving at half past five to begin the four-mile walk that brought him back to the place where he worked during the rest of the week.

* * *

In 1917 Rudolf Höss, son of Catholic tradespeople, ran away from home because he couldn't stand to sit and watch the war go on without him. He was sixteen years old. When he returned from the war, his parents were dead. That released him from his vow to become a priest but cost him his inheritance, which had been tied to that vow. An uncle was there to make sure that conditions were met. Höss traveled eastward, moving (illegally) into the Baltic area with the Rossbach Freikorps. He kept close ties to that Freikorps until 1923, when he was sentenced to five years in prison for his part in a *vehme* murder.* (He later became commandant of the Auschwitz concentration camp.) When he was released from prison in 1928, he joined the Artaman League to learn farming.[14]

> During my first days there, I met my future wife. Filled with the same ideals, she had found her way to the Artamans along with her brother. At our very first meeting, we knew beyond a shadow of a doubt that we belonged together. There was a harmony of trust and understanding between us, as if we'd grown up together. Our views of the world were identical, and we complemented each other in every way. I had found the woman I'd longed for during my long years of loneliness. That inner harmony has remained through all of our years together; it remains with us today, undisturbed by the vicissitudes of everyday life, by good and bad fortune, or by any other outside influence. Yet there was one thing that always made her sad: I kept the things that moved me most deeply to myself, never revealing them even to her.[15]

The above paragraph, a serenade to noninvolvement, seems chiefly motivated by an impulse to reveal nothing concrete about the reality of his wife. When a "harmony" cannot be affected by anything, neither "good" nor "bad fortune," then it is immutable, existing only as an idea. That idea appears to be one of unity, of "harmony" and "belonging together." "Our views of the world were identical," he says, and "we complemented each other in every way." This seems to be an attempt to describe some fantasy in which Höss and his wife (she, too, is nameless) are a single being.

The fact that "the [nameless] woman" is the one he "longed for during all his years of loneliness" hints that she may represent someone else who,

---

*Murders ordered by secret tribunals after the manner of the dreaded Westphalian *Vehmgericht* of the Middle Ages. (Trans.)

earlier on, had been *the* woman for him. This woman, the mother, is described by Höss at another point as his "home" (*Heimat*).

The actual wife is mentioned only in the final sentence of the quotation, and then in the most brusquely distant way. He cannot bring himself to "reveal" to her the things that "move him most deeply," and that has been a source of constant sadness for her.

Höss's paean to unity addresses the notion of a particular relationship to women, in which the image of the wife is made to coincide with a different image that remains hidden.* The brother at the side of the chosen woman, noted in Niemöller's earlier account, turns up again here with the same function. The brother at the sister's side seems to attest to her special suitability for marriage. Sisters who sail with their brothers, or travel with them to join the Artamans, can be expected to be virgins.

By stressing that his wife found her way to the Artamans with her brother, Höss, we sense, is defending himself against the potential charge that he has fallen in with a woman who is experienced with men (a "whore"). This woman is a virgin—that's the important point.

* * *

Ernst von Salomon tells how he met his first, and only, love:

> I fell in love. I plunged into a bottomless chasm of savage longing for death, and at the same moment I was hurled toward the burning sun of an intense affirmation of life. One nod from her and I'd have been ready to blow myself, my house, the city, or the world sky-high. I bought a copy of the little volume *Mozart on the Road to Prague* in matchbook-cover format and wrapped it in twelve narrow-lined pages of poetry I had written for HER. Thinking that I would soon have to support a large family, I decided to work overtime writing dividend certificates. God alone knows how hard that was. My colleagues at the office were astonished to see me clean-shaven every day. When I received my first overtime check, I sent HER a gold chain. Then I had a dream-suit made for myself. Ten years later, by the way, this woman became my wife.[16]

Even this SHE remains nameless. After this brief detour, Salomon's narrative blithely returns to its former path, focusing mainly on his almost symbiotic friendship with Kern, one of the murderers of Rathenau. His thoughts stay with Kern until Salomon is given a five-year sentence for his role in planning the assassination. Released from prison, he goes to HER home:

---

*Later on, at the Nuremberg Trials, Höss will tell the American psychologist assigned to the proceedings, Dr. Gilbert, about his "alienation" from his wife and the "infrequent desire" of either for sexual intercourse. (*Nuremberg Diary*, p. 251ff.)

> She was visibly startled when she opened the door. She led me
> silently through the hallway into the room. She set the table for
> tea. . .When she glanced over at me, I staunchly held back any
> feelings of sympathy.[17]

That's all he has to say about HER. The same evening he goes out to a cafe
with his brother, who has turned up as a matter of course (unannounced, in
other words) at her home. They go without HER.

His "love" for HER had fed him violent images, opening up the "bottomless chasm of savage longing for death" and hurling him toward "the
burning sun of an intense affirmation of life." The resulting impulse was to
"blow everything sky-high."

The danger of destroying others, and of self-dissolution, originates in
this "love." Salomon's thoughts seem to revolve around an idea he calls
"woman," but which has a very different meaning—something that comes
to the fore in his observations after leaving prison:

> The strangest thing of all was the women. They had nothing in
> common with the women in my prison dreams. Their faces
> seemed naked and boring, just as monotonous as their long,
> uninteresting legs. The only things that reminded me of the
> dreadful torments of my cell were the wrinkles their shiny silk
> stockings made at the knee. They alone seemed alive.[18]

A fetishistic object, the wrinkles of stockings at the knee, is the only thing
capable of exciting him, though not pleasurably. The memory of
"torments" is what stirs him, while nakedness and long legs—two attributes
usually considered sexually stimulating—leave him indifferent.

* * *

> I was a single man approaching forty. I knew quite a few eligible
> girls, yet when I really thought about it, I knew that what I
> wanted was to pursue the youthful dream of love that still lived
> inside me. Economic obstacles no longer stood in my way. Un-
> fortunately, however, other factors had produced such serious
> conflict with my father that I could not bring any young woman
> into the family.

Those remarks on page 106 of his memoirs represent General von
Lettow-Vorbeck's first attempt to come to terms with the problem of
"women." The initial foray must have exhausted his energies, since he
returns to the topic only after an eight-page digression on military matters:

> I suffered setbacks in my personal life as well. After reconciling
> with my father, I wanted to propose to the young woman who

had filled my imagination from the time when I was a lieutenant.
I had completely withdrawn from her to allow her total freedom.
Now I learned that she had just gotten married. I was
crestfallen. I had no success in attempting to win the hand of
another woman. Her heart was no longer free. Despite the
discipline of my military duties, there were times when I felt
quite crushed.

He does not reveal the source of the "serious conflict" with his father,
nor how it was resolved. He says nothing further about what it meant to
have "times when" he was "quite crushed," either. Indeed, the qualifiers
"quite" and "there were times when" raise doubts as to how "crushed" he
actually was. In the same way, he does not say who the women in question
were. After that brief allusion, Lettow drops the matter as if he had already
said too much.

Lettow has a lot to say about other things, however. He indicates, for
instance, that the rigor of his military service functioned as a facade, and
that the woman who filled his imagination for twenty years had no need to
exist anywhere else. The phrase "to allow her total freedom" means just the
opposite: as far as he is concerned, she hadn't the slightest freedom. The
phrase could be turned around to read "to allow *me* total freedom"—not to
pursue other women, but to escape the one he has internalized.

In Wilhelmshaven I met a women to whom I was immediately
drawn. She was married, though—a Gordian knot. Yet
everything worked out wonderfully.[19]

This bait is dangled before us for sixty pages, until the fish is finally
landed in the chapter, "Marriage: My Time in the Army and the Kapp
Putsch":

I was surprised that I hadn't heard anything from a woman
I had been friends with. Then I found out she had been divorced
for some years and had lovingly looked after my aging parents in
Berlin during the hardest years of the war. That meant she could
not have forgotten me. I was now forty-nine and thought the
time was right to leave the single life behind. It was March 2,
and on March 6 I was to report to Field Marshal von Hindenburg in Kolberg. I felt sure I'd be transferred immediately to the
Baltic. There wasn't much time for getting married, so I sent a
brazen telegram to my future wife in Flensburg, saying that I expected her at my parents' house in Berlin right away. Lieutenant
Christiansen, who in 1915 had sent a ship laden with war
matériel to our rescue in East Africa, was with her when my
telegram arrived. Thunderstruck, she showed him the telegram.
He kissed her hand emotionally. . .

I went to my parents' house and revealed my intent to
marry. When my future wife cabled that she would arrive in
Berlin on March 4, I scheduled the wedding for March 5. To
prevent her from delaying her trip to Berlin, I never told her that
I had marriage in mind. . . .

When I met my wife at the Lehrter Station on the evening
of March 4, I told her that I would marry her at 11 A.M. on
March 5. Struck speechless by this announcement, she adamantly
refused.[20]

The road to this general's bed seems to run directly through his parents'
living room. It is loving attention paid to those parents that prompts him to
think of this woman when considering marriage. He recognizes that right
away: "That meant she could not have forgotten me." His telegram does
not say that he "expects" her in Berlin, but that he expects her (a
command!) at his parents' home in Berlin. Unlike the woman (who is she?
his childhood sweetheart? the one from Wilhelmshaven?), the parents are
informed of Lettow's intent. The wedding takes place as a matter of course,
but not in church. If the Lettows can't go to the church, the church will
come to the Lettows:

The ceremony took place as planned, at 11 A.M. on March 5,
by my father's bedside. Wearing the Iron Cross-First Class he
had won in 1870, he sat erect, with my mother beside him in her
wheelchair.[21]

The sacrificial lamb in that horrific Prussian wedding is the woman. He
treats her just as he had treated the one who had "filled his imagination" for
twenty years. He is more strongly drawn to the Baltic campaign than to
her.*

The woman is expected to begin living within an image and a myth. She,
Madame Nameless, is now the wife of Lettow-Vorbeck "Africanus," the
hero of East Africa, the man who returned unvanquished from the great,
lost war. The mere mention of Lettow's name in connection with a woman
is enough to impel Lieutenant Christiansen to kiss that woman's hand
"emotionally." Lieutenant Christiansen, for his part, is an honorable man.
He knows Lettow from the war and spends time with ladies only to prevent
them from traveling in bad company.

The omission of the woman's name is made all the more striking by the
fact that Lettow-Vorbeck is otherwise so good with names and dates. He
knows a multitude of people, whom he nearly always mentions by name.

---

*The East African hero displayed his splendid military nature by traveling one day later to
Field Marshal von Hindenburg in Kolberg, where he was placed at the head of a Freikorps. (Colonel Reinhard, *Die Wehen der Republik*, p. 101.)

Even the young girl chosen to present him with an official bouquet on his return from Africa has a name: Lotte Heckscher.

Dates are no problem, either: Lieutenant Christiansen, 1915; telegram to Flensburg, March 2; to Hindenburg, March 6; wedding ceremony, 11 A.M. on March 5; meeting his wife at the Lehrter Station, evening of March 4; announcement of the wedding on March 5 at 11; and the Iron Cross, 1870.

All that gives the impression of an ingrained habit acquired on the general staff, of a life that is planned and reviewed, constructed like a military campaign: short, clipped field reports; expressions like "first class!" or "a piece of cake!" She alone remains nameless, dateless, outside history.

Twenty pages later, we discover in passing that she has a daughter and twin sons from her first marriage. When the first son of her second marriage is born, Lettow writes about the "baptism of *my* little Rüdiger."[22] Only the son evokes such emphasis on Lettow's own paternity. When a girl is born in November 1923, "a daughter has been added to the family."[23]

The wife dies. Lettow writes an extended obituary, finding words for the woman now that she is dead. The obituary, the longest section of the book devoted to her, is annihilating:

> I never came to terms with my wife's death. She was so
> vivacious, warm, and happy, that no one who came into contact
> with her could remain indifferent. Almost everyone she met felt
> drawn to her and basked in the sunlight she radiated. It was that
> way in the social whirl she loved so much: at gatherings of the
> colonial Germans; at the countless teas she gave in her beloved
> winter garden in Bremen; or when employees from Karstadt or
> some other firm visited her. Without trying, she was the natural
> center of attention. It was the same way in Waterneverstorff,
> when she would invite droves of refugees from the East for
> coffee and cake in our room . . . In Hamburg, where we ex-
> pected to spend our autumn years together, she gave our new
> home the stamp of her personality and the exquisite taste she
> had inherited as a descendant of the Goethe-portraitist Tischbein.
> When she departed from us, it seemed as if she were still alive
> and might walk through the door at any moment.[24]

"She loved the social whirl": that was it. The rest of it simply says that she was a superb representative, a quality her husband admires, since it enhances the esteem the world owes him in any case. Her "exquisite taste," being inherited, is only partly attributable to her. Lettow adorns her with the male names of Goethe and Tischbein, just as Rossbach had embellished the memory of his second wife with Schiller and Heinrich George.

The absence of real relations between Lettow and his wife is underscored by the fact that he ventures to speak of her at length only after her death. (Not only the wife is treated in that way; *his* two sons are fully appreciated only after they have fallen in battle.)[25] The result of all this is that the reader begins to grow uneasy whenever Lettow devotes more than one sentence of praise to a family member. That person will soon be dead, we conclude. And we are right.

Some massive, suppressed aggression seems to be contained in those obituaries: a "wishing-to-death," The words, "When she departed from us, it seemed as if she were still alive" might be interpreted as a confirmation that her death has made little real difference.

Once Lettow has discharged the genteel duties of eulogizing, he generally turns to a description of some hunt. (Admittedly, there are hunts after almost every other event in the book.) By the end of his autobiography, we are well informed in at least one respect: we know when, where, and what Lettow has shot.

* * *

Naval lieutenant Manfred von Killinger, a farmer's son who became prime minister of Saxony in 1933, secretly picked out his future bride one Easter day. In his memoirs he calls himself "the bogeyman," or simply "Peter."

> Before boarding the ship, he spent his Easter leave at the Lindenhof. A lot had changed. Only one sister was still living at home. One sister had gone off to teach school in the capital; two others had gotten married. The sister who was still at home had invited her friend Gertrud over for the holiday. Some years before, Peter had spent a few days with Gertrud's parents at their cabin in the Erzgebirge.
>
> He'd liked her even then, but, my God, she'd become a beautiful young thing in the meantime! He must have been blind back then. Peter was quite enchanted. She was bright and unspoiled, practical, well mannered, unaffected yet firm in her beliefs. There was nothing halfway about her. For her there were no compromises: something was either decent or it wasn't. That's how she led her life, and that's how she judged other people.
>
> There's the one for you, Peter thought. She'd make a splendid wife for a soldier. But there was plenty of time for that later.[26]

It would be difficult to pass up a woman who is not only "unaffected," but is also able to measure reality according to two uncompromising principles: "decency," or lack of it. All he needs now is the proper moment to inform her of his plans. That moment arrives:

> There was an unexpected break in training. Peter had a few days before he would be called back. What should he do? Without knowing why, he felt a sudden urge to see the girl who had captured his heart. With quick resolve, he wrote to announce his arrival and set off for her parents' home in the Erzgebirge. He spent several blissful days with Gertrud in the beautiful summer weather.
>
> One morning a call came from Gertrud's brother in the capital. He announced that he and other doctors had been told to report for duty. That evening they learned that the kaiser had ordered a general mobilization. To think that "the bogeyman" had almost missed the war!
>
> Taking his leave of Gertrud, the bogeyman asked, "What now?" She just stared deeply into his eyes. He took her head in his hands and kissed her on the mouth. "What now?" she said. "If you come out of the war in one piece, bogeyman, we'll get married."
>
> Peter removed his signet ring from his finger, handed it to her, and said, "And if I don't, wear this in memory of me." Not a single tear. She didn't bat an eyelash, though he sensed that she was struggling inwardly. Peter looked forward to having such a valiant German wife some day.[27]

He, on the other hand, doesn't seem so brave. He waits until the final moment to open up to her. He is clearly less afraid of the war than of confessing his love; and, in fact, he might still escape by not coming back alive. The story goes on:

> When the torpedo boats had to return to the docks for overhauling, "the bogeyman" made a quick decision to go on leave. How much longer should he wait? How much longer would the war go on? No one could tell. Gertrud, his bride-to-be, was in complete agreement. Within a few days, the arrangements were made and they were married. They spent a few weeks of undiluted bliss at the very spot in the Erzgebirge where they had first found each other. After that, Peter had to return. Gertrud stayed for the time being with her parents. The constant comings and goings of the torpedo boats were no kind of life for a young wife. Gertrud realized that.[28]

She at least is informed in advance of the wedding date; she even agrees to it. Beyond that, she is an object of convenience; he has time for her between training sessions, or when his ship is being overhauled. He lets her parents, rather than her, know when he wants to visit. Everything is done on the spur of the moment. The man is certainly a fast operator, though it takes him a while to turn up at the home of the woman he loves.

No sooner does he settle down with her than his trust in her seems to wane. Has he done so much damage to her uncompromising decency in "several weeks of undiluted bliss" that he is now afraid to leave her unattended in port while he goes chasing after Limeys?

Gertrud stays with her parents. It's safer that way, as Gertrud herself acknowledges. As for the constant "comings and goings" of the torpedo boats . . . no, that's not for her.

At last, the war is over. Yet:

> "I took an oath, father. I turned my torpedo boat over to the enemy without a struggle. I lowered my flag without a struggle. I have sworn to avenge myself on the people who were responsible for that. Those scoundrels will never rule Germany."
>
> Once again, there was a long pause in the conversation. Everyone sensed that Gertrud must speak next. She did. "I know what you're thinking, Peter. You're thinking about the Freikorps that are being set up everywhere against the Spartacists. I could tell you to stay here and let others risk their necks, but I won't do that. Absolutely not. I'll stay here on the Lindenhof and learn to make myself useful. But what good is the farm if the Bolshevists are going to burn it down some day? No good at all. The bitter truth is that the soldier, the decent soldier, has to fight again now. No matter who holds political power, now is the time to grit your teeth and save Germany, and us, from the Red flood. You'll have plenty of time to worry about what happens after that. When you're no longer needed there, come home and we'll start over again."
>
> Peter stood up and kissed his wife. "Bravely spoken," the father said. "I was thinking the same thing, but I didn't want to influence you. You're right, it's time for soliders to speak again."[29]

Peter is so glad to be off again that he immediately kisses his wife in front of the others. No doubt she is also looking forward to having more freedom around the farm. Although they will be apart, they are united in their struggle against the "Red flood," he as a decent soldier, she as an honest laborer.

Lieutenant Martin Niemöller.   General von Lettow-Vorbeck.

Killinger goes on to lead the Assault Force (*Sturmkompanie*) of the Ehrhardt Naval Brigade. After the brigade is dissolved in May 1920, he joins the right-wing underground. He continues his activity there until November 9, 1923, when the failure of Hitler's Munich Putsch temporarily puts an end to his life among other males.

> "The bogeyman" came home again and took charge of the farm. A second little girl, Renate, had now joined her older sister Brigitte.[30]

Not one word about his wife, not even when the third child is born:

> Tiny Peter opened his to the world on the Lindenhof. He did not have to concern himself yet with the political battles that were raging in Germany.[31]

Wife Gertrud, on the other hand, devotes herself all the more to such concerns. At the close of the story, she confesses:

> If I had it to do all over again, I wouldn't have married you if

you'd chosen any other path. We German women can't put up
with weaklings. We need real men, not dishrags.[32]

Anyway, that's how the man describes it.[33]

* * *

So much for our brief review of seven marriages in Freikorps circles, all
of them described from the husband's point of view. I have cited almost all
of the references to wives from the accounts of Ehrhardt, Rossbach, Killinger, and Salomon. Höss speaks more frequently of his wife, but in a manner that is qualitatively similar to that of the passages I have quoted. Lettow
and, in particular, Niemöller also mention their wives more frequently,
though only after the marriages have taken place. The wives remain
marginal figures. They are representatives (Lettow); child-bearers; silent
supporters of their husbands (Niemöller); observers.

THE HISTORICAL CONTEXT AND
THE NATURE OF THE MATERIAL

Who were these men, and what became of them? Ehrhardt and
Rossbach commanded their own Freikorps. Lettow-Vorbeck was a
Reichswehr general who oversaw Freikorps operations in Hamburg and
Mecklenburg. Like Ehrhardt and Rossbach, he played a leading role in the
Kapp Putsch, whose most immediate impetus was the Ebert-Bauer govern-
ment's threat to dissolve the Freikorps.

Lettow-Vorbeck, Ehrhardt, Rossbach, Killinger, and Niemöller were
"senior" officers, in the sense that they had risen through the ranks before
the war (unlike many of the younger officers, who had not gone through the
typical officer's training program of the Prussian monarchy). These men
were monarchists and extremely mistrustful of the "republican" army.

Salomon came straight out of the academy. He had missed action in a
war in which he would dearly have loved to earn his first laurels. The
Freikorps offered him a welcome opportunity to become a man after all, at
the trigger of a machine gun.

Höss was a young noncommissioned officer who had fled to the
military from school, without learning any other trade. For him, as for most
of the men who had tasted even a little power during the war, the military
was the only peacetime alternative to "starting from scratch."

In sum, we have an older officer (general); four younger, middle-rank
officers (three lieutenants and a captain); a cadet (officer-in-training); and a
corporal. Such were the military ranks of the seven husbands.

Now to their origins. Hermann Ehrhardt's family home was a Baden rectory. Rudolf Höss was the son of Baden tradespeople, Martin Niemöller of a Westphalian pastor. Gerhard Rossbach came from a state-owned tenant farm in Pomerania. Paul von Lettow-Vorbeck was the son of a Junker living east of the Elbe. Manfred von Killinger was from an estate in Saxony, while Ernst von Salomon hailed from a family of Prussian officers.

These seven men are representative at least of the leadership caste that gave the Freikorps its particular style. The majority of officers in the "white troops" came from families of estate owners, pastors and other university-trained people, or military officers. Some were also sons of civil servants, or of independent tradespeople of the lower and middle ranges. The only underrepresented group here are the sons of small farmers, who formed a considerable part of the Freikorps.[1] By contrast, the Prussian military academies—breeding grounds for an officer type steeled in discipline and obedience to the kaiser—are disproportionately well represented. Lettow, Rossbach, Salomon, and Killinger all had the benefit of such training.

After the Freikorps were dissolved, the intricate network of the nationalist underground and secret societies expanded, forming the core of a "black army" in response to the Versailles treaty's limitation of regular German armed forces to 100,000 men. What were our seven up to?

Rossbach became one of the chief organizers of the "labor communities" (*Arbeitsgemeinshaften*) movement, which was concentrated in Mecklenburg, Pomerania, and Silesia.[2] It provided a cover for whole bands of Freikorps soldiers who tried to survive the awful, warless years after May 1920 by working on the land, as foresters or in similar occupations. One Freikorps commandant, Major Peter von Heydebreck, tried for instance to establish a lumber company in which he was the boss and his former troops the workers.[3]

The weapons of the Freikorps had never been handed in. Their novels are permeated with a constant fear that weapons stashes will be betrayed; they are riddled with stories of desparate attempts to hide weapons under cover of night, with accounts of arms theft, trading, and smuggling.[4] Weapons were dug up and removed from their oiled wrappings as the occasion demanded: against Poland in Upper Silesia (1921); against French occupying forces in the Ruhr Valley (1923); and later, on behalf of the SA.

Rudolf Höss began as a member of one of those "labor communities." Later on we find him with the Artamans. There he meets Heinrich Himmler, who will open the door to Höss's career in the concentration camps. The Artamans were a *Landbund* (land league) that waged an ideological and practical struggle for the "purity of the German soil." Their aim was to drive Polish seasonal workers—a necessary labor force at the time—from estates in the region east of the Elbe. According to Höss, they met with partial success by organizing unpaid "labor outings" (*Arbeitsdiensten*) during the harvest seasons.

Like so many officers who were horrified by the republic and sought refuge in some counterbalance, Niemöller moved to the country to learn to work the land. His move was not under the aegis of one of the "labor communities." Niemöller viewed farming as a serious occupation, not some transitional phase. He rejected the reality of the republic so thoroughly, in fact, that at the close of his agricultural training he was completely surprised to discover that his officer's pension, a considerable sum, had been so eaten up by inflation that he could no longer buy the farm he had been planning on.[5]

The SA and SS were later to feed heavily upon these "rural resources." Another of the Freikorps successors was the "Organization Consul," or OC, with Lieutenant Ehrhardt at its head. Its specialty: political assassination. Since the proceeds from this were inadequate, OC members supplemented them with occasional work, embezzlement of organization funds, laundering of capital through a bank established by Ehrhardt, and the like. These activities are almost never mentioned in Freikorps novels or biographies; only occasionally in legal transcripts from the Weimar years; a little more frequently in the works of Emil Julius Gumbel, a Berlin professor who zealously tracked down and documented contemporary evidence of the "white terror."[6] Gumbel's was a dangerous enterprise. In all likelihood, he managed to stay alive only because the nationalist underground appreciated having an establishment figure around to record and publicize its bloody deeds.

The OC seems to have been a direct descendant of the Ehrhardt Naval Brigade. It can take credit for the murders of Erzberger and Rathenau. Kern and Fischer, who dispatched Rathenau, were officers in the Ehrhardt Brigade, as were Schulz and Tillessen, Erzberger's murderers.[7] Ernst von Salomon, a onetime member of the brigade, received a five-year sentence as an accessory to Walther Rathenau's murder. The man who ordered the assassination of the foreign minister, Manfred Killinger, escaped without a scratch and, as we saw earlier, was able to take possession of his farm in 1923.[8]

Escherich, a head forester, tried to establish an armed nationalist organization with regional subdivisions on the model of the German army. His outfit achieved notoriety as the "Orgesch" (*Organisation Escherich*), an organization with which most nationalist conspirators had some kind of contact,[9] but which quickly collapsed under the weight of its myriad competing ideas and factions. Although each of these supported the overthrow of the republic, each faction also wanted sole power for itself afterward. Martin Niemöller was among those who were affiliated with "Orgesch."[10]

Among our seven husbands, we also find representatives of the "*vehme* murderers," whose deeds made bloodcurdling headlines in the republican press, especially after 1923. The *vehme* murderers were Freikorps soldiers, members of secret nationalist societies, or of labor communities. They administered their own form of justice by executing comrades suspected of treason—in particular of betraying arms caches. Although the name suggests otherwise, there were in practice no "*vehme* tribunals." Murders took place on the order of the relevant leader, or by agreement among a group of men who had identified a particular "suspect." Often enough, it was private disagreements that gave rise to the act.[11] When an outside enemy is lacking or out of reach, armed male brotherhoods are liable quite literally to set about tearing each other apart.

Rudolf Höss was in prison from 1923 to 1928 for his part in a *vehme* murder. And Salomon's only motive for releasing one "traitor" he had beaten close to death was exhaustion.[12] The prevailing attitude toward such murders is evident in Arnold Bronnen's account of a car trip he took with Rossbach:

> An ancient beech forest encircled ebony pools. From the heights, as the road rolled restlessly up and down the mountainside, we would catch sight of the Oder Valley, with its retinue of jagged church steeples. The adjutant sat silently behind us, while at his side our mutual friend fixed his lascivious gaze on the landscape, searching out possible sites for the *vehme* murder we might have to undertake. That's the way he was. He could never let such things rest. And in this case, he gave the area an A1 rating.[13]

Vehme murders only began to capture the headlines when it became fairly clear that the danger of a military coup had passed. The forces of right-wing nationalism—the "incurable militarists" who had always been acceptable to Weimar governments when it came to "protecting" the "republic" against the Left—could thus be publicly denounced without fear of retribution. *Vehme* murders provided an ideal pretext for taking the "White terrorists" to task, without touching on such issues as the Socialist party's (SPD) role in the defeat of the worker's revolt of 1920. *Vehme* murders exposed "reactionaries" in their own lairs, betraying each other, stealing from each other, slaughtering each other. Here they could finally be exposed. . . . And at this point, the judiciary was able to strengthen its hold. There were even a number of convictions, whereas until then virtually every Freikorps soldier responsible for killing workers, leaders, or members of left-wing parties (USP, KPD) had gotten an acquittal or minimal sentence.[14] Were not their crimes committed, after all, in defense of the fatherland and in the service of the government (of which Ebert was then the head)? Certainly the republican press used *vehme* murder stories (sometimes in the form of serialized novels)[15] as a way of "coming to terms with" the White terror.

Ten years later it became clear that these murders had been an inadequate object on which to focus attacks on the nationalist underground.

A final date worth noting is November 9, 1923, the day of the abortive coup in Munich, which has entered German history books as the "March on the *Feldherrnhalle.*" (Americans refer to it as the "Beerhall Putsch," because it begin in the *hofbräukeller*.)[16] That day marked the end of the first stage of the attempt to establish a new order in Germany—the "Third Reich"—that "which was to come" before the soldiers, who had suffered defeat but had never been "beaten in the field," sank into "the slimy mire of bourgeois life."[17]

On that November 9, Rossbach and Killinger were in action with Hitler in Munich. Lieutenant Ehrhardt stood with his troops at the Bavarian border, ready to march on Berlin. At the last minute, however, his ally, Bavarian Prime Minister Kahr, defected (under pressure from the army). Ehrhardt's troops never marched. Shots were fired at the putschists, whose ranks included Ludendorff. The "movement" claimed its first sixteen martyrs and acquired a cult object: the swastika flag carried in the putsch was raised to the status of a "blood banner." Throughout the 1920s, the seal would be set on SA initiations by the touching of that banner in solemn often nocturnal rituals.

It is possible to list a number of uprisings in which our seven participated. From 1904 to 1907 Lettow-Vorbeck and Ehrhardt had taken part in the near annihilation of the Hereros in Southwest Africa. (Even today, the West German press still refers to Namibia—not infrequently—as "German Southwest Africa.") Lettow then fought against the "Boxers" in China, and against the workers' revolts in Hamburg and Mecklenburg. Ehrhardt fought for the same cause in Berlin, Braunschweig, Munich; Rossbach in the Baltic region, Berlin, Munich, Hamburg, and Upper Silesia; Höss in the Baltic, Munich, and Upper Silesia. Even Niemöller's name must be included here: in March 1920, he led a corps of students from Münster against workers in the Ruhr Valley. Opponents in the Baltic were first the forces of the Russian Red Army, then Latvian and Estonian republican troops; in Upper Silesia, Polish communists and nationalists; on German battlegrounds, the insurrectionary proletariat and its allies.

The multifarious activities of the seven men cover almost the full spectrum of causes fought by the Freikorps and their successor organizations in the postwar period. These men represent the typical backgrounds and the typical perseverance that would later inspire the Nazi propaganda machine to award them the honorary title, "First Soldiers of the Third Reich." Certainly their activities covered a wide spectrum. Referring to the "Technicians' Emergency Service" (*Technische Nothilfe*), "notorious" for their role in strike breaking, Alfred Sohn-Retel has written: "With the Baltic campaigns, this constituted one of the formative elements of Nazism.[18] And although this is certainly true, the two groups need not be so sharply differentiated; there are indications in the annals of the Freikorps that Freikorps soldiers themselves played the "strike-breaker role" in the years 1919-21.[19]

* * *

Not only autobiographies, novels, and eyewitness accounts by men in Freikorps circles (whom I shall from now on refer to as "soldier males"), but also their own actions (centering on the "White terror") and novels written about them, all give expression to a common historical period: the time between November 1918 and November 9, 1923. Although at first glance it might seem that the republic, after a period of stabilization, had emerged victorious by 1924, it was in fact the case that, in those five years, the German revolution was defeated and the cornerstone laid for the subsequent triumph of fascism.

The literature to be cited here falls into three categories. The first consists of texts produced through 1923, which were intended to function as propaganda in contemporary struggles. From 1924 to 1928, there was less "nationalistic" and almost no Freikorps literature; interest in it declined appreciably in the Weimar Republic's stabilization phase. A new boom began in 1928, spurred on by the return of older fighters from prison, exile, or the drudgery of occupations they had never truly wanted—as well as by the growing strength of the German Communist party (KPD). There was a need for new literature to expose the terrors of Bolshevism. Signs of economic crisis in the offing promoted a renewed interest in guns as decisive instruments in domestic politics, a renewed attraction to the protection afforded by aggressive leagues of men. More and more, national socialist partisanship supplanted the rejection and hatred of political parties that had characterized literary production up to 1923. At the same time, preliminary battles were being waged for hegemony in the nationalist camp. This period was to last until 1933.

After 1933, a third boom period produced a number of heroic chronicles of the "movement." Most important, it was at this stage that Freikorps novels acquired their key figure: the hero who begins consciously pursuing national socialism as early as 1920. The new *political* soldier became the hero of the novels, as opposed to the dashing young officer who took pride in knowing nothing about politics. Thus after 1933, novels began to outnumber biographies. Biographies would have to have been severely contribed in order not to conflict with the fascists' official version of their rise to power; and much would need to have been deleted to escape the displeasure of their masters (though these were the masters whom the Freikorps had wished for). For my own study, however, these periodizations have been of little significance, and will be pursued only when they relate to other strands of my argument.

It must be almost self-evident that war novels by writers like Ernst Jünger and Franz Schauwecker are indispensable for an understanding of the events of the German revolution (as the years between 1918 and 1923 may be called). They will be examined particularly in relation to the construction of a male type who finds life without war and weapons unimaginable.

Memoirs written after 1945 are another, smaller resource category. They are principally works of concealment and self-justification. Rossbach, for instance, reworked and published his memoirs as late as 1950 (claiming never to have been a Nazi, always to have opposed Hitler, etc.). Again, they will be drawn on only when my own problematic so demands.

Most centrally, we will look at the nature of the "White terror" and one element within it, the language of the soldier males. The question here is not so much what such language "expresses" or "signifies,"[20] as how it functions, its role in the man's relationship to external reality, and its bodily location. The relationship of human bodies to the larger world of objective reality grows out of one's relationship to one's own body and to other human bodies. The relationship to the larger world in turn determines the way in which these bodies speak of themselves, of objects, and of relationships to objects. How does "fascist language" speak about those relationships, and why?—that is the direction of my inquiry.

My decision to undertake an analysis of the soldier male's relationship to women was not made in advance. It did not originate in theory, nor have I grounded it in theory after the fact. That decision grew from reading the source documents, especially the peculiarities of passages in which women were mentioned. Those passages reveal strangely ambivalent emotions. They vacillate between intense interest and cool indifference, aggressiveness and veneration, hatred, anxiety, alienation, and desire—ambiguities interesting enough to pursue. The work starts here and takes some unexpected turns, always keeping in mind the matter of the "White terror." New turns in the argument will usually (though not always) be given some theoretical justification as they occur.

In reading and setting down my thoughts, I discovered that the material resisted the traditional categorizations of research on fascism.[21] Rather than abandon that discovery, I have made it a central part of my methodology: the material has taken precedence over interpretations.

* * *

November 9, 1923, was a turning point in the history of the *völkisch*/nationalist/militarist movement. It scattered the movement into prisons, bourgeois life, and other countries. Salomon and Höss languished in prison under conditions less favorable than Hitler had in Landsberg, where his private secretary Rudolf Hess was in the cell to transcribe the fiery speeches that would later appear as *Mein Kampf*. (Hitler did not *write* a single word of the book.[22] I shall have more to say on this point later.)

By means of brief prision interludes, Rossbach found his way to the arts. He formed a singing troupe with whose help he sought to preserve awareness of true German culture at a time of reduced interest in political discussion. Their travels brought him notable success—playing for foreign visitors.

Killinger paid visits to Gertrud on her farm. (She is mentioned by name, a singular exception to the rule.) Niemöller began studying theology in Münster. Lettow recounted his African adventures on the lecture circuit, wrote books about them, and occasionally represented banks and business firms. With moderate success, Ehrhardt tried to keep his brigade together underground.

For the time being, the movement was dispersed. Röhm, following his release on probation from five months of pretrial detention, began building up his "Front Exiles" (*frontbann*). In 1925 he refused the leadership of the SA because he found the continued maneuvering between rival nationalist groupings uncongenial and because Hitler's position seemed unclear. Röhm took an excursion into "respectable circles," traveling to Bolivia in 1928 as an officer and quickly entering the army's general staff. There he was as much a forerunner of CIA trainer-advisers as was General Seeckt in China, who after his dismissal from the German army presided over Chiang Kai-Shek's general staff.

After his part in Munich, Göring, too, went into "exile," first in Austria and then in Sweden. Somewhere along the way he encountered the "drug" that would later be his constant companion.[23]

If that seems like a heavy defeat, remember that by the end of the 1920s all of those men would be back in the thick of the action. By contrast, the armed German working class suffered a *final* defeat in 1923. The German Communist party's resolve to seek the path to power without an armed struggle was firmly set; it led them to surrender to the national socialists in 1933 without a fight.

What happened to our seven men after 1933? Two became high-ranking Nazis. After a stint as an SA group leader, Killinger became prime minister of Saxony. Höss was appointed commandant of Auschwitz after serving in numerous concentration camps. Rossbach and Ehrhardt found themselves in the wrong factions during the struggle for power. Rossbach was relegated to a sinecure, a job as a company representative. Ehrhardt, warned in time about plans for June 30, 1934—"The Night of the Long Knives"—escaped into Switzerland.[24]

Salomon became a writer and a reader for the Rowohlt publishing firm. He brought out an anthology on postwar history, *The Book of German Freikorps Fighters*, then hibernated in the film studios at Babelsberg and

Geiselgasteig. The Nazis were too stupid for his taste, and "fairytale films were a neutral country."[25] Lettow lived on his general's pension as a sympathetic well-wisher.

What about Martin Niemöller? The retired naval lieutenant and later church president was an exception in this circle, as can be seen from the fact that though, until now, he has seemed to belong to the same category as Höss, he found himself the latter's prisoner in Sachsenhausen concentration camp. In retrospect, Niemöller can justly be called a republican and a democrat. He presents an interesting case. Why did a person like him, who by his own admission detested the 1918 republic, who was in close contact with naval lieutenant von Loewenfeld—leader of a murderous naval brigade that Niemöller almost joined—take a different route? He did go "back to the land" at first, but did not go on to join the SA. Instead he began theological studies, notably in a branch that defended freedom of choice in the fact of Nazi pressures. Niemöller declined an invitation to join the army.[26]

The question is, what prevented him from becoming a Nazi bigwig? If an answer to that question were possible, it might throw light on the character of those who were the "First Soldiers of the Third Reich."

BIOGRAPHICAL TRADITION

It seems to be the way of men to keep silent about their (private) women in their (public) biographies. Almost all the readers of my unfinished manuscript, at least, could think of a variety of writers who followed that precept. Should our analysis not then take into account cultural norms? Indeed, it must. A lot of things cannot be taken literally. Memoir writers also want to justify themselves—to their comrades, to themselves, to the public, to "literature," to history. If a city seems more captivating than a woman in their writings, that is not necessarily a confession; if sexuality is hardly mentioned or left out altogether, that says nothing about the true meaning of sexuality or women where these men are concerned. That's just the way these things are written. You don't saddle the reader with feelings about the woman in your life, and the way to a general's bed does inevitably pass through his parents' living room. All of that is cultural history and not specific to the Freikorps.

Perhaps even terror is not "Freikorps-specific" or a "fascist" specialty, as it might at first seem. Men's "reserve" where women are concerned certainly follows a convention, though not necessarily a friendly one. Concern for the women's own lives is certainly not its impetus.

To put it another way, these familiar conventions do not constitute a barrier against terror. In fact, we need to ask how much terror they themselves contain. We will be examining a series of phenomena that move along the hazy border between "outright terror" and "mere convention." Is there a true *boundary* separating "fascists" from "nonfascist" men? Is it useful to apply the term "fascist" only to ardent party members and functionaries, and to regard the remainder as deluded, opportunistic, or forced into compliance? Or is it true, as many feminists claim, that fascism is simply the norm for males living under capitalist-patriarchal conditions?[1] Those questions define our inquiry into boundaries of the concept of fascism; they will always be somewhere in the background of our investigations.

A further word about biographical tradition. To Ernst Blüher, one of the founders of the *wandervögel*, that tradition was anything but naive convention. Quite the contrary: commenting on the autobiography of Carl Peters, a German colonial in Africa, Blüher noted:

> I realized after reading the very first chapter of this interesting work that it had carried me into the midst of *my own* problems. The book is very personal, more than one would expect; and *women* play almost no role in that personal content. Even mothers are given short shrift . . . We see before us one of those indefatigable conquerors and organizers; one of those men-of-action and politicians who has nothing to do with women; one who needs male society, the constant company of men, an endless cycle of making and breaking friendships with them.[2]

Blüher has every reason to dwell on such things. He was an open propagandist for male clubs and the only form of physical love he considered appropriate to them: male-to-male (He rejected "homosexuality" as a pseudoclinical concept.) For Blüher, elimination of women was a goal of paramount importance. It is he who gives a name to this norm on which culture is founded: "male society." Whether male society is an essential component of capitalist reality and whether the latter ought to be—or even has to be—regarded as productive of fascist reality is another question that we shall bear in mind.

PARTINGS

Married men were a minority among the soldiers. More the rule were junior officers who deserted their "girls" when the fatherland called. "We couldn't have the young girls hanging onto our coattails, so we went off heroically even when our contribution did not seem absolutely crucial." So said Rudolf Mann, an orderly in the Ehrhardt Naval Brigade.[1] Whenever

1916 postcard series for soldiers at the front.

"comrades" were gathering somewhere, those who were at heart true soldiers would drop everything:

> Inner discipline helped them to overcome their outward splendor. Even the man in yellow shoes, tuxedo, and straw hat—an outfit which he felt to be festive and which he had worn to his engagement party—was a soldier.[2]

The man thus described by Bronnen in his book on Rossbach reported in the summer of 1921 to the "border patrol" in Upper Silesia. The last "real" battles before then had been in the Ruhr, in March/April 1920, shortly before the dissolution of the Freikorps. Opportunities for battle were increasingly scarce; not so women eligible for proposals of marriage.

Peter Mönkemann, hero of Tüdel Weller's Freikorps novel of the same name, falls in love with a woman who corresponds precisely to the "princess of his dreams"; she returns his affection. Yet the call of the soldier is irresistible:

> When he turned out the light and went to bed in his sparsely furnished hotel room, he thought of his princess. The temptation was overwhelming to go home, see her, make love to her. He dedicated three minutes of exquisitely painful thoughts to her;

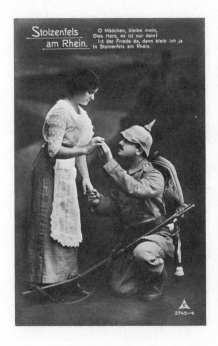 

then he cried out "No!" and forced himself to think about the Freikorps and the little major.[3]

What is more, his thoughts obey him. The movement toward soldiering is depicted as a movement away from women:

> There was a young stormtrooper
> Commanded by his fate
> To leave his wife and child behind,
> And leave without a wait . . . [4]

These partings are joyful; the man enjoys them:

> My theoretical work in Hamburg during the war gave me little contact with the actual craft of warfare. For that reason alone I had no second thoughts about tearing myself loose from wife and children and marching into the jaws of the Bolsheviks.[5]

This is how Baron von Steinaecker, a lieutenant commander, announces his decision to do battle against the Red Army in the Baltic. He is about to treat himself to a previously untried pleasure. The "jaws of the Boksheviks" seem to hide delights that women cannot provide; therefore "no second thoughts."

BRIDES

And if the bride, the fiancée, the "princess," refused to wait and took another?

> Who could blame her? She was in the first bloom of youth and yearned for life, while he knew only his fatherland![1]

"He," in this case, is Freikorps commander Captain Berthold. The man who understands the bride so well is Count Truchs, cavalry captain, in Dwinger's novel *Halfway* (*Auf halbem Wege*). "She yearned for life." Right, but for *that* life she didn't need the captain.

Peter Mönkemann is similarly let down. When he returns to marry his "princess" after more than five years of voluntary fighting in the "aftermath" of the war, she bursts into tears instead of flying into his arms. She has taken another, a businessman, and "she knows she has lost a paradise."[2] That paradise was the love of a man whose itchy trigger fingers kept him from touching her for five long years during which time not a single bullet aimed at the fatherland's enemies left the barrel of his pistol. The novel closes with a homily to Germany's future greatness and its prophet, Peter Mönkemann. Love of women and love of country are at opposite poles.

One of Berthold's crashes—to which he remained invulnerable.

Captain Berthold was one of the great "national heros" of the Freikorps. He had gained renown as a fighter pilot and had been shot down and severely wounded several times. He refused invitations to join the general staff. He is depicted as a man with a compulsion for the front. He came out of the war with a *pour le mérite* and an arm that was crushed almost beyond use. Berthold's wounds had never healed because he always discharged himself prematurely from the hospital and went back to the front. Even after the war, he did not allow himself time to recover. As soon as he heard of plans to fight the Red Army in the Baltic, he organized a Freikorps: "Berthold's Iron Legion." The diseased arm didn't affect his ability to command, and as Count Truchs reported, the man had a heart:

> He had a fiancée even before the war—I was one of the few who knew about that. He would permit himself to marry her before victory had been won. When the war was lost, though, he found that he could not ignore his promise. He asked her to remain patient until he was no longer needed by the revolution.[3]

In the words of a well-known song, "The water is wide." In this case, however, every effort is made to avoid crossing the gulf that separates the lovers. In fact flight from the fiancée seems to be one of the driving forces behind Berthold's repeated returns to arms.

To men for whom death for the fatherland apparently had a powerful unconscious significance, a woman who cannot wait the warrior's return is, in the last analysis, unimportant. In the end it is Berthold who does the suffering. *He* does not permit himself; *he* cannot ignore his promise to marry; *he* must ask her to be patient, while she—assuming he survives all that suffering—merely has to wait for him to marry her. The only goal she is allotted in life is that of becoming Mrs. Berthold. As long as she remains within that framework, she is Berthold's angelic bride—speak only good of the dead. The moment she begins to develop a life of her own, she disappears as if by magic from the narrative, never to be mentioned again. From the start, indeed, she is no more than a fiction. She never appears in her own right; she is only spoken *about*.

In Thor Goote's "documentary novel" *Comrade Berthold* (*Kamerad Berthold*), the reader is surprised on page 256 by the existence of a fiancée who had up to then been absent from the tale.

> For fifteen minutes he worked without looking up. Then, seeing the image of the young woman again, he leaned back once more. For weeks it had haunted him; much as he tried, he couldn't shake it loose. "A woman . . . My comrades would probably laugh if they knew how I agonize over a young thing who has just left the family nest!"

(She, too, is given no name.)

> He spent all his time gazing at her picture, feeling a strange sense of contentment radiating from those eyes. The transformation he had undergone through her made him a happy man. Life could not go on without this girl standing at his side, if only in thought.[4]

It *is* only in thought and it is only the *image* that has worked this supposed transformation. Berthold is the same fighter as always, only a little more worn down, a little closer to death, a little more worldly-wise. His arm is worse and defeat in the Baltic is at hand. It looks as if the fiancée is introduced here to associate Berthold with a particular fictive image of woman before he dies. That association will allow the myth of "Iron-Man Berthold" to become fixed in the memory of his comrades.

What is striking here is Berthold's conviction that only a German war victory, or at least a victory over the republic, will enable soldiers to become lovers and husbands, Germany must first attain the status of a "nation" if any of its soldiers is to "know" anything other than "only his fatherland." Since the representation of his personal sexual life is so closely bound up with concepts like "fatherland" and "nation," these concepts must be intimately related to the man's body and to its ability to make love to women. Germany's status as a non-nation drives a powerful wedge between the soldier and the marital bedchamber.[5] His male self-esteem is dependent on the status of Germany, *not* on his actual relationship with a woman.

After the "movement's" 1933 triumph, Dwinger—himself a Baltic veteran—filled several thousand pages with a hymn to the Freikorps fighters. We find him here reveling in elaborations on the theme of womanless warriors:

> "Haven't you ever been in love?" Werner abruptly asked.
> Truchs shrank back, retreated into silence. Finally, he whispered,
> "Yes. . . but she died—as my bride." He said nothing for
> awhile, then added, "I would like to love again. I sometimes
> have a dim feeling that new life awaits me there, new
> commitment—but I'm too old for that now. I'm too tired."[6]

Captain Werner, the man who asks the question so "abruptly," is hardly a stranger to the problem:

> "Now tell me, my dear Werner," he said at a staff gathering.
> "Reckow's letters made me think of asking whether you have
> ever?. . ." "Ever what?" Werner asked distractedly. He was
> storing away a bundle of papers, hunched over his work as
> always and pedantically folding each item. "Sighed, kissed, made
> love," Killman laughed. "No," said Werner matter-of-factly.
> "That's what I thought," Killman confirmed as he sauntered
> over to Wolter.[7]

Next Killman asks the same question of the rest of the officers. Not one of them is married or has designs on a woman. The commander himself is not asked; there is no need:

> "Do you really need to ask? Are you such a poor judge of
> character? He has no idea there are such things as women. He
> never had one, not even in the cadet corps. No, he believes in
> the old saying: 'Swear an oath to the black flag alone, and you'll
> have nothing else to call your own!' That's really true of all of
> us, or at least it should be," he pondered on. "Freikorps men
> aren't almost all bachelors for nothing. Believe me, if there
> weren't so many of their kind, our ranks would be pretty damn
> thin!"[8]

Real men lack nothing when women are lacking. That belief gives a particularly repulsive edge to Dwinger's "sympathy" for men whose women have died and left them. A sympathy that barely conceals this method of eliminating women from his writings. Behind the seeming benevolence of his question, "Who can blame her?" there is contempt; for the only life worth living is in the company of Berthold or one of his men. When Werner "matter-of-factly" denies that "he had ever . . ." he is denying the "fact" of female existence. In his remarks about the "good old boy" who doesn't know "there are such things as women," Dwinger brings his denial of women to a head under the pretext of a harmless joke.*

Denial of women is only natural, and therefore worthy. Dwinger plays dumb by having his warrior Pahlen philosophize: "Freikorps men aren't almost all bachelors for nothing. Believe me, if there weren't so many of them, our ranks would be pretty damn thin!" "Believe me" is an order; it demands that anyone who wants to join the troops should leave women behind. The men one meets there don't need women.

Dwinger lets women die or drop out of the picture before they can reach the status of wives, that is, before they can "belong" to a man. He doesn't kill these figures off himself; he assigns that task to the Reds, who provide the image of evil for his larger worldview.** Whenever Dwinger has no further use for women in his construction, he makes ideological capital out of their deaths:

> "I had such a beautiful young wife . . . the Reds beat her to death while I was off at the front. But I've avenged her already and will keep avenging her. I'll send thousands after her to their graves, like kings of olden times."[9]

The "beautiful young wife" serves as a pretext for murder. Wild, young Pahlen may have been indifferent to her while she was alive. It is clear now where pleasure is to be had: in "vengeance." Pleasure that contact with the beautiful young wife did not provide. The avenger's formulation also seems to betray the fact that the idea of seeing his wife with other men is a relatively pleasant one. It is striking that he intends to send the murdered "Reds" *after* her to their graves. Is the oath of vengeance really directed at the wife herself? Isn't the text really saying something like this?

> I had such a beautiful young wife. She went to bed with other men while I was off at the front. But I've avenged her already

---

*After 1933, Dwinger wrote expressly to serve the interests of the fascist state, which needed men like him to perpetrate acts of terror in the domestic class struggle and to carry on its necessary war with other nations. He consciously articulated themes that in the writings of the other frequently cited authors seem to have slipped into the text almost of their own accord.

**The device is a product of the inauspicious tradition of the bourgeois Bildungsroman and has since become the rule in "pulp novels." Characters who have served their purpose within the author's intended ideological framework are suddenly torn from the action (by floods, accidents, auto wrecks, communists). The rigid systems of rules governing such novels prevent the authors from simply abandoning characters whom they no longer need for their (didactic) demonstrations; instead they must be "bumped off."

and will continue to avenge her for to me she is dead. Let her
make love to anyone she pleases. I'll deliver the lovers
myself—as corpses. I'll send thousands into her bed, turning it
red with their blood, as was the custom among ancient kings. I'll
find ecstasy in killing.

To read the text in this way is, in the first instance, to resort to conjecture and to the exaggeration of certain of its features. It remains to be seen whether such a reading is justified. The end of the quote seems, however, in one sense to legitimate this way of reading. Although it was by no means customary to send "thousands" to their graves in the wake of "ancient kings," a number of such kings did indeed have their property—and hence also their wives—interred alongside themselves.

DE-REALIZATION

A change of scene. After the war. A man and woman in a lecture hall:

I'm sitting next to her at the lecture. She is bashful. Assiduously,
she applies herself to noting the fact that the home of the
original Germanic tribes was probably on the lower Danube, or
somewhere or other. How should I know? I hear her breathing
quicken, feel the warmth of her body, and smell the fresh scent
of her hair. Her hand rests carelessly almost at my side. Long,
narrow, and white as freshly fallen snow.[1]

Under the man's gaze, the woman is transformed into something cold and dead. The man is Michael, in Goebbels' post-World War I novel of the same name, who gazes at the hand of his beloved Herta Holk. Like so many women in these novels, she has the ability to evaporate as the story progresses.*

Relationships with women are dissolved and transformed into new male attitudes, into political stances, revelations of the true path, etc. As the woman fades out of sight, the contours of the male sharpen; that is the way in which the fascist mode of writing often proceeds. It could almost be said that the raw material for the man's "transformation" is the sexually untouched, dissolving body of the woman he is with.

To soldiers returning from battle, women seem to have lost their reality. Lettow-Vorbeck (Africanus) stops over in Italy on his journey home. He visits a museum:

---

*Of course, a professor of literature was right in pointing out to me that this is merely traditional imagery: white skin/snow, gleaming teeth/pearls. Goebbels was a good student of literature.

LOISEAU-ROUSSEAU DIE PERLE

This picture hung over her parents' bed for as long as she could remember—
according to the General Lettow-Vorbeck's daughter.

> In Rome, I was struck by the charming sculpture of Mars in
> repose. He has put aside sword and shield and is smiling wist-
> fully as Cupid strokes his knee, eyeing him impishly. Colonel
> Trench has told me in Southwest Africa how overwhelming it
> would be to see white women after years of colonial warfare.
> Mythology had captured the ancient relationship between Mars
> and Venus with complete psychological accuracy.[2]

Leaving aside the fact that this is a beautiful example of the pomposity
of Prussian officers' pronouncements on culture, it is striking that Lettow
unceremoniously substitutes a museum *statue* for the "white women" Colonel Trench had talked about. What is more, it is the statue of a *man*, Mars
in repose. The relationship between Venus and Mars seems to Lettow to
have been "captured with complete psychological accuracy" for the simple
reason that there is no Venus present; for Cupid, who strokes the knee of
Mars, is a boy.

It is not sinking into the arms of real women that was one of the recurrent fantasies of the exhausted soldier in the trenches, but marching home
through columns of jubilant women. In that, he was later to be
disappointed:

Returning from the field, the Bremen Regiment looked forward to parading into the city with full honors, as promised. Instead of bouquets and pristine maidens in white, they were met by machine guns and, in the first moment of shock, were disarmed.[3]

Pristine maidens in white: like Lettow's statue or Goebbel's snow-white hand.

HANDS OFF!

Whenever the possibility of sexual relations with women arises in these accounts, the writer takes pains to point out that nothing actually happens. Munich, May 1919. Searching for billets after the defeat of the republic of workers' and soldiers' councils:

> No lover of luxury, I stood firm against the entreaties of a rich and charming widow from the Leopoldstrasse. She would enter my study to ask senseless questions, then make eyes at me.[1]

Instead, Rudolf Mann stayed "at the home of a baron," where his bed "was freezing." Women—like heating—are "luxuries," at least when they are real, "charming," and "widows." Yet in retrospect Mann could rave as he recalled *images* of women ("Oh, yes . . . and then there were the girls . . .") and fantasize about "fabulous quarters" with women, whiskey, and cigars.[2]

In the only reference to women in another report, we read:

> beyond that, we gained a true appreciation for the people of Munich, kindhearted, upright folk whose female representatives in particular spoiled us beyond reason.[3]

"Female representatives"—"gained a true appreciation." Their coffee and cakes may by all means be downed in celebration of victory—as long as a quick getaway is assured.

> We talked at length on that wind-whipped dike . . . we talked of many different things, but our secret whispering always ended on the topic of war and revolution. In the end, she shook herself and said, "Ah, there you go again. I'm freezing and we have to get home." I was annoyed that I'd spent all my time with this girl talking about those things, but that's how it was this time and almost every time.[4]

The perception of the "wind-whipped dike" obscures the image of the companion, who is simply "a girl." The route of defense against feminine enticements travels from "secret whisperings" to "war and revolution."

"That's how it was this time and almost every time"—and this is how it often is, in many variations in the texts. The affect that appears destined for the woman as love object takes a different turn, finds an image of violence, and couples with that:

> I plunge my gaze into the eyes of passing women, fleeting and penetrating as a pistol shot, and rejoice when they are forced to smile.[5]*

Jünger plays on one such coupling here. A pistol shot and a young girl's smile are brought into association, as if that were the most natural thing in the world.

On the evening of a one-day leave from the war, Ernst Jünger approaches a woman on the street in Brussels. She is married to a worker who is away at the front. He is invited into her home:

> It was an hour of oblivion stolen from the war. For that hour I am her husband; I have escaped from the circle of fire and sit in peace with her before the fireplace, hand in hand. Tomorrow, yes tomorrow my brain may be shot to flames. So be it.
>
> As we part at the threshold, the wind and rain blowing through the door into the hallway she says, "Je ne t'oublierai pas." I will not forget you. She sounds genuine. I cross the bridge back into the city, my hands in my coat pockets and my head lowered. My spurs rattle each step of the way.[6]

He then meets a fellow soldier and they go together to a tavern. We are by now worlds away from the laconic simplicity of a comment by Brecht on two strangers who find themselves spending the night together in the same room: "and then love broke out between them."[7] The moment of parting: as if he had to defend himself against the warmth of her breath, he feels "wind and rain blowing . . . into the hallway" as she talks, just as Salomon prefers to perceive the "wind-whipped dike" as opposed to the movements of his companion's body. Jünger snatches "an hour of oblivion" from the war (a loss which that war can surely take in its stride), not a night shared by two warm, living bodies. How is he to handle this woman? In holding hands with her, he deprives her of sensuousness, placing her within his fiction of a male-female relationship. This fraternal gesture, an adolescent defense ritual, both keeps her at a distance from his body and banishes the fear of having his desire returned by the girl, or vice versa.

---

*"I have such sweet and pleasant dreams/of my darling and the slaughterhouse." Those are lines from a Swiss military song sung by the provision detachments: a butcher's song. (Bächtold, *The Life and Language of the Swiss Soldier* [*Aus Leben und Sprache des Schweizer Soldaten*], Basel, 1916. p. 39.)

Walking hand-in-hand is, among other things, a sign of the incest taboo between brothers and sisters.

The pompous declaration "I am her husband" makes him seem even more pathetic. And how easily he slips from the world of his desexualized idyll to the Eros of warfare: "Tomorrow, yes tomorrow my brain may be shot to flames." The scene closes with a further image of violence, a little more restrained this time: "My spurs rattle each step of the way." Those are cold and threatening sounds, omens of bloody contacts.

Jünger was not essentially a cold man. One glance at his evocations of warfare is enough to show the immense trouble he takes to write of the "encircling fire" of the front as a series of gigantic eruptions of the senses. Yet the house of a Brussels working-class woman is presented as a haven of refuge from the "encircling fire." Being with the woman actually frees him—momentarily at least—from threatening, erotic thoughts. The class difference between them plays its part in desexualizing the experience. Outside of a brothel, Jünger, or indeed any other officer of the Freikorps or the Imperial Army, would certainly not have got too close to a working-class woman—at least not with benevolent intent. This woman has a husband at the front, a comrade-in-arms. Jünger might shoot the man, but not deceive him. He speaks of him sympathetically.

> I picture him clearly, this simple *poilu*, and feel like a brother toward him. No doubt he feels the burden of war as much as I

do. We might soon be facing each other across the battlefield, quite close, without knowing it. Only our bullets, whizzing overhead, will almost touch.[8]

There are resonances of empathy between Jünger and the (absent) husband, but with the wife, there is only oblivion.

Thor Goote's Captain Berthold turns down a similar opportunity for a quiet, peaceful time with a young French woman:

> Rudolph Berthold stands in the twilight, the fragrance of the last roses wafting through the door. It swings open: Is everything all right, does he need anything else? The words drop gently, resonating.
>
> The girl steps up to him. Leaning against the window, he perceives her outline dimly in the darkness of the room. He sees those eyes, senses that this girl is not hostile.
>
> He remains where he is, his hands gripping the windowsill.
>
> It is the last night of summer, the last night of fleeting youth—of youthful abandon! It would be good to forget everything, to press his face up against that of another. . . .
>
> The heavy scent of the garden drifts into the room. The front is a distant irritation, then moves closer, a clear sound of blasting.
>
> The girl stands there, her head bent as if under some load. His eyes open wide, Berthold stares past that face, yet sees it. His hands tighten around the wood, but still he feels this young woman who asks each evening whether he wants anything else, and who will leave as gently as she has arrived. . . .
>
> His voice is hoarse. "No, thank you. Everything is in order!"
>
> The girl takes a deep breath. For an instant it seems she is about to take another step toward him—the last step separating them from each other. The girl raises her hand, but only to say gently, "Bon nuit." Then she is gone from the room.
>
> Berthold stands motionless.
>
> Rumbling deeply, bomber squadrons speed toward the enemy.
>
> "You must fulfill your destiny, not evade it!" he tells himself.[9]

At least three motifs here have counterparts in the Jünger text. Berthold "senses that this girl is not in any hostile mood." His formulation implies that the opposite would normally be the case. Jünger's impression of the working-class woman's parting remark (it sounds "genuine") implies

French postcard (1914). "Wilhelm, you shine upon night battles and witness how others win the day."

something more; women, he assumes, will lie as a matter of course. In the Goote text, too, the retreat from a possible sexual encounter leads into an image of violence: "Rumbling deeply, the bomber squadrons speed toward the enemy." Finally, Jünger talks of an "hour of oblivion," while for Berthold, "it would be good to forget everything." Bodily love with a woman is associated with forgetting, and women are a means to that end.

These men look for ecstasy not in embraces, but in explosions, in the rumbling of bomber squadrons or in brains being shot to flames. Berthold, having successfully escaped a woman, is reminded by sounds from the front that his "destiny" cannot be evaded in the same way. It is at the front, not in bed, that any future encounters will take place. The extent of Goote's distance from the reality of love relationships becomes clear in his failure to inject any semblance of sensuousness into his writings. He becomes either ridiculous ("the words drop gently, resonating"); sentimental ("the last night of fleeting youth—of youthful abandon!"); or trite ("the fragrance of the last roses wafting"). Not to mention the fact that the woman, if she were more French reality and less German fiction, would probably have said "bonne nuit."

And what kind of conception of the female body is expressed in the formulation, "His hands tighten around the wood, but still he feels this young woman . . ."? Not "thinks of," but "feels." In defending himself against potential intimacy, Berthold transforms the female body into an inanimate object. Hands tightening around an object usually indicate fear of losing control, of fainting, or, conversely, of letting go and striking out—or perhaps even, in this case, the fear that bodily contact produces a lightning flash, a body blow.

VISIONS

Captain Hans Rodenhelm, in Erich Balla's *Fighting Men* (*Landsknechte wurden wir*) is made to finish a glass of rum and fall asleep before the author allows him brief contact with a woman:

> The glass was empty, his head sank down onto his arm.
> And then—the strangest of experiences. Was it reality or a
> vision? He never found out.
> A soft, comforting hand runs tenderly through his hair. A
> gentle voice caresses his ear. "Don't be sad anymore, big
> brother, everything will be fine from now on. I'm here and I
> love you. I'll give you anything, anything your heart desires; just
> don't be sad anymore."
> An arm wraps itself around his neck, soft and warm. The
> drowsy sleeper feels the breath of a kiss at the back of his neck.
> He longs to spread open his arms and draw in the comforting
> happiness that surrounds him, but, exhausted as he is, paralyzed
> in his astonishment, he cannot lift even a finger.
> "Stay with me," the voice goes on. Slowly, his rigid body
> begins to slacken. He raises his head, but blinded by the glare of
> the candle, quickly drops it back down again. When he looks up
> again, in the shadow of the half-open door he momentarily sees
> the daughter of the family with whom he is billeted—so clearly,
> it can't be a dream. Her eyes are fixed on him with an expres-
> sion of infinite love and sadness. She waves a hesitant good-bye
> and then the door quietly closes.
> As he ponders that strange apparition, Holz comes to wake
> him up.[1]

Holz is a man. "His absolute matter-of-factness and sober pragmatism are infectious." Rodenholm feels sure of himself again. "And it's good to know that my nerves are under control again." And so:

> Farewell, sweet dream from a sweet fairy-tale land. I hear the
> call of men and men are right to call when weapons are heard
> clashing in the land.[2]

The only part of the vision Rodenholm sees clearly is the woman leaving the room. To the apparition, moreover, he is "big brother." (One kind of door, then, is closed *before* she leaves the room.) Yet he feels such a strong yearning for this sisterlike woman that she must be made to appear in a vision.

Albrecht, the hero of Franz Schauwecker's *The Nation Awakes (Aufbruch der Nation)*, does not shake off his nocturnal visitor quite so easily:

> The night brought with it an oppressive, enervating presence. It crawled forth from the corner of the room, closed all the doors, and stayed with him until morning.

The presence is a dancer he dimly remembers meeting somewhere. She sings the same song, over and over again: "Moon, from what paradise do you come on wings?" In the end, she looks at him and he sees that she recognizes him too:

> In her glowing smile, quite silent, is a bewitching mixture of love, triumph, passion, and promise. She begins to laugh as she had sung, from somewhere deep in her throat: a warbling laugh, a tinkling bell announcing some celebration.
>
> He can contain himself no longer. He draws her close, for she belongs to him and he cannot let her go. She does not offer the slightest resistance. Bending her body almost imperceptibly, she glides over to him. . .what else can she do? After all, she belongs to him and her place is with him.
>
> They lie next to each other. She lifts her arms and her dress slips off. Underneath it she is naked. Her nakedness assaults him with a sudden glowing shudder, a gust of wind across a placid lake. He says nothing, but with a jolt his breath rushes into his blood, filling it with pearls of pure, quivering bubbles, a gushing froth, just as the blood of men shot in the lungs leaves them lying yellow and silent like corpses, while the blood spurts endlessly, gurgling and seething at every breath—breath which they heave up, groaning, as if by a block and tackle, the air is so heavy and leaden.

From her nakedness and his own pearl-filled blood, he is drawn by some magnetism toward the blood of men shot in the lungs—an image from which he can scarcely tear himself away. In the end, he has recourse to some general reflections on love, through which he is able to approach her once more:

> The room is lit up with the whiteness of her skin—a light that is pale and velvety, suffused with the scent of linden and elder trees caught in a light rain. Her voice whispers and rustles among the leaves, where bees buzz with their burdens of honey and pollen. The distant rumble of the front is a constant

background, an endless staccato fire of cannon, firing loads of iron and powder, sending up smoke and noise. They collapse, still whispering, moving eyes and hands, groaning and groping. Then, suddenly, they are dead and silent, where before they had been alive and screaming. "There, there," she sighs into his ear, "you're with me; it's only me here next to you."

She is shocked by her own words and her breathing becomes anxious. Has she said too much? Has she frightened him off? He doesn't respond. He is silent and unmoving. Swiftly she raises her head and searches convulsively for his face. She wants to look at him, see his face. But before she can see him, he pushes her back, gently, irresistibly. She feels that gentle power as a knife thrust of horrible sweetness. She tries to fend it off, but can't. Dizzy with tenderness, she slides into a purple daze. Her head spins faster and faster. She tries to stop it, but she is grasping at moving walls of smooth crystal: she cannot get a grip. Yet she doesn't need to hold herself up: the dizzy motion carries her. With a long, flowing sigh, she lets herself drop into the swirling whirlpool. In an instant, it lifts her up and carries her away.

He feels something overpowering, a cramp, a flaming essence of body and soul; it surrounds him like the scorching impact of fire out there in the trenches. It breaks over him and rises up within him, this glowing explosion, a fiery seed planted in his heart, a bursting star.[3]

Schauwecker's text might help explain what it is that so regularly makes · this desire, which begins by seeking satisfaction in woman as object, take flight before it achieves its goal, the affect displacing itself onto some other ideational representative. For Schauwecker actually breaks free of that pattern, though not before he has reproduced it three times over. His first attempt leads only to a representation of "men shot in the lungs"; his second, to the two of them lying "dead and silent"; the third to a "knife thrust of horrible sweetness." Yet finally he reaches her, and she him, to dissolve in a "swirling whirlpool" and a "glowing explosion." What these two experience is identical to the process of "being surrounded by the scorching impact of fire out there in the trenches."

Those are *not* metaphors for orgasm. This is no transition, it is an ending; not tension-and-release, but tension-and-explosion. In Schauwecker's vision, the scales are finely balanced between fear of, and longing for, that ending. Perhaps desire finally tips the scales here—whereas with other writers it might be anxiety.* In all of these texts, could it be that

---

*In this sense, the relationship between the protagonists Albrecht and Gertie in Schauwecker's *The Nation Awakes* (*Aufbruch der Nation*) is different from those in other

the fear of dissolution through union with a woman actually causes desire to flee from its object, then transform itself into a representation of violence?

Schauwecker's text also gives some indication of the possible nature of the love object that is the target of his at once pleasure-seeking and anxiety-ridden desire. The fantasized object cannot be clearly distinguished from the fantasizer. She "belongs to him," she seems to be a part of him. When she says, "you're with me; it's only me here next to you," she is shocked at herself, as if she has said too much. Are we dealing here with a *forbidden* love object? Is she someone he is permitted to know, but must not be allowed to recognize? Spending the night in one room with her, he feels *incarcerated*. She is an "enervating presence" that "crawled forth from the corner of the room" (she does not come from outside): she "closed all the doors and stayed with him until morning."

There are echoes here of descriptions of symbiotic relations with women, in which the man feels trapped and from which, under certain conditions, he never manages to free himself completely. Are the wives left nameless because they are somehow associated with the object of these visions? Is that why women aren't allowed to appear in clear, concrete form, leading lives of their own?[4]

ERASING THE STAIN

General von Lettow-Vorbeck was once forced to defend himself against rumors that he was a ladies' man. The occasion was a sea voyage to join his troops in Africa:

> Prince Wilhelm of Sweden boarded with his retinue, out to hunt lions in Kenya. My table mate was a Danish woman, Karin Dinesen. She was engaged to Baron Blixen-Finecke, another Swede who owned a coffee plantation in Kenya and who intended to marry her when she arrived in Mombasa. We struck up a friendship. Her Somali servant boy, Farah, had traveled to Aden to meet her, and I presented him with a portrait of a horseman, instructing him to give it to his boss-woman as a wedding gift. Inscribed on it was the following well-known poem:
>
> > The greatest paradise on earth
> > Is found astride a horse's girth,

works mentioned here. It is almost a love story; yet everything changes when Albrecht goes off to war. We see Gertie less and less, and toward the end of the novel—it's been a long time since they've been in contact—she appears to him through the machine-gun housing as a kind of ghost, and he "knows" that she is dead.

> In the health of the body,
> Or at the breast of a lady.

She was an intelligent, highly cultured woman who was later to shoot a good number of lions. We corresponded up until the war.[1]

Again, the first striking feature of this passage is Lettow's almost caricatural thoroughness in recording the names and origins of the people he meets on his voyage. In contrast to Lettow's wife, even the Somali servant boy is honored with public recognition of his first name, Farah. Lettow's attention to detail has two clear functions here. First, the woman comes from a respectable family and is therefore above suspicion; second, she is much more of a "boss" than a "woman"—a fact which she proves by shooting "a good number of lions." Her enjoyment of this explicitly male pastime leads Lettow to remark that she is "highly cultured." The notion of being cultured has close affective associations with shooting and fighting, both of which are also masculine categories. Yet the real key to this tale lies elsewhere. Years later, Lettow reads the book *Out of Africa*. Its author is none other than that Danish woman, Karin Dinesen. He notes that "I too am mentioned in it." The inscription on the portrait is, however, misquoted. Dinesen writes:

> The greatest paradise on earth
> Is astride a horse's girth;
> And the health of the body
> At the breast of a lady.

I found this a little hard to swallow: it moved me to renew my contact with her. We laughed long and loud about her "German."[2]

The idea that someone he knew might read Dinesen's book and gain a false impression of his sexual outlook, or perhaps even his sexual behavior overseas, apparently haunted Lettow until he received written confirmation from Dinesen that this Danish German was not penned by him. Her letter could then be produced as evidence in situations of potential embarrassment. There is more in play here than simple prudishness or questions of morality; we are dealing with the warding off of a *threat*.

In an account of his days in the army, Lieutenant Ehrhardt recounts how he once succeeded in exposing a navigation officer who pretended to be a paragon of virtue. Sailing along in a boat one night ("We were shooting birds in the moonlight"), he spots the "noble paragon" in another boat with a Swedish girl. "From that point on, his reputation was ruined," he writes, adding that "some have a passion for hunting and others for other things."[3]

Frisian girls awaiting Hindenburg in Klanxbüll.

If the episode was humiliating for the other man, for Ehrhardt it is a tale of triumphant revenge.

As a high-school student, Ehrhardt had been interested in photography. His habit of proudly showing young women around his darkroom gave rise to certain rumors. When one of Ehrhardt's teachers suggested in front of the class that there might be some connection between those darkroom visits and Ehrhardt's failure to learn his vocabulary, the young man struck him. He was expelled from school. The fact that his father, a strict pastor, approved his son's behavior in this instance shows how monstrous the reproach must have seemed.[4]

To return to Lettow and his concern for his public image; on a visit to his brother and sister-in-law's in Flensburg, when he was about fifty years old and at the height of his renown, an extraordinary sight meets his eyes. Behind a row of "young ladies dressed in white," he spots a sign that reads "Mate with Lettow-Vorbeck for 20 cents." He completely loses his composure. Perturbed as he is, he sits through the speech of welcome without hearing a single word. When it is over, he is relieved to learn from his sister-in-law that his stepdaughter is the author of this notice. So much does she admire him that she has named her buck rabbit Lettow-Vorbeck and is now peddling its prowess to interested rabbit-keepers at twenty cents a head.

The general is staggered to think that his potency might be traded on the open market—and at bargain-basement prices. He calls it "the most perverse experience of my entire life."[5]

Dwinger, meanwhile, invents the character Feinhals to represent the "stain" men pick up from running after women. Feinhals is no regulation soldier; though his job is to look after the horses, he is something of a jack-of-all-trades. Feinhals's true forte, however, is spying on Reds. He is constantly chasing women, but somehow never catches them:

> He toddled off toward the stables, but not without first stopping
> in the chicken yard. There he saw a bright, pleated skirt flapping
> in the wind. Soon enough, his comrades heard him happily
> crowing.[6]

Dwinger makes him into a big baby who "crows" at the sight of a woman's skirt and who gives his comrades-in-arms endless excuses for the sparring they so enjoy. Once, when he can't get to sleep, for example:

> "Maybe he and that blonde girl . . ." the student tried to say.
> "The blond girl!" Feinhals angrily shot back. "You old
> snotnose! If you want my opinion, she's a silly goose!" "Aha!"
> said Pahlen, continuing to probe until he finally hits home:
> "We've got wind of your little game."[7]

In short, anyone caught dealing with women has blown his cover; he is hit by his companions and bleeds.*

When he was still young enough to play Cowboys and Indians, Manfred von Killinger (Peter, in his autobiography), once captured a schoolmate's sister, Else and took her to his secret cave:

> As they sat together among the fallen leaves, Peter said, "Well
> now you have to be my squaw. We bandits take pity on women
> and treat them well. We steal precious stones and jewels too, to
> give you as presents."
>
> Peter had never thought too much of girls, and he couldn't
> stand the boys who flirted with them. Now that he and she were
> sitting together in the cave, though, he thought those boys might
> have the right idea after all. This Else was a damned pretty girl.
> He found himself wanting to kiss her.
>
> "Hey, Else," he said. "Now that you're a squaw you
> belong to me, because I'm the chief. We have to seal our union,
> so you have to give me a kiss."

Else refuses at first, but gives in when Peter promises that next winter he'll go skating only with her.

> Peter peered through the opening and listened to make sure

---

*In Dwinger's novels *The Last Riders* (*Die letzten Reiter*) and *Halfway* (*Auf halbem Wege*), Büschen, the boy in charge of the horses, is the only exception to that rule. He gets the blonde girl Feinhals had written off as a "silly goose." Büschen is not so much a soldier in heart and soul as the others. He turns to farming, and a farmer needs a woman—to be his maid. (*Halfway*, p. 552)

no other Indians were sneaking around to watch them. The coast was clear.

Then he took hold of Else's blonde head and gave her a kiss. Else didn't move a muscle.

"Good," Peter said. "Only don't tell a soul about this; it will be our secret. Now I'm going to tie you to a tree and call the others. I'll say you didn't like me, so I had to sentence you to death."

"It's just a game, isn't it?" she asked nervously.

"Of course."

He pulled out an old clothesline and made Else stand against a tree. Peter tied her up to the tree so she couldn't move at all. Then he let out his war cry. The other Indians hurried over. They were more than a little surprised to see Else tied to the tree.

With iron countenance, Chief Winnetou growled: "She has scorned me. She is a spy for the 'Bloody Hand.' Let her die a martyr's death at the stake."[8]

Peter feels constrained both to cover his sexual tracks and to take revenge on Else for allowing herself to be kissed. Killinger goes out of his way to show that Else is truly afraid. He also builds three guarantees of Peter's safety into his story. The first is the assurance that no one is watching. The second is the fact that Else doesn't move a muscle; she certainly didn't seduce *him*. Finally, her passivity is underscored by having her tied so tightly to a tree "that she can't move at all."

That story is not significant in and of itself; its significance lies in its inclusion in Killinger's autobiography. The adult Killinger, prime minister of Saxony, takes pleasure in the image of Else at the stake. To extort a kiss and then punish the object of extortion, is to say that she was at fault for being so enticing. Any woman who is neither whiter-than-white virgin, nor statute, vision, nocturnal apparition, princess, becomes a threat that must be warded off, for instance through the discipline of the military march. We learn this from the way in which Captain Heydebreck, later commander of a Freikorps, proudly describes the attitude of his troops during their retreat through Belgium in November 1918:

> The demeanor of the troops was exemplary. On my orders, they marched that long march through the streets in tight formation, a corps of merciless avengers, the honor guard of destiny. Not one woman, not even prostitutes, had the audacity to approach them; they would have trampled everything and everyone underfoot. In Prussian goose step, they marched past me through the square in front of the city hall. They halted and stood firm there, a rock amid the surge of the gaping masses.[9]

What massive resistance to the mere possibility that women might be on the streets while Heydebreck's troops marched through! Not to mention how unlikely it would have been for those Belgian women to have thrown their arms around the necks of a successfully defeated occupying force. What is it, then, that Heydebreck is defending himself against? Is it the women who, for no justifiable reason, he automatically turns into prostitutes? Hardly. More likely it's just the opposite, namely, the idea that the soldiers themselves might approach the women, now that they had no war to win anymore and no hope of pay to underwrite asceticism. Once again here, an affect once set in motion, reverses itself and sets off in another direction, to emerge as a wish for destruction: "trampling everything and everyone underfoot" is the response that Heydebreck believes he may expect from his men. "Everything" is the evil of defeat, "everyone," the women—as if they were to blame for the lost war. It is *women* that this "corps of merciless avengers," this "honor guard of destiny," seems to grind underfoot as it marches. The men "halt" and "stand firm," a phallus against the dissolution that surrounds them, remaining hard against the onslaughts of surging womanhood. The women would love to have the "audacity to approach" the troops, but they dare not. Those boots are made for "trampling."

If the erotic woman is the terrain of warfare, then in Schauwecker's *The Nation Awakes* (*Aufbruch der Nation*), the soldier Aberhlf fights a hopeless battle on that terrain. He steals bread from his division and brings to a French beauty:

> a fabulous fortress of blossoms, curls, and flashing eyes; Verdun in miniature, so to speak, and in its way just as unnerving, just as pale and fragile and dizzying as its larger counterpart.[10]

Aberhof deserts to that fortress and comes to a bad end.

FORMS OF DEFENSE

The preceding sections have brought to light a number of recurrent forms of defense, through which an affect avoids contact with women. The abrupt curtailment of a movement toward woman produces thoughts and images related to acts of violence. The idea of "woman" is thereby coupled with representations of violence, as for instance:

> I . . . sit in peace with her before the fireplace. Tomorrow, yes, tomorrow my brain will be shot to flames.[1]

And the image of other men interposes itself, repressing that of the woman:

> seeing the image of the young woman again . . . For weeks it had haunted him . . . My comrades would probably laugh if they knew . . .

The man withdraws by becoming passive, "playing dead":

> He longs to spread open his arms and draw in the comforting happiness that surrounds him, but, exhausted as he is, paralyzed in his astonishment, he cannot lift even a finger.

An idea, a symbol, an attitude, a standpoint—any of these can intervene between man and woman and take their places:

> Women? . . . Are there such things? "Swear an oath to the black flag alone, and you'll have nothing left to call your own!"

Women are robbed of their sexuality and transformed into inanimate objects:

> How overwhelming it would be to see white women after years of colonial warfare . . . (a remark prompted by the viewing of a sculpture—and a male one at that).

Yet the man may become similarly lifeless. "As if I were long dead". . . . the fragment of a song that Gerhard Scholz, the main protagonist of Hanns-Heinz Ewers's *Riders in the German Night* (*Reiter in deutscher Nacht*), can't get out of his mind. It had been sung to him by his mother.[2]

In the case of wives, there is always some male "guarantor" in the background to testify to their sexual purity and the suitability of their origins. Three of the women here were vouched for by "brothers," a guarantee that is doubly valid when those "brothers" are also friends of the husbands. An allusion to the father vouched for the purity of two other wives. The image of another woman was saved from tarnish by the names of Schiller, Friedrich, and Heinrich George; another, by Goethe and Tischbein. In the latter case there was also an officer, Lieutenant Christiansen, whose reputation as an officer and a gentleman was well known from the war.

A SOLDIER'S LOVE

To say that these texts were entirely devoid of eroticism would be untrue. Although descriptions of love scenes may be rare, they nonetheless occur. Hellwig, Dwinger's student, for instance, has a sweetheart:

> . . . tentatively he drew his fingers across the surface of her breast, wondering at the easy, full-blooded pulsing of the powerful arteries underneath.[1]

His sweetheart has "soft lips" and a "sinewy body."

Kossarew, an immigrant Russian anti-Bolshevist serving in the same Freikorps, "sucks" the lips of a loved one in a kiss, while his own lips bring forth

> the rapid sounds of all manner of caresses. In a silent exchange, he drinks in the breath of his beloved and tenderly offers her his own.[2]

Another soldier with his beloved:

> "How warm you are," he said with devotion, "how full of life, how sweet your breathing. . . . What comes after you will not be breathing; it will be cold forever. . . . It will be like this, the way I feel it now, in this silent moment when I can feel your breath."[3]

The use of expressions such as "arteries" and "full-blooded" may already have alerted attentive readers to the fact that the love objects in all three of these cases are horses. The first shows a student with an officer's horse:

> The horses of the staff guards stood nearby, and with them the animals of the staff themselves. Truch's horse, his long-legged "Psyche," turned the slim neck whose soft skin was reminiscent of crushed velvet, and stared across at him, its ears bent forward. "What a horse!" the student thought with admiration." Just like its master! Just as tall, just as noble, just as gentle . . . and yet like him it's been through the entire campaign, wading through horrible swamps, living for days on end on nothing but the straw from thatched roofs. Our cold-blooded nags were long dead and gone, but this noble creature kept unswervingly on. Even if it had a tongue to speak with, it wouldn't have complained!"
>
> Hellwig stood entranced. He searched his pockets for a piece of bread and walked over to the stall of the dark-brown animal. He felt something akin to envy as he leaned against her sinewy body and she took the bread from his hand with her soft lips. He tentatively drew his fingers across the surface of her breast, wondering at the easy, full-blooded pulsing of the powerful arteries underneath.[4]

"Long-legged"—"slim neck"—"soft skin . . . reminiscent of crushed velvet"—"noble." Nowhere in all the memoirs of these soldiers, nowhere in the novels glorifying their battles, are women spoken of or perceived in anything like these terms. It would be unthinkable in these circles for a man to stand "entranced" before, or make advances to the woman of his desires. That would bring a death sentence; the author would have the man in question killed off in the next battle.

It is more than conceivable, however—as in the case of the student, Hellwig—for one man to think of another man in loving terms. Dwinger's use of language makes little effort to conceal the fact that the sexual advance toward the horse, which looks, "just like its master . . . just as tall . . . noble . . . gentle," is really directed toward that master, Count von Truchs, the secret object of his devotion. (The horse, it should be noted, is invariably "masculine." Kossarew reports that he regularly saluted his old horse[5]—and no soldier would salute a woman.)

EXCURSUS ON "HOMOSEXUALITY" AND
WHERE WE GO FROM HERE

Are we then dealing with "homosexuality"? As a catchword, it seems appropriate here, but does this really get us anywhere? A number of writers have identified homosexuality as an essential component of aggressivity among soldier males. "Latent" homosexuality in particular is seen to create enormous reserves of energy by suppressing drives, which in turn demand release in aggression. Wilhelm Reich, for example, writes:

> During the war it would be observed that those who had strong heterosexual commitments or had sublimated fully, rejected the war; by contrast, the most brutal, gung-ho types were those who regarded women as toilets, and who were either latently or manifestly homosexual.[1]

Freud seemed certain that, in comparison with heterosexual love,

> homosexual love is far more compatible with group ties,* even when it takes the shape of uninhibited sexual impulses—a remarkable fact, the explanation of which might carry us far.[2]

Freud was unable to explain that "fact"; nor did he offer any material evidence in support of it. How far then can it be deemed to hold true? There might be some justification for taking these kinds of assumptions as a point of departure, as assertions to be proved or disproved, if only we had some sort of theoretically grounded understanding of what the term "homosexuality" might mean; if only there were some agreement about the form of social behavior, love relationships and preferred activities, possibilities for satisfaction of drives, forms of pleasure and unpleasure, communication structures, modes of thinking, feeling, and acting that might be expected from the type of person who is labeled homosexual, or latently homosexual. In the existing literature, however, we search in vain for any such general consensus.

Opinion also differs concerning the degree to which the cultural forms of capitalistic-patriarchal society may (or should) be seen as institutions of compensation for a more pervasive, latent homosexuality. Conceptions of homosexuality are so diffuse, so much a product of defensive processes— even among analysts themselves—*that we are forced to assume that the concept provides anything but a real understanding of what homosexuality is. It sets in motion a series of prejudices, false ideas, and personal-defense

---

*Freud gives the name "mass commitments" (*Massenbindungen*) to the organizational dynamics that occur in hierarchical institutions (e.g., the army, the church). The quotation here refers to the army. For a critique of Freud's use of the term "mass" in this context, see Elias Canetti, "A Critique of Freudian Methodology," in volume 2 of *Crowds and Power* (*Masse und Mache*).

mechanisms, to reach the strained-but-safe conclusion that homosexuals are always first and foremost the *others*. They are aliens, or even enemies, who are nothing like ourselves. They can be pinned down with a term like the "tough guy," whom Adorno had in mind when he added the following to his stock of aphorisms: "Totalitarianism and homosexuality go together."[3]

Within the context of Adorno's own system of values, this assertion can be seen to amount to an annihilation of those who were the victims of this totalitarian disease. To direct an accusation of this kind against Adorno appears particularly justifiable in relation to a proviso of his own insertion, in which his masculine allegiances come to light. For him the "tough guys," despite their alleged hatred of effeminacy, are "in the end . . . the true effiminates." Are we then dealing here with competition among males to determine who is the "real man"? Is effeminacy the worst imaginable shame?

Let's take another man, Brecht. In his journal entry of May 27, 1942, he noted:

> sitting for an hour one afternoon with feuchtwanger in his beautiful garden. he says they now have hormone injections in the army that remove all traces of homosexuality (though they have to have boosters every few months). now the army won't be any fun even for homosexuals.[4]

As men who enter army life of their own free will, homosexuals are once again seen as enemies here. (Strangely enough, the army doesn't like them either.) And what of Brecht himself? He was always reluctant to say anything that might betray his feelings for the people he had most to do with; yet in what may be the most candid entry in his journal, he calls Lion Feuchtwanger, the man whose garden provided a backdrop for weighty discussions on art and politics, a "true friend."[5] The repression-machine of the Feuchtwanger-friend Brecht must have been working pretty well for him to accept unconditionally that "all traces of homosexuality" might be swept aside by this kind of medical intervention.

At the very least, then, we may say that the attitudes of all these anti-homosexuals contain elements of masculinism. They are expressed with a self-confidence that emphasizes difference; with a kind of self-satisfaction at possessing qualities that are decent and "manly," as opposed to the horrible, perverse desires for which inoculation is the only cure. Decent men can get by with clever, materialist discussions on the difficulties of writing the truth, or even with the joyous birth pangs of powerful aphorisms.

The two authors cited above, though personal enemies, were engaged in a common struggle against prejudice; nonetheless, the passages quoted

---

*See the controversy between R. Reiche and H. Stierlin over Charles Socarides's *The Overt Homosexual*, in *Psyche* 26 (1972). More about that in volume 2.

Bertolt Brecht with Oskar Maria Graf in New York.

should suffice to show how fraught with prejudice the problem of homosexuality remains, even among the "enlightened."

For me there is one further reason to dispense with the term "latent homosexuality" as an explanation for specific modes of behavior. My aim here is to dissociate myself from a practice that has become widespread in psychoanalytic writing, particularly nonclinical psychoanalysis, in which psychoanalytic theories are applied to areas outside therapy. The prevailing tendency to bring certain determinate phenomena under the umbrella of a psychoanalytic concept—a procedure in which individual concepts are isolated from their contexts and evolutions within Freudian practice, from their relationships to very specific symptoms, from their functions within Freudian theory as a whole, and so on—this tendency leads to a number of somewhat arbitrary abstractions.* Even writings that attempt to gain a "handle" on psychoanalysis through theoretical science (as in Lorenzer) or through *Ideologiekritik* (the critique of ideology, as in M. Schneider), display an unmistakable tendency to reduce the phenomena under investigation to the most all-embracing of concepts possible. (As a rule, the mode of conceptualization here must be critical of Freud, while still remaining Freudian.) The malleability of the conceptual constructions which then emerge entices readers who have no chance to test their psychoanalytic knowledge against actual practice, to manipulate them in a way that bears little relation to phenomena in the real. Those constructs, which do a better job of ignoring real phenomena than of abstracting them, are particularly attractive to students who are not in clinical science, but who want to add psychoanalysis to their arsenal of theoretical tools ("approaches") and are not about to question such applications. The various attempts to sacrifice Freud-the-practicing-physician to Freud-the-philosopher belong in the same category.[6]

This widespread flight from concrete reality has become almost a reflex reaction. Its apparent goal is to dispel contradictions within social reality before they have a chance to make themselves apparent. That, of course, is highly inimical to psychoanalytic understanding, which proceeds through association and strict attention to detail. Too hasty a rush to reduce phenomena to a single concept functions as a massive obstacle, rather than a key to the perception of reality.

With all this in mind, I have attempted to avoid supporting my own prejudices with quotations from psychoanalytic writers and have tried instead to present typical specimens of the writings of soldier males, sticking closely to the text in every case. In the following pages, I will not attempt to apply any one psychoanalytic system to fascist texts; I will however look at psychic *processes*, such as the nature of the soldier males' object relations; or the type and intensity of his affects;[7] or, in relation to phenomena that we have in part already discussed, his typical psychic defense mechanisms.

In this way, I may be able to represent more closely the course of development of my own understanding, which evolved step-by-step as I read the books, rather than from any preconceived theory. The advantage for the reader will lie, I hope, in not being constantly surprised by the introduction of terms from some psychoanalytic system whose context is generally unfamiliar. A second advantage is that the material itself takes on a concrete shape for readers who, as victims of the injunction prevailing in Germany against learning about fascism and its antecedents, may be relatively unfamiliar with this material. Furthermore, the reading process will not be interrupted by passages of "universal" interpretation—an omission that should allow the readers' own critical faculties to be brought into play, and remove any obstacles to the formation of her or his own feelings and thoughts on the texts by some "know-it-all" author.

A SOLDIER'S LOVE (CONTINUED)

The soldier males' defense against women as love objects should by now have become evident. It is time to ask who, or what, these men *do* love. Are

---

*Or, especially in the case of academic "psychoanalytic literary criticism," to a kind of evaluation of writers' personalities that is on a par with interpretation of meaning in old-style German literary criticism.

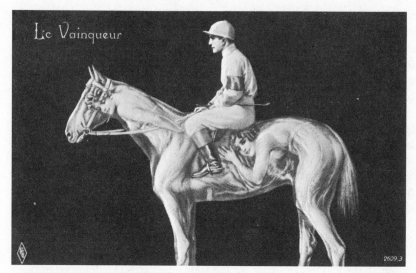

Le Vainqueur

French postcard.

there any objects with which they have relations that they themselves would recognize as love relations? Let us first return to the seven husbands who were introduced at the beginning. In his early childhood, Rudolf Höss had a great love of animals, in particular his pony, which is named Hans. As for his two sisters, who "were always strangers to me," their names are never revealed. His parents moved to the city when he was seven; the pony stayed behind.

> to my extreme regret there were no stables, no animals. Later on, my mother would often tell how for weeks I was almost sick with longing for my animals and my mountain forest. At the time, my parents did everything to rid me of my excessive love for animals. Nothing worked. I would look for any book I could find with pictures of animals, crawl off somewhere, and dream about my animals.[1]

Of his time as commandant of Auschwitz, Höss writes:

> If ever anything happened to disturb me, it was impossible for me to go home to my family, so I would mount my horse and gallop away the images of horror; or I would walk through the stables at night to find consolation with my darlings there.[2]

Manfred von Killinger adds the following preface to his book *The Joys and Sorrows of Life in the Putsch* (*Ernstes und Heiteres aus dem Putschleben*):

In writing this book, I was often reminded of my "Little Tiger." Of whom? Of a creature who loved me, whose great eyes gazed after me, questioning, when I was forced to leave him. I held his head in my hands and kissed his nose, and I cried. I am not ashamed of those tears. Little Tiger was better company than human beings; he was unable to speak.[3]

Martin Niemöller restrains himself from using that particularly ticklish term—the word that is so carefully avoided in descriptions of relationships with women—until he can use it to designate his feelings toward the first two parishes committed to his charge. "My first love," he says, "belonged to them!"[4]

Lieutenant Ehrhardt:

Even as a young boy I loved anything that could be used for shooting; and I bought my first pistol, which wasn't much to write home about, with pennies saved from the breakfast money I received for my walk to school from Weil to Lörrach.[5]

Ernst von Salomon:

I love unbroken people: men. The kind who have no problems; the kind who are self-contained, powerful, calm.[6]

Rossbach never mentions love, nor does Lettow-Vorbeck, though for the latter hunting is "a very great pleasure,"[7] just as it is a "passion" for Ehrhardt.

Some other love relationships: "How I loved my native village" (from Rudolf Berthold's diary).[8] "If you love Leipzig, enlist in the Leipzig volunteer Regiment" (from a 1919 enlistment poster).[9] Killinger talks of the "two-fold love of the homeland soil and of the community-of-blood (*Blutsgemeinschaft*)."[10] And then there are the men, the troops:

I think of the stalwart Thirty-eighth Homeguard Infantry
Brigade with the deepest love and pride. . . . (Crasemann)[11]
Captain von Flotow loved his cadets and his cadets loved him.
(Salomon)[12]
After three years of war, this regiment is as good as it ever was.
That's why I love these men and stand up to fight, like a mother
hen for its chicks, whenever blind ignorance threatens to tear it
apart. (Franz von Epp)[13]
"I could kiss our people," Bismarck wrote to his wife in 1866.
They were far worthier of love in this far more terrible
war. . . . (von der Goltz)[14]

Epp and Goltz were generals. Epp was the leader of a Bavarian Freikorps that was particularly active in the defeat of the Munich socialist republic in May 1919, and in putting down the March Revolution of 1920 in the Ruhr Valley. Von der Goltz was commander in chief of German troops in the "Baltic enterprise." Crasemann was press officer for the Maercker Freikorps.

> I simply can't live without my people . . . I can't live without my corps. . . . I have no other training, no wife or children, only my men. . . . What place would I have in the world without my soldier's greatcoat; what good would I be in this world without you? (Dwinger's Freikorps-commander Mannsfeld).[15]

The end of the relationship to the troops is thus depicted as the end of all relationships. There are resonances of suicide here.

"Young manhood was their only flame and intoxication," says Jünger of those men who would not at any price be anything other than soldiers.[16] As the leader loves his men, so the simple soldier loves his superior. "And so far as a warrior can love, he loved that man, his Langsdorff." (Donat, Dwinger's prototype of the brutal, professional fighter.)[17]

That type of bond, love for the leader, appears in one form or another in almost all of these writers. Love and battle:

> When blood whirled through the brain and pulsed through the veins as before a longed-for night of love, but far hotter and crazier . . . The baptism of fire! The air was so charged then with an overwhelming presence of men that every breath was intoxicating, that they could have cried without knowing why. Oh, hearts-of-men, that are capable of feeling this! (Jünger)[18]

What was all of it for?

> We are guided by our love for the German people and fatherland. (Lieutenant Ehrhardt).[19]
> Out of passionate love for our poor people. (Rudolf Mann)[20]
> For the abandoned German people . . . to whom we were devoted with a modest, passionate love. (Heinz Schauwecker)[21]
> We were left with a belief in Germany, with a love for its unfortunate people. (Mahnken)[22]
> Or simply: "love of the fatherland." (Höss)[23]

In countless different forms, then, the activities of these men in postwar Germany—their own part in the struggle against the revolution—are brought into association with the word "love." Perhaps a final example. This one is a journal entry Rudolf Berthold made at 8 P.M. on the evening of September 13, 1914:

> An hour ago I received the Iron Cross, Second Class. Other than

His Excellency von Bülow, I am the first in our army to wear that simple, solemn mark-of-distinction. . . . I kissed the Cross.[24]

A kiss that forges a lasting association out of this momentary and unexpected affinity with the commanding general, His Excellency von Bülow.

The type of man we have before us "loves":

—the German people, the fatherland
—the homeland soil, native village, native city
—the "greatcoat" (uniform)
—other men (comrades, superiors, subordinates)
—the troops, the parish, the community-of-blood among fellow countrymen
—weapons, hunting, fighting
—animals (especially horses)

Aside from the animals, all of the love objects on the preceding list are ones we've encountered previously in connection with movements of resistance to women as potential love objects.[25] In other words, these men claim to "love" the very things that *protect* them against real love-object relations!

The only human objects appearing here are men and male organizations.* It would be *possible* to draw the conclusion that something like homosexual libido must be in play here. If however I do *not* draw that conclusion, then this is because it seems to me that the *general* difficulty of establishing any object relations** is such a dominant theme in the material dealt with so far, that the whole matter first requires closer inspection.

When these men give their own reasons for their resistance to all that is feminine, they tend to point to the experience of war:

How can women understand us, when they gave nothing, when they shared nothing of our experience during those years of torment?[26]

Those words are spoken by Thor Goote's Captain Berthold as he stands watching his troops dancing at a ball. Or:

---

*Niemöller's "parish" is the only grouping that is not exclusively masculine. He parts company with the others in that regard.

**In psychoanalytic literature, a person toward whom drives are directed is designated an "object." For further discussion of terms such as "object relationship," I refer the reader to the *The Language of Psychoanalysis* by Laplanche and Pontalis. They outline the origins of each concept, along with its function in the thinking of Freud and his most important successors. Whenever I criticize psychoanalytic terminology (as when we come to "projection"), or whenever a term becomes particularly important for my argument, I will discuss it in the body of the text.

Rossbach and Hauenstein, alias Friedrich William Heinz.

> We soldiers are in the habit of respecting only those who have
> stood their ground under fire. That is why many of us inwardly
> turn away from women, even when outwardly we can't do
> without them.[27]

That explanation should be treated with caution. These men's resistance
to women may have been reinforced by the war, but it was hardly *created* by
the war. The origins of their attitudes may be found in the prewar,
Wilhelmine period.

A short anecdote told by Dwinger, for example, reveals the extent to
which anything connected with the term "Prussian" comes to be directed
against, and to exclude, women. Dwinger is referring here to General von
Watter, who led the army and Freikorps divisions against the workers'
rebellion in the Ruhr in March/April 1920:

> He refused to permit his orderly to polish his wife's shoes,
> for instance, giving as his reason: "A soldier is placed in my
> charge by the state. It is theft from that state when he performs
> work for anyone other than me!"
> "For heavens sake!" Wolter cried out.
> Truchs answered with a faraway look in his eyes, "That's
> what it means to be a Prussian!"[28]

Women have nothing to do with the "state." A state employee is a
slave, of course, but he is a slave of a man and himself a man. As such, he is
closer to the state than even the wife of a general. Women are on a par with

members of colonized races, the most prominent among whom still appear only on the level of white shoeshine boys.

WOMAN AS AGGRESSOR

There is something about women. Their image often appears in association with the eerie, the uncanny. The first reference to a woman in Ernst Jünger's *Battle as Inner Experience* (*Der Kampf als inneres Erlebnis*), for instance, reads:

> Cautiously we circled around the burned out ruins of wealthy estates, vaguely fearful of bumping suddenly into the ghosts of those who had been torn from their peaceful existences.
> . . . What might be hiding in the darkness of the cellars?
> The corpse of a woman, floating with tangled hair in black groundwater?[1]

There is no compulsion for him to conjure up the image of a dead women here—except perhaps the compulsion of his own fantasy.

Women also appear as agents of destruction. F. W. Heinz was a member of the Ehrhardt Brigade and OC; leader of a "self-defense" organization in Upper Silesia and of a Stahlhelm unit active against the French in the Ruhr in 1923. After 1933, he was a director of the Reich Literature Council and in 1938 a member of the circle around General Witzleben, who planned the removal of Hitler and a return to monarchy under Prince Wilhelm, eldest son of the crown prince.[2] Heinz ascribes the defeat of Polish troops in a 1921 battle near the Annaberg to the influence of women (he never actually saw the troops in question):

> Those 20,000 men were firmly encamped around the big cities, where they gradually degenerated in a stupor of shared whiskey bottles and dissolute womanizing.[3]

Neither did Bogislaw von Selchow, a naval lieutenant during World War I, "see" the objects of his writing. (After his time in the navy, von Selchow began studying in Marburg, where he commanded the Marburg Student Corps, which acquired a certain notoriety for murdering fifteen captured workers near Thal in Thuringia.) Describing a bullfight he attended during his time as a naval officer in Mexico, he writes:

> Now came the surprise: the protagonists of the fourth act were women. Young, beautiful amazons whisked gracefully into the arena. . . . For an instant, even the bull was taken aback by so much beauty. He caught the scent of women. . . . It wasn't a

pretty sight. The noble animal didn't deserve that. A fight? Well and good. But theater? No, he was too good for that.

In the end, one of the women singes the bull's hide with a firecracker:

The bull raised its mighty head. Who did that? The bull sensed the indecency of what had just occurred. . . . The silver amazon fled across the sand, but the bull, its honor wounded, was quicker. Would she reach the *tablas*? Breathless silence. The bull has her on his horns. He tosses her high into the air. A blood-drenched mass, silver and blue, lies in the sand.

At that point the bull is finished off by a real man.

Silently we went on board.
"Beasts," someone said.
He meant human beasts.
"I feel pity."
"For the bull?"
"No, for people who have never been anything but spectators. I envy the bull. Is there anything more glorious than a brief, untroubled life that comes to an end in a few moments of supreme heroism?"[4]

The bull—taken aback by beauty, catching the "scent of women," sensing the "indecency" of what is happening, "its honor wounded"—all at once its feelings are those of von Selchow, enraged at the appearance of women armed with lances. His satisfaction at seeing a "blood-drenched mass" that could no longer "whisk gracefully," is undisguised. The device of introducing tension through the phrases, "Would she reach the *tablas*? Breathless silence," serves to heighten the pleasure of seeing the female transgressor destroyed. She got what she deserved, while the bull displayed "supreme heroism." Slipping into the persona of the bull (as sacrificial victim), von Selchow commits a deeply satisfying, cold-blooded murder.

As a rule, there are two forms in which women appear as threatening, enervating, indecent, or aggressive:

Yet there were whores roaming about on the streets behind our troops at the battlefront. They waddled up and down the Friedrichstrasse whenever we were shooting from among the linden trees. With their aura of unutterable strangeness, they would throw themselves at us as we lingered for a short break in the shelter of the houses, still in the grip of the laws of a turbulent battle, the enemy still fixed in our sights. It wasn't their whispered propositions that seemed so intolerable; it was the easy, matter-of-fact manner in which they groped at our bodies,

bodies that had just been exposed to the ravages of machine-gun fire.[5]

The "whore," who with her "easy, matter-of-fact manner" does not recognize the soldier as abandoning a sexual activity when he drops his machine gun, is one manifestation of the woman as aggressor. The other, also described by Ernst von Salomon, has "blueness" as its distinguishing mark. This kind of woman appears en masse, as in this antimilitary demonstration against the Berthold Freikorps in Hamburg:

> Shaking their fists, the women shriek at us. Stones, pots, fragments begin to fly. . . . They hammer into us, hefty women dressed in blue, their aprons soaked and skirts muddied, red and wrinkled faces hissing beneath wind-whipped hair, with sticks and stones, pipes and dishes. They spit, swear, shriek. . . . Women are the worst. Men fight with fists, but women also spit and swear—you can't just plant your fist into their ugly pusses.[6]

The women who awaken that strong desire in Salomon are working-class women. Woe to the man who falls into the "filthy clutches of the Hamborn hussies";[7] there will literally be nothing left of him. "Whores" and "working-class women" are hard to tell apart. In a construction such as that of the "Hamborn hussies," they are made identical.

Returning from a tour of a working-class stronghold, the Ruhr Valley, Dwinger's spy, Feinhals, can report:

> The wildest of all were the women. I now believe everything we were told about Berthold's people! And there were always enough of their kind on hand—in that respect, they were better prepared than we were.[8]

(What they had heard was that Berhold's men had been scratched to pieces by a hundred raging women.")[9]

In Thor Goote's "documentary novel" about Berthold, the women go one step further:

> Women pounce on him, spitting, scratching, biting. . . .
> Women, shrieking, twist his arm-of-a-thousand-pains from its socket, tearing off his chain, stabbing his chest and back, kicking his body. "Spare my people," is his final moan. Then, shred by shred, the women rip the clothes from his body. Shots ring out.[10]

Hurrying to the scene of the murder that same evening, Goote notices the "little bracelet" worn by Berthold "gleaming on the arm of a prostitute" indicating her guilt.[11]

The clearest expression of the identification of proletarian women with whores comes from Hans and Berta Krafft, the model German couple in Zöberlein's novel *A Dictate of Conscience (Befehl des Gewissens)*:

> The gentle eyes in the lewd faces of those half-grown children told clearly enough where they had come from. Passing by, they heard one brazen imp loudly boast, "This floor is still too cold." And with no shame in front of the passersby, the other young scoundrel laughed, "It would be much nicer in bed, don't you agree?" The first boy lamented precociously, "If only the old folks weren't always watching."
> Hans and Berta exchanged shocked glances. "That's how they make proletarians," he said. Berta shuddered as if confronted with some hideous revulsion, then answered, "I suppose they'll grow up to feel completely at home in the company of pimps and streetwalkers."[12]

Soldiers are often seized with a "hideous revulsion" when they come into contact with the proletariat. This is Salomon, once again, describing house-to-house searches for arms in Berlin:

> two women were still lying in bed when we entered, each of them with a child. One of them let out a shrill, gasping laugh, and the others crowded around her door. The corporal came closer. Quick as lightning, she lifted the blanket and her dress;

smooth white cheeks let out a resounding snort. Recoiling before them, we heard the others begin screeching, laughing uproariously, slapping their thighs, they couldn't get enough of laughing, even the children were laughing.[13]

Major Delmar encounters something very similar during the "taking" of a brothel that happens to be caught immediately between the two fronts in one embattled industrial region:

> Only one of them, the redhead, dared to plant herself naked in front of me, laughing in my face. Her full breasts bounced up and down as she laughed. The aereolae were big and brown. The sight of her disgusted me. The red she-devil must have read my thoughts, for suddenly she turned around with a loud screech and presented me with her behind, slapping it all the while.[14]

The description of the proletarian woman as monster, as a beast that unfortunately cannot be dealt with merely by "planting a fist" in its "ugly puss," hardly derives from the actual behavior of women in situations such as those described above (even here, they are hardly let off lightly). Rather, it can be traced to an attempt to construct a fantastic being who swears, shrieks, spits, scratches, farts, bites, pounces, tears to shreds; who is slovenly, wind-whipped, hissing-red, indecent; who whores around, slaps its naked thighs, and can't get enough of laughing at these men.[15] In response to some secret need, this monster is identified with the proletarian woman—an idea formulated most clearly in the following example from Delmar:

> "Hatred is the most purely proletarian of emotions!"
> "It is perhaps to that sinister truth that we may look for explanations when we read of the mutilations of our wounded in battle reports from the first weeks of the war. Almost without exception, it was the women and girls of the industrial population who practiced such cruelties. They were much rarer in agricultural regions. Those outrages were called forth by the release of every vengeful instinct in the hearts of women who, by force of nature, had become devoid of all feelings."[16]

The clearest indication that Delmar is not speaking factually here is to be found in his spontaneous "knowledge," at the sight of allegedly mutilated corpses, that this is the work, "almost without exception," of "women and girls." He feels persecuted by proletarian women whose hearts, "by force of nature," have "become devoid of all feelings." He then ascribes to them the intent to "mutilate" men (himself included).

When the fighting starts, even in predominantly rural areas such as Latvia, it is "women from the indigenous Latvian working-class population in particular" (Hartmann)[17] who figure large as perpetrators of butchery.

Delmar traces the "natural" lack of feelings of these women to their sexual behavior:

> In sharp contrast to bourgeois society, we encounter an attitude toward the value of virginity here that suggests a complete dissolution of the spiritual foundations of modesty.[18]

The proletarian women is *shameless*. This is the same conclusion reached by Goote's Berthold while on leave at home, when he visits the wife of his working-class spotter, Jupp, to report Jupp's death:

> He turns into the narrow, gloomy street, but sees no one standing in the entranceways.
>
> There is just one woman, who snatches a postcard from the mailman's hand with anxious haste—as if she were in hiding.
>
> He climbs the strange, steep steps in the gloomy staircase. Second floor. Third floor.
>
> Finally he sees the door and the ceramic nameplate they had tried to find once before by lighting matches that broke in the excitement.
>
> As he bends down to read the name, he hears a man's voice behind the glass door.
>
> "Why in the world did I ever come here?" he thinks. He gropes his way down the rickety staircase and back onto the street.[19]

The proletarian woman is a whore. At a pinch, a proletarian man like Jupp may act as a comrade, so long as he is a useful member of male society within the military.* Only then is he able to cast off the dark shadow of menace that attaches to women from the cheerless city quarters just beyond the town boundaries. The women are threatening, because, among other reasons, they are not virgins. The sexual experience that nationalist soldiers sense in them seems to release a particularly powerful fear. That fear is brought into association with the word "communist." Delmar again:

> In women, the first theoretical realization of communist ideals always has to do with the sexual drive.[21]

In his Freikorps novel, *Peace and Order* (*Ruhe und Ordnung*), Ernst Ottwald, later a member of the German Communist party, draws the same conclusion. He reminisces:

> for that matter, the terms "cathouse," "bar," "criminal," and "communist" are inseparably and inextricably connected in my mind.[22]

---

*"The bestial blood orgies of the night shifted next day to a rally against the 'hyenas of the revolution,' organized by the leadership of the revolutionary strikers." (Heinz's Berlin journal entry of March 3-4, 1919.) Men: daytime; women: night.[20]

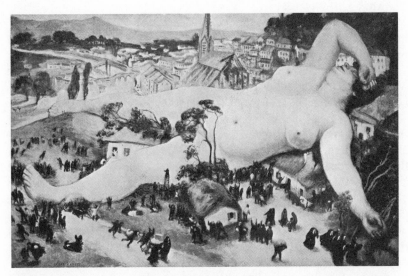

"The Horror," Jean Veber (1904). The body of the Fourth Republic blocks the men from the path to the church and offers herself as access.

The same "inextricably connected" concepts are introduced again in Zöberlein's graphic descriptions of Katja, depicted as the woman who really pulls the strings of the Munich workers' and soldiers' councils. She arranges an orgy:

> At last the proletarians can be party to these pleasures. Had he but known that life could be this splendid! Just look at that Katja; she has the devil in her oriental Russian body. Every curve and every movement is a provocation. She laughs with each and kisses with all. Her front is covered by a transparent silk ivy leaf, and her back is bare. . . . He has much yet to learn, if he is not to lose touch in the new society proclaimed by the republic. . . . Long live free love! Come to me, Katja! She coos with laughter and curls up in his paws like a cat. Grinning, Sigi turns off the light.[23]

("Throttles the light" is more like it.) Zöberlein will reveal nothing more: the indescribable is consigned to darkness. His fear of any more concrete description must be considerable. And indeed, how *can* he describe something that may well never have existed in the light of day; or, if it did exist, was very different from anything implied by the terms "free love" and "communism" here?

Revulsion at these monsters-of-the-imagination, "proletarian women" and "female communists," is no doubt related to sexual ideas that are charged with even more intense anxieties, so great that they cannot be expressed. "Proletarian woman" seems to be the name for a horror that is in fact unnameable in the language of soldier males. Just what that horror might be, remains unclear.

One thing is clear, however. These men make no attempt to track down whatever it is that poses the threat. Why should they, when they already purport to know what it is: (female) communism.

The process of naming is of great significance, characteristic as it is of the formation of all the central fascist concepts, at the core of which there always lies some displacement of the kind seen above. Thus the language of the fascists may be seen to take on some of the features of a secret language—though it protects itself from "decipherment" by appearing so utterly inane. Self-styled critics from the bourgeois intelligentsia (like the German Communist party in the 1920s) all too readily accept the implications of that inanity, namely that it is something not worth troubling themselves with. The bourgeois intelligentsia withdraws with an aloof smile on its own complicit lips, while the communists set their faces in the woodcut mould of strongman Stalin, who at least could have been depended upon to wipe out these kinds of nuisances.

Erotic male-female relationship — violent, unfeeling woman — threat to the man — dirt, vulgarity — prostitution — proletarian woman — communism

RIFLE-WOMEN (*FLINTENWEIBER*): THE CASTRATING WOMAN*

The fantasized proletarian woman who awakens such fear in hardened soldiers has another peculiar quality, evident for instance in the following example from Dwinger. The passage deals with one of the many contrived narrative deaths for which an ideologically appropriate perpetrator must be found. The cavalry officer, Count Truchs, whom Dwinger portrays as a kind of last champion of dying age, decides not to apply for a regular army post when the Freikorps era ends. The future perspective outlined by Captain Werner, according to whom the soldier must now become a political animal if the "national cause" is ever to triumph, is anathema to Truchs. (Werner is the central bearer of Dwinger's ideological position: in 1919, he already knows precisely what the Nazis will project back into the past after 1933 as correct political behavior; accordingly, he always does the

---

*The term *Flint weib*, used today as a pejorative description of a woman with a gun, a female soldier or, by extension, a woman of apparently violent or aggressive tendencies, has its roots in the term *Flinte*, originally a seventeenth-century flintlock rifle. *Flinte* was used from ca. 1919 on to designate guns of any description; in nineteenth century colloquial usage, it also referred to the penis, or to prostitutes—Trans.

1848. In the corners of the picture are symbolic representations of the republic, communism, the parliament, and the priesthood (repose). The inscription: "You are fools, all you four. Whatever you are looking for, you will find here."

right thing.) Since Truchs refuses to play ball, he has no further practical value for the movement. The only remaining requirement is for him to make an exit in a way that benefits the movement. While riding out lost in thought to meet his death, he falls into the hands of a small band of workers:

> There was a young woman among them, Truchs noticed with amazement, a young factory girl, her face aflame. "Throw down your sword!" their chief repeated. "Never!" replied Truchs once again. . . . "Shoot him down then!" said one man, breaking the silence. . . .
>
> "No!" the woman screamed. "He's a fancy one; we want him alive."

Truchs is shot in the left arm, then the right. But he keeps a grip on his sword, first in one hand, then the other, before collapsing on top of his dead horse, Psyche.

> "Look at him making himself comfortable!" shrieked the woman.
>
> "Look at him! He's still sneering at you. . . ."
>
> "I'd be interested to know what I've done to you," he said quietly.
>
> Aren't we a fancy dog!" she cried down at him. "With that damn monocle, I suppose you're an aristocrat!"

"So that's all I've done?" Truchs asked, astonished.

She spat at him by way of an answer, but she was too far away. . . . Then the girl pulled a pistol from under her apron, stepped up to the edge of the cliff, and held the pistol to his stomach.

"I can't listen to this stinking corpse anymore!" Her coarse words were punched out through gritted teeth.

She shoots.

His head grew heavier. It wanted to sink down slowly, sink onto Psyche, onto her soft skin. How good that would feel. The pain raged and hammered into his arm; deep in his abdomen, he felt as if he were being sliced with knives.

The woman jumped onto his face, grinding his monocle, that accursed symbol, over and over again into his eyes with the heels of her rough shoes.[1]

When his comrades find his body, Captain Werner guesses, "Perhaps he even fell into the hands of women—in our time, our century, it has even come to that."[2]

The central point in the construction of this murder is that the woman castrates the man. There is also an implication that she is a whore; the fact that she is the only woman traveling with six men is clear enough indication.[3] The weapon she uses to castrate him is initially hidden; the pistol is pulled unexpectedly out of her apron, as if it were a concealed . . . penis?

The same motif is even clearer in a report by a journalist with the upper middle-class newspaper, the *Kölner Zeitung*, on the condition of Freikorps soldiers—who during the Ruhr uprisings had been officially accepted into the army. This report dates from March 25, 1920, when the fortress of Wesel was about to be taken by the workers. The soldiers are depicted after a night of retreat and escape in fear for their lives. The reporter finds them on a farm near Wesel, where the wounded are quartered:

Two hussars lay tossing and groaning on the straw in the stables. A lancer, a tiny little man, wept like a baby, his eyes still full of the horrors he had seen in Hamborn and Dinslaken. The whole lot of them had lost any nerve they might have had; they saw only images of severed heads, ears, noses; of young girls tortured to death; of Spartacist women riding shaggy horses, hair flying, two pistols in each hand. It was said that Wesel and all the farms surrounding it had been taken by the Reds. Only the Wesel citadel was still being held by a small force; they were surrounded, and doomed to an inevitable death at the hands of the Spartacists.[4]

"The War." Henri Rousseau.

This report strikes me as particularly revealing. It clearly reproduces a product of fantasy, inasmuch as there were no such things as Spartacist women who rode around on shaggy horses. To this extent, then, the report shows these images of armed women to be a product of the soldiers' fear of death.

The emphasis on "two pistols in *each* hand" suggests that something more, or at least other, than mere pistols is intended here. The whole appearance of the "Spartacist women" supports the hypothesis that we are dealing with the fantasy of a threatening penis. Hair flying, packing pistols, and riding shaggy horses, the women present an image of terrifying sexual potency. It is a *phallic*, not a vaginal potency that is fantasized and feared.

The activity of the women consists in castration. Heads, noses, ears—anything that protrudes is *cut off* by them. Viewed in this perspective, it becomes easier to understand von Selchow's hatred for the woman who approaches the bull with a lance.

In his history of the Freikorps, Nazi-chronicler von Oertzen cites another newspaper report, from the *Vossiche Zeitung* of March 12, 1919. The reporter records a conversation he had with an unnamed sector commander of a White brigade. Among other things, the captain is quoted as saying:

> We recently discovered a hand grenade under a woman's skirt. I couldn't have the woman shot, because out of fear of her husband she . . .[5]

He breaks off there. His account is evidently intended to voice a fear of the armed woman; to locate the position of her weapon ("under her skirt");

and to place that weapon in a sexual context ("out of fear of her husband"). In actual executions, the reverse situation in fact prevailed; women who fell into the hands of Freikorps soldiers were shot, often precisely on the grounds that they had hidden weapons under their skirts.[6]

It looks very much, then, as if these men are likely to assign a penis to a certain type of woman (the "proletarian whore"), whose penis they fear as an instrument of castration. The men experience "communism" as a *direct* assault on their *genitals*.

The same experience is evoked time and time again; it becomes almost a standard theme. The most fertile terrain for its development is provided by the battles in the Baltic, where rumors were rife of armed Red Army women on the warpath after men. Thor Goote:

> the worse thing is not to die from a head wound, as this boy has just done; it is far worse to be captured by this bestial enemy, to suffer the most drawn-out, bitter, and tortured death imaginable at the hands of sadistically grinning rifle-women.[7]

> the dead continued to scream, though they were already cold. They will scream into eternity, those twelve savaged men of the Iron Legion, each drenched in black blood between hips and thighs, each with that terrible wound with which the bestial foe has desecrated defenseless wounded men.[8]

A miniature portrait of one of these women in repose is offered by Dwinger:

> To Laizis's right sat an older girl, one of the so-called rifle-women. Her small eyes were encircled by deep black rings. Her bloated body lay stretched across the table; her fingers, themselves also armored with rings, toyed with a revolver. The commissar addressed her by her first name, Marja.[9]

Aside from the revolver, she is adorned with a further penis-attribute: the fingers "armored" with rings. And like Katya, the Munich Russian and revolutionary, this rifle-woman has a name: Marja.

Married women remain nameless so that they do not take on the contours of figures in concrete reality. Their fictionality allows men to continue to associate or equate them with representations of other, unnameable, forbidden women. The lack of a name also seems to guarantee that there is no penis. The fact that the rifle-woman, the woman with the castrating penis, is expressly named suggests that the name itself has a sexual and an aggressive quality; that it functions, then, as a penis-attribute. Just like waitresses, barmaids, cleaning women, prostitutes, dancers, and circus performers, the rifle-women are given only first names. Women who have only

"Mélusine découverte par son mari," from P. Christian's *Histoire de la magie* (Paris, 1870).

first names are somehow on offer to the public; whether movie stars or servants, they are somehow prostitutes. They usually come from the bottom rungs of society; their origin and status do not bear the stamp of a family.

All of that makes them, on the one hand, objects at the disposal of men; whereas on the other, they are footloose, powerful, dangerous—especially in times of disintegrating political "order."

In acquiring a first name, they are branded with a stamp whose meaning is unmistakable. There isn't a single named female in any of those novels and biographies who doesn't turn out to be a "whore," or who is unsuited to be the hero's wife for some other reason. Unless, of course, she is either vouched for by her brother, named in connection with some respectable family, or introduced as a friend of a sister.[10] Leaving one's own wife nameless, then, is a powerful piece of magic.

Zöberlein's Katja is another woman armed with a rifle. A meeting of the Munich Red Army's general staff:

> Wearing her stained, silk morning-gown, Katja came over to join the men, who stood around the map, yawning. She leaned over them, still drunk, slurring her speech. "Well Sigi, what's the story with my women's batallion? We want guns, grenades, revolution! Blood and vengeance! Cowards and dogs; Katya will

show you the meaning of revolution!'' She scratched at them
with imaginary claws, her face wearing the expression of a tiger
that has tasted blood. ''They'll scream and shake with fear, and
slowly, slowly bleed to death. And then . . . shoot them all
down with machine guns, shred them to pieces and pulverize
them with dynamite.''[11]

Katja's speech here should warn us against any attempt to contain the
vengeance imputed to women in the single term, ''castration.'' ''Shred them
to pieces and pulverize them with dynamite'' implies something else. It aims,
first of all, at the *total* annihilation of the men of the Right. At this point, it
can focus on a method of killing that cannot be explained by a mere intention to castrate. This may prove significant.

In Nazi propaganda, attempts were made to give the idea of the
Flintenweib a veneer of authenticity. In E. F. Berendt's 1935 *National-
Socialist Primer* (*Parolebuch des Nationalsozialismus*), we read:

It is well known that there were rifle-women behind the Red lines
who were under orders to stop the troops from falling back, or
if the retreat could not be stopped, to shoot at their own people.
The rifle-women were the sort of cruel furies only Bolshevism
could devise. While the heart of one of the men of the Red
Guard might be moved to pity at the sight of suffering in-
nocents, those women were bestialized and devoid of all human
feeling.[12]

Even worse than the worst male communist, is a female communist.
Dwinger has his ''Marja'' proclaim:

''I stand nature on its head. With me, rivers flow uphill.''[13]

She is a natural catastrophe, a freak. The sexuality of the proletarian
woman/gun slinging whore/communist is out to castrate and shred men to
pieces. It seems to be her imaginary penis that grants her the hideous power
to do so.

The words with which General Maercker addresses the men of his
Freikorps can be seen to emerge from the same context.

''Rosa Luxemburg is a she-devil. . . . Rosa Luxemburg could
destroy the German Empire today and not be touched; there is
no power in the Empire capable of opposing her.''[14]

The rifle-woman in Ekkehard's *Storm Generation* (*Sturmgeschlecht*) is
also proletarian, evil, and a whore; but she is something else, too. Berlin,
1919 . . . street fighting . . . a woman cries out from a window for help:

By God, that woman is beautiful! Her fear makes her stun-

"Salome," by Franz Stuck.

ning. She seems strangely familiar to Warttemberg. Then he
remembers. Images return to him: the old woodcuts in the Warttemberg family Bible up in grandmother's room. They look like
this, those Old Testament women. Ruth, Esther, the woman who
demanded the head of John the Baptist—Salomé. And just like
Salomé, this young woman stands up there in the window with
her bare arms raised above her head, a narrow, glittering ribbon
around her hair and forehead.

"Careful, Hans!" Warttemberg roars to him. Fear constricts
his throat. He has no idea why.

It seems to him as if he can see all that will come to pass:
dark and inevitable fate.

"I am holy Democracy. I await my lovers." Drawing by A. Willette (early nineteenth century).

That "fate" is an ambush, to which eleven of the twelve men in the detachment fall victim. Warttemberg, the only one to escape later, sees yet one more facet of this Biblical beauty, before the scene in which he staggers back to his brigade, a bullet in his left arm and his dead friend slung across his shoulders. (At the close of the novel, he will marry the friend's sister, Elisabeth Bramwede.)

> Salomé, Ruth, Esther: she stands there, a half-flight above him.
> Tight, tucked-in skirt; left hand planted on her hip; right hand
> brandishing a pistol. The woman who enticed them to come up,
> with her shouting and crying.[15]

The beautiful Jewess—a special case of the woman with the penis? The problem of the castrating woman becomes increasingly complex as other incarnations of the woman with the penis are added to that of the rifle woman. Geza Roheim, for example, describes the witch as the most common form of the woman with the penis, as a defensive construction against the anxiety generated by the erotic woman, the woman capable of orgasm.[16] For Canetti, too, the "real sin" of witches is "their sexual association with the devil."[17]

Benjamin once ridiculed the notion that there might be grounds for astonishment over the rise of fascism "in this advanced century," Brecht noted, "as if it were not the fruit of all centuries."[18]

Can we not then trace a straight line from the witch to the seductive Jewish woman? Is the persecution of the sensuous woman not a permanent reality, one which is not primarily economic in origin, but which derives from the specific social organization of gender relations in patriarchal Europe? (The extent to which "fascist" reality is, may be, or must be rooted in the changing organization of male-female relations; the extent, then, to which even terror may be understood as the "fruit" of a specific type of male-female relationship—or nonrelationship, as the case may be: this will be considered more closely in chapter 2.) The erotic woman is a living example of nature perverted—here we already begin to sense the proximity of fascist conceptions of race.

Erotic woman — unfeeling woman — vulgar woman — whore/proletarian woman/Jewish woman (witch?) — woman-on-the-attack — woman with a penis/weapon — castrating/flaying woman — bloody mass — communism

THE RED NURSE

The Freikorps soldier's fantasy of the rifle-woman seems to present itself to him as concrete reality in the figure of the "Red nurse." In all the struggles of the workers' Red Army against the army and security police in the Ruhr, these women were always to be found near the front lines.

In his description of the participation of working-class women and girls in the struggles of Red Army men, Erhard Lucas stresses that "until 1914, the emancipation of women was not a fundamental or important goal in the consciousness of the workers' movement."[1] The reluctance of workers to elect women to political bodies (e.g., executive councils), inherited from the social-democratic tradition, makes it all the more surprising, according to Lucas, that,

> working-class girls were active everywhere as a matter or course,
> going off to battle with their men—boyfriends, fiancés,
> husbands—or in some cases, quite independently.

"The Fruits of the French Revolution." English drawing from the period following the French Revolution.

World War I had promoted that independence among women, by forcing them to take jobs in industry while running the family without help from men. Erhard Lucas again:

> There probably wasn't a single city in Germany that did not see confrontations, at some time or other, between women standing in long food lines and the police. For the first time, women held independent demonstrations (against meager food rations, low wages, etc.).

After the war, however, the importance of women's new modes of public behavior was neither recognized nor supported by workers' organizations. Lucas notes, for example, that even under the authority of the executive councils, "it was apparently taken for granted that women would be paid less than men for the same work." This may have been one reason for the reluctance of fighting women to present themselves as equal partners with their men at the front.

> They apparently needed some rationale for their participation, since they all called themselves nurses, whether or not they had the relevant training.

Thus in the context of armed confrontation among men, these women appeared to reinforce the image of the "proletarian woman" with which the Freikorps soldiers approached them. The role of nurses was seen as a form of camouflage, opening up possibilities for an "unmasking."

On a visit to the staff of the Schulz Freikorps in Wesel, press representatives from Münster picked up the following information:

> The mobilization of so-called Red Cross nurses is characteristic of the moral turpitude of the Red troops. These medical detachments are recruited exclusively from the ranks of prostitutes, especially from Oberhausen.[2]
>
> Brothel inmates are put into service as Red Cross nurses.

This is taken from Liaison Officer Mittelberger's official report to the Defense Ministry of March 27, 1920.[3]

His allegations relate to an actual decree issued by the Oberhausen Executive Council, an organ of the insurgent workers, according to which "Harmony Street" (the "Eintrachtsstrasse"), a red-light district known far beyond the town boundaries of Oberhausen, was to be shut down. A measure that was in fact hostile to prostitution, and that aimed to expel prostitutes from the town, was then interpreted by the military as proof of the opposite, namely that the Red Army was well disposed toward prostitutes and as "putting them into service." More than this, the Red Army is presented as recruiting its medical aid *exclusively* from the ranks of prostitutes. To the soldiers, then, Red nurses were best seen, indeed *had to* be seen to serve as prostitutes.

A second step in the "unmasking" of those "nurses": they are equipped with arms that they never really carried. When the official newsletter of the Army District Command, April 1, 1920, reported that "a portion of the Red Cross nurses is being armed with carbines,"[4] its report was not based on any firsthand knowledge of the situation in the Ruhr.

By this point, the military had been successfully pushed back from the Ruhr region. The Army District Command newsletter was forced to piece together its "hot-off-the-press" information from espionage reports, rumors, its own preconceptions about the enemy, and from reports in newspapers outside the Ruhr region, whose sources were equally unreliable. The carbines were a fiction that fed on such sources; the women must be armed and *couldn't* be anything other than prostitutes.*

---

*"Because newspapers often don't reach the troops, the newsletter is the only means of orientation and information for our people. Forwarding offices are therefore requested to provide for quick distribution of the newsletters." An announcement in the newsletter of Army District Command VI, March 28, 1920. Not a single issue of the newsletter fails to give reports of the Reds' terrible cruelties—reports which, after the defeat of the uprising, proved to be fabricated.

What was more, these women had men: men who didn't leave love behind them just because they had "taken up arms." The men of the military responded with a mixture of disgust and . . . envy? One army reporter writes:

> The farthest outposts of the Reds stood atop Daberg Mountain, a historically strategic site for Western enemies of the city of Hamm. . . . In any camp beyond that point, wild scenes could be witnessed of Red bandits strutting back and forth, "every inch the world revolutionary," surrounded by those most repulsive of characters, the Red "nurses." These women in- dulged even unwounded warriors with prophylactic attentions; and as for the men, the spring season was in their blood. They did it right there in the fields and forests.[5]

That officer's defenses against sexual activity in women are so strong that, even in the face of contrary evidence, he clings to the notion of the freedom of male decisions from female influence. It is "the spring season," rather than the "attentions" of the women, that gets into the "blood" of the men.

The fact that the Reds do the unmentionable "it," "right there in the fields and forests," reduces them to the level of animals. The officer on the other hand is raised to a height from which he can watch them coupling, not without excitement, and then shoot. This perspective may correspond to the way in which he views his own sexuality. The emotionally charged formula- tion of the "spring season," though meant negatively, in fact simply expresses his own experience of sexuality—as the onset of a sickness. He *ex- periences* the Reds' lovemaking as an instance of being overcome by nature; of falling victim to something that has nothing to do with oneself; as with animals, it is "in their blood." To the extent at least that they are victims of "the spring season," he seems to understand those men down there. But when instead of repressing the sickness, they give in to it and take up with those "most repulsive of all characters," the nurses, his finger touches the trigger.

The thing that irritates him most is precisely the sympathetic notion that the women "attend to" their men, even if the men aren't wounded. This is what makes them whores. Prostitution is equated here with a voluntary erotic relationship between a man and a woman, where the man is neither sick nor mortally wounded, where he is driven neither by animal instinct nor by duty. For such men, there is help at hand:

> One such woman lay behind the bushes, in the most tender embrace with her lover. A grenade had caught her off guard in the practice of her true profession.[6]

Here Major Schulz, a Freikorps commander, attests with satisfaction to

Major Schulz.

the destruction of an idyll of the kind seen above. The erotic male-female relationship is given its true meaning by the grenade. From beneath the surface, its essence emerges: a bloody obscenity. The sight must have been deeply pleasing to the major: how otherwise could he talk of the "most tender embrace" in the face of two bloody, mutilated corpses.

An intimate connection between love and destruction similarly characterizes a comment handed down to us by Captain Rodermund on women in the Red Army:

> Women marched in their midst, with red kerchiefs and red armbands with white crosses; women who surely hadn't come along to carry out the work of good Samaritans.[7]

No, these women were relentlessly on the lookout for love. From the soldier's viewpoint, then, the "true profession" of working-class girls and women at the front was clear from the start. The soldiers' image of them has a longer history than any press conference remarks by Freikorps staff members, or "reports" in the circulars of Army District Commands. The latter merely served to *reactivate* a belief in the existence of armed women who were out to castrate men.

The official communiques of military leaders were, nevertheless, extremely significant for the actual behavior toward women of soldiers marching into the Ruhr Valley. What those "reports" did, in the end, was to provide black-and-white "evidence" of the existence of these horror-story women, thus laying the foundation for the *actual* use of force against them.

Victims of murder, no longer in a position to write their own history, have no means of defense against being retrospectively branded as criminals by their murderers. Thus in 1929, Hans Schwarz van Berk added a new twist to the characterization of "Red nurses":

> Escaping to the marketplace, the women changed their clothes in broad daylight, to become the kind of Red nurses whose wiles will further demoralize the workers' army.[8]

The women had "escaped" from a prison. At nine years' remove, the fascist sees the Red Army, a man's army, as an ally against those women. The Nazi historian von Oertzen shows the same empathy for the Red men. He regrets that:

> In particular, the countless women and prostitutes in the battle sectors and behind the front—most of them disguised as nurses—made for completely impossible conditions.[9]

Thus women are to blame for everything, both for communism and for its defeat. They are even to blame for the failure of the Kapp Putsch, which for naval officer Schmalix was adequately explained by the fact that the task of typing out appeals to the people had been entrusted to Fräulein Kapp and one other woman.[10] No putsch could have succeeded in the face of this kind of blunder.

ON SYTHEN'S GROUND—WHERE MYTHS ABOUND

It is at Sythen Castle, a site of contrast, at once myth and concrete reality, that the nature of the Red nurse is made to unfold in the most telling terms. Sythen Castle: again, it is Hans van Berk who writes its story:

> All hell had broken loose at Sythen Castle, near Haltern. One might be tempted to see all this as a fantasy from some sophisticated anti-Bolshevist film from Hollywood had it not taken place in the straitlaced land of the Germans. The walls of the castle were bursting with hand grenades and clubs. Door panels and cabinets had been left gaping open; the chapel altar reduced to a pile of rubble; vestments, chalices, and crucifixes subjected to treatment reminiscent of the Thirty Years' War: the storerooms turned into troughs and watering holes. Visits were even paid to the servants' rooms. Hand grenades sent up gushes of water in the fish ponds, throwing silver fish bellies into the air. There were forty nurses rummaging through the wardrobes

and linen closets, scrambling for the best items, parading naked with them in front of the mirrors. One "nurse" gave the servants a tongue-lashing. "Girls! Starting today you're no longer servants, you're young ladies!" By that evening the "young ladies'" brooches, watches, and chains were missing.[1]

Van Berk takes a great deal of trouble over this portrait of alleged scenes at Sythen Castle; yet he was no more an eyewitness than was Captain Schneider, who used the goings-on at Sythen Castle as the basis for a series of newspaper articles as early as April/May 1920—at a time when the shots of the kangaroo courts were still ringing in the ears of workers from the defeated uprising. Schneider wrote for the *Berlin Daily* (*Berliner Tag*); the *Buersche Zeitung* caried his articles in the Ruhr. To produce his account, Schneider had contented himself with stringing together a few of the most commonplace insults:

> whores dressed up as nurses. Every one of them steals, robs, plunders and ransacks from kitchen to cellar . . . constant comings and goings throughout the night, doors splintering, cabinets cracking open. Naked women stand by the wardrobes, trying on the countess's clothes. Hordes of them, a hundred or more—around forty of them "nurses"—lie around on the floors and in the guest rooms. Men and women alike, all of them blind drunk.[2]

A comparison of the two accounts shows the chapel, vestments, crucifixes, hand grenades in the fish pond and rooms, brooches, watches, chains, etc., to be the work of van Berk, the product of his own destructive desire in the process of writing. From those two "reports" on the same set of circumstances, witnessed by neither of the two authors, we may now glean some evidence of the characteristic features of their mode of writing.

Even a simple comparison of the accusations made against the nurses has shown most of them to be fabrications. Yet in both texts they take the same direction, as if following the same hidden pattern. In that respect they are identical.

Both authors write as if they had been on the scene at the time. Indeed they seem to commit these actions themselves, in the very process of writing about them. "Doors splintering and cabinets cracking open." There is no distance there; the writer stands in the very midst of events. He does not report; he is emotionally *there* in deed and action. Writing itself seems to be a procedure for channeling off aggression: the evidence given by the texts (which testifies *against* the nurses) stands in direct opposition to the affect expressed (*in favor of* destruction). In other words, these men are describing what they would have done if they had been the Reds; or what they themselves actually *did* when they were billeted in castles with army or

Freikorps troops. Maybe what we have here is less a case of pure "fabrication" than a use of spurious names and dates.*

For the reader with psychoanalytic knowledge, the passages quoted here and in previous sections will have flicked on a little mental light marked "projections." True enough, there are projections in play here. Van Berk's hand grenades exploding in the fish pond of Sythen Castle stand as a classic example. At the time of the events, March 1920, the castle was occupied by one of seventeen Red Army strategic command units.** It is absurd to think that armed workers, faced with a decisive battle against army and Freikorps troops, and under the watchful eyes of a strategic command unit of the Red Army, would have tossed their meager supplies of hand grenades into the fish pond of some castle.

By contrast, there are passages in Freikorps literature in which that same fishing method is regretfully acknowledged to be customary practice among Freikorps soldiers:

> and the River Aa fed us with its fish. On many occasions, and in
> defiance of orders, they were wrested from their element by
> means of hand grenades thrown into the water. This fishing
> method was one of the vices that could not be bred out of our
> people! (Baron von Steinaecker)[3]

It seems to me unlikely, however, that it is solely or primarily the defense mechanism of projection—whereby desired or actually performed acts are repudiated and ascribed to another—which is working to distort the writing process. If I ask myself why van Berk and Schneider chose Sythen Castle, out of all possible sites, as the location for their "anti-Bolshevist film," I come up with a different answer. Clearly, it's the *castle* that interests them. Their theme seems to be "Reds-in-the-*castle*." Why should this be the case? They doubtless saw it as perfectly legitimate for the Freikorps—who were interested after all in *retaining* the monarchy—to billet themselves in castles. "Reds-in-the-castle," on the other hands, were a sacrilege, a perversion, a synonym for society turned upside down.

In dreams, thoughts or perceived images of "castles" often refer to or are associated with the womb. "Castle" carries the connotations "mother," "noble woman," "pure, high-born woman."[4] In this context, it seems to be the *body* of the pure woman that becomes an arena for the display of excesses committed by the Red nurses/whores in van Berk's and Schneider's accounts. Their texts thus present the alleged events at Sythen Castle in terms of a paradigmatic movement between two opposing images of women. On the surface, they depict an episode from the 1920 workers' uprising in the Ruhr Valley; the subterranean theme, however, is one of

---

*The same applies to most of the articles in the Army District Command newsletter.

**It was the only one in a building of that kind. The others were located in schools, guest houses, etc. (cf. Lucas, *Märzrevolution*, II, 70-74).

"*proletarian* whores and their menfolk laying waste to the *aristocratic* body of the mother."

Two realities (at least) are represented simultaneously here; their relation to each other is that of parasite and host plant. The parasite (which has reality as an idea but is not depicted directly) envelopes the host (the events represented) so completely that the host almost disappears. The objects of representation—men of the Red Army, Red nurses in Sythen Castle—are just about permitted to retain their names; their living reality, however, is devoured as nourishment for a preconceived idea on the part of the writers. Here, "projection" seems to me an inadequate term to describe a process in which perceived reality is annihilated in order to preserve the life of an ideational representation, a process of annihilation that seems to proceed from some as yet indefinable compulsion characteristic of these authors, and from the reduction of ideational representation to certain determinate paradigms.

For the moment, we need only note that this particular mode of writing *always* produces texts about the author himself, and that it is as such that we will most often be reading and understanding the texts under review. At the same time, we should not ignore the portion of external reality that they *do* contain; to varying degrees, they are also texts *about* the object of representation. Yet in the same way that none of the relationships to women examined in the preceding pages bear the stamp of object relations in the psychoanalytic sense, the linguistic usage of soldier males does not enter into the kind of relations to its represented objects that would allow them to be fairly represented.

The objects, or configurations, onto which these preexisting representations are parasitically grafted ("cathected") can be identified in the text as those most saturated with significance. They are full of life, full of history, of extreme affective intensity. "Women," "rifle-women," "communism," "whoring," "castration," "castle," "hand grenades," and "countess"—all create possibilities for very intense affects. That seems to be their distinguishing characteristic. One way or another, they guarantee the "high life," life lived to the full.

> They rampaged through the palace in great swarms, lying in the baronial beds with the rifle-women, using the baroness's rococo salons as lavatories, the Venetian mirrors for target practice, and the Steinway grand as a table for their revels, feeding the fires with the contents of the old libraries![5]

This is Dwinger, writing about "Reds" in a palace in the Baltic area. It isn't called Sythen, but Sythen it is. Or again:

> *September. Jakobstadt.* I visited Kreuzberg Castle. It was totally plundered. The floors were so covered with excrement, the walls with obscene inscriptions, that it could have been put on show to

foreign journalists as an example of the excesses of Bolshevism.
The Korff family vault had been broken into; the corpses had
been thrown out of their coffins.[6]

The Baltic officer writes as if he himself had seen the corpses lying
there, as if he had witnessed them flying through the air. Walls smeared with
excrement and desecrated graves: some strange pleasure seems to be
associated with seeing the inner regions of the "noble woman" in this state.

All of the objects and configurations of which the language of these
men incessantly speaks have a definite air of fictionality about them.
Historical events are experienced and reported as if in a delirium; but it is a
highly controlled, selective delirium. Their feelings, their touch, their
language descend on a relatively small number of densely signifying objects
and configurations, each of which is invaded by, enveloped in fantasies.

Once again, the process seems to resemble a defense mechanism, or, in
this case, a safety device. Of all the multiplicity of details and contradictions
reality offers, they extract so *few*, and almost always the *same* ones, that
their "choice" appears as a compulsion.

This host-parasite relationship engenders specific paradigms for
transmuting, as opposed to perceiving, external reality. It can perhaps be
said to function as a kind of security lock, which automatically snaps into a
preordained position whenever the multitude of impulses from perceived
reality (both "internal" and "external") becomes too confusing or too
threatening.

It is the historical-social-political dimension that these men invest with
their fantasies and affects. The impulse to enter that dimension seems,
however, to originate more as a tactic of evasion than from any positive attachment. What concerns them are the grand themes. In their writings,
something at least as large as the fate of the fatherland always has to be at
stake. They feel closer in spirit to the mythical Nibelungs than to afternoon
teatime. That preoccupation with large-scale politics, with the destinies of
the race and humanity, implies a negation of the small, the close-at-hand, of
microhistory. By moving outward to broad horizons, to the public and the
social, they attempt to avoid the private, the intimate, the individual, or,
more precisely perhaps, the singular.

That should immediately warn us that we won't get very far here with
the "subject-object" dichotomy. I think we can agree that their fantasies
can't be called "objective," but it's just as wrong to label them
"subjective." What they share is a strong family resemblance; following a
set of paradigm, they are in many cases almost identical. Aside from that,
they are clearly anti-individualist, antisubjective. *Their language is as
uninterested in the object as it is in the subject*; it seems indeed to be penned
by *fictive* authors, by *one single* fictive author. What we see at work here can
best be described in terms of a process: the fascist process of appropriating
and transmuting reality, recorded stage by stage in the writings of these

authors. Their records are no more or less "objective" than any other manifestation of reality, whether it be "psychic," "economic," or any other kind. This is the point at which I part company with the fallacious opposition between "subject" and "object," and thus with one of the basic assumptions of all communist theories of fascism, including that of Wilhelm Reich.

We should also note two further provisos that run counter to current basic assumptions. First, neither defensive fantasies nor paradigms for the transmutation of reality seem here to be class-specific. Movements of defense, such as the one that triggered the "sensuous woman" complex in the men, are not only found among fascist or Wilhelmine officers. M. Rohrwasser has established their presence, though in milder form, in the so-called proletarian mass novel of the 1920s.[7] To make the point even clearer, any male reading the texts of these soldier males—and not taking immediate refuge in repression—might find in them a whole series of traits he recognizes from his own past or present behavior, from his own fantasies. (Any man who categorically denies this might want to verify it by asking the present, or past, women in his life.)

To what degree, then, did a specifically masculine organization of life—in short, "patriarchy," of which more later—use fascism to ensure its own survival? Here the notion that its survival under fascism was organized by capital, in particular by capitalist-class "fractions" from heavy industry, is neither to be dismissed, nor do I wish to move it to center stage. It seems to me that this whole dynamic has already been adequately explained[8] and that the only necessary point of criticism in formulations of the primacy of economic determinants is their claim to totality.[9]

The second proviso concerns the nature of the unconscious and repression. Whenever the word "communism" is mentioned in our sources, not as the collective organization of social production but as a fear of being castrated by a sensuous woman armed with a penis, its usage is so overt and deliberate that, as far as I'm concerned, we really can't talk about an *unconscious* displacement, or an *unconscious* fear. On the contrary, it strikes me that concealing the kinds of thoughts we've been discussing, the ones traditional psychoanalysis would call "unconscious," is the last thing on earth those men would want to do. They're out to express them at all cost. The "fear of castration" is a consciously held fear, just as the equation of communism and rifle-woman is consciously made. All of this leads to the conclusion either that the men are repressing precious little, or nothing at all (in which case they may be collectively banished to the realms of the perverse and the psychotic);[10] or that there are areas of real repression, of actual desires and fears, that are never touched for example in dream analysis, however admirably suited its language may be to the discovery of repression on the level of psychic representation. If the latter were the case, the unconscious would not be even minimally in play.

The implications of all this are profound. As far as I can see, the conclusion that must emerge from a reading of our textual sources is that the oppositional pairs "subjective-objective," "conscious-unconscious" (of thought and action), "proletarian-bourgeois," "communist-fascist" fail to provide useful criteria for understanding the texts. Yet those were my own analytical tools when I began this book. If I had applied them, they would have disguised the reality of the texts. Until now, it seems, fascists themselves have been questioned too little about fascism, whereas those who claim to have seen through fascism (but who were unable to defeat it) have been questioned too much.

Freud once commented that doctors have a tendency "to dismiss patients' assertions as gross exaggerations." He went on to say, "In my opinion the patients are once again nearer to a correct view than the doctors; for the patients have some glimmering notion of the truth while the doctors are in danger of overlooking an essential point."[11] Regrettably, most theorists of fascism have acted toward fascists as those doctors did toward their patients.

THE WHITE NURSE—COUNTESS OF SYTHEN CASTLE

The attributes ascribed to the "castrating woman" are uniformly negative: her wickedness is all-encompassing. She seems to realize this herself somehow, because she tends to want to be something other than what she is, something "better"—a "young lady," as in van Berk and Schneider, who have their nurses parade in front of mirrors in the clothes of a countess. Similarly, after the ransacking of a castle, Dwinger's riflewoman, Marja, sits astride her horse "in the lace dress of a countess."[1] Zöberlein's Katja wears fur coats, or dresses in a "transparent, silk ivy leaf."

These women want to be noble, beautiful, and rich. Because they aren't, they ape the external appearance of the noblewoman: perverted nature's aim is, obviously, to pervert society. Yet in doing this the women become show girls, instantly recognizable as mere imitations. They could never fool a "real man." At the same time, their presence points toward the existence of "positive" women whose positions are considered worth occupying by the "negative" ones. Sythen Castle has a countess:

> And as we stride through the ruins, the faithful servant delivers a
> shocking account of the days of suffering the castle's inhabitants
> were forced to endure. He tells of the trials of the count, who
> escaped death only by the skin of his teeth. He paints a picture
> of the brave woman who held out in the midst of brutish hordes,
> in order to salvage what could be salvaged. Bearing herself

> proudly, she never lost her courage, and the others were inspired
> by her example.[2]

We see before us a different kind of woman, a heroic mother figure. She is a
genuine countess, clearly above any suspicion of whoring.

Pure mother figures of this kind seem to represent a type that is
diametrically opposed to the castrating woman. Whenever the former are in
trouble, we are called upon to empathize. (In reality, it is clear that nothing
much happened to them, other than their having to bear the sight of
"brutish hordes" of workers for a few days. On the other hand, Red nurses
who fell into the hands of soldiers never had the slightest opportunity to
demonstrate their "proud bearing" and staunch courage, as we will see.)

One woman stylized as a mother figure in this way was the wife of the
doctor in Stoppenberg, a suburb of Essen. On March 18, 1920, a force of
about twenty security police used the doctor's villa as a redoubt against
armed workers. Although the encounter ended in victory for the workers,
both the doctor and his wife survived unharmed.[3] In a number of reports,
however, it is emphasized that the woman was *almost* killed by the workers
when they were forcing their way in to the house. Rodermund, for instance,
writes:

> They stood the doctor's wife, whom they found inside the house,
> against the wall and spat on her, relishing the mental agony she
> had to endure through their continual threats to shoot her.[4]

This woman, as in the previous example, is subjected to a purely
"mental" agony, which is itself only a product of the authors, Schneider
and Rodermunds', imagining what might (or should?) have happened to
her. Dwinger makes a little more of the battle for the villa of the Stoppenberg physician:

> The doctor merely shakes his head. Prinz now notices his wife, a
> pale-faced young woman who, like him, is binding wounds
> without stopping. Together, they carry the wounded into the
> cellar. The wife spreads every blanket she can find over the stone
> floor, and they bed them down on those, one after the other.

As one of the besieged security policemen is about to leave the villa for
negotiations, "the doctor squeezes his hand, the woman presses it to her
bosom, and then he drags himself upstairs." Here the doctor's wife clearly
adopts the position of the mother in a parent-child configuration. Finally,
the house is stormed:

> Two of them tear the woman loose from her husband, shoving
> her across the bodies of the wounded and aginst the cellar
> wall. . . . The woman finally sinks down unconscious, perhaps
> saving her life by fainting at that point.[5]

This version of events contains some interesting clues for further analysis. What is the woman actually doing? She is applying bandages, transporting the wounded, spreading blankets on the floor, setting up a makeshift field hospital. *In other words, she is a nurse.* And whom is she taking care of? Her own people. She is married, not a whore; even her husband puts in an appearance to prevent mistaken suspicion from falling on her. Together, they constitute the parents in this passage; in the role of caring mother, she watches over the sick and wounded. Overall, then, she appears as a fantastic incarnation of a nurse *of the Right.* She too only narrowly escapes a threat that, in fact, has been conjured up for her by the author. Her life was only "possibly" in danger.

And finally, the very epitome of this female figure is encountered by Lieutenant Gerhart Willmut in Dwinger's Baltic novel. Willmut has been taken prisoner and is wounded. The Latvians in the Red Army have thrown him into a dark dungeon, where he lies in a state midway between waking and unconsciousness:

> When he awakes for the third time there really is a woman kneeling behind him, holding his head in her lap and looking down into his eyes, at the blood trickling from his mouth. Her face is extraordinarily beautiful, but indescribably pale, almost white. From that face come the gentle words, "Have they tortured you?"
>
> He moves his shoulders a little, tries to part his blood-encrusted lips. "Not yet," he whispers. She strokes his forehead with her long, cool hand. "Tell me," she says.

Willmut tells his story.

> Finally, she says, "You'll have to die."[6]
>
> "Yes," he says, with such unaccustomed calm that he barely recognizes himself, the exuberant Lieutenant "Mutwill" ("Courage wills," as his comrades jokingly called him.) "I never really believed it would come to this, though I always knew it was possible," he continued. "But for it to be like this. For me to . . . for it to begin with . . ." Without finishing, he sat up abruptly.

"For me to". . . be allowed to experience this? to *have to* experience it? The first way of completing the sentence would allow the situation to appear as unexpected fulfillment, while the second would refer to horrors still to come. Dwinger no doubt leaves the dots to leave both possibilities open. Is she love, or is she death?

Next Willmut asks the apparition, that "almost white" face from which gentle words "come" and that speaks—as Dwinger points out twice—in a peculiarly "melodic voice," as if she might just have something with which he could . . .? (Again, the dots.)

"No," she says, softly.

"You don't want to!" he moans. "I can see that. . ."

She interrupts him in her melodic tones. "Do you really
think I'd let you beg for it?"

What he wants is something to kill himself with, but Dwinger makes
sure that the question of love is also kept alive.

He sinks back again, biting his bloodied lips. "You mean,
you've already been . . ." he asks, eyes closed.

"Not until tomorrow morning," she replies calmly. "The
Latvian woman already offered me to the Mongolian, but he
only said he had no time for such things." Her eyes are averted
as she speaks; her beautiful lips don't move.[7]

The "Latvian woman" is none other than our old rifle-woman friend,
Marja. She even seems to be in charge of organizing the obligatory rape
scenes. The Mongolian, on the other hand, had no wish to play along, as we
discover a few pages further on, when he bursts into the room, packing a
pistol in each fist. Instead of shooting he hands one of them to Willmut,
who by this time has absorbed enough vitality from the apparition to evade
death. The behavior of the Mongolian is attributable to his fear of Marja,
whose approach is announced by the sound of her silk dress dragging along
the floor (the hissing of snakes). The "Mongolian," who turns out in the
end to be "white," shoots her in both arms, at which point German comrades arrive on the scene to save the day.[8] Here again, the mother figure has
escaped a highly threatening situation *by the skin of her teeth*. She remains
pure.

Now back to the cellar. Rescue is not yet at hand, and the apparition
has not yet assumed material form. Who is she? First of all, a mother.
Dwinger stresses that Willmut has "boyish hands"; and in a pause in the
conversation, she "begins to stroke his forehead again, from the middle outward toward the temples." A mother with a child in her lap.

It is in this pose that they consider how to kill themselves. Surprisingly
quickly, Willmut agrees to strangle her. To spare him any unpleasant consequences, however, she refuses to go along with this.

For a long time they say nothing, just gaze steadfastly at
each other: she down at him, he up at her. How warm her hands
are at this moment, he thinks happily; before, they seemed cold
to me. A sort of glow rises up unexpectedly in his breast,
threatening to choke him as it runs upward, to break into a
burning stream in his eyes. "Finding you here," he stammers
helplessly. His next words seem unconnected. "I'm still so
young, you understand."

Then the heat wells up into his eyes, stopping for a brief
moment behind the lids, then pouring finally, uncontrollably,

"Jumbo." Poster on the stationing of black French troops in Germany (after 1918).

down his face. Yet not a single sob shakes his young body; there are no spasms to disturb the flow of his tears as they stream out in one great, peaceful, redeeming current.

The "heat" wells up and erupts here into a kind of ejaculation. Fulfillment comes from the dissolving of personal boundaries into a stream of tears, and from the return to the mother's womb.

> Taking her hands from his forehead, he wipes the tears from his eyes, all with the repetitious motions of a child.
> "Who are you?" she suddenly asks.
> "Lieutenant Gerhart Willmut," he answers dreamily. "And what's your name?" he asks tenderly in reply.
> "Sandra, Countess Fermor," she responds quietly. Again she starts to wipe away the tears that he begins to shed once more.
> "Don't cry," she whispers. "Don't cry."[9]

After they are rescued from the cellar, all of this is erased. Never again will Countess Sandra Fermor and the lieutenant touch each other, though her remaining with the troops means they won't be separated:

> "You'll need a nurse, and I've had three years' experience in the field."[10]

Mother, sister (-of-mercy, nurse), and countess all in one person. Such is the holy trinity of the "good" woman, the nonwhore. Instead of castrating, she protects. She has no penis, but then she has no sex, either. Her body is "completely enveloped in a white apron, her pale face sternly framed by the white cone of her Russian cap." Willmut is no exception in succumbing to her charms:

> When a dying man from the Second Squadron was laid down in front of her and, at the sight of her, called out in a failing voice for his mother, the student actually saw her smile.[11]

Otherwise, her face remains a cold (nobly beautiful) mask. It draws itself up into a smile only when its bearer, as Mother Death, is preparing a bed for one of her adopted sons.

Up to this point, three heroic mother figures—the countess of Sythen Castle, the wife of the Stoppenberg doctor, and Countess Fermor—have exemplified the concept of the "good woman." As mother figures, they offer their "sons" either protection, or a model for bearing up under suffering. All of them narrowly escape rape, or threatened death, at the hands of the Reds. There is no allusion to any love relationship they might have, and they have no children of their own.

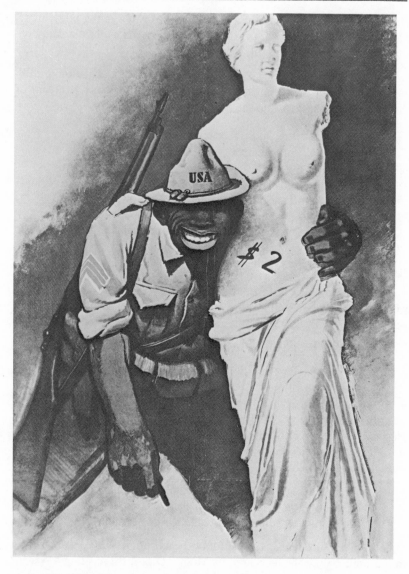

Italian World War II poster, on the arrival of the Americans.

We are led to ask about their husbands. The countess of Sythen Castle had one, Count Westerholt. During the period in which Captain Schneider worked as a journalist for the Berlin newspaper, *Der Tag*, Westerholt was shot and killed. Red sailors were suspected of being the perpetrators. The propaganda effect was enormous. Here is Captain Schneider:

> The sympathies of the whole region are directed toward the victim's wife, for the tribulations that she had undergone. We should remind our readers that the countess was forced, during the "visit" of the Red Guard to Sythen Castle, to endure alone the whole raging anger of a bestial people.[12]

That death considerably enhances the countess's martyrdom, of course, as well as her usefulness as a vehicle for particular operations in the articles of Captain Schneider. Now that she has no protector, the newspaper reader is called upon to assume that role. In other words, the story is constructed to make the killing of Reds a reparation paid to the mother figure, a kind of courtly tribute. The task in hand consists first of restoring her honor, in order to assume the vacated function of her protector—at least in fantasy. The killing itself was of course quite real; for the military courts-martial, then, rumors of alleged crimes committed by Red Army fighters could be highly expedient.

There was a second rumor that contradicted the first. Closer scrutiny of the circumstances surrounding Count Westerholt's murder raised the suspicion that a soldier in the regular army might have been the guilty party. The matter was, however, rapidly hushed up; it died a quiet death. (In May 1920, the murder of a count by a representative of the "Right" would have come at an inopportune moment for any state institution, since it would have undermined the credibility of their own offensive against insurgent workers.)

By 1925 a chance discovery revealed that this had indeed been a right-wing murder. In the June 1926 issue of *Socialist Politics and Economics* (*Sozialistische Politik und Wirtschaft*), Heinrich Teuber reports how Georg Rehne, a soldier in the Reichswehr, was seen on May 1, 1920, wandering around with a loaded carbine in the Borkenberger Woods near Haltern (the site of Sythen Castle). He happened upon a man dressed in green, Count Westerholt. The count suspected Rehne of being a poacher, but when challenged, Rehne refused to give his name and pleaded with Westerholt not to make trouble for him with his company. Westerholt insisted on returning to camp with Rehne and filling out a report. Carelessly, he allowed Rehne to walk behind him. After some five or six minutes. Rehne felled him with a shot in the back of the neck. It was only the next day that Rehne learned whom he had shot. It was particularly convenient for him that the murder was atributed to the Red Army.

By August 1925, Rehne had left the army and was working in a print shop in Oldenburg. He confessed, was arrested, then denied everything. Later, however, he admitted his guilt to a cellmate who turned out to be a police assistant sent there to spy on him. On December 2, 1925, Rehne was sentenced to death. The judgment was upheld by the third Penal Senate of the Imperial Court on March 25, 1926.[13]

Count Westerholt's death was particularly conducive to the construction of myths around the figure of the "countess of Sythen Castle." It was that death alone that allowed her to operate as a "white countess," robbed of her husband by the Reds. It was taken for granted that the perpetrator was to be found in the Red Army. We have here, then, a fine example of the way in which the military and the judiciary function in accordance with the reality of their own preconceived ideas. Criminal investigations are immediately dropped when suspicion is cast on a man from their own ranks: the case becomes uninteresting, "unreal." The same will not be true by 1925, when the Weimar Republic, by this time in a period of stabilization, will by no means be averse to passing sentence on the occasional representative of the Right.

Let us return to our second countess, Sandra Fermor. She, too, had a husband whose death rendered her untouchable. It's for his sake that she refuses Lieutenant Willmut's offer:

> "When you first met me, it had only been one week since my husband was killed before my very eyes by the Bolshevists. . . . I had only been married to him three months, but my love for him was greater than words can express. . . . There is only one thing I can do to thank my husband for all he gave me during those three months, and that's to live only for him until the end of my days, to be with him alone in all my thoughts . . . My hands, my body, my lips belong to him. . . . He has perished . . . my noble home has perished, as I would perish too. . . . I cannot be happy, Willmut, for his sake I cannot. . . . Neither could I ever help you, for ever since that day I've been dead—no more than an empty husk. No one will ever breathe life into me again."[14]

As far as any love relationship goes, the heroines with dead husbands are no longer available. It's better not to fall in love with them. A few pages later, Lieutenant Willmut is hit by the bullet that has his name on it. Knowing that death had already stroked his forehead, he threw himself *too* courageously[15] into battle.

The third woman, the Stoppenberg doctor's wife, seems an exception to the rule. Not only is her husband alive, but he also takes part in the action in the scene in which she appears. Yet one peculiarity does emerge: Dwinger casts the doctor as a man sympathetic to the workers' cause, who is initially unwilling to give any assistance to the security police after they have barricaded themselves in his villa.[16] Since he cooperates only under coercion, the doctor carries a certain taint—a taint that is all the more significant for having been fabricated by Dwinger himself.

> The real physician, a certain Dr. Kondring, served as an in-house practitioner for a Stoppenberg mining concern. In other words, he was anything but sympathetic to the workers. The security police had definite reasons for choosing his house as a munitions depot; it was the same house that provided telephone contact with their command center in Essen. A left-wing doctor? Not a chance.[17]

The fact that Dwinger makes him out to be a leftist, while making the wife the heroine of a scene of tragic suffering, suggests he's trying to drive a wedge between them. The reader is given the impression that the woman has wound up with the wrong man; at this point, then, she too can become the object of any latent protective desires. She, too, has something of the heroic self-sufficiency that can stand up under the threat of "Red terror." It is not as a potential *lover* that we are encouraged to desire her; what is more, Dwinger can kill another bird here with the same stone, since the Reds can be made to appear all the more inhumane for behaving so despicably toward their own ally.

The "countess" dimension seems to be missing from this example—though perhaps not altogether. The wife's "pale face" alone may be too flimsy a piece of evidence; but the fact that the head of the security police is named "Prinz" seems to me to suggest that she, his "princess," belongs more firmly in their camp than in that of her left-wing doctor husband. After all, it was Prinz's hand that she pressed to her bosom in parting. (This reading does not contradict the notion that the doctor and his wife are "parents" of the security police. It merely modifies it, in that, while both of them remain parents, the mother now takes precedence over the tainted father. The son, it is hoped, will turn out better.)

The husbands of our three representatives of the "good woman" image are either dead or flawed. The dead husbands have been killed off by the Reds, while the flawed one is a little too Red himself. When all is said and done, the women stand alone; this is what equips them to be heroic mother figures, countesses, "white nurses." They are made to appear strong, but at the same time they need to be protected from outside enemies. Thus any enemy of their enemies is able to present himself as a protector (while at the same time retaining a "chivalrous" distance, in order not to awaken the dead husband).

The fiction of a mother-son relationship that is at once sexual and asexual is arrived at through a process of desensualization, of what might almost be called a draining of life from the mother, and a wounding of the son, both of which mitigate the repellent character of the incestuous fantasy. She is already among the angels and he is injured (castrated). Both are sexless and in need of help.

A closer look at the role of the son reveals more of the explosiveness of this relationship. For it is the sons themselves, not the Reds, who eliminate the fathers from the "family" configuration (their death being reminiscent of dreams in which the parricidal urge attains its goal through the father either dying or being murdered by an enemy). Yet the love object, the mother to whom parricide was intended to grant access, is never attained. The son never succeeds in taking his father's place. For him and the mother as well, the new path leads only to celibacy. It is a route strewn with pain and suffering, which may even lead to death.

One aspect of the "parricide" also affects the mother. She is deprived of her husband and given no one to replace him with. We seem to be dealing here with some kind of concealed aggression toward the mother. She is forever denied any further earthly satisfaction. Her face hidden behind a marble mask, she occupies a prominent place in the gallery of the angels—and this in her own lifetime. Why would the sons want to take revenge on their mothers? We can see that even apparently harmless manifestations of the mother-son relationship, like that between the white nurse and wounded soldier, might also be screens for latent aggression toward the mother. Has the mother committed some sin, sexual or otherwise, that the son sees as worthy of punishment?

These authors, after all, are anything but unaggressive in the constant games they play with the threat of rape from which most of these women only narrowly escape. The beast, once loosed, is always capable of going one step further (and indeed threatens to do so, in the case of Sandra Fermor at least). The plundering of the castle may then function as a means of maintaining the threat of rape as an ever-present possibility.

MOTHERS

There are perhaps further insights to be gleaned from the way in which the writers' own mothers appear in their works. They seem to be seen from two different perspectives, the first being that of the small child. Let us look at a few examples, beginnng with Ernst Röhm:

> My mother is the best mother, and the best woman, in the
> world. As her youngest son, and as one who loves her above all
> else, I can say no more than this.[1]

(And indeed, he says not a single word more on the subject.)
Peter von Heydebreck:

> We three children clung to our mother with an infinite love, and
> even today, we still compete in vain to hold the first place in her
> affections. The times when she would tell us stories about the life
> of Jesus, read us fairy tales, or sing folksongs with us, are some
> of my most beautiful childhood memories. There's only one
> thing she would do that particularly displeased me, and that was
> insisting I wear an overcoat in winter.[2]

Lettow-Vorbeck:

> The villagers thought of her as their guardian angel. Her whole
> outlook on life was serious . . . intelligent, firm-minded, and
> helpful. And her deep religiousness stayed with her to her very
> last breath.[3]

Rudolf Höss, on his return from the war:

> For the first time, I truly felt the loss of my mother. I had no
> home anymore! I stood there, feeling abandoned, completely on
> my own.[4]

Hermann Ehrhardt's mother protected him against his father's
harshness:

> One winter night I stood forgotten outside in the snow for four
> hours, until my mother finally announced that I'd had enough
> punishment.[5]

And another time:

> My mother entreated, "But the boy has already put up with
> enough fear and terror; otherwise, he'd be lying in bed now in-
> stead of running away. Let him get a good night's rest first.
> Tomorrow he'll understand better what a stupid thing it is that
> he's done."[6]

Manfred von Killinger, thrown out of cadet school for his part in night-
time drinking excursions, describes his homecoming:

> My mother took her boy's head in her hands and gave him a
> kiss. She had already forgiven him, without having to hear the
> father's story. She knew her son and knew he was incapable of
> doing anything improper.[7]

The picture is clear enough. The mother protects; she is an angel, a
home; she is loved. The religious streak, already emphasized by Heydebreck

and Lettow, is occasionally pronounced enough to stand as a separate element—in which case, the encomium is liable to read like that of Maximilian Delmar to his mother:

> The shimmer of the eternal light, falling onto the image of the madonna on the altar, revealed to me the sweet mother of my life. To her alone I say, "Amo! Amo!" Only she is capable of healing, of saving our suffering humanity. Only she can pry humanity loose from the machine-satan of this godless age.[8]

This second aspect is most often emphasized when it is as adults that the sons talk of their "mothers" (quotation marks since in many cases they are not talking about their own mothers).

Martin Niemöller:

> As the bells rang in the New Year on that New Year's Eve of 1919, my mother-in-law stood by an open window, crying to herself as she gazed down along the Wupper Valley. The death of her oldest son had all but broken the heart of this uncommonly strong woman, but it took the distress and humiliation of the fatherland to break it completely. "Martin, do you think things will ever be as they once were in Germany?" I opened my mouth to answer her, and even today I don't know how I could answer as I did; for my own plans were not based on any expectation of change for the better. "There can be no doubt about it, mother!"[9]

Lettow-Vorbeck, describing a friend's mother:

> I also learned a lesson from his aged mother, who refused to break down, even in the face of the shattering news of the death of her son, the last of an ancient line. She became a living example for me of the belief that there is nothing so hard that it cannot be endured!

The Prussian outlook on life.[10]

With the words "life requires actions, not tears," General von der Goltz pays homage to the attitude of a Baltic woman:

> Her adolescent children at her side, a widow stood tearlessly beside the bier of her murdered husband. "Germans don't cry," was her explanation.[11]

The mother of First Lieutenant Paul Scholz, hero of Hanns Heinz Ewers's *Riders in the German Night*, is seen in the same harsh light:

> And yet even this news failed to break his mother. Although the war had devoured four of her sons, she still survived. She was

General Goltz.

destroyed by something ridiculous by comparison; Lorraine, in being overrun by the French, had become the very cesspit of society.[12]

The society, that is, that had given her husband employment. Is it his loss of a position, or is it Lorraine that kills her? Whatever the case, she certainly outlives her sons.

It is not the men's own mothers who are honored in these terms; these writers are reluctant to place themselves in the position of object of the mother's heroism, as the son deserving of pity. "I had a comrade," goes the song . . . and *he* had a mother."[13] At the same time, their own mothers are permitted to show an occasional sign of suffering:

> Mother didn't have it easy with my choleric father. She certainly didn't always agree with his overly strict behavior toward their sons.[14]

Here Lettow-Vorbeck hints that the same strictness may have precipitated her own premature death. The protectress and sufferer are united in one and the same person.

Even the "good mother" is, then, a split figure. One side of her (their *own* mother) is loving and protective, especially of children against their fathers; the other side (mothers of comrades, etc.) is hard. The latter appear as mothers-of-iron, who don't even bat an eye lid at the news of the death of the sons they have sacrificed so much to raise.[15]

Both characteristics, gentleness and harshness, are respected by the sons, though they are sparing in the words they use to honor them. If fewer words are devoted to mothers than even to wives, then the words that are

Lettow-Vorbeck in the arms of his mother.

used are more grand. Mothers are "good angels," "the best of all women," "homes" that can be loved "infinitely" and "above all else" (as only Germany can otherwise be loved).

More than this, the traits of the mother coincide precisely with those of the white countess/nurse we encountered in the previous section. In both, a loving, caring side is posed in opposition to a cold, distantly heroic side.

Looking more closely at hymns of praise to the heroism of the mother-of-iron, we find confirmation for our suspicion of a hidden aggression. Like the countesses/nurses, the mothers derive their heroism from the attitudes they exhibit when they lose their sons or husbands; it is striking that no one lifts a finger to ease their suffering. Suffering is not only taken for granted, it's expressly admired.

Yet there is also a hint of something more in these passages. "The death of her oldest son had all but broken the heart of this uncommonly strong woman"—a formulation that clearly conveys more than pure sympathy. Would the writer be sorry to see her heart broken? Are mothers, like fathers, destined for death? When Lettow has his friend's mother live out the saying, "There is nothing too difficult to endure," isn't there an undertone in his triumph that says, "Yes, she should suffer and do nothing but suffer. This is what she deserves!" And who is the real object of aggression in the following prison episode, in which Salomon tells of a minister

> who once stood in the pulpit and proclaimed that the prisoners were not solely to blame for their misdeeds. It was the bad example they had been set: that was it. Even as children, he said,

they would have witnessed their mothers performing indecent acts with the lodger.

Salomon:

> Afterwards, I demanded that the director force the minister to get back up behind the pulpit and make it clear that, whatever else he may have been thinking of, he didn't have my mother in mind.[16] (The minister apologized later in Salomon's cell.)

Is Salomon's aggression not directed against his mother here? Without any clear grounds, he is spontaneously moved to associate his own mother with the minister's charges of indecency—and all under the guise of defending her purity. Are we not perhaps dealing here with a *threat* issued from the son's cell, warning the mother not to get involved with a lodger (and *any man* might well be regarded as a lodger)? Salomon clearly feels an intense need to ward off this fear that his mother might have been capable of any such involvement.

Lieutenant Willmut's readiness to strangle Countess Fermor (before the Mongolian has a chance to do so . . .) is also striking in this regard. Is it just possible he would have enjoyed doing it? Although Willmut himself is the nominal sufferer—his life is rebuffed—the final conversation between him and the countess can easily be read as her death sentence:

> "What do I have left? Nothing at all, not even
> God . . . Oh, can you tell me, Sandra, where our God has gone to?"
> With crystal clarity, she asks, "Which one?"
> He looks up in amazement, takes a step closer. "You mean, even you have lost Him? Even you have no more God?"
> "No," she answers distinctly, "The old God is dead, I think, for all of us who had eyes to see with. But I do have a god. He can help me more than the old one."
> "And his name?" Willmut whispers.
> "Restraint!" she softly replies.[17]

This time she is no longer speaking in a "melodic tone" but "distinctly," "with crystal clarity." What we have here, in other words, is the reverse of idealization: an attempt on the part of the son to take his mother's life. She is no longer to exist for herself or in relationship with others. She is to be only a heroic still life for her son: *nature morte*.

In Rudolf Herzog's novel *Wieland the Blacksmith* (*Wieland der Schmied*), the wife of the protagonist, Thorsberg, dies right at the start of a plague that is "inundating" Germany (the revolution). Thorsberg is a doctor and, more important, a doctor committed to the fight against this so-called plague. The body of his wife, who is introduced as "Frau Minne" (Lady Love), is equated with the profaned body politic of Germany. She is the mother of two children (son and daughter) who, along with Thorsberg, form the heroic trio of the novel.

> Next morning he subjected his wife to a long, thorough examination. When he had finished, he knew that she would die a slow death.
>
> From that time on, his eyes became brighter and clearer whenever he looked at her, his voice took on a happier and more confident tone whenever he spoke with her, all to bolster her faith in living.[18]

Are we simply to label this sham and pretense, or is the passage not openly expressing the wish that she *should* die? Dead, she is not without her uses. The husband returns, now and then, to the site she now occupies:

> He stood there unmoving, his gaze penetrating the heavy slab, the oaken coffin lid, to reach the transfigured face of this long-suffering woman. He stood there unmoving, holding long conversations with her.

The children too:

> They make a vow at her graveside: "Sword of honor, we will always be faithful, Lady Love."[19]

The author quite clearly *wants* the woman to exist in the novel only as a corpse, a sufferer. Therein, it seems, lies her only value for him. Accordingly, he kills her off and blames the "plague" for her death.

The image of the mother seems, then, to be deeply divided within itself. Even she apparently harbors an evil side that is better concealed and that becomes a target for her son's aggressive impulses.

Are the only good mothers dead mothers?

What is the sons' aggression directed at? Two things, I think. First, it aims to take away the mothers' husbands, and the mothers' aliveness too, the warmth of their human suffering in the face of misfortune. They are left husbandless and turned into cold beings. To that extent, the sons' assaults are directed not only at the mothers' sexuality, but at the availability of their warm, human intimacy, their *motherliness*. Both of those things seem to threaten the song.

In the preceding section, one thing that stood out in the "return-to-the-womb" episodes was the carefully constructed distance of the womb the sons were returning to. Every means was employed to rob the situation of its sensuousness. The place Willmut returned to was more reminiscent of the cold of the grave than the warmth of the maternal lap. In every one of the representations of motherhood cited in this work, this motherly warmth has been split off and put aside.

This splitting off is a defense mechanism. It saves the splitter from being swallowed up by what he detaches from, by the "bad object." Could it be that making the mothers as cold and hard as steel betrays a fear of *intimacy* as something terrifying, and of a mother's *warmth* as something in which a son might easily perish?*

We can now return to our first point relating to mothers and their husbands. The son must be directing some aggression toward the father, since the father is the only person who stands in any possible relation to the mother. (If it were some other man, the entire configuration would change: the mother would then become a whore, rather than a mother.) It is almost as if the father should never have been permitted to touch the mother, as if his having done so were the precise reason for his death at the hands of the "Reds." This in spite of the fact that the fathers must already have touched their wives at least once, when the sons themselves were *conceived*.

That raises some important questions. Are the sons out to negate the fact of their own conceptions? Do they *want* different fathers, wish they *had had* different fathers, or wish they'd *never had* any fathers at all? Do they wish to have been virgin births? Or to have given birth to themselves?

One thing is clear; the literature in question is a literature of sons.

---

*The "separation" of women into "good' and "evil" aspects has been frequently discussed, though generally in a very superficial way. In *The Authoritarian Personality* (*der autoritäre Charakter*) (Adorno, Brunswick, et al.), for instance, the model analysis of a man named "Mack" reads: "How is the rejection of women to be reconciled with the fact that Mack idealizes his mother and intends to marry a girl with a "tremendously nice personality'"? Here it must be considered that "Mack" actually has two conceptions of women: the "bad," weak, dangerous, exploitive, sexual woman who drags one down, and the "good," wholesome, asexual one who gives. It is the former with whom one dares to have sex relations (as in the aftermath of a New Year's party). The latter is described mainly by contrasting her with the former; she is not interested primarily in a "good time" or in "spending fellows' money," or in anything "sordid." Undoubtedly the imagery of this "good" woman derives in part from the imagery of the mother, "who devoted her last strength to us kids." (*The Authoritarian Personality*, p. 803)

The first problem with this formulation is that it overlooks the fact that *both* images of women are ultimately derived from the mother. Freud demonstrated that long ago. For the boy who grows up with bourgeois moral values and understands what his parents are up to in the bedroom, it is an easy step to associate what he sees his mother doing with what prostitutes also do. (Freud, *Gesammelte Werke*, VIII, 73, and XIV, 418)

A more fundamental weakness of such conclusions is that they fail to destroy, and may even create, the impression that good things happen to "good" women, and only bad things to "bad" ones. Of course, that isn't even true in the novels. What happens is that the "good" woman is simply killed off *in a different way* from the "evil" woman. Idealization, or "devivification," is another form of killing. In the figure of the "evil" woman, it is probably not only the sexuality of the mother that is being denied ("prostitution"), but perhaps also her "lethal" essence.

Everything is seen from the perspective of the sons, who have to come to terms with the world, their mothers, and also with sisters (real sisters or nurses).

Whether heroes or chief opponents, fathers are categorically denied a voice in these books. To a remarkable extent, they are simply dispensed with. Even the generals whose reports appear here—Lettow, von der Goltz, Lüttwitz—write as *sons*, as antirepublican rebels. They write as the sons who have survived the disgraceful abdication of their father, Wilhelm II, and who now intend to make up for his errors. Their father has failed them, and now they are stepping forward to do battle for his succession before Mother Germany. Patriarchy secures its dominance under fascism in the form of a "filiarchy"—that much is clear. Nothing but sons as far as the eye can see—Hitler too is one of their number.

"The kaiser should have died at the head of his capitulating army." This is the reproach on the tip of every tongue; often it is directly voiced.[20] The fact that he failed to do so (and that many older officers opportunistically declared themselves in favor of the republic) has completely destroyed the credibility of the patriarchs. Now it is the turn of sons.

SISTERS

The white nurse doesn't exist only as a mother figure, or "white countess." Just as often, she appears as the wounded man's "sister." A perfect example appears in Thor Goote. His "Comrade Berthold" is made to return several times to the field hospital, where the "Sister Franziska" who takes care of him also happens to be his real sister. She invariably turns up wherever her brother is lying wounded. This woman too is on better terms with death than with love:

> Sister Franziska wears a white cornet over her wavy dark hair and a white apron over her blue-and-white nurse's uniform. A wave of iodine accompanies her as she walks . . . She searches in his eyes, though without staring at him.
>
> She doesn't need to ask. She knows those eyes. Day after day, she sees that unspeakable look in the eyes of the men who are carried here to die, or to steal a few months away from death.

She is disinfected. She exudes a "wave of iodine." That wave seems to be directed exclusively at her brother. She follows his movements and he shapes her life:

"I'm taking the express train out tonight, Franziska!" His sister sees him laugh again for the first time. She doesn't ask where he's going. Where else, except toward the front?

He still has two weeks' furlough left, and already Christmas decorations are being sold on street corners . . .

But she doesn't talk about that.

She busies herself with making the tea, buttering the bread, cooking. This may be the last time I see him, she shudders. And he means so much to me!

Yet she doesn't ask him for anything. She doesn't try to hold onto him. You really can't hold onto anything, after all, and you shouldn't cling to anyone . . . .

She sweeps him with a look of pain, smiles as his gaze meets hers. She must stand by him! Not hold back! Share his suffering! This is the finest thing any woman can do, and no woman can do more.

That is her destiny, even though it was never part of her childhood dreams. I will fulfill that destiny, she thought, just as he never runs away from his![1]

"And he means so much to me!" He is everything, but not quite everything. He is the loved one who prevents her from having a lover. What about him? Sometime later on, we find him looking pensively at a photo of his "fiancée":

Next to it stands the small picture of his sister. Yes, until now Franziska has been my confidante. She has cared for me night and day without shirking; hers has been a true sacrifice . . . He picks up his sister's picture. Why can't all women be like you, so calm and unquestioningly reliable? There she stands, in her blue-and-white striped uniform, with that smile on her lips that wants to offer happiness, yet can't conceal from those who know her the pain and death she has seen wiping out young men year after year. And how warm her hand was in mine when she first found out about the girl who is my happiness.[2]

A number of things fall into place here; the veils begin to lift. Whenever Berthold thinks about the girl who is his "happiness," it's his sister he has in mind, rather than this fictitious "fiancée." He gives himself away with the question, "Why can't all women be like you?" A second question is implied here: why can't you be some *other* woman, one who is not kept apart from me by the incest taboo? The incest taboo enforces the invention of the "fiancée." The two photos that stand next to each other on the table are of one and the same woman. It is the *name* of the sister that necessitates her

Berthold's sister Franziska (1932).

Berthold as commander of the Iron Legion (1919-20).

duplication, since one Berthold can't love another Berthold. Now we also know why the fiancée "leaves" him, without ever making an appearance.

She existed only to lift any suspicion from his relationship to his sister, making it a "brotherly" one.

Mothers and sisters seem here to have been revealed as the true love objects of these men. The words of the incest taboo have written "the water is wide, and they cannot get across." We now also have a way of understanding why "good" women have to be husbandless, why they have to be pale as death. It is their very suffering, their attitude of sacrifice, the traces of self-denial on their faces, that give them their deathlike beauty. Why? Because the sons/brothers want it that way. They may produce one Red outrage after another as pretexts, but it's clear enough that they are the ones who want to see the "mask" on these women. The mothers/sisters are called upon to demonstrate that they, too, are consumed by suffering because they are unable to fall into the tender embrace of the sons/brothers. This is the only embrace that the sons/brothers believe the women really want. In short, it is the sons' merciless jealousy that has the husbands killed off (by the "Reds") and makes martyred angels of the mothers and sisters.

If anyone brings the white sister into close proximity with the sensuous woman, the "whore," the brother then explodes. Manfred von Killinger, who took a friend of his sister's as his wife, tells the following story from his days as a naval cadet:

> Some of the cadets, all members of a separate clique, were always telling stories and bragging about women. Peter would smile contemptuously. "And how about Mr. Chastity himself?" one of them sneered, "What are you afraid of? I thought you were always so plucky."
>
> "There's no pluck involved in what you're talking about. And I would do it if circumstances demanded."
>
> "It's not something for little children; you'd do better staying a greenhorn."
>
> Peter was angry. He would show these fellows that they couldn't get away with calling him some kind of inexperienced sissy.
>
> But he had been seen when he went on shore leave. One of the clique asked mockingly, "Well, how was it? Did you have a good time?" "Good time? Anyone who comes from a good home and has sisters doesn't think of that as having a good time. I just did it because you have to try everything once. At least now you weaklings can't impress me anymore. I have tried the game you play with dirty women, and it's left me with nothing but a foul taste in my mouth."

> "Quite right, for a man with sisters," one of them sneered.
> Without a word, Peter stood up, walked over to him, and slapped him in the face.

A duel ensues.

> Two dueling swords were honed, and under the watchful eyes of two arbiters—the staff physician and his intern—the "bullfight" began. Peter was calm, knowing that he could rely on his fencing expertise. When the command to start was given, they heard only a single smack. Before Peter's opponent had even taken in the command, the whole left side of his face hung in tatters.
> There was general satisfaction with the outcome of the "bullfight." Only the intern was dissatisfied; he thought it had all gone too quickly.[3]

"For a man with sisters": this is the key phrase. For him, no other woman is needed; the sister is contained within every other woman he may meet. This is precisely the problem that confronts Killinger; he is unable to distinguish his sister's body from the body of a prostitute in a brothel. In other words, the sister isn't just a white counterpart to the Red whore; in some strange way, she can also become identical with her. As a punishment for voicing the notion that Killinger might have encountered his sister among the "filthy women," the sneering cadet had his face demolished.

With his *Riders in the German Night*, Hanns Heinz Ewers has devoted a novel of almost five hundred pages to the "sister-nurse-whore" complex (with a dead mother in the background). The text deserves closer scrutiny.

The women in the narrative are, first, Pia, a sturdy old nurse, an eternal virgin beyond all sexuality, who is always on hand when wounds cry out for iodine, or wounded men for maternal care. Pia is particularly fond of Lili, another nurse. Lili is a Baltic woman and former countess who has been violated by the Reds. She is the only surviving member of a family whose property has been razed. She is found by German soldiers, lying on a dungheap; they take her away with them. She joins them initially in armed combat, rather than as a nurse. She is ready to shoot down any man who might remotely be seen as connected with her rapists. But she is also a whore, available to any man who is not either Latvian or Russian. A rifle-woman of the Right, in other words.

To make an end to that its hero, First Lieutenant Gerhard Scholz, buys her in an auction. A moment later, she comes "to herself" again. He, it turns out, has won her only so that he can drag her out of the "mire". She lives with him until the end of the Baltic campaign, but they are separated during the retreat.

She stays with Sister Pia and trains as a nurse. With Pia she goes to Munich, works for her high-school diploma, and makes plans to study medicine. The events in Upper Silesia intervene in 1921. German Freikorps soldiers need nurses. Pia is given leave by the hospital head to travel to Upper Silesia. Lili, who has now obtained a German passport under the name *Lili Ignota*, accompanies Pia. In Upper Silesia, she encounters Gerhard Scholz again. He still loves her, but has been prevented from contacting her, since their parting, by the unhappy plight of the fatherland.

Lili's thirst for vengeance remains unquenched. Her assent becomes crucial in the decision to shoot a young turncoat, Karl Friedrich Peters. A *vehme* murder. Much later, this decision turns out to have been made on the basis of an error of judgment; it brings Gerhard Scholz six years in prison, and leads to his total collapse.*

The novel opens with the 1921 *vehme* murder in Upper Silesia; the rest emerges only gradually. Thus without the reader's being aware of it, Lili's first act in the novel is one that will later lead the hero into misfortune. A preview of Lili's demise: she throws herself into the Seine, believing she has brought nothing but bad luck to the man she loves.

Pia is almost always close at hand when Lili is in trouble. During Scholz's trial, they sit together in the courtroom, stroking each other's hands for comfort.

Scholz's mother is already dead when the novel begins. The loss of three sons she was able to overcome, but Lorraine being ceded to France . . . etc. (see above). The mother is present in the novel through her voice. Her lovely renditions of songs by Brahms, Schubert, Schumann, Loewe, and Wolf pervade her son's memories. In moments of peace, when Scholz lies dreaming, the echoes of these songs return to him; he begins humming them, or even singing them. At such times "mother" is with him again.

Once, as he lies in the grass somewhere in Upper Silesia, awaiting Lili's first visit since their unexpected reunion, he sings to himself:

As if I were long dead.[4]

He sings himself to sleep, and when he awakens his head is in Lili Ignota's lap. He has continued to sing in his sleep, and Lili has understood: "As if I were long dead." Lili Ignota, countess, former rifle-woman and whore, now become nurse, sets herself the task of merging herself with the dead mother, and thus of taking her place in Scholz's eyes. Will she succeed?

These two "sisters" are accompanied by a third: Scholz's real sister, Käte. She is in love with her brother and is *fully conscious* of her incestuous

*Ewers's novel was patterned on the life of First Lieutenant Paul Schulz, who was given a six-year sentence as a *vehme* murderer. Schulz, one of the leaders of the Black Reichswehr, participated in sabotage raids against the French in the Ruhr Valley in 1923. See H. and E. Hannover, *Politische Justiz*, pp. 160-74.

desire.⁵ Later on, when the brother is in prison, she makes an overt attempt to seduce him. On Christmas, she manages to get into his cell under an assumed name. She has bribed the guard, and he uses her coat to cover the peephole from the inside as he leaves the cell. Scholz fails to recognize his sister's intent, but is surprised by the extraordinary friendliness of the guard. Käte unbuttons her dress and pulls Scholz down beside her on the wooden bed. He remains cold—he blames her overheated condition on the temperature inside the cell and suggests she open the window.⁶

In the battle over Gerhard Scholz, Käte and Lili are rivals. They are always somewhere close at hand, particularly in the main part of the novel, which describes resistance against separatists in the Rhine and Ruhr regions in 1923. Lili appears as Scholz's fiancée (though there are no allusions to sexual relations during this period); Käte as the secretary of a wholesale merchant, who is on excellent terms with the Franco-Belgian occupying forces and has introduced Käte to their most important reprsentatives. Through him she obtains open access to key sources of information. Her work has more far-reaching effects than Lili's; yet she has a reputation in the town as a hussy, a whore, a sow for the French.⁷ Through her relationship with Toul, a Belgian colonel, she is able both to prevent the death of the man who loves her, officer Peter Lannwitz, and later to pry her brother Gerhard loose from a Belgian prison.

In the second instance, false promises and subterfuges no longer worked. She was forced to pay a visit to the colonel's bed. (Lili has already tried the same thing with Toul and failed.) Neither is she spared the attentions of the merchant Lambert. On one business trip, she is so exhausted from overwork that he has to carry her to her bed in the hotel, where she promptly falls asleep. He climbs in beside her. She never even notices.⁸

Her first husband had been in the war with her eldest brother, Paul. During one spell on leave, Paul brought him home to the Scholz family; on their last day there, Paul found his friend in bed with Käte. They had fallen in love and intended to get married. Paul raised the roof, insisting that they get married immediately; but it was Sunday and they were both due back at the front the next day. A few days later, Paul and his friend were killed in an air crash. Fortunately Käte was not pregnant, and the whole affair was closed.⁹

Thus even Käte fulfills a kind of nurse function; she eases the predicament of men who are *politically* wounded. Circumstances may make her appear as a "whore"—but it's all for the good of Germany—and her brother.¹⁰

Her love for her brother is so exclusive that she can't go through with her engagement to officer Peter Lannwitz, even though she is extremely fond of him. He asks for her hand and she gives it. They sleep together, but her mind is somewhere else and she is unable to feel his caresses. Perhaps it makes him happy, she thinks. She writes him to announce that it simply won't work. It's not his fault, but unfortunately . . .[11]

Käte can only sleep *once* with a man. After this, she has to face the fact that he is not her brother. Lili has seen enough through all of this; she claims that Käte loves no one but Gerhard, and, what is more, that he returns her love; this causes a rift between herself (Lili) and Gerhard. The rivals, acknowledging their mutual animosity, resolve to remain friends. After all, aren't they fighting for the same cause and the same man?[12]

Since Scholz the man cannot be in love with Scholz the woman, he turns increasingly to Lili and expresses surprise over Käte's strange behavior toward him. He doesn't know exactly what she's been up to with the French and Belgians, but he can guess. Shall he treat her as a whore? (All of these thoughts are only implied; they are well beneath the surface.'[13] If he ever found out for sure, he would of course have to put an immediate end to the whole affair.

Lili alternates between the positions of mother and sister in relation to him. Sometimes he feels in her presence the way he used to feel with his mother, whose ability to see right through him had always disturbed him.[14] Then, in one key scene, Lili transforms herself into both Scholz's mother and his sister. Scholz has just been released from prison, thanks to Käte's sacrificing herself to Colonel Toul. He and Lili are discussing the possibility of going off to study in Berlin, but she has lost interest in medicine.

> "What, then," he asked.
> "I'll sing," she replied. "I'm told it can be of use to train one's voice. Would you have any objection?"
> "None at all," he emphasized, "assuming you need my permission in the first place. You realize, don't you, that my mother used to sing? We children would listen at the door."
> "Yes," she said, "children like to do that." She lifted the blanket a little and asked, "May I come to you?"
> Her fingers tenderly caressed his cheeks. "Red ribbons," she whispered. "Whipmarks . . . seven, eight, nine. I love you! Your wrists! Both of them rubbed raw! That's from the handcuffs, isn't it? Ugly wounds. Does it hurt? I love you."

She, as "mother," loves all of his wounds. But inside, something is eating away at her:

> And yet she wanted to say, "I wasn't the one. It was she, the other woman, she alone, Käte. Not I. She did it. She alone.
> And she wanted to say, "I, I'm the one. I did it for you, I, your sister! I am your sister, and I did it. Because I love you, dearest, that's why I did it. It's me, Käte. I love you, I love you." She trembled and whimpered, glowing under his kiss.

"I am," she whispered, "I am."[15]

Although she never actually says any of these things out loud, it is as if brother-son Scholz has nonetheless heard her. That same night, Lili Ignota, the woman who can have no name of her own, who must give away her body in exchange for other names, is made pregnant by Scholz.[16]

Later, when Scholz is in prison, she learns all of the songs his mother used to sing.[17] Despite all this, she has a miscarriage. It seems that the children of former whores (or of incestuous relationships) are not to be allowed to come into this world.[18]

She wants to have a child, but feels she never will. She takes up residence in Paris, where she hopes to find some way of having Scholz pardoned. In the Jardin du Luxembourg, she is often to be found watching a woman whose own tender gaze rests on a child in her baby carriage, but who attempts to hide the baby from the gaze of others. One day Lili discovers that the carriage has been empty all along.[19] She herself is the woman.

The ultimate failure of her efforts to obtain Scholz's freedom is something we learn of only from vague indications in her suicide note.[20] She has by now jumped into the Seine. It seems that she has made a mistake at the last minute; she tried to use Käte's method to free him, but Käte's work was simply beyond her.

As soon as she hears of Lili's death, Sister Pia hurries to Paris, where she finds the body in an anatomy class:

> The anatomy professor had used her to give a lesson. She had then been dismembered, parts of her going to every student.
> Sister Pia offered money to the anatomy students to gather all the pieces together. Only the left foot was still missing; it was simply nowhere to be found.[21]

Pia has Lili pieced together again, then arranges her funeral. Lili's circuitous route has led her to become the victim of a dismemberment fantasy on the part of the author, Ewers. Following his belated revenge on the former whore (a piece of her for every student), there ensues her reassemblage into a good woman. That "limb" that remains missing (the "left foot") is the imaginary penis which she had always carried around with her and which had caused her to climb into so many of the wrong beds.* We will soon meet her again as a *castrated* woman, dead and white.

Without her brother, meanwhile, Käte becomes increasingly melan-

---

*This is a consistent component of mythological fantasies of dismemberment, as for instance in the myth of Isis and Osiris. The part that stereotypically remains missing when the body is reassembled functions as a sign of castration. See Rank, *Das Inzest-Motiv in Dichtung und Sage* (Leipzig and Vienna, 1926), pp. 285ff.; and Mannhardt, *Germanische Mythen* (Berlin, 1858), pp. 57ff.

choly. The visit to Scholz's cell described above occurs after Lili's death. Scholz can make no sense of one line from Lili's suicide note, "Now you have only Käte." He simply does not understand. "Gerhard, not a soul here knows I'm your sister," Käte had pleaded then.[22] He finds the whole situation disturbing.

When his illness earns him a rehabilitative leave, he doesn't visit Käte, or even write to her. His valet from the war years nurses him back to health. His word of honor vouching for his return, Scholz is finally permitted to spend a few weeks in Italy. There he meets a Scottish lady, who pursues him unsuccessfully. She claims to be in love with him, but he avoids her. Only on the last evening do they strike up a brief conversation. She refuses to believe he could be capable of murder. He somehow manages to sense she is different from the high-society tramps who have consistently rejected him during his stay on Capri; yet, touched as he may be by her advances, he nonetheless feels too German to give in to them.[23]

When he reports back to the criminal police in Berlin, they make a laughingstock of him. How could anyone be stupid enough to return voluntarily to prison? That business of the word of honor had been merely for show. They had really wanted to give him a chance to abscond. Unfortunately, they now had no option but to lock him up again.[24]

Scholz meanwhile had been counting on an amnesty, which he had previously been led to believe might be forthcoming. Terrified now, he turns heel and runs from police headquarters. He actually manages to escape, and the story goes crazy. On his way to the police, Scholz had been musing on certain passages from Heraclitus and had felt a sudden need to see what Heraclitus actually looked like, at least in plaster. He had gone into a shop and found . . . Lili in plaster. A death mask had been made of her face and was now being peddled far and wide as The Unknown Beauty of the Seine—a hot item. The woman who owned the shop had made a point of indicating that the drowned woman had allegedly been a prostitute. And there she was, hanging on the wall for all to see. Scholz had bought two masks,[25] and now, fleeing from the police, he remembers that he has left both of them at police headquarters. He goes back to fetch the masks. Although he waits until lunchtime, when the building is more or less empty, he is spotted and put under arrest.[26] (The fact that he could have bought new masks is never so much as considered. It seems that impressions of the purified Lili cannot be left lying around at a republican police station.) It is thus out of some compulsion that Scholz in effect voluntarily returns to his cell.

It is here that he learns, soon afterward, of Käte's gruesome end. During the time when she was walking out with Colonel Toul in order to save her brother Gerhard from a Belgian prison, a German youth had once called her a "French tart"! He had taken note of her face, and later recognized her

on the street. The *Völkisch* youth group to which he belongs are admirers of
Gerhard Scholz. They put her on trial. She refuses to defend herself or give
her name. They cut off her hair, administer a laxative, then march her off
into the woods:

> "Jump to it, sweetheart," their leader says. "You'll find a
> pig's wallow down there—the sort of place a prize slut like you
> belongs!"
> She stood there on the country road, helpless, immobile.
> "Get a move on, fairy princess!" the leader warned, "Into the
> woods with you. A bit of movement will soon warm you up. A
> sight for sore eyes, you are—with your bald head and shit all
> over your dress!" The other boy gave her a whack across her
> fanny with his switch. "Move it, you whore, before I have to do
> it for you!"
> She turned around and felt a second lash across her left
> breast. The pain bit into her. She let out a shrill scream.
> "What are you doing, man?" the leader bellowed at him.
> "Be careful!"
> "Sorry," the boy said. "It was a mistake, I was trying to hit
> her rear end again! Now let's get this over with. Come on, run!
> Run!"[27]

She wanders around aimlessly in the woods for a few days, not daring
to show herself. She is finally apprehended; taken for a mad woman, she
dies in an infirmary, of pneumonia.

. . . Victory

Her brother Gerhard, realizing that everything she'd done had been for
his sake, casts a spell on himself in the St. Ré penitentiary. However, he
finds the lads' actions above reproach; indeed he commissions his own attorney to take over the defense of his sister's murderers. Afterward he lays
her to rest inside himself, as a saint:

> She appeared to him, not wanting his name, Gerhard Scholz, to
> be mentioned in the same breath as that of a French hussy. She
> acted as she had on that day, sacrificing herself for him. Bearing
> all the shame, all the torture—for him. For his sake she had
> descended into madness and for him she died. Käte, his sister.[28]

The two women (sisters/sister-nurses) are relentlessly pursued by the
author's rage for destruction because they aren't absolutely "white."
Although they are sisters/lovers of the hero and actively fighting on the right
side for Germany's future, they have to die: their first men were not their
only men.

World War I poster. For public consumption, "white" women aren't given names like Käte or Lili. They are called Homeland—Mother—Soviet—Liberation.

World War I poster. "Liberation."

World War I poster. "Victory."

Lili's first man was the one who raped her. Käte's fell in battle before they had a chance to marry. In each case, we are dealing with crimes punishable by death, for which the women must atone. The practiced reader of these texts comes to recognize the pattern as soon as any such character is introduced. In this case, however, I was a little unsure. The women have an unusually strong presence in the novel. Ewers spares no linguistic expense to place Käte/Lili's efforts on behalf of Germany and of First Lieutenant Gerhard Scholz in a heroic light. But to no avail. In the end, it becomes clear that the entire book is laid out as evidence that *no* amount of effort, however well intentioned, can ever remove the "whore's taint" from the sister/lover. Only death can restore her "whiteness."

Scholz nonetheless gets his woman. True, for a while he suffers bouts of nausea and wants only to die, but then the Scottish woman begins tending to his needs. Through her connections with the British ambassador—the fact that he is a relative prevents any doubt arising as to her methods—she obtains Scholz's release.[29] Numbed, mute, and apathetic, he allows her to lead him away, even letting her touch his hand. Finally, he begins speaking again. We are told of his first five words to the Scottish woman, who has been the agent of his rebirth. Those words are cause for great hope. "The words of a German,"[30] he says after listening to her talk for a long time. What she said is never related, and so she is allowed to remain alive. Any concrete statement from her would render her *more real, more alive*—and as we have seen, those are mortally dangerous attributes.

It may have been precisely Käte's and Lili's political effectiveness that made them so dangerous. Rebuilding the country is men's work. Those "sisters" helped out far too much and wanted far too much. Any move on their part is suspect, even the "right" one.

The dead, white mother wins out over the erotic sister. To evade the latter's enticements, Ewers/Scholz has to divide, then reduplicate her in the persons of Lili and Käte. The result of that division is that Lili is set against Käte; both are weakened, divided, and destroyed.

The Scottish savior comes from afar as a noble, white mother figure (returning from the realm of the dead). It seems doubtful whether her relationship with Scholz may be termed incestuous, given that the mother figure serves less as love object than as "home," or principle of sanctuary—a principle that safeguards the man against incest with the sister. It is a fine line that divides "white sisters" from "whores"—and although that border is almost invisible, in the end it is a sharp one. Anyone who tries to cross it dies. Anyone who tries to efface it is made to pay a penalty: the penalty of a sword-slashed (*Spaltung*), and anyone who infringes that border will confront the person producing this splitting with a part of what he holds repressed. Through immediate punitive action, the repressed material is relentlessly returned to its allotted place.

MARRIAGE—SISTERS OF COMRADES

For marriage to be possible, it must almost always follow the same model. The writer's own sister is pledged to a comrade-in-arms, good friend, or other respected male; and his sister becomes the writer's wife.

> It was a difficult time: six months of fever and blood poisoning, and eight operations. But the ways of the Lord are wondrous. That accursed field hospital was crucial in changing the life of someone very dear to me. My sister, coming from Tübingen to take care of me for a few weeks, met the man I admired most among all my doctors.
> Two years later, he and she were united in a very happy marriage.[1]

It's this configuration that allows the marriage of Freikorps-commander von Heydebreck to be called "very happy" before it's even gotten underway. She marries a man the brother respects, and that acts as a guarantee.

In the opening section, "Seven Marriages," the husbands displayed a striking preference for marriages of that kind. In three cases, they married sisters of male friends or comrades. Two of the others chose women who could be associated with the names of "spiritual brothers" (Schiller, Heinrich George, Goethe). The seventh man married his sister's girlfriend, entrusting her to the care of his stalwart German father during his time away at the war.

I haven't been able to find evidence of a single wedding that wasn't "secured" in one of the ways described above. Ironically, marrying a woman whose name is never mentioned makes it possible to marry a name; only here that name, that known, familial quantity, may simply be "sister," or the name of another man (the bride's father or brother). It can never be a woman with a name all her own—just plain Lili.

This configuration has both an incestuous and a homoerotic aspect. First, the incestuous. Through the identification with a comrade, a legitimate sexual connection to the writer's own sister is created. As for the homoerotic, the brother is loved through the medium of the sister. Both men, brother and husband, are united in her.* The sister and brother form an identity, with the same name, same flesh, same familiar territory.

Yet the really decisive aspect of this configuration is its third one: recoil. Affection plays a much smaller part here than antipathy. The man recoils.

---

*Wilhelm Reich tried to explain the practice among soldiers, cadets, and others of visiting brothels together, on the basis of a hidden goal, which was finding one's comrade, the other man, in the person of the prostitute and having intercourse with him through her. See *Die Funktion des Orgasmus*, p. 167 (referring to Boehm, 1922).

He recoils from erotic woman, that unfamiliar, nameless flesh, that living territory of *becoming*. And he avoids any man who behaves toward her in anything other than a brotherly fashion.

This marriage does not then seem to establish any relation to an object; it seems rather to constitute an escape from particular possible objects. If we take this union with a woman who falls into the category "sisters of comrades" and compare it with all that ethnology has to say about marriage practices, we are struck by the fact that it is based not on economic or political considerations, but wholly upon *psychic* grounds. It is a marital type that can be filed under "defense mechanisms." For that very reason, I doubt that we can talk about latent strivings toward incestuous or homoerotic love objects in such cases.

The same applies to the preference for marrying virgins—of which "marriages to sisters of comrades" is a special case. Those marriages are not directed toward a female love object, but away from the threat that emanates from female objects. (Where there is love, there is also communism and castration.)

In that sense the "sister," viewed as a love object, serves to define the *limits* of possible object choices. Anything beyond her name is uncharted, dangerous territory, yet she herself is taboo. What this all comes down to, again, is that no object seems attainable and no object relations seem capable of being formed.

What about the mother? Once the sister-as-impossible-love-object has been successfully renounced (and marrying a friend's sister seals that success), the mother appears to draw the man/son/husband back under her spell. As the white countess/nurse, she seems to return from the realm of the dead to hold him once again in her shadowy clutches.

It's fair to say, then, that the man never reaches beyond the sister, nor frees himself from the mother.[2] At the cemetery, after visiting his wife's grave:

> Lore hangs onto his arm. "Do you still remember, Helmut, how you used to walk with me when you were a brand-new lieutenant? I was so proud. Two old aunts took us for a couple, instead of brother and sister."
> "Come on, Lore. That was twenty years ago."[3]

THE LADY WITH THE LIGHT

We can see now that the "white nurse" is given a preeminent role in the psychic security system of the men. She is the essential embodiment of their recoiling from all erotic, threatening femininity. She guarantees the maintenance of the sibling incest taboo, as well as the connection to a caring mother figure, who transcends sensuousness.

Her presence in the war makes her even better suited to her role. Aside from nurses, women hardly existed for soldiers in the First World War. They knew about nurses either as patients themselves in a military hospital or from comrades who had returned from one. The nurse's *image* haunts nearly every one of these texts.

> All of them were older nurses, but to every one of the young men they seemed incredibly clean, bright, white, delicate, and young.[1]
>
> They looked as appetizing as fresh fruit wrapped in tissue paper, and their faces looked rosy-white under their white cornets. Most were Frisian women, blond and delicate.[2]

Schauwecker pretentiously packs the white bodies of his imaginary nurses in tissue paper. The cruder witticisms of the troops dip them into a more acidic desexualizing agent. To the men, they are "carbolic babies" (Karbol mäuschen),[3] who won't deny any wish to a suffering soldier. Carbolic acid was a common disinfectant in the field hospitals. Whether in tissue paper or carbolic acid, though, the nurses are disinfected sweethearts, that is, parodies of sensuous women.

The image of the nurse moves back and forth along a scale ranging from coolly ministering mother to enticing, erotic sister. As a "carbolic sweetheart," she is closer to the erotic sister/prostitute end of the scale. The sister/nurse teases and seduces, while the mother/nurse rejects and offers care. She gets her way, as Jünger points out so well:

> Though I'm no misogynist, I was irritated by female nature every time the fortunes of war tossed me into some hospital ward bed. From the manly, purposeful, and practical action of warfare, you plunged into an atmosphere of vague emanations. The detached objectivity of the Catholic nursing orders was a welcome exception.[4]

As we know, one of the most pervasive male fantasies in our society concerns sexual relations with nurses. It crops up in war films, in reports about nursing, and becomes a standard theme in novels. It is that staple food on which, for example, Hemingway's *In Another Country* feeds.* Equally well known is the fact that nurses refuse to conform to the images of them projected in male fantasies. It may be less well known that they are

---

*His nurse dies in childbirth, after being made pregnant by a recovering soldier.

seldom pressed to do so either—except, perhaps, by doctors.[5] When all is said and done, the patient doesn't desire the nurse as a person, but as an incarnation of the caring mother, the nonerotic sister.* Indeed, that may be the main reason nurses are called "sisters" in so many countries.

The hospital situation is highly conducive to that fantasized (non)love scenario. The wounded man is almost never alone, and his wounded state usually impedes his lovemaking ability. He is given into someone's care, degraded from his status as sexual object. To be a hospital patient is often to be deprived of individual rights, particularly in field hospitals. A man may find himself reduced to the status of a powerless child.

Yet the ideas and demands of our soldier males seem paradoxically to have been better served by precisely that powerlessness. Here they were better able to focus their needs for mother-child and sibling relations onto the sister-nurses.[6] Men who try to turn those into sexual relationships are not destined to live long. In Thor Goote's *We Shoulder Life* (*Wir tragen das Leben*), Peter Ohlstädt falls in love with a nurse named Luise. A week before his scheduled release from the field hospital, he deliberately breaks his arm. Yet postponing his departure doesn't help him at all. From that moment on, he can't stand it when Luise is near him and he gets drunk every night. Luise, for her part, wants nothing to do with him.

> I couldn't go on like that. There was so much fear lodged in my gullet that I was embarrassed in front of everyone. And at night, a bald-headed vulture with sharp claws sat on my bed. Night after night.[7]

---

*As part of a music-class assignment to make up your own songs, a twelve-year-old elementary school student from southern Bavaria came up with the following in 1974:

> Sister, I need medicine or else I'll die. Quick, medicine!
> Sister, I need a doctor or else I won't be long for. Quick, a doctor!
> I was standing on the avenue, just to get a look at you,
> When everything became a zoo. I couldn't even move my shoe.
>
> Sister, I have to get out or my life is in doubt, I have to get out!
> Sister, I need a cigarette, a cigarette 'cause I'm not okay yet.
> Then for a few hours I was gone. I didn't know what was going on
> Till I saw Sister dear, then everything got clear.
>
> Sister, you're a sex-bomb, such a sweet blonde, a real sex-bomb,
> The ambulance brought me into this place
> But it's the leaving I just can't face,
> 'Cause you look so good, I'd stay forever if I could.
>
> Sister, what your miniskirt hides
> Might be the biggest shock
> Of my nine lives.

English postcard from World War I. "The Star That Shines Above the Trenches at Night."

Ohlstädt confesses this to his friend Helmut, the novel's protaganist. He is so afraid of the mere possibility that the nurse may approach him that he symbolically castrates himself (broken arm), then hallucinates the castrator (vulture) on his bed every night. Alcohol is his third device for preventing Luise from approaching him during his hard-won reprieve. On New Year's Eve, 1918, immediately after the confession to Helmut, Ohlstädt shoots himself, even though his friend has already absolved him ("You stuck it out at the front, didn't you?").[8]

Nurses belong equally to all patients. They are creatures that blossom when everyone else is suffering:

American nurses parading in front of United States President Wilson.

Led by a young nurse, the sick prisoners celebrated their arrival with a howl of redemption. It was a sight that made the heart stand still, an impression that left us speechless, a sacred vision of the helpless collapse of men freed at last from torment. One thing that will never leave my memory is the image of that lovely young nurse, overcome with joy, leading her indescribably wretched patients out into the light, toward their liberators, in a calm and almost maternal manner.[9]

This is the climax of Captain von Medem's impressions of the conquest of Riga in an official military report to the General Command of the Sixth Reserve Corps, dated August 15, 1919. His superior, Major Bischof, was so impressed that he borrowed the description verbatim in his own account of events from the "Baltic enterprise."[10] ". . . into the light, toward their liberators." The liberators are men, and the woman is one of the principal mainstays of their "freedom."*

Without realizing it, the Red nurses were skirting a real precipice. One can almost feel the rise and intensity of the soldiers' rage at the sight of those

---

*Today, she leads a splendid existence as an agent of male dominance in medical novels (and a less splendid one in the hospitals themselves). "She handed medical superintendent Kissinger the sterilized scalpel. With a shudder she realized she was witnessing a glorious hour for humanity. This operation in which for the first time an entire planet would be severed with a single incision."

"His deepest wound." This and the next four illustrations, drawings from Magnus Hirschfeld's *Sittengeschichte des Weltkriegs*. Miss Cavell was a director of a nursing school in Brussels during World War I. She arranged for injured British soldiers to escape back to England. German occupying forces shot her for "spying." Extant photos show her in the dark suit that befits a director of an institution, not in a nurse's uniform.

"most repulsive of all characters" serving the workers. That was committing a monstrous crime against the soldiers' image of the purity of nurses/sisters and the asexuality of mothers. What they saw was prostitutes slipping into nurses' uniforms they didn't deserve to wear, then openly making love to those criminals. It was a mockery of the soldiers' sacredly unattainable, incestuous desires. The soldiers' safety devices were being dynamited; perverted nature was being helped to stage a breakthrough. And it was all being done with that irritating nonchalance, that abysmal recklessness, that the workers and those women always showed toward the feelings of the soldiers. With great pains and under duress, the soldiers had learned how to erect within themselves the protective idol of the suffering woman; and now those people were laughing, making love, and not suffering one little bit (at least not from lovemaking or laughter.)

The response:

> a hand grenade surprised her in the practice of her true
> profession.

Recent feminist research on the history of European medicine has demonstrated that even more is concealed behind the figure of the white nurse. The research has shown that it took centuries of struggle to force women healers and their knowledge of "folk medicine" out of medical practice, then replace them with academically trained, professional male physicians. Witch-hunts were, among other things, a means for achieving that goal. All that remained for women was midwifery.[11]

"An angel in all but power is she!"
"Un ange,—mais une force!"

THE MURDER OF MISS CAVELL
INSPIRES GERMAN "KULTUR."

In the middle of the nineteenth century, there was a new female assault (the first target being the military hospital), which was closely linked to the name of Florence Nightingale, the "angel of the wounded men." In *Witches, Midwives and Nurses*, Barbara Ehrenreich and Deirdre English write:

> At first, male doctors were a little skeptical about the new Nightingale nurses—perhaps suspecting that this was just one more feminine attempt to infiltrate medicine. But they were soon won over by the nurses' unflagging obedience. (Nightingale was a little obsessive on this point. When she arrived in the Crimea with her newly trained nurses, the doctors at first ignored them all. Nightingale refused to let her women lift a finger to help the thousands of sick and wounded soldiers until the doctors gave an order. Impressed, the doctors finally relented and set the nurses to cleaning up the hospital.) To the beleaguered doctors of the 19th century, nursing was a godsend: Here at last was a kind of health worker who did not want to compete with the "regulars," did not have a medical doctrine to push, and who seemed to have no other mission in life but to serve.[12]

In other words, a nurse is also a castrated doctor. As the "lady with the lamp," she first appears on male battlefields during the preliminary skir-

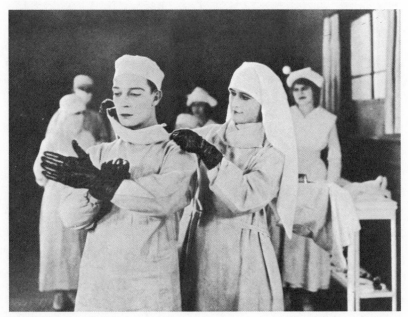

Buster Keaton in "Daydreams."

mishes of imperialism that will lead to greater wars: Nightingale in the Crimean War; Dorothea Dix in Union field hospitals during the American Civil War.[13]

> . . . genuine aristocrats. They were refugees from the enforced leisure of Victorian ladyhood. Dix and Nightingale did not begin to carve out their reform careers until they were in their thirties, and faced with the prospect of long, useless spinsterhood.[14]

The ladies with the lamps placed far less value on medical training than on the formation of character. Florence Nightingale—whose name must have been assigned to her by some male providence—objected to the establishment of a formal nursing "profession," with formal training and examinations. "Nurses," she claimed, "can no more be examined and certified than mothers."[15]*

---

*No more than prostitutes are examined and certified. Freud relates the dream of a "well-respected, highly cultured older woman" who offers her services to the military field hospital, but does it in a way that tells everyone she means "services in bed." A reminder that the juxtaposition of white nurse and prostitute meant something even to bourgeois women who entered the "Nightingale service." (*Gesammelte Werke*, XI, 137ff.) There were many such women in World War I; cf. Hirschfeld, *Sittengeschichte des Weltkriegs*, I, chaps. 3 and 5. Quite a few of those wrote biographies and novels as well.[16]

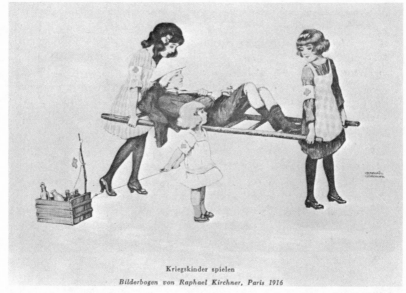

Kriegskinder spielen
Bilderbogen von Raphael Kirchner, Paris 1916

"Children of War at Play." Drawing by Raphael Kirchner (Paris, 1916).

In a historical sense as well, then, the white nurse is an emblem for the bourgeois woman's renunciation of her *female* body. The nurse's is a dead body, with no desires and no sexuality (no "penis"). She unites in herself the opposing poles of mother and sister, burying all of their dangerous enticements inside: the fiction of a body, which men need in order not to feel threatened.

All of that is signaled, in the end, by the nurse's uniform. "White" signifies untrodden ground; no stream of red has ever been let loose within that uniform, never a stain on its fabric.* The nurse is a blank page and condemned to remain so, if she is to function as a terrain for male fantasies.**

One man did in fact write on that page, by allowing himself to fulfill his incestuous desire for his sister. He reports an episode of premarital "sexual intercourse" (his phrase), the only one I could locate in these books that was not followed by the death of the "sister." The man is Rudolf Höss. Stationed during wartime in Palestine, Höss lies wounded in a military hospital in Jerusalem, the city of miracles:

---

*The husband of one of Freud's women patients poured a pot of red ink into the bed after an unsuccessful wedding night. (*Gesammelte Werke, XI, 269*) Thus it seems to be precisely the man who has been incapable of any release, who sees the red stream as a sign of major events.

**Just as the "whiter than white wash" is a "territory" for endless housewife/industrial fantasies in which all traces of life are hallucinated away. (See "The Body as Dirt," chapter 2 of the present work.)

RED CROSS OR IRON CROSS?

WOUNDED AND A PRISONER
OUR SOLDIER CRIES FOR WATER.

THE GERMAN "SISTER"
POURS IT ON THE GROUND BEFORE HIS EYES.

THERE IS NO WOMAN IN BRITAIN
WHO WOULD DO IT.

THERE IS NO WOMAN IN BRITAIN
WHO WILL FORGET IT.

English poster from World War I.

Warum ~~CDU~~ wählen:

Almuth von Holle, 27, OP-Schwester, 4400 Münster

„...weil ich Angst vor dem Sozialismus habe."

"Almuth von Holle, Nurse." Poster for the German congressional elections (1976).

Even my own mother couldn't have taken better care of me than that nurse did. Gradually I noticed, however, that it wasn't only maternal love that moved her to offer me so much tender care and attention.

Until then love for a woman, for the opposite sex, was something unknown to me. Of course, I'd heard a lot about sexual matters from my comrades' conversations, and soldiers talk about those things in a fairly straightforward way. Yet I myself was still a stranger to such desires, perhaps for lack of opportunity. Besides, the strains of existence in that theater of war were hardly conducive to any sort of affectionate feelings. Because I'd resisted any show of tenderness since I was a young boy, I was confused at first by her tender caresses, her holding me and supporting me longer than was necessary. Confused, that

is, until I, too, entered love's magic circle and began to see the woman with new eyes. At every stage, the affection I felt was exquisitely unfamiliar, as was the sexual union she quickly guided me toward. I myself wouldn't have had the courage to initiate this first sexual experience which, in all its charm and tenderness, became a touchstone to which I would return throughout my life. I could never discuss such things in a trivial way. Sexual intercourse without the deepest affection had become something unthinkable. This protected me against flirtations and brothels.[17]

Flirtation = brothel; yet one visit from a woman of this kind renders a man immune to both.

The passage comes from a forty-five-year-old death row inmate. What reason would a man like that have for holding anything back? He had watched more people die than he could remember. He had ordered and directed their deaths. He had been shaken, but he had held out to the last: the duty of an SS man. On *that* level at least, nothing human was alien to him. Now seeing his own death before him, he confesses his earliest love for the first time, in words that could hardly be more helpless or unreal. *Nothing* in that passage is based on experience. "Exquisitely unfamiliar"— "at every stage"—"all its charm and deepest affection"—"love's magic circle"—the body itself is never brought into play, neither would he have confessed even to that fictitious love if he thought he were going to stay alive. The dream of his lifetime was having that white nurse/Virgin Mary appear to him in the Jerusalem military hospital. It was a dream dreamed by seventeen-year-old private Rudolf Höss, the man who earlier would have given anything to avoid becoming a priest, or to be allowed to become a soldier. His first sexual experience "became a guiding principle for the rest of my entire life." Realizing the fantasy acted like a cork, bottling up any further possibilities for real love relationships.

Also drawn by that "guiding principle" was the fiction of the wife he had really married. ("I had found the woman I'd longed for during my long years of loneliness.") The nurse visited him in prison every day. How could his wife make up that headstart? "Yet, there was one thing that always made her sad: I kept the things that moved me most deeply to myself, never revealing them even to her." *Least of all* to her. The moment she (the wife) became a real person, all of those beautiful fictions would have to die. And without his symbiosis with the Mother of God Rudolf Höss would never have been able to stick it out at the gas chambers to the bitter end, when everything else he'd believed in was falling apart around him.

AN ASIDE ON PROLETARIAN REALITY,
PROLETARIAN WOMAN AND MAN OF THE LEFT:
THE REALITY CONTENT OF THE PROJECTIONS

It is clear that the Freikorps soldiers' projected image of proletarian women is a distortion. We still need to ask, though, how much the actual behavior of those women may have contributed to the image. How did they act toward the soldiers? Were there aspects of their behavior that fit in with the men's way of seeing?

Anyone who feels solidarity with the women and tries to combat the soldiers' views by stylizing the women into industrious, comradely, charming companions will be sorely disappointed. One set of projections isn't going to defeat another.

Interestingly, one of our sources of information on workers' lives (in Hamborn, in this case) was penned by another Baltic nobleman. Count Stenbock-Fermor, after fleeing the Baltic area in 1919, worked from November 16, 1922, to December 20, 1923, as a miner in one of Thyssen's pits, near Hamborn.* As a high-school student, he had taken part in the Baltic Territorial Army's battles first against the Red Army, then against Latvian and Estonian republicans. After working in the mine for a year, and living four to a room in a workers' hostel, he began to see proletarians and communists from a new perspective. His book, *My Life as a Miner* (*Meine Erlebnisse als Bergarbeiter*), published in 1929, depicts him as a participant-observer of the living and working conditions of the proletariat. The values he places on what he observes are often determined by the outlook of his class and caste, but that's what makes them so useful at this point. Here is Stenbock-Fermor on sexuality in Hamborn:

> Aside from questions of wages and politics, stories about women were one of the favorite topics of conversation. A feature of these stories was their devastating lack of a sense of morality. The men talked about their wives in the filthiest manner and told of their intimate relationships with the wives of their comrades. I overheard one miner telling a hewer, "Hey you, Anton! Last week, when you were on night shift, I slept with your old lady!" The hewer answered serenely, "Do whatever you want, boy, just don't let me catch you at it or you won't be worth two shits!"
>
> I was standing close to the cage one morning before our descent, when I heard a young fellow behind me call out to the person directly in front of him. "I took my shift off yesterday and went over to Hans's to f——— his old lady." A hoarse scream went up at that point. A tall, black-bearded man threw himself onto the speaker, and with the words "You miserable, goddam, lowdown dog, stinking pig!" beat him about the head until he was staggering like a drunkard. At that point I had to climb in, so I couldn't follow the rest of the fight. I heard that the black-bearded man was the husband. When the shift was over, I saw both of them, the husband and the "friend of the household" peacefully walking along and having a friendly conversation. Boxing the man's ears had put an end to the matter!
>
> Things like that happened every day. Many of the married couples took in single men as boarders, and I was told it was very common for a boarder to start up a relationship with the

---

*"Financial need and probably a certain lust for adventure—I was studying engineering in Strehlitz/Alt at the time—induced me to earn my living temporarily as a manual laborer." (p. 5)

women of the house. That would usually happen when the husband worked a different shift. The husbands didn't consider peccadilloes of that kind especially tragic, generally accepting them in silence. Beatings or even stabbings occurred only when the guilty parties were caught in the act, or when things became too obvious in some other way. Even then, though, peace was quickly restored and grudges never held.

The living conditions of the miners were as bad as could be imagined. . . . Naturally, these deficiencies had the most detrimental effect on the rising generation. Living at such close quarters in tiny rooms, from infancy onward the children witnessed their parents' marital relations. And since the parents had heavy work to contend with all day long, no one worried about the children. Left entirely to themselves, they would be up to no good on the streets.

I often saw very small children playing on the streets, swearing at each other in the filthiest language. At fifteen or sixteen, most of the girls already had their "boyfriends." The number of illegitimate children was shockingly large. Although there were no brothels in Hamborn, street prostitution was rampant and venereal diseases were terribly widespread.[1]*

Fermor's statement about the "shockingly large" number of illegitimate children needs to be corrected. It holds true only if he is referring to illegitimately *conceived* children. As far as illegitimate births go, statistics for the period 1900-1913 show Hamborn as below the average for all cities in the Prussian provinces, and even for most rural areas.[2] This is because, for a number of reasons, a marriage almost always took place when there was a baby on the way. The girl's parents could rid themselves of another hungry mouth that was generally not bringing in any money, while the boy could give up the life of a boarder to set up his own household—a route by no means open to all, given the district's considerable surplus of men. A boarder marrying the daughter of his host, or so-called board-farmer (*kostbauer*), was the most frequent of all marriage rites. Often the marriage was all but inevitable, simply because the lack of other space forced the boarder and host's daughter to sleep in the same room.[3]

As I have already mentioned, Fermor lived in a workers' hostel. He says nothing in his book about personal relationships with women, giving the impression that during his year as a miner, he never spoke to any woman alone. As he tells it, his leisure time was filled up with "culture." He would

*Because of the significant role fear of syphilis played in the sexual lives of these men (more about that later), statements about the spread of venereal diseases that are not based on medical statistical reports have to be denied on principle. There was "street prostitution," but it didn't evolve until the post-World War I era. See E. Lucas, *Arbeiterradikalismus*, pp. 70ff.

read Spengler and Nietzsche, or go to the theater in nearby Duisburg (the original Faust!). His book also recounts a more extended discussion he had with politically active workers. That discussion shows that it is precisely the great importance he assigns to art, philosophy, "culture," that prevents him from accepting the political demands of the proletariat, especially when the topic of power is broached.[4] For him the notion of culture, or better, a "feeling" for culture, is linked to the rejection of female sexuality and a preference for certain male social circles. For much as he values these discussions, nowhere is he further from the proletariat than in the description of their sexual relations ("devastating lack of a sense of morality"). The workers' struggles against hunger, exploitation, and housing shortages are things he can appreciate and support. He has no doubts about their solidarity, even admiring it. Yet their sexuality is alien to him.

Additional information about sexuality in the boarding-house system comes from the reports of a pit foreman named Werner, who worked both in Silesia and in the Ruhr Valley:

> Among miners in the Ruhr district, there were three distinct
> forms of board: "half-board," "full-board," and "full-board-
> plus." With half-board, the price of the room included lunch
> and morning coffee. I paid 28 marks for that. You had to buy
> your own bread and fixings, which cost about the same again.
> With full-board, the price of the room was about 50-60 marks
> and covered everything. With full-board-plus, the price was the
> same, but the lady of the house was thrown in, too.[5]

Werner adds that "full-board-plus" was seldom arranged in advance, but in practice was almost "the rule."[6] Sexual relations between boarder and "lady of the house" were encouraged by the husband's frequently different work shift, by the confined physical space, and by the often considerable age difference between husband and wife. Girls were generally married off very young, while men usually held off until they had put together some savings and were no longer just starting out in their jobs. A boarder would often be of about the same age as the host's wife, and both of them ten to fifteen years less worn out by a life of misery than the man of the house. In other words, sexually the boarder and wife were often better matched than the married couple.

Yet it wasn't those external factors that played the biggest part in forming such relationships. Nor was it the scarcity of women, which under other systems of production, as we know, can lead to very different results—for instance, rendering the woman taboo for anyone but the husband, as happened during the colonization of North America.

The really decisive factor is the conspicuous absence of any Christian-bourgeois sexual ethic. Among the workers, the set of circumstances bourgeois law defines as "adultery" does not provoke either condemnation of women or murder attempts against male rivals. Jealousy and wounded pride don't generate the havoc that the Wilhelmine bourgeois world might have expected in such cases. Sexuality appears as a natural part of everyday life, more matter-of-fact than eating. That doesn't apply only to the Ruhr. Here Werner writes about Silesia:

> Silesian miners, earning very little in the ten to twelve-hour shifts that were customary then, saw intercourse with women as the poor man's only pleasure. Their talk constantly turned on that theme. Friends my age, or just a few years older, would very often tell, without embarrassment, what had happened to them on wild nights in the weaver villages in Tannhausen, Wüstegiersdorf, and Liebau.
>
> Since I was of the same mind as my comrades, I took it for granted that I should go have a look around those villages as soon as possible, so I could have a good time, too.
>
> I would often travel over with my friends on Wednesdays and Sundays. I wouldn't get back until next morning, with barely enough time to don my work outfit and get to my shift.
>
> The combination of mines employing large numbers of young fellows, and textile and ceramics factories employing so many girls, is the reason why Waldenburg district always shared first place in the statistics on illegitimate births.[7]

In this district, where there was no shortage of women, and many of the young men lived with their parents—we aren't dealing with the Ruhr Valley, where artificial resettlement had occurred at an incredible pace—we can easily believe there were a large number of illegitimate births. Nevertheless, the sexual mores depend less on the region than on class.

Even those two accounts by Fermor and Werner are enough to show that there was no basis among workers for the types of fantasies we have come to associate with the men of the White Guard. Above all, the tribulations of puberty didn't weigh so heavily, and hopelessly, on proletarian youths. They apparently didn't depend for their lovemaking on fantasies concerning the constitution or the function of the human body. They were not victims of a celibacy enforced until well into their manhood years. From a sex-economic standpoint, this is not nearly as "devastating" a moral turpitude as Fermor's hours of lonely lovemaking with culture, where the body's thrills had to be brought up from the depths of Nietzsche. Now that *is* a sad ethos.

None of this says anything about psychic processes within those sexual relationships, or how humane they were, or how equal men and women were within them. There is little reason to deduce, as Wilhelm Reich sometimes did,* that sexuality among the proletariat was a freewheeling affair. Confined living space, hunger, limbs battered from work in the house or in the mines, crying children, weariness, apathy, a hurting vagina, sickness, and alcoholism are extremely poor aphrodisiacs, but they were the constant companions of proletarian life.

In a 1913 dissertation about a group of 500 Hamborn working-class women, women's rights advocate Li Fischer-Eckert focused on those whose situations she considered most favorable:

> In the lives of these women, everything comes down to a single question. What will we eat and where will we get clothes? That question stalks the women from early morning until late at night, from the washtub to the stove, from the garden to the sewing machine and into the barn. Only by expending all of their energies are they able to avert a total defeat—the collapse of the family—in the endless guerrilla warfare that rules their lives, a war of attrition between income and expenditure. Yet it isn't only physical stamina that succumbs to this battle. Just as bad, and maybe even worse, is the way in which in the endless drudgery to satisfy the family's external needs any personal life the mother may have had suffers. She forgets how to take her own self into account. In the end, she is no more than a mechanical tool. Like slaves in ancient Rome, she is valued as a piece of property, has no rights, and can't imagine herself as anything different. And those are the women who are best off (all without jobs!) in Germany![8]

In women whose situations were worse, Fischer-Eckert noted overwhelming apathy, growing out of a despair of living conditions ever improving. Nearly all of the women stated that they weren't living in the Ruhr Valley of their own choice and that their dream was to be able to move out when they were older. Where to? Where there was "plenty to eat."[9] According to Fischer-Eckert, only families with no more than two or three children could hope to stay above the subsistence level if they were very thrifty. Just under 80 percent of the families questioned had four or five children, however.[10] In times of unemployment, lockout, or strike, the situation was often aggravated beyond the endurance even of families accustomed to unhappiness and deprivation. Fermor records numerous suicides of entire working-class families after a lockout of several weeks in 1923. (It was carried out by Thyssen to force the workers to return to the eight-hour

---

*"The worse the material conditions of life are, the less restrained does genitality become." (*Die Funktion des Orgasmus*, p. 169) The rest of the section on the social import of genital strivings is considerably better, though.

shift; that is, to give up the last remaining gain of the revolution, the seven-hour day.) An elderly communist worker, particularly well liked by his workmates, was one of the last, Fermor tells us, to resume work under the conditions dictated by Thyssen. He did so only because his wife had threatened to leap out of the window if the children had to go on starving any longer.[11]

We can imagine a whole series of reasons leading to sexual relationships between working-class women and boarders. First, a certain nonchalance about the significance of "love." Then there was the hope that the boarder would make himself a bit useful around the house, by bringing the children presents once in a while or sharing his relatively more plentiful resources with the family during times of starvation. Although affection, sympathy, and pleasure for pleasure's sake may have been in play, probably more often it was an uninvolved, brutish, and even desperate groping for the flesh of another human being, a chance for contact with some other living thing. In the semifeudal, petit bourgeois, small-farm milieu of the Freikorps soldiers, women like that didn't exist. The reality of working-class women didn't match the actual experience of soldier males, but it may well have fit in with the horror stories they were fed about erotic, aggressive, "masculine" women. The war had freed working-class women from the housewife's role they had known beforehand. Forced to become sole providers for their families, many entered the factories. They had organized antihunger demonstrations and ransacked display windows. They had had to learn how to deal with the owners, whether the issue was wages or the cost of renting factory-owned housing. They had conquered traditionally male terrain and now bore themselves in a corresponding fashion. They were changed, alien.* Alien even to their own men, it seems. There is a peculiar note of irritation even in writings that profess solidarity with women by giving a prominent place to what they accomplished. Here, for example, is an

---

*The measures taken by the Nazis at the start of World War II showed how much they feared having women in the work force. In fact, they apparently blamed women for the collapse of the "Home Front" in 1918. In arguing for the retraction of a plan to increase the number of women in the work force, Secretary of State Stuckart wrote on May 9, 1940: "The compulsory recruitment of women for work purposes is particularly disposed to influence the mood of the populace. . . . This recruitment of women must be approached with great caution. Mistakes in this area can have dangerous consequences not only for the mood at home, but for that at the front." Thus, in the "blitzkrieg" era, the percentage of women in the work force dropped by 3 percent. That was accomplished by providing state support payments to women who would otherwise have had to work. As the war dragged on, this policy became increasingly untenable. "Of a total of 35.9 million employed in 1944, every second job was filled by a woman, and every fourth by a foreign worker. (Behrens, pp. 133ff.; Eichholtz, pp. 81, 83, 85; and Kuzcynski, p. 282. See Tim Mason, *Zur Lage der Frauen in Deutschland, 1930-1940*, pp. 129ff.)

excerpt from Heinrich Teuber's article, "Miners' Wives" ("Bergmanns-frauen"), 1927:

> The spatial confinement in mining districts promotes a solidarity among women and men who are on strike or locked out. The same thing is difficult to muster in occupational groups living in a more scattered community. It isn't rare for women to take an active role in men's battles, where they often accomplish more than the men through picketing and related assignments. Once a woman has gotten fired up about the legitimacy of her demands, she almost amasses such enormous energy that it puts most men to shame. In the process she may often give free rein to her temperament, but at the same time she calmly takes the consequences into account.
>
> During the general lockout of the Ruhr miners in May 1924, whole companies of female pickets assembled. Armed with sticks and moving along secret paths, they intercepted those men prepared to give in and go back to work, and drove them back to their homes. When the night shift changed, it was a strange thing to see the women marching out of their villages with burning lanterns, ready to surround every mine within a large radius.[12]

So a lantern-lit procession of women at night is "a strange thing." And he writes of "secret paths." "Temperament" is used where, with men, we would probably have found the word "courage." Most important of all, the woman "calmly" takes "the consequences into account," where a storm of protests might be expected from men. Clear enough, then: the women are alien beings, different from men.

To the Freikorps soldiers, proletarian women must have seemed in many ways superior, self-assured, and provocative. In particular, they were superior to the mothers and sisters they knew from their own families, who, if they worked at all outside the home, expended their energies in charitable activities on behalf of the military, and thus in demonstrating their sexual abstinence. Working-class women, by contrast, clearly led lives that were not abstinent. They must have breathed new life into the soldiers' repressed sexual desires. Here were women who could be had by men. The catch was, they could only be had by *other* men. These women were made of flesh, not corsets and bodices, yet their flesh was unattainable. Who were they there for? The answer was, men who, however different they may have been from each other, had one point in common: they were nothing at all like the military. All of the writers who spent some time in working-class areas agree that workers and their wives hated anyone wearing a uniform. On the basis of his own experiences in Hamborn, Fermor calls that hatred

"pathological." The response, when Fermor suggested that a worker ask a policeman for directions to a meeting was:

> I'd rather drop dead from searching around too much than say one word to a bloodhound like that![13]

Anyone wearing a uniform must be an oppressor. That was all there was to it.

Just how was a proletarian woman supposed to react to men whose entire habitus was alien, whose "manhood" was half-brutal and half-comical? How should she react, especially, to those pimple-faced Freikorps types fresh from high school, or a military academy, or who had run away from small farms or college drinking-fraternities, all so that they could elude the never-ending woes of puberty in the company of soldiers? Those boys didn't know up from down yet!*

Others among the soldiers had gone off to war at eighteen and now had four years of male companionship in the trenches behind them. True, they may have swooned over some field-hospital nurse or gotten drunk in some brothel on a leave, but what else did they really know about women? Freikorps officers were mostly under forty, still young enough, according to the unwritten code of the Imperial Army, not to be suspect for remaining single. They were just as unlikely to have had any sexual contact except with prostitutes, or occasional dalliances with daughters of middle-class parents, girls they set out to use from the start.

Try to imagine one of those gentlemen, or young boys, approaching a young working-class woman who is relatively unrestrained sexually, clicking his heels as he extends her an "invitation" to a dance and, indirectly, to sexual intercourse. How can it ever work? He is used to laying his money on the table and buying a woman, in which case he knows that he can behave with the inconsiderateness of a proprietor.[14] Or else he is used to taking the long way around; only here he can't go through with the proper bourgeois sexual foreplay by inviting a working-class girl to the casino, introducing her into "society," or going off with her to Duisburg for a night at the theater. With a working-class woman, he doesn't even *feel like* taking that detour. How else, though, can he express what he's really after? Calling a spade a spade is out of the question, since his only vocabulary for sexual relations is either pejorative—designed for communication among males—or stilted. He finds

---

*"As a seventeen-year-old soldier, what had I learned about life? I knew how to kill people, run around with whores, tell dirty jokes, ransack houses, and keep myself free of fleas." That's Stenbock-Fermor describing himself in the Baltic State Army days, in *Deutschland von unten*, p. 113.

"The First Kiss" (ca. 1910), from Schidrowitz's *Sittengeschichte des Proletariats*.

Photo from Mitau in the Baltic (1919).

Bottrop, 1919. A squadron of the Thunderbolt Freikorps, better known in the Ruhr Valley as the Deathbolt Freikorps.

Light machine guns belonging to the Schlageter Company of the Heinz Storm Troop.

Upper Silesia 1921
Swastikas on steel helmets,
Armbands red, white, and black,
The Ehrhardt Brigade
Is the name of our pack.

(First stanza of the brigade's anthem)

that he is simply too stupid to carry on any kind of conversation with a female member of that despicable substratum.*

It doesn't take much imagination to see that *any* reaction by working-class women to the stiffly erect Germanness of the soldiers was interpreted as a total desecration of their masculine ideals—even when the women didn't start out by laughing at them. Now those same men were standing around on the streets with their guns and cannon, attempting to teach the proletariat how to live right. They were male mannequins, tin soldiers, bright-eyed and immature, with no inkling of the problems of an industrial population. How could they measure up to a working man, who sweated and slaved to feed his dependents and improve living and working conditions in the district,** while those unemployed militarists killed time playing with their guns and taking food from the mouths of the working population?[15]*** The only part of their "masculinity" remaining was brutality, and that made contact even less likely.

That stereotype of the imperial age, the young lieutenant who is the heartthrob of all the girls, may have had some basis in reality in smaller garrison towns. In urbanized working-class settlements, especially the Ruhr region, other rules applied. Heinrich Teuber describes the situation before 1914 as follows:

> Even the Prussian military government felt the contrast between its animated toy soldiers and the cheerless army of Ruhr workers.
> For that reason it kept the two groups far apart. There wasn't a military garrison in the entire coal-mining area.**** The

---

*Many of the men can hardly have had any sexual experience with women. That's probably not the only decisive point here, though. In *Family and Aggression*, David Marc Mantell reported no particularly high level of sexual abstinence among two hundred Green Berets who said they had participated in terrorist campaigns in Vietnam. There was significantly high agreement among them, however, on being "left cold" by their first sexual contacts with women. They had been disappointed by their lack of feeling, which then became habitual, though it never stopped them from chasing women. (Frankfurt-am-Main, 1972, pp. 215-33)

**According to Christa Reinig, "This is a Theweleitian fantasy, with the author's personal stamp of approval. As in all left-wing fantasies, money plays no role here. The money was in the soldiers' pockets. The working men could get hold of it easily enough, though, by renting out their 'old ladies' to the 'male mannequins' and 'tin soldiers' for an hour. If working-class women had any remaining desire for proletarian solidarity, they got no thanks from working-class men for it. Even today, a worker will never try to completely humiliate another worker by swearing things like 'You soldier!' Or 'You capitalist!' He'll just say, 'You old woman!'" (*Schwarze Botin*, December 1978). At least where the 1919-20 workers' uprisings are concerned, I really doubt that the same rules applied then as apply "even today." Yet I see now that the charge that I am idealizing "*the* working man" by contrasting him with the military is justified.

***For that reason, in Berlin they were given the name "Suppe Garde" (Soup Guard), a nickname prompted also by the name of one of their instructors, a certain Herr Suppe.

****A minor correction. From 1899 on, Mülheim was the garrison city of Infantry Regiment 159.

cities north of the Rhine—Essen, Gelsenkirchen, Bochum, Dort-
mund—were the only Prussian cities free of military occupation.
Still, once in a while they had a chance for a quick look at the
troops: every time there was a major strike among the workers.
The last occasion for that was as recent as 1912.[16]

What we have is mutual antipathy, the workers not liking the military
and the military avoiding the workers. The military was uninterested in
training an army for civil war in regions contaminated with social
democracy.

There was thus no peacetime tradition for working-class women falling
in love with lieutenants.

The manifest differences between working-class women and soldiers,
especially the women's comparatively unrestrained sexuality and self-
assurance, only reinforced the soldiers' existing belief that these women were
threatening. Most importantly, however, these fantasies assumed a shape;
they became concrete by attaching themselves to actual women. Excitement
was heightened by the real proximity of the women, which seemed to make
it possible for them to become preferred objects for the men's
"dischargings."

To what extent did the women's actual behavior contribute to the image
the soldiers had of them? To a very considerable extent, I think. It is no
mere "projection," at least, when the soldiers equate proletarian women
with prostitutes. They do that with the help of a very simple, very "normal"
procedure: judging what they see not in its own right, but according to their
own criteria. Both bourgeois and to a large extent also "Marxist" science do
the same thing, since they can't begin anything until they've made the facts
harmonize with their own preconceived notions.

What do the soldiers do, then? They judge the proletarian women as if
they were *their own sisters*. If their own sisters did what the proletarian
women and girls do, without a doubt they would be prostitutes. Their
military brothers would have to treat them accordingly, casting them out.
The strange step in this process is the one that enables the soldiers to view,
and treat, working-class females as if they *really were* their own sisters. They
are *exchanging* the perceived object for another one. They replace the sexually exciting working-class woman with a member of their own family. I
think that clearly suggests that there is a partial identity of the two objects
that makes the exchange possible; that is to say, the soldiers are really replac-
ing the working-class woman with a similarly sexually exciting member of
their own family, who in most cases seems to be a sister (not a mother).

It could also be said that they "familialize" the working-class women,
while "eroticizing" and "proletarianizing" their own sisters. For a number
of reasons, their own sisters are well suited to that kind of operation. The

body of a sister (often older) is frequently the focus for an adolescent boy's first voyeuristic sexual experiences, precisely because the sister, as an un-suspecting member of the same family, isn't as careful as other girls about concealing her body from her brother. She may even get some enjoyment out of being looked at, especially if her developing breasts finally provide some visual evidence that she is different from her brother. Over and above this, the sister represents the domestic servant at the mother's right hand; and in the brother's eyes, the moment she begins having relationships with other men she becomes a prostitute, because she really belongs to her brother. The prohibition on physical lovemaking turns her into one of the "white sisters" we've encountered in preceding sections. Her other, erotic aspect—the "Red sister"—can't be allowed to exist anymore, except for the purpose of fulfilling the brother's fantasized desires. By refusing to hide their sexuality, working-class women are behaving exactly as the soldiers/brothers would secretly wish their own sisters to behave toward them. And to make things even better, some of those women are actually called Red "sisters." The problem is that their love is directed toward other men, and that can lead to charges of infidelity and prostitution, always on the assump-tion, of course, that the woman running around town with a man on her arm is one's own sister.

What leads to this substitution of one object for another? I am reminded here of Charlie Chaplin in an Alaskan cabin during a snowstorm, running round and round the table, trying to dodge the ax of the other gold miner. He is out to slaughter Charlie, for he is so hungry he sees him as a gigantic chicken.

Could it be that the soldier's appetite for love is so large that he can't suppress it any longer when he spies sexual nourishment in the form of working-class girls? That in place of the real stimulators, he hallucinates the object that always used to make him similarly excited: his own sister (though she is hazy and blurred). In that case, the soldier's attacks against working-class women, could be seen to be directed at the specter of his sister going around with another man, as revenge against the sister for denying him love.

The connections suggested here are particularly evident in a letter writ-ten by Max Zeller, student and sergeant in a rifle battalion. Dated April 2, 1919, the letter was sent from somewhere in the Ruhr Valley to the military hospital where Zeller had only recently been a patient. Beginning "Dear Sisters and Patients," the letter reads:

> During the entire battle I thought of nothing but you nursing
> sisters in Station A. The reason is that we shot ten Red Cross
> nursing sisters right at the start. Each one of them had a pistol
> on her. Shooting at those disgraceful characters was a real
> pleasure. You wouldn't believe how they begged and cried! But

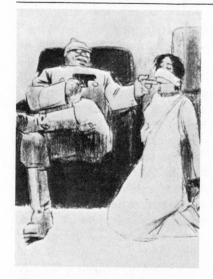 

"Germany has conquered Belgium."   "How lewd they really are." (Paris, 1915)

French newspaper caricature on the German occupation of Belgium during World War I.

anyone caught with a weapon is our enemy and better know it. We were much more generous even to the French on the battlefield. Now, how are things at the hospital? The people around here give us everything.[17]

It is with the image of the white sisters before his eyes that he shoots at the red ones. Yet his aggression is directed in essence against the white nurses (i.e., his real sisters) for having aroused him sexually (in his boyhood or during his time in the field hospital), without allowing him any means of discharging that originally pleasurable stimulation.*

The mere sight of women who are clearly less hostile toward sex is enough to reactivate the man's undischarged stimulation. His excitement is intensely physical, not just a series of mental images, and it gives him momemtary access to fantasies in which he and the white nurse are sexually conjoined. Until now he has repressed those fantasies or kept them to himself, revealing them, as Höss did, only in the fact of inevitable death. At the same time, his aggression is aimed at his own bodily arousal and its attendant fantasies; for they carry him back to a situation from which he has always feared there would be no escape. The new women don't give him any physical outlet either, especially not in the context of armed class struggle in which they meet. That's why the aggression is discharged at them *on*

---

*In volume 2 it will become clearer that he, too, had a part in denying himself that "means of discharging" the stimulation.

impulse. The women's "crime" consists in reminding the soldier of a desire he is prohibited from satisfying. It is, moreover, not only "in essence" that aggression is directed against the whtie sisters, but also in extremely concrete ways. It reaches them in the form of the letter Max Zeller sends to the field hospital. The letter is clearly an open warning to the nurses: beware the consequences, should you ever dare to do what your "Red" counterparts are doing. The white nurses could not, and did not, belong to their brothers and were therefore subject to a general sexual taboo.

What is called "projection" is anything but mere delusion. It would be easy enough to apply the scapegoat theory here, except that the connection between the real object of aggressive intent and the substituted object is more than just arbitrary. It is a real, living, sexual presence—not a "projected one"—that carries working-class women into the soldier's field of vision. I find the term "projection" highly misleading for that process, which I prefer to call a *hallucinatory object-substitution*. What the victim of the substitution contributes is a similarity with the initially intended object.

We haven't discussed why the level of arousal is so great that it generates what we would call a hallucinatory perception (more about that in volume 2, chapter 4). An even more puzzling question is why the affect seems almost to have skipped a step. It would seem "logical" for the soldiers to react to being sexually aroused by the Red nurses by deciding to rape them on the spot. Yet that *hardly ever* occurred, either in novels or in fact. And so we are left to wonder why a onetime desire to love has mutated into a desire to kill, rather than discharging itself through rape as we might have expected.

As an illustration of the way in which soldier males were rejected by women from their own social circles, we should take a look at the following proclamation, written by Fräulein Schobacher from Kempten:

> Women and girls of Bavaria! Each one of you should hear your
> own name being called whenever our planes are roaring over
> your hometown! Listen for that call from on high! Do you want
> the communist madness to endanger your most intimate domain,
> as happened to your sisters in Munich? Do you want criminal
> hands to tear the white linen out of your closets, all those
> treasures you so lovingly sewed and collected? Or open your
> bedroom chests to steal all of your precious belongings and
> cherished mementos? Do you want your house reduced to a heap
> of rubble? Do you want your flower garden to become a mass
> grave for your murdered loved ones? One look at poor Russia
> will prove my words true! No! Of course you would never want
> those things to happen. Then help us! You, too, have the power
> to prevent those atrocities! During the war you showed that you

could be silent heroines, and in politics you showed that you
could be understanding companions for your men. Your votes
helped to elect the legitimate government of Bavaria. Let's turn
that voice to action again, by sewing the edelweiss of the
Freikorps onto the clothes of your husbands, brothers, and
fiancés. There is power in your voice! Use it to proclaim to one
and all, "Join the Swabian Freikorps!"[18]

The readiness to ship "husbands, brothers, and fiancés" off to the civil war, where they can protect the women's sexual integrity, is so apparent here that it must surely contain a lot of aggression toward the men. Schobacher's fear that male communists might soil her white linens could be read as a desire for something like that, done by one of her own men: is the "so lovingly sewed and collected linen" not meant for use after marriage? It is. Yet a proposal by one of her own boys is not what is to be expected. As far as her own men were concerned, their women were "white," no longer fit objects for the men's sexual desires. The heroic gesture of sending the men off to battle is partly revenge as well: If I'm consigned to spending the rest of my days guarding a closet full of white linen, you can go bleed to death in the war—you're not much good for anything else.

* * *

The proletarian man's relationship to proletarian women, and women in general, is also ambivalent. Particularly in men who have begun to rise above the mass of proleterians, through advancement in their jobs or in workers' organizations, there is an increasing tendency to reject the less restrained sexuality of working-class women. Werner, a man promoted to the post of pit foreman, often refers proudly in his book to his own liberated morality. Here he is reporting on his marriage:

> I had no experience with marriageable women and had never managed to carry on a successful love affair. I didn't have any sisters or other female relatives who might have conveyed the mentality of the opposite sex to me. Then again, I was mindful of my father's request that I not marry too soon. And honorable young maidens held me in some disdain—as I did them also. I just didn't stand a chance with them. For one thing, I was no Adonis, and for another, my views on morality made me seem like someone who had no inhibitions whatsoever. Similarly, I could never take seriously women who considered themselves "God's gifts." I simply had no time at all for young women like that.
>
> While visiting a Silesian who was in charge of distributing explosives at the Hibernia mine, I got acquainted with his wife, a woman originally from Weisstein. She was amply endowed with all of the traits I valued most in people. She was hardworking, dutiful, decent and forthright in her thinking, and she identified with the working people. She was attractive looking, an excellent cook, and her house was sparkling clean. There was a seventeen-year-old daughter living in the house. I proposed to her, and the engagement took place on Christmas, 1901.[19]

He chooses a spotless "white" maiden for himself. She is introduced by a colleague's untainted wife, and she comes from his own homeland, Silesia. Once again, we see the distinction between the kind of woman you have a good time with, and the kind you marry.

The woman he marries belongs to the category for whom he had previously had "no time at all." As a wife, she ceases to be viewed as a sexual being. What comes to the fore, instead, is her ability to perform the chores that are expected of a wife. Too much of a delight in sexuality might get in the way of those. So he marries a "white" woman. Until then, his relationships with women had been for pleasure only. In marriage, though, his relationship to his wife becomes that of an employer and master.

Michael Rohrwasser has produced a study of women in so-called proletarian novels of the 1920's, *Spotless Maidens, Sturdy Comrades (Saubere Mädel—starke Genossen)*. He found that accusations of sexual depravity among working-class women were often simply parried in these novels with similar gibes at bourgeois womanhood.

In Gisela Zenk, daughter of a factory owner, K. Grünberg creates a monster much like the ones soldier-male writers make of proletarian women:

> They found themselves in a dimly lit hall. From somewhere or other, a heavenly music of the spheres came wafting over, so melancholy that it made him cry. The priestess was kneeling before the stone altar, her white robe flowing behind her. With a newfound solemnity, he too knelt down. When the priestess rose, he recognized her as Gisela Zenk. "This is how a German girl gets married," she said, at the same time laying a shining dagger upon his heart. Then he saw himself lying on the stone altar, his blood bubbling into a glass bottle that Gisela was holding up. When it was full, she raised it to her lips . . . at that point he woke up, completely horrified and bathed in sweat.[20]*

Looked at in isolation, a passage like that is hard to distinguish from corresponding ones in fascist texts. The fact that Gisela Zenk castrates the man only in a dream, rather than "in reality" as in Freikorps novels, is unimportant in the end. Text remains text whether a character says he is reporting facts or reciting a dream. If the tendencies we've been discussing seem relatively harmless in proletarian novels as compared with fascist

---

*The process of turning women from the enemy class into monsters also has its converse in Grünberg (how could it be otherwise?). Mary, a proletarian girl, becomes a kind of Blessed Virgin of the Proletariat. She dies a heroic death on Maundy Thursday. (See Rohrwasser, p. 86; Grünberg, p. 326)

novels,* that's because in proletarian novels the central concern is not the *aggressive removal of women from the scene of the action.* It remains nevertheless a tendency—even quite a strong one. To put it another way, in such novels a woman can still be sacrificed for the good of the party; but she doesn't have to die one of those gruesome deaths that fascist novels seem to consider prerequisite for restoring order to the world. In addition, many proletarian novels are at least a little progressive in their content.**

The poverty of this proletarian literature is brought home to us when we realize that not one of the novels contains the kind of detailed, narrative account of life in a proletarian city that we find in the "memoirs" of Count Alexander Stenbock-Fermor—who certainly didn't set out to write proletarian literature. What appears as the "partisanship" of his writings doesn't result from any political orientation on his part; it's just that the reality he's describing comes down on the side of the workers.

In any case, "proletarian" literature of the 1920s does no justice at all to the new experience of political power gained by proletarian women in the course of the war and revolution. Unfortunately, it was hardly any better for women in the reality of the postwar years. Women were not elected to executive councils, and they were still paid less than men even in instances in which workers' organizations themselves set the wage scales. The men were back again, taking up "their" old posts everywhere. Things were no different within the Red Army in March 1920:

> Remuneration in the Red Army is in accordance with the terms of the March 22nd bulletin: 165 marks for front-line troops; 40 marks for local service; 30 marks for female personnel.

That, for example, is excerpted from a proclamation issued by the Duisburg Executive Committee, which at that point was made up exclusively of left-wing communists.[21] On the treatment of women in the Red Army, something of special concern to us here, Erhard Lucas writes:

> A number of the leaders were unhappy with the presence of women and tried to remove them from the combat units. The reasons given for this were inconsistent and not always clear. Sector Commander Gräf thought that one medical orderly, male or female, for every two Red guards meant that there were too many medical personnel. He proposed to headquarters in Marl that all of the nurses be excavated back to base. On March 31, headquarters responded by ordering all the women nurses from task force and assembly points to Marl, where a

---

*Having read Rohrwasser's comments on J. R. Becher in his dissertation manuscript, I wouldn't make the same claim. Indeed, why use the word "proletarian" here at all? There weren't any proletarian novels; what we have instead is just inferior bourgeois literature.

**Although as insignificant as any content ever is.

decision regarding their future disposition would be made. Gräf's rationale: "It is impossible, in the long run, to discipline[!], pay, and provide rations for such an enormous network of nurses."[22]

Headquarters is addressing some very real problems there. Even if the women had been willing to give up their pay, the rations would have remained a heavy burden for the army. All the rest, though, is simply a psychic defense against women. Surprisingly, no thought was ever given to the possibility of arming the women.* Erhard Lucas again:

On March 24, Combat Leader Kuhn ordered the heads of his units to send him married nurses under twenty-one years of age, and unmarried ones under twenty-five, to be discharged.[23]

On March 31, Leidner issued a corresponding order for the entire Red Army from Mülheim:

"All female medical personnel, with the exception of professional nurses, are to report immediately to their home bases for discharge."

Kuhn and Leidner apparently saw the women's presence as detracting from combat readiness.

(The order to discharge single women under twenty-five may be interpreted as a sexual precaution.) And as if that were not enough:

The municipal commandant of Duisburg, Münsberg, was quite open in his hostility to sex. He boasted to an employee of one Berlin boulevard newspaper that he was ready to race to the front in his car the minute he heard that "carbolic sweethearts were running around in the trenches." He added that he would walk up and down the trenches "with my revolver in one hand and my flashlight in the other." "I'll issue an order," Münzberg went on to say, "that making love at the front is punishable by death. That kind of thing disgraces the sanctity of our cause." The Duisburg Executive Committee even suspected the presence of prostitutes and issued an order that "any unauthorized person caught behind the front lines will be shot. This applies equally . . . to females of doubtful character. . . . Anyone with knowledge of demoralizing activity of that kind is obligated to report it."

---

*In contrast, there were references to individual armed women in the camps of the white troops (Wrangell, p. 71); military activity on the part of white nurses (Pitrof, pp. 108ff.; von Brandis, *Baltikumer*, p. 271; Engelhart, *Ritt nach Riga*, p. 143); a white rifle-woman (Brandt, *Albert Leo Schlageter*, p. 19); the use of women as spies (Glombowski, p. 48; Major Weiss, p. 75). All of these are Freikorps sources.

Accusations of prostitution also came from the Red Army leaders themselves, in other words. Their remarks, reproduced in Nazi anthologies about the Freikorps fighters, served as an alibi for the Nazis' extreme misogyny, since they were seen as proof that the Red nurses had actually been prostitutes, and that sensible left-wing men had been equally unwilling to put up with nonsense of that kind. This interpretation immediately became standard. As early as 1920, a journalist calling himself "Spectator" offered this account of the "days of terror in the industrial region of Rhineland-Westphalia":

> You also had to watch out for the female "medical assistants," who are said to have been more numerous in many battle sectors than the soldiers. Their humanitarian ministrations were extended even to the able-bodied during lulls in the fighting; in fact, their shameless activities went too far even for their own leaders in Duisburg. The leaders threatened women running around there without authorization, with death, should they be caught.[24]

Now that is a form of communism even a fascist can go along with.

Erhard Lucas's treatment of the events is a model of the cautious approach leftist historiography still takes toward this complex of issues. On principle, he approves of having women at the front. The battle "concerns the women, too," goes his rather rationalistic argument, "why shouldn't they be there?"[25] But what of lovemaking at the front? Although Erhard doesn't speak out against it, in the sentence, "Naturally, in the Red Army the two sexes sometimes went so far as to engage in sexual intercourse," the intent to see lovemaking as a matter of course is openly contradicted by his distant, legalistic language. Is he secretly afraid that if he expresses himself in a more positive way, he might be taken as an advocate of prostitution? Is that where he gets the defensiveness to decide, "I will not go into the (highly debatable) ruling of the Oberhausen Executive Council here"? The reference is to the evacuation of Oberhausen's red-light district, Harmony Street, "which was aimed at forcing the prostitutes out of the city." Erhard Lucas confines himself to "pointing out how slanderous it was for the military to connect the two things, that is, the eviction of prostitutes from Oberhausen's Harmony Street . . . and the presence of women and girls in the Red Army."

Where the guardians of the moral conscience of the workers are concerned, we might also want to point out the misogyny that led them to issue such a totally useless, superficial, and bureaucratic order in the midst of an armed struggle. The purpose of rumors put about by the military was indubitably "slanderous," but even if the rumors were true, what would the basis of this "slander" have been? Would communism have been discredited by having prostitutes fighting for its success?

The contradiction that runs through Lucas's entire account even enters into his relatively belligerent statement that bourgeois papers outside the rebel regions wrote about the Red nurses "using such a malicious, indignant tone, you feel as if the bourgeoisie's own irrational hatred for prostitutes is being mobilized, and Red Army women are effectively turned into social outcasts." Although Lucas's analysis is on the mark, we need to ask whether there is such a thing as a *rational* hatred of prostitutes. The problem is simplified when we realize that for the military, the bourgeois press, and the minds of individual soldiers, proletarian women were more or less the same as prostitutes. Should we wish to "defend" them against that accusation, it would make little difference whether the Oberhausen prostitutes were really at the front or not. The problem's only true relevance is in connection with the need, or desire, to humanize sexual relationships within our own ranks.

To return to the debate: if the women of Oberhausen really were at the front, what would have been so wrong with that? Wouldn't their bandages have helped the wounded? Wouldn't their embraces have comforted the men? Would sleeping with them have destroyed military discipline or eroded fighting strength?

Lovemaking may "weaken" men who are afraid of women, but it tends to "strengthen" other men, above all by intensifying their desire to live. Wouldn't that be a stronger aid to victory than the desire to die? Or to kill? (If you weren't fighting for a cause you believed in, of course, that same desire would act as a powerful impetus for running away; but in March 1920, the Red Army of the Ruhr workers had no such problem.)

As the class struggle comes to a head, a "prostitute" switches her work site in order to fortify the fighting men. Now, couldn't that be seen as a fragment of a concrete utopia, as proof that as the bourgeoisie fades out of the picture, so does prostitution? (Even without bureaucratic evacuations of "Harmony Street" red-light districts.)

That kind of reasoning didn't seem to be very much in vogue—at least among a number of leading figures on the left who behaved in a way that wasn't very much different from clergymen. As a historical-dialectical materialist, Lenin could say in a conversation with Clara Zetkin that prostitutes were "double victims of bourgeois society, first of its accursed property orientation, and then of its accursed moral hypocrisy." As a man, Lenin had to add:

> Grasping that fact is something totally different from—how shall I put it?—organizing prostitutes to form a separate guild of revolutionary fighters and putting out a trade newspaper for them. Are there really no female industrial workers in Germany

left to be organized, leafleted, and drawn into your struggles? We're dealing here with a malignant growth.[26]

Only after the last female industrial worker has been "organized" and "drawn into" the communist cause, can the first prostitute ("double victim") become the beneficiary of a "trade newspaper." That's a genuine patriarchal leap within Lenin's dialectical thinking (to use Eisler's words). It never even occurred to Lenin (naturally) that in Marxist theory "prostitution is only a *particular* manifestation of the *universal* prostitution of the *worker*,"[27] including the female worker, or that, in the right form, a trade newspaper for prostitutes might just have more to say about the situation of the average female industrial worker than the party's propaganda sheet. Yet even the Marxist formulation negates femaleness; Marxism is revolutionary in an economic, rather than a cultural, sense. As a footnote to this episode, Lenin also asked Clara Zetkin to bring that "talented woman communist in Hamburg," the one who was writing for prostitutes, back from her deviant path.

In real life, Brecht also acted in a peculiar way where prostitutes were concerned. Prostitutes were indispensable for the milieu of his first works—city streets. The way in which he wrote about them was anything but negative. But ever since 1975, when the Suhrkamp Verlag press and Brecht's son Stefan (along with an eager handful of pirate presses) have allowed us to look into Brecht's diaries for the years 1920-22, we know that as a young man Brecht was not especially magnanimous about the "prostitute problem," at least not when he himself was physically involved in it. When the Augsburg actress Marianne Zoff was pregnant by Brecht, whom she loved, and was being pursued by the industrialist Recht, who wanted to marry her, she opted for Recht. When he heard about her decision, Brecht wrote in his diary:

> Then I went out and dictated a letter, a note, telling her she was carrying my child and leaving me, though I had asked her to stay with me until the child was born. (April 30, 1921)[28]

He must have considered his offer generous. (We don't know to whom he "dictated" the note.) The whole episode finally ends in an abortion. Brecht:

> Marianne Zoff has taken leave of her senses. It began with her running round with men and ended with the corpse of a child in a doctor's bowl. That whore didn't deserve to have a baby—mine left her because her heart was impure!
> I dragged myself home, feeling as if I'd been hit over the head. The vulgarity of it all! I could strangle that whore! It's the filthiest thing I've ever been through, but it's something I know

so little about. A thousand times I said to her, you can't do that. Not *you*. And this is how she repays me. Now she can go jump in a lake. *Without* the extra burden. That's the way she wanted it! Everything else was just playacting under the stage lights, to the tune of coffeehouse music. *This* is what she *really* wanted! I've never seen such a naked display of the prostitute's bag of tricks, of her romanticism. So that's how a pregnant whore unloads! And to think I wanted to place that cracked pot in my room, when it was dripping with the discharges of every man around! Being abandoned, seen for what she is, unmasked, abandoned—that's the reason for her frightened rage and desperate hope of a new and outrageously powerful situation that might still be able to wrestle, trick, steal her away from prostitution. Get away from me! Away! Away! Let her be used as a whore now! Throw her to that other man! Leave her for R.(echt)![29]

And so on. True, Brecht was hurt and furious when he wrote that. But that's exactly the point. Whenever a man begins to *feel*—and he feels a lot when he's furious—all else is destroyed. The woman who used to have a name and was "the most beautiful woman in Augsburg" has ceased to exist. All that remains is "that whore," a "cracked pot."

We are seeing a man whose woman no longer wanted to be an image. (He had often called her a "Maori woman" before.) The image becomes filled with life (a life that is perhaps unpleasant), and suddenly the man is crying that he's been deceived. The product is not as advertised. There's nothing left to do now but "throw her to that other man."

On a theoretical level, both of them—Brecht and Lenin—have all the answers on the issue of prostitution. The moment their personal love relationships or work for the party are affected, however, understanding goes out the window. What surfaces in its place are powerful emotions from a previously hidden antiprostitute syndrome, emotions that completely contradict the men's intellectual insights. In Brecht's case, they surface with truly unexpected venom.

What do the "prostitutes" really have to do with all that? When socially acceptable paths of self-realization are closed to many women, the institution of the mistress blossoms. It helps some few women gain influence and power, as is shown, for instance, in the history of European courts. It may also win them a comparatively pleasant life and a certain amount of independence. What choice is there, when all other roads are blocked?

For North American black women, for example, brothels for a long time provided the only means of achieving at least a degree of independence (as well as a possible pathway to premature death). Weren't German proletarian girls in a similar position at the turn of the century? The prospects of "making a fresh start" elsewhere on savings from the brothel were probably not as remote as waiting for a well-heeled husband to appear.*

How else were women to escape the mortal dangers of factory work, or a lifetime of killing poverty? Can the oppressed be blamed for refusing to wait for victory in the class struggle to put an end to their degradation? Hardly. And how can we condemn them, even though we know that the road they take is not going to lead them to their goals?

In a 1911 essay by Hugo Luedecke, "German Red-Light Areas" (*Deutsche Bordellgassen*), we read that the brothel is the last stop along the "downhill path of so many household servants."[30] (Luedecke had done most of his research in the "Mire" (*Schlamm*), Halle's red-light district.) Stuttgart police assistant Henriette Arendt names the most frequent stopping-off points on the road to professional prostitution: servant, factory worker, waitress.[31]** Parent-Duchalet's research on Paris comes to the same conclusion.[32] According to the 1926 yearbook of the Vienna Police, of 1,097 registered prostitutes about 70 percent were either servants, factory or unskilled workers, or seamstresses.[33] An article in the *Westminster Review* estimates the number of prostitutes in London in 1850 at 10,000, "most of them seamstresses."[34]

It has frequently been demonstrated that the typical master of the Wilhelmine bourgeois household thought that a kind of right to sexual access went along with hiring a servant girl. He would often encourage his sons to have their first sexual experiences with the servant girls, when the

---

*Who could have guessed that the hope was illusory? The police would be waiting in the new city (according to Ettlinger) where even—or very likely just those—women who had given up prostitution were registered under the prostitution laws, which enforced weekly check-ins, compulsory examinations, and so on. For more about the difficulty of shaking off the status of "state-controlled prostitute" and getting free of the morals squad, see Luedecke, in Krauss Antropophyteia IV, pp. 286ff.

**Under the guise of "adoption," there was heavy trafficking in proletarian children in Germany. They would be adopted by "foster parents" and later delivered to brothels. Henriette Arendt fought that trafficking. A letter on the subject reads as follows:

To Municipal Police Headquarters:
It is our fervent wish that Arendt be so swamped with day-to-day business that she will find no time "to spend long hours going through the personal columns in the daily papers." That is not what the city council hired her for, aside from the fact that those adoption stories are a well-known evil. The problem with Arendt's sensationalist scribblings is that she regularly takes advantage of her official capacity as "police assistant of Stuttgart," bringing the entire city of Stuttgart into disrepute, as if everything she finds is unique to Stuttgart. —It doesn't matter at all to me, but it is a widespread source of displeasure that she, more than anyone we've ever seen, is constantly digging up material designed to bring our existing society into disrepute. Any other police official would be in a position to do the same; but the others are more tactful and better versed in the responsibilities of their office.

boys were still too young to visit brothels.* From the very beginning, therefore, relations within society created a tendency to equate the servant girl with the prostitute.

Once the servant girl had been seduced, most often under the impetus of "abundant alcohol consumption, lack of family restraints, and a natural need for love,"[35] there followed the sobering experience of being abandoned, being comforted by the next lover, and so on and so on, until she finally "succumbed" to prostitution. That sounds very schematic, but is probably what happened. Other than marrying, there was little opportunity in Wilhelmine society to escape this milieu.

The significance of this situation for proletarian women becomes immediately clear when we discover that, of 495 Hamborn working-class women questioned by Fischer-Eckert, 343, or 70 percent, had been servant girls before they married. Only two, a deaconess and a kindergarten teacher, had been able to achieve relative independence on the basis of their professional training.[36]

What we are seeing here is not the persistence of the "right of the first night" (ius primae noctis); rather, it is the extreme vulnerability of "lower-class" women to constant assaults on their bodies by "gentlemen." That is the norm of societal relations.**

The leaders of the workers' movement (Bebel, Engels, et al.), only too well aware of this direct process of prostitution, believed that the main weapon against it was the stable proletarian marriage.*** "Indeed, it is in the interests of both sexes to secure an honorable place for women. Make it possible for every adult male to establish a family, and prostitution will simply disappear." So it was declared at the Congress of the International Workers' Association, Geneva, 1866.[37]

That suggestion gives not a single thought to the status of women. It is evidently aimed simply at getting "prostitutes" off the streets and trans-

---

*The same thing happened in indirect ways. Karl Meboldt, author of the polemic pamphlet *Modern Marital Imprisonment* (Leipzig, 1904), relates how a servant girl slipped into his bed simply because it was winter and she couldn't stand it anymore in her unheated room. He was thirteen and very pleased. See Regler, *Das Ohr des Malchus* (Cologne, 1958), pp. 19 and 21.

**A parody of the leaflet, *Servant Girls' Protest*, circulated in Halle in 1900 to lighten up dinnertime at men's clubs:

Point 4. We wish to rest on a wide democratic foundation.

Point 5. . . . above all, we want a male member standing before us as director.

Point 8. As ever, we shall patiently endure the pressure of men.

Point 9. We will come together in Hairburg.

(and so on) in: Krauss, *Antropophyteia IV*, p. 158.

***Roswitha Burgard and Gaby Karsten *The Fairy-Godfathers of Feminism*, (*Die Märchenonkel der Frauenfrage*). Bebels's and Engels's pertinent remarks on the subject extensively cited and critiqued—though perhaps too much of today's knowledge and assumptions is turned against those "pioneers."

"Awake, Proletarian!" Street poster (1918).

forming prostitution into its universal, "indirect," bourgeois form. It is accepted without challenge that the status of the "female worker" actually leads to prostitution.

General as it may be at times, I think that this brief outline of the relations between the proletarian woman and prostitution is enough to show how inadequately the authors cited here behaved toward this "problem." The entire complex of prostitution strikes a sensitive nerve in the patriarchal man, including the patriarchal man of the left. At stake are the purity and integrity of his sacred "organ," together with its outgrowth, his brain, itself also reaching ever upward. The patriarchal man of the left avoids the dangers of female sexuality (through castration or syphilis) by decreeing that in the class struggle there may be both men and women, but only one sex, that of the wage earner, which is to say, none at all.

We are confronted with a remarkable phenomenon here, namely, that in their comments about prostitutes and women in general "reactionary" and "revolutionary" men are able to find some common ground. Their deeply ingrained, shared "maleness" seems to be the soundest basis for overcoming otherwise unbridgeable political and class differences. The men are bonded together by their deep-seated fear of the vengeance of women. And even if that fear turns out not to be seated so "deeply" (in the unconscious, for example), capitalist-patriarchal society makes sure tht the image of the socially emasculated wage earner conflicts with that of the Old Testament God, even in the mind of the working man, who was also supposed to have been created in His image. The same conflict rages even more wildly in the bourgeois male. He sees himself as a fictional amalgam of all the confusion and contradictions of his historical possibilities, so much so that women don't stand a chance of attaining human status for him.

The urge to see women in images seems irresistible. After establishing that the problematic of the two sexes won't be dissolved with the abolition of class divisions, Ernst Bloch, for instance, reaches this conclusion about women:

> The pervasive ambiguity will remain, that ferment of confusion and involution, half-resolved, falsely resolved, or unresolved, for today's society to pass on to some future one.

Aside from the fact that it posits the ridiculous fiction of the "enlightened man" as the antithesis of femaleness, the passage is acceptable, if only because of its relative vagueness. In his next sentences, though, Bloch reduces the "ambiguity" that is woman to "concepts." He plasters the open potentialities of the word "woman" with labels from the lumber room of patriarchal historical fantasies:

> She is something gentle and wild, destructive and merciful, a flower, a witch, a bronze goddess, and a model of hard work. She is a maenad and a commanding Demeter, a ripe Juno, a cool Artemis, Minerva the muse and much, much more. In music she is the capriccioso (violin solo in Strauss's *Heldenleben*) and the prototype of the lento, of peacefulness. Finally, spanning the two in a manner beyond any man's comprehension, she is the bridge between Venus and Mary.

Not that Bloch himself wouldn't have known that these labels were "alienating commodity-categories." In spite of that, he felt able to use them as "real" descriptions of the "forms" taken on by that "confusion" that is woman.

Bloch preferred to think of women as creatures with future promise. As if all that is repressed must wait until some future time to achieve any degree of being-alive, to deserve a name of its own, and to be treated as having a *real* life of its own.

> A woman's real potential is more nebulous than a man's, but since time immemorial and in every vision of feminine perfection, it has also seemed more promising. It is rooted more deeply in established fantasy.[38]

Behold: it is women who contribute so much of the raw material for the concept of "hope." This may be the most benign way of disembodying them, but that is nontheless what the passage does to them. Here again they are made into building blocks not for the emerging kingdom of soldier males, but for the human society of tomorrow.

In a letter from Marx to Engels, a remarkable distinction is made between males and females. Jenny von Westphalen, Marx's wife, has just given birth to another daughter, once again disappointing her husband's hopes for a son. Marx writes that "yesterday morning, between six and seven, my wife was delivered of a bona fide traveler—unfortunately of the 'sex' par excellence."[39] Of *the* sex, in other words. As if there were only one.

It's hard to say exactly what is *meant* by that, but then again, it doesn't matter all that much. What's important is that Marx casually sets up a contrast between maleness as something asexual, and sexuality per se, as embodied in the term "woman."

It is the privateness of these remarks that makes them so interesting. Marx would never have published them. An essential element of sexual relations is the public silence on how they are determined. Indeed, it is precisely this that is the basis of their unquestioned and unexamined effectivity in *published* theories.

Almost no research at all has been done yet on the effect gender relations, as power relations, have had on impeding the development of more humane relationships between human beings throughout history. (In chapter 2, we'll introduce a little material on that.) A ruling caste (not just "class") has written history, and it's precisely not the history of actual relationships to the "sex par excellence."

Unlike that between the classes, the contradiction between the sexes is not intrinsically antagonistic (meaning, among other things, that a man has more free play for his behavior than a capitalist does). The phenomenon of the orgasm is probably adequate proof of that; no orgasm has ever taken place as the result of two classes embracing each other. Here, contradiction seems less likely to be resolved by a "battle of the sexes" than by the desire to create situations that make human orgasms possible. Oppression is not necessarily contained within *every* communal enterprise.

Later on, we will see that one of the primary traits of fascists is assigning greater importance to the battle of the sexes than to the class struggle, even in their *conscious* thinking. They view the class struggle as an irrelevant issue, one that can easily be taken care of by the establishment of the folk-community. (*Volksgemeinschaft*).

Groupings in which work on the male-female contradiction is once again made to await the triumph of socialism are not only continuing the negative tradition of labor-movement parties of the 1920s, they are also reestablishing a framework for the forms of communication and dominance that typify male bonding and brotherhood: dogmatic monologues ("Long live the phallus!"); bureaucratic centralism; self-satisfied denunciations of enemies and deviating friends; intrigues; exclusions; and, along with that, a

"Who's stamping out fascism? A socialist youth of indeterminate gender." Poster on the defeat of fascism (Italy, 1945).

Actresses of the 1930s, from part 2 of
Oskar Kalbus's *Vom Werden
deutscher Filmkunst* (Altona-
Bahrenfeld, 1935). Lois Chlud.

corresponding insensitivity to any realities that do not approximate their
own.

I don't want to make any categorical distinction between the types of
men who are the subjects of this book and all other men. Our subjects are
equivalent to the tip of the patriarchal iceberg, but it's what lies beneath the
surface that really makes the water cold.*

ATTACKS ON WOMEN

Women who don't conform to any of the "good woman" images are
automatically seen as prostitutes, as the vehicles of "urges." They are evil
and out to castrate, and they are treated accordingly. The men are soldiers.
Fighting is their life, and they aren't about to wait until that monstrous
thing happens *to them*. They take the offensive before these women can
put their horrible plans into practice. Here is Captain Ehrhardt, describing
his brigade's march into Braunschweig:

---

*In the series *Moral History of the World War* (*Sittengeschichte des Weltkrieges*), edited
by Hirschfeld, progressive bourgeois medicine and psychiatry attempt to digest the events of
the war. They talk about "dark, vengeful feelings of degenerate femininity," as well as the
opposite, namely, rape "that is lustfully received by the woman who is defeated in love." The
authors, all good liberals, distance themselves from the gung-ho soldier, but share his hatred
of women. (pp. 272, 300, 304, 306)

Carola Höhn.

The advance went smoothly, with no resistance except for a minor incident outside of Gliesmarode. The women from the cannery had stationed themselves there. Safe in the knowledge of the soldier's duty to spare the female sex, they swore, spat, and raised a ruckus. One of my officers assembled five mounted orderlies and carried out a small police charge. That pacified even communism's female element. The street was cleared.[1]

Ehrhardt's orderly officer, Rudolf Mann, describing the same scene:

The communist's women and mothers-in-law massed in droves outside of Gliesmarode, all in colorful kerchiefs, sackcloth aprons, and wooden shoes. Workers from the cannery.

(There were no mothers of communists present, as far as Mann was concerned.) On the matter of the "police charge":

It was like a wolf among sheep. The priceless scene of the Amazon guard's headlong flight made us laugh so hard, we almost fell off our horses. One young maiden ran blindly into a water-filled ditch.[2]

Using the word "maiden" at that point is what excuses everything; women are whores in any case and wetness is their natural element.

Mother and son (1935).

A mopping-up expedition in Munich, reported by Manfred von Killinger, storm-troop leader in the Ehrhardt Brigade:

> I am presented with a slut. The typical bad girl from Schwabing. Short, stringy hair; seedy clothes; a brazen, sensuous face; awful circles under her eyes.
>
> "What's the story with her?"
>
> She slobbers out, "I'm a Bolshevik, you bunch of cowards! Lackeys of princes! Split-lickers! We should spit on you! Long live Moscow!" Whereupon, she spits into the face of a corporal.
>
> "The riding crop, then let her go," was all I said.
>
> Two men grab hold of her. She tries to bite them. A slap brings her back to her senses. In the courtyard she is bent over the wagon shaft and worked over with riding crops until there isn't a white spot left on her back.
>
> "She won't be spitting at any more brigade men. Now she'll have to lie on her stomach for three weeks," said Sergent Hermann.[3]

Which is to say, for three weeks she won't be able to practice her "true profession." The passage was no doubt intended as a proof of Killinger's extraordinary humaneness. "The riding crop, then let her go," is a show of mercy. She deserved something worse than that.

In Herzog's *Comrades* (*Kameraden*), the wife of Volker Hagen, a soldier returning from the war, is also lucky:

"A slovenly slattern who measured the war by the men she
bedded and not by the blood her husband shed. She roamed
around wherever life was freer and wilder, leaving her young boy
to go to seed at home. When we got back home eight weeks ago,
Hagen found his child in rags and his wife in silk stockings."

"Then he reached for his leather hunting-belt," said the old
man grimly.[4]

But Hagen didn't take it with him. He just took the boy and left the wife.

Ottwald quotes a speech General Maercker gave to the Freikorps and
short-term volunteers during the Kapp Putsch in Halle:

"It's a well-known fact that women are always at the head
of these kinds of riots. And if one of our leaders gives the order
to shoot and a few old girls get blown up, the whole world starts
screaming about bloodthirsty soldiers shooting down innocent
women and children. As if women were always innocent." We
all laugh.

"Gentlemen, there's only one thing to do in cases like that.
Shoot off a few flares under the women's skirts, then watch how
they start running. It won't really do much. The magnesium in
the flares will singe their calves or behinds, and the blast flame
may burn a few of the skirts. It's the most harmless device you
can think of! So, gentlemen, no more warning shots! Flares between the legs will do the job best."[5]*

Inscribed above all these examples is the phrase, "Mercy before
Justice." People have died for far lesser crimes. Writing of the seizure of
Helmstedt in April 1919, Maercker notes in his memoirs:

Through a regrettable accident, nurse Ida Sode of the
Marienberg convent was shot in the head while observing the
battle from the bell tower of the convent church.[6]

That laconic comment settles the matter for him.** Even a white nurse
cannot be sure of her safety. Why did she have to be watching? As a rule,
though, no secret is made of the intent to kill:

A truck with a field kitchen on the back and flying a large red
flag had blithely driven into Rasefeld from Wesel. Petty officer
Oehlke brought it to a halt with a hand grenade. It explodes

---

*A credible account. Maercker himself writes that he recommended "star shells and the
like." (*Vom Kaiserheer zur Reichswehr*, p. 164)

**Maercker's press officer, Crasemen, embellished the story to read that a woman and
her child, tied to a car by the communists ("A devilish tactic"), had fallen victim to bullets.
(p. 40)

right on top of the car, killing the woman sitting in the field kitchen.[7]

The tale is told in the past tense. Only the killing itself was put into the present by Ulrich von Bose, a former captain on the general staff and chief general staff officer of Loewenfeld's Third Naval Brigade.

Munich, May 1919. The Reichswehr has secured victory. Now come the informers. Their services were welcome, except—as we learn from Zöberlein's *A Dictate of Conscience*—if those who wanted to inform were women:

> "They can scream and howl, for all I care." With that, Lindner kicked them out onto the street.

A working-class woman gets caught between the fronts, again in Munich, 1919, when Zöberlein gloats over the fact that she is shot by her own people, the Red Army men:

Dita Parlo and Willy Fritsch in *Melody of the Heart.*

Look! My God, some mad woman is running out of the house and across the street! She doesn't hear everyone screaming, "Get back! Get back!" With loud sobs, she rushes up to the child who is lying next to the dead soldier, drops to her knees, and draws the limp little body to herself. The soldiers' guns are lowered again.

The woman kneels directly in the line of fire; writhing, sobbing shrilly, she presses the child to herself. "Fritzl, my dear little Fritzele!" She can't accept his death, but she must. "My dear little Fritzele!" She is wracked by hideously penetrating sobs. She raises her skinny fist toward the sky, trembling with impotent rage. "You murderers! You murderers! You . . ."

Zing, zing, zing. A whole pack of bullets zips past. The woman is hit. She falters, trying to cry again, but this time the sob is more like a sigh of deliverance. Then the mother falls on top of her child, next to the soldier who had tried to save it.[8]

It is not until a few pages later that more devious motives for this woman's death are revealed, when Zöberlein's hero, Krafft, finds two of his old wartime comrades in the ranks of the Reds. Having taken refuge in an attic, they are discovered by Krafft, who confronts them with their crimes. Seeing the error of their ways, they repent. Krafft doesn't take them

Trude Marlen.

prisoner; in fact, he goes to visit the home of one of those old friends. There we learn that it was this friend's wife and child whose deaths had just been contrived by Zöberlein. Now we see the reason for that: it allows the old friend to switch over to the "correct" side of the class front. There is no wife around anymore to seduce him into considering himself proletarian, no child to scream in hunger, and no "skinny fist" to hold him back from becoming a good fascist. The death of his wife and child atones for his political blunder.

Dwinger gets even more enjoyment from attacks of that kind, if that is possible. To carry them out, he sends his most preeminent woman-haters and the best of his warriors, Donat and Pahlen, into action:

> "They're probably spitting there again," thought Donat, knitting his brow. Suddenly, he saw a mouth before him. It wasn't really so much a mouth as a bottomless throat, ripped wide open, spurting blood like a fountain.
>
> Old Donat was right. They certainly were spitting. But the men of the brigade didn't take it lying down. Quick as lightning, they turned their carbines around and ground them into those spitting faces.[9]

The pleasure in annihilating women climaxes in the murder of a communist who is also the mother of two children. A house-searching party

Bavarian drawing of Lola Montez, beloved of Ludwig I.

finds her in a dwelling that has been denounced as the Berlin hideout of the communist Radek.

> "You're murderers!" she screams mindlessly, "house-breakers, bloodhounds, mercenaries! What are you doing here in my house? I'm a communist, if you want to know. Do you want to kill me too, the way you did Rosa Luxemburg?"
> "Not you," Pahlen says, "Radek!"
> Hearing that, she laughs hysterically, throws up her hands in a strange kind of ecstasy, then promptly spits in front of them. "Just try to find him. He's smarter than you, you damn Noske hounds! Bloody White Guard troops!"
> Donat grabs her by her upper arms, stifling her shrieks and turning them into pitiful whimpers.
> "It's about time you shut your goddamn foul mouth of yours!" he says hoarsely, shaking her like a feather pillow in his hammerlike fists.[10]

For the moment, she escapes; the noise wakes up her children, "a handsome five-year-old boy and a tiny girl of three." Suddenly, they are standing in the room. Donat meets up with her later, though:

> "Clear the streets, as far as the back of city hall!" The response he gets is laughter, which builds into animallike howling. "Come on over here," yells a woman standing right in front of Donat, "so we can beat you to death like we did the others!"
> "What others?" Truchs wonders, momentarily unnerved.
> Then he raises his sword and calls out loudly again. "I'm

"Deutsche Hiebe und Spanischen Grundbesitz" (a German beating on Spanish property).

telling you for the second time to clear the streets immediately.
After the third warning, the shooting starts!"

"You wouldn't dare!" the woman shrieks, and, as if she
were conducting an entire chorus, each of her words is followed
by a howling that seems to issue from the throats of animals.

Donat racks his brain. "Haven't I heard her before?"

Finally, with the cold detachment he might have shown in
some dinner-table conversation, Truchs says, "I'm telling you for
the last time to clear the streets right now!"

"You won't shoot!" the woman screams, echoed by her
mocking chorus.

"Take aim!" Truchs says.

"Right into them this time," Donat thinks, grinding his
teeth together. The human wall presses forward, as if about to
attack. A rain of spittle hits the soldiers, hitting Truchs too in his
long horse-face, dripping slowly down onto his service coat and
sticking to his ribbons.

"Get away!" Donat bellows.

The spitting woman, an image of the Megaera, stands before
the barrel of his gun—his sight is pointing straight into her
mouth, into the center of that slobbering hole, so wide open with
hysteria that he can even see the gums. "Get away!" he screams
again, as if afraid of himself. It's really her. Now he recognizes
her.

"Fire!" roars Truchs.

It's the same as it was at the *Hallesches Tor* (Halle Gate).
Everything turns suddenly to frenzied flight. Yet Donat sees
nothing of this. He sees only the woman who was standing there

Dorit Kreysler.

Christl Mardayn.

before him a moment ago. It threw her onto her back, as if she had been blown over by some gigantic wind. Is that thing at his feet really her? That person without a face? The head isn't really a head anymore, just a monstrous, bloody throat. "I warned her," Donat thinks to himself, trembling. "I warned her. . . ."[11]

When the square is cleared of bodies, Donat recognizes the two children among the dead. He carries them off in his arms.

The women's crime seems to be that they excite the men too much and that the men cannot stand this inner turmoil:

With their screams and filthy giggling, vulgar women excite men's urges.

Let our revulsion flow into a single river of destruction. A destruction which will be incomplete if it does not also trample their hearts and souls.[12]

The women have to go. "You can't just plant your fist in their faces," Ernst von Salomon had complained, yet once these inhibitions are overcome, the treatment can be even more thorough. In the attacks, there is a sense that a long pent-up rage is finally being loosed on its target: at last! A sigh of relief seems to run through the text. Part of the instinctual energy

Inge List.

Hilde Weissner.

we've seen bottled up until now is finally discharged. At long last, the libido can seize upon an object—these women with their sanctimonious faith in the soldiers' obligation to spare them. The ability to attack and destroy them—this is a bursting of bounds, a liberation. At last these men can penetrate to the truth behind the joke that "women are always innocent" and can carry out the appropriate sentence.

The women themselves are responsible, of course. They are known to be ringleaders; they block streets and pathways with their filthy whores' bodies. They are "old girls," "informers," "megaeras," communism's female element that showers the soldiers with a "rain of spittle," screeching, shrieking, giggling all the while and thinking themselves safe in the soldiers' "duty to spare them." Whatever this "Amazon guard" gets is only its just deserts. The soldiers feel they are the legitimate ones to carry out punishment, because the women seem to have directed everything against them.

All of the ills we've seen perpetrated by the "evil" part of the divided woman—becoming prostitutes, filthy animals; castrating and murdering men; donning the "white" nurse's uniform to avoid being recognized as a "rifle-woman" (woman with a penis); trying to live in the reflected glory of the "pure" mother/sister, but then besmirching and perverting her image— all of the strands seem to converge here into one massive knot of justification for the frenzied pleasure the soldiers take in persecuting these women.

"Tommy's dream." British World War I poster.

The following deduction can now be made: *terror against a woman who isn't identified with the mother/sister image is essentially self-defense.*

The threat posed by women is so great that it is an inadequate defense merely to divide them into two components, an asexual-nurturing one and an erotic-threatening one. The threatening element has to be *annihilated* as well. Even the "good" component doesn't escape unharmed. Whereas the "evil" woman is beaten or killed, the "good" woman is robbed of life, rendered lifeless. The affective mode of self-defense in which this occurs seems to be made up of *fear* and *desire*.

SEXUAL MURDER: KILLING FOR PLEASURE

Case #1. After a hard-fought battle, Freikorps troops occupy a Latvian village and conduct a house-to-house search:

> Two women in heavy sheepskins and bast shoes have a special trump card in their hands. Nothing, they believe, will ever happen to them, for they can prove that they took in, and even patched up, a wounded German soldier.[1]

Without that proof, who knows what might happen? The women are lucky they have something to show, though it's not going to help them in the end. What an infantile delusion, to think that they can fool German soldiers. The wounded man, whose "teeth have been smashed in, splitting his gums," mumbles "cellar."

> There they find the horribly mutilated corpses of five German soldiers. All have had their eyes poked out and their noses, tongues, and genitals cut off. The faces and uniforms show clear signs of brutal kicking. A few of the arms have been broken as well.
>
> For a moment, a deathly silence reigns in the cellar. Then a single, piercing howl erupts from the lips of the men who are standing amid the corpses. An elemental sound from the deepest depths of nature, its roar expunges all trace of humanity from the human body. It wakes the beast and sets it on the blood trail. Overcome by a common resolve, two or three men storm upstairs. The dull thudding of clubs is heard. Both women lie dead on the floor of their room, their blood exactly the same color as the roses blooming in extravagant profusion outside the window.
>
> The act was sudden, but unjust. The women were aware of the horrors in the cellar, of course, and had probably even given

complete assent to the fate that befell the poor wounded men, but they hadn't carried out the evil deed.[2]

Balla's remorse at the injustice is not very great. The two creatures in those "heavy sheepskins" may not have been wolves, but they were Latvian women and, on those grounds, deserved beating to death. It's important to note that the murderous beast is presented positively. Only women, then, are not permitted to become "animals": man may (and should?) do so. The involuntary nature of their deed is expressly applauded. And what need is expressed in the perception of the women's blood as "exactly the same color" as the roses outside the window, or of the flowers as blooming "in extravagant profusion"?

Case #2. German soldiers are on the lookout for "spies," that is, Latvians collaborating with the Red Army:

> In the beginning we kept a very close eye on "Red Marie," a young woman with lush, shimmering red hair. She had a noble figure and the wild grace of a free-born animal, and she stirred men's senses whenever she appeared. But Red Marie's response to all the attention and approaches was a mocking laugh, provocative and humiliating at the same time. She was clearly trying to make fools of the German spy-hunters, too. Almost every day she went into the woods alone. Before disappearing into the brush, she casually glanced around, as if to make sure that the coast was clear. Yet every time the German soldiers followed her in, she would be picking berries or lying under some tree, lost in thought. And if she spotted her pursuers sneaking up on her, she would break out again into that infamous laugh, as if relishing a successful ploy. They would simply let her go in the end. Why look like fools over and over again? To hell with her!

Lieutenant Bewerkron finally unmasks her. He accidentally discovers a telephone wire on the forest floor. Following it,

> he came to a halt, speechless. There, in a ditch fitted out as a telephone booth, sat Red Marie, stark naked. In her face, deathly pale with fright, two incredibly large eyes flickered.
> "Shoot!" she cried. "Why don't you shoot? I'm finished anyway!"
> But Bewerkron didn't shoot. He mechanically engaged the safety catch, just to have something to do, just to break the spell of this incredible situation. "Excuse me, please," he said. It was a helpless stammer. "I was just trying to . . . I didn't realize . . ." More than that he couldn't muster.

A warm ray of hope entered the woman's eyes. The fear of death loosened its tight grip. With a tentative smile, she extended her hand to the young man. "You're a good person. You won't do anything to me, will you?" Half-stunned, Bewerkron sank down onto a dirt mound that had been covered with an old, torn horse-blanket. Quite overwhelmed, he contemplated the marvel of this hour.

Then the telephone rang. Short, short, long . . .

The noise brings the lieutenant back to the "reality" of the war. He orders the woman to get dressed.

Marie obediently stands up and puts her clothes on. "Excuse me," she says with a hint of flirtation, "but it was so hot today and I wasn't counting on any company."

Bewerkron sits there like a frozen icicle, then they climb out of the ditch. The lieutenant knows he's committing a crime punishable by death, but he can't help himself. He's determined to save this woman. And there, suddenly, a patrol springs up before him.

Bewerkron is praised. "Congratulations, lieutenant, on catching that stinking carcass in the act." Then official procedure has to be followed. He reports to the captain.

The captain had himself put through to divisional headquarters in Riga. The Riga connection came through between a lost hand of *Grand ohne Vier*, and an unfinished hand of *Null ouvert*.* It ended with the matter-of-fact order that the spy should be shot. . . .

With this, Marie's image faded from the minds of the men in the room—what was she after all but a leaf falling from a tree?—and the excitedly awaited *Null ouvert* began again. It was an extremely tricky game that demanded total concentration.

Around midnight, Bewerkron crept over to the little wooden cabin in which the woman was imprisoned. He told the guard he had to conduct another interrogation.

He soon found himself standing opposite Red Marie in the dimness of the shabby room. Sitting on a plank bed, she stared at him, wide-eyed, transfixed. "Oh, I knew you'd come! Now everything will be all right!"

Grand ohne Vier and *Null ouvert* are variations of *skat*, a well-known German card game. Played mainly by men, it was a popular pastime among German troops in World War I.—Trans.

"The Lascivious Nymph," F. Mirwald (Munich, 1906).

Pulling him down onto the bed, she wrapped him in her caresses, hotter and hotter. —Slowly, very slowly, they returned to reality. Now poor Bewerkron would have to get a firm grip on his heart if he were going to carry out his errand of mercy.

"Listen," he said with an unwavering voice, "I've come to tell you that I'm going to rescue you, without a doubt. But first you have a hard trial ahead of you. Tomorrow morning at five they'll take you into the woods, and then—well, they probably

told you about that already. Now, listen carefully! I'll be giving
the command. It goes, 'Ready—aim—fire!' They'll shoot, too,
but nothing will happen to you. Now keep telling yourself that
tonight, after I'm gone, won't you? Absolutely nothing will
happen to you! On the command 'Fire!' my people will turn
their guns upward and shoot into the air. Get away into the
bushes then, and you're saved."

Around Red Marie there shone the powerful glow of her
good fortune. She pulled the young officer's head to her breast
and laid her cheek against his hair. Then she kissed him, tenderly, trustingly.

The next morning at half-past five, the firing squad stood in
a small forest clearing. The birds were singing, insects buzzing,
and it was a joy to be alive. Red Marie stood against the trunk
of a sturdy oak tree. They hadn't tied her hands, or bound her
eyes. She stood there posed like a queen, without a trace of the
fear of death. Her gaze rested, brightly and steadfastly, on the
ashen face of Lieutenant Bewerkron, who presently opened his
mouth and very softly ordered, "Ready—aim—fire!"

The report of the salvo whipped through the forest. For a
moment, Red Marie stood upright against the trunk of the oak,
then her body slowly sank to one side. Even as she fell, her eyes
remained faithfully fixed on the young officer.- - - -[3]

In the Bewerkron-Red Marie relationship, the peculiar coupling of love
and death emerges most clearly. We need to ask whether this example really
departs from what we've seen so far as much as it might seem at first glance
to do.

Case #3. This deals with the death of Marja, the rifle-woman, after she
has fallen into the hands of Dwinger's Mannsfeld Freikorps. The male protagonist is Pahlen, whose father, mother, and sisters—a baronial family
from the Baltic—are being held captive by the Latvians. They may even be
dead, though at the very least the rumors say they have been tortured in
Mitau. Pahlen falls into a trancelike state:

Pahlen seems not to have heard. Stubbornly, he continues:
"Was this woman in Mitau?"

The tall man, bowing slightly, answers with restrained
politeness, "She was a resident in Mitau and also accompanied
them on the Baltic campaign." "Thank you!" Pahlen coolly
responds. Bowing with the same politeness, he quickly follows
the two soldiers, who are about to carry the woman behind the
barn, where the other captives have been herded together. He

"Crocodile Hunting in the Colonies." Drawing by A. Willette.

stops them. "Listen, you two. How would you like a thousand marks?"

They drop the woman and look at him in bewilderment. "A thousand German marks?" one of them asks. The other one laughs, "An offer I'd never refuse!" "In that case," Pahlen says softly, his face a frozen mask, "you'll have to beat this woman to death. But not with those clubs of yours. Use that little Cossack whip that's hanging from her wrist."

"I'll be damned!" the one man says. "That won't be easy!" the second man declares, scratching behind his ear.

Pahlen pulls out a wallet that still gleams with the imprint of a seven-pointed crown, its edges worn smooth with use, and hands them a large bill. "There's nothing to be afraid of. It's not against orders. She's murdered so many people that this is simply a punishment for her crimes."

"A rifle-woman then?" the first one asks.

"A genuine rifle-woman!" Pahlen nods absent-mindedly.

The first man laughs and licks his lips. "Then everything's in order. We'd have done it even without the bill. "One of the famous rifle-women, is she?" He repeats, shaking his head as he stares at her. Then they bend down again, grab her by her shattered arms, and haul her brutally away. Pahlen takes one last look at her face; she seems fully conscious, yet it is distorted by an animal hatred. Curses spring from her protruding lips, pouring forth with every breath she takes.[4]

". . . Progress."

As the cavalry riders of the squadron move off, they are treated to the following scene:

> Moving along the stream, they are astonished to see it blocked by the bodies of Bolsheviks. The soldiers must have been given an order—or else this never would have happened—to toss all of the wounded into the water. Langsdorff's whispered inquiries meet with the expected(!) response. Someone did deliver the order, but no one knows the messenger's name. The last body they ride past seems to be that of a woman. But it's very hard to tell, since all that's left is a bloody mass, a lump of flesh that appears to have been completely lacerated with whips and is now lying within a circle of trampled, reddish slush.
>
> As Pahlen rides past it, he takes out his gold cigarette case, lights one up, and draws the smoke deep into his lungs. Then they break into a trot.[5]

The next mailbag brings the news that Pahlen's parents and brothers and sisters are still alive. "Ah, almost dancing on the spot, he reads the note a dozen times."[6]

Hauenstein, alias Friedrich Wilhelm Heinz.

That *absent-mindedness* in the very act of murder—was I responsible? Was I not? Was that bloody mass really the same woman?—must have some particular significance.

Case #4. Here the author is *against* the killer in terms of national allegiances—he is a Pole killing a German woman—but *with* him as far as the deed itself goes. Only Friedrich Wilhelm Heinz's depiction of the (alleged) murder gives it its character as a sadistic killing:

> The Polish pillagers were loaded up with crates of cigars. An older, heavyset woman was running along behind them, begging the squad leader, in a torrent of Polish, to release her son. A blow from a fist distorted her features. She staggered. In falling, she knocked a cigar crate out from under the arm of one of the Poles. "German sow!" the Pole howled. He began slamming kicks into her. Soon a second man braced his foot against the curled-up figure, pressed the barrel of his gun into her, and fired. The woman writhed up, shuddered, then lay still. Her abdomen was crushed, a pulp of blood and excrement, cloth and flesh. Her hands groped the empty air; her nails scratched at the cobblestones; her lower jaw opened and shut a few times. The woman was dead.[7]

* * *

Representations of murders committed against women frequently end on this peculiar note of satisfaction ("—and there was peace again in the land"). It pushes feelings of disorientation and horror that also surround the event into the background. The dominant emotion is a passionate rage that will not leave its object until the object lies dead on the ground. This highly unaccustomed release of emotion indicates that psychic defenses have been lowered or dropped altogether. The function of those defenses—of individual "defense mechanisms"—is, on the one hand, to prevent both the conscious mind of the individual and of other social subjects from having access to repressed desires and clusters of fear-charged drive. On the other hand, the individual protects himself against the force of forbidden excitations, against emotional intensities which he is incapable of "working over" and which might lead to feelings of "inundation." (It is precisely this which partially accounts for his suffering.) Since the defenses have been relaxed in the case in hand, allowing emotions of considerable intensity to break through, we can expect to get a better look at the features of things that are otherwise hidden from us.

Strikingly often, it is specific *parts* of the female body that are attacked: the mouth, the buttocks, and the entire area beneath the woman's skirts. *Mouth*: a woman is punched in the mouth; she is clubbed in the teeth with a rifle butt; a shot is fired into her open mouth. The mouth appears as a source of nauseating evil. It is "that venomous hole" that spouts out a "rain of spittle."

Buttocks/abdomen: kicks in the behind, lashes with riding crops on the naked "back," "singeing the behind," shooting flares under the skirts. The "bare cheeks" from which Salomon made his working-class woman "snort," and the redhead who, "with a loud screech, showed her behind" to Delmar, both underscore the way in which the object both attracts and repulses men's attention. The boy who lashes Käte Scholz's naked breast with a whip offers his friend the excuse that he had meant to hit her "rear end," but she had turned around. This suggests an antithesis between the breast and buttocks. The breast, as a "maternal" organ, should be exempt from attack; the buttocks which the beleaguered women desperately require for the practice of "their true profession," makes a perfect target.

Attacks on women are carried out on horseback, with whips, boots, rifle butts, and bullets. Bare-handed attacks almost never happen; a single "slap" is the only instance in all of the cited texts.

Why mouth and buttocks, and why those specific instruments? Freudian dream interpretation might at first seem to provide an answer.

Mouths can symbolically represent the vagina,[8]* and the spittle pouring out of them, its secretions.[9]** It is possible that all the objects with which the attacks are carried out might stand for the penis.[10]***

Following Freud then, we might conclude that we are dealing with attacks or murders committed against victims with whom, in symbolic terms, the perpetrator is engaged in sexual intercourse.

The female buttocks can also be seen to represent the vagina, at least under certain preconditions. In "Sexual Theories of Children" ("Infantile sexualtheorien"), 1907, Freud interpreted the displacement to the buttocks of the attraction to female genitalia as an attempt to ward off the fear of castration, created when young boys saw the "castrated" genitals of women (their mothers, mostly), as well as an attempt to evade the imaginary penises concomitantly assigned to women.[11]

The "animallike" qualities that, in the view of men at least, are attached to erotic women could also be fitted into this analysis. In our texts, the castrating woman was called a "human beast" and a "bestial enemy." On the Russian woman Katja, Zöberlein saw "fingers like claws" and "a face like a tiger that's been licking blood." Before firing into the women demonstrators, Donat hears a "howling that sounds as if it comes from the throats of a thousand animals." Balla's Red Marie has "the wild grace of a free-born animal," whereas Marja's face is "distorted by an animal

---

*And, moreover, not just symbolically. I hardly think that pricks, for example, experience mouths as "representations."

**Which, however, are also real secretions, with a nonsymbolic, sexual function.

***The penis is also put to use in nonsymbolic ways as a weapon. Is Freud's understanding of sexual symbols not perhaps based on the positing of a particular type of sexuality as the "real" sexuality (namely, sexuality that involves the mutual use of two sexual organs that have matured to become central foci)? The concept of "representation" would then derive from the fact that "deviant" sexual realities were not recognized. Relegated to the realm of the "symbolic" or the "perverse," these realities provide material for interpretations or for therapy. The notion—indispensable for Freud's theory of the libido—that human behavior is in the broadest sense sexual behavior, seems to me directly to contradict the theory of sexual symbols. Behaviors are either sexual, in which case they are of themselves (not symbolically) so; or they aren't sexual, in which case they can't represent sexual acts and are something completely foreign to sexuality. And so, the theory of symbols seems to be grounded in an arbitrarily narrow conception of reality (and one that opposes the libido theory as well). Thus Freud himself would seem to be responsible for the regrettably popular game of deciphering symbols, still very much in vogue among people who have no real idea of psychoanalysis. An example would be Hans Scheugl, who looks at film within the framework of "neurosis," and to whom all films are the same: carriers of symbols that need to be decoded. Under the heading of "latent homosexuality," for instance, Howard Hawks is made out to be a represser. A familiar story in Germany: the Left, who find no meaning in images, but still want to go to the movies and live a little, write books to fill the void into which films used to fall in the eyes of this country.

"The Transformations of Sleep." "He spied a woman resembling the Gertrud whose name we mentioned so painfully at the beginning of our story." From Grandville, *Un autre monde* (1844).

hatred," and so on and so forth. "These women were brutish" is the most frequent stock characterization of them all.[12] Freud writes:

> Wild beasts are as a rule employed by the dream-work to represent passionate impulses of which the dreamer is afraid, whether they are his own or those of other people. (It then needs only a slight displacement for the wild beasts to come to represent the people who are possessed by those passions. . . .) It might be said that the wild beasts are used to represent the libido, a force dreaded by the ego and combatted by means of repression.[13]

Do "sensuous" women really arouse these men so much that they lose control of their libido, "feared" as it is "by the ego" and "combatted by repression"? Is this libido structured in such a way that the men are forced to kill, where others would love? Should acts of murder like that really be seen as failed attempts at love? That argument would be supported by the absence of any direct assaults upon the genitals during the murders; as the "real" targets, the genitals might succumb to repression and, therefore, be lost to both consciousness and linguistic expression.

There is some evidence that speaks against such an interpretation. To begin with, the men weren't only writing or dreaming. They were killing with weapons, not symbols. Their victims were living human beings. Questions on the nature and origin of that lethal violence are completely overlooked by "translations" of latent *contents* into manifest ones, or decipherment of symbols—even in cases where the symbols have been "correctly" read.

"Translations" like that don't explain anything. They simply point toward something (here a conflation of killing and loving that still remains to be defined), but I think they also obscure something. It is precisely this something that specifically characterizes these occurrences.

Let's take a closer look at the manifestations of violent erotic advances:

—a "club" thrust into a "hole"
—a "wolf" among "sheep"
—being gored by a bull's horns
—flares sent underneath skirts
—whipping the naked buttocks (repeatedly)
—"trampling" women with kicks to the abdomen and buttocks
—being beaten into a "bloody mass" with a whip
—a bullet in the mouth
—numerous "simple" shootings
—being beaten with a rifle butt, or ripped apart with a hand grenade

It is striking that most of the attacks seem to be aimed at producing a *particular condition* in the female body. It's as if the writers were taking great pains to make their victims look exactly like the castration wounds perpetrated by frenzied rifle-women on their dead comrades—wounds that they describe with almost lascivious delight. "Drenched with black blood between hips and thighs," is the way Thor Goote "saw" the wounds. And what do the women look like, after the men have gotten through with them? "Just a monstrous, bloody throat" remained where there had once been a face, as Donat sees it, "trembling." Von Selchow's female bullfighter: "A blood-drenched mass, silver and blue, lies in the sand." ". . . a bloody mass, a lump of flesh that appears to have been completely lacerated with whips and is now lying within a circle of trampled, reddish slush" (Dwinger's hero, Pahlen). Killinger's "bad girl from Schwabing" is beaten "until there isn't a white spot left on her back"—the point seems to be to make everything red.

Other examples: "The magnesium in the flares will singe their calves or behinds," says Maercker's character Ottwald. Yet an assault of that kind can cover the entire lower body with burns. Rudolf Mann's "wolf among sheep" inflicts a similar bloody wound (or at least this is latently contained in the image). In Salomon's description, the tortured women lie "naked and cut to pieces in the filth of the street."[14] And then there's the German mother Heinz has killed by the Poles: "Her abdomen was crushed, a pulp of blood and excrement, cloth and flesh." ". . . slowly, slowly bleed to death. And then . . . shoot them all down with machine guns, shred them to pieces, and pulverize them with dynamite," Katja, Zöberlein's mouthpiece, had demanded. The proletarian lovers Major Schulz found behind a hedge, where they had been "surprised" by a hand grenade, must also have presented a picture of a "bloody mass." For Balla: "Both women lie dead on the floor of their room, their blood exactly the same color as the roses blooming in extravagant profusion outside the window."

There are two distinct processes at work in the acts of murder. The assault itself can be seen as a symbolic sexual act. It destroys the sensuous woman's genitalia, which for the soldier males, as we've seen, are the source of a castration threat—especially the penis he fears is located there. On that level, the murders of the women appear to be castrations, arising out of the men's own fear of being castrated. In this psychodynamic process, the dominant motif is *defense*. The wound into which the women is transformed appears here as a castration wound.

It's the second process, however—the pleasurable perception of women in the condition of "bloody masses"—that seems to deliver the real satisfaction. The assault itself is probably more a means to this end than an end in itself. In Freudian symbolism, there is nothing that corresponds to the sight of a "bloody mass," nor are there any other references to it in his writings.*

---

*Because I don't know everything of Freud's writings, I have relied on the "comprehensive index" (*gesamtregister*), which lists nothing of this nature.

It's as if two male compulsions were tearing at the women with equal strength. One is trying to push them away, to keep them at arm's length (defense); the other wants to penetrate them, to have them very near. Both compulsions seem to find satisfaction in the act of killing, where the man pushes the woman far away (takes her life), and gets very close to her (penetrates her with a bullet, stab wound, club, etc.). The closeness is made possible by robbing the woman of her identity as an object with concrete dimensions and a unique name. Once she has lost all that and is reduced to a pulp, a shapeless, bloody mass, the man can breathe a sigh of relief. The wound in question here goes beyond castration, in which one can at least still identify the body to which the wound belongs. What we are dealing with here is the *dissolution* of the body itself, and of the woman as bodily entity as well as love object.

It is only after she has been reduced to this state that her sensuousness meets with an almost appreciative tolerance. The "red roses" of her sex *only* blossom from the wounds on her dead, deformed, opened-up body. Whatever it is about the sensuous woman that excites these men lies beneath the surface, under her skin. It looks very much as if the killings are conceived as corrective measures, which alter the false appearances of the women so that their "true natures" can become visible.

In the episode between Lieutenant Bewerkron and Red Marie, Balla performs the same corrective in reverse on Red Marie. The mechanism is particularly clear in this case since—himself a former Baltic Freikorps commander—is less intent than other writers on suppressing his theme: the attraction of men to Red Marie's sexuality. Nonetheless, what he describes is by no means a love scene. Only at the moment when Red Marie's death is a *fait accompli* are the bodies allowed to come into contact.

Now, the stages of the transformation. Naked in that ditch, working as a spy for the enemy, Red Marie is an evil, erotic woman, untouchable for Bewerkron. In the telephone, which rings at the very moment of his arrival, the enemy and the menace of Marie (her "penis") are present. Next comes the cabin. Bewerkron has an official duty to perform; one of his own men stands guard in front of the cabin; Marie's death has already been decided on. At this point, Balla grants Bewerkron a few caresses ("hotter and hotter"), very much like the ones Höss received from his nurses in the night. Here, too, Bewerkron is completely passive. Here, too, the process of desexualizing and derealizing Red Marie begins immediately. Almost from the first moment, she has a kind of halo ("Around Red Marie there shone the powerful glow of her good fortune"); then, suddenly, she becomes one of our nurturing mothers. "She pulled the young officer's head to her breast and laid her cheek against his hair. Then she kissed him tenderly, trustingly."

We see her at the execution as a heroic "white countess":

> She stood there posed like a queen, without a trace of the fear of death. Her gaze rested, brightly and steadfastly,* on the extremely pale face of Lieutenant Bewerkron.

Then the shots. The blast, an old magician's trick, and—miracle of miracles!—Red Marie joins herself to Bewerkron. She enters into him. "Even as she fell, her eyes remained faithfully fixed on the young officer.- - - -" In the course of those four hyphens, the inexpressible occurs. Bewerkron and Red Marie, who has just turned into a white Marie (Mary), are conjoined. Even before the shots are fired, she had been robbed of all life. Bewerkron's merciful deed was to draw every last vestige of sexuality out of her, until she was dead.

As in the previous cases we've seen, the action here simultaneously (or successively) serves both as defense *and* wish fulfillment. First the *fear* is overcome, then the *desire* is satisfied. The "object" falls victim to the process.

The way in which fear and desire manifest themselves in men deserves closer scrutiny. Let's first take fear, which is depicted as fear of castration. That fear is triggered by the chaos of stimuli which emanates from the erotic woman and which the soldier male cannot "work over" since it threatens to destroy him. For him, its point of origin lies in the female genitalia, to which a persecuting phallus is somehow attached. This idea has some similarity with the mythological construct of the Medusa's head, which for several millenia has haunted the emotions of men, who fear for the most "elevated" of their possessions. It would be surprising if it weren't conjured up here, too. It appears to Horst Warttemberg in the streets of revolutionary Berlin, after the Jewish woman has lured him and his comrades into an ambush:

> Again he hears the metallic-sounding laughter of Ruth, Esther, Salomé: a face as lovely as those of the Old Testament women. And it seems as if, in that mocking laughter, a mask is being lifted from another face that appears behind it: the head of the Gorgon, Medusa.[15]

Freud offers an interpretation of the reaction that head triggers:

> The sight of Medusa's head makes the spectator stiff with

---

*The double emphasis on "steadfastly" (*unverwandt*) at such a critical point is noteworthy. Using Freudian clues for decoding the meanings of dreams, one could almost read the opposite into this, namely, that she was "related" (*verwandt*) to him. In that case, the red-white sister antithesis would reverberate in the transformation of Red Marie. Dwinger's Lieutenant Willmut and Countess Sandra Fermor had also gazed at each other "steadfastly" (*unverwandt*). See p. 93 above.

terror, turns him to stone. Observe that we have here once again the same origin from the castration complex and the same transformation of affect! For becoming stiff means an erection. Thus in the original situation it offers consolation to the spectator: he is still in possession of a penis, and the stiffening reassures him of the fact.

This symbol of horror is worn upon her dress by the virgin goddess Athene. And rightly so, for thus she becomes a woman who is unapproachable and repels all sexual desires—since she displays the terrifying genitals of the Mother. Since the Greeks were in the main strongly homosexual, it was inevitable that we should find among them a representation of woman as a being who frightens and repels because she is castrated.[16]

The reaction of stiffening noted in the first paragraph of the Freud quotation turns up frequently in our sources—most clearly in the case of Balla's Lieutenant Bewerkron. He sits there "like a frozen icicle." In other words, he transforms himself into an erect penis, repelling all advances. As Pahlen pays out a thousand marks for Marja's murder, his face is "a frozen mask." Each time he gives an order against the women assembling in the street, Cavalry Captain Truchs raises his sword; and he refuses to drop that sword when he is later shot by the "working-class woman." Platoff, waiting for Marja to appear, "slowly lifts the hammer, gazes fixedly through the sight, in the direction of the doorway." (This procedure doesn't necessarily improve his aim.) Lieutenant Willmut in the same situation: when "the cold iron lies hard against his fingers, all of a sudden he is icily clear again." Whenever they sense the approach of a woman, the men become hard, clear, icy, iron, rigid.* Or, further, Truchs's last command before the order to fire, which he finally issues "with the cold detachment he might have shown in some dinner-table conversation"? "The tall man, bowing slightly, answers with restrained politeness," and then Pahlan "coolly . . . bowing with the same politeness."

It seems indeed that the overall stiffness of the soldier male's language and behavior fit into the Freudian complex. The eternally stilted, cool, formal conduct; the ceremoniousness; the stiff distancing even from "good" women—all could be seen as manifestations of the attempt to ward off castration. The cool silence regarding their wives of the six husbands introduced at the beginning, turns out to be a heightened defense against fear, as do the men's efforts to keep the wives from penetrating too far into their own tales of adventure or the stiff attitudes they adopt in the presence of women.

---

*See the ads for Bommerlunder *schnaps* and Stoltenberg, the politician: "The great, clear one from the north" (since abbreviated by Franz Josef Strauss as "the Northern Light").

Lieutenant Markmann.

It is not difficult to find further examples in the texts as, for instance, the patrol that suddenly "springs up before" Lieutenant Bewerkron, just as he is in danger of succumbing to Red Marie. Or saying that Bewerkron would have to "get a firm grip on his heart" in order to reveal the basis of his deception to Red Marie. Or, last but not least, the "Frederickan goose step" that allows Heydebreck's soldiers to become a "rock amid the surge" when confronted with the threat that the prostitutes might "brazenly" approach them.

The stiff military pose is of no use—indeed is often detrimental—in actual armed combat, and to those with a happier sexuality it appears laughable and repulsive. A demonstrative attempt to defend against castration appears to be *one* of its causes—not the ultimate one, as we shall see.[17] The process of "stiffening" occurs *prior to* the attacks; it is the man's initial reaction to the sight of the Medusa. In brief, before killing the woman the man deanimated himself, so that he can master his fear.

Before looking at the peculiar state of pleasure experienced during and after the attack, I want to say something about the second part of the Freud quotation concerning the Medusa's head. It is a formulation from the later works of Freud, showing that throughout his life he never abandoned the view that the thing that terrified men so much (especially "homosexual" men) was the "castrated" state of the female genitalia. That assumption is particularly enraging for women who refuse any longer to be persuaded that the vagina is an organ of "lack," while the prick is one of "fullness." They

Polish drawing (ca. 1919).

are right of course.* Indeed, men who have loved and been loved by women, should be similarly enraged. In an act of pleasurable lovemaking, how is the vagina inferior or castrated? Is it any less potent, say, than the phallus?

Even those men who see the vagina as a "Medusa's head" aren't afraid of the vagina's castrated condition, but of its castrating potential. In fact, it ought to be apparent to any unprejudiced observer that what men who fear vaginas must really be afraid of is the vagina's ability to take the male member into itself (to devour it, to swallow it up). For whatever it can take in, it can easily keep for itself. With the fiction of the "vagina dentata," men have given concrete expression to that fear, in a horrifying perversion of the very attribute that lends the vagina its *potency*. It is precisely this potency that Freud is energetically suppressing when he repeatedly holds up the *penislessness* of the vagina as a male nightmare. We'd be better off asking ourselves why Zöberlein sees his "Katja" with a "bloody tiger's mouth." It's not because it's been "bitten" that the "Medusa's head" is so terrifying, but because the head itself can bite, a fact that is visible in most of the ancient representations, in which the throat is as much a source of terror as the snake coiffure. It's less a wound than a sharp mouth that impels a man to stiffen with fright: it's not so easy to bite off an icicle. Yet even an icicle melts simply by being touched, and so the bone must become hard and keep its distance if it is to survive.

What about the snake coiffure? Is it a sign of castration? Just the opposite. How did all of those phallic forms find their way onto the Medusa's head? Not because the head was *missing* something, but because it had retained something: all of those pricks that tried to suppress female potency. There is the same terror in Pallas Athena's virginity. She has not been robbed of her potency yet, and pity the man who tries. His "member" will be kept as a trophy—and she can cut off as many "members" as she has pubic hairs. It is in no sense, as Freud thinks, the castrated genitals of the mother that she displays as a deterrent; it is the symbol (attached to her by men themselves!) of man's fear of her uncastrated, horrifying sexual potency.

This is where the terror of the Medusa's head comes together with the fear of the rifle-woman's castrating "penis." She, too, is in possession of a

---

*They're not necessarily right to relegate all of Freud to the garbage heap or to pick out only the passages that expressly deal with femininity. The latter are seldom defensible and have become easy to criticize over time. Freud's mode of thought, conversely, isn't the least bit misogynous; for any research into human feelings can be of use to women. The broad condemnation of Freud within the masculine society in which he was writing can in part be traced to the fact that, in the eyes of men in positions of dominance, he wasted is life on "women's nonsense." The pleasure principle, even if Freud did at times accord it the name of "man," is in no way patriarchal. Or are there women who would say it was?

trophy, only because she has stolen it. And even with "rifle-women," it's not just *a* phallus—but *the* phallus—that hangs from their belts. Haven't we already seen "Spartacist women" galloping across our path on shaggy mounts, naked, hair flying, and two revolvers in each hand? That was the "Medusa" in action.

On the level of defense against castration, then, the man reacts by stiffening. But if the satisfaction of perceiving a particular state in the victim ("bloody mass") turns out to be the true goal behind man's "symbolic acts of sex," the ultimate aim of the castration defense seems to be to produce a specific state in the man himself. It is as if he were not really there when he murders, as if he were overcome by a sudden *absence*.

After he has fired, Donat no longer *sees* what is happening on the square. All that's there is a dead woman, but she doesn't seem to have been killed by his bullet. "It threw her onto her back, as if she had been blown over by some gigantic wind. . . . Is that thing at his feet really her?" He himself had been preoccupied the whole time with an effort of memory. Where in the world had he seen her before? He seems to be repeating some earlier process. The shot was fired almost without any help from him, in response to the command to shoot.

When Pahlen sees Marja the "rifle-woman" in captivity, he no longer *hears* what's going on around him. Yet he is stubbornly pursuing a goal. He too doesn't do the killing himself; he pays two anonymous men to do it. When they ask him for a reason, he answers absent-mindedly. His reaction to seeing the victim is like Donat's. It "seems" to be a woman's body lying in the slush, and it has "apparently" been lacerated with whips (though *he* had ordered the killing). The troops that move off after the killings are "astonished" to see that the stream is blocked with the bodies of Bolsheviks. The corpses are Bolshevik, that much they know. But who put them there?

Balla's men no longer *speak* when they find the corpses. "For a moment, a deathly silence reigns in the cellar. Then a single, piercing howl erupts from the lips of the men . . . An elemental sound from the deepest depths of nature, its roar expunges all trace of humanity from the human body. It wakes the beast and sets it on the blood trail." They are beside themselves. An explosion has burst their boundaries as human beings. "The dull thudding of clubs is heard." The perpetrators: anonymous men, "overcome by a common resolve."

Heinz ("Georg") can no longer *stand* when he sees the German woman who's been killed by some Poles. Yet he can't take his eyes off her, either. A procession draws near:

> Georg, finding it difficult to stay on his feet, leaned against a lamppost and stared alternately at the dead woman and the advance party, with the priest and altar boys. A hand knocked his

hat off his head. The hat rolled over to the woman and settled in the pool of blood.[18]

That kind of impudence would usually cost the perpetrator his life, but not here. After all, it helped Heinz to establish a closer association with the dead woman. Georg's hat is lying in the blood; he just stands there staring. Where is he?

The color has drained from Bewerkron's face before he gives the command to fire, a comand he, most unusually, issues "very softly." Red Marie's gaze rests a moment on that ashen face before her body slumps down "slowly . . . to one side." Who performed this evil deed? We know only that "the report of a salvo whipped through the forest." Bewerkron and Marie are united by her gaze: "Even as she fell, her eyes remained faithfully fixed on the young officer - - - -" Was this an execution, then? Not at all. "The birds were singing, insects buzzing, and it was a joy to be alive."

How much of this is real and how much hallucination? Corpses lie all around, but how did they get there? Here lie two lovers, "surprised" by a grenade. The woman in the street falls victim to a "fusillade of bullets." "Through a regrettable accident" nurse Ida Sode falls from the tower when Maercker pulls into Helmstedt. Von Selchow leaves the job to a Mexican bull.

It's only when enemies—Bolsheviks, Poles, etc.—are named as the perpetrators that murders are carried out *directly*. Such people are deliberate, sadistic killers. "You won't get away from me again, they hear Marja laugh." The Pole shoves the gun barrel into the woman's body and "fires." Or again, a Red Army man kills a Baltic countess, shooting her "from his saddle, with a bullet into her pale-skinned head, just below the parting of her blonde hair, in the center of the magnificent curvature of her forehead." (The latter observations are, of course, those of the noble Dwinger, not the brutish Latvian.)[19]

The soldier male murders differently. He's not altogether present. One might say that he is *intensely absent*. He doesn't really murder. True enough, there's some kind of blast, some order or other, a shot, and there are the bodies lying in their blood. Yes, the men pulled the triggers, but not as an act of will; they were *somewhere else entirely* in their minds . . . but where?

The perception of the "bloody mess" doesn't take place within a relation of observer to observed object in which both are clearly separated from each other. The mode of perception is not "I" see "that thing out there." Instead, perception occurs as if through a veil. It's hart to say what is seen, and what is hallucinated. As a "bloody mass," the victim loses her outlines and her character as an object. The same thing happens here to the perceiving *subject*. He, too, finds himself in a state of dissolution. This process, in which both the killer and his victim *lose their boundaries* and enter a union, and in which the predominance of hallucinatory perception puts the man into a trancelike state, seems to be the ultimate aim of the attacks.[20]

PRELIMINARY FINDINGS

Processes such as the dissolution of personal boundaries, and associated disturbances of object relationships, are difficult to describe using the concepts of psychoanalysis as developed by Freud. The reason is that the older Freud became, the more he moved the whole question of the origin and function of the "ego" as a psychic agency into the forefront of his theoretical considerations. That development occurred between *Beyond the Pleasure Principle* (1920) and *The Ego and the Id* (1923). Freud thereby laid the foundation for the lines of research that would later become known as ego psychology and opened up a different path for psychoanalysis from that which, as we will see, would have been necessary for the analysis and treatment of the phenomena under discussion here. Certainly, the results of our investigations so far suggest that the "ego," in the Freudian sense of a mediator "between the world and the id"[1] exists only in a very fragmented form, or, indeed, hardly at all, in soldier males. There is some question whether it has ever really been formed in them at all.

The reasons that impelled Freud, sometime around his sixty-fifth birthday, to put forward a theory of the psychic apparatus structured according to agencies (ego/id/superego) are not to be sought in any new discoveries he made at this time. We are dealing here with reformulations of the familiar, shifts in emphasis within psychoanalytic hypotheses, and, ultimately, with Freud's decision to organize into a simple *system* the multiple and contradictory hypotheses generated in the flow of research.

Now, people aren't born with an ego/id/superego structure; it has to develop within them. The decisive questions are where, when, and how that happens, and whether it always happens.*

Freud's answers to those questions are as follows: this structure evolves within the father-mother-child family triangle, through the "normal" decline of Oedipus complex between the second (or third) and the fifth year of life. The family, the Oedipus complex, and the child—already experienc-

---

*This is the difficult legacy left by many an aging sage to succeeding generations—doubtless a kind of revenge of the elderly. Yet Ulrich Sonneman has shown the compulsion to systematize overriding the evidence of actual research even in the young Freud's thinking (*Negative Anthropologie*, pp. 73ff.), whereas Laplanche and Pontalis correctly stress that various different notions of the ego are present in Freud's work and remain so even after the formulation of the "second theory" of the psychic apparatus (pp. 185ff.).

ing the world consciously and *speaking*—thus occupy the center of the Freudian theory of the origins of the "ego." There, the "ego" differentiates itself out of the "id" through a series of identifications.* The psychological process of identification is therefore given considerable weight in Freud's second theory of the psychic apparatus. Most important, the transformation of the original, incestuous object-cathexis of the parent of the opposite gender into an identification with that parent is seen by Freud as the key process within this development.[2]

Relationships within that triangle, as well as others derived from them, are relationships between subject and object, between whole persons with clearly defined boundaries and names, between one "ego" and another. "Incest," within the family constellation described here, is a relationship (or the prohibition of a relationship) among people with definite contours: a son wants to sleep with a mother, putting him in competition with a father, whose revenge on the son is the threat of castration, which causes the son to renounce incest in order to retain his filial phallus. At the same time, the son identifies with the father, transferring his object-libido to some other woman chosen in the image of the mother, or to a sister and through her to a friend of the sister, or to the sister of a friend, who is also a son like himself, and so on and so on. Or rather, not on and on, for this is where it ends.

For the men we are dealing with here, there is no such end. They want something other than incest, which is a relationship involving persons, names, and families. They want to wade in blood; they want an intoxicant that will "cause both sight and hearing to fade away." They want a contact with the opposite sex—or perhaps simply access to sexuality itself—which cannot be *named*, a contact in which they can dissolve themselves while forcibly dissolving the other sex. They want to penetrate into its life, its warmth, its blood. It seems to me that they aren't just more intemperate, dangerous, and cruel than Freud's harmless "motherfucker" Oedipus; they are of an entirely other order. And if, in spite of everything, they have a desire for incest, it is, at the very least, with the earth itself ("Mother Earth"). They are far more likely to wish to penetrate "her" in some violent act of "incest," to explode into and with her, than wish themselves in the beds of their flesh-and-blood mothers.

Here we are faced with something that cannot be subsumed under the heading of "Incest," or the concept of "object relations." What we have here is a desire for, and fear of, fusion, explosion. In parallel fashion, the fear of rifle women cannot (as we have begun to see) simply be reduced to the concept of "castration anxiety." What we encounter instead is a fear of total annihilation and dismemberment.

*A psychological process in which the subject assimilates some aspect, property, or attribute of another and is transformed, wholly or partially, after the model the other provides. (Laplanche and Pontalis, p. 205)

Accordingly, a simple "translation" of textual symbols remains unsatisfactory. The symbolism that figures in Freud's dream interpretation is itself attached to person-to-person object relations and predominantly to familial ones. Laplanche and Pontalis stress that:

> Whereas the symbols discovered by psychoanalysis are very numerous, the range of things they symbolize is very narrow: the body, parents, and blood relations, birth, death, nudity, and above all, sexuality (sexual organs, the sexual act).[3]

What we have here, on the other hand, are situations in which bodies, parents, blood relations, and any other human beings cease to exist as objects with boundaries. In their place, however, there are *states* of perception and emotional intensities that are never worked over by consciousness. They are hallucinatory, intoxicated states.

According to the findings of more recent psychoanalysis, the phenomena that appear here in place of Oedipal ones—the fear of/desire for fusion, ideas of dismemberment, the dissolution of ego boundaries, the blurring of object relations—do not originate in the Oedipal triangle, but in a dual relationship. It is the relationship between the child and the first person who takes constant charge of it, usually the mother. This relationship not only predates the father-mother-child Oedipal triangle, but is also fundamentally different from it.[4]

If we were to give a very general description of progress in psychoanalytic theory and therapy since Freud, we would have to single out two areas in which most of it has taken place. They are child analysis and the treatment of psychoses, both areas that Freud neglected, or, rather, disliked. We've since learned why. The disorders of infants and psychotics did not develop under the influence of the Oedipus complex. From the perspective of the topography of the psychic apparatus in Freud's second theory, they either lack the psychic agency known as the "ego," or else that agency is extremely disturbed. Michael Balint pinpointed this as the main reason for the failure of analysis with such patients.

> Our technique was developed for patients who experience the analyst's interpretations as interpretations, and whose egos are strong enough to absorb the interpretations and, in the words of Freud, to "work through them." We realize that many patients are unable to do this and that these are the very patients we have difficulty with.[5]

With patients who don't have access to an (Oedipal) ego of that kind, the *linguistic* process of analysis can't get off the ground. The "ego" isn't present because their development was disturbed when they were children, at a time when—psychologically and physiologically—they neither had, nor were, "egos." Experimental research with children has shown that the perceptual and neurological functions that allow children to think of themselves and describe themselves as "I" don't evolve until sometime between the ages of two and three. (Piaget, Spitz, and others)[6]

The period preceding this, especially the first year of life, has been called the "symbiotic phase" by child psychologist Margaret Mahler, precisely because during that period the child exists in a kind of symbiosis with the nurturing mother or, more rarely, the mother-substitute. The child is not yet able to feel, or perceive, its own boundaries. It experiences itself as united with the body of the mother.[7]

Through the dialectical process of extricating itself from that symbiosis, the self-perceiving ego of the child evolves. In the same moment as the child perceives its mother as an object located outside itself, it also perceives itself as an *object distinct from the mother*. In other words, it becomes an "ego," a *subject*, by learning to see itself as an object. (An object in the mother's eyes, and in the child's own eyes in front of the mirror.)[8] And so, the ego doesn't simply differentiate itself out of the id, as Freud tells us; it differentiates itself out of the mother-child symbiosis, a dualistic union.[9]

If the separation-individuation of the symbiosis is disturbed, the inevitable consequences are severe disturbances in the functions of the ego, preventing it from ever developing correctly, as well as severe disturbances of the capacity to form object relationships. (The range of possibilities preventing a child from escaping the symbiosis runs from the extreme of the "hard" mother, who never properly accepts her child or thrusts it away from her too soon, to that of the "soft" mother, who will never let the child out of her embrace.)[10] Michael Balint calls this arena of early relationships the "field of the basic fault."

> The main characteristic of the field of the basic fault are: (a) that all the events occurring in it belong to an exclusive two-person relationship—there is no third person on hand; (b) that this two-person relationship is very peculiar, entirely different from the familiar human relationship on the Oedipal level; (c) that the dynamic operating in this field does not take the form of a conflict; and (d) that the language of adults often proves useless and deceptive when it tries to describe events in this field, where words no longer have their conventional meanings.[11]

What seems important to me here, aside from the emphasis on the dual relationship, is the remark that the dynamic operating in this case does not "take the form of a conflict." Balint goes on to say that it "assumes, rather, the form of a mistake in the basic structure, a fault, a lack that demands to be compensated for."[12]

The sequence under discussion does *not* go like this: I can't reach my mother because my father bars my way, so I have to repress the incestuous desire for my mother and suffer as a result, since I don't want to give up incest. That would be a conflict. Instead, we have this: there's something wrong here, something threatening. Why is everyone so unreal, pressuring me and pressing in on me? Am I truly "I"? What's going on here? Everyone had better get away, or I don't know what might happen. . . . It would take a basic structural fault to force the patient to perceive even an unthreatening reality as threatening in this way.*

In light of all this, it becomes less difficult to answer the question of the origins of the phenomena under discussion here. The inability to form object relations, the disintegrated ego states, the *absences*, the hallucinatory perception, the coupling of defense-and-attack mechanisms—all these point to origins within the field of basic faults.

The acts of murder the soldiers enter into, for pleasure and to counteract fear, likewise strike me less as defenses against the threat of castration than as attempts to compensate for the fundamental lack of which Balint speaks.

There is general agreement that in patients of this description, the agency of the ego, within the framework of the Freudian ego/-id/-superego model, is unformed or defective. This has serious consequences for the overall validity of the Freudian conception of analytic technique and theory.

After all, the "ego" plays a central role in the operation of psychic mechanisms. It not only controls the energy cathected in object relations; defense and repression are also functions of the ego, according to Freud.[13] What, then, if that ego doesn't exist or is only fragmentary? Who or what sets defense mechanisms in motion? How does repression now function? The forms of defense in these men are, as we have seen, coupled with forms of pleasure production. This is unusual.

And what about repression? Considering how frequently quasi-incestuous relationships were constructed in the texts of our authors, it was striking how little effort was expended on concealing them. It seemed to me, in fact, that many of the writers actually put their "incestuous desires" on display. There didn't seem to be much repression in play there. The same was true of castration anxiety; the only thing preventing it from becoming

---

*Defects originating in the field of the basic fault are considered, in the older terminology, "psychoses." The latter term is subject to some controversy, though. My purpose is not to determine the boundaries of "psychosis," or the relationship of that term to the term "schizophrenia," or whether either term is at all useful as a designation for the illnesses in question. The fundamental distinctions between those illnesses and the Oedipal conflicts that were Freud's chief interest are not my concern here. If I occasionally use the terms "psychosis" and "psychotic" later on, I will be referring to Balint's theory of the basic fault, as well as to Mahler's concept of impeded "individuation" during the process of emerging from the symbiotic phase.

an explicit theme was the failure to express terms such as "incest" and "castration" openly.

This is hardly surprising, since to a considerable extent repression is a function of the developed ego. What is repressed, and therefore considered "unconscious," in "Oedipal" patients surfaces in the *consciousness* of "psychotic" patients. They *do not* repress, or rather, they repress something *other* than the fears and desires to which the names "incest" and "castration" have been given.[14]

This fact carries grave consequences, in turn, for the Freudian notion of the unconscious. In traditional psychoanalysis, the kind of material that has been discussed in this first chapter is considered an expression of unconscious desires, which to some extent at least result from previous repressions. It seemed to be a basic task of therapy, therefore, to render the unconscious conscious and allow repressed material to be experienced; to interpret it and work it through with the patient; to enable the patient, in the process of analysis—through transference to the analysis—to release the affects belonging to the repressed desires.

Yet what if everything the analyst is inclined to interpret is not the least bit "unconscious" in the patient? If "incest" and castration anxiety constantly haunt his fantasies, daydreams, and diary entries, and if there is no affect stirring inside him, how can the analyst come to speak about (i.e., "interpret") that configuration?

Can we blame Freud for not being particularly fond of such patients? Hardly. Nor can we blame him for leaving their treatment—to the extent that they ever wanted analysis, which in most cases they didn't—to others. The situation is complicated by Freud's decision to formulate his second theory of the psychic apparatus as if such people didn't even exist. He seems to have had such little regard for them that they were completely left out of his ego psychology in the end. As far as Freud is concerned, in *The Ego and the Id* Oedipus mounts his throne once and for all, proclaiming his exclusive rights to existence.[15]

Perhaps even that would not have been too bad, were it not for the following fact: the type of people who are not susceptible of "treatment" within such an ego theory must have been particularly numerous in Freud's day. I do not mean to such an extent that the asylums were full of them, but I am thinking rather of the multitudes of people who would have agreed, for example, that the Jews (or whoever else) had to disappear from the face of the earth, of all the people who felt sure that someone or other had to die so that they could live. They can't really have been such normal, Oedipal types. Oedipus doesn't go that far.

On the other hand, it would also be wrong simply to define these men as "psychotics." They do not, in fact, seem to possess the Oedipal form of the "ego," and yet they are not, for that reason, in any way "unadapted to reality," nor do they have "weak egos" or any other such disorder. After all, they were triumphantly effective in founding their very own empire of the future. In many respects, they were extremely successful; their mode of writing is controlled, in a manner which "psychotics" would hardly be capable of, as if a watchful ego were ever occupied in maintaining correct grammar and the proper chronology of events. By what type of ego, if it is not the Oedipal, do these men stabilize and control themselves?

Michael Balint has now suggested viewing Freudian ego psychology as a "limit-case" of ego psychology.[16] One might ask then: could it be that this limit-case arose out of a movement of defense, out of a historical defense against the terrifying phenomena that were coming to light so clearly among Freud's contemporaries? (Freud himself was a Jew, of course, and thus had every reason for defense against certain phenomena, particularly because he wanted to stay where he was and yet have nothing to do with politics.)

Two Frenchmen, the psychiatrist Guattari and the philosophy professor Deleuze, have criticized Freud's Oedipus construct in general for its defensive character and, in particular, for its concept of the "unconscious." Whereas analysts of the "basic fault" school object that Freud's notion of the "unconscious" is inappropriate for certain patients ("psychotics"), Deleuze and Guattari question whether it applies to anyone at all. Is there anyone, they ask, who has an "unconscious" that is associated with the name "Oedipus."[17]

The Swiss analysts Parin, Morgenthaler, and Parin-Matthey were able, for example, to demonstrate that the Oedipus complex, in the Freudian sense, doesn't exist among the African Dogon tribe.[18] Since then, a broad consensus has emerged that Oedipus is a predominantly European phenomenon which Freud inaccurately declared to be a universal human structure. Deleuze and Guattari go one step further. They dispute the very idea of a structure of the unconscious. They don't contest the existence of the Oedipal structure, but ask whose structure it is.* The names of Oedipus ("incest" and "castration") originate, in their opinion, in society, not in desire or in the unconscious.

What then, is the "unconscious," in their view? Their answer is basically no different from Freud's. Their starting point is also an energy that strives to manifest itself in the world, to discharge itself, to achieve pleasure. Unlike Freud, however, they refuse to bring this *productive force* of the unconscious—or desiring-production, as they call it—into association with names such as "incest," "castration," etc.

The unconscious, they argue, knows no names or persons; nor does it know any parents or have any memory. It neither produces images nor does

---

*"We even believe what we are told when Oedipus is presented as a kind of invariant. But the question is altogether different: is there an equivalence between the productions of the unconscious and this invariant?" (*Anti-Oedipus*, p. 53)

it have anything to do with any expression or meaning.[19] For the unconscious, there is no preferred object, either, not even the mother. Whole objects and persons are in no sense preferred objects of desiring-production.[20]

What, then, does the productive force of the unconscious direct itself toward? Here Deleuze and Guattari have recourse to the child analyst Melanie Klein's theories of the significance of part-objects for infants.[21] An infant does not perceive the mother who feeds it as a totality, "mother"—all analysts now agree on this point. It has various points of contact with various parts of the mother's body, of which oral contact with the breast during suckling is the most important. In other words, the child establishes its first significant relationship with the outside world by way of the part-object "breast."[22]

Deleuze and Guattari consider this kind of object relation consistent with the mode of production of the unconscious. It does not require *whole* persons for its productions. It achieves satisfaction when parts of itself are joined to parts of other objects, forming transitory productive connections that are afterward dissolved so that new productive connections can be formed.

Deleuze and Guattari call this mode of production *machinic*.[23] The unconscious is a desiring-machine and the body parts, components of that machine. In suckling, the sucking mouth and nourishing breast form a sucking-pumping machine, which continues to run until hunger is satiated. For Freud, the pattern is different: *son* Sigmund suckles at the breast of *mother* Amalie, who is later recognized as the *wife* of the *father*, Jakob Freud, and a triangle is constituted in which the son becomes "Oedipus."

It will strike most of us as strange that a process as fleshly and fluid as suckling should be described in terms of "machines." As bourgeois individuals, we have been brought up to think of ourselves as totalities, and unique ones at that. To the bourgeois mind, this conception of self accords precisely with the notion that we cannot be anything like "machines," "mechanically" produced or producing, or even "products of mass production." Even those who prefer to be seen as part of a collective system of human production would object to being considered machine components. In short, machines and human beings are opposites in our thinking, rather than things that might have something in common.

Deleuze and Guattari use the term in another sense. It's not the person, the totality that they perceive as "mechanic." For them, the "machine" is something prepersonal (i.e., unpersonal). It is an assemblage made up of moving parts that have the capacity and impetus to form new machines with other parts, then to dissolve those connections in order to form still other productive connections with other parts and so on. The unconscious is a molecular force.[24] Deleuze and Guattari make it explicitly clear that the word "machine" is not serving as a metaphor here.[25] It is used to refer to a function: the mode of functioning of the unconscious, which in the first instance wants nothing other than to *produce*. Its content is "the desire to desire,"[26] and what it produces is reality.[27] This productive force, this "desire to desire" is directed toward all the part-objects and objects within reality.* No one and nothing enjoys and privilege of being the true object of unconscious desire. Consequently, for Deleuze and Guattari, there is no such thing as incestuous desire, either.[28]

We can see now that what we're dealing with is an attempt to produce a description of the possibility of object relations, which takes its orientation not from whole objects, but from the theory of part objects. Thus the concept of the machine begins to lose something of its initial repugnance and mystery.** When Deleuze and Guattari claim that the unconscious functions and produces as a desiring-machine, what they are saying here is, precisely, that this is its *human* mode of functioning.

It follows from this that:

> The unconscious poses no problem of meaning, solely problems of use. The question posed by Desire is not "What does it mean?" but rather *"How does it work?"* . . . It represents nothing, but it produces. It means nothing, but it works.[29]

The Freudian concept of the libido, as a sexual energy that seeks to attain pleasure by making connections and achieving releases of tension, might fit in with this interpretation of the "unconscious"—but not the names Freud assigns to "unconscious" desires (e.g., "incestuous desire"). How does Freud come to associate "incest" with the unconscious? A glance at Freud's theory of the origins of culture will tell us. It all begins for Freud when the (Oedipal) individual, after successfully renouncing incest within the family and identifying with the parent of the same gender, begins searching for substitute objects in the outside world of social reality. There, through a lengthy process of libidinal denial and transformation, which Freud calls "sublimation," the individual learns to dispense with the immediate satisfaction of desires. A portion of the eros is applied to efforts of a social nature, which benefit humanity, help to build human culture, etc.—all of this happening, in the last analysis, because the incestuous object had to be successfully renounced. It was because I could not take possession

---

*Drives and part-objects are neither stages on the genetic axis nor positions in a deep structure. They are political options in response to problems, entrances, and exits, impasses that the child lives politically—that is to say, with the whole force of its desire. (Deleuze and Guattari, "Rhizome" in *Ideology and Consciousness*, Spring 1981, p. 58)

**The notion of "montage," as it appears particularly in French Surrealism, is closely allied to the concept of machinic desiring-production mapped out here. Montage is similarly unconcerned with totalities and with meanings. It uses familiar components to invent new functions.

of the mother that I became a social being, sublimating and creating culture.[30]

In Freud's account, "incestuous desire" is repressed and made unconscious; it continues to have effect indirectly. Deleuze and Guattari reverse the causality in this process. They begin from the premise that "no psychic operation or transformation" is needed to cause Desire to cathect reality outside of the family. Desire orients itself *directly* toward the social arena.[31] "Incestuous desire" and other desires develop in a child in accordance with the conditions of the society in which it is raised. If it is born into a family in which, under the dominance of monogamy, the mother is given a particular role as a sexual object, and if the family sees to it that the child has very little contact with reality outside of the family, the child will be forced to direct its desires toward something within the family. That doesn't leave much to choose from. The process is intensified if the child is given a taste of the forms of social repression that predominate outside the family. If too few of its desires can be realized there, and if its desiring-production is impeded because the organization of social reality denies the type of production it desires, then the child is thrown back upon the family and will once again try to find objects for its desire there. And so, the story doesn't go; because he couldn't take possession of the mother, he subjected the Earth to himself (Freud). It goes: because he wasn't allowed to use the Earth and produce, he went *back* to his mother. In this scheme of things, "incestuous desire" is not a primary desire at all, but a form that Desire assumes because of the repression to which it is subject in society.[32]

According to Deleuze and Guattari, "incest," "parricidal desire," and the "desire for castration" are socially determined distortions. Desire takes these names when its productive force, the "desire to desire," is repressed powerfully enough to enter into sociofamilial bondage. Through the *post facto* coinage "Oedipus," Desire acquires names that were not originally its own, and the "unconscious" a structure that it does not possess. These names and that structure retroactively introduce guilt and shame into the individual:

> The law tells us: You will not marry your mother, and you will not kill your father. And we docile subjects say to ourselves: so *that's* what I wanted![33]

In this way, the unconscious is made out to be something which wants what cannot be permitted, and which pursues aims that need to be repressed. The result of this operation is that the unconscious becomes a locus of chaotic, "socially unacceptable" desires; it is in this form, regrettably, that we encounter it in the late Freud.[34]

Clearly, this operation results in the maintenance of the status quo. If this is the true form of Desire, then dispensing with its fulfillment is at least made that much easier. Ashamed of one's desires, one atones by obeying the laws. In the process, the unconscious—as Deleuze and Guattari understand it—is *itself repressed*; in place of the "desire to desire," there appear the false names of Oedipus. The unconscious is rendered incapable of functioning and producing in accordance with its own forces and laws, until it can do no more than "merely 'represent' what a repressive apparatus gives it to represent."[35] In the end, Desire continues to exist only as *displaced* desire.

The chief criticism leveled by Deleuze and Guattari against Freud is that he invariably saw as the unconscious itself what were in fact representational forms of social repression, encountered in analysis on the level of displaced desire. They don't dispute the aptness of the names he gave to ideas he considered significant, such as "incest" and "castration." Yet, by declaring these to be formations and modes of expression of the unconscious, Freud himself contributed to the repression of the unconscious as a productive force that explodes the framework of authority of every society.

> And there is the essential thing: the reproduction of desire gives way to a simple representation, in the process as well as theory of the cure. The productive unconscious makes way for an unconscious that knows only how to express itself—express itself in myth, in tragedy, in dream. But who says that dream, tragedy, and myth are adequate to the formations of the unconscious, even if the work of transformation is taken into account? . . .
> It is as if Freud had drawn back from this world of wild production and explosive desire, wanting at all costs to restore a little order there, an order made classical owing to the ancient Greek theater.[36]

The form of interpretation psychoanalysis is thereby consigned to is incapable of penetrating to the unconscious. It is forced to borrow its concepts from itself, and in the end it is the interpretation "by means of which the conscious makes of the unconscious an image consistent with its wishes."[37]

If we take this criticism seriously—and I see no reason not to do so—we are left with two arguments *against* considering traditional analytical complexes, such as incest or defense against castration anxiety, to be unconscious. First, for defects originating within the field of the "basic fault"—as they seem to do among our male subjects—the bipolar opposition conscious/unconscious (in the Freudian sense) plays a minor role anyway, since the repressing "ego" is present only fragmentarily, if at all. Second, and more seriously perhaps, it seems as if latent ideational representations such as "incestuous desire" are *never* unconscious, neither are they ever "Desire." Instead, they seem to lie in the preconscious, where they stand not for the unconscious, but for social repression.

What then are our men really repressing? How does their unconscious really function? What does it actually desire and what does its production really look like?

* * *

Let's review the mode of production of our writers' language once again. It too cannot be grasped simply by revealing its "unconscious" contents. It is not primarily characterized by its specific use of a typical symbolism, nor indeed by any kind of *expression*; we are not even dealing here with projection.

Making clear what that language cannot do is revealing in itself. It cannot describe, or narrate, or represent, or argue. It is alien to any linguistic posture that respects the integrity of its object or takes it seriously. The language seems just as incapable of forming "object relationships" as the men who employ it. (The language neither lies nor tells the truth; those are irrelevant categories.)

What does it do, then? It consistently *employs* the postures mentioned above (e.g., "narration," "argumentation"), but only as empty shells. It seems to me that the process that is really specific to it is a different one, a process of transmutation. The linguistic process is inherently a process of production, one that appropriates and transforms reality. What is striking about our male writers is that the particles of reality taken up in their language lose any life of their own. They are deanimated and turned into dying matter. They are forced to relinquish their life to a parasitic, linguistic onslaught, which seems to find "pleasure" in the annihilation of reality. Reality is invaded and "occupied" in that onslaught.* The language of occupation: it acts imperialistically against any form of independently moving life.

It is, above all, the living movement of women that forces it immediately into a defensive-aggressive stance. It either screens itself against their existence (e.g., wives, "white" mothers, and sisters), or destroys them (e.g., proletarian women, "rifle-women", and erotic sisters and mothers). The emotional force and sexual intensity emanating from women seems unbearable, incapable of being worked over by this language.**

Mechanisms of defense and attack are not the only things at work in that language. (Projection is a simple defense mechanism.) In relation to the self, those mechanisms act as survival mechanisms. In relation to objects, they act as annihilation mechanisms. Both these latter are coupled together,

---

*In published critiques of "standard themes," "clichés," and linguistic "models," the reality-destroying character of this linguistic process is overlooked. Such critiques tacitly set these things up in opposition to the positive concept of "originality," rather than against life-creating *production*.

**It will become clear in chapter 2 that "women" is a code word for the whole complex of nature, for anything at all having to with "feelings" and the unconscious.

Levien and Leviné, proponents of the Munich soviet republic, as shown in numerous Nazi publications.

operating in one and the same action. They are two effects of a single process.

Human productions as a rule invest their objects with life. It is the living labor of the artisan that allows a table to be created from a tree,* the worker's living labor that forges a tool out of raw metal; the "mother's" living labor that enables a newborn infant to become a person. The production of our men acts conversely. It divests social products, both people and things, of the life that has entered into them, especially in war. Their mode of production is the transformation of life into death, and dismantling of life. I think we are justified in calling it an antiproduction. This antiproduction has a destructive and a creative aspect. It builds new orders from a reality that is devivified.

The process of destruction is marked by two successive states. "Perception" is followed by an assult. Even perception itself is an act of destruction, since it doesn't really "perceive" at all. The men's gaze is constantly on the hunt. It is searching out any movements within reality that communicate a threat. We can visualize this process more clearly by comparing it to the operation of a camera. A camera admits light and produces living images. The eyes of these men, conversely, admit nothing. When they catch sight of real movement, they block out the light—the eyes narrowing to mere slits—then emit beams of their own that cause the viewed object to appear

---

*This has amused quite a few people who don't realize that a table can be more alive, or deader, than a tree, depending on the work that has gone into it. They have branded me a vitalist philosopher (*Lebensphilosoph*).

distorted. Their eyes operate rather like spotlights. The image that is formed from the sharply illuminated real objects resembles a police photo. In police photos, people appear doomed not to remain much longer among the living, as if they were already under a death sentene. The police photographer acts as if he were going to produce a photograph. In reality, he destroys his subject's physiognomy in the glare of his spotlight. Soldier males train that same gaze on reality. They record the living as that which is condemned to death.*

In its second stage, the destruction is completed. The men turn their weapons on the illuminated object, because it brazenly continues moving around in the spotlight's glare, instead of quietly crawling off into some corner or taking its own life. Instead of a camera and cutting-table (living image and montage), they work with a spotlight and machete (dead image and dismemberment.)**

Yet like the police photographer, they insist that what they have produced is a photo. That's one of the functions of the dates they're always naming, of chronology as an organizing principle, of running to contemporary history for material, of their faultless use of schoolbook grammar, and of naming names that are vouched for "by the whole world." All of that creates the impression that they are capturing "reality" in their sentences in a proper ("photographic") manner. Is it their fault if there are so many terrible things out there?

The real source of terror is the light they themselves cast onto reality. As if magnetically attracted, their eyes hunt out anything that moves. The more intense and agitated the movement, the better.*** When they spot such movement they narrow their eyes to slits (defense), sharpen their vision of it as a dead entity by training a spotlight on it (deanimation), then destroy it, to experience a strange satisfaction at the sight of this "bloody mass." Their writing process works in exactly the same way.

We can speculate from this that it is above all the aliveness of the real that threatens these men. The more intensely life (emotions) impinges on them, the more aggressively they attack it, rendering it "harmless" in extreme cases. That is one side of the process, its destructive aspect.

---

*In the afternoon I walk back into the city, into the flood of its awakening activity. With the heightened awareness of the city dweller, I stride through the bustle as my brain cuts the surfeit of changing images to pieces, with ease and precision." (Jünger, *Der Kampf als inneres Erlebnis*, p. 66)

**Wim Wenders combined both processes into one when he wrote that Alois Brummer used the camera like a meat grinder. (*Filmkritik*, ix, 1970)

***See the striking frequency of the word "observer" (*Beobachter*) in the names of "*völkisch*" newspapers in the 1920s. *Völkischer Beobachter* (launched by Dietrich Eckart), *Niederdeutscher Beobachter* (published by Friedrich Wilhelm Heinz), *Westdeutscher Beobachter* (founded by Robert Ley, a subsequent leader of the "Labor Front", etc.—all were merged into the *Völkischer Beobachter* after 1933. It's clear that what this becomes is the gaze of the central (state) organ.

What happens on the "creative side"? Reality, robbed of its independent life, is shaped anew, kneaded into large, englobing blocks that will serve as the building material for a larger vista, a monumental world of the future: the Third Reich. In constructions of this kind, with their massive exteriors and solid forms, everything has its proper place and determinate value: the "army" and "nation," "German-ness," "rifle-women," "mothers," "Sythen Castle," "workers," "nurses," and, above all, soldiers.

The monumentalism of fascism would seem to be a safety mechanism against the bewildering multiplicity of the living. The more lifeless, regimented, and monumental reality appears to be, the more secure the men feel. The danger is being-alive itself.*

As an addendum to this preliminary description of the mode of production of soldier males, we need to point out that their mode of writing is no different in principle from their mode of action. The way in which reality is appropriated is the same on either level.

* * *

As far as I know, Walter Benjamin is the only critic who addresses fascism, and fascists, without assigning any significant role to the reproach that they are blinded to reality.** The others never tire of finding fault with the "unreality" of the fascists' fantasy worlds, the "irrationality" of their behavior, or the "subjectivity" that gives rise to errors in their political theories. These reproaches— and they are no more than that—judge fascism not by its reality, but on the grounds that it hasn't seen fit to comply with the maxims of its critics, to behave "rationally," for instance (which is a completely arbitrary demand).

The rational-irrational opposition has an outright violent effect when coupled with the subjective-objective opposition. This coupling was primarily responsible for distorting the view of fascism held by the German Communist party (KPD) in the 1920s and 1930s, as well as that of its present-day

---

*When Walter Benjamin characterizes fascism as a "parody of revolution" and its *modus operandi* as an "aestheticization of politics," he is assigning it a unique mode for producing (i.e., destroying) reality. It is still too early for us to examine Benjamin's theses; an analysis of his thought will follow later. Along with Benjamin, Georges Bataille should be mentioned here. Unfortunately, I was unfamiliar with his essay "The Psychological Structure of Fascism" (1933-34; German edition, 1978) when I began writing. Bataille sees fascism arising out of the same "heterogeneity" that produces revolutions. He describes the conditions under which movements growing out of that heterogeneity can, and inevitably do, become pillars of social "homogeneity."

**Empires can be built only on, and out of, dead matter. Destroyed life provides the material for their building blocks. A human present, or future, cannot be constructed in the manner of a building. The problem—power as thought and intention—is contained in the very notion of "building." Walls can be built, but not socialism (however many times Wolf Biermann may assert the contrary). The future and present of humankind must be lived by human beings in the process of producing life.

(voluntary)* successors. The latter "explain" fascism as deriving from the laws of motion of capital and, alongside that "objectivity," allow for a few "subjective factors" to take up the (considerable) remainder of the burden of explanation.

In its crudest and most widespread form, this line of thinking calls anything related to social production "objective," "rational," "real." "Subjective," "irrational," and "unreal" are the labels for anything that merely occurs in human beings, in the "psyche," impeding the victory of the rational and "objective" process that of course leads inexorably toward socialism.

In truth, these bipolar opposites are related to another opposition—that of negative and positive—and to the distinction between "right" and "wrong." They are evaluative terms, for the most part negative judgments. It is systems, not knowledges, which they sustain; and the systems they come from are obsolete. Like some glacial deposit from the European Enlightenment, they lie scattered in the conceptual landscape of science, blocking reality from view, preventing the development of new concepts that might correspond better to processes in the real, and serving as barricades in the struggle waged by ideologues and defenders of the bourgeois ego (including the unwitting variety) to stave off their own demise.

There are even some people who believe that thinking based on the opposition of subject and object was invented by Marx. (After all, why should they be any different in claiming Marx for themselves?) They are still arguing about what constitutes "correct" and false consciousness, for instance. Yet, consciousness must always be false if it is set in opposition to the "unconscious," emotion, and human affectivity—and as a rule, it is. "Correct" and "false" exist as potential distinctions within axiomatic systems. The science of human beings should learn to renounce such distinctions and introduce others, for instance, distinctions based on modes of production or degrees of aliveness. "Living," "dying," and "killing" are distinctions that are more adequate to reality, easier to make, and more useful (but more dangerous).

Still, even psychoanalysis had—and to an extent, still has—difficulty relinquishing the opposition between the so-called fantasy world and the so-called real external world in order to understand fantasies (of any description) as one reality among others.[38] Any attempt to label one phenomenon of human existence "more real" than another is *arbitrary*. People who do so anyway are employing an arbitrary definition of reality.

Deleuze and Guattari's response to all this is that "there is only one kind of production, the production of the Real."[39] In the present situation,

---

*At least the German Communist party can point to its historical dependence on the party of Stalin and to the fact that the Third International of that party prescribed how fascism was to be "assessed" and combatted. What alibi do Kühnl and his comrades have?

that matter-of-fact sentence is cause for relief; it clears a whole mountain of coarse, theoretical rubble from our path:

> The objective being of desire is the Real in and of itself. There is no particular form of existence that can be labeled "psychic reality." As Marx notes, what exists in fact is not lack,* but passion, as "natural and sensuous being."[40]

In other words, there can be no such thing as a production that is more real than real productions themselves; and the producer is simply a human being, not a person who is sometimes more human, sometimes less human, depending on whether s/he is producing more "subjectively" or "objectively," more "consciously" or "unconsciously."

> There is no such thing as the social production of reality on the one hand, and a desiring-production that is mere fantasy on the other. . . . The truth of the matter is that *social production is purely and simply desiring-production itself under determinate conditions.*[41]

That leads us to ask why, under certain conditions, desiring-production can turn into murdering-production. This is one question that is appropriate to the reality of fascism. Any question is inappropriate if it takes the form of recriminatory laments, in which the masses are assumed not to have "seen through" fascism, to have rejected communism for no other reason than their own slow-wittedness, or because they are attracted—for real, "objective" reasons—to fantasies alien to reality. Accordingly, Deleuze and Guattari (justifiably) see even Wilhelm Reich committing the error of:

> creating a distinction between rationality as it is or ought to be in the process of social production, and the irrational element in desire, and . . . regarding only this latter as a suitable subject for psychoanalytic investigation. . . . He therefore necessarily returns to a dualism between the real object rationally produced on the one hand, and irrational, fantasizing production on the other. He gives up trying to discover the *common denominator or the coextension of the social field and desire.* In order to establish the basis for a genuinely materialistic psychiatry, there was a category that Reich was sorely in need of: that of desiring-production, which would apply to the real in both its so-called rational and irrational forms.[42]

If we admit that there is a specifically "fascist" mode of producing reality and view that as a specific malformation of desiring-production, we also have to admit that fascism is not a matter of form of government, or

---

*Meaning that it is not lack that creates desire. In *that* function, "lack doesn't exist."

form of economy, or of a system in any sense. In this sense, an analysis of fascism becomes necessary for reasons above and beyond its hideous political *effects*. We need to understand and combat fascism not because so many fell victim to it, not because it stands in the way of the triumph of socialism, not even because it might "return again," but primarily because, as a form of reality production that is constantly present and possible under determinate conditions, *it can, and does, become our production. The crudest examples of this are to be seen in the relations that have been the focus of this first chapter, male-female relations, which are also relations of production.*

Under certain conditions, this particular relation of production yields *fascist* reality; it creates life-destroying structures. I think that has become apparent, just as it becomes apparent that fascism is a current reality whenever we try to establish what kinds of reality present-day male-female relations produce. (Even the authors of school textbooks, who have taken it upon themselves to extol the virtues of freedom in this land, see the family as the "germ-cell of the state," not as a site for producing living life.)

Freud circumvented this problematic, as we noted, when he formulated his second theory of the psychic apparatus. He secured his retreat by inventing the notion of the "death drive,"[43] according to which human aggressiveness no longer appears to be a specific mode of reality production, but a biological given of the species.

In my opinion, however, he had evaded the "problem of fascism" far more effectively beforehand. How did he come to develop his theories, as a rule, on the basis of *male* children? Simply because he himself was a man? What was he really saying when he "openly" confessed, late in life, that he didn't know much about "female sexuality"?[44] To my thinking, that is less a "comment" on "female sexuality" than on the fact that he viewed "female" and "male" sexuality as two seprate phenomena. As if the *nature* of "male" or "female" sexuality had any real significance, as opposed to the relationship existing between them. Relations between the sexes are socially organized and controlled, the object of laws. They are not simply "sexual." A man doesn't have "this" sexuality and a woman "that" one. If it seems possible today to make empirical distinctions between male and female sexuality, that only proves that male-female relations of production in our culture have experienced so little real change for such a long time that structures have arisen whose all-pervasiveness tempts us into regarding them as specific to sex. But if male-female relations of production under patriarchy are relations of oppression, it is appropriate to understand the sexuality created by, and active within, those relations as a sexuality of the oppressor and the oppressed. If the social nature of such "gender-distinctions" isn't expressly emphasized, it seems grievously wrong to distinguish these sexualities according to the categories "male" and "female." The sexuality of the patriarch is less "male" than it is deadly, just as that of the subjected women is not so much "female" as suppressed, devivified—though, sustaining less damage from its own work of suppression, it also contains the more beautiful possibilities for the future.

In perceiving sexuality more as an attribute of sex than as a relationship between the sexes, Freud once again substituted an expressive force for a productive one. He hit upon Oedipus as an *expression* of "male" sexuality under patriarchy. How exclusive an expression of that one, "male" sexuality Oedipus is, and how little Oedipus characterizes the mode of production of human sexuality per se, are things that Freud himself was indirectly forced to concede when he couldn't manage to locate such a structure among even the youngest of his girl patients. Yet the model was (tentatively) put forward as one that applied to all of humanity.

This criticizing of specific features of Freudian psychoanalysis makes me rather uncomfortable. I really hadn't planned on taking up a position (a very fashionable one by and large) on the anti-Freudian front. An anti-Freudian bent, of the kind found in the two authors quoted above, didn't rise up within me until I began a closer reading of the texts under discussion. More and more, I realized that where our male subjects were concerned, the Freudian categories criticized here were fanning the air.*

The same thing applies in part to Wilhelm Reich, since in his theoretical and systematic formulations he generally moves on the terrain of Freudian categories. Reich's incessant Oedipalization of his clinical material is especially conspicuous in *Character Analysis*; he tries to force the tight manacles of the late-Freudian ego/id/superego topography onto behavioral modes that clearly break the Oedipal mold.[45] And when we read how Reich defines the "phallic-narcissictic character type"—a category he coined and into which (according to the Reichian definition) the men in question would predominantly fit—it becomes obvious that this concept is totally inadequate for the phenomena he is trying to describe. He lumps together so many different things, in the end, that the "phallic-narcissistic" formulation becomes not only arbitrary, but downright nonsensical:

> Almost all forms of active male and female homosexuality, most cases of so-called moral insanity, and, moreover, many cases of erythrophobia and manifestly sadistic male perverts, belong to the phallic-narcissistic character type. Productive women very often fall under this category.[46]

---

*I hope that my objections haven't misled me into a replaying of that tired old game in which another young hopeful enters the field against one of his "spiritual fathers." I have no intention of dissociating myself from the inspiration I have gained from Freud's writings, more than from any other psychoanalytic texts.

Many an astrologer is surely more scientific than that. It seems clear to me that concepts from the psychoanalysis of the "basic fault" might have enabled Reich to carry his observations and experiences through to their theoretical conclusions, yet these were not available to him. Even his vehement attack on Freud's death-drive hypothesis, for instance, struck only at the construction of the "death drive" in isolation, ignoring the ego/-id/-superego topography on which something like a "death drive" would have to depend.[47] After all, the ego/-id/-superego topography implicitly exalts the value of "external reality," which helps create the "ego" (positive concept: "reality principle"), while devaluating the unconscious, which becomes the site of chaos, of *forbidden desires* whose realization is not only impossible, but undesirable as well.[48] In this system, human destructive potential no longer comes from "external" reality, but much more from within humans themselves. Something of the order of the death drive is therefore inherent within the Freudian ego/-id/-superego topography, and the role of the social frustration of desire in causing destructive behavior is considerably reduced. But as we noted, Reich attacked only the "death drive," while appropriating the Freudian "ego" concept in its entirety for his character analysis. Although I'm not in a position to offer extensive proof at this point, I think that Wilhelm Reich's psychoanalytic terminology was basically outmoded or, more specifically, always off-target because of its internal inconsistency. The inconsistency comes from the fact that, in many respects, Reich had ventured far from Freud in his conception of human psychic processes, without reflecting that distance in the concepts he used, which were consistently borrowed from Freud.[49]

For instance, in the debate previously outlined as to whether the "libido" (i.e., the "productive force of the unconscious") turns toward all of reality immediately, or only after successfully renouncing familial objects, Reich assumes a counter-Freudian stance precisely corresponding to the one we've seen in Deleuze and Guattari:

> Sexual desires naturally urge a person to enter into all kinds of relations with the world, to enter into close contact with it in a vast variety of forms. If they are suppressed, they have but one possibility: to vent themselves within the narrow framework of the family. Sexual inhibition is the basis of the familial encapsulation of the individual as well as the basis of individual self-consciousness.[50]

Once again, Reich fails to draw the inevitable conclusion that he should question the concept of incest as an unconscious desire.

His basic findings break through the Freudian framework in every case. His definition of character as a type of body armor, if formulated in psychoanalytic terminology, would demand a concept of the "ego" divergent from Freud's.[51] His sexual theories are far removed from Freudian prudishness. For Reich, sexuality is never a Latin libido or a Greek life principle;* it is the pleasurable mingling of human bodies, the force that produces life-affirming reality. He makes an important contribution to psychoanalytic technique with his writings on the analysis of psychic resistance in patients undergoing therapy.[52] He flies in the face of Freud by insisting that material surfacing in patients should not be interpreted immediately, if the patient's resistance is so great as to suppress any affect belonging to the idea expressed, in which case, interpretation would only increase the patient's reserve toward the analyst. He insists—even when this controversy leads to a break with Freud—that his suggestion accords with Freudian deliberations.[53] In the realm of psychoanalytic theory, he remained something of an unloved star pupil of Freud. Analysts such as Melanie Klein, Michael Balint, and Margaret Mahler criticize Freud by introducing new psychoanalytic concepts, which have begun to free analysis—to an extent more radically—from the chains of the Oedipal categories.

It was Reich who started the shock waves, however, by violating a different taboo. He let politics into the analyst's office and sent psychoanalysis out into the streets—this time German streets, not village paths in Africa.** (That's why even today he is still ignored by the more refined ladies and gentlemen of science. Now we can all see what they were maintaining their silence about.) I'm not saying anything new here, of course. Still, it can't be admired sufficiently that at a time when analysts were transforming themselves in droves into amateur ethnologists, expecting progress in the human sciences to come primarily from the study of "savages" still living in a "pre-historic" site, while declaring Europe to be the continent of culture and civilization, that at such a time one of their number refused to follow his contemporaries into that flight. Reich did things exactly the other way around. He idealized the Trobriand Islanders as examples of perfected natural humanity, in order to turn back to Europe with the realization that the "savages" were here, in his own country, where fascism was on the verge of victory.[54]

Reich is at his profoundest as a thinker when he refuses to accept ignorance or illusion on the part of the masses as an ex-

---

*He scoffed at "proponents of the death drive, who, now that they could talk about 'thanatos' instead of sexuality, were becoming increasingly abundant and respectable." (*Die Entdeckung des Orgons*, p. 99)

**In that respect, Reich resembles another lone wolf and bourgeois revolutionary of his day, Hanns Eisler. Eisler did with Schönberg's inventions something similar to what Reich did with Freud's: he attempted to introduce them into the revolutionary actions of a proletariat engaged in a struggle for its own liberation. Reich and Eisler did what the Galileos of this world don't do; they revealed the new secret to their "inferiors." Except that those to whom the secret had been revealed wanted no part of it—they weren't allowed to by their immediate superior, the party. Contemporary comrade Brecht *didn't* write any plays about that.

planation of fascism, and demands an explanation that will take their desires into account, an explanation formulated in terms of desire: no, the masses were not innocent dupes; at a certain point, under a certain set of conditions, they *wanted* fascism, and it is this perversion of the desire of the masses that needs to be accounted for.[55]

That's how Deleuze and Guattari pay tribute to Reich's formulation of the question in hand, and I think they're right in choosing exactly that point as the nucleus of their praise for him.

Among Reich's own explanations there are some pithy utterances of genius, such as the statement that fascist sensibility springs from a mortal fear of orgasms—a formulation that nonchalantly sweeps Freudian concepts aside.[56] Many times, though, he is unable to break free of that very same conceptual system. Reich is often vague, especially concerning details, for the reason suggested by Deleuze and Guattari, namely, that he never resolved the apparent contradiction between class interests and human desire.[57] Reich saddles fascist material with interpretations that are more demonstrations of his own thinking than descriptions of the fascist mode of destruction of reality.*

Yet a more "immediate," political reason may have been responsible for keeping *The Mass Psychology of Fascism* at a certain distance from its fascist material. Reich lost his entire archive when he emigrated; he was therefore forced to piece a lot together from his head. That's comparable in difficulty to a long-distance diagnosis of a patient. From my own acquaintance with the texts in question, I know that I almost automatically tend to "apply" Freudian concepts to the soldier males (as I write about or rather *of* them) unless I have the original fascist texts right in front of me.

I don't know how anyone who doesn't think, feel, write, and behave like these men can ever retain a grip on the contents of their writings, especially the affects. It's of the same order of difficulty, I think, as the oft-reported and oft-lamented problem of retaining in "consciousness" the events of the concentration camps.

And indeed, consciousness is not the proper place for "preserving" memories of fascist atrocities, or, perhaps, the events of human history in general. When we read, and reread, texts—i.e., look at history over and over again—they begin to correspond to our own unconscious. The pathway to knowledge might just be that of refusing to repress our unconscious and allowing history (fascism) to be "lived through" by it, in such a way that our

---

*Reich's texts often give an impression of tremendous haste in any case, especially *The Mass Psychology of Fascism*. It's as if the book were written simply as a quick explication of what Reich already knew in his own mind. Much of his writing therefore has more the effect of a swift unburdening—time was closing in, after all—than of a process in which the material and thinking have sufficient time to be developed.

understanding of history finally comes about *through the experience of our own unconscious.* That suggestion will make historians' hair stand on end, but it comes from one of them, a Parisian professor, Alain Bensançon:

> In its sphere of activity, research hits upon the most interesting facts within the psyche of the observer himself. It is a matter of laying hold of the observer's own unconscious, not that of the patient. Only to the extent that he allows the distortion to come to light and settle in his unconscious (without transferring it back to the patient again), can he examine it with all of the requisite care. He can really understand his patient, in a psychoanalytic sense, only by recognizing in himself the reactions triggered by the patient . . . This assumes that the historian's ego can fearlessly withstand the unrestrained circulation of fantasized scenarios and the affects associated with them . . . It is a matter of paying attention to the emotional stimuli and disturbances that influence the operation of the psychic apparatus, by way of our relationships to the texts in question, and to our overall personal histories. The task is to listen to oneself as well as the other person; to inform the anxiety attendant on the research, and attaching to the function, that an interesting truth is about to rise up and approach; and to unmask that truth.[58]

The same thing can be stated in another way. It will not do to conceive of fascism—or any other historical object—as something alien and opposed to the individual self. Or, in the words of Walter Benjamin: "It is not enough simply to know the thing you wish to destroy; to complete the task you have to have felt it."[59] Yet this is precisely the impression one often does not gain from Reich. He writes *about* fascism as the shining, enlightened rationalist:

> The enlightener thinks in opposites. To expect dialectics from him is perhaps unfair. But is it unfair to expect from the historian that insight into the appearance of things which sees beauty even in the most profound disfigurement? Historical discovery through negation is an absurdity.[60]

I myself consider it unfair to use Benjamin's criticism against Reich; it certainly applies to him only in part. Yet it strikes me that there is a good deal of truth in it, just the same. I may have to apply that criticism to myself in the end. . . . In any case, up to this point I've hardly been able to see the "beauty even in the most profound disfigurement."

* * *

One finding that begins to emerge: along with capitalist relations of production, a specific male-female (patriarchal) relation might belong at the center of our examination of fascism, as a producer of life-destroying reality. A second finding: in and of themselves, the Oedipal categories of psychoanalysis don't seem capable of apprehending fascist phenomena.

Beyond that, a series of questions has arisen—questions resulting from the confrontation between the material of fascism and prevailing views of it, as well as from the attempt to allow that material to take its own effect, rather than repressing it with overhasty explications.

If the terms "incest" and "castration" are no more than *names* for a *displaced* desire, then what is really being *desired*? If incestuous "desire" (like everything else that defines the Oedipus complex) is not an object of repression, but actually takes part in repression, as a repressing agent, then what is really being repressed? If all that we find in the Oedipal system are representations of repressed desires, then what does desire itself look like and how does the unconscious function? What is its mode of functioning in soldier males?

If the unconscious doesn't express anything—that is, if it doesn't speak through dreams, myths, and art in images, symbols, and meanings—what, then, do its productions look like? And if everything appearing at the "level" of expression and representation is not unconscious, what, then really is unconscious?

By what means does an unnamed threat light upon the victims of its terror, if not through mere projections? How does the scapegoat become a scapegoat—or is it not a matter of "scapegoats" at all when women, Jews, and proletarians are being persecuted? If projection turns out to be an insufficient explanation, what kind of perception exists in these men?

What about the "egos" of the men? According to Freud's second theory of the psychic apparatus, the Oedipal ego is formed through various identifications and renunciations within the family triangle, after which it is able to make certain object choices. The ego, in *that* form, doesn't seem to be present in soldier males. What kind of ego do they have, then? Their ego (and its objects) pass through states of extensive dissolution. What is the source of its "reality adaptation"? (After all, the Nazis did come to power.) Is it enough to understand those states of dissolution as regressions? And if so, to what state are they regressing? If not, what's really going on?

Finally, what about psychic defense? It seems to be not only a defense, but also the positive pursuit of the goal of some drive. Does it coincide with known defense mechanisms, which are presumed to arise out of the ego(!), or are we dealing with an entirely different phenomenon?

Last but not least, do the avoidance of erotic women, the fear of them, the terror directed against them, and the attraction to male bonding, especially in the military, have *anything at all* to do with homosexuality?

IPAC (International Psychoanalytic Congress), Jerusalem, August 1977.

So that we can come closer to answering some of these questions, in the next chapter we will pay more attention to certain bodily states depicted by the men themselves, particularly their fears and pleasures during "states of dissolution." From there on, we'll take a lengthy excursion into the bottomless abyss. We'll be moving into the water, and all else that flows there.

Chapter 2
Floods, Bodies, History

AGGREGATE STATES OF THE BODILY INTERIOR

The Red Flood

> The raging stream is called violent
> But the riverbed that hems it in
> No one calls violent.[1]
>
> (Brecht)

"The wave of Bolshevism surged onward, threatening not only to swallow up the republics of Estonia and Latvia, neither of which had yet awakened to a life of its own, but also to inundate the eastern border of Germany."[2] W. von Oertzen on the Baltic situation at the end of 1918.

Bolshevism seems to be a kind of ocean that surges onward in waves, inundating and engulfing. Wherever the "Red flood"—also the title of a novel by Wilhelm Weigand, about the Munich socialist republic—was sighted, the cry of "Land under!" pierced the air. "The Reds inundated the land";[3] so says a certain Hartmann, volunteer in the Baltic Army, which "for a time was the only one to stand up to the Red wave" in the Baltic region.[4] "In the east, coming from the Baltic, the Red wave surged onward" (Walter Frank).[5] The Freikorps have rescued Germany "from the Bolshevistic flood . . . and ruination." (Weimer-Borchelshof)[6] In Upper Silesia, Germans troops struggle to dam up "the raging Polish torrent" (von Osten).[7] "The stream of insurgents pours like the Great Deluge over the Ellguther Steinberg Range as far as Oberwitz, against the makeshift front of the German" (Eggers).[8] The Freikorps were in the Baltic area[9] "in order to stem the all-destroying flood that was slowly advancing toward the west"[10] (Wagener, a captain in the Iron Division). The Freikorps soldiers, volunteer dockworkers of the nation, were racing from every quarter to the border areas. "The side of the ship of state that faced east was in the greatest danger. This was where the water gushed through its ribs and plates" (Rudolf Mann).[11]

A knee-jerk interpretative reflex would lead us immediately to say that political events are being described here as natural processes, and that everyone knows this is what reactionaries always do. Yet we would be saying no more or less than that the phrases quoted above were "false"; were we to be asked why, our answer would be, "in an attempt at disguise." In other words, this interpretative reflex reacts to sentences of that kind simply by proclaiming them "lies" or "nonsense," adding perhaps, as a corrective, that politics are not nature, and those fascists should be ashamed of themselves.

Yet do these words truly "lie"? The powerful metaphor of the flood engenders a clearly ambivalent state of excitement. It is threatening, but also attractive: the flood approaches! Strong emotions are in play, and those don't lie. (Comrade Schottenhammel[12] steps forward: "Captain, Sir, you're getting worked up over nothing. This is not the Great Deluge, just the Red Army. . . ." "That's what I'm saying you idiot! We'll all be drowned in the Red flood!")

What are they really talking about? And why floods, torrents, raging water; why do they not say, for instance, "the Bolshevists advanced like the fourth Ice Age," or like a "hurricane," or an "Asiatic sandstorm"? None of these would sound convincing. But why not? And why do the Bolshevists in particular flood in so terrifyingly, but not the Imperial German Army in its invasion of Belgium, or the Freikorps in the Baltic region? The latter march in dry and solid, an army of dam-builders with a song on their lips.[13]

It is not so much the metaphors of flood that are important here, as the specific use to which they are put. This particular use of language causes many things to flow: every brook and stream, "après nous le Déluge," still waters; floods of papers, political, literary, intellectual currents, influences. Everything is in flow, swimming upon this wave or that, with or against the current, in the mainstream or in tributaries. Drifting along . . . scum . . .

Our soldiers, conversely, want to avoid swimming at all costs, no matter what the stream. They want to stand with both feet and every root firmly anchored in the soil. They want whatever floods may come to rebound against them; they want to stop, and dam up, those floods. "The attempt to disperse a wave of Red insurgency was once again successful."[14] (General Lüttwitz on the occasion of the Freikorps' entry into Munich, May 1919). Or (Salomon): "Another day of extremely heavy fighting ensued . . . before the Red flood was finally flushed away."[15] Nothing is to be permitted to flow, least of all "Red floods." If anything is to move, it should be the *movement* (i.e., oneself)—but as *one* man; in formation; on command as a line, a column, a block; as a wedge, a tight unit. Death to all that flows.

But what is the source of that flowing, and of the peculiar attraction exerted by the flood on the soldiers? Ernst Jünger once wrote: "To the foot soldiers, it [life] was a storm cloud above the vastness of the night."[16] A storm cloud may pass over, or it may discharge itself in thunder. The latter is the more likely. The flood from the cloud wouldn't catch them unawares; it is there from the beginning, locked up, ready to break loose (when there is a crashing collision).

Salomon says that even as a cadet under the monarchy, he sensed that "within the old order, the new flood was rising before every dam, threatening to pulverize its petrified forms of life."[17] The expected flood was "threatening," all right, but it was also invested with positive traits. Salomon is no unquestioning defender of "petrified forms of life."

We find a similar ambivalence in Lutz Rossin: "The grave-diggers of Germany had wielded their spades for the last time, piercing through the ancient dam of traditional state authority: an artificially created tumult flowed in a broad stream through Germany."[18] While Rossin condemns this development, he nevertheless causes the flood to flow powerfully, "in a broad stream." What got to him most was the act of piercing through. The movement it triggers is reiterated in the sentence; it is carried across, and beyond, the colon. (Why is it that children love to put up hastily constructed dams to block the streams of rainwater collecting in gullies, then wait for the moment when the dams break, let the flood rage again, only to build new dams and watch them break again, and build and wait again, until the water—which does not always flow—has flowed away completely?)

What Rossin does find repugnant is *the thing* that flows. "The Red flood brought all of the worse instincts to the surface, washing them up on the land."[19] The flood can be localized more specifically. It seems to flow from the inside of those from whom the constraint of the old order has been removed. Something comes to light that has hitherto been forbidden, buried beneath the surface; the "worst instincts," true enough, but *powerful* and exciting to watch. For a moment at least, one is *powerless* and hypnotized in the face of those floods—as if *defenseless*. ("Shall we build a dam?"—"Yes, tomorrow; but first we must collect ourselves.")

The dam had broken in the West:

> The whole world poured out over Germany: Americans and New Zealanders, Australians and Englishmen, Portuguese and French. The bitterest pill to swallow was the stationing of blacks everywhere by the French: Moroccans and Senegalese negroes, Indochinese and Turks.[20] (Dwinger)

The notion of external invasions combined with internal dam ruptures seems to make it possible to subsume Germany's defeat in the war, and the revolutionary changes in and around Germany, under the image of the flood. Drives liberated by these invasions and ruptures abandon the riverbed to which they had been forcibly consigned by Wilhelmine society, to flow freely over their banks. Jünger's "storm cloud" and Salomon's "new flood" equally clearly contain a reference to processes occurring within the two men themselves. (In childbirth, too, streams of water and blood—red floods—are released before the baby is delivered. Pharoah's daughter actually *did* pull Moses out of the river—though the name of the river wasn't "Nile.")

November 1918. The retreat through Belgium. The dissolved ranks of German soldiers, who are by now refusing to take orders from the militarists, appear here as a flood that is carrying along something terrifying and new, something previously hidden. Here is Captain von Heydebreck, later a Freikorps commander:

> There began a time of heavy trials. On the very next day we encountered the flood that had washed through Lüttich for almost an entire week. Day and night, column after column, uninterrupted, thousands upon thousands racing and chasing through the streets, or simply lounging around. Carriages so full of them that the horses often collapsed; motorized trucks overcrowded, fighting for places. The same scene at the railway station. Each man thinking only of himself, and everyone else be damned. A psychosis of fear dissolved any bonds of solidarity, a fear or arriving too late, now that others had set about making a good life for themselves back in Germany. Only the field kitchen kept the remnants of formations together. The flood washed onward, day in and day out, howling, screaming, swearing, several columns at once, passing each other, blocking the street. Where on earth did they find those quantities of red cloth?[21]

This is a time of trial for Heydebreck. Will he succumb to the temptation to hurry home and make a "good life" for himself, to make a living perhaps from some profiteering scheme—for it is to *his own* thoughts that he gives expression here, not to those of the soldiers racing homeward—or will he stand firm against the enticements of the flood? He'll stand firm, of course. That's clear from the start. But that doesn't mean he has to completely suppress a certain enthusiasm for the confusion that spills out around him. "Where on earth did they find those quantities of red cloth?" There is astonishment in that question and admiration. They have *dared* to do this! Where did they find it? Perhaps they had it all along, perhaps it was folded up and hidden away, maybe even forgotten. Not it appears unfurled: the banner of their desires, a red flag. For an instant, Heydebreck senses that he too has such a banner: then the floodgate closes, and he is once again a rock amid the raging sea. The flood is abstract enough to allow processes of extreme diversity to be subsumed under its image. All they need have in common is some transgression of boundaries. Whether the boundaries belong to a country, a body, decency or tradition, their transgression must unearth something that has been forbidden.

This is when the flow begins, inside and out, exciting and frightening at the same time. The closer the flood is, the more dangerous it seems. Thus the German streams, which flow most freely during the civil war, are particularly dangerous. Most dangerous of all, though, are the floods within oneself, like those that washed over Horst Wartemberg, hero of Ekkehard's novel *Storm Generation* (*Sturmgeschlecht*), in the "Breughelesque hell' of that era:

> General strike. State of siege. Sees only Germans with hate in their eyes. Hears only curses and swearing. A gigantic, filthy-red wave breaks over him. He feels he's drowning in it.[22]

Nothing but red cloth: "Strikes"—"hatred"—"curses"—"swearing"—against whom? Against the authorities he has so far complied with (without striking, with suppressed hatred, secretive curses, and swearing); and complied to such an extent that the mere sight of a different practice is enough to make him dizzy. He saves himself by a kind of loss of consciousness. The "gigantic, filthy-red wave" that breaks over him has really sloshed up inside him. He threatens "to drown" within himself. Much like Heinz Schauwecker:

> Meanwhile, shame and betrayal, filth and misery rose higher and higher around us; we could practically have drowned in it. The bitterness of living through a mindless revolt, with its shameless self-complacency, forced the love of life right out of us.[23]

The flood is close at hand, then, either in oneself or on the outside. The men seem to relate every actual or imminent flood directly to themselves, each one to his own body. The terrain of their rage is always at the same time their own body; this feeling is found in every single utterance associated with the "Red flood."

The excitement peaks when the Red wave actually reaches the body (i.e., when it kills):

> The sergeant slowly drags himself down the iron staircase, unbolts the heavy gate, and steps out into the square with his arms up. In an instant, the Red wave sweeps over his corpse and storms up the stairs like a pack of wolves, lips dripping saliva.[24]

. . . and Dwinger is swept right along with them. His emotions are with the movement of attack, with the wave, with the stream of salivating lips that has been set free—by Dwinger, though he also "condemns" it. He lets his political enemy carry out the forbidden act.

Roden does the very same thing. At the deathbed of his Captain Berthold in Harburg:

> Hour after hour goes by. One attack follows another. When the depleted brigade has used up its last cartridge, Captain Berthold has the white flag hoisted. He wants to negotiate. Alone, unarmed, he walks over to the rebels. A few seconds of silence, then the wave breaks loose—tearing down, beating, kicking the body of this lone man in the midst of the raving masses—tearing him to pieces—letting him drop with the brutish scream of the unleashed beast. ———[25]

An uplifting moment, fading out with proper solemnity in three emotion-filled dashes. The sympathetic reader is to be gripped by an excitement that arises from the precise fulfillment of expectations. The man is torn to pieces: so be it.

What's really going on there? In both instances a lone man, the leader of the moment, steps up to face the "Red wave." He is beaten, all alone, and swallowed up. The authors in both cases have an affective investment in the wave, but also in the man. Or, more exactly, it's the *process* as a whole—"Heroic, Defenseless Man Devoured by Red Wave"—that is important to them.

Their attention is riveted on the moment when the dam bursts, the moment when the liquid crashes up against the solid and destroys it. It is as a result of this act that something really begins to *flow*: the blood of whoever has been killed. To collide with a red flood means death; the solid dissolves (whether the flood comes from within or without).

Within this process, the desire for collision seems to be as strong as the fear of it. The desire for "contact" is realized, in the sense that this desire instigates collision; the fear is realized, in the sense that the collision ends in death. The result, therefore, is not a friendly amalgamation of both elements, but the annihilation of one. In other words, instead of a river of love, a stream of blood begins to flow.

"Blood, blood, blood must flow/Thick as a rain of blows."[26] This was a favorite song of the fascists; and it seems to me to express their supreme dictate, in the form they themselves liked to give it. (The singer of the song can specify whose blood should flow as the occasion arises: "to hell with the freedom of the Soviet republic"; to hell with the freedom of the Jewish republic"; and so on.)[27]

It should come as no surprise that the historical events in Essen and Harburg did not occur in the way portrayed by Dwinger and Roden; we already know the extent to which these men pattern external events after their own affective needs. What is of interest, however, is the degree to which events are distorted; interesting too are the actual events themselves.

Dwinger's "Red wave" was a group of armed workers who, on March 19, 1920, while fighting off the Kapp Putsch, captured the Essen water tower, where forty-six Kapp sympathizers from the civil defense forces and security police were entrenched. The battle over the Essen water tower "was often cited in bourgeois, and later national-socialist, historiography as a prime example of the 'Red Army's' sadistic atrocities" (Erhard Lucas).[28] Today, it can stand as a "prime example" of the characteristic features of that historiography. True, the besieged Kappists had displayed the white flag; but then, disagreeing among themselves about the prospects for further resistance, they had opened fire on the slowly advancing workers. This fact was later actually confirmed in a court of law (quite something, in the context of the Weimar "Republic"). That verdict notwithstanding, the Essen water tower boasted, until very recently, a memorial plaque that listed the names of all who had fallen at the tower in the battle for Essen as victims of the "Red terror."[29]

In the case of Berthold, the victim of the "Red flood" was not simply a fabrication (as it was in so many other instances). He actually was killed by workers in Harburg. The circumstances aren't entirely clear, but one thing is certain: the "famous shot" was fired (by whom?) not as he was offering to negotiate, but, as happened so often, after the subsequent surrender of the "Bertholders." In the ensuing confusion, Berthold and several of his soldiers were killed. Had the workers really behaved as a "raving mass," there would have been more deaths, in which case the distinction drawn by the workers between officers and troops—something that even Salomon stresses in his account of the situation—would have to have been dropped.[30]

Considering that Berthold's "Iron Legion" was an active putschist unit that the workers knew to be on its way to Berlin to topple the republican government,[31] considering, too, that the Bertholders were known to have fired into crowds on previous occasions,[32] the restraint of the workers is nothing short of astounding; for the rest of the troops were allowed to escape.[33]

Street of Blood

In Thor Goote's *Comrade Berthold*, we find the eponymous hero sitting and licking his countless wounds in his parents' parlor—a forest ranger's home—at Christmas, 1918. The war is lost; the monarchy is no more; a revolution has taken place. He can't get in to the Christmas spirit. His parents watch his suffering. The father wants to help, but his son isn't listening:

> Rudolf Berthold presses his fists together, but his own voice is strange to him. He hears himself speaking, yet sees only the red street of blood that runs toward him.[1]

It isn't the blood of the recent war that pursues him. This blood comes from the future; it is coming *toward* him. It had to do with the anticipated terrors of the republic. The "Red flood" is at the gates. The "red street of blood" is one he himself will (probably) have to pass through.

News of the 1914 declaration of war had elicited a similar image from Ernst Jünger:

> Reeling, deranged, the masses flooded through the streets
> beneath the crest of the monstrous wave of blood that rose up
> before them.[2]

This "wave of blood" also comes from the future; there is no way to go but through it. But what is its source? Are we dealing with a clumsy attempt to portray all of the blood he expects to flow in the forthcoming war?

For the nationalist playwright Lissauer, the onset of the war offered an occasion to compose pamphlets spreading dark prophecies. An example:

> Men rose up, fire in their blood:
> "We see. We know.
> Smoky vapors sun and moon with darkness bring to woe,
> Blood is in streams and seas all to flood."[3]

It's hard to discern any grammatical connection between "streams," "seas," "blood," and "flood." They will come; that much is clear. In the title of the pamphlet "People's Whitsuntide" (*Volkspfingsten*), Lissauer creates associations with the Resurrection. The whole complex of this future flowing of blood seems somehow connected with the expectation of a birth.

In another work, a play about Thomas Münzer, Lissauer draws a connection between the blood that will flow in the civil war and menstrual blood. He has one bloodthirsty peasant call out to another one, who would rather negotiate: "The maiden is loath to turn her bed red; but, maiden, it's the time of the month."[4]

Two salient ideas are expressed here. Fighting occurs as surely and as regularly as menstruation, and therefore it's due right now. Second, menstruation itself presupposes an act of violence. The text seems to be saying: "The battle within you has already taken place, maiden; why now hold back the blood? It's the time of the month, maiden."

The folklorist Hans Bächtold, who has made a study of "soldier customs," notes this war prophecy of 1912:

1911: a fire year
1912: a flood year
1913: a blood year[5]

When 1913 turned out not to be a "blood year," it became a "good year" and "1914, a blood year." The prophecy could then "come true." No matter what, a "blood year" had to come.

The sequence fire/flood/blood turns up again in Eberhard Wolfgang Möller's "Cantata to a Great Man" ("Kantate auf einen grossen Mann," 1935):

> Ever faster mankind sees, and fainter,
> Flood to flood, and brook to brook, escaping,
> And himself amid the raging waters,
> Endlessly and restlessly departing.
>
> And he vies with burning firebrands
> To find a place where he may rest his head.
> Flaming falls the flame from walls. He stands
> And now he sees: the stream is red and blood.[6]

The colon in the final line makes it clear that the stream's being "red and blood" is tantamount to a logical consequence.

We may assert then that blood is a potential final stage of the flood. (It might just be that the "Red flood" is *always* a river of blood.) The river of blood appears in connection with ideas of war: civil war, internal currents and struggles, birth, and menstruation. In every case, blood is expected to flow.

Boiling

The floods, waves, and torrents are not always in the form of free-flowing streams. Frequently they are confined, raging within vessels of various descriptions. It was the revolution, Salomon felt, that "transformed the city of Munich into an enormous cauldron, where thick blood and thin beer bubbled up wildly together."[1] "Everything is simmering indiscriminately and mindlessly in a single pot, to make the stinking brew we call German fate."[2] Those lines were sent from the Naval Ministry by Hans Humann to his friend von Selchow, who entered them in his diary. "Can you not hear the poison of conspiracy, the seed of a new revolution, boiling away in this massive cauldron; already it scatters its scalding foam from place to place, spreading strikes and unrest?"[3] For Wagener, a captain on the staff of the Iron Division, this is how the "boiling wave" of Bolshevism may be heard approaching.[4] For Hollenbach, hostilities on the part of the Hamburg proletariat were cause for "admiring the seething soul of the people (*Volkssele*)," and "delighting in the spatterings of the foaming brew."[5]

To F. W. Heinz, the period 1918-23 "threw the militarist Freikorps and their Spartacist opponents into the boiling conflict of a witch's cauldron";[6] this was "the boiling chaos in which we sought and found the essence of the era."[7] Preparations had been under way from 1914 to 1918: "The war had blown the lid off the volcano of the old, encrusted values. All the peoples of the earth had been thrown into the crucible of a great conflagration."[8] Jünger experienced this as the "storm warning for a global change. . . . Then the stars roundabout will be drowned in a fiery glow; idols will splinter fragments of clay; and all the molded forms will be melted down anew in a thousand blast furnaces."[9] Evidently this is a cyclical process, if everything is to be "melted down anew."

Scene: the city. "The atoms whirl around in the boilers of the metropolis."[10] Dissolution: "There was no more firm order, no more firm values" (Salomon).[11] Likewise succumbing to fluidity was the former guarantor of that order, the government: "The men who were washed up to the top in the maelstrom of the revolt, like scum in a boiling soup." (Salomon)[12] Rudolf Herzog saw "greasy cauldrons fighting to grab themselves a place at the fire. Blood-red banners marched through the land; behind them thronged the vulgar multitudes, in the company of fanatics and utopian dreamers."[13]

It is the war, the different states of the republic, but above all the civil war, the *revolution*, that is manifested in the image of a gigantic process of boiling and liquefaction. The times are hanging over the fire (as a pot, a kettle, a massive kettle, a witch's cauldron, a greasy cauldron, the boilers of the metropolis, the crucible of a great conflagration). With the heat of a thousand blast furnaces, that fire is causing the old order, the old people, the entire world, to bubble, boil, foam, and melt.[14]

For Ernst Jünger, this is a "global change." All that's solid becomes hot and fluid (all that's masculine, feminine?). Dissolving human bodies appears to be the real work of the revolution. Freud suggests that we see pots, kettle, vats, and hollow spaces in general as "representations" of the womb—the body of the mother.[15] And if we put aside the traditional familialism[16] of psychoanalysis, our own bodies, the body of the metropolis, the body of the earth, and so on: all of these come into contention as potential vessels for this seething process.

Is the whole earth turning into a uterus that will give birth to something terrible and new? Is that uterus the unconscious? Freud did, in fact, call the id "a cauldron full of seething excitations."[17] Does that mean what we have here is a terrible eruption of the "global unconscious"?

Exploding Earth/Lava

Finally, the anthropomorphized body of Mother Earth is presented as the cauldron that is threatening the soldier's body with scorching floods.

Civil war in the Ruhr Valley:

> In front of them, the earth bursts open with drumhead-rupturing thunder; beside them, with deafening booms; behind them, with thudding explosions. They suddenly feel as if they are standing on shaky ground, as if the earth were no more than a thin skin under which a gigantic cauldron of blazing fire was blazing up. Every second, that thin skin bursts at some point, shooting copper-red lava toward the heavens with enormous force from out of the fissure. Strangled with fear, a few of them wonder what would happen if it suddenly opened up here, right here under my body, which snuggles so trustingly up against its coolness—(Dwinger).[1]

In this "grenade fire," the tension isn't between the opponent who shoots and the victim who seeks cover; at the heart of the experience is the tension between the soldier's body and the surface of the earth he presses himself against. The surface feels human (skin) and it reacts (to feelings such as "trust") in a human way. To the soldier, "it . . . lies right here under my body." He is "snuggled" up against it; short of penetration, no greater intimacy is possible. The soldier lies waiting amid the contradiction between the coolness of that skin and the body's internal heat, which would cause him to perish. The active party is the "earth." The "fissure" has already opened up in front of him, beside him, and behind him; the only place left is *under* him. Or should we say, the only place left is under *him*? The grenade fire doesn't decide whether or not it will open up, nor can the soldier himself open it. *It opens of its own accord.*

This is no longer a matter of the war. The war simply creates a means for expressing the desire for—and fear of—being swallowed up by the earth, in a form that is not socially unacceptable, and that indeed may even be welcomed.*

---

*For contrast, compare a passage from Remarque's *All Quiet on the Western Front.* The earth as the giver of life: "From the earth, from the air, sustaining forces pour into us—mostly from the earth. To no man does the earth mean so much as to the soldier. When he presses himself down upon her long and powerfully, when he buries his face and his limbs deep in her from the fear of death by shell fire, then she is his only friend, his brother, his mother; he stifles his terror and his cries in her silence and her security; she shelters him and gives him a new lease of ten seconds on life, receives him again and often for ever.

Earth!—Earth!—Earth!

Earth with thy folds and hollows and holes, into which a man may fling himself and crouch down! In the spasm of terror, under the hailing of annihilation, in the bellowing death of the explosions, O Earth, thou grantest us the great resisting surge of new-won life. Our being, almost utterly carried away by the fury of the storm, streams back through our hands from thee, and we, thy redeemed ones, bury ourselves in thee, and through the long minutes in a mute agony of hope bite into thee with our lips." (pp. 36ff.) Here the thrill of "frightened happiness" comes after the danger; in Dwinger, from the danger.

Here, too, fitting the process within the concept of incestuous desire would be an inadmissible case of reductionism. The overwhelming power of the dissolving, devouring body and the man's passivity, his "thrill" (of fear and desire)[2] are what dominate the process. The potential for *physical*, and not simply hallucinatory, dissolution is close at hand. Ego boundaries and bodily boundaries: where are they in this process? Do they still exist? Are interior and exterior still distinguishable? Is it the earth that bursts, or the man himself, through the fiery stream of internal lava that follows an eruption of drives. In the following grenade explosion, what is "internal," what "external"; "subject" and "object"; cause and effect?

> The smoke shot up like a surging wave of black sludge, scum, and sprayed clumps of earth, lumps of rock and ice, a fivefold death with a tornado of howling splinters and the hissing gas of explosive material. His eyes glared wide open; his heart opened wide, then, burning, contracted with a sudden detonating violence. . . . O God, was this the earth that had dissolved into a sloppy mush, a bog, fired vertically into the air by the gas and pressure and molten river released from its interior, a deluge of filth and vomit?[3]

The grenade couldn't have produced this "deluge" if it hadn't existed before hand as a "molten river" in the earth's interior. The earth can dissolve of its own accord (as it also does in Dwinger). We are witnessing an eruption here; the grenade strike only sets it off. Is the eruption external or internal? It is his heart, after all, that "burns up" and contracts "with a sudden detonating violence." (Yet he has not in any way been hit.)

The grenades only release streams that have been flowing in concealment anyway, whether in the "earth" or in the man's own body:

> Right beneath the visible world, the immensity of the un-
> fathomable begins: a numbly glowing, fluid ocean of ebbings
> and floods, of incalculable forces of pressure and tension (Erbt).[4]

The "visible world" is in the first instance "earth" ("We gained an inner composure *on* the land"). The *underlying* "immensity of the impenetrable," the "earth's interior," is however immediately equated with the man's own interior. "Happy the soul in which the inscrutable peacefully reposes."[5] That "peaceful repose" is endangered from without and from within. Outside, there is the "Age of Steel," which has produced the proletariat, Marxism, and the "upheaval"; at the same time, all of this is somehow *inside* the person:

> Yet when the inner grip is broken, when the heart is drunk with
> the desire to press on beyond the tangible, when we set out,

Cover of a novel (1921).

armed with the hammer of ideas and the yardstick of numbers, to enter upon that mysterious realm and, drawing inspiration from its fearful flame, so that we may speak the inexpressible and grasp the inconceivable—then come upheaval and ruin, the torment of dismembered souls. We flutter away in fear, like the night owl that has mistakenly flown into the glaring noonday sun.[6]

The feeling of extreme disjunction expressed in the image of the night owl in the glaring noonday sun is more the speaker's feeling of disjunction with himself than with the outside world. The "upheaval" comes from within; it results from the intoxication that suffusses his heart and "enters upon that mysterious realm." It is an intoxication of *consciousness*; he is working with the "hammer of ideas" and the "yardstick of numbers." It concerns a person's attempt to know himself, his own "interior." The "fear" therefore stems from his contact with himself, from the encounter between two otherwise painstakingly separated personal realms, which are only inadequately described with the antithesis "consciousness-unconscious." The person is split into an inner realm, concealing a "numbly glowing, fluid ocean" and other dangers; and a restraining external shell, the muscle armor, which contains the inner realm the way a cauldron contains boiling soup. The bubbling contents want to get out; every one of the cited conjurations of war and civil war is toying with the possibility of that hot, locked-up flood's erupting.

Within the images of the cauldron containing blazing fire, copper-red lava, molten river, sloppy mush, fearful flame, etc., the man's own body appears, but also a larger, external body (the metropolis or the earth, primarily). The evil of that "witch's cauldron," the big city, also seethes away in his own insides. The political "order" holding the metropolis in check, for instance, appears to have the same function as the body armor that "bottles up" his own seething interior.* The exploding earth and rebellious metropolis owe their terror primarily to the fact that they embody the potential for—and may violently bring about—an eruption of his own interior. When this interior becomes too powerful, or when the larger, external body (the earth) opens up, or when the metropolis bursts its bounds of order, so that its interior reaches the man's body, the latter is destroyed. In violence and pain, the bodies flow together; their boundaries are exploded: ripping drumhead, eyes wide open, detonating heart. The exploding grenades allow the soldier to *experience himself*; he senses his identity with the detonating explosives. He dissolves into fear: the "torment of dismembered souls, "the night owl" on its mistaken flight, the heart "burn-

---

*Cf. the German term *Kesselschlacht*, literally "kettle" or "cauldron-battle," in which peripheral armored divisions proceed against surrounded troops, then destroy them.

ing'' that violently contracts; the feelings of "strangulation" as he waits for the earth to open up. And this as we remember, "right here under my body, which snuggles up so confidently against its coolness."

The more passively he is exposed to the events, the more overwhelmed he is by fear—the fear of dissolution. He doesn't want to "go down," but "it's stronger than we are." The fear is even greater when he sits inside one of the threatening bodies, as was the case with troops waiting below ground to meet an assault:

> Like slime, fear crawls around inside us with a thousand tentacles locking every fiber in its sucking arms. Absolute feeling, it dissolves the world and ego into a blackish broth with only a few fiery spots burning through here and there. It's as if we were naked and blindfolded on an executioner's block, twisting among sadistically leering eyes, with braziers, sulphurous sparks, and white-hot tongs hissing all around. All thought evaporates then in the stinging flames of emotion (Jünger).[7]

"Every fiber," even the most minute unit of solid matter, is encompassed by "sucking arms." The ego dissolves. It loses all perception (their eyes are blindfolded) but is itself open to view (naked). It is punished (on the executioner's block) and, at the same time, exposed to the enemy's view, for his delectation. In every detail this reads like the converse of the feelings the soldier has when he kills. There he actively transgresses his boundaries; here he himself becomes the victim of a similar process.

In the last analysis, even the term "fear" isn't appropriate for Jünger. It isn't broad enough to encompass what he feels:

> It is stronger than we are. A nebulous thing lies within us, driving its enigmatic being across the troubled waters of the soul at times like those. Not fear—we can scare that into its burrow by staring sharply and derisively into its pale countenance—but some unknown realm in which the boundaries of our sensibility dissolve. Only now do we recognize how little at home we are within ourselves. Something slumbering deep down, drowned out by frenetic daily routine, rises up and, before it has even taken form, flows away into gloomy sadness.[8]

Something nebulous, across the "troubled waters of the soul." The "sharp, derisive" look with which the officer usually distances himself from his objects, is of no use here. The very place from which that view might be obtained, swims and dissipates in the "unknown realm" of the man's interior, where is not "at home." The fluid element of the interior does not simply flow; it flows *away* into "gloomy sadness."

"Never lower the flag," the commander inscribed on his chest.

Or, it explodes: "At times he may sleep, but when the earth quakes, he sprays boiling out of every volcano,"[9] writes Jünger of the "spirit of war." He lives in *every interior*;[10] every vessel is a potential volcano, particularly the human body.

Warding Off the Red Floods

In chapter 1 I described the way in which soldier males freeze up, become icicles in the fact of erotic femininity. We saw that it isn't enough simply to view this as a defense against the threat of castration; by reacting in that way, in fact, the man holds himself together as an entity, a body with fixed boundaries. Contact with erotic women would make him cease to exist in that form. Now, when we ask how that man keeps the threat of the Red flood of revolution away from his body, we find the same movement of stiffening, of closing himself off to form a "discrete entity." He defends himself with a kind of sustained erection of his whole body, of whole cities, of whole troop units. Jünger: "Only steely individuality could hold out there without slipping into the whirlpool."[1] Von Osten: "Only the larger cities towered as islands of Germanness, above the raging Polish flood!"[2]

"All over the country the groundwaters rose up, expelled by the forces of Hell. Above this murky flood, only the German cities still towered, isolated, threatened, slowly sinking" (Bronnen).[3] "Around the periphery of the German sphere of influence . . . the Polish flood surged with mixed success." (Lieutenant General von Hülsen).[4] Troops as a "rock amidst the raging sea,"[5] against the enticement of the prostitutes of Lüttich" (von Heydebreck).

Whether it is the man himself, a city, a rock, or a periphery: the aspect of *towering up* is decisive in warding off the flood.

> Glowing red from the wild flames of the uproars,
> Our own land—and chased by the lash of hate,
> Like a gloomy tide around the cliff that lonesome soars.
> From East and West it breaks on us of late.[6]

(Third stanza of a poem celebrating the "induction" of *wandervögel* troops into the Freikorps at Rogau, March 25, 1919.)

> Annaberg*—The name awakens memories of untold suffering,
> gravest danger, and hellish torment. Untold misery flooded
> through the regions of the Reich. German brothers and sisters
> threatened to drown in a sea of distress. Annaberg! At thy foot,
> the dreadful torrent scattered (E. F. Berendt).[7]

> The flood swelled threateningly all around the isolated
> Lichtschlag corps (Mahnken).[8]

First and foremost, it was the soldier who towered up, followed by the cities and mountains (such as Annaberg) that he conquered; but intellectual greats can also fill the bill—if, for instance, the man threatened by the flood is a schoolmaster:

> Once, young miss, there was an age of heroes. Some great
> man—a Salzmann, Pestalozzi, Fichte, Herbart—would give his
> era a watchword, a sense of direction. That heroic age is over.
> We live in the days of the masses, the flood, the inundation.

---

*The Annaberg, a mountain in Upper Silesia, was the site of a Polish position stormed by Freikorps troops during the fighting in May 1921. Although the action ended in military defeat, "Annaberg" was the greatest partial victory up to that point and became a central myth in the early history of the movement. "Annaberg" is a symbol of the "what might have been" character of the Freikorps. Eggers (1935): "The German rebels' act of sacrifice was denied practical success. Its success in the realm of the soul was that much greater, however" (*Der Berg der Rebellen*, P. 272). Even the "soul" seems to qualify as a towering structure—of which more later. Something else that towered up for Germany: Helgoland.

Freikorps memorial on the Annaberg.

> Now it is in millions of minds that the new ideas are born
> (Erbt).[9]

We've already seen that these antithetical formations can't be reduced to an opposition between phallic and Medusan. It has however become equally clear that they embody a specific opposition between "maleness" and "femaleness." We may be able to tell what that opposition looks like, once the nature of all the flowing and dissolving streams that spill up against the saving heights is clearer to us.

Rivers—especially large, mighty ones—often come from far away; it isn't easy to discover their sources. It's easier to see whence they flow. To locate some of the sources of the streams flowing here, we'll have to swim upstream, "backward," taking a more extended raft-voyage through European, and even the whole of human history. It will be some time before we

"Do what you must, conquer or die." The tower of Saaleck Castle, where Fischer and Kern, the murderers of Foreign Minister Rathenau, hid out after the deed (1921). In a fire-fight with the Prussian police, Kern was killed and Fischer shot himself.

René Magritte, "Le Château de Pyrénées." (c) Georgette Magritte, 1986.

have landed back at our narrower theme: fascist language and its relation to the White terror.

The schoolmaster seeks asylum from the desires of those millions by holding himself erect among the "great men," the last bulwark against the flood of the masses. Somehow, it seems to be his model of an enormous penis that prevents him from recognizing the "inundation" as a chance for his own liberation.

Heroic spirit is not the only thing that tempers the blood of heroes: "The wretched border-state formations,* nurtured back to life by aid from England and France, now needed the blood of German soldiers to stand up to the Red flood" (Gengler).[10] The blood of soldiers is "phallic" blood, a cliff, a summit.

On the basis of his clinical practice, Reich reports that soldier males often in fact suffered from sustained erections.[11] Fear of the flood therefore has a decided effect not only on their language but on the structuring of their bodily feelings as well. Powerful forces must be at work.

The defensive passages are consistently organized around the sharp contrast between summit and valley, height and depth, towering and streaming. Down below: wetness, motion, swallowing up. Up on the height: dryness, immobility, security. The pattern of events within these passages: what's down below is smashed against the summit, or dammed in by it.[12]

STREAMS

All That Flows

"Who does not feel in the flows of his desire both the lava and the water?"[1] Deleuze and Guattari pose that question in *Anti-Oedipus*, referring to every person in whom the flow of the streams of desire isn't, and hasn't been, impeded. Perhaps the best evidence that this is no mere metaphor is the fact that Wilhelm Reich attempted to describe the pleasurable feelings of orgasm as a "streaming" (*Strömen*) and the abatement of physical tension as a "streaming away" (*Abströmen*).[2]

One look at the history of medicine, psychology, philosophy, or biology is enough to show that attempts to understand human functioning with the notion of "flowing" are part of a long tradition. In Jean Starobinski's book *Literature and Psychoanalysis* (*Literatur und Psychoanalyse*) there is a chapter on the "History of Imaginary Streams." It attempts to trace the path of that effort through European history from the time of Descartes.

> For a long time, as we know, the psychology of movement proceeded from the notion of vital spirits, which *flowed along* inside

---

*He has Lithuania and Latvia in mind.

the motor nerves, as if within hollow tubes. . . . Descartes developed an entire hydraulic system in that regard, which was thought to provide explanations of the phenomena of movement . . . The motor nerve is a tube . . . It is not the tube that is considered valuable, but the stream flowing through it . . . it is the very same stream that comes out of the great reservoir of the coronary chambers, in order to effect movements of the most diverse kinds.[3]

Starobinski's account describes how the advancing knowledge of the natural sciences, particularly physics, brings about changes in the way the bodily fluids are viewed. There are attempts, for instance, to equate the nervous stream with the magnetic flow and to see "all the elements of a galvanic battery"[4] in the lamellae of the cerebellum.

The Austrian Mesmer ("according to him, man is immersed in an ocean of 'fluid-matter'") doesn't see streams solely in the human interior. He introduces "the theory of a stream of interpersonal relations," thereby establishing links, according to Starobinski, with the humor theories of Ficino and Paracelsus.[5]

"Pierre Janet was completely justified in dividing science after Mesmer into adherents and opponents of the flow therapy. . . . Adherents of the flow therapy believe that a physical force is communicated between the magnetizer and the magnetized object. Opponents . . . find the main explanation in the psychological processes occurring within the patient."[6] A distinction begins to arise between the positions of "exo-fluidism (in which the stream, or fluid, passes from the magnetizer over to the patient)," and "endo-fluidism . . . in which nervous energy is depicted as a substance in motion," which "remains permanently contained within the individual." Psychoanalysis is linked to the second position, building "on the model of a *restricted* fluidism."[7]

Psychoanalytic patients are hardly the object of a magnetizer or hypnotist; they have to enter into their own streams. Even Breuer and Freud's initial outline of a psychoanalytic theory is in this tradition. In *Studies on Hysteria* (1895), they write:

> Or better, let us imagine a widely ramified electrical system for lighting and the transmission of motor power; what is expected of this system is that simple establishment of a contact shall be able to set any lamp or machine in operation. To make this possible, so that everything shall be ready to work, there must be a certain tension present throughout the entire network of lines of conduction, and the dynamo engine must expend a given quantity of energy for this purpose. In just the same way, there

is a certain amount of excitation present in the conductive paths of the brain when it is at rest, but awake and prepared to work.[8]

It is always those two elements—an energy or "current" (stream) and a motor—that are said to constitute the "soul." In fact, they are the dual components of every real machine; there is always a moving, variable current—an electrical, gaseous, or fluid stream—that sets the parts of the motor in motion.

Freud at first latches onto the idea of a stream, only to abandon it later on. According to Starobinski: "From 1900 on, the stream for Freud is no longer an 'endo-cerebral stimulus' (still strongly emphasized in his 'outline'), but the libido, the *drive*."[9] Freud begins to suspect that certain biochemical reactions are active in the experience of pleasure.

To the extent that, now as then, there exist no natural-scientific explanations for these processes, the debate over the nature of bodily processes involved in psychic occurrences is impossible to resolve. Yet this is immaterial for an understanding of the distinctions among attempts to describe the workings of the libido. For, in every case, those attempts are indeed based totally on a form of knowledge: the knowledge, that is, of the experiencing of one's own bodily processes.

When Wilhelm Reich described the pleasurable feeling of orgasm as a "streaming-away," naturally he was attempting to find a term that would do justice to his own orgasmic feelings. Similarly, Freud must have started out from his own bodily sensations when he proposed that the somatic processes in the pleasurable release of tension be seen as chemical in nature. Both men found sufficient confirmation of their experiences in other people to be sure of their cases. We can't claim that either of them was "wrong." In discussions of sexual satisfaction, Freud seems to speak of sublimating processes, and Reich of *orgasmic* ones. It's no accident that the necessity of sublimation is given a crucial role in Freudian views on sexuality, whereas the necessity of genital satisfaction occupies the same position for Reich.

For Reich, the feeling of streaming also establishes the link between human beings and the life energy of the external cosmos. There is a remarkable statement on that same feeling in Freud's late essay *Civilization and Its Discontents*.[10] In a letter to Freud (whose friend he considered himself), Romain Rolland had complained that Freud's assessment of religion "had not appreciated the true source of religious sentiments." Here is Freud's recapitulation of Rolland's argument:

> This, he says, consists in a peculiar feeling, which he himself is never without, which he finds confirmed by many others, and which he may suppose is present in millions of people. It is a feeling as of something limitless, unbounded—as it were, 'oceanic.'"[11]

Freud's response is resolute: "I cannot discover this 'oceanic' feeling in myself." Yet he was interested enough in the subject to devote almost eleven pages to it. On the "feeling of an indissoluble bond, of being one with the external world," he finds that "to me, this seems something rather in the nature of an intellectual perception." He refuses to concede that the ego lacks definite boundaries, except in an inward direction. "But toward the outside, at any rate, the ego seems to maintain clear and sharp lines of demarcation." If the Freudian "ego" fades at all, it fades into the "id." Toward the outside, it is a boundary, "clear and sharp." But there is an exception:

> There is only one state—admittedly an unusual state, but not one that can be stigmatized as pathological—in which it does not do this. At the height of being in love, the boundary between ego and id threatens to melt away. *Against all the evidence of his senses*, a man who is in love declares that 'I' and 'you' are one, and is prepared to behave as if it were a fact. [The emphasis is mine.]

There is something sad in this assertion. Freud has to stress that being in love should not be considered pathological. And, as if that weren't enough, he then goes on to define the *height* of being in love as a state in which the greatest potential for the dissolution of boundaries between two people can be realized. He chooses this state rather than that of bodily union, in which it is surely *in accordance with* "all the evidence of the senses" that the border between "I" and "you" is blurred.

In adults, that is, the only infringements of boundaries recognized by Freud are in fantasy, though he goes on to concede that vestigial, infantile feelings of lack of differentiation from the external world may come into play, binding a person to the world in a kind of "mass of sensation"(!)[12]

To explain the presence of "what was originally there along with what was later derived from it," he chooses the image of the city of Rome, whose present-day appearance shows visible traces of millennia of architecture. He follows this—incredibly—with a two-page treatise on the building of Rome, in which we learn a number of things about the Aurelian and Servian walls. Although taking flight in thought isn't Freud's usual métier, we are left here with the impression that it is.

In brief, if the feeling of streaming exists, it behooves the adult to lose it in the "ego feeling of maturity." Freud fends off Rolland's suggestion on the "source of religious needs":

> The derivation of religious needs from the infant's helplessness and the longing for the father aroused by it seems to me incon-

trovertible. . . . I cannot think of any need in childhood as strong as the need for a father's protection.

It is abundantly clear from this that Freud once again simply bypasses the phase in which the child's paramount need and longing are for *maternal* protection. Childhood doesn't begin for him until about the time when the little Oedipus is complete and identification with the father has been secured.

To complete the picture, at the close of the section, Freud quotes another friend, whom he calls "omniscient." The friend claims to have found, in a number of yoga practices, a physiological basis for many of the axioms of mysticism. Freud's reaction to his friend's (by no means outlandish) postulate is the following concluding remark:

> But I am moved to exclaim in the words of Schiller's diver (*Taucher*): "Let him rejoice who breathes up here in that roseate light!"

Freud strives to go *upward*; for him that whole oceanic business is somehow under water, dark and threatening.* With his seemingly harmless remark about "oceanic feeling," Rolland appears to have struck a nerve; he has provoked a side of Freud that is openly *afraid* of the possibility of limitlessness in humans. Amazingly enough, his fear is expressed in relation to a feeling Rolland assumes to be a happy one.

In an interview recorded by the analyst Kurt Eissler in October 1952, at the behest of the Sigmund Freud Archives, Wilhelm Reich took up precisely that point.[14] It is evidently at the heart of Reich's divergence from Freud:

> Freud was an intellectual individual. He believed in the over-
> powering role of the mind, i.e., of the intellect as against
> emotions. You know his basic attitude toward emotions. Not
> that emotions are bad, but you have to get them out of the way.
> You have to control everything. Your intellect and your mind
> must be masters of the emotions. But that attitude came into
> conflict with the direction that the work in genitality took, in
> which the emotions are involved, the "streaming," the feeling in
> the body. Freud rejected the existence of so-called "oceanic feel-
> ing" (*ozeanische Gefühle*). He didn't believe in such a thing. I
> never quite understood why. It is so obvious that the "oceanic
> feeling," the feeling of unity between you and Spring and God,
> or what people call God, and Nature is a very basic element in
> all religion, in all religious feeling to the extent that it is not sick

---

*"No fire, no coal/Can burn as hot/As secret love/Of which we know not." Freud was able to do more with this manifestly different, and more widespread, notion of "love" than with "streaming."

and distorted. Freud rejected that. And I regret to say, I had the feeling that *in the process os subduing his own aliveness, his own biological aliveness, he had to restrict himself, to sublimate, to live in a way he didn't like and to resign.* I had the feeling that he, somehow, couldn't accept the concept that is behind all good religion. Do you get my point? All good religion. I am referring to the biological activity in your organism that is part of the universe. He rejected it. And I know he didn't like it. Now, my work developed in just that direction. In the schizophrenic, for example, the streaming they feel, the emotions they feel, that's all very real. And somehow, Freud couldn't follow that. His work became intellectualized. And, to my mind, that was a part of the bad development that took place. He was caught in words. He was caught in words.[15]

Reich-lovers and Reich-haters may now strike up a common chorus about Reich the crazy old man; that's their affair. To me, however, it's clear after reading this interview, that "Reichians" are just as caught up with distorting and dogmatizing Reich as Marxists are with Marx. The Marx of the Paris manuscripts wasn't "Marxist" yet, and the elderly Reich in the U.S.A. was no longer "Reichian" enough. His disciples, strictly forbidden from reading his later writings, banish him anew each day—that is an aside.[16] I no longer believe that the elderly Reich was mad, at least not in the sense of *non compos mentis.* True, in the interview about his relationship to Freud, he talks in an unbroken stream. Some may find that mad. Yet he speaks with great clarity about points of agreement and disagreement with Freud; in fact, he speaks more openly than ever before, because he is perceptibly speaking without tactical intent.

And Reich never tires of pointing out that it was Freud's resignation, his turning away from the aliveness of life, that finally led him to reject Reich. What is important to hold onto here is the fact that Freud rejects the feeling of the "streaming" of pleasure. Reich's *Function of the Orgasm* was published by Freud (1927), true enough, but received no notice in his own works, even though the quarrel with Reich had not yet begun. Freud wanted nothing to do with "oceanic" feeling, or the pleasurable union of the ego and the universe. Like streaming, the machinic element also disappears form the Freudian conception of the psychophysical functioning of humans. It survives only as a *metaphor* in the terminology of the psychic *apparatus,* which is, however, no longer an actual apparatus, but a kind of stratified model in which various levels—the id, ego, and superego—are built up from the "bottom" to the "top," like the floors of a house. In the cellar the unconscious, the id, "presides" like some anarchistic theater producer. The parents are on the top floor. With the one creating all kinds of havoc below and the other pulling wires from above, both parties work upon the poor

"The Creation of Steam." Wilhelm von Kaulbach's cartoon for an industrial hall mural (ca. 1880).

ego, an actor playing himself on the ground-floor stage, who must both master and simultaneously represent his own social role. This, as Deleuze and Guattari complain, is the model of a representation, not a production.

Their *Anti-Oedipus* attempts to reintroduce the categories of production into the functioning of the human unconscious. When the concepts of flowing and the machine are brought into play to wash away and dissolve that rigid (theatrical) puppet, Oedipus, to transform his clockwork mechanism into the spinning of a toy top, then this is at once a playing with bewildering terminologies and, more significantly, an attempt to reinvest the theory of the human psyche with a dimension that had been pushed into the background by the systematizing thought of the later Freud: an understanding of the human unconscious as a force of production; an understanding that what it produces is not a special "psychic" reality, but social reality per se.

It is the desiring-production of the unconscious whose streams pour out over the "body without organs" (matter that has not yet been socialized, "nature"), in order to produce, populate, and change that body in accordance with the flowing of desires. Desire splits off and joins; streams of desire join up with other streams, then separate from them again. The unconscious is a flow and a desiring-machine, the human being a system of couplings, with which s/he can couple onto, and uncouple from, continuing processes: "Now what?"—"So that's what that was"—Now what?"—those are the questions and the stations of desire. Through the stream of desire's connections with objects, institutions, continents, and other bodies, new desiring-machines arise and begin to function, opening up territories, crossing borders, then breaking up again or destroying themselves. They produce new relations, new objects, the self, human social life. It is movement with goals, but no end: "Now what?" . . . "And what after that?" . . . "So that's what that was" . . . "Now what?" . . . and so on.[17]

Readers who find all of this unfamiliar, confused, and suspect should hold onto their suspicions. There will be a lot more streams flowing in this chapter, and at the end it will perhaps be easier to see whether all this amounts to anything or not.

I'd like to remind the reader that this section began with a fear—the fear of the "floods" and "lava" that are capable of erupting from within soldier males—and that this feeling should be taken seriously and its origins explored, no matter where that may lead us.*

It should again be stressed that it was not until late bourgeois society developed a notion of culture centering on the sharply delineated "individual" that the machine and streams were set in opposition to the human body, whose functions were now understood to be capable of "schematic" representation in geometrical figures such as pyramids and triangles. Cut off from most forms of production, these individuals (in whom the social process appears to be merely *represented*) have believed (and still believe) in their difference from "machines." To know nothing about machines and not to get one's hands dirty has been considered a mark of distinction and a privilege by at least six generations of German bureaucrats and politicians; the same is true of their ability to pull themselves together, to control outpourings of emotion, or to not have any in the first place. In the bourgeois German vernacular, consequently, awareness of flowing and of the machinic in human productions lives on only in a negative, defensive form:

---

*If the attempt to describe the activity of the libido, the desiring-production of the unconscious, or whatever it may be called, as "flowing" or as the work of a "machine," is somehow unsatisfactory, not up to the demands of stricter conceptual systems, then this is an unavoidable handicap. Or maybe not: every assumption about the "unconscious" to date has been "speculative," whether we give more emphasis to its "chaotic-instinctual" nature, like the later Freud; or begin, as Lacan did, with the premise that it is structured like a language and therefore functions like one; or, with Deleuze and Guattari, see an energy in the unconscious which wants to "produce," to flow, to discharge itself, and with respect to which everything "chaotic" is external at first, i.e., social anarchy and its injection into the system of representations. They all have the same starting point: observations about their own bodies and the bodies of others. The right-or-wrong distinction is less germane than questions of how the various hypotheses operate, what results they give, and how well they can be worked with. Furthermore, they are not at all strictly separable. What we find are partial deviations from other writers, emphasizing or rejecting specific features of their theories. Common to all of them is a focusing of interest on the unconscious and its functional modes—that's what really distinguishes them from other, nonpsychoanalytic theories.

in words such as "ejaculation" (*Erguss*) or "copulate" (*verkuppeln*). The first is uncontrolled; the second immoral. Marx had hoped that modern industry would bring with it "a fluidity of function, universal mobility for the worker."[18] We know that that has not happened; still, the fact that the technical innovation most responsible for preventing it, the assembly line, is also known as "production flow" is a perversity that should give us pause for thought at the very least.

Everything connected with machines and mechanisms in bourgeois linguistic usage is saddled with negative valuations that are diametrically opposed to the actual nature of the mechanical and machinic. Thus, we say that movements are "mechanical" when they are characterized by an absence of consciousness and interest on the part of the person carying them out. "Mechanical" is more or less synonymous with "dead," or "apathetic." Yet the very same middle-class citizens find beauty in the mechanical gestures of the circus juggler. Here, though, the mechanical effect is brought about through concentration, not lack of it. In a similar way, the steady, mechanical pace of a bicycle racer prompts the sports reporter to talk of the beauty of his racing style—because the machine in question, the bicycle, is constructed for the purpose of allowing the rider's abilities to be expressed and realized. These and other examples demonstrate that machines of this kind seem only to be built where no production is taking place: for sports events, moon landings, war, and leisure; but *not* for factories or even dental patients, not to mention the gynecologist's office. We may conclude that an artificial division, or actual opposition, of humans and machines holds sway within the realms of production. The responsibility for that surely doesn't lie with the machines, but with those who finance them, who have planned and built them in a way that allows the principles of antiproduction to be introduced into production. This is what gives rise to the ambivalent images in Fritz Lang's *Metropolis*, in which workers hang onto the machines, shuddering as if the machines were implements of torture, or to the images in Chaplin's *Modern Times*: both show the machine as the monster, rather than the capitalists, who created the "monster."[19]

The negativization of the "mechanical" in the bourgeois vernacular and in bourgeois thinking in general, corresponds, therefore, to the negativization of the machine in the capitalist production process. Thus a new relation becomes evident: the hostility between worker and machine, set up by the capitalist, is identical to the hostility the bourgeois ego reserves for the productive force of its own unconscious. This hostility is dictated by the social compulsion to become an "ego" of that type in order to remain bourgeois. The bourgoisie's fear of having to become "workers," should they cease to meet the social demands of their class, can thus be seen to spring from the bourgeois ego's fear of coming in contact with its unconscious, of being condemned "to the machines."

The formulation of the later Freud, "Where id was, there ego shall be,"[20] can thus be seen as a program for eliminating the machinic and the flowing from the productions of the human unconscious: shutting down and draining. Indeed the idea is formulated word for word in Freud's comparison of the process of ego formation ("culture-work") to the draining of the Zuider Zee.[21] The person capable of being described by the ego-id-superego topography would in this case be conceived as a dry grave, the final resting place of streams and desiring-machines. This ties in with an assumption whose validity will have to be proved later on: that the *concrete* form of the struggle against the flowing-machinic productive force of the unconscious has been (and still is) a battle against women, against female sexuality.

Given that the channeling of streams and shutting down of desiring-machines became constituent elements of Freudian psychoanalytic thinking, it seems obvious that Freudian concepts have only a limited capacity for describing the psychophysical processes leading to the struggle to suppress female sexuality (and to suppress the productions of the unconscious in general). I'll therefore begin by trying to gather support from writers who haven't closed themselves off to feeling "the lava and the water in the streams of their desire," and letting them flow. In the writings of these authors from various continents and societies, particular bodies of water find a home, and the reader is free to drift along on them for a while, or offer resistance, as s/he wishes.

> Say, you are in the country, in some high land of lakes. Take almost any path you please, and ten to one it carries you down in a dale, and leaves you there by a pool in a stream. There is a magic in it. Let the most absentminded of men be plunged in his deepest reveries—stand that man on his legs, set his feet a-going, and he will infallibly lead you to water, if water there be in all that region.

It is *precisely* the most absentminded of men who will find his way to water, we should add, if that is the element in which desires flow. But it affects everyone.

> thousands upon thousands of mortal men fixed in ocean reveries. . . . But these are all landsmen; of weekdays pent up in lath and plaster—tied to counters, nailed to benches, clinched to desks. How then is this? Are the green fields gone? What do they here?
> But look! here come more crowds, pacing straight for the water and seemingly bound for a dive.[22]

The same compulsion is felt by Isaac himself, narrator of Melville's

Moby Dick. He has to go down to the sea at regular intervals; if he stays on land too long, he will start knocking people's hats off.

> Yet the springs their word forever keep:
> The water continues to sing in its sleep.

—The emotions of Eduard Mörike, a rural pastor in the Swabian town of Cleversulzbach.[23]

> Let them come, the ovaries of the water,
> Where the future stirs its tiny head

—of Aimé Césaire, an African revolutionary from the Antilles.[24] For the North American poet, Walt Whitman, a view across the wide expanses of the USA fails to bring fulfillment.[25]

> O something unpro'd! something in a trance!
> To escape utterly from others' anchors and holds!

Mayakowski:

> Break free of those played-out Caspian waves!
> No going back to Riverbed-Russia!
> > We want to
> Dance and raise hell
> > with the Mediterranean waves,
> Not in rotting Baku, but in bright Nizza.[26]

That was his hope for the Soviet Union—in vain. The riverbed called Stalin began his rise in Baku and never set eyes on the Mediterranean. For Solzhenitsyn in the *Gulag Archipelago*, it was literally streams of prisoners that Stalin channeled into the camps, those enormous gullies where life and desire trickled away.

> The hatred of life, of everything that runs or flows freely . . .

It was to combat this hatred that Henry Miller, German by heritage, living by choice in France, passported United States citizen, and cosmopolitan Jew issued his streams of words:

> They cut the umbilical cord, give you a slap on the ass, and presto! you're out in the world . . . a ship without a rudder.[27]

> . . . Stop it now! If you mention
> Landing again, I tell you,
> I'll jump overboard, right before your eyes.[28] (Saint-John Perse)

> Ocean, I don't think the earth
> Has any voice to answer with
> That sounds as happy as you. (Rafael Alberti)[29]

Or the Chilean revolutionary Pablo Neruda, whose verses overflow in praise of waters:

> . . . Your profound energy
> Seems to glide onward, never exhausting itself;
> Seems to return to its own peace.
> The wave that rushes out from you,
> Consubstantial arch, stellar spring,
> Was, in crashing, only froth,
> And rolled back to arise anew, unconsumed,
> All your strength returns to be a source
> . . . .
> The universal basin quakes with your salt and your honey,
> The hollow space encompassing all waters,
> And you are lacking nothing.[30]

Thus the flowing of the libido is sung. Its most fundamental principle is to land, then drift freely along again; to have no prescribed goal, because everything is its object. The waters flow to every shore and from every shore. Out of that comes an assurance (more than an intimation) of happiness: "And you are lacking nothing."*

> Lord, ain't don't got a bone in his jelly-back.
> Floating every day and every night, riding high,
> then there's a rest, sometimes the wind ain't right.

> (Jimi Hendrix knew: With the Power of Soul)

It is the desire for a life free from lack—or writing extravagantly in the knowledge of abundance (as Bataille would say)—that permits writers from different societies and regions to arrive at such similar ideas when trying to describe states, or expectations, of happiness. They are rooted in a feeling they must all have felt: the actual experience of nonlack in the streaming of pleasure through their own bodies.

> Desire causes the current to flow, itself flows in turn, and breaks the flows. "I love everything that flows, even the menstrual flow that carries away the seed unfecund," writes Henry Miller in his ode to desire. Amniotic fluid spilling out of the sac and kidney stones, flowing hair, a flow of spittle, a flow of sperm, shit, or urine that is produced by partial objects and constantly cut off by other partial objects, which in turn produces other flows, in-

---

*These are just a few examples, chosen more or less at random. Anyone who swims through the libraries of the world's literatures (as Herman Melville reported doing in order to fish up everything about whales) will find an infinite number of waters, whose flowing is that of desire. I've included more of these in the Appendix.[31]

terrupted by other partial objects. Every object presupposes the continuity of a flow, the fragmentation of the object (Deleuze and Guattari).[32]

The streams of desire flow in *real* streams, *real* physical processes: in the stream of sperm, the stream of tears, the stream of warmth that autogenic training teaches us to direct toward our various extremities; and in the streams that flood through our musculature during orgasm. (Starobinski opens himself up to criticism here. He dispenses with real streams in a single sentence, naming only blood, lymphatic fluid, bile, and pus, so that he can enter "the realm of imaginary streams without dealy.")[33]

And it isn't only *the* body in, on, and out of which things flow, but its parts—partial subjects, or "organ-machines" (as they are called in *Anti-Oedipus*). These processes are not initiated by the body, or the person, as a whole:

> Doubtless each organ-machine interprets the entire world from the perspective of its own flux, from the point of view of the energy that flows from it: the eye interprets everything . . . in terms of seeing.[34]

and so on.

The Oedipal triangle, its vertices defined by the father-mother-child configuration, uses the lines connecting those vertices to superimpose itself on the current of streams. It cuts off streams, channels them, directs them toward father/mother without allowing them to get there. Sublimation: a highly ramified canal-and-drainage system. Yet:

> Flows ooze, they traverse the triangle, breaking apart its vertices. The Oedipal wad does not absorb these flows, any more than it could seal off a jar of jam or plug a dike. Against the walls of the triangle, toward the outside, flows exert the irresistible pressure of lava or the invincible oozing of water.[35]

The streams don't need an "ego" to act as a dam and mediator. In Henry Miller's experience:

> and my guts spill out in a grand schizophrenic rush, an evacuation that leaves me face to face with the Absolute.[36]

In *Crowds and Power* (*Masse und Macht*), Elias Canetti talks about a "mythical primitive age . . . when transformation was the universal gift of every creature and happened all the time. The *fluidness* of that world has often been emphasized. You could change yourself into anything at all, but you also had the power to change others. Out of that universal flowing emerged individual shapes that were simply fixations of specific transformations. . . . The *process* of transformation, in other words, is the oldest shape there is."[37]

"Encounter on the *Autobahn*." From the November issue of *Atlantis* magazine (Zurich, 1936).

"Being at the mercy of the alien" was part and parcel of this process. In the resultant fears, Canetti saw the reason why an "urge for permanence and hardness" had to arise in humans.[38] But did it really *have to*? Canetti's terminology is contradictory here. What can *alien* mean to someone who is in constant flux? Wouldn't it just be an *Other*, a renewal each time (though perhaps threatening as well)? Even the term "transform" seems unfortunate, since it presupposes a definable, *true* nature, which a person can move away from and back toward. Rather than a "process of transformation," the "oldest pattern" would be a flowing between two transitory points: "Now what?". . . "So that's what that was". . . "Now what?"

It seems unlikely that a human desire itself would limit the flowing of its streams or the fluidity of its form—Canetti ignores the attendant *pleasures*—in order to assume a fixed, confining external shape. It seems far more likely that the rigidity and permanence of bodily boundaries and psychic systems have been set up by external social constraints and natural adversity—a dam built around flowing desire by hostile forces.

We can perhaps concede to pastors of the ego that this dam also protects us and that we need it. Still, we have to ask what it is protecting us from. Is it the adversities of the outside world or something within ourselves? ". . . and my inner being pours out in a massive schizophrenic eruption," spilling me perhaps into the waiting arms of a clinical physician, with his insulin needle? It is this that I can and must fear and protect myself against. But what if the dams are meant for the essence of the eruption itself? What if they have been erected against our own innermost flows, because those flows are seen as some lethal *evil*, rather than as pleasure?

In narrative literature of the nineteenth century, there is a remarkable proliferation of characters whose "inner" (true) and "outer" (social) natures are divided. Characteristic of this kind of split is the antagonism between the "inner" and "outer" natures. Dr. Jekyll, the promising young scientist, is about to abandon his risky experiments along with his other youthful sins, in order to enter into a love-marriage with a general's daughter. But after drinking the potion that exposes his inner being to the outside world, he is transformed (the notion of transformation fits in this case) into Mr. Hyde. He has to become Mr. Hyde, because otherwise social convention would delay the redeeming union with his beloved *too long*. In any case, Mr. Hyde abandons himself to the inner stream that will bring about his death.[39]

The stream flows *within*, as it does in our fascist texts. But in this case *contact with onself* produces not fear, but pleasure—albeit a pleasure deriving from "evil." The millstream *flows*: it is no "numbly glowing, fluid ocean." And Hyde isn't the night owl "that has mistakenly flown into the glaring noonday sun." Robert Louis Stevenson allows him to reach, and to *relish*, the stream of evil and of intoxication in a fully conscious state. This is something the villains of English and German romanticism have in common. It's a *game* that gradually becomes more serious, until finally the transformation is irreversible and the outcome is death—immersion in the dead sea of evil that first felt like an ocean of freedom.

In the fascist texts, we saw that any contact between "inner" and "outer" realms—any boundary transgression—immediately shuts off consciousness, producing a trancelike state. Dr. Jekyll descends to his inner streams as an *ego*; by contrast, Jünger, Schauwecker, and Dwinger's eruptions occur *as if of their own accord*, triggered with the help of the war. The men are at their mercy. Dr. Jekyll's dilemma seems like a preliminary stage of this later state. The decisive element of Jekyll is his splitting. The bodily exterior and its borders form a cohesive totality; they have ceased to be an arrangement of loosely connected part-objects, a transit system for streams en route to the production of social reality. The inner stream is seen as something *sinful*, as the evil "that was originally inside of me." It is only fitting that it should be penned in.

Almost always, it is scientists who are made to transgress *inner* boundaries and discover they've gone "too far." Others who go too far are those who violate *outer* boundaries. Rather than being transformed by some potion, they discover to their horror (after planning and constructing an actual creature, a machine that is the human being of their dreams) that they have given form to the "evil" within themselves, which immediately sets out to destroy both their lives and itself. This is what happened to Mary Shelley's Dr. Frankenstein.[40]

Odd, isn't it, that just when natural scientific theory and practice are advancing more rapidly than ever before in human history, the literatures of contemporary societies produce a string of scientists who come to ruin by immersing themselves in that far-reaching stream of knowledge and discovery? What taboo have they violated? In every instance, it is the taboo against extending their research to human beings—to themselves and their own bodies. They run up against the forcibly maintained religion of capitalism, which decrees that human beings should remain an unfathomable mystery (where their potential for freedom is concerned). The only thing open to investigation is human exploitability.

The contradiction runs as follows: the process of primary accumulation in industry opens up the borders of a hitherto unknown human productive potential, setting in motion streams of money, commodities, and workers, and propelling itself forward on the streams of sweat and blood of workers and non-European peoples. Running parallel to that is a process of *limitation*, directed against the evolution of human pleasures. Deleuze and Guattari call the first process *deterritorialization*—the opening up of new possibilities for desiring-production across the "body with organs"—and the second process *reterritorialization*, which is the mobilization of dominant forces to prevent the new productive possibilities from becoming new human freedoms.[41] We'll look next at the course taken by reterritorialization in bourgeois history as a whole; that is, at how anything that flowed came to inspire the kind of fear we have seen in our solider males.

To begin with, the work of reterritorialization constructs human subjects as *masters* of the machine—as directors and channelers of their own, and of social, streams. This is a reactionary undertaking, for the object of such efforts is their own unconscious: production is blocked here, while streams of money flow on.

Those who hear the machines that are ticking away within themselves, who open up and make the connection to their own streams of desire, and who dream of a new human being at a time when the emergent class is busy exploiting the old one—these are the condemned, the damned. Witness Jekyll, Frankenstein, or Jules Verne's clockmaker Zacharias, whose soul is a mainspring that confers immortality, and who dies when the deveil robs him of it.[42] Witness Ambrose Bierce's Mr. Moxon, who is murdered by the chess-playing machine he has built, after defeating it in a game. There are many others: sorcerers' apprentices, killed by the streams and machines they have set loose.[43] "That kind of thing should be left to the Creator," that is, to the entrepreneurs.

More on the subject of deterritorialization/reterritorialization:

> For capitalism constantly counteracts, constantly inhibits this inherent tendency while at the same time allowing it free rein; it continually seeks to avoid reaching its limit while simultaneously tending toward that limit. Capitalism institutes or restores all sorts of residual and artificial, imaginary, or symbolic territorialities, thereby attempting, as best it can, to recode, to rechannel persons who have been defined in terms of abstract quantities. Everything returns or recurs: states, nations, families. That is what makes the ideology of capitalism "a motley painting of everything that has ever been believed." The real is not impossible; it is simply more and more artificial. Marx termed the twofold movement of the tendency to a falling rate of profit, and the increase in the absolute quantity of surplus value, the law of the counteracted tendency. As a corollary of this law, there is the twofold movement of decoding or deterritorializing flows on the one hand, and their violent and artificial reterritorialization on the other. The more the capitalist machine deterritorializes, decoding and axiomatizing flows in order to extract surplus value from them, the more its ancillary apparatuses, such as government bureaucracies and the forces of law and order, do their utmost to reterritorialize, absorbing in the process a larger and larger share of surplus value.[44]

The real is not impossible; it is simply more and more artificial. Even the production and maintenance of life are not impossible; they simply take place more and more often in illness. Here is Margaret Mahler, reporting on her young patient "Teddy":

> He was preoccupied with the fear of losing body substance, of being drained by his father and grandfather, with whom his

body, he believed, formed a kind of communicating system of tubes. At night the father-grandfather part of the system drained him of the "body juices of youth." Survival depended on who was most successful in draining more life fluid from the others, he or the father and grandfather part. He invented an elaborate heart machine which he could switch on and connect with his body's circulatory system so that he would never die.[45]

Let the juices flow, in spite of all the father-grandfather (and other) systems for extracting them.

Let's stop for a minute. It should be possible now, I think, to develop some idea of what is at stake in fending off the communist surge and the Red floods. For the soldier-male dam, none of the streams we've mentioned can be allowed to flow. He is out to prevent all of them from flowing: "imaginary" and real streams, streams of sperm and desire. Even taking pleasure in the stream of evil (the kind that flows in Mr. Hyde) is impossible for him. All of these flows are shut off; more important, not a single drop can be allowed to seep through the shell of the body. One little drop of pleasure—a single minute flyspeck on the wall of a house, or a single escapee from a concentration camp—threatens to undermine the whole system (the system of dams). Those drops are more than mere metaphors; they are harbingers of imminent defeat ("we're going under").

But human beings live in, and on, flows. They die when streams dry up. What no longer flows is consigned to death:

> I wanted to swim in the fullness of life,
> In the estuaries that were most open to the world,
> And when people slowly withdrew from me,
> Closing paths and doors, preventing
> My hands, born of springs, from touching
> Their painful nonexistences,
> I went from street to street and river to river,
> From place to place and bed to bed,
> And the salty mask of my countenance crossed the wasteland,
> And in the last humble houses, without
> Lamps, without fires,
> Without bread, without bricks, without peace, *alone*,
> I wrapped myself, dying, in my own death.[46]

Pablo Neruda managed to recover from that death. What about Gottfried Benn? The nonchalant formula of his renunciation in his "Ptolemy" ("Ptolemäer") reads: "Make peace with yourself and occasionally gaze at the water."[47]

A stream that has disrupted, rechanneled, perverted. A stream of suffering:

In Dahomey,
On the Congo,
Along the Nile,
My song had the slow cadence
Of gentle love,
The sweet flow
Of good omens,
And the easy pride
Of fresh-fought battles.

From the southern islands
To the Nile,
My song extended
Like a crystal stream.
But for three hundred years
Black ships with sharp keels
Cut through all the waters
Of my quivering sounds.

Poisoned hopes,
Corpses of love,
Skeletons of dreams,
And ashes and slime
Fell from the black ships,
Changing the course of streams
That ever since have run
With terror and homesickness,
From the Atlantic islands
To the Mississippi.
And to never-ending sorrow.[48]

Roussan Camille. The drying up of streams—their transformation—is a bodily sensation, the ending of a sensation, the transformation of a feeling:

for really and truly, seriously, literally:
my feelings are a craft with upturned keel,
my imagination a half-buried anchor,
my drive a broken rudder,
and the tissue of my nerves a net drying on the shore![49]

Confirmation of the fact that where flowing ceases, death appears. Not some metaphorical death, but a real, physical one. The body whose parts no longer set any streams in motion, and in, on, across, and out of which nothing flows anymore, is a body that has died. Simone de Beauvoir wrote that orgasm in old age is like an ebbing away.[50]

Lucien Coutaud, "Plage de Cheval de Brique" (1955).

Flows have no *specific* object. The first goal of flowing is simply that it happen (and only later that it seek something out). Writers have seldom given names to the streams in and on which desires flow toward unknown human futures. They are oceans, rivers, springs, surges, or simply waters, the endless movement of this matter without form. Less often do we read of the Pacific Ocean, the Nile, or the Congo. When these names are added, they are less descriptive of a site than of a history—desire enters historical territory, it becomes "political," takes on a name, the designation of a desire, such as the "played-out Caspian waves" for the movement of the Russian Revolution, which Mayakowski desires to infuse with the "dancing and surging" of the waves of Nice's shores. For the Haitian Roussan Camille, the distance from the Congo to the Mississippi is a political distance, signifying the long road of dead dreams taken by the blacks on their abduction from Africa. Aimé Césaire's "future," stirring its tiny head in the "ovaries of the water," is one of anticolonial revolution.

> When the moon is obscured
> By the clouds,
> It continues to shine on the water.
> That is the beauty in these
> Troubled times.[51]

These lines, by the aging Hanns Eisler, are dedicated to socialism in the German Democratic Republic ("L'automne prussien"). Like a light mirroring itself, socialism shines upon the Prussian waters, where socialists aren't nearly as much at home as "fish in the sea."

Phylogenetically, human life emerged from the water, just as every individual human still does. A fetus develops within the amniotic sac of the mother's womb; and wherever a human society is a friendly body of water enclosing the individual, life is good. The liberation of China and Southeast Asia from American-European-Japanese colonialism was achieved by soldiers whose motto was that a "fish in its own waters" is stronger than all the search-and-destroy weaponry of the centers of capitalist power, and all the technological know-how of their murder industries (except where total annihilation is the goal).

Vietnamese soldiers in the stream of their people's desire. American GIs in the stream of money, or shooting up the heroin that washes away fears of the enemy *wave* for the duration of an assault, only to lose its effect little by little. . . It's the rush—that first overwhelming streaming of the stuff through the arteries and the body, the inundation of consciousness with pleasurable sensations—that every addict says is the experience to which he must return. Never again to be a rock amid the raging sea.

But political names don't determine the nature of desires; they simply attach themselves to them:

> It is quite troublesome to have to say such rudimentary things:
> desire does not threaten a society because it is a desire to sleep
> with the mother, but because it is revolutionary. And that does
> not at all mean that desire is something other than sexuality, but
> that sexuality and love do not live in the bedroom of Oedipus,
> that they dream instead of wide-open spaces and cause strange

flows to circulate that do not let themselves be stocked within an established order. Desire does not "want" revolution, it is revolutionary in its own right, as though involuntarily, by wanting what it wants (Deleuze and Guattari).[52]

Nowhere in the texts we have quoted does desire aim to affiliate itself with an *ego* having distinct properties, a distinct totality with names like Neruda, Césaire, or Miller; nor does it simply aim for identity with some process calling itself the "Russian Revolution." Desire wants more than that; to be a "played-out wave," a surge, a flow, the very element in which life moves.

If the cited passages have any common aim, it might be to reverse the Freudian demand: "Where ego was, id shall be," or "Where dams were, flowing shall be." (Although they would avoid the term "*id*," partly because of its unfamiliarity, partly because they would know it comes from the rocky landscape where the "ego" holds sway and the "cliffs of castration" stand; also because their river is not the "Chaos" or "Acheron" that glimmer in the later Freudian "id," but the joy of freedom.) "You oceans of love sleeping within me! I feel you, fathomless ones, beginning to stir, preparing unheard-of waves and storms." This "ego" (Neruda's) does not respond by saying "I want to board a solid ship, put on my oilskin, head into the southwester, reef the sails, go into the cabin, and plot out the course that will take me into the peaceful bay, the harbor." On the contrary, a different process is applauded here: dive right in, be dissolved, become nameless—and not just in a regressive sense. What we see here is a breaking out, a crossing of boundaries to discover new lands and new streams (not a returning to the womb!), deterritorializations, unconnected to any "former homeland" or any new one.

Capitalism brought about a comprehensive deterritorialization; in the course of its evolution, it dissolved every previous order and code (religious, scientific, philosophical), altering their functions and rendering them obsolete. It opened up new worlds, made new areas accessible, created new avenues for the deployment of human bodies, thoughts, and feelings, even for escaping from the existing order. Like every dominant force that wishes to remain dominant, feudal capitalism (followed by bourgeois capitalism and the bourgeois state) took up the task of blocking new possibilities, obscuring their existence, chaining them up, redirecting streams for their own benefit, "codifying" them in a way that served dominant interests, yet allowed subject peoples to retain the illusion of newfound freedom.[53]

Under no circumstances could desires be allowed to flow in their inherently *undirected* manner. Word of the ability to tie themselves to *any* object, then abandon it to form new ties in a powerful movement of affective intensities, couldn't be permitted to leak out. *Goals* had to be found, desires had to be channeled.

The new overlords, interested in the flowing of desire, at least insofar as it might bolster the flow of currency, looked then to the possibility of encoding. Streams of desire were encoded as streams of money, and circulation replaced free trajectories. The end result: a strictly limited number of infinitely capacious counting rooms under private ownership; and for the rest, the shackles of wages and the lure of (state-controlled) gambling operations. How quickly did the promise of America as the land of limitless opportunity become synonymous with the unlimited chance of making money! The sad thing wasn't so much that the slogan "From dishwasher to company boss" was ideological or untrue, as the fact that desire had been reduced to that narrow ambition.

From the flowing of desire to the flowing of money. What precisely this involved was captured by the Donald Duck cartoonists (producing under the name of "Walt Disney") when they gave supercapitalist Uncle Scrooge the ability to swim around in his reservoirs of gold treasure. On one occasion his perennial adversaries manage to rupture the dam; the stream of gold coins spills thunderously out onto a dry riverbed. The victors don't have the heart to deny the old miser his last wish, which is to take a final dip in his river. Inspired by the sight of the old man frolicking in the stream of gold (a fish in water), they jump in after him and break their necks on the hard surface.

A further form of encoding is of greater interest to us here; it is older—probably the oldest form there is—and underwent many changes

Postcard (Riga ca. 1906).

before being shaped by the gradual ascendancy of bourgeois society in
Europe. I'm referring to historical changes in function to which women have
been subjected in patriarchal male-female relations. Under patriarchy, the
productive force of women has been effectively excluded from participating
in male public and social productions. What has happened to that force?
For one thing, it must have trickled away in direct slave labor for men. But I
don't think that form of absorption explains everything, or that the function
of women is confined to being portable power packs for men (as Borneman
claims).[54] It seems to me that women were subjugated and exploited in more
than simply this direct fashion. They were put to worse use, namely, by
themselves having to absorb the productive force of men belonging to the
subjugated classes of their eras—all to the benefit of the dominant class.
What I have in mind here will become clearer, once we have come to understand the following: in all European literature (and literature influenced by
it), desire, if it flows at all, flows in a certain sense *through women*. In some
way or other, it always flows in relation to the image of woman. (It is far
rarer for it to flow *aimlessly* as a desire for freedom, as in the recently cited
examples.)

In their primary role as "powerhouse," women simply don't exist in
Western literature. (The same is true of other producers of surplus value: the
slave in ancient times, the peasant in the Middle Ages, the modern worker.)
In their secondary role, as a force of absorption, however, they have been a
central concern—perhaps *the* central concern—of that literature. It is
usual—and rightly so—to speak of a history of the female *image* in Euro-

Drawings by Paul Kamm during World War I.

pean literature, and of a history of the men who made it. Somehow, that image lives in water. Let's see *how* it flows there:

> Rocking like the white algae
> On the sea's gently poured
> Surface, she glides about, and
> Leaning into the tide, splits
> The water's swell ahead.
> Above her rosy bosom,
> Beneath her delicate neck,
> A great wave parts.[55]

That's from Mörike's "Aphrodite on a Discus" ("Aphrodite auf einem Diskos"). From the time of Hesiod to the present, the foam-born Venus, Aphrodite, Anadyomene (who arose herself from divine loins and water)[56] has been swimming over white seas of paper, the desiring-territories of those who write. . .

> (Only what is unfit to see
> Is covered by a dark wave.)[57]

Love: the stars stand
Guard over our kisses.
Seas (distant Eros)
Surge, and the night surges,
Climbing round beds, round chairs,
Before the Word was lost,
Anadyomene,
Eternally from shells. (Benn)[58]

Nymphs, naiads, nixies. The Little Mermaid, the beautiful Lilofee, Undine, the Lorelei. The other side of the coin: with love comes fear.

I think the waves in the end
Devoured captain and ship;
The Lorelei and her singing
Are what caused them to slip. (Heine)[59]

The water rushed, the water swelled,
A fisherman sat by,
And gazed upon his dancing float
With tranquil-dreaming eye.
And as he sits, and as he looks,
The gurgling waves arise;
A maid, all bright with water drops,
Stands straight before his eyes.

. . . .
Couldst see how happy fishes live
Under the stream so clear,
Thyself would plunge into the stream,
And live forever there.

. . . .
The water rushed, the water swelled,
It clasped his feet, I wis,
A thrill went through his yearning heart,
As when two lovers kiss!

She spake to him, she sang to him,
Resistless was her strain;
Half drew him in, half lured him in;
He ne'er was seen again. (Goethe)[60]

Of course you must lie on your back
As usual. Let yourself drift.
Don't swim, now; just act as if
You were part of some mass of flotsam.
Look up at the sky and act as if

Postcard (1905).

You're being carried by a woman and all is well.
Without stirring things up too much, the way God acts
When He takes a swim in His rivers in the evening.[61]

That was the young Brecht, writing about "Swimming in Lakes and Rivers" ("Schwimmen in Seen und Flüssen").

Did you grow up, sister, on the coast,
That now your eyes are raging like the sea,
And now your breasts are like two waves
That never tire of cavorting?

. . . .
Or did you grow up in the golden sand,
Along the riverbed, among the water's roots,
That now your arms around my neck
Are two small springs, thirsting for freedom?[62] (Davico)

Your soul is the image in the murmuring water, where
Your fathers bowed their dark faces.
Hidden movements merge you with the waves,
And the whiteness that makes you a mulatto is just
A bit of foam, spittle cast upon the shore.[63] (Roumain)

Waters of love, quite different one from another, but always female—whether from Europe, Africa, or the Americas (I can't speak for Asian literature). It's no accident that the writers of romanticism and of the nineteenth century (especially the latter half) rarely create these associations between women and bodies of water. True, the "woman-in-the-water" may turn up in their works, but if she does, she bears the name of Ophelia.

How much of this is pure phantasm and how much real experience? Or is it all just a shimmering specter, a name hiding other names?

> O River, my River in the morning radiance!
> Receive, receive
> This yearning body,
> And kiss its breast and cheek!
> (Already she is feeling round my breast,
> Cooling with love's passionate shudders
> And jubilant song). (Mörike)[64]

> I love her with almighty force.
> Nothing can stem my love!
> It is a raging waterfall
> Whose torrent cannot be dammed. (Heine)[65]

And when I rock myself in the boat of your hips
Happiness reigns at home my soul is homeless. (Czechowicz)[66]

> We parted on a coast in the region of Riff.
> The ship was leaky too. I was sated:
> Still pale from loving, we gazed into each other's eyes.
> For weeks afterward, the sea seemed flat to me. (Brecht)[67]

> They lie in the grass
> A man and a woman
> They eat oranges, they trade kisses
> They trade their foam like waves. (Paz)[68]

> And I took her along to the river. (Lorca)[69]

A stream of promises
Flows down from your hair,
Pauses at your breasts,
And finally forms a syrupy lake on your body,
Shaming your firm flesh of nocturnal mystery. (Guillén)[70]

. . . so that my wave might break in her wave and carry us back drowned to the shore, in the flesh of shredded guavas, in a chastened hand, in lovely algae, in flying seeds, in a bubble of light, a memory, a prophetic tree. (Césaire)[71]

Mural by Lothar Bechstein. From the journal *Kunst im Dritten Reich* (1937), edited by Albert Speer.

so marvelously impersonal. *It was one cunt out of a million, a regular Pearl of the Antilles,* such as Dick Osborn discovered when reading Joseph Conrad. *In the broad Pacific of sex she lay, a gleaning silver reef surrounded with human anemones, human starfish, human madrepores* (Miller)[72]

Here is the song of the whole world's love;
Here, between the thighs I worship, Madeleine,
All love murmurs, as the sacred song of the sea
Murmurs all within the shell. (Apollinaire)[73]

It was an enormous cunt, too, when I think back on it. A dark, subterranean labyrinth fitted up with divans and cosy corners and rubber teeth and syringes and soft nestles and eiderdown and mulberry leaves. I used to nose in like the solitary worm and bury myself in a little cranny where it was absolutely silent, and so soft and restful that I lay like a dolphin on the oyster banks. A slight twitch and I'd be where there were mossy round cobblestones and little wicker gates which opened and shut automatically. Sometimes it was like riding the shoot-the-shoots, a steep plunge and then a spray of tingling sea crabs, the bulrushes swaying feverishly and the gills of tiny fishes lapping against me like harmonica stops. In the immense black grotto there was a silk-and-soap organ playing a predaceous black music. When she pitched herself high, when she turned the juice on full, it made a violaceous purple, a deep mulberry stain like twilight, a ventriloqual twilight such as dwarfs and cretins enjoy when they menstruate. It made me think of cannibals chewing flowers, of Bantus running amuck, of wild unicorns rutting in rhododendron beds. Everything was anonymous and unformulated, John Doe and his wife Emmy Doe; above us the gas tanks and below the marine life. (Miller)[74]

Beetles crawled under us; hosts of
Ants broke joyfully in on us,
Perhaps to bathe between stomach and stomach,
Or wander around between leg and leg. (Bierman)[75]

But the river—there must be rivers once in a while. I'm nuts about rivers. Once, in Rotterdam, I remember— — —. The idea, though, of waking up in the morning, the sun streaming in the windows and a good, faithful whore beside you who loves you, who loves the guts out of you, the birds singing and the table all spread, and while she's washing up and combing her hair all the men she's been with and now you, just you, and barges going by, masts and hulls, the whole damned current of life flowing through you, through her, through all the guys before you and maybe after, the flowers and the birds and the sun streaming in and the fragrance of it choking you, annihilating you. O Christ! Give me a whore always, all the time! (Miller)[76]

There was always some shit left on the stick. While I was working on all that in analysis, always with strong feelings of shame, I recalled a scene from over a decade earlier. The memory, surely a prelude to my recovery, helped clear my mind. A woman and I were lying next to each other after making love, under an open, sunny window—an Arcadian image—and drinking red wine. She picked up my flaccid root, just to see what it felt like, raised her wine glass, and baptized the thing—its happy life, its legitimate, spotless existence. A lot of grim, puritanical self-hatred dropped off of my penis at that moment (or at least became more bearable); and a presentiment of freedom and legitimate belonging rose within me, something analysis could tie into. (Tilman Moser)[77]

> In the mussels and snails
> Of all the world's oceans,
> My songs of love
> Are imprisoned. (Martins)[78]

I dreamed nights that you and I were two plants
Growing together, our roots intertwined,
And you knew the earth and the rain as well as my mouth,
For we are made of earth and rain. Sometimes
I think we will sleep below in death,
In the deep, at the bases of statues, and gaze
Upon the ocean that brought us here, for edification and love.

My hands were not hard as ice when they first knew you. The
Waters of other seas passed through them as through a net.
                                                    But now
Water and rock guard seeds and secrets.

Love me, sleeping one who, lying naked on the shore,
Looks like that island: your perplexed love, your astounded
Love, hidden in the hollows of dreams,
Is like the motion of the sea that surrounds us. (Neruda)[79]

Female geography. A map of the world:

> For you are Woman in my mind, my speech, my body,
> Mother of all living things, of crocodiles, of hippopotamuses,
> Of fish, of birds, of iguanas; mother of instincts, nursemaid
>   of harvests,
> Powerful woman!
>
> Water open to the rudder, the keel of the pirogue,
> Congo, my woman of the wild thighs, of long arms gently
>   wrapped in sea roses,
> Precious woman of Uzugu, oily body with skin of diamond night.
>   (Senghor)[80]

Yours is the sign of the primeval forest;
You, with your red necklaces,
Your armbands of beaten gold,
And in that dark caiman
Swimming in the Zambezi of your eyes. (Guillén)[81]

They did not see Adinas' velvet form
Swimming nude in the whirlpools of the rivers

. . . .
They did not see Adinas' dancing beauty
Flare up in the Caribbean Sea

. . . .
They did not see Adinas flaring up
In the winds of the Caribbean Sea. (Telemaque)[82]

An equatorial belt slung round her hips,
Like a little earth,
The Negress strides forth, the New Woman,
In her thin snakedress. (Guillén)[83]

From the Leucadian cliff
I plunge into the white foaming ocean tide, burning with love!
(Mörike)[84]

Fadeouts: fan dances—
A swarm—the herons are blue—
Colibris—garlands of pacific ocean—
Around the dark places of Woman. (Benn)[85]

my woman with the Val d'Or throat
like a rendezvous deep in the bed of an untamed stream
with breast of night
my woman with breasts like ocean molehills
my woman her breasts ruby melting pots. (Breton)[86]

"The Elbe at Dresden":

Ah, the river betrayed us then
The truth that everything flows.
The earth turned under us
As we held a kiss

. . . .
The river sang to us. This was our song:
Everything flows, everything flows.
My love, my love, now I'm alone.
The stupid river brings the message home:
Everything stays as it is. (Biermann)[87]

Symbolic representation of water, by Ziegler. Center section of a tryptich that hung over the mantle in the Führer Room of the "Brown House" in Munich (after 1933).

From *Kunst im Dritten Reich* (1937), ed. Albert Speer.

As long as

      you don't see

Love the Redeemer

          above the Neva's whirlpools,

Poitevin, "Les Dableries Erotiques" (1832).

You too shall

wander

unloved

Row!

Drown between bricks! (Mayakovski)[88]

A river without end, enormous and wide, flows through the world's literatures. Over and over again: the women-in-the-water; woman as water, as a stormy, cavorting, cooling ocean, a raging stream, a waterfall; as a limitless body of water that ships pass through, with tributaries, pools, surfs, and deltas; woman as the enticing (or perilous) deep, as a cup of bubbling body fluids; the vagina as wave, as foam, as a dark place ringed with Pacific ridges; love as the foam from the collision of two waves, as a sea voyage, a slow ebbing, a fish-catch, a storm; love as a process that washes people up as flotsam, smoothing the sea again; where we swim in the divine song of the sea knowing no laws, one fish, two fish; where we are part of every ocean, which is part of every vagina. To enter those portals is to begin a global

Hieronymous Bosch, from "The Excesses of the Monks" (1562).

journey, a flowing around the world. He who has been inside the right woman, the ultimate *cunt*—knows every place in the world that is worth knowing. And every one of those flowing places goes by the name of Woman: Congo, Nile, Zambezi, Elbe, Neva ("Father Rhine" doesn't flow—he is a border). Or the Caribbean Sea, the Pacific, the Mediterranean, *the* ocean that covers two-thirds of the earth's surface and all its shorelines, the irreproachable, inexhaustible, anonymous superwhore, across whom we ourselves become anonymous and limitless, drifting along without egos, like "masses of rubble," like God himself, immersed in the principle of masculine pleasure.

What is really at work here, it seems to me, is a specific (and historically relatively recent) form of the oppression of women—one that has been notably underrated. It is oppression through exaltation, through a lifting of boundaries, an "irrealization" and reduction to principle—the principle of flowing, of distance, of vague, endless enticement. Here again, women have *no names*. Only one, "Madeleine," somehow slips into the cited texts.

Exaltation is coupled with a negation of women's carnal reality. No single real woman is now of any use for the noble aims and Edenic pleasures of her creative masters, who may dedicate their deeds to a woman—ever since the fourteenth century, the image of an immeasurably perfect and all-deserving "Beatrice" has always hung somewhere in the firmament—but they are resolved to carry them out *without her*. The various forms of "devotion" to women have passed themselves off as philogynous, yet the at-

Ad from the *New York Times* (19 June 1977).

titude they adopt seems in essence to be a secular offshoot of the Catholic cult of the Virgin. It extends even as far as to Henry Miller, who, on the one hand, is one of its frankest critics, but, on the other, introduces dissatisfaction into even the most liberated lovemaking by fixing men's hopes on the arrival of some woman in whose vagina the oceans of the world quite literally flow and by saddling women with corresponding expectations of performance. There is still more of transcendence in the "juices" he writes of than of the real wetness of the women who have made love to him. Transcendence

Upside-down cover of *Männerbuch*, by V.E. Pilgrim et al. The photo they used is from an album by the Who.

and competition. We sense that the depersonalization of women here, the dissolving of their boundaries, is a consequence of the extreme abstractness of a desire that lacks adequate objects. And the only things preventing desires having adequate objects are barriers of domination. The link between the female image and the notion of wish fulfillment derives from these barriers.

It is not a real, living woman who appears here in relation to desire—though the man in question may have chosen a specific woman to embody his ideas—nor is it a real work of art. German dramatist Georg Büchner (an exception) actually permitted a woman to complain about that process. He was one of the few writers who didn't approach his public holding an elevated, overly expansive image of women:

> Lena: Am I like the poor helpless fountain, forced to reflect every passing image in my silent depths? Flowers are free to open or close their cups to the morning sun and the evening wind. Is the daughter of a king less than a flower?[89]

Sexuality and water go together in Büchner's writings too, but he allows a woman to discuss them. She is the prostitute Marion, one of Danton's "priestesses of the body":

> But I became like an ocean, devouring everything and burrowing deeper and deeper. I saw only one counterpart: all men, merged into *one* body. It was just my nature, and who can get around that? He finally noticed. He came up to me one morning and

Max Ernst, "Seelenfrieden" (Peace of mind), from *Une semain de bonté.*

kissed me as if he were trying to suffocate me. His arms tied around my neck. I can't tell you how afraid I was. Then he let me go, laughed, and said he'd almost done something stupid. I should keep my dress and wear it. It would wear out by itself soon enough, and he didn't want to spoil my fun in the meantime, since it was the only one I had. Then he left. I still didn't know what he wanted. That evening I was sitting by the fire: I'm very excitable and feelings are my only connection to the outside world. I sank into the glowing waves of the sunset. Suddenly a crowd came down the street, children in front, and the women were looking out their windows. I looked down: They carried him past in a barrow, the moon shining on his pale forehead, his hair wet. He had drowned himself. I had to cry—that was the only crack in my life.[90]

This is a singular event. For once it isn't the man who fantasizes, losing his ego in the waves of a woman. Büchner has the prostitute speak as if she were the pleasure principle itself: "I'm just one thing in the end: an uninterrupted yearning and grasping; a fire, a stream."[91] But this pleasure principle moves her lover to seek refuge in death—a watery death. She isn't condemned for that. Danton responds: "I wish I were part of the ether, so I could bathe you in my tide, so I could break on every wave of your lovely body." The wave Danton is referring to here belongs explicitly to both bodies. In their fusion, they are depersonalized and made alike. This is no "ego" battling the flood; it is a pleasure that transcends names. Odd, though, that Danton is ready to acquiesce to his own death. He is bored with the struggle for power. Lacroix expresses it this way: "Lazy through and through! He'd rather be guillotined than deliver a speech."[92] Is there some connection there?

Very Early History: The Woman from the Water

In her impressive work *The Descent of Woman*, Elaine Morgan establishes a link between women and water that is anything but mythological. Her book attempts to rewrite the history of "man's" evolution. Why?

> Smack in the center of it remains the Tarzanlike figure of the prehominid male who came down from the trees, saw a grassland teeming with game, picked up a woman, and became a mighty hunter.
> Almost everything about us is held to have derived from this. If we walk erect, it was because the Mighty Hunter had to stand tall to scan the distance for his prey. If we lived in caves it was because hunters need a base to come home to. If we learned to speak it was because hunters need to plan the next safari and boast about the last.[1]

And "her"?

> Most of the books forget about her [the woman] for most of the time. They drag her onstage rather suddenly for the obligatory chapter on Sex and Reproduction, and they say: "All right, love, you can go now," while they get on with the real meaty stuff

about the Mighty Hunter with his lovely new weapons and his
lovely new straight legs racing across the Pleistocene plains. Any
modifications in her morphology are taken to be imitations of
the Hunter's evolution or else derived solely for his delectation.[2]

Faced with so many blatantly androcentric interpretations of the
available evidence on the process of becoming human, Morgan refused to
accept the whole "Tarzan yarn." While searching for the fundamental
changes that made apes into humans, Morgan discovered that it was "she,"
the female ape, *and none other*, who had taken that final step. She took it as
an escape route that led to the sea. Africa, toward the close of the temperate
Miocene period:

> After a couple of million years of this peaceful existence the first
> torrid heat waves of the Pliocene began to scorch the African
> continent. All around the edges of the forest the trees began to
> wither in the drought and were replaced by scrub and grassland.
> As the forest got smaller and smaller there wasn't enough room
> or enough food for all the apes it had once supported.[3]

They were forced to retreat to the plains, where they were no match for
their numerous predators. This was especially true of mother apes, who were
impeded by the slow development of their primate babies. In short, they
died out. ("I yelped myself when I first reasoned myself into this
cul-de-sac," Morgan writes.) But the continent also had coasts, and along
those lived the very same frightened, hairy, nonspecialized human apes of
the Miocene type:

> She also couldn't digest grass; she also had a greedy and hector-
> ing mate; she also lacked fighting canines; she also was
> hampered by a clinging infant; and she also was chased by a car-
> nivore and found there was no tree she could run up to escape.
> However, in front of her there was a large sheet of water. With
> piercing squeals of terror she ran straight into the sea. The car-
> nivore was a species of cat and didn't like wetting his feet; and
> moreover, though he had twice her body weight, she was ac-
> customed like most tree dwellers to adopting an upright posture,
> even though she used four legs for locomotion. She was thus
> able to go farther into the water than he could without drown-
> ing. She went right in up to her neck and waited there clutching
> her baby until the cat got fed up with waiting and went back to
> the grasslands.[4]

Morgan sets out to prove that for the next twelve million years or so,
these creatures remained in and near the water, evolving fundamentally into

the human type ("Australopithecus") whose remains would eventually identify it as our earliest ancestor.[5]

A synopsis of her arguments. In the water, there were few dangers and adequate nourishment: shrimp, crabs, mussels, seal species, birds' eggs. Among the things that developed in the water were an *erect posture* (head above water) and a *smooth skin*. Every land mammal that entered the water abandoned its hairy coat in favor of a subcutaneous fat layer of the kind that human beings—alone in the genus of primates—still have today. The generally accepted theory holds that human fur disappeared because it became too hot. (Morgan: "The more you think about it, the more impossible it becomes to believe that hunting man discarded his fur to enable himself to become cooler and *at the same time* developed a layer of fat, the only possible effect of which would be to make him warmer.")

Other developments included *living in caves* (always plentiful along coastlines) and *using tools*—at first for opening mussels, the way sea otters use stones to this day. Furthermore, hair remained only on top of the head (above water, for protection against the sun), and "the vestigial hairs that remain on the human body . . . are arranged quite differently from the hairs of the other primates. . . . The arrangement of the hairs follows precisely the lines that would be followed by the flow of water over a swimming body." In Morgan's opinion, women's hair grew longer in order to give infants who were swimming around in the water something to hold onto. The old coat of body hair disappeared, meanwhile. And strangely enough, "in the later stages of pregnancy it still happens that the proportion of thin hairs on her scalp becomes relatively smaller and the proportion of thick hairs relatively greater."[6] In sum:

> All the developments that otherwise appear strained, and improbable, and contrary to what we know of normal behavior among primates and other quadrupeds, in these circumstances become not only credible and understandable, but natural and inevitable. Many features carelessly described as "unique" in human beings are unique only among land mammals. For most of them, as we shall see, as soon as we begin to look at *aquatic* mammals, we shall find parallels galore.[7]

For Morgan, the specialized anatomy of women is particularly indicative of a life in and near the water. How did the breasts and enlarged buttocks originate? The male response, she notes with irony, is that sex needed to become sexier.[8] Morgan herself sees more immediate reasons. The breasts enlarged for the sake of the nursing infant, which, with the disappearance of the mother's fur, would otherwise have been far too distant from the nipples as it lay in the crook of its mother's arms.[9] "The fact is that the Tarzanists, as well as forgetting about the females, are constantly forgetting about the infants."[10] And what about the buttocks?

When she first took to a littoral life she had nothing in the way of padding there. Her vagina was in the normal quadruped position, just under where her tail would have been if she had one; it was normal also in being exposed, flush with the surface for easy access. . . . But sitting on the beach was a very different matter [from sitting in trees]. . . . If it [the buttocks] evolved . . . as a protective feature, then the female ape would need it more. The male had only one orifice instead of three,* and that was a rather less sensitive one; besides, he didn't have to spend time sitting around holding the baby, which as long as it was breast-fed she would have to do.[11]

The "waves" of the female body came directly from the sea, then, and from the mother-child relationship.

The elaboration of the buttocks had consequences for copulation, in conjunction with the inward displacement of organs (a process that is characteristic of all mammals returning to water). The vagina *migrated* farther inward and forward. The traditional primate coupling stance—mounting from behind—became increasingly difficult.[12] Again, Elaine Morgan:

Why did Homo sapiens develop the largest penis of all living primates? . . . Why did he switch from rear-mounting to a frontal approach? . . . Once again, if you are asked to believe that man's sexual approach has any possible connection with an aquatic phase in his history you might at first find it hard to swallow. But once you begin to realize that practically *all* land mammals use the rear approach to sex, and practically *all* aquatic mammals use the frontal or ventro-ventral approach, then you are bound to suspect that the connection must be more than fortuitous.[13]

I'll set aside the sexual dilemma associated with that development for the moment, in order to spell out where else Elaine Morgan is heading with her line of reasoning:

If I may for a moment be thoroughly anthropomorphic, most of the species that go back to the water seem to get no end of fun out of life.

She cites some examples, including otters and penguins, "and dolphins, if you believe the people who know them best, are the gentlest, gayest, most attractive creatures on the face of the planet."[14]

---

*Anus, urethra, vagina.

Morgan attempts to distinguish the peaceable, life-affirming traits that were acquired by humans in that aquatic era—ascribing them for the most part to female protohumans—from traits that were picked up later on land. Here the hunter finally enters and temporarily dominates the scene, bringing with him male bonding and warfare (which, she agrees with Lionel Tiger, is a *function* of male bonding).[15] Her book ends with the words: "All we need to do is hold out loving arms to him and say: 'Come on in. The water's lovely.'"[16] She doesn't mean that women should once again be confined to their sexual functions; instead, she is voicing a desire for a life lived under the sign of a female pleasure principle that will hold out *water* against male aggression.

In his attempt at a genital theory, psychoanalyst Sandor Ferenczi also speculates on the connection between femaleness and water.[17] He begins with an era vastly predating the one Elaine Morgan discusses, namely, the era in which living species first evolved out of the water.[18] Ferenczi suggests that before there were any living organisms on land, there was no copulation involving penetration. The latter arose only after the drying up of the oceans forced aquatic animals onto the land. Before that there was no need for a womb to protect progeny, since spawn could swim in the water. And water dwellers had only a single "exit" for everything, from excrement to sperm. Fertilization took place through simple contact with exposed, accessible organs. On land, a battle over water erupted: Ferenczi suggests that females were forced to submit to being penetrated by the erectile penises the males had developed and to being "turned into oceans." From then on, the female interior was forced to serve as a substitute for the lost aquatic existence. Ferenczi concludes that *"amniotic fluid is a sea that was 'introjected,' as it were, into the mother's body*, in which, as embryologist R. Hertwig says, 'the delicate, vulnerable embryo carries out movements and swims *like a fish in water.'"*[19]

According to this view, even today male penetration of the female is a striving for the aquatic life abandoned in primitive times. Inadvertently, Ferenczi found himself well on the way toward weakening and washing away the psychoanalytic theory of symbols when he established that *"mothers should actually be seen as symbols or partial substitutes for the ocean, not the other way around.*[20]

First comes *la mer*, then *la mère*. First streams, then their lesser equivalent, incest: shallow brooks recoded into mommy's bed.[21]

Yet even here, in its very beginnings Ferenczi sees violence invading the sexual act. That violence was reinforced, according to Morgan, when males had to learn to approach females *frontally*, now that the vagina could no longer be reached through the customary procedure of mounting from behind. (Females at the time still went through cyclical periods "in heat".) This union of sexuality and violence is absent in other mammals. For them, the sexual act is brief, uncomplicated, and pleasurable.

"How on earth did the human species come to lose, mislay, and/or generally louse up such a simple straightforward process?"[22] She concludes that women were totally unprepared to admit men frontally. On the contrary, all of their experience said that such an approach could only be aimed at "ripping out their entrails." The women put up a fight, but instead of releasing them the men threw them onto the ground. Frightened to death, the women signaled their submission and seeing that gesture of humiliation, the men let them go: "it was impossible for him to go on clobbering a member of his own species that was giving clear indications that it had stopped fighting back."[23]

At this point, the species was again threatened with extinction. But as we know, what died was not the species, but the human capacity—still *compulsory* in other animals—to release a victim whose subjection has been made apparent. Males lost the ability to react to the gesture of submission; unrelenting, they pressed on regardless.

It follows that the males who learned this earliest were able to reproduce most prolifically.[24]

This view, if correct, implies a truly lethal juxtaposition of male copulatory behavior and the unlimited application of violence. Fortunately, history advances in contradictions, and that applies here as well. Morgan concludes that to placate and "persuade" women (there was no language yet), the whole social apparatus of intimate behavior—delousing, fondling, petting, kissing, warming—was integrated into the human act of lovemaking. (The same behavior exists among apes and other social animals, but there it has *nothing at all* to do with copulation.) In other words, the human capacity for love grew out of the introduction of violence into human copulation.[25]

Morgan's book offers a response from anthropological and behavioral research to questions of the origins of human (male) aggression. For once, it is a response that doesn't succumb to the kind of biologizing and depsychologizing that is so characteristic of behaviorist thinking. Morgan's main accomplishment has been to free the available evidence on early human history from contradictions, incongruities, and prejudices, and then to integrate it into a new system. In contrast to the previous findings of the male sciences she cites, her new findings have the simple advantage of plausibility and the aesthetic advantage of not being forced.

I have presented Elaine Morgan's views in considerable detail, because the insights they offer are indispensable for anyone concerned with male-female relations and gender difference. They show the way in which sexual dimorphism has manifested itself in a process that was centrally both natural *and* social from the very beginning. As the example of the female showed, the very form taken by the human body is the result of a natural process and of a social production. The ocean and the mother-child relationship produced the female body, just as the male body acquired its heavier musculature, strength, and speed through subsequent involvement in hunting and warfare.*

Woman: Territory of Desire

The end products of these processes have been both highly durable and highly mutable. Their mutability has increased in the course of history, with the acceleration of processes of social transition. Femininity in particular has retained a special malleability under patriarchy, for women have never been able to be identified directly with dominant historical processes, such as those that gave rise to bourgeois society, because they have never been the direct agents of those processes; in some way or other, they have always remained objects and raw materials, pieces of nature awaiting socialization. This has enabled men to see and use them collectively as part of the earth's *inorganic body*—the terrain of men's own productions.

Behind every new frontier that is opened up, the sum total of all female bodies appears: oceans of animated flesh and virginal skin, streams of hair, seas of eyes—an infinite, untrodden territory of desire which, at every stage of historical deterritorialization, men in search of material for (abstract) utopias have inundated with their desires. It's easy enough to see that this territory was (is) unsuited to the discovery of a freer existence, and it's just as easy to see that men in power were not the ones who would enter it with that in mind. Their global voyages took place in a very different geography. Rarely did they mistake the bodies of women for that of the earth.

But what of other men? Take Odysseus for example. Having lent his indispensable assistance in the battle to subjugate his archenemy, Troy, Odysseus is dispatched on a journey around the world. It is not difficult to imagine who among the Greeks might have been delighted at his departure, who then was inconvenienced by his fame and power. He is made to encounter more than the usual run of women: the siren's song without its bitter finale, Calypso, Circe—a few decades spent in exotic paradises in the bliss of untouched nature. Then comes the inevitable drifting back toward home and hearth, where Penelope patiently awaits his return, with the roasted boar, and her own body, in readiness. She is one of literature's saddest figures, keeping herself busy for eons by fending off robust young men with a representation of Odysseus' phallus, so stiff that only he can bend it. And the reason for all this? Had he taken the direct route home, Odysseus' return might have been termed a *quest for power*; as it is, we now see his wife as the goal of his roundabout route.

---

*Both Morgan and Lionel Tiger are well aware of the fact that long-distance swimming is the only competitive sport in which women remain superior to men in speed and stamina.

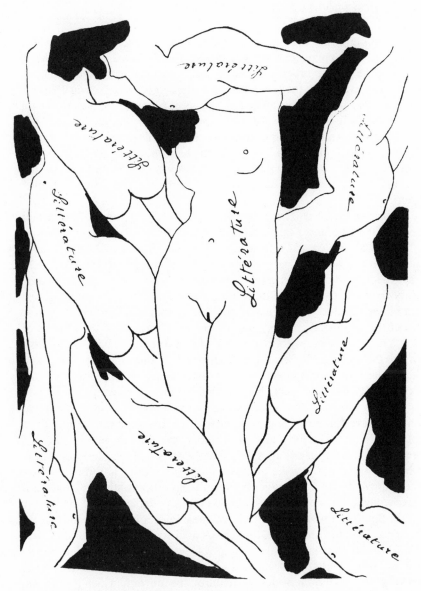

Francis Picabia, title page of *Littérature* (1931). (c) Spadem, A.D.A.G.P.,
Paris/V.A.G.A., New York, 1986.

And what of the ideals of the courtly Middle Ages? Subduing the
Orient, converting the infidel, slaying the monster, uniting the realm, and
finally defeating the pope—what was it all for? To allow men to wind up
composing love songs beneath the window of some courtly damsel (his
"one-and-only"). What an abasement of male desires. And why? All for the

sake of some higher-born male, a prince or emperor for whom the whole world had been conquered; some demigod who pocketed everything while blocking the path to productive possibilities—the same path psychoanalysts would later identify as the one that leads to the Mother. Again, why? So that the demigod, his men now dubbed as knights of his own round table, would gesture lightly in the direction of the ladies: "Take her, Prince Valiant. She's yours now." And that "one-and-only-one," well versed as she was in waiting, would prove in the end to be the most difficult of all obstacles—unless of course she was stolen away at the last moment, so that the global journey, the quest for the horizon, could start all over again. . . .

Percival, on his quest for the Grail, is suddenly reminded of his distant beloved when he sees a fallen drop of blood eating into the snow.

The Catholic church offered up the body of the Virgin Mother Mary, more heaven than ocean, as a territory for licentious desires. It is possible to trace the process of sexualization of that body through legends surrounding Mary from the twelfth and thirteenth centuries onward; the same process can be seen in the lyric poetry of the later minnesingers, in which, as any run-of-the-mill literary history will tell us, the "image" of the Mother of God tended to merge with that of the adored secular woman.[1] From now on, the body of the Mother of God increasingly became a secular body, and the secular body began to take over the function of the body of Mary.[2] The secular body didn't remain fictional; real women were employed to give form to its function. In the period that most concerns us here, the initial phase of development of bourgeois society, the first such women were those attached to the bourgeois courts of the Italian mercantile capitals of the thirteenth and fourteenth centuries. With the expansion of the European world, which followed in the wake of exploration by seafaring adventurers, these were supplemented by images of women from other continents—the black slave woman, the woman of the almond eyes, the Indian squaw, and above all the South Sea maiden. Collectively, these images began to construct the body that would constitute a mysterious goal for men whose desires were armed for an imminent voyage, a body that was to be more enticing than all the rest of the world put together. It was the fountain men drank from after crossing the arid terrain of their adventures, the mirror in which they sought to recognize themselves.

This process had numerous advantages for the ruling group, few for the conquering hero, none at all for women. The hero subjugates the world (its potential for new freedoms being kept secret from him), only to discover that image of woman still shimmering on a distant horizon. Yet rather than turning against his lord, on whom he remains dependent and who will soon send him on a new voyage of discovery (or deny him money for such a journey), he steers on toward the ultimate prize: the lap of his beloved, who

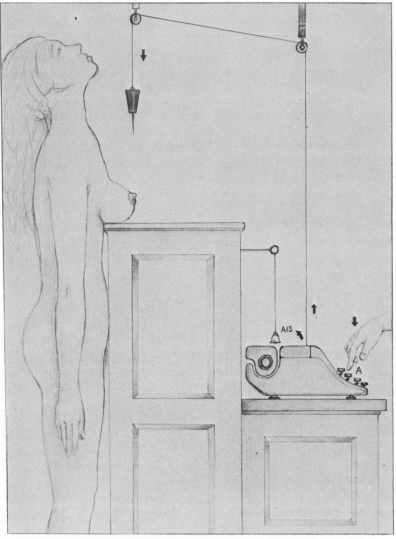

"Her eyes sweep . . . into the past . . . into the future." Plate 4 of the series "Irrwischsonate" (Will-o'-the wisp sonatas), from Günter Brus's *Irrwisch* (Frankfurt: Kohlkunstverlag, 1971).

may or may not wait for him in one of the many rooms of his master's palace. His guiding principle:

> Here is the place of a hundred thousand pleasures,
> Where love is given over to delight.
> In this small vale the man is gently wooed,
> Who many a foe with flame and sword subdued.[3]

A poem that might have been penned by some life-loving prince—as a toast to be spoken to his men.

Second, and more important, holding out the "high-born" woman as a partial reward for the higher-ranking retainers of princes prevented these men from setting out together with women, as equals; from leaving the European terror behind them, to found new, more human settlements elsewhere.

It should, of course, be pointed out that the despotic rulers who wanted to find a sea passage to India were more likely to send out killers than they were to send out men who dreamed of women. In other words, these images of women were addressed not so much to the conquerors, as to all those men who went on voyages of discovery and who could have used the opening up of the world to draw conclusions displeasing to the despots: for instance, that the new territories could be settled instead of merely exploited. Not such a far-fetched idea. Yet the despots didn't so much fabricate images of women as profit from them. The task of fabrication fell to the explorers themselves, and it wouldn't be wrong to conclude that they may not have performed it of their own free will (of which more later).

Divide et impera—divide and rule. This motto of the Roman Empire applies under patriarchy, not only to the division of the people as a means of their subjugation, but also to relations between men and women. The maintenance of inequality between the sexes, its perpetual renewal and exacerbation, has always been an important part of the work of the dominant group.

In this context, it seems to me that women's productive potential, still relatively unformed and not yet absorbed into social forms (particularly in the higher echelons of society), must have been admitted into areas of social production whose products served to uphold the system of dominance. They were allowed to enter that system as representations of a fiction of abundance ("Paradise regained in the body of a high-born woman"), which arose from the encoding of the body of the earth, "unproduced" nature, with the fiction of a boundless and all-fulfilling female body. (As we will see later, it was not only in the work of artists that this encoding took place.) Maintaining relations of dominance—the "divide" half of the motto—was assured through the establishment of the experience of *lack* as the basic component of real male-female relations of production; for the image of woman and her living reality can never be made even approximately to coincide with each other. Relations of production have thus become relations of anti-production, within which and out of which inequality and oppression are engendered, creating a reality that constricts and reterritorializes.

The *fictive* body of woman has become an imaginary arena for fantasies of deterritorializations, while actual male-female relationships have continued to serve, and have been actively maintained, as focal points for

From Poitevin's "Les Diableries Erotiques" (1832).

the implementation of massive reterritorializations. Exotic women, and women of the ruling class, have provided the raw material for those fictions. Women belonging to the oppressed classes, by contrast, have provided the material for male fears. These latter women have been victims, rather than images; they have been persecuted, not exalted.

The witch-hunt, for example, can be seen as part of a larger crusade accompanying the expansion of the medieval European world, a crusade that was directed against female sexuality in the subordinate classes. The fact that historians have persistently overlooked or ignored what is often clear evidence of the real nature of witch-hunting is one of the strongest arguments for the contention that history is written from the standpoint of its masters, and that the masters in this case weren't simply "bourgeois" or "capitalists," but also men.

The most highly evolved and effective form of encoding the earth's body as the body of infinite womanhood seems to consist in the even narrower conceptualization of the body of *all women* as the body of the mother—incest as a substitute for further exploration. Out of this substitution comes Oedipus; its precondition is the installing of monogamy as social convention. Oedipus is the son of monogamous parents. First, though, he is a son; the Oedipus complex is a son complex. (Thus it can simply be taken for granted that daughters aren't subject to it.) And Oedipus is a suffering son (as is Jesus, or Siegfried). Strange how often a suffering son stands at the center of patriarchal religions, myths, art works, or scientific constructs.

Could it be that Deleuze and Guattari are right in claiming that the Oedipal construct sprang from the mind of Laios, the paranoid despot who feared his own son would depose him?[4] He certainly had reason to be fearful; the son did want at least a piece of his realm, or of a different one. (He already had the mother. If she loved anyone, she loved him, not the despotic father.)

The despot rules over two domains: first the mother and (through her) the subservient bodies of all women in the realm; and then the body of the earth—the land, the city, with its production and its wealth. But how is he to escape a son who worships the indivisibility of power? He has the oracle proclaim that his unborn son will desire to practice incest and to murder his father. A son who desires such things is not to be wanted, even by the mother; thus he will be exiled. The problem in the end is that the young boy believes the story. He forgets the world, begins to hate his father and to pursue his mother. He wins her hand and the realm along with it; but the curse of the gods is cast upon him. He is blinded and forced into exile. His brother Creon, the exact reincarnation of the father, takes his place in the succession, thereby rescuing patriarchal law. Oedipus appears here as the invention of a father who is out to save his own skin.

There are striking parallels here with the function of images of women. These too appear as "springing from the mind of the despot," who is intent on protecting his position of dominance from potential social rebellion among his "sons." These parallels seem even more significant when we consider that both secular female images and the "Oedipal" ego were made possible by the same process, namely, the awakening development of bourgeois society in the eleventh century.

ORIGINS OF THE ANTI-FEMALE ARMOR

Early Bourgeois History: The Expansion and Contraction of Bodies and the World

Norbert Elias offers a clear and thorough analysis of this development in his two-volume work *The Process of Civilization* (*Der Prozess der Zivilisation*). The central theme is the mode of development of the bourgeois individual. Elias focuses primarily on that development in Germany; Rudolf zur Lippe has examined the same process, through the changing significance of dance, in Italy and France from the fourteenth to sixteenth century. His work, also in two volumes, is entitled *Mastery of Nature in Humans* (*Naturbeherrschung am Menschen*).

It escapes neither author that the new human being who emerges from that process is, first and foremost, a new *man*. Yet they fail to draw the

Christoph Fugger and other heads found on our currency. More about the relevant
history in A. Hauser's *Sozialgeschichte der Kunst*.

necessary conclusions from this; women remain mere appendages of the
development in question. Since neither author sees the male-female relationship as a relation of production, both can safely ignore the productive
energy of women. What I have in mind, then, is not just to sketch out their
descriptions of how the "civilized" ego evolved, but to relate that to the part
played by women in the process. It seems to me that the new male ego could
never have developed as a ruler-ego, one that was isolated from women and
opposed to them, without the (admittedly enforced) cooperation of women
themselves.

It is the central dialectic of this process that the powerfully expanding
world of medieval Europe stands opposed to an increasingly self-confining

individual. The man who initiates and implements processes of expansion ("*deterritorialization*") is converted by these processes into a sharply defined entity: a kernel of energy and enterprising spirit; a tough, armored ship that can be sent out to seize and "order" the world according to the European perspective. The man puts on a coat of "armor" (a key word for Elias). A lengthy process of "self-distancing," "self-control," and "self-scrutiny" ensues—a "subduing of affect," an opposition of "interior" and "exterior," of near and far. The development of perspective is the clearest expression of this process. Perspective is the triumph of an artificial view of things, an illusion built upon a specific preconception, a way of seeing that is more the work of the brain than of the eye.[1]

As Lippe tells us, "The unity that serves to encompass diversity is that of a geometrically reconstituted perception on the part of a fictitious eye."[2] Today, after the experiences of colonialism—the European subjugation of the world's peoples from the perspective of a European center—we can finally see that anyone who talks about *perspective* is really talking about a *focal point*, an *ego* to which everything else becomes subordinate. In the last analysis, that person is talking about subjugation and imperialism. How did this come about?

The major expansion of boundaries began in the eleventh century. "Under the combined pressure of land enclosures and population growth, society expanded not only outwardly but inwardly to a certain extent as well; it began to differentiate itself, to add new cells and form new organs: the cities." (Elias)[3] Land was cleared on a larger scale, and those who cleared it battled over the right to use common lands, and the forested places and fishing grounds surrounding the settlements. It was possible to travel greater distances; the invention of the snaffle allowed the horse to be used as a means of transport. The result was that numerous functions were dispersed from the closely controlled domain of the manor. Grain, for instance, was now transported to water mills for grinding. Through a series of uprisings, cities gradually won greater privileges and, finally, self-government.[4]

Elias repeatedly stresses that fact that the process of self-limiting ego formation and the centralization of state authority are not to be seen as separable. In other words, the "ego" became a kind of microcosmic centralized state authority, with the same division into *public* and *private* functions.[5] Ethnologist Mary Douglas points out the same connection, saying that "the physical body is a microcosm of society, facing the center of power, contracting and expanding its claims in direct accordance with the increase and relaxation of social pressures."[6] The resultant tendency, which Elias does not consider as important, was for the body to extend its boundaries in times of social expansion and decentralization. Relaxation of social constraints, necessitated mainly by a considerable widening of distances,

became a potential source of new freedoms for the human body. Every new trade route disclosed a novel pleasure; every new object from some foreign land held the possibility of a new feeling. Pepper took its place alongside the salt of the earth. Paprika and silk: those were once words for new sensations.

What about the corresponding processes of contraction? First, the circulation of money was introduced. According to Elias, the longer the "human chains" separating production from consumption, the greater the need for money, a "common standard" of exchange.[7] As a result, money came to control these human chains. Second, the guilds placed strict controls on handicrafts and trading.[8] Third, even at this point the early bourgeois citizens began their messianic mission of suppression. They impeded the movement of runaway serfs into the cities by demanding high fees for the right to municipal citizenship.[9] Through extensive persecutions of heretics, the Church attemptd to halt the spread of deviant teachings and, with notable success, to reintegrate dissidents (e.g., Franciscans and Dominicans) into the body of the Church.[10] The age was one of longing for "renewal," and though that renewal was carried into practice, there was a parallel effort to shackle innovation. So much for the history books. They don't tell us how the possibilities and practice of new freedoms of the human body were restricted and made subject to the wills of rulers, because they never address that question in the first place.

Two contradictory developments related to women come to mind here, the first having more to do with the *image* of women. During the process of relaxation of constraint occasioned by the demise of medieval society, the image of Mary, Mother of God, slowly converged with that of the noblewoman of courtly literature, while the latter was gradually replaced with the image of an attainable woman—both images being cautiously sensualized in the process. At the same time, there began a protracted reign of terror against the actual expansion of sexual pleasures. Its first target was women of the subordinate class, but its real target was the threatening possibility of pleasurable male-female relations of production in general. Persecution on both fronts would have been a mistake. Divide and rule: *she is the witch, he the bewitched.*[11] It is enormously important to grasp the fact that even in the fifteenth and sixteenth centuries—the "enlightened" phases of the Italian Renaissance and of German "humanism"—the emergent bourgeoisie offered no more than token resistance to witch-hunting.[12] The problem wasn't one of weakness; the bourgeoisie simply wasn't interested, because the women being burned were not *its own*. By about A.D. 1500, the bourgeoisie had grown powerful enough to finance kings and emperors, elect its own candidates to the Church, and establish secular schools in almost every city. It would have been easy to put a stop to the work of the inquisitors, had the bourgeoisie wanted to do so. The fact that it did not indicates that the Inquisition must have had its uses. Along with the other forms of terror they spread, the inquisitors were highly successful in consolidating inequality in male-female relations—a basic prerequisite for the greater controllability of the populace.

Expansion and Contraction, A.D. 1500: The Ocean Wide and the "God Within"

After 1230, the decentralization of medieval society, brought about through a process of internal expansion, began to gather momentum. The last Hohenstauffen emperor, Frederick II, was unable to maintain central authority in an empire that had grown much too large. His authority collapsed, and a long phase of rule by mutually antagonistic principalities began in Germany. It would take three hundred years for those principalities to evolve into tiny *central powers*, each with its own governmental and judicial bureaucracy.[1] This process was not finally completed until after the Counter-Reformation, following the Peace of Augsburg in 1555.[2] For the interim period, Elias's statement is largely applicable: "There was no central authority powerful enough to force people to exercise restraint."[3] One thing Elias overlooks here is the Inquisition. It may not have been able to preserve the centralized empire, but it was certainly capable of maintaining its own centralized jurisdiction.[4] It shouldn't surprise anyone that the Inquisition arrived on the scene at precisely the moment when the empire was disintegrating. The annals of the year 1233 record the first murder of an inquisitor in Germany.

Although the Inquisition took central command of violent attempts at reterritorialization, it was only partly successful in containing the vast tides of expansion that ripped apart the medieval order. Far too many streams had been unleashed for them all to be coaxed back into the lap of the Church—the *one* Church. The period from 1415 to 1430, for example, saw the first successful peasant revolt (of the Hussites in Bohemia).

From about 1400, extensive collections of *Schwänke* began to appear in German literature.[5] These were brief sexual narratives, equipped by this date with only token moral endings. Their heroes—priests, itinerant students and tradespeople, farmers on their way to market—usually had occupations that brought them in contact with people from all walks of life. In most cases, they would encounter women whose husbands happened to be temporarily absent; and when night fell, one woman or man was as good as another. The new pervasive social mobility expressed itself as a new sexual mobility.* At no time since has so frank and unaffected a sexual literature been written in Germany. (Writing on the literature of the fourteenth and fifteenth centuries, Frenzel and Frenzel comment that "the status of women fell."[6] Confusing the reality of women with the image of the sublime woman in that way is standard practice among literary historians. When they talk about "the status of women," their real concern is not with flesh-and-blood human beings, but with their value in the currency of images.[7])

At this point, according to Elias, the elaborate system of "self-restraints," which the developed bourgeois ego later learned to direct against its own desires, was not yet in force; or rather, its evolution was still confined to small sectors of the population. In the absence of direct intervention by external authority, people had little reason, and probably lacked the ability, to set up barriers against possible new, pleasurable expansions of bodily boundaries—even when their lives depended upon it. "At the close of the Middle Ages, a bodily frenzy spread through Europe, from Sicily to the Lower Rhine, in the form of the 'dancing madness,' or 'St. Vitus' dance.' People danced themselves to death."[8] Lippe sees this as a "craving for physical self-awareness" in reaction to the medieval suppression of drives. The Plague, one of the great vehicles of the dissolution of boundaries, must also have played its part here.[9] Even the fifteenth-century bourgeois "ego" was affected, as Elias tells us:

> Much of what strikes us as contradictory: their intense piety,
> their violent fears of hell, their guilt feelings, their atonement,
> the immense outpourings of joy and gaiety, the sudden flaring
> and the irrepressible energy of their hatred and their
> aggression—all of this, as well as sudden shifts in mood—is in
> reality symptomatic of a single ordering of emotional life. Drives
> and emotions were brought into play more freely, more directly,
> and less secretively than later on.[10]

The same applies even more clearly to peasants of the period. At this stage they were still effectively "dammed in" by direct, external coercion, rather than by any system of "self-restraints." It was these people who were most active at the time of the early bourgeois revolution, from about 1450 to 1550. While the invention of printing broke down the barriers to ownership of the printed word, tables of the movements of the sun, moon, and planets, published in 1474 by the Nuremberg mathematician Johannes Müller, began to open up the oceans. On the basis of Müller's tables—which Columbus

---

*Often represented by the mobility of money. See the many tales about the odyssey of a marked gold coin through a variety of pockets. It is stored next to beautiful bodies, lost in dark crevices, and finally turns up, rich in experience, back with its initial owner ("it could almost have happened to you, you know?").

"Flora," Jan Massys (1559).

used—a ship's position could be calculated without reference to coastlines.[11] The earliest extant globe, the *Erdapfel* (literally: "earth-apple") of a Nuremberg merchant Martin Behaim, dates from the very year in which Columbus "discovered" America. "America" is not drawn onto that globe, having little importance yet. More important was the knowledge that the earth wasn't a saucer with an edge one could fall off of. The ocean didn't lead through hell; it was navigable.

What would happen today, when the average ego is considerably more "stable" and repressive apparatuses are far more intricate, if the existence of some sparsely populated, quasi-paradisiacal planet were confirmed? The directions for getting there couldn't be hidden away forever in some steel-plated safe, nor could the means for financing the venture. In order to keep the buses rolling up with full loads to the factory gates the system of terror would have to be stepped up sharply; new forms of reterritorialization would be needed.

So, then, there were other shores beyond the limitless ocean; and the old chains of Europe were beginning to loosen, unleashing a realizing of desires greater and more intense than ever before in the history of the world. Even heaven, the "supreme object," had begun to dissolve; like the newly discovered continents, it too seemed sparsely populated, inhabited by none but a few harmless natives of divine lineage. The discovery of America carried with it the discovery of the human body. Opening up what was far away raised the possibility of opening up what was close at hand. A new knowledge dawned on the horizon: in the world, there are only human beings and nature; only the self among many others, and whatever you choose to make of that. There were despotic rulers too, of course, but not by any divine right. Their power was restricted to the reach of their armies, and that was that. There was no need to believe in anything beyond that; so why not pick oneself up and stake out one's tents where there was no church, no tax collectors, and no witch-hunters? Why wait? (Leonardo drew up workable plans for flying machines and a submarine.)*

In the face of these prospects, the kind of repression that had nurtured capitalism in its infancy could no longer be organized. Dams had to be erected—and plenty of them. The weapons that had beaten down the peasant revolts were no longer sufficient. Neither were the witch-burnings, though they continued apace (*The Witches' Hammer, Der Hexenhammer*, appeared in 1487). The more visible freedom of women was directly combatted in a simultaneous attempt to prevent a more general unfolding of human pleasures in relations between the sexes, which might have allowed those making the new discoveries to become free human beings.

Something different was also needed, however, for men who might be led into temptation. A new boundary was drawn by a handful of such men,

---

*Foucault is probably right in assuming that the opening of frontiers was not converted immediately into new bodily freedoms. He sees another process in the foreground. "For people in the fifteenth century, their dreams, the phantasms of their madness, and freedom (even when it is terrifying) have more attractive force than the desirable reality of the flesh" (*Wahnsinn und Gesellschaft*, p. 39). In support of his insight, he summons Bosch, Breughel, Dürer, and the extensive "literature of fools" (*Narrenliteratur*) of the period, as for instance Sebastian Brant's *Ship of Fools* (*Narrenschiff*) of 1492; but he overgeneralizes in saying, "The world sinks into a universal madness. Victory belongs neither to God nor the devil; it belongs to insanity." (Ibid., p. 41)

Foucault ignores the new sexual experiences and expansions, clearly evidenced in such collections of *Schwänke* as The Story of the Pastor of Kalenberg (*Die Geschicht des Pastors vom Kalenberg*)—a result, perhaps, of his relying too much on "high art" to read the trends of the era. But it is precisely in Dürer and the other painters he names that the process of ego formation is far enough advanced for perspective finally to triumph over the madness of the late-medieval age, and for a new, *rational* insanity to win out over the distorted insanity of the grimace. Its triumph is already evident in these artists; we don't have to wait for Erasmus, as Foucault claims. Although intermeshing and intermingling still took place among the populace, these painters had already perfected the isolating male gaze—the same gaze that is trained by the money changer and his wife on the gold scales in one of their paintings.

first for themselves and then for many others. For a short time it seemed likely to lead them to the stake, but then, in the form of a "new morality" (*neue Sittlichkeit*), it drew solid walls around a new way of life. Luther and the reformers stepped out of the wings, blueprints for dam-building under thier arms. Once again, the forces of reaction surfaced in the guise of a rebellion against existing authorities (authorities that were more or less dying out anyway) and set their traps.[12] Secure in the support, not so much of St. Paul as of local princes, Luther made his offer: the God within, in exchange for the rejection of the pope. This no doubt offered distinct advantages for those groups that were already making a home for themselves in the increasingly powerful independent principalities and for the part of the bourgeoisie which, having allied itself with the nobility, now hoped to be able to cease troublesome payments to the Church of Rome. But what of all those others who were already in open rebellion (the Anabaptists, for example, whose rebellion had begun in 1534-35)? They would have set sail without God or private property, and no pope could ever have hoped to track them down.*

Deterritorialization: the ground had been dug out from under traditional codes. Not surprisingly, the existing order was weakest at the periphery of the known world. In England, the land at the very edge, church and monastery property had been secularized as early as 1530. But it was also in England, removed as it was from the reach of Catholic armies, that the most rigorous reterritorializations set in. The country not only turned Protestant but became the largest exporter of the latest European innovation: the God within. (The blow that later severed Mary Stuart's head from her torso also represented a historical rupture, opening the way for the U.S.A.—an English-speaking, puritanical America.) The New World was conquered and settled by English Puritans, the most constricted frontier-breakers the world has ever known. Chained fast to the hearts of the conquerers was the new God with his new rules: private property in abundance and an abundantly chaste body hold a correspondingly abundant promise of heaven. Later the chain was loosened a little; it moved over into vest pockets in the form of the pocket watch, the new instrument of constraint that permitted even the most minute units of time to be exploited more intensively.

In rapid measure, the world was transformed into private property. Anyone who left the launching pad of Europe for the vastness of the New World did so with the idea of acquiring a parcel of unclaimed private property across the mighty ocean. Free-flowing desire found its haven in the log cabin, a European parental hearth transported into the wilderness, in which

---

*Marx writes that Luther "transplants the priest into the human heart" (*Nationalökonomie und Philosophie*, cited by Kofler, p. 279). Because in the process in question the God of heaven gradually dies, leaving only an "inner" God (in the form of "conscience" and the profit motive), it is fair to speak of a "God within." This God has become wholly masculine; all the feminine components (e.g., Catholic adoration of Mary) have been removed and similarly secularized, in the image of woman.

everything *remained* "under lock and key" and "guarded." Even here, the streams were blocked. Conclusion: You're the same wherever you go, the world has already been parceled out, so you might as well stay at home.[13]

Indeed most people were forced to stay "at home"—or at least, in their native lands: for it was the streets that they inhabited, not workplaces or dwelling-houses. In his history of madness in Europe, Michel Foucault notes that England was the first country to consider placing the insane (in other words, from the sixteenth and seventeenth centuries on, people who were not working) in institutions. The first internments occurred in 1575.[14] In 1622, two years after the *Mayflower* put to sea, a pamphlet attributed to Thomas Dekker noted that "many communities consign their paupers, and those able but unwilling to work, to begging, knavery, and thieving, so that the whole land is plagued as a result."[15] A royal commission formed in 1630 was more emphatic: "For these people live like savages, and are neither married, buried, or baptized; and it is this licentious freedom that has caused so many to find pleasure in vagabondage."[16] This situation was countered at first with institutions called "houses of correction," which later evolved into "workhouses." Foucault stresses that the first such institutions arose in the large industrial centers; he could have added that most of these were also ports—like Bristol, which established the earliest workhouse in 1697, or Plymouth, which followed suit in 1703. (The first German *Zuchthaus*, 1620, was also established on the periphery of the country, in the port of Hamburg.) "Barely a hundred years after the ship-of-fools vogue, we can trace the literary theme of the *house-of-fools*." (Foucault)[17]

Monogamization

Foucault also demonstrates the monstrous proportions assumed by the practice of confinement in the seventeenth century; it became a central instrument of stabilization in the bourgeois absolute state.[1] Fully 10,000 of a Paris population of around 100,000 were interned at one point.[2] It was not so much the insane as the single and jobless who were placed in asylums in an attempt to safeguard public order and decency, particularly in times of economc crisis.[3] Married people were expressly excluded as far as possible. Marriage was clearly tantamount to an oath to uphold the state's notion of order, as well as an agreement to work and forgo the vice of idleness.[4]

The slow implementation of monogamy began in earnest in Germany during the fifteenth century, in conjunction with the Italian Renaissance. It was a reterritorialization process that complemented, and went hand in hand with, the persecution of witches, a process in which any sexuality that had survived the attempts at its extermination was to be encoded anew.

It is often assumed that monogamy was introduced because the bourgeois male, who was in the process of slowly developing into a capitalist, was interested in keeping whatever wealth he had amassed intact, so that even after his death it could continue to work along the pathways he himself had marked out. To this end, he needed a successor, a fully legitimate son, to carry on his work. And to have that son, he needed an unquestionably legitimate mother—his wife, the new "one-and-only."[5]

It doesn't take much imagination to see that this construct is excessively flimsy. To achieve the desired effect, all that would have been needed was an appropriate modification of the laws of inheritance—a sociojuridical problem, then, the difficulties of which stand in no meaningful relation whatever to the centuries of effort invested in its eventual solution (i.e., in the implementation of monogamy). It is, moreover, nothing short of absurd to think that the new life's work of the bourgeois wife should have consisted only in guaranteeing the legitimacy of the heir. A bourgeoisie specializing in world exploitation would hardly have allowed itself to squander the productive forces of femininity in this way.

It is rarely directly economic factors that are operative in the restructuring of the relation between the sexes. What is, however, often very directly operative is an attempt to secure relations of domination that not only impinge directly on, but could also be said to realize themselves in, that relation. This is true in the present case. As social structures expand and become more mobile, the system of external limitations and constraints begins to lose its force. At this point, the social framework comes to need internal boundaries for streams of desiring-production to wash up against: reservoirs, canals, drainage systems. In other words, if people are to perform the new functions required of them—but are to remain at the same time capable of being subjugated—they have to be given new bodily boundaries.

The new scion of the bourgeoisie, for example, had to be able to look beyond the surface of things, to plan ahead. He had to be able to distance himself from objects, other humans, and his own emotions; to learn to wait for the right moment to act; to acquire diverse knowledge; to live in the awareness of being his father's successor. In short, he had to perceive himself as a citizen and a man. A human being of that description couldn't simply be decreed by law; he had to be "modeled" (Elias's term for the process). And more and more, the modelers were the parents in what was evolving into a nuclear family. Elias:

> This is not without a certain hint of paradox. As social existence places greater demands on individuals to reform, regulate, restrain, and conceal their instinctual lives, and as the conditioning of young people becomes proportionately more difficult, the primary task of inculcating the requisite social habits for handling drives devolves more and more on the intimate circle of the nuclear family, that is, on the father and the mother.[6]

From volume 1 of R. Alt's *Bilderatlas zur schul—und Erziehungsgeschichte.* (Berlin: Volkseigener, 1971).

The chief "modeling" processes, as Elias shows, were the development of a capacity for self-distancing—that is, a psychic splitting of individuals from their affects[7]—and a constant advancing of the thresholds of shame and embarrassment, of the "limits of filthiness."[8] This produced the bodily splitting of an individual into *inner* and *outer* physical realms, with the skin forming an increasingly sharp borderline. The term "armor" is no mere metaphor in this case. The nuclear family became an internal boundary of early bourgeois society, guaranteeing that the "ego" it engendered would view the world as a place of ends and purposes, an arena for the realization of predetermined interests. This boundary was well suited to the purpose of averting fantasies of the world as an almost infinite, barely explored body—a body inviting the spread of human desiring-production with its unknown pleasures. If the father was a good businessman and the mother a good agent of the father's wishes—which she became by being rewarded as his one-and-only—then the son who heard of foreign shores learned not to ask whether life was beautiful there, only what he could get out of the place.

All of this happened very slowly. "As late as the sixteenth century, and in the most respectable bourgeois families, we often hear of a man's legitimate and illegitimate children being raised together." (Elias)[9] That much public acknowledgment of the boundlessness of the stream of sperm was finally too much; it gradually disappeared from bourgeois life. Here too

(Berlin: Volkseigener, 1971).

Luther appears as one of the champions of progress, and not only with his formulations of marital commandments and prohibitions. Once again, he hauled in the chains with a gesture of rebellion: he married a nun. Monogamy could now come marching in, festooned with the popularity of anti-papism. To the "God within" was added the "woman within." She was active within the confines of the home, within the extended borders of the male ego—borders against the world of all other flesh and against the flowing of all the rest of the world outside. In the school plays which Luther himself, among others, had encouraged, and which functioned from 1530 on as a means of demonstrating to schoolchildren the proper way to live, one of the principal figures was the Biblical Susanna, the very model of the faithful wife.[10]

The new drive toward monogamy wasn't confined to Germany; it was characteristic of any social unit that could be seen to be developing along bourgeois-absolutist lines. Running parallel to the centralization of state powers was a centralization of the responsibilities for modeling and shaping the new, centered ego, within a family type which, for the first time, could be neatly represented by the triangle that would engender Oedipus, the supposed hero of the whole story (at least according to a number of sons whose own familialization clearly proceeded with particular success). In Germany itself, the movement toward centralization was largely absent. Since, from

"To the Councilors of all the Cities in the German Land" (Martin Luther).

1555 onward, Catholicism and Protestantism coexisted as official state religions, it was left to local princes to decide which of the two would be valid in a given area. As a result, the rift (or rather, the many rifts) that ran through Germany became wider and more deeply entrenched. Developments in France allow a better reading of the implications of the process of centralization, especially in terms of the function accorded here to the process of centralization, especially in terms of the function accorded here to the "high-born" woman.

Centralization and the "White Lady": The Geometricizing of Bodies

In volume two of *Mastery of Nature in Humans* (*Naturbeherrschung am Menschen*) Rudolf zur Lippe gives a detailed description of the Circe ballet that was performed at the French court of Henry III at the close of the sixteenth century. Lippe has access to a primary source, the original description of the ballet (1582) by its choreographer, Beaujoyeulx.[1] The ballet's plot centers on the subjection of the sensuous siren Circe to the new principles of state authority. The ballet aimed "on one hand, to portray the forces and groups opposed to modern, centralized disciplining powers in France as Circe's victims; and on the other, to paint the king as victor and liberator."[2]

> The royal ballet was a direct ritualization of the contemporary
> mythos, in the sense that the reigning monarch personally
> reviewed the progress of the plot as he would a parade.[3] . . .
> The purpose of this ritual . . . was not only to taboo Circe as a
> venial agent of sensual frenzy. Circe was meant to represent
> longing in general ("le désir en général"), the conjunction of the
> divine and the sensuous ("meslé de la divinité et du sensible"),
> and she had "quite diverse effects, leading some of her victims
> to virtue and others to vice."[4]

It wasn't simply a question of overthrowing the "longing in general" that surfaced in the person of Circe, but of dissecting and transforming it as a force of production.

Lippe says that "under the form of rule that is equated with masculinity and a humanity endowed with reason, Circe, the embodiment of a 'generation universelle', gains a right to exist in a position of subordination."[5]

A more elevated position was assigned to Pallas Athena:

> The reason why she [Pallas Athena] should have become the key
> figure in the struggle is elucidated in the mythology of her birth.
> She was born not of a woman or a body, but from the head of
> Jupiter. "That great god engendered me from his divine mind."
> She is correspondingly able to promote and protect human
> theoretical intelligence.[6]

Lippe fails to investigate the cranial birth any further. While emphasizing that the king himself (Henry III) danced the part of Jupiter in the ballet, he misses the larger point: namely, that the principles of the new rational state have arisen out of a bachelor birth from the brain of the ruler at its center, without the carnal participation of a woman. All the magic of nature, all the pleasure and sensuousness associated with Circe, have been removed from the offspring of this new life. Nature is there to be exploited;

anything that promises pleasure in nature is attacked, through an attack on the sensuous woman. Rarely is that permanent process whereby domination is secured under patriarchy as palpable as it appears in this case.*

Even the part of nature that is to provide the raw material for power under the new regime is represented in the ballet by women—and not just any women. The duchesses of the French provinces and Queen Louise herself dance before the king, as naiads clad in white. They perform in the midst of lavish scenery: a garden with a fountain.

> The naiads are water nymphs from that same fountain; that is, they are the purest and most characteristic forces of a country represented as a garden with a fountain. The social position of the actresses serves both to confirm that notion and to signify that the forces they represent are on the side of the crown. Their lovingly orchestrated appearance here is the first occasion on which royal power is deployed against the accursed principle of nature.[7]

Lippe is doubtless too entrenched in the tradition of the Frankfurt School to articulate what is really happening here: a public dramatization of the subjugation of female forces of production, in accordance with the wishes of the court. The newly constructed edifice of the bourgeois-absolutist state is founded upon the restructured sexuality of the "high-born" woman, who is to become a model for all women. The flowing of the streams of desire is captured and held in a fountain; it bubbles up to please man in his own garden. It is desensualized, "white" water, perfect for irrigating the new ordered state. The patterns of the dance, deprived of all carnality, are a model of canalization: "The dance consists of twelve persons, who form twelve different geometrical patterns in front of the king."[8] In the *grand ballet* that ends every pass, all of the dancers turn their gaze toward the king. They group themselves into squares, circles, even triangles, symbolizing the new forms that are working to dominate nature, with the

---

*Adorno and Horkheimer are on the right track when they state that "as representatives of nature, women in bourgeois society have become an enigmatic mix of irresistibility and impotence" (*The Dialectic of Enlightenment*). The particular wording of that statement can be ascribed to their feeling for individuality and to their urbane politeness (toward those in power). To these men, the world is so much a game that women still merely *represent* the oppression that has been and continues to be directed against them. As a living part of the "nature" in question—as "nature" itself—women aren't fit objects for refined thought. The oppression of women is simply a male fantasy, something representational. Here the bourgeois woman really does become a "representative"—though not of "nature." Whether she surfaces as an "enigmatic figure" in the arts, or as a female Maecenas in the intellectual circles of the early (thirteenth-fourteenth century) bourgeois courts of Italian merchant capital, she is made to represent male dominance. It was not in any sense "nature" that women represented, but power (though not power that was their own).

"Study," Dante Gabriel Rossetti (ca. 1860).

help of the "natural sciences." Beaujoyeulx's description shows that that was precisely the intent. It seemed, he says,

> that/everyone believed Archimedes could not have grasped/the geometrical proportions better than the princesses and ladies/demonstrated them in this ballet.[9]

What is being practiced in the ballet is the geometricization of the body itself, in counterpoint with the "geometricization of perception." (Lippe)[10] This stage in the erosion of the coastlines of femininity remains almost completely preserved for us today in the concentric layout of the castle or palace gardens of the seventeenth century.

Symbolic representation of marriage
(Germany, 1504).

We should point out one further significant aspect of the ballet that Lippe overlooks. While the naiads are forming the base of the triangle and bowing to War, Queen Louise herself stands at the triangle's apex.[11] Thus, even the individual woman's subjugation to man (as his wife) is dramatized. Here, the reigning king and queen themselves can be seen to be propagating the notion of the bourgeois nuclear family, through the enactment of a court ritual. The bourgeoisie is not yet fully evolved, yet it has already infiltrated absolutism to this extent. And oddly enough, it is the figure of the triangle that is chosen to dramatize that fact. (Oedipus is growing apace.)

Solo with Accompaniment: Falcon and Medusa, or "Let There Be Ego"

Lippe has shown how the dance medium in particular has been used since the Renaissance for the conscious cultivation of new images of the body. The peasant population, on the one hand, had set about casting off the chains of the disintegrating medieval order with the wild capers, the grimacing and grotesqueries of some cataclysmic carnival. (Bakhtin's concept of the carnival as a massive inversion of the old order in revolution[1] seems better suited to describe the features of this kind of bursting of boundaries than Foucault's notion of *folie*.)[2] The new ruling group meanwhile began to practice the measured step; their new public face fulfilled what Lippe calls a "function of ostentation."[3] At the Italian courts, symmetrical dance forms, in which several groups danced simultaneously, came into being shortly after 1450.

Parmigianino, "Self Portrait," (1524).

Here, there arose a tension between any given movement and its mirror image, through the identical repetition of that movement by the other person. Movement was simultaneously set in opposition to, and united with, itself, enclosing a space that became the locus for a *process of self-representation and mimetic self-reflection.* (Lippe)[4]

That process is strikingly similar to the process of infantile ego change, as we have come to understand it today. The child's reaction to its own mirror image is decisively important for observing the latter process. The child's gleeful reaction in the second half of its first year of life—the "symbiotic phase"[5] in Margaret Mahler's terminology—led Jacques Lacan to conclude that it is perceiving its own image as that of its mother.[6] Its rejoicing comes from the feeling of happiness in not yet being separate from the mother.* René Zazzo has shown that this behavior changes markedly between the ages of two and two-and-one-half years (Mahler's "individuation" phase),[7] when the child's predominant reaction ranges from confusion to actual fear of its own image. It may not be overstating the case to claim that the child experiences terror in the moment of its individuation, as it comes to perceive itself as an isolated, "lonely" being, a subject robbed of all of its previous, protective undifferentiatedness. In *Psychoanalysis of the First Year of Life*, (*Psychoanalyse des ersten Lebensjahres*), Franco Fornari sums it up in this way:

> The child's own image, in becoming a true self-image, engenders
> a kind of alienation within the self that it contains and
> represents, by inducing the self to place itself on an equal footing
> with every other object . . . The price of this subjectivization,
> which we know as self-consciousness, is therefore
> objectivization.[8]

In the ritual court dances of the fifteenth century, the same operation of objectivization was carried out by the dancers on themselves. This was a public, rather than private, ritual, and it established new public obligations. Instead of using mirrors, the dancers invented symmetry.**

It was precisely this process, in which one dancer's movements were mirrored exactly by another, that isolated individuals from each other and allowed them to perceive their difference. As they traced out their symmetrical figures in the measured steps of the dance, a new supreme object appeared above them to replace the old God: the abstract conception of the new European subject. It took concrete form as a submissive subject, following prescribed lines of action. Lippe again:

> They tried to fit their movements to the vision of their objective
> contemporaries, rather than appropriating their own bodies
> through firsthand experience. The body was instead made subject
> to the same principles that were being employed to appropriate
> the objective world.[9]

---

*This reaction seems to be more independent of the circumstances of development than is, for example, the well-known "eighth-month anxiety" (*Achtmonatsangst*), in which the child reacts with horror and fear to the "strangers" who force upon it its first sporadic perception that it is distinct from its mother (S. F. Fornari's *Psychoanalysis of the First Year of Life*, pp. 20ff.). Max Benjamin T., barely nine months old, plays in front of the mirror but shows no trace of eighth-month anxiety. "Normally" this would be a sign of a disturbed separation from the mother. But we have found that the same thing happens in most cases in which both parents, or several adults, are looking after the baby on a regular basis. Eighth-month anxiety, then, appears to be not so much a developmental stage in the process of individuation, as an expression of the (usual) isolation of the mother-child relationship at the time of the baby's first feelings of individuation.

**One of the reasons: they didn't have big enough mirrors. Not until early in the seventeenth century were techniques available to produce mirrors sufficiently large to reflect whole bodies. Then came the large mirrored halls of the French kings.

The observation of individuation in modern infants—themselves products not simply of natural laws, but of the historical development described by Lippe—most aptly support his remarks on dancers at the Renaissance courts; and they show him to be right in one of the daring conclusions he draws. He assigns special importance in his book to the *posa* (pause) in dance, though it played a subordinate role in the writings of dancing masters of the era in question. Only one of these, Domenico, gave it a more extended treatment. *Posa* is the term used for a hesitation that occurs *in the midst of moving* from one dance step to the next. Domenico writes:

> Within each bar one stops for an instant, as if one had seen the Medusa's head (as the poets say); that is, after completing a movement one freezes as if turned to stone for this instant, and in the next resumes moving, like a falcon beating its wings.[10]

Lippe sees that hesitation as "the index and focus of a change" in which *"that aconceptual medieval unity of human beings acting in concert was dissolved, without any immediate transition into rational conceptualization having been made.*[11] This is all very abstract, and like most statements of its kind it overlooks what is happening to femininity. Thus Lippe is at particular pains to argue away the Medusa:

> Indeed Domenico talks not of reflection and consciousness, but of a paralysis that interrupts the succession of movements for an instant. He even cites the head of the Medusa, as if the paralysis were impossible to describe except in terms of fear.

But Lippe isn't happy with that. In a model act of "bachelor birth," his own mind is delivered of the following observation: "Consciousness arises precisely by entering into the movement of its contents, in order to survey itself as a whole, at a higher level of truth."[12] When the moment arrives to recognize that what is being abandoned here isn't just an "aconceptual unity" among people in the Middle Ages, but the possibility of a state in which women and men intermingle as equals, this man sets about inventing a "higher truth" of consciousness, from which he can survey himself "as a whole."

The result? What Lippe sees represented in the petrification of the *posa* is a memory of the immediately preceding movement, a "mimetic learning." He refuses to give serious consideration to Domenico, for whom the *posa* is more the expression of some fear. Yet everything points to the conclusion that it is man's fear of reverting to something that might prevent him from soaring off toward a new form of male domination, on the high-flying "falcon" of his notion of the phallus. He is afraid of falling back into a state of intermingling with the opposite sex—a state in which his own power would dissipate. Falcons have an aversion to moist surroundings. And a further point: the male-female opposition set up in the images of "falcon" and "Medusa" turns up again in the course of the dance. Lippe emphasizes that set roles requiring virtuoso dancing were reserved for men, while the slow, ornamental parts were given to women.[13] In other words, the symmetrically spaced women were a version of the Medusa brought to order; the falcon taking flight was the man. His flight became truly *modern* if he managed to learn the lesson that "in a piece for four voices, one was chosen to set the pace and hold out against the distracting influence of the others."[14] (An exercise in perspectival training for the advanced masculinist, centralized, competitive ego of around 1500.)[15]

Germany was less highly developed and less resplendent than France; it had no sufficiently self-confident, autonomous city-states for symbolic events to be staged as exercises in the collective acquisition of new bodily limits. The new falcon, forced to explore other possibilities, hit upon some that were more appropriate to the internally divided state of Germany. Luther tanned his own hide with a whip, in an attempt to acquire the kind of armor the Western "ego" now needed as a habitation. This method caught on—perhaps more than all the rest of Luther's innovations put together. The body was now kept in check with pain; the whip migrated into the hands of an "educator." When he approached a woman, this kind of man was already a hard, solid ship, incapable of experiencing mingling with another body as a pleasurable expansion and reordering of boundaries.

Some of the Principal Features of Reterritorialization Through Women and Images of Women

Whether affecting women or men, all of the processes in question were processes of reterritorialization. They traveled (and were therefore initiated and controlled) from the "top" downward. We shouldn't deceive ourselves as to the significance of individuals in all of this, either; even in the case of Luther himself—cast by bourgeois-Protestant historiography as one of the West's first great heroes of the ego—it is possible to show the extent to which his behavior expressed the interests of his most powerful contemporaries. His attack on the Roman Church, or rather the success of that attack, was made possible only by the fact that in Germany of the early sixteenth century there wasn't a single socially relevant force—neither the majority of the princes, nor the bourgeoisie, nor the peasantry—that wouldn't have opposed the Church, that is, the papally allied regency of Charles V.[1] Again, the new ego was established from the top downward; it began to develop much later among the peasantry. The "top-to-bottom" direction of this ego formation is obvious enough to incline Elias to see all that is new in history as traveling from the top down, as if always invented by each new ruling group. He largely misses the point that this kind of development has the character of a shackle upon any new behavioral possibilities that appear among the people and threaten traditional forms of power.[2] Yet it is precisely this process that produces the compulsion for "new things from above" to disguise themselves domestically as rebellion, while externally they can present themselves directly, and immediately, as imperialism.

The year 1521 provides the most geographic illustration of these dual aspects of a single development. While Luther, the Little Monk, was delivering his famous lines to the Diet of Worms ("Here I stand; I can do no other"), another of Emperor Charles V's subjects—this one seemingly more obedient—stood before Tenochtitlán, the Aztecs' capital in Mexico, intent on reducing the city to rubble and ashes. Two hundred thousand Aztecs "discovered" the new way of death. The man responsible for those deaths, Hernán Cortés, "could do no other," either. He was reaching out for the new, external god of Gold.

Thus the expansion of the European world outward beyond old boundaries found expression in imperialist drives against "primitive peoples." I submit that this corresponded to an inner imperialism that took as its territories lands formed from the subjugated nature of female bodies. Just as the external gold was mined from the body of the world's peoples, these *internal* variety (the new male ego with its new freedoms) was extracted from the body of subjugated femaleness. The patriarchal bougeoisie, arming itself for a new departure toward world domination, depended equally on both forms of subjugation. (*Both* is really a misnomer, since they were aspects of a *single* process. Just as human productions cannot be divided into a desiring-production on the one hand and a "material" production on the other, so also can men in power not be seen to have made that distinction in the process of establishing and consolidating their power. It was two aspects of a single conquest that set up white masters over the colored nations of the world and placed the dominant male ego of the emergent bourgeoisie in a position of domination over women in his own society. He would continue to employ those women as the colorful raw material for shaping the images and setting the boundaries that were so necessary to secure his domination.

Since women were excluded from processes leading directly to the production of surplus value, they remained less sharply defined, more malleable. Productive processes define those who are engaged in them quite precisely, allowing (or forcing) them to assume an identity with relatively firm outlines.[3] The more "malleable" (untapped, or contradictorily organized) productive force of women became something in the nature of a reserve army, which could be used as a stopgap whenever the men in power at any given time felt threatened by other males. (If the threat seemed to come from women, it was combatted directly.) In their other function, women served as building blocks for internal, movable barriers in the masculine-European system of domination—barriers against which any centrifugal forces that threatened to reach more far-flung frontiers could break.

In the seventeenth and especially the eighteenth centuries, all of these frontiers and boundaries shifted considerably. To understand how this occurred, we should perhaps briefly review the main features of the process as they have emerged so far. We have seen how the noblewoman was gradually eroticized, in conjunction with a violent de-eroticizing of the common woman. In the course of that eroticizing, the bourgeois male gained access to a female body that had previously existed only as an image: the transcendent body of the noblewoman. The noblewoman herself is made the possessor of the erotic body for two purposes: for lovemaking *and* for the representation of the power of her overlord, whose commercial wealth made the secularization of her celestial flesh possible. This development was kept from getting out of hand by confining women to a representational function and by monogamizing the male-female relationship.

Among the people, the (slower) consolidation of monogamy had a different function. Here it wasn't a limitation placed on a process of sexualization; on the contrary, it was the final stage of a campaign for the total elimination of sexuality—the "lesser of two evils." Monogamy surfaced here as the new code for a new set of circumstances within which access to the body of the opposite sex, which had for a brief time been relatively easy, was now to become more difficult for both parties. What had been accessible was now made unattainable because it harbored a potential for new freedoms. Alongside the "divine" one-and-only (inaccessible to the man of low breeding), an "everyday" one-and-only appeared (as a boundary for that same low-born male).

In bourgeois society, the more the absolute distance between the top and the bottom of society decreases (as it has done since its beginnings), the lower that image of the "high-born" woman sinks (most particularly as a result of that image being put on *display* by high-born men), to become sedimented in the fantasies of the "low-born" man; thus lack is instituted anew in male-female relations. For the more or less socially impotent male who is the sad hero of this tale, the image of the high-born woman inevitably comes to represent the pleasure of the high-born man. The commoner will never experience that pleasure, since SHE will never be attainable. In other words, the closer the high-born woman comes by displaying her enticements to the man of lower position, the more the sight of her makes him feel his social castration as a sexual castration: his prick is too short, he can't get it up high enough. By means of this highly effective mechanism, his relationship with any real woman can be ruined, since she can never measure up to, and will always be a poor substitute for, dreams of pleasure associated with the image of the high-born woman. In his own mind *he* can never measure up either, since castration tends to be total (relative castration is no easy matter). He is then likely to develop an extreme form of penis envy with respect to the only phallus that can "measure up": the phallus of his master.

He uses the fiction of a sublime phallus as a bridge to reach the woman sublime—and yet in reality he has neither. Both the phallus and the woman are then likely to figure large within the inventory of his masturbation fantasies.

Since attempts to reterritorialize move from "top to bottom," associated changes in processes of encoding can always be observed first among the ruling strata. Whenever fundamental changes "result" in those areas that historiography has traditionally labeled "the history of manners" and passed on to specialists.

The "One-and-Only" and Doubts about the Nature of Reality: Armor on Two Fronts

Elias offers an extensively researched analysis of court society in a book of the same name (*Die höfische Gesellschaft*). The scene is France, twenty or thirty years after the situation we saw portrayed in the Circe ballet:

> In the first and second decades of the seventeenth century in
> France, the publication of a lengthy serialized novel elicited con-
> siderable response within the emergent circles of court society.
> For a time, this novel was the literary focus of a form of cult,
> generating discussions, games, and other social
> diversions. . . . The novel in question, *L'Astrée* by Honoré
> d'Urfé, is a product of an era in which even nobles raised in the
> tradition of the independent warrior and seigneur began to
> realize that the balance of power had shifted irrevocably in favor
> of the occupant of the throne and his representatives. In other
> words, the power of central government had grown at the ex-
> pense of those local and regional ruling strata that had previous-
> ly been able to be more autonomous.[1]

The cult around *Astrée* offers exemplary evidence to support the argument that those social forces that had lost a direct battle for the power of
government were both driven back into a realm of marginality and offered
reparation in the form of a new and palpably more proximate image of
woman.[2] What is more, it was the defeated parties themselves who invented
that image:

> In the civil wars, Honoré d'Urfé had fought on the side of the
> Catholic League against the Protestant armies of Henry of
> Navarre, the later Henry IV. D'Urfé had been captured, re-
> leased, recaptured, and finally forced for a time into exile. He
> was a member of a wealthy, locally esteemed family of provin-
> cial nobles who had close ties with Italy, the court of Savoy, and

the higher echelons of the Church. He was cultivated in the
mode of the Italian and French Renaissance. Although no cour-
tier himself, he had been trained in courtly manners. He belonged to the camp of the vanquished and was now making his
peace with the king.[3]

In *L'Astrée* as in the Circe ballet, sensuous and "white" women are
placed in opposition; yet in *L'Astrée* the women's social positions have been
completely reversed. At the court of Henry III, as we saw, the dramatic part
of the supreme "white" woman was still played by the queen herself, who
used that role to propagate submission to her husband and to central
authority; in other words, to propagandize for monogamy. Circe
represented a sensuous female pleasure principle, untamed by any central
authority or by any husband. Thirty years later, when the centralization process had been completed, the court had no further use for this kind of propaganda. The task of propagating a new morality that could enchain
desiring-production was shifted elsewhere; it "fell" into the hands of the
vanquished social group. The victors—the court with its central
authority—were now able to develop a less inhibited sensuality of the
privileged, a sensuality in which restraint was no longer necessary as a means
of safeguarding power. Thus in *L'Astrée* the nymphs (ladies of the court)
are seductresses who threaten the new ideal of the vanquished: the love-
marriage.[4] Shepherdesses and shepherds (members of the subordinate
stratum of the nobility, to which d'Urfé himself belonged) attempt to
demonstrate the superiority of the love-marriage and defend it against the
erotic enticements of the nymphs.[5] The novel is openly critical of court life.
In one scene Galatée, a nymph, tries to wean the protagonist, the shepherd
Céladon, of the "folly of faithfulness." Elias believes Galatée to be modeled
on the first wife of Henry IV, Marguérite de Valois. There seems to be a real
possibility that nymph and queen were indeed identical; Marguérite herself
has left to posterity a short story in which a shepherd makes no attempt to
resist seduction by a high-born lady, indeed the very highest-born of ladies.[6]
Yet d'Urfe's open criticism of the court, the king's willingness to have
L'Astrée dedicated to him,[7] and the queen's attempt to conceal the tendencies he attacks, only serve to render Elias's interpretation, that we are
witnessing a "continuation of the struggle through other means,"[8] uncon-
vincing. It seems to me more likely that the opposite was occurring, namely
an acquiescence to subordination (in the familiar form of petty rebellion).
Acquiescence of this kind is visible, for example, in the way in which an
earlier objective set originally by the now dominant sector of the
bourgeoisie—the desexualization of the bodies they aimed to dominate and
the consolidation of monogamy—is here taken over by the subordinate
stratum (against whom monogamy was still being used thirty years earlier as

a weapon in the ritualized struggle of the court dance). *L'Astrée*'s "thinly disguised polemic against the ruling court aristocracy"[9] was in fact welcomed by the court, as a tribute to the power it had now secured; after all, *L'Astrée* offered an object lesson to the lower orders in the behavior the court expected from them. (It was increasingly the bourgeoisie that provided a market for books on the "proper" way to live). In short, the defeated stratum relieved the court of the burdensome task of propagandizing for something it needed for the stability of its rule, but did not intend to practice. Why did the vanquished take up that burden? Because they had no other choice. They were no longer great lords, but they were still minor lords. The only way to hold onto that status was to begin working for the great lords. This is a typical course of action for a faction that has been defeated, but remains relatively powerful within the social hierarchy. Elias aptly describes such factions as "strata fighting on two fronts" (*Zweifrontenschichten*).[10]

Yet Elias's assessment of the space in society assigned to the defeated, as an area of free play in which certain criticisms could still be voiced, seems to me fundamentally misleading. He writes:

> They laid aside their swords and built themselves a play world, a
> mimetic world in which people dressed as shepherds and
> shepherdesses could live out the apolitical adventures of their
> hearts, above all the sorrows and joys of love, without coming
> into conflict with the constraints—the commandments and pro-
> hibitions—of the harder, nonmimetic world.[11]

And yet it was in this "playworld" that new modes of social behavior were tested, popularized, and finally forced into circulation. Out of all this "playing" came new laws to regulate civil life; the process was "apolitical" only in the sense that it no longer involved any direct battle for state power. The new image of woman presented by the ruling stratum to those whom they intended to maintain as subjects was the image of the "one-and-only." The only way to win her was with love—a love immune even to the benefits of a brief affair with the queen herself. Galatée, the nymph, elucidates those (political) benefits to the shepherd Céladon; but he declines to contemplate enjoying them. It could not have been made any clearer than this that the reader should also forgo the pleasures that Céladon forgoes here.[12] When a man's eyes were riveted on the one-and-only (who had by now slipped a little further down into the world), his attention was diverted from political power: "This representative of a middle-ranking nobility embodied a love-ethos that was to become a widespread ideal amongst the middle ranges of the bourgeoisie."[13] Soon the "one-and-only" would be available on the bourgeois marriage market, and put on display in bookstores and theaters.

At first glance the new love relationship, based on mutual trust between male one-and-only and female one-and-only, appears to have brought about the greatest possible intimacy and equality (or at least to have brought such a possibility into sight). In fact, however, the relationship concealed unexpected new problems, which arose out of the state now arrived at by the European ego. In the "self-distancing thrust"[14] Elias sees occurring in the sixteenth and seventeenth centuries—"thrust" being an unsatisfactory term, though it serves Elias's purpose in stressing the intensity of the process—a split occurred within human beings, decisively altering their relationships to themselves and to "reality." The nature of the relationship between reality and illusion became a pressing problem for humanity. It was no longer obvious "what was real, actual, objective, or whatever one chose to call it, and what was merely human thought, artifice, illusion—in short, what was 'subjective' and in that sense unreal."[15] Elias makes it clear that this troublesome dilemma was an *inevitable* by-product of the advancing process of self-distancing within the individual. The dilemma arose when the affective link between persons (the bourgeoisie and court at first) and their environment was broken. People ceased to exist within a panoramic environment, an uninterrupted sequence of immediate events; instead, human beings for whom the outside world was now a thing, the object of deliberate goals and purposes, learned to confront the environment as perspectivistic subjects. To achieve their goals and purposes, they needed a highly developed, highly controlled arsenal of behavior that would permit them to perceive and subdue the "objective world" with increasing efficiency. But as their affective relations to the external world were increasingly obstructed, parceled off, and made "instrumental," people became more and more puzzling to themselves. The more precisely they came to "know" objects—that is, to fit them into ordered, axiomatic systems—the more clouded their perceptions of themselves became. Up to this point, human emotions had poured out over the earth's body in a relatively uncontrolled, intense, and perilous fashion, allowing people to *experience* themselves; now the emotional "ground"—in the truest sense of that word—had been pulled out from under their feet.[16]

In fact this whole problematic is related to a specific change in the mechanisms for self-control that are deeply embedded in human beings—a change which led to the development of an armor that made them feel "separate" from the rest of the world and prevented them from finding convincing arguments to show that what penetrated that armor was not just an illusion, not something invented or added by them, and therefore real.[17]

With Descartes' formulation of the ego, which is because it "thinks," the observation of the self as a means of confirming one's own existence moved to the forefront of rationalist philosophy. This development created undreamed-of opportunities for men in power, in their "divide-and-rule" assault on human beings. The sexes had already been split asunder; now individual human beings could be divided internally. The man belonging to the social elite was particularly implicated here, since he was the first to develop the type of "ego" that made this internal splitting feasible. But the splitting of the "ego" was predicated on the cementing of the sexual division within society: this "ego" could only have been carved from the denial of any possible equality between intermingling bodies—a fact that Elias and a number of other historians fail to recognize.

This dividedness, this potential confusion over the state in which the subject finds itself, is, I believe, the beginning of an opposition between the "inner" and "outer" realms of the subject, which laid the foundation for a phenomenon recognized by modern researchers to be instrumental in producing the disconnected bodily state known as schizophrenia: the *double bind*. A double bind is a situation in which a person is simultaneously subjected to two commands or demands, each unavoidable, yet each contradicting the other or precluding its fulfillment. Added to that, the double bind makes it impossible to perceive that contradiction and thus either to adopt a critical, or some other metacommunicative stance in relation to it—"metacommunicative" in the sense of reacting to the *nature* of the demands made, not to their contradictory "contents" or "messages" (to use the terms adopted by these writers).

As one might have feared, the inventors of the very useful term "double bind" (Bateson, Jackson, Haley, and Weakland),[18] tended from the very start to familialize the concept. Since therapy takes the realm of the family as its point of departure, it is perhaps not surprising that theory too names the family as the most obvious birthplace of the double bind. The persons assumed to be making the contradictory demands are, first, the mother (as someone who makes contradictory demands on herself), then the mother and father. The alleged victim is the schizophrenized child, who obediently submits to the double bind (or *relationship trap*, as Bateson and others also call it) by splitting and tearing itself apart, so that it can fulfill both terms of the contradiction. If the child doesn't fulfill them, it faces death-by-withdrawal-of-love. One way or the other.

As we shall see, it is not strictly necessary to limit the notion of the double bind in this way.[19] It seems to me that there may be a whole series of double binds, or relationship traps, that arose out of the new divisibility of the human subject and became entrenched within the power structures of patriarchal capitalist society.[20] There is evidence of one such double bind in the new love relationship (between shepherd and shepherdess) promoted by d'Urfé in *L'Astrée*. Elias maps out the ramifications of this bond of unshakable love very nicely:

> The main theme is the passionate emotional bond between one
> unmarried young man and one unmarried young woman. This

bond, which can find its fulfillment only in marriage, is exclusive in the highest degree. It is this man's desire for that woman and no other and, conversely, the woman's desire for this man. In other words, the ideal of the love-bond presupposes a high degree of individualization. It precludes even the most transitory love-relationship between one of the partners and a third party. Yet because the two people in question have highly individual mechanisms for self-control, producing highly differentiated armored defenses, the strategy of courtship becomes more difficult and protracted than before. The young people in question are also so socially independent that their mothers and fathers can do very little to combat the force of the love-bond, even if they object to the choice of partner. In fact, that is what makes the courtship so difficult and dangerous: the two young people have to test each other. The game of love is influenced not only by the half-involuntary, half-deliberate masking of their emotions, but by their awareness of that masking and their reflections on it. What is really going on behind the partner's mask? How genuine and how reliable are the other person's feelings? . . . In a case like this, the young woman and the young man are forced to rely entirely on their own judgment and feelings.[21]

Here then the notion of "relying on one's own judgment and feelings" is propagated at a moment in history when, as we have seen, the ego is extremely uncertain of the reliability of its own judgment and feelings. Just when people had begun to wonder whether their feelings could claim any basis in reality and to fear that emotions were nothing more than insubstantial conceits, one such emotion—trust—moved into the center of male-female relationships. The relationship trap here consists in the demand that one should "have faith in one's own feelings," without knowing how to recognize or understand them, or which feelings belong to whom, or even which feelings one has oneself. (It is not difficult to see how quickly this situation can lead to a madness of mistrust, of oneself as well as others. The installation of a new divisive element has created a new potential for domination.)*

---

*Beginning in the fifteenth and sixteenth centuries, thought and experimentation were directed more and more toward the birth of a new test-tube human being (*homunculus*), or toward the rebirth of the self through meditation. These endeavors, which were at the very heart of the alchemists' "internal combustion processes" and the mystics' exertions strike me as reactions to the entanglement of male-female relationships. Among other things, they are attempts to create a new reality by circumventing the female body—to engender the world from the brain (as we saw happen in the Circe ballet at the court of Henry III). I had intended to describe the processes of *rebirth* and *bachelor birth* (which are important for fascism) in one of the chapters of this book, but this field proved extensive enough to warrant a separate study. I shall however have a little to say about this in volume 2. The catalog for an exhibition of "Bachelor Machines" (Venice, 1975) also contains some good material and passable articles on the subject.

Homages paid to the "one-and-only" are a good indication of how quickly and thoroughly she became the object of specific male desires, rather than a human being in a relationship between equals. One example is to be found in *Ännchen von Tharau* (Annie of Tharau), a wedding song that became popular in East Prussia sometime around 1650 and soon became known across the whole of Germany.

> Annie of Tharau I want as my mate.
> She is my life, my wealth and estate.

(All things the man would certainly miss if he had to do without them. What she is not is a person in her own right, a female self.)

> Annie of Tharau, my treasure, my goods!
> You are my soul, my flesh, and my blood.[22]

It would be insufficient to say that the woman in this case is simply a piece of property. She is rather a part of the masculine self that has been placed outside of him and now needs to be reincorporated. She is at once the medium for the desires of the male self and the name of the desired object. Soul-flesh-blood/wealth-estate-treasure-goods: coupled not for production, but joined together under the sign of antiproduction (lack as the guarantee of attachment).

> Sickness, grief, affliction, and pain,
> These the knotting of our love shall remain.

As if sensing the violent element—(the chains)—in this attachment (where emotion is absent and the defense against intimacy dominates), the writer seems to choose the ugliest word he can find to describe it in the song: knotting (*Verknotigung*). And as soon as the knot is tied, the woman is transported to the distant horizon; separation fantasies reign supreme even in the wedding song. The "one-and-only"—now a derealized every-woman—is ensconced in the near distance of permanent lack:

> And if you were suddenly parted from me,
> And lived where the sun people rarely could see,
> I would follow you still, through woods and through seas,
> Shackles and dungeons and armed enemies!
> Annie of Tharau, my light and my sun,
> I wrap my life around your own.

Follow? His pursuit will yet become a persecution and at the same time a movement of flight.*

---

*The song also demonstrates nicely where most of the products that anthologies label "folksongs" have come from in Germany: from the top down to the people. In imperial and fascist Germany, this song was made the common property of almost every German housewife, right down to the proletariat.

Sexualization of the Bourgeois Woman in the Seventeenth and Eighteenth Centuries

Up to this point—about the middle of the seventeenth century—efforts to implement monogamy and construct the bourgeois nuclear family were coupled with a desexualization of the people in question. Only the image of the noblewoman (an unattainable woman) had been sexualized in any fundamental sense. An intimacy ordained from above was accompanied, as we have seen, by a growing emotional distance between women and men, and a severing of people from their own feelings. The attempt to encode male desire with the image of the "one-and-only" seemed successful enough, but the end product of the process was neither particularly attractive nor particularly stable. No doubt this form of codification of male-female relations proved inadequate for preserving power during the great dissolving of boundaries in the century preceding the French Revolution of 1789—the era of the so-called Enlightenment. Unless the man's relationship to that "one-and-only" were made more enticing, all of the painstaking work of monogamization might be dissolved in the streams of a new desire for knowledge within a bourgeois world that was vigorously emancipating itself from absolutism. We know that the eighteenth century has entered history books as the "Gallant Age," even "The Woman's Century."[1] If those names were truly justified, then it would be almost impossible to understand how the nineteenth century became so completely a man's century. What happened to all of that progress made by eighteenth-century women? Didn't it amount to anything? Or is it the case rather that eighteenth-century women were partly permitted, partly coerced into a behavioral latitude that could be taken away from them at any time—a friendly semblance of freedom that has ensnared a number of interpreters? The contradiction is often contained in the very terms of tributes paid to women's new status, as when Elias writes:

> Marriage gains a special character in the absolutist court society
> of the seventeenth and eighteenth centuries, since it was in the
> construction of this society that the man's dominance of the
> woman was for the first time almost totally broken. The social
> power of women approached that of men; women played a large
> part in determining social opinion; and whereas society had
> formerly considered only men's extramarital relationships
> legitimate—those of the socially "weaker sex" were more or less
> harshly condemned—now women's extramarital relationships
> also became socially legitimate within certain bounds, in accord-
> ance with shifts in social relations of power between the sexes.[2]

The passage argues just as well for the opposite of what Elias is trying to prove. Women's "almost total" freedom from men's oppression refers here

"Phallic portrait" (late 18th century)
of Voltaire.

Rousseau.

only to the right to sexual escapades and certain other activities in an arena
Elias calls "social opinion." That in itself should have aroused his suspicion,
since social opinion is the very arena in which the civil reterritorialization efforts of the dominant groups took place, alongside more direct oppression
by the police, the army, and the judiciary. In other words, Elias is able to
reach his conclusions only by failing to ask what new form of male-female
relations had arisen and what kind of reality was being produced within
them (examining changes in the position of woman alone is never enough).
Furthermore, he says nothing about the continued exclusion of women from
all other areas of social production. How, then, can he infer that male
dominance had been all but broken?

Elias probably got that impression from the sudden, unmistakable
change that occurred in attitudes toward the sexuality of bourgeois women.
The drive toward monogamization and desexualization, which persisted
throughout the period from the fifteenth to the seventeenth century, was
halted in the eighteenth where bourgeois women were concerned. Most centrally, it was halted with respect to women of the upper nobility, for whom it
had, in any case, largely served as propaganda for the bourgeoisie and had
been dropped when the lesser nobility and bourgeoisie relieved the women of
the upper nobility of this specific function.

My first supposition about the purpose of this deliberate operation—we
will soon see that this is what it was—was that the "one-and-only" had to be
made more attractive if the fragile concepts of monogamy and the nuclear
family were to survive the prerevolutionary awakening of the bourgeoisie.
But there is another development to consider: the absolutist courts were

Le Comte d'Artois.   Mirabeau.

gradually losing their exclusivity. Wealthy middle-class citizens, higher officials, prominent scholars, and artists were making themselves at home on
the dance floors of the courts—especially in the numerous small courts of
German principalities, since here a bourgeois public sphere able to compete
with its aristocratic counterpart evolved later, for instance, than in France
(not to mention England, where the bourgeois revolution had ended—in
compromise—as early as 1688). As a result, the bourgeois public sphere, insofar as it existed, began to merge with that of the court. This meant that
noblewomen and bourgeois women encountered each other more and more
on the same dance floors, in the same social arena, although the hierarchical
distinctions between them had not yet been eradicated. As the female
representatives of coexisting, yet mutually hostile classes, these women
entered into a battle on the level of ideals, and the arena of that battle was
their sexuality. It is clear who had to be changed first, in order to have a
fighting chance: the bourgeois women. It is also clear what advantage the
noblewomen held: their "freer" sexuality, which had long been a weapon in
court intrigues and was an instrument of power and pleasure there.

This change favored the ruling group, insofar as the emerging public
sphere of social, scientific, and political life was encoded with a sexualized
femininity.[3] The two volumes on the "Gallant Age" in Eduard Fuchs's
History of Manners (*Sittengeschichte*) provide a wealth of information on
how this happened. To enhance their sexual attractiveness, women were
completely transformed by a process that began with the rearrangement of
their bodies. The body's external appearance is not immutable; the contours

"Self-examination." Copper engraving by Voyez (late 18th century).

of the flesh, being highly variable, can be manipulated in any number of ways; so too can posture and movements. Enter an array of helpful devices: laces, fabrics, colors, infinite modifications of the hair and speech (the modulation of which can be considered part of the external appearance). The goal of all this reconstruction is "beauty":

> *Beauty* is an exceedingly pleasing shape and highly agreeable arrangement of the female body, deriving from the correct proportions, size, number, and coloring of the limbs, and bestowed on

the female sex by God and nature, though progressively enhanced as well by individual finishing and the application of artificial improvements.

An excerpt from the *Ladies' Lexicon* (*Frauenzimmerlexikon*) published in 1715.[4] Books of this kind were introduced as manuals that urged women to learn the new role that gentlemen expected from them. And from start to finish, these manuals were normative. They demanded "correct proportion" and explained in detail what that "was." The *Frauenzimmerlexikon* listed "thirty components of complete beauty," as "required by a certain French writer." Along with the obvious ones, like

3. Not too fat, not too thin
14. A gracious smile
21. Small, reddish ears not standing too far away from the head

There were some outright pieces of artifice demanded of women:

6. A delicate skin, underlaid with tiny blue veins
22. A long, alabaster neck
30. Tiny, narrow feet, well-proportioned and facing outward

And (19) "a lovely, agreeable speech" from a mouth exhaling (18) "pure and gentle breath."

But even this scale was unreliable for measuring the degree of beauty a woman had painstakingly inculcated in herself, for "in matters of beauty, nothing can be determined in a certain and absolute sense." What was needed was another person for her to please, and that relativizer was none other than "the taste and mood of the male sex." Once again, a double bind was lurking here: you could make yourself as beautiful as you wanted (had to) and still not be loved.

Each part of the body was subjected to specific norms—ideal requirements that vacillated with the publication of new prescriptive books, such as *Squires of Beauty* (*Leibdiener der Schönheit*) in 1747, or *Academy of the Graces* (*Académie des Grâces*) in 1760. Calves, knees, thighs, the buttocks, and especially, the size, coloring, and shape of the breasts were constant objects of precise male demands. Women were obligated to make sure those demands were met.

According to Fuchs, depictions of women in literature were largely "composites of the most highly prized charms of the era, which were then simply given the rubric of some specific name." In the seventeenth century, the favored names were "Sylvia, Albania, Lesbia, Arismene, Rosilis"; in the eighteenth, they became "Fleurette, Phyllis, Röschen, Luise, Minna, and Laura."[5]

"La Curieuse," French engraving based on P. A. Wille (ca. 1780).

The eighteenth-century names show the degree to which actual, bourgeois women had come to embody the ideal norms of men, male ideals of "beauty." "The female beauty had the voluptuous buttocks and lovely breasts of the ladies of England, the fiery glance of the women of Poland."

"Le Bouton de Rose," French engraving by Voyez, based on P. A. Wille.

Or this, from *Squires of Beauty*: "A perfectly beautiful woman must have an English face, a German body, and a *podex* from Paris."[6] The frequent appearance of English women as models in these catalogs shows the extent to which the female body served as an arena of competitive display in the

"La Comparaison." Color engraving by Janinet, based on a painting by Lavreince (1786).

contest between the bourgeoisie and the nobility. In England, where absolutism had been deposed, bourgeois women occupied the highest rank. Consequently, English women were "the most beautiful"; it was they who offered the best material for the bourgeois dream represented in these images of women: beauty instead of freedom.

"The most popular pictorial device of the cult of beauty was the comparison." (Fuchs)[7] This pictorial convention placed women in constant opposition to an ideal image, as well as to their own bodies and those of other

"La comparaison des petits." Engraving by Chaponnier after a painting by Boilly (ca. 1788).

women. The road to "beauty" thus did *not* pass through woman's experience of her own body: it was simply one more road to her constitution as object and representation (though it included sexuality in this case). Fuchs writes:

> In every one of its artistic representations, communal bathing in particular strikes us as nothing more than a mutual display of voluptuous beauty and a continuous hidden competition.[8]

Doubtless, communal bathing can appear in this way not simply because the meaning of an (artistic) product is never exhausted in the

"The Bathers." English engraving by Bartolozzi.

represented object or the "message" it conveys, but because the competition (even for the space within the picture frame the river has to yield to the bodies) is clearly apparent—not "hidden" but open. And it is hardly "art for art's sake" when feet or breasts become objects of rivalry or when two female bathers offer their rear ends for "comparison" with the perfect buttocks of some Venus carved in stone. The putative goal is voluptuous pleasure with the right man. Witness the entry for *lasciviousness* (*Geilheit*) in the *Frauenzimmerlexikon:*

> *Lasciviousness, called salacitas* by Medici, is a continuous desire and constant appetite for lovemaking in women, deriving from the fiery, succulent, delicate, and voluptuous structure of their bodily parts and inciting them, accordingly, to ever increasing lust.[9]

The same lexicon recognizes a *furor uterinus*—also called "mother's rage" (*Wüten der Mutter*) or "man-madness" (*Mannstollheit*)—that is produced by "an imaginary conceit of a beautiful male subject and denial of intercourse"—that is, by unquenched lasciviousness.[10]

Since the quotations come from a manual for adolescent bourgeois girls, we can safely assume that an effort was being made to train women to function sexually.[11] Young women were supposed to learn to feel the yearning within themselves; and if they felt no lasciviousness, they were missing the decisive attribute of femaleness.

Fuchs stresses that the process of eroticizing women occurred "in the consciousness [of society as a] whole. . . . There was no room for even the slightest questioning of the claim that a powerful epidemic of man-madness was conspicuously rampaging through the female population."[12] It's as if the process of witch-hunting had been turned on its head: bourgeois women were now commanded to do what the women of the common people had been burned for doing earlier. Bourgeois women were being fashioned into images of sex goddesses;[13] to the extent that they were allowed to be sensuous, they were expected to crave sex.*

It wasn't only the work of Kepler, Galileo, Descartes, and Newton—the "arrival of reason," as Jules Michelet claims in his 1862 work, *The Witch*—that caused witches to "disappear" in the seventeenth century. More likely, the dominant groups sensed that the breaking down of old boundaries by the new sciences would have to be countered in a new way. This is what led the Colbert government to prohibit its tribunals from hearing any accusations of witchcraft in 1672.[14] How would the new cult of beauty ever take root if women's bodies continued to be burned in public? The taint of evil had to be removed from the erotic, if eroticism (now appearing as a quality of the body of women from the rising social strata) were to serve its purpose, namely to fill the emerging bourgeois-absolutist public sphere with love stories, instead of discussions of how the princes could be driven from the face of the earth. Louis XIV, the absolutist appendage of his bourgeois regent, Colbert, set an example for this aberrant trail by chasing after "skirts" (Fuchs calls Louis an "erotomaniac").

The persecution of sexuality in women of the subordinate classes didn't end at this point, and neither did their real exploitation, but both ceased to be put on public display. Instead, internment in asylums (with an independent jurisdiction, like that of the Inquisition)[15] replaced public persecution; the manufacturing plants increasingly took over the task of absorbing female sexuality (and "breeding" surplus value); and the process of monogamization traveled "downward," having once again loosened its grip "up above" in the course of the sexualization of the bourgeois woman.

Male historiography tends to see this slackening of the "elevated"

---

*And their sexuality had to be centered on the opposite sex. The first books claiming that onanism led to insanity appeared at about the same time as the sexualization of bourgeois women. In *the Manufacture of Madness*, Thomas Szasz places the publication of the first book against onanism in the year 1716 (London). The renowned work by Tissot, the French medical "authority," appeared in 1758. Later, the persecution of masturbation entered the domain of psychiatry. What was occurring, then, was not a universal sexual liberation, but a specific new channeling of sexual functions: the massive persecution of masturbation (neologism: *Masturbationsirresein*, literally "masturbatory insanity") made it possible to harness the uncontrolled process of sexualization with an effective, new double bind.

"English Beauty." "Allegro," by Westfall. Portrait of Lady Hamilton.

woman's sexual chains at the end of the seventeenth and into the eighteenth
century as a consequence—in fact, as the crowning point—of the Enlightenment. It seems clear to me that it was also an *anti*-Enlightenment process
that was sustained by a double female sacrifice. Absolutist noblemen offered
the first sacrifice; they prostituted their women by "lowering" them into the
domain of the upper-bourgeois male's (no longer purely fictive) phallus.
Noblewomen began to haunt the minds and novels of bourgeois men as
lovers, and in more than a few gallant adventures these men got as far as the
women's chambers. The divine lords yielded up their women in order to
preserve their thrones. The second female sacrifice came from the

bourgeoisie: "Sexual pedagogy was carried out most intensely on the daughters of the petite and middle bourgeoisie," but they were told that "their charms were far too refined for the sensuous divertissement of Franz, the boy next door." (Fuchs)[16] In *Letters on the Gallantries of Berlin* (*Briefen über die Galanterien von Berlin*), we read:

> A mother who has a beautiful daughter will often undress her at bedtime, admire her splendid figure, and ecstatically proclaim to the little Medici Venus: "Oh, my dear little Minna, you shall surely marry a councilor or nobleman some day!"[17]

By 1782, when the passage was written, speeches like that were "often" given. Here is a mother in a later work:

> Dearest girl, when first you came
> Pretty hoods I made you,
> Fair of face and sweet of frame
> Softly I arrayed you,
> Saw you in my hopes a bride,
> Rich in wedded rank and pride;
> So my thoughts portrayed you.

But:

> Parties, cunning though their aim,
> Brought a conquest never . . .

And finally:

> Fools today come on apace;
> Dearest, give your fond embrace,
> Make one yours forever. (*Faust II*)[18]

Bourgeois mothers helped with the sale of their daughters' bodies in order to get a bit closer to the throne. The daughters' only chance to rise socially (outside of revolution) was by marrying an "upper-class" man.[19] As a rank that led instead away from revolution, this was a prototype of nonrevolutionary structural displacement within the power relations of a society. The displacement operated on the basis of female sacrifice.

In accepting these terms, the bourgeois man renounced revolution (by the grace of his lord, he would receive a morsel of power). He also renounced any human relation of production to the woman of his own class or stratum, by once again preventing her from becoming his equal. The reality produced within the relationship that did arise was characterized by sexuality as a market value, love as a technique, and a system of extramarital lovers as a logical consequence of the missing relationship within the marriage. Women had to be kept away from any work, including the work of raising

"In the Loge." French engraving of an earlier work by J. M. Moreau the younger.

children. Nursing infants was considered disgraceful, according to Fuchs: "Most women swallowed powders that were said to drive the milk out of the breasts within forty-eight hours."[20] Sometimes the marriage contract stipulated that the woman should be relieved of such tasks.[21] Breasts had a sexual value from which any other function might detract.[22]

Writers had all the work they could handle. After all, women had to be trained ("cultivated") for their new responsibilities—to be filled with images, and in the end to become images themselves. Women learned to dance, sing, and play instruments. Bourgeois men, not averse to striking Enlightenment poses either, rushed to demonstrate their own castration. A man was suspected of being an enemy of the state, and no true cuckold, if he didn't compose aphorisms, treatises, and gallant tales of the profound, sublime, true, real, unreal, mysterious, charming, finite, infinite, and unfathomable nature of the female sex. In illustrated magazines for women, men offered women verses, songs, pictures, worldly wisdom, and advice on love. That was indeed the whole purpose of the illustrated magazines. Above all, though, there were novels. "If novels were brought into every discussion of political, religious, and philosophical issues, they were almost indispensable for the delineation of sexual problems and theories." (Fuchs)[23] These novels (Fuchs calls them "manuals of sentimental love") appeared in the magazines in serialized form. Once the heroic and political elements had been eliminated, the world of the novel became an arena for frivolous adventures[24] (bourgeois literary historians, notably Frenzel and Frenzel, recognize this change but fail—predictably—to draw any conclusions from it). *The Cavalier Reeling through the Maze of Love* (*Der im Irrgarten der Liebe herumtaumelnde Kavalier*) is the title of a novel written in 1738 by Johann Gottfried Schnabel. Converting the garden of love to a maze seemed to be the assigned task of bourgeois- and noblewomen. Seen from a great distance—from the summit of the male historian's mind—that process might look like emancipation.

The Reduction of Woman to the Vagina and Her Enlargement into the Sea of Seas

Centering on the sexuality of women appeared in literature as a centering on their primary sexual characteristics. All that was valued in the depiction of women was their erotic physiognomy,[1] especially the breasts and, of course, the vagina, which appeared in titles of poems as *die Schooss* (lap, or womb). This brings us to the conclusion of one of the main trains of thought in this chapter: it was in the breasts and vaginas of women sexualized in this manner that global seas began to flow for men of the era.

> As an amorous wind drives the sails of my senses upon the shipless sea of her marble breast, I spy Venus swimming on two shells, the pure milk of grace adhering 'round her rubies.[2] (*Die asiatische Banise* [*Banise of Asia*], a novel written in 1689 by H. A. Ziegler)*

It isn't enough to say, as Fuchs does, that Venus has become mortal ("always a fully or half-clad lady of the salon"),[3] or that "we see the whole land filled with numerous mortal angels,"[4] as Baron Pölnitz wrote around 1700. Venus didn't enter the entire body; she simply transformed herself into a specific notion of the vagina. In his poem *Die Schooss* (1700), Johann

---

Banise is a woman's name.—Trans.

"The Novel Reader." Engraving by Westfall.

Besser illustrates this point at extravagant length. In what might appear a parody of the new punctiliousness of the sciences, Besser expends some 150 stanzas on an attempt to fathom the nature of the site he calls the "fountain-head of all delight." In a separate introduction to the poem in Besser's collected works (which were dedicated to Frederick I), his publisher recounts the celebrated history of the poem. He notes how much it had pleased the electoress (*Kurfürstin*) Sophie, who had received it through the good offices of Leibniz; and how, even before it was printed, the poem had wandered from her hand into those of countless ladies of princely rank, each one of these high-born ladies finding it equally enchanting.[5]

> As the magnet draws the iron unto itself with might,
> As toward the northern pole the needle lines its sight,
> The womb of the beloved is magnet and true north,
> Toward which the *whole desire** of feeling men goes forth.
> They say that Venus was, her nature to disguise,
> Not in the common way, but specially from the tides,
> Conceived and born within the helmet of a shell,
> Where she by ocean's froth was rocked and suckled well.

---

*The emphasis is mine.

Who lends this credence not, who Venus' doings weighs?
Yet since a lady's womb a shell's image o'erlays:
I hold when Venus first into the world was brought,
The thing from whence she came to ladies' womb she wrought;
That, when the goddess left her armored shell behind,
And wanting human hearts to be therein enshrined,
Within the wombs of women the shell she did contain,
And afterwards descended unto her home again.[6]

A sad state of affairs indeed: we read this tribute to the divine vagina of the electoress in a volume dedicated to her lord, the elector; written by the king of royal poets; and handed to the electoress by the great philosopher-scientist. The great lady is enraptured, and the great lord extends the poet's commission. In the numerous other womb-poems Fuchs cites, the vagina is always a sea of all delights that has been installed in a woman's body; the vagina is "a garden, drenched in the dew of voluptuousness," or "a haven of pleasure for the sugar'd fleet."[7] Above all, the vagina becomes the utopian site of an absence of lack. In the end, it doesn't matter in which woman that utopia is contained, as long as she is a high-born beauty.

No purple peach so soft and gently split,
No crevice in the world with such abundance (Besser)[8]

This is the site of earthly paradise. In another poem along the same lines, we read: "You fountain, never parched or frozen over."[9] Or "an abyss from which the world can fish out pearls." (C. F. Hunold)[10] The alleged sensuousness and frivolity of rococo is invalidated when women's bodies are made substitutes for the body of the earth, which the male "lover" then renounces.

'Mid stormy bolts I sail away
Across your new-discovered world,
Whenever waves around me spray
And foam onto the bed is hurled.
(Gottlieb Sigmund Corvinus)[11]

She is *greater* than the whole world. "In a word, it seemed as if nature had totally depleted itself for her benefit"[12] (Pölnitz, writing about the celebrated beauty Aurora von Königsmarck). A further example: the numerous geographies and ethnologies that appeared in the eighteenth century always opened with physical portraits of women from the countries in question. (Fuchs)[13]

* * *

But the time was not far off when men would begin to take revenge for the false promises held out by women's bodies. The sexualized woman

"La Comparaison." French engraving by Bouillard, based on a painting by Schall (late 18th century).

would become an erotomaniacal monster who was out to suck the marrow from men's bones. Sexualization would prove to be the prerequisite for turning upper-class, erotic women into witches, vampires, femmes fatales—as happened in the nineteenth century, when bourgeois states began to withdraw internal freedoms to suppress sexuality anew, to mold the unrobed and vulnerable woman into a "bell-shaped,"[14] secret erotomaniac. Underneath those skirts that reached to the ground, a terrifying penis would sprout: a snake; a dragon; an avenging father who, now that he had other uses for her, had taken his own woman out of circulation and locked her up. The bourgeoisie (in Victorian Britain, Wilhelmine Germany, or any of its other bastions) needed soldiers to fight the proletariat and to serve in the coming imperialist wars. And the easiest way to get soldiers is to remove women from public life, that is, from the very social space women had been *granted* in the eighteenth century. And if male-female sexuality were publicly persecuted, then bondings between males would form of their own accord.

Toward the close of the eighteenth century, it had already become fairly difficult to carry out the role of "being more than the world" in society. Only a virtuosa like the Marquise de Merteuil (*Les Liaisons Dangereuses*) could manage it, and even then only as a manifestly "evil" woman. She had to duplicate herself:

"Mary Magdalen," Felicia Rops (late 19th century).

We had six hours ahead of us; I was determined to make this a time of uninterrupted rapture for him and therefore tempered his storms with charming coquetry. Never, I believe, have I gone to such trouble to please; I was truly content with my own efforts. After dinner, I alternated between playing the child and the rational woman, now displaying reason, now sensibility, or even licentiousness. I enjoyed treating him like a sultan, leading him into his harem where I played all of his favorites. All of this came from the same woman, though to him it must have seemed as if each pleasure came from a new lover.[15]

Being all women at once: it was this quality that (in the end) doomed the "one-and-only" to failure, for the possibility of the charge "She deceived me" is contained in her construction from the very beginning.

German Classicism: The Woman-Machine and the "New Morality" as a Further Erosion of the Shores of Woman-Nature

The authors of German classicism responded to the sexualization of the bourgeois woman with a new morality, a new cult of the "one-and-only" and a new image of the high-born woman.

In Germany, as elsewhere, the bourgeoisie had become more powerful and more self-assured. Out of the aristocratic-bourgeois public, there evolved a new bourgeois public sphere which, though opposed to the courts, lacked the power to attack them in any fundamental way. What then happened was typical of power constellations of this kind. Attacks against the absolutist nobility began to center on its *immorality*, rather than its political hegemony.[1] On the grounds that the new freedoms were practiced in perverse form by the dominant class—in an atmosphere of social intrigues, diversions, and deceit—the men of the rising class, too weak for revolution, retracted every one of those new freedoms and began to fight them under the banner of a new morality. The women of bourgeois tragedy were killed off by their authors in an attempt to keep their bodies free of the taint of an aristocratic embrace; Lessing and Schiller used daggers and vials of poison to ensure that the bodies of bourgeois maidens remained undefiled. The class conflict was acted out through love stories. (Would noblemen have gone unnoticed if they hadn't fallen in love with musicians' daughters?) In the place of any real humbling of the nobility, there was an exaltation of bourgeois women—their persistent elevation into the titles of dramas. As dead or exalted figures, bourgeois women provided the building blocks of the classical aesthetic (whereas the writers themselves pined away in more or less unrequited loves for women of the aristocracy). Emilia Galotti, Luise Millerin, a gullible Kätchen, a charming Klärchen (appearing in a dream to Egmont as a goddess of freedom), an Iphigenia, forced to *reconcile* the world with itself, without first securing the liberation of women; then, once again, queens and female saints: Mary Stuart, surpassing the terrible queen (no *real* woman) in beauty and humanity; the Maid of Orleans, representation of the *sublime*; and on and on, each one more noble than the last, the noble forerunners of life-size, inflatable rubber dolls advertised in the Sears & Roebuck catalog (Chicago, Winter 1964/65ff.). A whole host of men—the intellectual lights of the age—who proved too weak to take hold of the new freedoms and implement them, who dodged the issue by inventing interesting images of women, gave these images properties that surpassed those of the real women they represented (thus they avenged themselves on the women of the aristocracy). Fixated on images of the sublime, men no longer needed to bring power relations so sharply into focus. At last, they could openly scoff at the French Revolution for drowning in blood, while they themselves remained so damnably humane* (or they could spill their crocodile tears).[2] They could dream on about some higher paradise, while the newly allied nobility and monied bourgeoisie, sprouting factory owners and military apparatuses, prepared to turn the country into a prison.

Streams were channeled—into factories and chancelleries. Streams of sweat became streams of money. See the world? Sure, but only as a soldier (well-drilled streams). Blood was allowed to flow (red-black-yellow, the colors of the flag), but even that was turned into a stream of money in a pre-

---

*That's what Goethe, "ironically," called his Iphigenia-figure.

"Die Freiheit" (Freedom), Alfred Böcklin (1891).

scribed riverbed—the same riverbed along which the first streams of tourists flowed. The sperm-stream flowed into the one-and-only. Streams of words on the freedom of the human race trickled away into images of sublime woman.* When Kofler says that German classicism "remained irretrievably caught up in the ethereal realms of humanist ethics and aesthetics,"[3] the

---

*"Inventing sweet images of women/Such as the bitter earth does not contain," is what the writer Gottfried Keller termed "the loveliest of all poetic sins." He was guilty of that sin himself, although he did rework *Green Henry* (*Der grüne Heinrich*), his best-known novel, in an attempt to hide traces of it. Those characters who elude previously encoded definitions, because their desire is not so easily deceived, are given a special coding; the curse of restlessness is placed on Ahasver, Don Juan, and the Flying Dutchman (the man who never stops searching, who never lands, is doomed to wander aimlessly). The figure of the dandy, conversely, seems to proceed by deterritorialization. He lets himself be carried along in the stream of urban humanity, coupling himself to the metropolitan-machine without tracing the multiplicity of the labyrinth back to a fictive female body. Even Paris is something like a "one-and-only"; though it doesn't stand for anything outside of itself, it has a concrete reality.

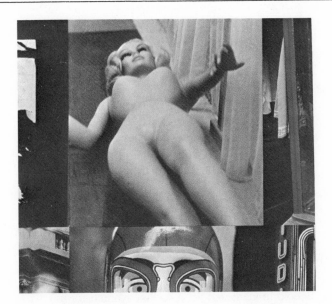

formulation misses the concrete element: classicism soared to those heights on images of women. (You need some concrete material even for rising up into the clouds.) The word "irretrievably" doesn't quite fit here either; images of women were, in fact, retrieved and used to excess in the nineteenth century as repressive models for bourgeois women; for them the principles of what Kofler calls "ethics and aesthetics" remained perhaps quite literally "overriding."

It seems that all those Gretchens, Kätchens, and Klärchens, sprang from the self-deception of impotent men (and that the "classical" writers' impotence in the face of woman was a social phenomenon, not a personal one). What did these men—officials, theater and newspaper people, professors—have to do with the aristocratic wives of wealthier bourgeois citizens?[4] Well, some of the men had once been private, household tutors. That wasn't such a bad vantage point from which to study the powerful, unless you happened to fall in love with your master's spouse. When a man worshiped his master's wife—by drawing her portrait, writing verses for her, and so on—he was exchanging his revolutionary potency for a few scraps of social power (prestige, rouge, small change, laurel wreaths) given by the grace of that master—and for actual impotence (since desire can't be fooled).

Life on the summit isn't only lofty and sublime; it is also dry. The seas continue to flow down below and become the enemy, that gnaws, as it were, at the peaks. There is exemplary evidence of this in the second part of *Faust*, the rhymed antecedent of Freud's *Civilization and Its Discontents*.

Helen. She follows Euphorian (= Icarus), the son she and Faust had together, into death. The stage directions dictate: "She embraces Faust; her bodily form vanishes, her robe and veil are left in his arms." Phorkyas to Faust:

> True, this is not the goddess you have lost,
> But godlike it is. Take the priceless gift
> To serve the flight in which you soar aloft;
> 'Twill bear you swiftly up above all dross,
> On through the ether, if you can endure.
> We meet again, far, very far from here.

Directions: "The garments of Helen dissolve into clouds; enveloping Faust they lift him on high and bear him from the scene."[5]

At the beginning of the fourth act, Faust lands in the "Mountain Heights" on this cloud. The cloud sails off to the east, disperses, and an image appears. Faust:

> In pillowed splendor couched, soft-gilded by the sun,
> Behold, a giant and yet a godlike woman-form
> And well I see, like Juno, Leda, Helen—so
> In lovely majesty it glides before my sight.[6]

(The woman from whose robes the cloud has arisen is so allegorically vague as to allow her image to bear the names of several *homologous* women.) And then:

> Now like the soul's pure beauty mounts the lovely form,
> Nor suffers change, but floats to ether far on high,
> And all that's best within my soul it bears away.[7]

It's easy for the man of culture to say that the "best within [his] soul" remained with the woman he abandoned. She was a way station. Only by re-nouncing love does he arrive at some destination: the work of culture. In the end, Faust is a colonizer, the bourgeois in power. And what does he want Mephistopheles to help him with?

> To hold the lordly ocean from the shore,
> To set the watery waste new boundary lines,
> And bid it wallow in its own confines.[8]

Faust becomes an ocean-dammer, a land-reclaimer. His beloved has hardly been consigned to heaven, and already nature is being subdued again down below; already it is being coupled with images of unfettered femaleness. Once again, women are being dammed up with the sea:

> A paradise our closed-in land provides,

Though to its margin rage the blustering tides;
When they eat through, in fierce devouring flood,
All swiftly join to make the damage good.

. . . .

With dangers thus begirt, defying fears,
Childhood, youth, age shall strive through strenuous years.[9]

It isn't as if the old bourgeois priest simply forgot to mention women here: they are objects of the process, not its beneficiaries. Their part in the process is not of this earth:

All things corruptible
Are but a parable;
Earth's insufficiency
Here finds fulfillment;
Here the ineffable
Wins life through love;
Eternal Womanhood
Leads us above.[10]

Those are the final words of the story, uttered by the *chorus mysticus.* Finis. The elderly Freud defined culture-work (*Kulturarbeit*) in exactly the same way: draining out the Zuider Zee, because the love object (the "mother") was unattainable. But that is a construct; women are unattainable only because they have been sacrificed. This is the starting point of sublimation, a form of male dominance over the earth, women, and men's own affects.[11] Culture could have arisen without that sacrifice, but men could not have remained dominant.[12]

The ineffable that wins out at the end of *Faust* is nothing other than a signed contract for dominance—a contract that bases male production on the division of the sexes and the subjugation of woman-nature. The gist of the pact is that Mephistopheles (who always speaks the truth about bourgeois society) assumes all responsibility for crimes committed by productive bourgeois men. Women are subjugated; the man (Faust) is exonerated; and the guilt is borne by the Evil Spirit, Dr. Faust's public Mr. Hyde. Faust has entered into a pact with his Doppelgänger, the external embodiment of his soul. The dear old man is able to slip into heaven at the last minute becaue the Doppelgänger, Mephistopheles, is busy ogling the behinds of some little angels, which he takes for the buttocks of juicy he-devils. Goethe's insidious joke—allowing the homosexual to break through—underscores the impetus for the pact: men's love of self and other men, which prevents their souls from reaching women.

*　*　*

Jean Paul handles the subject of women in a way that is different, more difficult to interpret:*

> Before she is worshiped as a divine statue, every beautiful woman is set on a pair of high-heeled shoes, as on a pedestal; she is also described as the first story, or ground floor, of the entire female building.[13]

And since he saw the women of his day, who were considered "divine statues," as having no other necessary or permissible function, he counseled the rest of the world to follow his lead. The heading of one of his early works reads: *Simple, yet well-intended biography of a new and pleasing woman of pure wood, whom I long ago fashioned and married.* In this work, he had no trouble explaining in detail why nothing would be lost if flesh-and-blood women were replaced by wooden ones. What would the real difference be, after all?

> If a wealthy man wants to give another wealthy man fifty thousand dollars, let him deliver the money as before through his daughter; only now she'll be made of wood.[14]

We can already see that Jean Paul didn't present his characters (images) as women. His subject matter was not so much women themselves, as the functions bourgeois society assigned to women around the year 1800:

> True, the princess wrapped up her portrait and sent it on ahead; and that is all the prince knew and loved—especially since, like every original, it was far lovelier than the living copy that was to follow. It was with this painting that the regent consummated his nuptials.[15]

Those two passages are chosen only to give an impression of a text that is almost impossible to quote as a body of coherent thought, since any coherence is too readily deconstructed in the ironic, relativizing mesh of his syntax to be isolated in quotations. There is not so much a construction of false images in Jean Paul's mode of writing as a process of dissolution.

His wooden woman is not an image, but a machine. And significantly, she is a nonimitative machine. That makes her different from other technological machines which operate like human beings and which, in the eighteenth century, begin to replace the *homunculi* that had grown (like Vaucanson's flutist)[16] from horse manure and virgin's blood. Jean Paul's "new and pleasing woman of pure wood" is a desiring-machine that is deprived of life only because living women have been degraded to objects of cheated desire. Imitating or exalting these women would have led desire out

---

*Jean Paul Richter (1763-1825), a noted German writer and, in fact, something like a Goethe-antipode!

into the desert, where streams—even abundant ones—immediately dry up without a trace.

Thus it was that Herr Kempelen's plan to construct playing- and talking-machines displeased Jean Paul, for this promised to take bread from the mouths of sportsmen, on the one hand, and women on the other. Besides, what would be gained by having machines do what human beings did poorly anyway? With that in mind, he asked whether Herr Kempelen

> might not have better served his honor and his virtue if
> he . . . had pondered hard and finally managed to create
> thinking-machines. For since so few professions make use of
> thinking, he would then have caused little or no harm, the more
> so because those few whom the rivalry of thinking-machines
> would seem to have deprived of a livelihood, would surely have
> died of hunger even without that rivalry.[17]

Jean Paul saw the social functionalizing of "high-born" women as a false mechanizing of their bodies (prepared speeches from robot-mouths, the striking of beautiful poses, etc.); and in the deployment of technological machines to ape the machinery of human musculature, he saw an unnatural—or at the very least, superfluous—application of technology. In his view, therefore, "high-born" women belonged neither in the theatrical machinery of the "sublime," nor in the machinery of contemporary sexuality. His remark that "until now, no platonic love for a living woman has been able to hold out longer than a coiffure," might have been directed equally against the classical propagandists of the cult of the sublime, or against the propagandists of sexualization.[18] From goddesses and screwing-machines to embodiments of monetary value; all these were better represented by wooden dolls . . . even if this did take one drug for the minds of sleepless thinkers out of circulation:

> It is the sad fate of women (and everyone) that when love is un-
> commonly platonic, it does not last. The greatest thinkers have
> sat up past midnight to ferret out the cause of this, but as far as
> I know, they haven't come up with anything.[19]

But had they come up with anything, they would then, like Oedipus—who ferreted out his own crimes—have been struck blind on the spot.

In the course of an "ordering" and centralizing subjugation of the land, the body of the high-born woman was geometricized into fragmentary, or-namental representations. This process was followed, it seems, by a false mechanizing of the productive capacity of the high-born woman (this time in the context of a nascent, machinic unfettering of economic production within bourgeois-absolutist society).

"The Machine," Jean Veber (ca. 1900).

Here too, then, it seems that a change in economic production and in the forms of dominance is cemented with a new, modern mode of control of women's bodies—for it is indeed renewed control (in the guise of freedom) that is at stake here. The multiple functionings of desiring-machines, which by nature couple partial drives with part-objects, are ruptured the very moment that the mechanizing of women begins (hence the use of the term "false"). Confined to particular social functions in the public sphere (judgments) and to the (hypertrophied) sexual function, women become totality-machines (*Ganzheitsmaschinen*) centered on the mouth and the vagina. (In most men's minds, they continue to exist as blabbermouths and fucking-machines.)

In the nineteenth century, the association of machinery with sexuality remained in effect, at least where the erotic woman was concerned. As a new campaign for the open suppression of female sexuality began to take effect, women were once again "withdrawn" from the public sphere. Factory machines and female genitalia were equally held back from bourgeois consciousness, becoming instead the stuff of ominous dreams. (They didn't enter the unconscious, though; they were revealed to a select audience and otherwise concealed.)[20]

* * *

We should bear in mind that none of the historical functions of women, none of the modelings of the female image was ever completely obliterated by its successor or through "obsolescence." As long as the body of woman continues to serve as a territory of desire in place of the body of the earth, which is withheld, there is no need for historical images to die away. Capitalism, once evolved, can reproduce and activate those images at will. (In the first chapter of this book, we had some living proof that these images never die.) That is precisely what Deleuze and Guattari are trying to stress when they describe capitalist ideologies as a random collage of everything that has ever been believed.[21]

One of the main reasons why forms of oppression that are no longer current can be reutilized is to be found in the constant dissimultaneity of developments within capitalism. Ernst Bloch, who pointed out the significance of this in *Legacy of Our Age* (*Erbschaft dieser Zeit*, 1935), confirmed the same view in a recent interview in the journal *Kursbuch*.[22] One of capitalism's principal strengths is indeed its ability to make its history current by artificially reconstructing it; for in the crosscurrents of those dissimultaneities, with the *technological reproducibility of history*, conflicts of the historical past can also be brought into the present. No past class conflict or gender relation will ever be wholly dead or unimportant, as long as the capitalist mode of production remains able to create the conditions for reintroducing it within the diverse territories of its own domain of power. Perhaps this is why hardly any of the possibilities for setting the oppressed against each other have been permanently consigned to history.

Into the Nineteenth Century: Crystalline Wave/ Concealed Woman—from Water to Blood

"These authors write like the final generation,"[1] Heinrich Mann* said of the German romantics (referring especially to those after 1813). The freedom-fighting spirit, whatever there was of it in Germany, fizzled out in the so-called wars of liberation, which ended in the defeat of the national enemy, Napoleon, but which also strengthened the power of princes and kings at home.[2]

The process of restricting the emancipatory potential of production—a process linked to the empowerment of the European bourgeoisie (in Germany, in league with the nobility)—once again made specific use of the territory of female bodies. The chief characteristic of this new usage was a prescribed concealment of women, in contrast to the public display of women in the preceding era. It soon became evident how firmly and successfully the codification of political and aesthetic utopias with the female body had already been anchored in men's feelings. Defeated and disap-

---

*The works of Heinrich Mann (1871-1950), celebrated writer and brother of Thomas Mann, include *Professor Unrat*, adapted for the screen as *The Blue Angel.*—Trans.

pointed, they returned to previous promises of freedom encoded on the female body and took their vengeance on that body itself.

As if women had been the ones to claim that their bodies were more than all the rest of the world, they were made responsible for the lie of sexualization. In the course of the nineteenth century, the erotic woman becomes the devouring demon. As if she had been the deceiver, as if she had promised rivers, springs, and wide oceans, she now meets her death by drowning. As a drowned corpse, she floats through the literature of the romantic period—and of all those that follow.[3]

In Lautréamont's song of the ocean, vengeance extends to the principle of flowing itself:

> Ancient ocean with your crystalline waves, you are laid out like the azure stains we see on the beaten backs of cabin boys; you are a monstrous blue beaten into the back of the earth.

After a colon, he adds: "I love this comparison."[4] "Crystalline waves" equal frozen flow. The limitless blue has become the color of a cruel delimitation of bodily boundaries. In place of "never landing," a whip.

All of the flows in which the body might have dissolved and discarded its armor are now stemmed. Held within all too narrow confines, desire begins to swirl in dangerous currents; under the mounting pressure, attention turns inward to processes of explosion, eruption, implosion.

After a time, Mary Shelley's Dr. Frankenstein can see human beings only as monsters thirsting after the blood of their neighbors.[5] The monster he constructs, in an attempt to create the perfect human being,[6] is the first in a long series of creatures that embody the evil streams of their creators' inner abysses—or more precisely, that *come* to embody those streams (the creatures can be made evil only by the world that afflicted their creators).

All of these streams, good and evil, begin to coalesce in the inner stream of the blood. Within the bodies of people who have come to view the dissolving of boundaries as a process of destruction, the blood slowly absorbs the energy of the dammed-up currents, which will later try to discharge themselves through fascism, as in the lava streams we encountered at the start of this chapter.

First, blood replaces water in declarations of love:

> Good night, dear angel! Oh! whether You are the one or not, open all the veins of Your white body and let the hot, frothy blood spurt from a thousand blissful fountains; I want to see and drink you like that, drink from the thousand springs till I am drunk and can mourn your death in jubilant frenzy, crying all Your blood back into You and mine in tears, until Your heart heaves once again and You have faith in me, because my blood lives in Your pulse.

Untitled drawing by Gibson (late 19th century).

This is Clemens Brentano,* writing in 1805 to Karoline von Günderode.

It would be nonsense to claim that the romantics were intellectual forerunners of fascism—there are no such forerunners. And no one ever becomes a fascist on the basis of things that were thought or written earlier; he evolves out of his own circumstances. Still, a number of romantic texts react to the damming up of flows in early nineteenth-century, capitalist-patriarchal society in a way that can help us to understand the reaction of twentieth-century fascists to the armor they were trained to wear.[7]**

Brentano's yearning for "fountains" of blood can still be understood as an act of love toward the specific body of a woman. He wants to unite with that body through the commingling of his and her blood. Here the affect has been converted into its opposite, but still clings to its original object. Most important, though, the affect is aware of itself. Romantic terror is premeditated; it is a triumph of consciousness (de Sade, Byron, Shelley, Maturin). Romantic "evilness" is intentional, calculated. When the fascist awakens from his destructive frenzy, by contrast, he does not believe he has really been evil.

As bodies (the sexes) were increasingly isolated from each other and from themselves (interior-versus-exterior) in the latter half of the nineteenth century, the connection with an object became more tenuous. In literature,

---

*Brentano (1778-1842) was a writer of the romantic period in Germany.—Trans.

**Other romantic works reveal very different reactions. Some of those can be found in Margaretha Huber's *Enigmas* (Rätsel), a marvelous book (illustrated by Magdalena Palfrader) that I have been wandering around in for a while and that will continue to occupy me for some time to come. Huber writes: "I peer into the mysterious realm of a lost way of thinking, the door to which romanticism opened just a crack." (Frankfurt, 1978)

the surging of the blood and fears of inundation were rarely tied directly to women anymore; their threat was communicated only through the affective intensity of passages in which men talked about imminent catastrophes.[8] The love object, withheld from men and negativized, had dissolved into an all-encompassing, threatening principle called (among other things) femininity. Externally as a Red flood, internally as an infernal maelstrom of terrifying desires, this principle threatened to deluge men and break them apart. (I'll stop here for the moment. Later on in this chapter, I'll have more to say on this whole complex as it arises in the texts of the soldier males themselves.)

Closing Remarks

I have attempted here to describe some of the changes that occurred in the history of bourgeois Europe in female-male relations of production, as well as the various concomitant processes whereby images of women were functionalized in specific ways; yet I have given no more than a broad outline. Every stage of the process in fact deserves extensive treatment. This broader outline is presented here only as evidence that the relationship of the twentieth-century soldier males to white and Red women (analyzed more thoroughly in the first chapter) is anything but an isolated or unique phenomenon. Rather, it represents a segment within the continuum of bourgeois patriarchy—and thus, in the present context, a segment within the genesis of fascism.

It should have become clear that both bourgeois and Marxist historiographies have largely failed to perceive (or have not taken seriously) the most important elements in this continuum: those elements, that is, within which male-female relations are used to secure power. In particular, they have ignored the installation of lack in relations of production between the sexes, of an artificially and forcibly induced inequality that continually remakes these as relations of antiproduction, spawning repression, hierarchies, the battle of the sexes, building blocks of fascist reality, social deserts in which children have been (and still are) forced to exist.

My second aim here was to demonstrate the extent to which the male body came in the course of these developments to be isolated from, set off against, and exalted above the female body, until as Faust the Colonizer it stood (active or merely watching) above an ocean waiting to be drained, and finally, as the fascist male, became a rock amid the raging sea (defending) or one of Jünger's men-of-steel (destroying) in the intoxicating whirlpool of reality. At this point, the mingling of human bodies became an unresolvable dilemma.

Historians have never been interested in what has really happened to human bodies—what bodies have *felt*. Yet until we have succeeded in reconstructing the development of our bodies in history, we will remain strangers to ourselves—confined to a haunted, enchanted, subjugated nature, unable to experience other bodies as equals, incapable of the physical (more than simply sexual) experience of communism. "The body doesn't incorporate ideas; it generates them," Frieda Grafe wrote in an article on the paintings of Friederike Pezold,[1] whose work begins to reconstruct the female body (her body) by dismantling it into partial fragments—"corporeal signs" that represent nothing at all, but that permit the body to regenerate itself through the contemplation of its own components.[2] "The body no longer serves to incorporate ideas or fantasies outside itself."[3] (In European history, the body has been forced to serve men's thinking in precisely that way.) Grafe continues: "This makes a positive object for women's thinking out of the things we have long been ashamed of (as we were taught to be): our directness; our lack of mental discipline; our vulgar materialism, expressed primarily through our close relationships to our bodies, whose impulses, if acted on, create disorder."[4]

It hasn't been easy to sow disorder within male theories and scientific systems, both because those theories themselves abstract from the body and because I too, as a man, tend to ignore the body as I write—the body, which never feels the same from one day to the next, while trains of thought demand to be continued.[5] Yet here and there, the effort may have succeeded—via detours or out-of-the-way routes through places where the narrow channels of male thinking are eroded or have never become entrenched—in rediscovering that which is forgotten and repressed, and transforming the desiring-production of the unconscious into the engine of knowledge.

As pathways to the experiencing and knowledge of the true fate of the European body, of its splitting into child and adult, into genders, classes, and fragments of itself, those detours through human bodies still need to be explored. Until we have done that, we can't really claim to understand the history of the people of Europe.[6]

SOME CHARACTERISTICS OF AN ARTIFICIAL RELATION: THE MAINTENANCE OF LACK IN RELATIONS BETWEEN THE SEXES

Preliminary Remarks

In the succession of changes that we have seen induced in gender relations in reaction to the historical potential for new freedoms, certain recurring themes have caught my attention. These themes may well point to specific mechanisms for securing power in European male-dominated class societies. To justify calling them mechanisms, we would have to be able to find evidence of them in each different displacement of power; and I do not wish to claim that we will always be successful. On the other hand, I am not going to limit myself to indicating the necessity for a far more ambitious investigation of history than the present context allows. A process does not have to be a mechanism, a rule, or a law in order to be real and (hence) to merit the attention of "science"—especially when the gaze science fixes on its objects is no less artificial or fictive than are, for example, centered perspective or other related male inventions and fantasies.[1]

> Your yearning means nothing to me.
> Phenomena pass;
> I am searching for laws.[2]

For too long, men have talked in this way; and to a certain extent, the man talking here is not exceptional. The errors of male thinking are not easy to cast aside, especially not those whose long history has caused them to become ingrained in the male body. One of those errors, certainly, is the tradition of freeing the thinking brain from the depths of the most pressing situations and sending it off to some (fictive) summit for a panoramic overview.

Calling for a new approach to knowledge is not the same as being able to create one, but that is no excuse for abandoning the hope or the effort. Even in the remainder of this work, rules, though they are not made into laws, carry more weight than phenomena. Perhaps a distinction can still be made, however, between knowledges that can be related only to other knowledges (most literary study is of this kind), and those that also recognize the experiences and feelings of readers—phenomena tied to the readers' own lives and to the existence of their bodies.

The Body of Woman as
Object of the "New Morality"

A few pages ago, I wrote of civil servants and petit bourgeois males in the era of German classicism, that they abandoned the revolutionary struggle to propagandize for a new morality. That seems typical of groups and strata that belong to the ruling class, but have not been allowed to exercise authority directly. We witnessed the same process in the relationship of the defeated decentralist d'Urfé to the court of the victor, Henry IV. D'Urfé began to criticize the sexual mores of the court after he had been vanquished in an armed struggle for power. The so-called heretical movements of the eleventh and twelfth centuries (Franciscans and Dominicans, for instance) aimed their attacks not at the Church hierarchy as a whole, but at the dissolute life of large segments of the priesthood, prostitution in the convents, and so forth. The "heretics" countered those transgressions with an ideal of physical asceticism, not one of revolution.[1] They, too, assailed authority with a new puritanism. (The same can be said of Christians in the late Roman Empire.)[2]

Sooner or later, all of these groups would gain access to power without a revolution. They would have a chance to train their new morality on social inferiors (though it had evolved in opposition to superiors). But for the time being, they focused their efforts on the bodies of women from their own strata, or on the images of high-born women (which grew out of an exaltation of women of their own strata). Asceticism and new moralities always seem to emerge from the groups Elias calls "strata fighting on two fronts." The power of such strata extends only downward; it is used against the sexuality of the general population rather than against the immorality of rulers.[3]

Evidence to support the claim that truly oppressed classes attack ruling classes because they deprive them of life (and not because of the obesity of those gentlemen or the harems they keep) can be found in the activity of the peasants at the time of their revolts (ca. 1525), or in proletarian life during the nineteenth and early twentieth centuries; in both cases, revolutionary activities coincided with freer sexual attitudes. For the most part, these groups did not respond to the sexual perversity of their rulers with a new morality (though their leaders frequently did).

Potential new freedomes often first become *visible* in practices within the ruling group itself. Since existing prohibitions are imposed by this group, its members are the first to violate those prohibitions when it suits them. That is one of the few freedoms reserved to a group whose relationship to other people is inherently perverse; it is marked by dominance just as are gender relations within the ruling group itself. Any freedoms appropriated by the ruling group must necessarily become perverse—to that extent, at least, its members remain human.[4]

But it is precisely here, in the perverse exercise of freedom, that their methods are exposed to the strata closest to them in the hierarchy of power. To a certain extent at least, these various strata occupy the same sphere of social intercourse. The contacts are personal, and so are the hatreds.

The conflicts that result here often had detrimental consequences for subordinate classes; for the "strata fighting on two fronts" become, as a rule, the most vehement critics of the dominant class—those who go so far as to abandon their own class (though often retaining the ideology of their stratum) and join forces with the oppressed. Here they—or at least some of their number—advance to the position of ideological leaders, from which they tend to continue the struggle for a "new morality"; that is, they demand that the oppressed now behave in accordance with the new morality.

A contemporary example of this is the bourgeois intellectual who abandons the bourgeoisie out of hatred for his own class, then demands that proletarians contest the legitimacy of existing power relations by becoming better people than their rulers. In making that demand, the intellectual assumes a function of direct domination consistent with that of the perverse ruling group he is trying to combat. He installs a hierarchical system of morality in the desiring-production of the oppressed. It is for this reason that revolutionary movements led by turncoats form "strata fighting on two fronts" so often sally forth under the banner of a new morality, and it is women who become the main objects of their endeavors. Being decent, upright warriors for the new world is enough for men; women have to be sexually pure also. Thus German social democracy, and later the German Communist party, combatted the sexual decadence of the seductive daughters of industrialists across the bodies of working-class daughters, who were now supposed to become holy virgins.[15]

The "new morality," then, assures the continuity of relations of dominance by transferring the structure of repression of female sexuality from one social formation to the next. Deprived of liberation, women within the new state once again provide the building blocks for internal boundaries against life. In the socialist movement, a categorical emphasis on struggles against the degenerate, shameless desires of the ruling class (against the czars, who were defeated, or against the bourgeoisie, who are about to be defeated) offers one means of obscuring its own struggles against female emancipation. Or, if we put that in more familiar terms: anyone who attacks the playboy in the capitalist instead of the oppressor is making a new pact with the devil. Thus the negative form of emancipation practiced by a "decadent" ruling class in the course of abdicating its power is assailed as moral decline, instead of being seen to signify the possibility of real freedom. Substituting a moral battle for a political one seems to me to be a typical method of selling out among members of the "strata fighting on two fronts." The end product is always a new, "revolutionary" morality, instead of an unfettering of the senses, an unfettering that will never occur without the unrestricted development of the productive force of women—which involves more than placing equal value on women's labor.*

In revolutionary movements, the tendency to encode political struggles as moral struggles arises in the form of a crippling contradiction (visible, for example, in the proletarian novel). By contrast, it is a characteristic of members of bourgeois "strata fighting on two fronts"—and of the peasant class, to the extent that they see the move from farm to factory as a step down—that they wage political battles almost exclusively as battles for "the

---

*I don't want to limit the productive force of women to the terms "productive," "force," or to anything we generally think of as specifically feminine—something, that is, which we do not yet know.

maintenance of morality," "the preservation of values," and so on; unquestioningly they now occupy the sexual battlefield their masters have abandoned to them.

The same is true of the men who are the subjects of this book. The relationship of officers to women that was described in chapter 1 can now be summarized. The men construct an image of a high-born woman ("white countess"). They then worship that image, which must be asexual. They persecute the sexuality of the "low-born" woman—proletarian, communist, Jew (= whore)—by first making her a prostitute, then murdering her; meanwhile lack is maintained in relationships with their own (child-bearing and asexual) women through their exclusion (as nameless wives) from social productions and from the confraternities of men. All of these forms of oppression—adoration, murder, exploitation—are related.[6]

As our meanderings through a number of tendencies in European history indicate, strata in which such forms of repression surface do *not* engage in struggles for economic power. The men fight for dominance within their own stratum (gained at the expense of their women and children) and (with the weapon of "new moralities") for power over socially less powerful strata. Capitalism's survival under fascism is due in part to the energetic efforts of the sons of "strata fighting on two fronts" to combat their own demise as patriarchs. Capitalism has been able to count on such men precisely because of their refusal to confront the issue of *economic* power. The diverse functions assigned to women in the process of securing power—the divisions achieved through women and images of women—are not products of any peculiar psychic "mechanisms"; they are simply repetitions within the individual of the social divisions into victim, beast of burden, image.

From the standpoint of psychoanalysis, "good" and "evil" women, "high-born" women, and "whores" all appear to be derived from the figure of the mother. The only logical conclusion is that those other women must somehow be present in individual "mothers" within "strata fighting on two fronts". And in fact, they are. These mothers are queens around the house, workers serving their husbands, whores for daddy. They are the ones whose bodies entice and repulse their children, who know nothing about their husbands' work, and on and on. "The mother" is never just one person (Freud's error), nor is she ever simply a *person*.

When very young children (nursing infants) suffer from lack of maternal affection—from waves of revulsion along the skin of mothers who are fed up with their infants and secretly reject them—they don't associate that suffering with the name "mother." In the first instance, the mother is no more than partial objects: breasts, hands, a face, a voice. Even as the all-encompassing, protective totality, she is not "mother," but much more: she is the outside world—the whole principle of the outside world. When the mother's attitude is negative, the child's cathexis of the whole principle of the outside world—the entire social realm of which the mother is a socialized component—is also negative. The child will cathect the absence of women able to offer emotional sustenance as the cruelty of society, the negativity of life. Later, this will allow the child to say that the world is evil, with the exception of its mother (because the "mother," as a name and a totality, is only constructed later on within the contest of *perceived* support). The mother figure, woven into a fabric of gratitude, comes to occupy a socially "good" role. She ceases to represent the extreme "evil" felt earlier by the infant. The destructive, persecuting aspects of the mother figure disappear without a trace: she is good; only the world (and internally, the ego too) is bad. In brief, forcing mothers to serve double duty as female bodies and social figures—inherently contradictory functions—has been the model process, the *matrix*, for misunderstanding the outside world and for turning object relations into phantom relations. The tip of the Oedipal triangle, which Freud called "mother," is a phantom.*

One Form of Female Sacrifice

A hierarchical system of female sacrifice has persisted up to the present day, becoming increasingly intricate. Under capitalist conditions of social production, it exists as a readily available weapon in the arsenal of technologies of power. All hitherto existing forms of dominance can be reproduced under capitalism "virginally" as commodities (through magazines, for example). No form of dominance is ever forgotten; any one can be reapplied, if need be, to the "random collage of everything that has ever been believed." In the system outlined earlier, a man who takes his master's wife, worships a woman from afar, or manufactures an image of a high-born woman is exchanging his revolutinary potency for a share of power in the existing society. The system would never have worked unless at least a small fraction of the desired bodies were made accessible; and indeed a number of bodies from images of the distant and the sublime were brought within reach—in the real bodies of women from conquered nations and races, for instance, or in the bodies of a limited number of women from higher classes (or higher strata). This process involves more than just converting low-born women into prostitutes for men of the ruling class and their auxiliary strata (as described in the first chapter). In smaller numbers, women from the higher social strata are also made available to men from the lower social strata: they perform the intermediary function of turning revolutionaries into social climbers. The same process is repeated through every class and stratum of societies that sacrifice their women in this way; the more highly differentiated their internal structures of dominance

---

*And thankfully so. Otherwise, we would be *nothing but* motherfuckers.

become—and none is more so than that of contemporary capitalist patriarchy—the more the process diversifies into an ever-expanding multiplicity of permutations.

We witness the worker fulfilling his dream of success by leading a daughter of the upper-middle classes to the altar. The devious working-class adolescent marks out a route to a career as social worker through the body of a female student. There is the civil servant's son whose thirst is quenched by the physician's daughter; the journalist son of a shopkeeper, who finds the right words for his boss's newspaper in the bed of the businessman's wife; the son of the lower-middle classes who falls in love with the woman with the noble name; the critical graduate assistant with whom the professor shares his spouse, but not his academic authority; the black rebel whose route to the liberation army is blocked by the body of his white mistress; and on and on. The power these men receive for their efforts remains indelibly stamped with their masters' insignia: it is borrowed power. For their part, the gods of the moment sacrifice their women in order to remain in power. In short, the persistence of female sacrifice is based on a set of complementary premises.

For the great mass of men, images of women sacrificed in this way are all that is needed; and these images are produced in abundance (far outnumbering the photos of politicians, for example*): the naked bodies of Brigitte Bardot and all those other women on whom deceived desire can—or rather is required to—feast its eyes. The spectrum of stars and cover girls omits almost nothing; in the end, the same desirous gaze is trained on flesh-and-blood women as was trained on the image. Above all, they are desired through the *look*. The body must not become a body; it is forced to remain an unattainable representation. Thus, America's male writers pounced on the dead body of Marilyn Monroe so they could make a new image out of the image that had been rendered unmistakably human by her suicide. They tried to add the image of a "soulful" Marilyn to the image of a physical one. That was a necessary step, in that she had just notified them that she was canceling the contract for patriarchal dominance.**

As banal as it may sound, radical renunciation of all high-born daughters and sublime mothers, of all attempts to worship elevated images of distant women is an essential step toward the emancipation of men—at least until these women themselves climb down from their sacrificial pedestals.

Eldridge Cleaver has described the tortured process of removing white women from the center of his thoughts and feelings, and the subsequent, supremely difficult step of learning to love and accept black women.[1] That process is not confined to the black-white constellation; it simply becomes

---

*Except on television, which tries to turn even politicians into sex symbols.

**Wouldn't rejection of images of women produced by men also imply a certain degree of caution toward the images women tend to produce of, and for, themselves? Wouldn't it imply a rejection of every exemplary model, every female photo on the wall? Particularly, I would think, photos such as that of Rosa Luxemburg. What good does it do to have men fucking the spirit of Rosa in their "politicized" women? Or to have women admiring Rosa's spirit in other women? Or to have women loving each other as bodies connected to the historical bodies of the women's movement? If yet more *images*, terminal stops, solid territories, are created to permit easy identification before the dissolving of boundaries (deterritorialization of desires, the partialization of the body) has even begun, then there is a danger that images will be replaced by other images (male by female images), instead of being erased by experiences.

in her public
image Marilyn is everything
we're told we want to be;
in her private life
she's everything we fear
we probably are.

Book publicity photo of Marilyn Monroe, streaked with red nail polish.

more evident when racial differences are there to reinforce other differences. In class society, the process extends in principle to every male-female relationship involving members of different social classes or strata, and even to relationships within the same stratum, to the extent that the latter is itself structured as a system of upward and downward mobility.

For a working-class son who successfully completes university training, perhaps even becoming a professor, it is perhaps even more difficult to marry a working-class woman than it was for Eldridge Cleaver to learn to love black women. The most common sign of upward social mobility is the acquisition of a woman from the social stratum to which the man has risen. (More often than not, mobility is only made possible by the sexual and financial sacrifice of a woman from the abandoned stratum). Acquisition of a "superior" woman also signals his renunciation of any attempt to change power relations within society. The price of owning an upper-class woman is submission to his own social castration. The man who takes this step will remain "potent" only as long as the system in which he "rose" remains potent. His prick—token of his superior social power—is only borrowed and glued on: a dildo in the name of the law. At the very mention of "revolution," these men hear castration. Any attempt to rob them of their dildo might expose the wound. The Law—that invisible monolith, that abstract condensation of all those abandoned, rock-hard pricks—must not be violated. "Present . . . arms!"

Thus to the men of the ruling group, all women appear as prostitutes. These men approach as brothel-goers or seducers, claiming their right of access to women of the lower classes; they have no obligations whatever toward these "whores." They come to buy, to plunder, or to offer patronage. At the same time, they offer up their own wives and daughters for auction as high-class virgins (or at least as "nearly new" commodities); toward lower-class men, then, they appear in the guise of the pimp. The woman's hymen is a social commodity, the final barrier obstructing the entry of a male social climber into a higher class or stratum. The woman herself is both virgin and prostitute: virgin for the buyer, prostitute for the seller. Thus the rising young hopeful sees the boss's wife as a virgin, but his own wife sees her as a prostitute. Both are correct: to the young man, she is a piece of virgin territory from an as yet unattained class or stratum; to his wife, she is a rich woman who, because she doesn't have to work, is free to become a high-class prostitute, to work then through her sexuality, to install lack as an everyday experience among the lower order. Not all of the sexual transactions that are possible, or required, within the system are necessarily implemented. On the contrary, a canon of rules exists precisely to prevent this from happening: the code of social decency. Yet, this code is what makes the whole system successful. Fixing desires within the channels of the code—anchoring the boss's wife as object of desire in the masturbation fantasies of men, or as threat in the fears of their wives—is enough to ensure the absence of revolt, an absence that is further assured by the failure of those desires to reach fulfillment and of those fears to be dissipated.*

---

*In this context, "making revolution" also means taking the "high-born" woman by force. That explains why on the day after a revolution is reported, bourgeois newspapers are

Desires and fears need to be channeled, but only to an extent that leaves their goals or their objects intact. As long as the image of another, "high-born" woman hovers behind the woman the lower-class man usually sleeps with, and behind every other woman within her normal reach; as long as his wife is afraid of being abandoned or deceived because she doesn't measure up to her "high-born" rival—the dominant class has nothing to fear. All of that simply oils the wheels of a repressive apparatus that feeds on the maintenance of lack in relationships between potential equals. Lack maintains the system, and needs to be created over and over again, so that like cannot come to like.

The Incest Commandment

The question of how lack—the incapacity to experience others except through fear, deceit, mistrust, or domination—is installed in individual subjects brings me back to the concrete situation of soldier males at the start of the twentieth century. In *Mass Psychology of Fascism*, Wilhelm Reich cites a text entitled *The Young Man and Veneration of the Virgin Mary* (*Marienverehrung und der Jungmann*), which highlights the "implementation of chastity" as a mainstay in the system of lack. Reich includes this passage:

> *To the young man, the Virgin Mary stands out as unrivaled grace, loftiness, and dignity,* the like of whom is not to be found in nature, art, and the world of man. Why have artists and painters devoted their skill and creativity to the Madonna again and again? It is because they perceive in her the most sublime beauty and dignity. It is a dignity and beauty which never disappoints. Here we have a mistress and queen, "to serve whom, for whom to exist, must be the highest honor for the young man. Here we have an exalted woman and bride of the spirit, to whom you can give yourself with the full power of the love which gushes from your youthful heart, without having to fear degradation and desecration."[1]

Besides nicely illustrating how historically superseded forms of reterritorialization can be artificially maintained (the cult of the Virgin versus the attraction of social revolution), this text focuses with some clarity on the notion of lack. Mary possesses traits (she is "unattainable") that are "not to be found in nature, art, and the world of man" (that is, nowhere). The young man's desire, then, is required to attach itself to something nonexis-

full of rape stories. The reporters are simply reporting what they would have done in a similar situation. It's not even the case they they are lying; they are merely translating the report of the revolution into their own system of relations, in which "revolution" means taking the boss's wife.

tent, something he will never be able to attain. Reich completely bypasses this element of the passage in his commentary. He all too readily follows the path indicated by the text itself (allowing us at this point to witness the Catholic church in perfect accord with one of the central dogmas of psychoanalysis). When the text says, "Inflict no wrong on a girl and remember that your mother too was once a girl,"[2] Reich takes up the point:

> Thus, in the emotional life of Christian youths, the Mother of God assumes the role of one's own mother, and the Christian youth showers upon her all the love that he had for his own mother at one time, that very ardent love of his first genital desires. But the *incest prohibition* cleaves his genital desires into an intense longing for orgasm on the one hand and sexual tenderness on the other hand.[3]

In other words, Reich makes the incest prohibition solely responsible for the incapacity of "orgasmic yearning" (*Orgasmussehnsucht*) to find a sexual outlet, as well as for the mystic leanings of the Catholic young man.

"But mysticism is nothing other than the unconscious longing for orgasm (cosmic plasmatic sensations)."[4] Experience teaches that any sentence containing the phrase "nothing other than" is probably fallacious or incomplete, and that maxim certainly applies here. "Cosmic plasmatic sensations" goes beyond mere *mysticism*. In the 1952 interview mentioned earlier, the elderly Reich himself made links between those sensations and the "oceanic feelings";[5] the texts of a Whitman or a Neruda on flowing have little to do with mysticism. Here, however, Reich, still the good Freudian, is quick to pin down the mother as the object of desire, thereby casting the incest prohibition as the central agency for the frustration of desire.

But the original Catholic text says something else. What cannot be found in nature, art, and the world of man" won't be found in mothers either; nor can all those streams of the world, in which poets long to float in open water, be dried up with the fulfillment of incestuous desire. The mighty flow of Mother Congo would lose none of its attraction; desire would continue to dive right in, drift along, float away. Reich is another victim of the trap analyzed by Deleuze and Guattari: mistaking the displaced representation of desire (incest) for the repressed desire itself. Yet desire is after more than the mother; the question is, how does it become fixated on the mother and thus become "incestuous desire"? Here a second process comes into play. Reich's choice of a Catholic young man is delicate sleight of hand; it allows him to avoid asking how the splitting that institutes genitality is brought about in Protestant young men—that is, in the absence of the cult of the Virgin. Let me, then, try to describe the form in which that process of fixation has most commonly affected sons of "strata fighting on two fronts" in twentieth-century Germany (up to about 1955).[6]

"Three Girls." Oil painting by Georg Schrimp (1932).

Think of all the crazy barriers adults interpose between children and sexual experience: the breaking off of certain conversations when children appear (conspicuous enough to arouse the children's interest in the very things they were not supposed to hear); the whispering behind hands; the meaningful looks; the evasion of children's questions; the manufactured lies; the inconsistency of their alibis; the frantic attempts to hide the genitals from the little ones' eyes; the horrified embarrassment when children ask the meaning of a forbidden word; the panic when they pick up something new; the hysterical "where did you get that from?"; the punishments threatening children who discover dark continents in the mutual exploration of their bodies—all this, for the young boy, has the effect of making a monstrous secret of the opposite sex, of installing the notion of a "mystery of woman," which does anything but steer his instinctual desires away from women.

On the contrary, what is said to be an education in chastity is primarily an education in pent-up lasciviousness: the establishment of a permanent state of unfulfilled desire. The boy is sexualized. His desire is—indeed is *required to be*—directed solely toward women. All of the growing boy's ideas, hopes, dreams, and plans must be focused and fixated on the conquest of that one object, woman. And the object *woman* is encoded as a woman within the family. She need not be the mother. In fact, this is where the sister seems to take on the great significance discussed in our first chapter. The image of the sister's naked body, seen for a brief instant at some point, eats its way into the boy (in the same way as does the image of the woman's body Mephistopheles showed to his greedy pupil).

The young boy is trained in puberty to the point of near madness to live his whole life within the structure of a fictitious before-and-after construct. "Once I've had a woman—*the* woman—then . . ." This "then" covers everything: guilt, fear, uncertainty, feelings of inferiority will all vanish; life will begin; I will be strong; I will defeat my father; I will leave him; my potential will unfold; SHE will belong to me, and I will protect her.

Out of that longed-for redemption comes the "meaning of life." And since redemption will never occur—it is predicated on misdirected desire—the German quest for the meaning of life, defined as attainable through a *single* act, will never end either. Franz Schauwecker tells the story for the pre-World War I era:

> We began to daydream about heroic deeds and far-off lands
> where we were the dragon-killers; about future days of honor
> and glory; and about women (just a little and always on the sly),
> whom we steadfastly regarded from a distance as goddesses with
> burning secrets in the folds of their garments and unnerving
> smiles—smiles that were sweet and terrifying at the same time.
> Behind our drawn swords, we all fell in love with one little girl
> who had a white sash-dress covered with tiny, pink and blue
> appliquéd flowers, and pigtails that were as thick as arms and
> reached down to the hollows of her knees. After playing Indians
> under the pine trees and junipers by the lake, we would dream
> about touching this girl's hand, then shudder, laugh a bit, and
> stare at her full, red lips. That was the best part: those hard,
> narrow, burning lips with the glint of her baby teeth between
> them. We would never have admitted this; in front of our
> friends, we laughed out loud about "the whole tribe" of girls.
> We bent over our Kary May* and buried ourselves in adven-
> tures, until such time as we were once again ensnared by our big,
> grown-up goddess with her knowing, frightening, blissful
> smile . . . she looked like a lady and was forever unattainable.[7]

Behind the far-off lands, heroic deeds, and Kary May, behind the little girl in her white sash-dress, stands the big, grown-up "goddess." Is she the mother? The description of her charms seems too intimate for that. More likely, she is the older sister or one of her girlfriends. But even she is "forever unattainable." Is that because of the incest prohibition?

And yet there can be no incest prohibition without incestuous *desire*. But as we now know, desire cries out for something else: "It isn't my mother I wanted. It was never her—or even simply a woman. I wanted to know the world, produce it, people it with my creations. I wanted to explore every possible connection, visit every site on earth and leave again." In that case,

---

*Author of widely read novels of the American West.—Trans.

what analysts label "incestuous desire" must somehow be installed in the subject from without, by society. And how is that "desire" installed? By means, it seems to me, of an indirect prescription, by the fixating of desire on the *mystery of Woman* (predominantly the sister in this case)—a prescription that merits the name "incest commandment."

At the end of the section on the marriages of soldier males, I said that these men never break free of their mothers or reach beyond their sisters. Now it becomes possible to indicate more precisely why. The (threatening) attachment to the mother remains, because, in all likelihood, dissolution of the earlier symbiosis was too abrupt to allow the boy to form an independent ego. The sister, however, remains a "boundary," by virtue of the incest commandment that is inculcated in the boy.[8]

The sister becomes a filter on the world, a mirage on its narrow horizons. The brother is driven toward her by powerful tailwinds from the blast-machines of pedagogic institutions (whose main medium is single-sex education, though they also implement other forms of differential treatment of boys and girls); and by all the many modes of parental behavior, which (where the boy is concerned) are there to fixate him on the mystery of the forbidden body, and to equip that body with magnets, labyrinths, narrow passes, and chasms: one-way streets.

It is the establishment of the indirect incest commandment in society that gives the incest prohibition its devastating effect (a purely social one). The incest taboo long ago ceased to have any economic function in capitalism. Should the boss's daughter and son see fit to marry each other, the process of monopolization can still continue undisturbed. Under capitalism, the incest taboo has been artificially resurrected only as an instrument to safeguard prevailing power relations. It is used to construct an effective double bind; with promises and enticements, an image of woman is foisted on a young man ("That's what you want"). In the image, the two opposing bodies of the sister and mother shimmer almost indistinguishably; in reality, both are kept out of reach, while the only women capable of becoming substitutes are maneuvered into a position of consistent refusal to fulfill any desires awakened in the young man. These women wouldn't contemplate allowing the sons and brothers who advance toward them to swim right into and through their bodies. The young girl (sister), in particular, is not sexualized as part of her education; contrary to the widely held belief, she is not trained for men.

No one paints a wonderfully mysterious yet horrifying picture of male sexuality for a young woman. Instead, she learns to look to marriage for her "salvation"—to the married household, that is, and not the marriage bed. If her desire were directed from the very beginning toward social existence and human production in its broadest sense, her future husband's initially more or less open attempts to see within her "the whole world," the culmination of his most intense desires, would seem ridiculous and trivial to her (instead of being taken, say, as a compliment). She would be unable and unwilling to assume her function as a filter on the world, a kind of transformer of male desires on their way to social existence. And so, her desire must be checked; her productive force transmuted into a force of antiproduction. This is achieved by teaching her to make demands on others (as opposed to taking action herself), demands that are addressed not to society or to life, but to men. Her demands for adequacy in a man are security, money, a home, a job, and children. With those requirements, she binds the man to social functions (a profession, for instance) that have almost nothing to do with his own desiring-production. The young man was originally shown a (veiled) image of woman with the inscription "Wide-Open Spaces"; now the woman sits him down under a motto in a picture frame, "Home Sweet Home." And lack is installed anew. The woman appears here as deceiver; the enticements of sexuality are revealed to have been dangerously misjudged—and new recruits are won for exclusive male groupings. Just as military armament, advertising, and administration function by skimming off and absorbing a portion of amassed social wealth or surplus value as a means of maintaining the lack by which the system stands or falls, so also the force of production of women is constructed into the system of power relations through functions of antiproduction, as a kind of agency of antiproduction within desiring-production itself.

This engenders a whole series of potential double binds, the core of which lies in the simultaneous incest commandment and incest prohibition: thou shalt covet (take) thy mother (sister), but thou shalt not be allowed to have either one.* Or, thou shalt love *women*, but only one *woman*. Thou shalt stay at home, but know the world. Probably the most perplexing of all is the sexualization of fantasies through the installation of the "mystery of Woman," coupled with a total ban on the practice of sexuality. The more antithetical constructs (whose terms are mutually exclusive, rather than dialectical or mutually relativizing) are built into human relations, the more easily human beings can be dominated and ruled. If any two stand in some mutual relation, one of them has already been caught in an inevitable trap.

Where, for example, the husband and social climber must submit to the laws and authority of the dominant class ("castration"), his ambitious wife learns to demand both social advancement *and* an uncastrated husband. Where the husband is required to retain his mother's image as his "one-and-

---

*Freud didn't overlook this important contradiction, but he Oedipalized (biologized) it. He ignored the socially determined, problematic nature of sororal incest; by changing the Wilhelminian commandment, "thou shalt," into a "thou shalt want" (referring to the mother), he invented Oedipus and the potential for sublimation. The phrase "Oedipus *wants* his mother" sets the stage for renunciation and transference; the phrase "a man *shall*" does not. Once again, it becomes evident that fascist man neither has, nor can have, any interest in sublimation.

18 bis 35
Frankfurt für
junge Erwachsene

Gell, da
guckste

Election advertisement, Frankfurt branch of the German Socialist Party (SPD), 1976.

only," the wife demands to be the "one-and-only" *and* demands that her husband rid himself of his mother's image. Even marital sex is caught in the grip of a double bind: the task of producing children is incompatible with the function of the "white" woman (whom the soldier male marries, as we know, precisely to fend off sexuality). In a system like this, any action is bound to violate some commandment or prohibition, engendering an oppressive and permanent sense of guilt.

Thus a woman from a stratum-on-two-fronts (the so-called middle class is hierarchically subdivided into many such strata-on-two-fronts)[9] is placed in the extremely contradictory position of presenting her demands to a man who is an advocate of the society that is oppressing her. (Yes, he must love *her*, and yes, he must be a revolutionary.) She speaks here, not with the voice of production, but from her existence as "being" (*Sein*). Aside from her function as domestic servant, she exists as a decorative representative (of men) and a sexual commodity; yet, as far as she is concerned, these functions together constitute her individual being. The mystery to which she aspires lies within the realm of male production: it is money. Only with the help of money will she be in a position to display the qualities she has learned and to carry out the functions that are expected of her. As a representative commodity, she is finally forced to love the customer paying the highest price—or promising to pay the highest price. On the level of representation, there is no such thing as production, only expression, manifestation, and "being" as commodity. As long as the woman accepts that position and uses it to legitimate her demands; as long as she does not become a process, a female producer liberating the streams of her desire and causing relations to flow, then, by the very nature of the demands she makes of men, she will consistently destroy the other term of the double bind, the other thing she wants from the man: his capacity to love. At the same time, the most acute double bind is within the woman herself. Although the acquiescent woman never shatters the framework of her social definition as worker, commodity, and representation, she still demands to be loved as a *person*. In other words, she continues to function as the means by which inequalities are introduced ("the wrong woman for every man," and vice versa).[10]

The Ocean in Woman—Escape from the Double Bind— Incest Prohibition/Incest Commandment

Since around 1700 and the beginning of the Enlightenment, writers such as those cited earlier have escaped these double binds by dissolving, liquefying, one of the terms: the monogamous "one-and-only." We can view this process as an intensified form of the struggle against an increasingly impregnable body armor, against an increasingly marked atomization of individuals in the early days of market competition. The writers applied the name "woman" to anything that flowed, anything limitless; in the place of God, the dead transcendence, they set the female sex as a new transcendence that finally abolishes lack. The earth became a limitless woman: life, thy name is woman; woman, they name is vagina; vagina, thy name is ocean, infinity.

In other words, they used, or misused, the fluidity—the greater malleability and as yet unspent utopian potential of femaleness, a desiring-production that is fallow, undirected, not yet socially defined, and thus remains in closer proximity to the unconscious; a life of emotion, rather than of intellect (that cruel, demarcating product of the constraints that beset men's bodies)—to encode their own desire, their own utopias, their own yearning to be free of boundaries, with the notion of an "endlessly flowing woman."

In this way, the writers were able to break free of enforced dichotomies, such as career advancement/castration, and also escape the type of relation described earlier, in which the woman functioned as an agency of absorption, a guarantor of lack in the production of the sexes. The men could even become political revolutionaries along this route; they were free to couple their desires to social processes. They learned to recognize those who drew boundaries and built dams as their enemies. Writers of this kind had little time for misogyny, but retained a certain ignorance of the reality of women,

René Magritte, "La Bagneuse du clair au sombre." (c) Georgette Magritte, 1986.

often in spite of numerous relationships with females. Since their notion of emancipation was predicated on the dissolution of women's boundaries— depersonalization, that is—they lost sight of the inequality that stamped their relations with women. Their desire for women did not arise in relation to actual women, but as a part of their search for a territory of desire. Hence, their desire remained oppressive. As they continued to measure every woman against an image of "woman," every woman ran up against a set of expectations that were not derived from her, but that she was, nonetheless, supposed to fulfill. If she did fulfill them, she transformed the man into a tender, grateful lover—but not for long, since the image in which he loved her encompassed far more than any woman could ever hope to be, and far less than any woman really is. (Analysts who insist that this is only the image of the mother are sad cases of stubborn blindness.) Relationships of this kind end, as a rule, when the man's production takes a new turn; he shifts the direction of his gaze, a new image enters his field of vision, and the previous incarnation of distant flowing loses her charm (Tucholsky: "The hole is the only intimation of paradise there is down here"[1]). Brecht, for instance, wished for relationships of about two years' duration, with uncomplicated separations and fresh starts afterward. All the fleeting male-female relationships that suffuse the biographies (and literary works) of productive nonfascists were (are) expressions of this code. After a period of intensity, most of the relationships end as abruptly as the began. No matter how much praise is devoted to her, the woman remains an image, a promise (though with the proviso that flesh-and-blood women manage to reflect the image for brief periods, lending it their bodies, thoughts, and feelings). This is the escape route of nonfascist men from the imprisonment of their bodily streams. It would be hard to find a clearer distinction between these men and their soldier-male counterparts.

> Oh, my love, if only you could swim . . .
> You wouldn't need me to be your ocean.

Floods of Love in Workers' Poetry (Supplement)

In the Reclam anthology, *German Workers' Poetry, 1910-1933* (*Deutsche Arbeiterlyrik 1910-1933*), love flows in nine of the ten poems under that heading ("Love").

> O ocean of desire I have sailed!
> O dark, mysterious, deep and yawning sea! (Karl Bröger)[1]

Longing flows from me like a divine and raging wave,
Carrying you, beloved, to isles of paradise. (Oskar Maria Graf)[2]

> When will you disclose the shining shores,
> So that my keel can furrow the dark tide—
> And your hand weave garlands out of flowers?
> (Christoph Wieprecht)[3]

> Beloved! My arms are drunken revelers
> Who know the taste of wine!
> Girl! Raging storm at sea! Hurricane!
> (Oskar Maria Graf)[4]

Although the streams are partly encoded through regressive associations with the "mother", although they are then channeled, made subject to a law, they are not forbidden.

> As the river streams to the sea, we flow toward you!
> In the same flowing turbulence you seek us out,
> And the same law that
> Joins two rivers,
> Joins us too.
> In coming home to Woman,
> We free ourselves, we free the woman.
> We come home to our mother, the Earth! (Heinrich Lersch)[5]

Worse than that, in the final analysis the woman is only a way station on the road to union with God the Father:

Your breath: scent as of radiant pines, wind of the world
wafting from your mouth. Have you come up from the fruitful
sea? Beloved! You eternal woman!

You speak my name: "Heinrich!" I am reborn out of that
sound. From your mouth our homeland rings as from my
mother's voice, sweet and familiar. In your arms I make a sacred
covenant between you, God, and myself. (Heinrich Lersch)[6]

Not raging, decoded streams, but a shallow brook reencoded into the
bed of mother. What we are seeing here is a damming-up process, one that
had certain consequences for Lersch: he was a fascist sympathizer after
1933. There are similarities here with Bröger, whose own waters were by
now beginning to seep away into poetic idyll:

You lie at peace, like the tide within the bay,
Sleeping deeply, woman, at my side.
Like a vessel resting at the harbor's mouth,
Its sails aglow with the pink of early day,
Your body breathes.[7]

Cited for contrast with fascist texts, these excerpts may tell us more
about the fear of flowing among soldier males than previous passages from
German literature of the seventeenth and eighteenth centuries, and more recent world literature.

After all, these poems were written by men who not only came from the
class that formed the main target of attack for soldier males, they were also
their contemporaries, both in time and social context. Reducing the distinction between them to one of superficial class antagonism is, however,
precisely what I set out to avoid. The opposition between the suppression of
drives and the affirmation of drives goes deeper; it does not simply divide
proletarian neatly from bourgeois; it runs through the bourgeoisie itself and
even through the ranks of colonizers, where it allows one of every thousand
to side with the colonized. The productive unconscious knows no classes. It
is not until we reach the level of representation, symbolization, substitution,
and displacement that everything to some degree bears the stamp of socially
available group fantasies.[8] It does not bear anything that can any longer be
called the stamp of the unconscious.

Nonetheless, it is on the basis of a distinction made unconsciously, an
opting for stream or dam (and not on the basis of any analysis of interests or
of class membership!), that the fascist sees anyone different from himself as
a "communist." "Girl! Raging storm at sea! Hurricane!"—this is enough.
Only a cultural Bolshevist could have written these words. To the fascist unconscious, the distinctions it makes appear accurate—a fact that Left consciousness refuses to perceive. The argument that a social democrat is not

communist, a communist not an anarchist, and that none of these categories has anything to do with Jews, has never had much effect. The fascist unconscious perceives an essential sameness in all of the categories (and in the many others that made the spectrum of concentration-camp prisoners so diverse that Rudolf Höss tried to classify them like so much exotic fauna.)[9] We would risk devaluing the most reliable instrument of perception available to humans were we to blunt the sharp edge of categories defined in the unconscious by calling them "projections."

The fascists were not projecting when they singled out Friedrich Ebert* from the Left for a certain grudging admiration.[10] They sensed that this man (whom Erhard Lucas fittingly describes as presenting a "brow of iron" to all demands from the Left[11]) would not allow a single drop of the stream to seep through; he would not rest until he had crushed all attempts to form soviets, to socialize particular areas of production, or to organize a republican army. Ebert's first love was his organization, the Party. The party in power: large, rigid blocks; dams.** (Like Ebert himself, the individual social democrat could always be counted on to serve as a dam in times of crisis.)

The phrase "Red flood" wasn't just a nightmare dreamed up by the Right; there were indeed members of the Left who identified with it. In their attempt to promote a general strike, the Stuttgart Council of Workers and Soldiers put out a newspaper in January 1919 entitled the *Red Flood*.[12] In an article published by the Essen branch of the German Communist party (KPD) on March 26, 1920—the armed insurrection had just passed its peak—an unnamed writer asked:

> Who and what is the government? A thin plank in a raging sea; a backdrop that will be put aside tomorrow.[13]

(Lucas suspects that the writer in question was Wilhelm Pieck, who was living in Essen at the time, on assignment from KPD headquarters.) At a rally four days later—the workers' defeat was already becoming apparent—Nickel, president of the Mülheim Council of Workers and Soldiers, made the following pronouncement:

> From this industrial region the fiery-red wave of revolution [will] pour out over the whole world! There is no chance that we will sink. Our movement is like a gigantic, irresistible wave; it sweeps up everything in its wake.[14]

The speaker identifies with the violent side of that gigantic wave

---

*President of Germany in the first years of the Weimar Republic (1919-25).—Trans.
**In General Maercker's view, Ebert and Noske were the only two who "understood" the men of the Freikorps (Maercker, p. 75).

(anyone who opposed it was, therefore, right to be afraid). It can be no accident that these words were spoken by a representative of the Mülheim Council of Workers and Soldiers, a group that gained a certain ambiguous recognition by suicidally refusing to lay down its arms, even when the struggle against the German army and Freikorps had become hopeless from a military standpoint. Anyone who prefers the wave of death to the free-flowing wave has passed an important watershed: a decision against flowing desire, against human liberation.

Not so Brecht. During his refugee years, he talked of government as the regulation of flowing. He saw good government, however, not as dam-building (or even making cuts for dams), but as the leveling of obstacles that block the flow of streams.[15]

CONTAMINATION OF THE BODY'S PERIPHERAL AREAS

Dirt

Dirt is, first and foremost, anything that impinges on the tidy insularity of a person, on the person's anxiously guarded autonomy. This explains the individual's reluctance to let anything into, or out of, her/himself. Besides avoiding dirt associated with contact and secretion, people regard anything that is only ambiguously part of themselves as unclean. By analogy, they are disgusted at the prospect of contamination, heterogeneity. When confronted with such contamination, they become afraid of falling prey themselves to ambivalence and amorphousness, of losing themselves, of being harmed by a process of amalgamation, insertion, addition, extraction, seepage, or infiltration. That is why things like pumps, funnels, spouts, and pipes are always suspect, and why people so often name commingling and in-between states when asked for examples of dirt. This is probably also the basis for the indelible connection between dirt and the primary type of commingling: sex.

People's third fear, after contamination by dirt, is of decay. They turn away in fright when something at the bottom moves toward the top, or something at the top moves toward the bottom; also when a structure dissolves (or the reverse): a rotting mushroom, or a nose appearing on a knee. Along with the dirt of decay, finally, there is the dirt of the mass. As individual entities, people despise anything that throngs or sprawls, any mass in which they might become caught up and irretrievably lost.[1]

This cataloging of dirt into four main types—secretion, commingling, decay, the dirt of the mass—comes from Christian Enzenberger's *Expanded Essay on Dirt* (*Grösserer Versuch über den Schmutz*). The *Expanded Essay* is a clean book, even in appearance. Everything is set in blocks, with empty, uniform spaces in between. A lot of white.

Between each of the book's four sections stands a blank page, its only adornment a Roman numeral. The book jacket is also white, with the title in black. Absence of colors. (Anything visible is potentially filthy, and colors seem to be no exception. The case of white—the visible absence of all colors—is different, as Melville tells us in *Moby Dick*.[2] But white can also be described as the invisible presence of all colors, a clean heterogeneity.)

Enzenberger's method of stringing together diverse quotes, figures of speech, and texts of his own, with no textual linkage between them, could itself perhaps be called "dirty" (or "improper")—and he plays this up with ironic flourishes ("When is he going to get to the point?"). Yet by consistently employing a style that is indirect, distancing, and artificially associative (even in the quotes), he manages, more importantly, to consign the dirt he is supposed to be discussing to some unreal distant region (to whiteness).

He doesn't admit that the dirt has contaminated him or that it has contaminated him to the extent it actually has. He has, then, done a neat and tidy piece of work—and he is generally on target. He focuses on the "tidy insularity" of the person. He acknowledges that dirt is a category that has to do with boundaries, that small quantities of dirt produce major contamination but large quantities are no longer considered dirty, and so on. His book discusses the essential types of dirt, and perhaps all types. One of its failings may lie in the overly pluralist existence he assigns to the various categories of dirt (in an attempt to show how all-encompassing dirt can sometimes be). He seems also to have neglected the fact that dirt can sometimes be). He seems also to have neglected the fact that dirt usually comes from, or is associated with, living bodies—with their peripheries, where the solid can meet and mix with the amorphous, even (in fact, especially) in the process of decay.

In our cultural circumstances, moreover, the "indelible connection between dirt and the primary type of commingling, sex," isn't just one among many links. Because it is forced to serve as a code for so many other things, it ought to merit special consideration. The "tidy insularity" of a person must very often have to do with an insular detachment from sexuality. In the end, though, these are only marginal corrections (or perhaps errors on my part).

The only really surprising thing—and perhaps the only point of real criticism—is that almost any given passage from a fascist text has a "dirtier" effect than Christian Enzenberger's copious anthology. Let's then climb down from the heights of writing *about* dirt and move into dirt itself—into those moist (and "female") depths into which fascists firmly believe non-fascists want to transform the whole world. Let's move into

> that culture which uses theater, literature, and other forms of writing to mock and drag into the dirt all that is heroic, brave, soldierly, decent, moral; and that commends to our youth all that is pacifist, cowardly, immoral, lowly, base, and demoralizing. We are acquainted with the forces that lie behind this. They aim to undermine our family life, to prevent our boys and girls from maturing in strict morality to become a race capable of defending itself, all so that these forces can sit back on their moneybags and rule over a listless race.[3]

A "race capable of defending itself" threatens to become a "listless race"; the *heights*, which appear unassailable in themselves (heroic, brave), are eroded by the machinations of the shadowy *depths* (undermining, dragging into the dirt). The phallus seems to stand aloft, not just clearly, but also *honestly*. Honestly, that is, because deception seems to reside in the depths. The depths are not simply depths, either; they contain "underlying" forces that are ambiguous, chameleonlike. The depths take multifarious forms.

The Mire

> All the mire that the revolution in Germany had carried to the surface from the depths. (Major Bischoff)[1]

> It was the last golden remnant of the early war generation that had not been buried by the muddy tide of revolution or in the quest for comfort. (Zöberlein)[2]

> just as the wave of Marxist mire was cresting, a spiritually conscious core of German resistance began to form in Munich. (Rosenberg)[3]

The mire seems to follow revolution in the same way that a flood follows a broken dam. Something collapses to give way to the mire. The phrases "muddy tide" and "wave of mire" show how closely these belong together; before there can be the mire, there has to be a tide, a wave.

It is not weapons that stand at the forefront of defense. The phrases "golden remnant of the early war generation" and "spiritually conscious core of German resistance" seem to indicate that it is, rather, ideological constants that offer immunity from the mire; clarity of thought is what these men are after. Thus Jünger can demand that his "worker" (whom he considers the masculine successor of the foot soldier and warrior) remain distant from the "gloomy mire of partisanship."[4] Representing interests, making

Major Bischoff.

compromises, negotiating, reaching goals in roundabout ways, planning for the long run, or taking both sides into account: all these methods are contaminated, at once male and female, in short, mire. (Firmness is susceptible to erosion, it must be kept good and dry; even the merest splash of depth will soften it.)

The mire may also form internally, in which case it is called the "quest for comfort." (Zöberlein) This is a disease that comes with age and is unknown to the golden younger generation. Hence it is mostly these young men who form the Freikorps: "Here the roar of the blood was not choked by the mire of cowardice, or of pleasure that knows no danger." (Heinz)[5] The lure of such pleasure was not to be underestimated; even Iron Berthold had to struggle to fight it off. To avoid succumbing, he renounced all home leave, explaining in a speech to his men:

> "But what are its benefits?" he asked, jutting out his chin. "At best, a soft job somewhere." He shook his head. "If you want to press on forward, you cannot allow this mire of failure of the will to form inside you. The most humane way is still to go for the beast's throat, to pull the thing out by its roots. (Thor Goote)[6]

The desire for a field-hospital bed, for home leave: these are beasts threatening to destroy the man. His battle against them is one of mammoth proportions. A five-minute rest in a comfortable chair might mean defeat; it might be enough to generate the "mire of failure of the will" that turns the stalwart soldier into a coward, a jellyfish, a thing without contours. Anything that protects the man against the loss of his bodily boundaries, the loss of himself as a person, is defined as humane: pull out anything soft "by its roots."

The same affective context no doubt motivated Sergeant Schaumlöffel to join the Marburg Student Corps, which gained its particular reputation by murdering fifteen captive workers in the Thuringian town of Thal.[7] Although Schaumlöffel didn't mention the mire, he was fighting off the same temptations:

> And it is the hope of these German men that a sizable troop can still be assembled to fight for the unchanging values, to offer a triumphant defense against suffocation in flabby self-indulgence and capriciousness.[8]

Anything that is soft, pleasurable, or relaxing must be combated. In the never-ending battle a German man must wage to remain a German man, relaxation seems tantamount to capitulation. To abandon the struggle is to risk "suffocation"—a feeling that comes from within (not from strangulation). Salomon presents this feeling in the same context:

> The West threatened us mercilessly with the crushing blows of their billion-mark demands.* To return would have been to unleash the floods that had already swept over the dams of Poland; to submit would have meant death by suffocation.[9]

The mire of cowardice rises up in the throats of those who submit, causing them to suffocate in "flabby self-indulgence."

The Morass

> Remember the hour, dark and dank,
> When Germany into the Red morass sank?
> Germany sold out, Germany traded,
> Streets and squares in blood paraded:
> Remember it still?[1]

That is the opening verse of Otto Paust's "Song of the Lost Brigade" ("Lied vom Verlorenen Haufen"), his retrospective on the era of Freikorps battles. For Paust, the Germany of that era was one large Red morass.

The threats posed by the morass were different from those of the "Red flood." There was the danger of sinking (*versinken*); and there were people who deliberately intensified that danger, for instance "a government . . . that dragged the fatherland deeper and deeper into the morass." (Rudolf Mann)[2] To Colonel Reinhard, commandant of Berlin in 1919, it seemed that "political conditions were slipping into the abyss."[3] In March 1920, General

---

*He is referring to the massive reparations imposed on Germany after World War I.—Trans.

Haas ordered the military to march into the Ruhr, in retaliation against the workers. "Otherwise," he proclaimed, "within a few months we will sink without a trace into Bolshevism."[4] (*Without a trace.*)

On October 26, 1918, a wounded Rudolf Berthold noted in his journal: "I am forced to sit here while we continue along this precipitous path."[5] In an order to his troops, he declared:

> In my opinion, the only way to rescue our nation from the miserable morass of the present is to rekindle the fire of enthusiasm for national honor and national feeling in each individual.[6]

The whole era, the whole state of the republic, seemed to be a morass, an abyss. Everything seemed to be slipping almost inexorably toward that final resting place:

> The country is full of loafers and cheats, of men whom the turmoil of revolution has whirled to the top, into ministers' seats, who muddle and "lead" us ever downward, farther down the slippery slope, immediately into the morass . . . while Bolshevism stands and sneers. Peace, work, bread: we still lack these things and we are getting no closer to having them.
> (Rudolf Mann)[7]

Conditions had become fluid; even at the head of the state there was no longer anything solid. The men in the government were themselves part of the morass ("whirled to the top"), their authority mere presumption (they muddle and lead in quotation marks). The men of the revolutionary turmoil were no longer men; they were half-male, half-female monsters, amphibians who were constantly being dragged back under by one part of their being. An officer of the Ehrhardt Brigade cannot bring himself to step onto the slippery slope, though the morass seems to exert a considerable attractive force even on him. There is something inexorable about the image of the slope (the only way you can go is down). The writer's emotions do not break the descent; they follow right along with the words "ever downward, deeper . . . into the morass." He might even have allowed gravity to take its course, had not the result, the sneers of Bolshevism, seemed too horrible. (Not only castration, but annihilation would have awaited him there.)

The officer senses the drive of contemporary events toward liberation, and part of him would like to go along. But because liberation is inextricably tied to the image of the erotic woman—who exists in his mind only as a castrating whore—the birth of the republic remains synonymous for him with the transformation of "Mother Germany" into a gigantic prostitute. All of the streams that were previously blocked have begun flowing across her body; they will soon flow out of her.[8] The officer must exercise restraint:

"What are you doing there, Papen?"
"I'm draining the Bolshevist swamp."
Photomantage by John Heartfield,
title page of a magazine for working-
class youth (1932).

claiming republican freedoms would be tantamount to touching that body, a
contact that would dissolve him. He must stand and watch the proletariat
careering down the slopes of his mother—of every woman—and surviving
the experience. The morass grows until it becomes endless. Mother Germany
has become a pigsty. A morass. The morass gives birth to new whores.

Berlin, 1919:

> For the moment at least, the Red flood in these parts has curdled
> in the form of a glimmering morass; and the naiads it bears
> show no surprise when men, in clandestine celebrations of
> victory, wink at them, or aim exploding champagne corks in
> their direction, as they dance *in puris naturalibus* in gleeful
> parody of the bloody shots fired this Christmas. Cavorting like
> so many octopi in the midst of this pungent morass, the men
> and women here obscure its waters with their tentacles; the water
> never reflects the stars. (Wilhelm Weigand)[9]

The allusion to the "stars" is not accidental here, for they are the
twinklings of pure mothers, of asexual women relegated to the distance of
the nocturnal firmament. (This also explains why Hans Baumann began his
Christmas tribute to German mothers with the line, "Sublime night of the
clear stars" ["Hohe Nacht der klaren Sterne"].)

"To perish in the morass of his animal being or to rise to a higher
worldview" is the alternative offered by Ekkehard to Ginsburg, a Jew in
whose "mongrel blood . . . the Aryan harmonies were first made to reso-
nate" by his love for a junker's wife. She is identified with the "higher

worldview": "Rarely has a plea for help to a pure woman resounded more fervently than during that night in Bredow."[10] It is all in vain; he founders. When races mix, the result is a morass. This is the home of the Medusa; her countless arms flail incessantly, never letting the water come to rest. For Weigand, the water is "glimmering" and "pungent"; the mixture, then, is also in the first stages of decay.

In more precise terms, it is not the entire body of a whore into which Germany is transformed. The morass that called itself the German republic is only the vagina of a giant whore—no doubt a menstruating vagina, since the morass is red. From this morass, all of the horrors of revolution emerge:

> Alongside ardent German fanatics, a mindlessly angry German riffraff; alongside Russian rabble-rousers, a bestial Polish contingent from the mines and factories of Lower Rhine-Westphalia. And among the nurses, prostitution as if some swamp had spewed them forth. Alcoholism and licentiousness in men and women. (Rudolf Herzog)[11]

The successful draining of swamps is evidently a very dubious claim to fame.*

---

*Yet those on the Left who are hostile to sexuality have been happy to make just such a claim. Draining the swamps of reaction and ridding the air of their awful stench have been favorite occupations of official Russian communism from the start. Or consider this: "As a communist organization, we would have been forced to join a feminist march that was traveling through the area playing pop music, decked out in costumes, splashed with colors, and spreading a vile ideological stench." This complaint was registered by the Communist League of West Germany (KBW) in the Frankfurt local supplement of the *Kommunistische Volkszeitung*, February 20, 1975. Draining the antiauthoritarian swamps, the swamps of the subculture, was the favorite catchword of the "Marxist-Leninists," who from 1969 on worked to transform the student movement into a rock-hard party of the proletariat. And I am truly appalled when I hear the East German professor Wolfgang Harich express the "melancholy" (*Spiegel*, May 19, 1975) that the present state of German literature causes him: "It [the melancholy] is due to the fact that, compared to its glorious past, German literature today threatens to degenerate into a rotten, stagnant swamp, from which the heads of at most a very few half-caste aspiring gods will still protrude." (Half-caste *Jews*? Poor Germany! Soon we will be dry ground again.) But as always, Harich finds himself in the best (literary) company:

> A marshland flanks the mountainside,
> Infecting all that we have gained;
> Our gain would reach its greatest pride
> If all this noisome bog were drained.
> I work that millions [of men] may possess this space,
> If not secure, a free and active race.
> [This is never-resting Faust, expressing his final wishes.]
> Such busy, teeming throngs I long to see,
> Standing on freedom's soil, a people free.
> Then to the moment could I say:

If it dries out a little, the morass becomes simply "filth." This is the *mot juste* for the republic in more peaceful times:

> Those who are not dead, or languishing in prison, or leading unsettled lives across the border, have bored holes for themselves in the filth that covers every living thing. Many have become enfeebled and gone to wrack and ruin, while many others have reorganized in new forms to wage bitter struggles in new places.[12]

Slime

Slime seems to be a variant of the morass, perhaps its surface. It coats the entire republic. "Look out for yourself. Prison may indeed be the best way to escape the great slime that covers us,"[1] wrote one man, an opponent of the republic's existence, to his imprisoned friend Salomon.

Just as unsparingly,

> the pacifistic, perverse slime of degenerate literati poured across the land, profaning and desecrating all the treasures of German culture, all the values of the German soul, and dragging everything healthy and rooted into the dirt. (Heinz)[2]

Even generals, to the extent that they made peace with the republic, became slime: "An attempt by the *slime* to gain power. Ecclesiastical slime—bourgeois slime—soldier slime."[3] This note from the diary of Colonel von Epp in spring 1930, refers to attempts by the Catholic Center party, other moderate parties, and army generals in the mold of Groener and Schleicher, to set up bourgeois coalition governments. Von Kahr earned the same reproach for failing to explain to the putschists how his last-minute decision to abandon the Hitler Putsch of 1923 was that of a man of "German conscience." He might have prevented "everything pure from being

> Linger you now, you are so fair!
> Now records of my earthly day
> No flight of eons can impair—
> Foreknowledge comes, and fills me with such bliss,
> I take my joy, my highest moment this. [He dies.]

"No flight of eons. . . ." Fascist rulers weren't the first ones whose gaze "tallied up the millennia," as Benjamin put it (*Letter from Paris (Pariser Breif)*). This is the gaze of the patriarch, surveying the last remnants of uncultivated femaleness, the last little "swamp"—annoying despite its size, "infecting all that we have gained." And from Trotsky to Hanns Eisler, the communist male mentality has passed such drainers-of-ourselves on to us as part of our humanistic "cultural legacy." They defined the social-democratic cultural life of the German Democratic Republic, and they continue to define the cultural life of the GDR today . . . the classics . . . Yechhhhh! If we want to find out who is to be drained next, all we need do is read one of the "leading" newspapers, which are always running an actual list of the kind of "swamp" that is threatening most severely the rocks on which our country's security is built.

F. von Epp.

overrun with evil slime, as so often happens in Germany.'' (Gronnen)[4] Pacifism, backdoor politics, bourgeois modes and manners, this is where the hard begin to soften. Franz Nord writes:

> What the soldiers feared was not future battles or future dangers, but their dark, ominous forebodings of a tenacious bourgeoisie immersing everything in its slime.[5]

Dwinger called the politicians of Berlin "Berlin slime-toads."[6]

Pulp

Pulp seems more closely related to mire. *Pulp* appears whenever the will to fight collapses:

> Hindenburg rescued wartime Germany from the Russian storms. Hitler rescued *postwar* Germany from the Bolshevist wave! And more: from national collapse, from being mashed to a pulp![1]

What Jünger feared most in the pulp was its hybrid character. He would rather have died than come in contact with anything soft and moist:

> surely we are closer to enemies of pure breeding than to any pacifist or internationalist. And surely we are achieving something more important, by killing each other here, than if we were to coalesce into some great pulpy mishmash.[2]

Like surging, soldier blood, *race* is a phallic concept. The front does not in the first instance divide classes, parties, or other interest groups. It is the race that struggles against the pulp, the rock against the raging sea: a battle of the sexes, a battle to fend off castration. When that battle becomes hopeless—when, as in Germany after 1923, there is no more front—the world loses its reality:

> They [Freikorps soldiers] became alienated from a world they perceived to be rotten, blurred as if beaten to a pulp, unspeakably implausible. (Salomon)[3]

The only real thing was fighting. (You couldn't be a man without fighting, and being a man was the only way of being alive.) When there is no more fighting, no more being a man, life ceases and everything (the man, the world) becomes a pulp.

"Behind"

The moist dirt wasn't only "below" (*unten*), it was also "behind" (*hinten*). The military base and home (*Heimat*) were *behind*. (From the perspective of the front, "home" was a wholly negative term, especially toward the end of the war.) Anything not part of the front was *behind*. During the war, "the military base was soaked like a sponge with deserters and wheeler-dealers." (Heinz)[1] And after the war, "the base dispersed on looting raids, surfacing again in the seething swamp of corruption surrounding the new authorities." (Heinz)[2]

With the "stab in the back,"* both home and military base reached out to sully the front itself. "The cowardly, mutinous homeland has ground our honor into the dirt along with its own." (Berthold's diary)[3] Above all, the worst kinds of hybridizations were taking place back *behind*.

> The strong ones, the healthy ones, the fellows with marrow in their bones were fighting and dying out there. Behind the front, hordes of stinking softheads and flat-foot Indians ran around desecrating the race! (Thor Goote)[4]

Goote is expressing a number of fears here. First, what is the point of all the fighting if he comes home to find that "softheads" have taken all the available women. Men of this kind turn everything they touch to softness. Soft children: no more soldiers. His second fear: those who have stayed behind are ignoring us. Worse yet, they shit on us, kicking up a "stink" in the rear, while our buttocks are still clamped tight shut. Third: those soft,

---

*The "stab in the back" (*Dolchstoss*) refers to the claim that German authorities betrayed the nation by surrendering in 1918 while the German army remained undefeated on the battlefield. Right-wing forces (especially Hitler) advanced this claim to discredit the Weimar government.—Trans.

useless skunks dare to call themselves our superiors! And fourth: this may be the end of the race. The elevated phallus that helped us to stand erect, now begins to falter, dragging us and our honor "into the dirt."

As long as the front still stood, distinctions could be made:

> They gradually came to despise everything and everyone behind the front; for they had recognized that they alone held the fate of Germany in their hands. (Schauwecker)[5]

The only people still left "behind the front" were the shirkers, the dodgers, the ones who hid in the latrines while the men at the front risked their necks.[6] The military collapse changed all that. Now these men, too, had to go "behind," into that despicable anal zone. And since they weren't returning victorious, they were forced to identify with the dirt (or at least step into it).

In brief, a spongy, seething swamp could also—or was likely to—be produced when what was *below* mixed with what was *behind*.

Shit

Just as Jünger had a preference for "purebred enemies," Goote too would rather have seen

> Tommies who love their fatherland, though they are my enemies, than the so-called Germans who, after squatting behind the lines like cowards, are now trying to do their sticky business with profits from the collapse of the nation.[1]

The "collapse of the nation" clearly refers to shit, the result of "squatting behind the lines like cowards." In the aseptic language of adults, "doing one's business" (big or small) is a common euphemism for eliminating excrement from the body's lower orifices. The phrase "their sticky business" leaves no doubt about the nature of the substance in question; these cowards are in the process of turning shit into gold, and we'll be getting the short end of the stick again, because it's been drilled into us that we would rather die than touch excrement. (Anyone who has been schooled in cleanliness remains a soldier even in the midst of collapse.)

The collapse may have been concocted "behind" the front, but at the actual moment of collapse it was the enemy that spread over the defeated soldiers like shit. F. W. Heinz has captured that moment:

> The collapse of Germany reared its ugly head, as a superior force flowing out, khaki-brown, from the dusk of August 9, under the shadow of fighter planes, amid the din of grenades and the clanking of armored transports, to crush the hastily formed front. The war was lost.[2]

The front was equated with an anal sphincter that could no longer hold anything back; the war was "going" in its pants; the enemy, contained up to this point, broke over and out of the soldiers as a "flowing . . . superior force." Here the collapse becomes a process taking place within the soldiers' own bodies and leaving them soiled. (The German language makes the same connection when it uses *Durchfall*—"falling through"—to mean both flunking an exam and involuntarily emptying the bowels.) This may explain the feelings of shame and humiliation so many officers recorded when they heard the news of the capitulation and the kaiser's abdication. At that moment, they stood before their country as grown-up men with "loaded" pants, exposed to the malicious eyes of all.

It was no shame to be inundated by the raging Red flood; in fact, that was a fate worthy of heroes. But the collapse was an offense to honor, and something that no defensive reaction could repair; the weapon had been ripped from the soldier's hands. The first thing that lifted the soldier male above all this filth was his staunch adherence to principle, his national consciousness, his sense of responsibility to the nation as a whole. The absence of such principles, cowardliness, had evidently allowed the "failure" (*Durchfall*) to occur in the first place. Thus it is characteristically in connection with the notion of incontinence that the *Sonderbündler* appear in Rudolf Herzog. (The *Sonderbündler*, or "separatists," lobbied in 1923 for the formation of an independent Rhenish republic that would develop close ties to France.) Here is Herzog's description of these perpetrators of crimes against the nation:

> A wave of excrement rolled across a Rhineland paralyzed with fear, stifling its final remnants of resistance, its final cries for help . . . And this wave of excrement rolled over the great and glorious cities of the Rhine, and when it paused and bubbled up, it was red with the blood of brothers. It rolled on toward the villages, hungry for corncribs and cattle stalls, and the farmers saw their possessions being swept away to nourish the alien *Sonderbündler* brigades.[3]

Here Red flood and mire, rebellion and national collapse, have coalesced into a single stream of blood and excrement. The origins of this wave are closely connected to processes that occur (could occur, have occurred, threaten to occur) within the human body. The Rhineland is conceived of as a human body. The final remnants of resistance, the final cries for help are the unsuccessful self-defenses of a body that has been "ravished" by the wave that was "hungry" for it. The horrible simultaneity of flood and mire (rebellion and collapse) conjures up the typical verbs for both things: "swept away" and "stifling." And for civil war: "bubbled up." Every terror is mixed in here. The body is "paralyzed with fear."

"Through the Body . . ."

Thus all the dirt of the new regime was perceived through the body and the senses:

> On the contrary, the filth of profiteering welled up to monstrous proportions, while the racketeers' claws and tentacles wound more and more relentlessly around the hungry throats of the people . . . To the broad masses of the nation, the government smelled rotten. . . . For many, the aura or morality surrounding the government gave off a stench that grew worse by the minute. (Freimüller)[1]

The man is standing in the filth, disgusted, exposed to claws and tentacles and nauseating stench. What an age this is, when "wheeler-dealers are tossed up by the muddy tide, finally to stick fast in some position of state power."[2] The whole world has turned sticky. The "dung-heap stench of revolution" penetrates Lieutenant Ehrhardt's nostrils.[3] Then there is Dwinger's Captain Werner: "I can take it no longer. It lies beyond my exhausted powers to drink in more of the morass each day."[4] And in *Memoirs of a Freikorps Student* (*Erinnerungen eines Freikorpsstudenten*), Hans Schauwecker delcares: "Meanwhile shame and betrayal, filth and misery rose higher and higher around us until we could have drowned in it. The bitterness of living through a mindless revolt, with its complacent absence of shame, was enough to deprive us of any enthusiasm for life."[5]

They were right in the middle of it, and it was forcing its way into them. Freimüller responded with the following concise formulation of the tasks of good government:

> It must restlessly probe the spirit and body of the people; it must listen to the nation's heartbeat. The moment its penetrating eyes perceive muddy obscurity, the moment its punctilious nose smells stinking excrement, the moment its attentive ears detect the ominous roar of an impending storm-wave, it must raise its arm with ruthless, burning zeal, never resting until the mire has been swept away, the filth expunged, until the roar of the approaching storm-wave has finally died away.[6]

The government's task is to get rid of any "dirt" that settles on the "body of the nation." This is all!

To the men of the Right, Left and Right were divided by the different boundaries they drew between dirt and cleanliness. "The cow-pie thoughts and the mental excrement of the whole materialist-rationalist-social democratic-Bolshevist scandal economy of the modern era will not be of even historical value to future generations."[7] This is how Lanz von

Liebenfels anticipates the triumph of the nonshits in the Third Reich in his *Racial Mysticism: Introduction to Aryan-Christian Secret Doctrines* (*Rassenmystik: Einführung in die ariochristliche Geheimlehre*), 1929.[8] Liebenfels offers an open declaration of a common penchant among "nationalist" writers for lumping together liberals, social democrats, communists, anarchists, syndicalists, etc., whose internecine battles are declared to be deceptive, diversionary maneuvers. Even a writer like F. W. Heinz, whose analyses of social conditions and political processes are exceptionally "rational" for a fascist, draws the line at this point: "The rest of the press concluded in chorus, and even the democratic press of Ullstein and Mosse offered proof, that their [the leftist press's] writers were intimately acquainted with the excremental language of the subhuman rats who were now beginning to surface."[9] The crucial phrase is "intimately acquainted" (*innig vertraut*); the "excremental language" is felt within and through the body, in those nether regions from which all of this had to surface in order to become visible.

The construction of the "subhuman" (*Untermensch*) can also be more easily understood from this perspective. A subhuman is a human of the nether regions, a person who is human even below. Men of the Right are human only on top; it is impossible to be a human being below. (This explains why men lie on top during sexual intercourse and why psychoanalysis, staunchly echoing the social code, ascribes strong "female tendencies" to men who prefer to be underneath. An acquaintance once used the term "the wrong way up" in a conversation, to clarify the notion of "progressive lovemaking." This might indicate something of the complexity of describing behavior in which the kind of sexual denial common in our culture does not predominate. Women are always "on the bottom.") Everything good comes from the top.

Rain

And yet not everything that comes from the top is good. On the contrary, anything that *flows* from above is particularly horrible:

> The persecution at home—from quarters that considered us
> thorns in their eyes—reached its peak. They were pouring
> veritable troughs of dirt on the heads of our Kurland fighters.
> (Ihno Meyer)[1]

How do these troughs come to be "up above," when dirt usually dwells in the depths? To begin with, this dirt had attained a social status that was considered "superior"—which explains why most of the floods of dirt rained down from the press. Lieutenant Ehrhardt characterized the articles printed about him by "the repulsive guild of mudslingers and honor-cleavers" (honor could be *severed!*) as a "rain of excrement."[2]

The men were particularly defenseless in the face of this curse. "The press, spitting out its crippling poison a millionfold each day" (Zöberlein),[3] was frightening precisely because its effects were so debilitating. The situation Heinz describes is also one of relative defenselessness: "A torrential downpour of curses, threats, and abuse assailed us from the outside."[4] (He was sitting in prison at the time and lived in fear of being lynched by a mob enraged at the murder of Rathenau.)

What possible defense could there be against rain that was being poured out of troughs up above? One was helpless, a child exposed to the whims of adults. That, in fact, seems to me to be the crucial point: the "big people," the grown-ups, were up there. The tone of the following complaint from Ernst Jünger makes that very clear:

> To kill people is nothing: they will all have to die one day. But it is wrong to deny them. No, to deny them is wrong. The worst thing isn't that they want to kill us, but that they continually inundate us with their hatred, that they never call us anything but Boches, Huns, barbarians. This is what makes us bitter.[5]

Jünger, the man of culture, feels he is not being taken seriously, that he is not being treated like a man, that his qualities are being "denied."

Not being recognized for what they are, or consider themselves to be, is one of the basic torments children experience at the hands of their parents and from the adult world as a whole. Adults are up "above"—more than this, they *look down* on their children. (The child withdraws, abashed by their ridicule, like a dog they have drenched with water.) When does their patronizing start? Most often, when children begin to express an interest in the areas adults keep to themselves. These are the areas the children have learned to recognize as "dirty" places, the places where "dirty" things happen—especially the genitals. The knowledge that adults nevertheless play their games with those forbidden objects and in those forbidden places (in the forbidden area of the house, the parents' bedroom) fills the imagination of every bourgeois child. Adults somehow have the right to dirty themselves under certain conditions. When they react defensively, with shocked evasiveness and above all with ridicule, to children's desires, or to pointed questions, the children equate those reactions with the forbidden dirtiness. The harmless remark "you'll understand when you're older," delivered with a superior smile, appears to the child as a form of defilement by the adults to whom they are helplessly subjected.

Cadets in the military academies used a kind of hissing to defend themselves against the similar intrusions they were subjected to by instructors:

> If any superior dared approach us to drip his honey into our ears, we would relentlessly employ the method of shushing. (Rossbach, cited by Bronnen)[6]

Infiltration by "Communist Subversive"

Hamburg. July 23

For three months, Günter Wallraf was our co-worker. After infiltrating Gerling (and other firms and institutions) under an alias, he infiltrated BILD. The court order allows us to call him a "Communist subversive" with impunity.

His habits were chewing on grass and leaves, tippling an occasional Ballantine's scotch in the morning, spooning down vitamins, and swearing when he lost at ping-pong. He was always bent over and could never look anyone straight in the eye. His whispered "Yes, sir" came more often than needed.

He said he had worked for an ad agency in Düsseldorf and wanted to try his hand at journalism.

His story was as phony as the name he gave: Hans Esser. He had an identity card made out in that name so he could approach readers and officials as a reporter. A female voice answered his telephone with a curt "Hello."

He spent his nights in a commune—nowadays we would call it a "communal living situation."

His disguise was as good as his income: 8455 marks in three months (he had a talent for writing).

He deceived co-workers who had accepted him as a genuine colleague.

Exactly one month ago he handed in his resignation, complaining of stomach pains. Since then he has slipped back into the darkness he crawled out of. No doubt he is writing down all the experiences he claims to have had in the Hannover editorial office of BILD.

Our phony co-worker is probably gushing joy by the bucketful. Good for him.

At least he quit smoking while he was with us. He was too busy for that.

A cadet had to learn to tolerate all kinds of drill, but he did not have to put up with this.

Here Jünger begins to stammer like a misunderstood child who feels he is not being given his due by the French (his opponents in the masculine struggle). When he says, we are ready to die, he means, we are men, just like you! Then why are you treating us like children ("Barbarians," "Huns," "Boches")? "*This* is what makes us bitter."

These writers feel themselves being drenched "from above"; they experience themselves once again in the situation of children—a situation that reactivates feelings of hatred toward the "grown-ups" of their childhood. The associated affect is so overwhelming precisely because reactivation of that hatred simultaneously conjures up the old situation of helplessness: they couldn't fight their parents. The fact that those parents ("grown-ups," the press, the French) adamantly refused to recognize the young boy, and later the adolescent, as a man, continuing to look "down" on the adult son as if he were still a child, left Jünger so embittered that he would rather have died than remain the object of the dirt that came raining down from up above. "I no longer intend to be spat on, shat on, and pissed on by those great pigs who think they can get away with anything. I am a man myself now. Away with those troughs of dirt!" And yet a displacement has now occurred. The people pouring out the dirt are no longer identified as the parents or their substitute authorities. The new defilers, neither parents nor authorities themselves, had simply claimed parental privileges as if that were the most natural thing in the world. It was other "children" who were doing the things these men themselves would have been severely punished for doing; what is was alright for parents to do, it was "dirty" for them to do.

The most important thing to remember here is that the men in question were defenseless, and to make matters worse, innocent. (They were no longer children, so why treat them as such?) They were being subjected to the greatest injustices.

Defense against the Morass, Slime, Pulp

The threat of the "flood" may be combated with "erections": towering cities, mountains, troops, stalwart men, weapons. Ideally, the "Red flood" should appear as identical with the Red Army; implicitly, it is always this. The flood is an armed, rebellious mass containing everything that will dissolve a man. The best deterrent? The weapon. The best way of keeping one's own camp under control? The ritual of the mass parade.

The threats posed by the morass, the mire, slime, pulp, shit, and showers of excrement are of a different order. The nature of these elements is unclear, more confused and heterogeneous. Since the morass is most like the flood (in terms, among other things, of its relative liquidity), it can also be combated with weapons, with the "Freikorps, death of the Red pestilence" (Paust),[1] or with an "ox-whip" (Herzog).

Beyond that, weapons aren't much use against the threat of sinking into a confused heterogeneity. The man within, with his "fire of enthusiasm," is to be called upon here to fight the "miserable morass of the present." This becomes evident in the case of the mire, against which only a specific type of inner nature, one that can generate ideological formulas for defense, is effective: "roar of the blood" (Heinz); "spiritually conscious core"

From Hans Roden's *Deutsche Soldaten* (*1935*). Monument on the site of an accident: "In memory of the eighty-one men swallowed up by the river during a military exercise on 31 March 1925." (A pontoon bridge on the Weser River collapsed.)

(Rosenberg); "golden remnants of the early war generation" (Zöberlein); "go for the [inner] beast's throat" (Goote).

The same is true of slime. "Look out for yourself"; otherwise, your only option will be to "become a stranger to youself" (Salomon). Hold fast to the "treasures of German culture" and the "values of the German soul" (Killinger); become nationalist enough to be immune to the slime: "Ecclesiastical slime—bourgeois slime—soldier slime"—Groener, Schleicher, von Kahr—are *men from the margins* of your own camp. Mire and slime form in places toward which the flood is already beginning to seep, places where dams aren't strong enough.

Pulp seems to signify an escalation of the threat; against this, nothing short of a Hitler is needed, or suicide, to avoid dissolution of the self into a substance of this kind (Jünger). That's the problem: if the man uses weapons against the mire, slime, or pulp, he is killing himself; for these substances are on and within his own body, in the places where his own dams have started to crumble.

Thus political enemies and the hostile principle of femaleness appear in the floods in much the same way—both of these flow as embodiments of the eruption of the soldier male's unconscious. Rebellion, rebels, the working masses, Poles in revolt, Bolshevism, the Red Army—all of these under the leadership, or with the decisive participation of women. Female practice: to do what is forbidden.

Fidus, "The Earth" (1893).

The morass appears to be the first stage in the solidification of the flood; as such, it is still relatively distant from the threatened men. Above all, it is the whore of a republic; ravished Mother Germany; a gigantic menstruating vagina, teeming with every imaginable creature; internationalism.

Mire, slime, pulp. On and through the men's own bodies, in peripheral areas that threaten to turn soft. Cowards. The military base, pacifism, self-interest, bourgeois thinking, the quest for comfort, pleasure that knows no danger, incontinence, "loaded" pants.

In the face of the cowardly man—the kind who allows his inner self to escape to the outside and who lurks even within the soldier male—the only defense is to "stand fast" (clamping the buttocks tight shut): to think of, and believe in, the nation.* At the center of this defense stands the prohibition against any kind of mixing (of men and women, of inner self and outside world).**

In the final analysis, there is no defense against cowardly men, the coward in men (alias "the pig within"), or the collapse. Soldier males are helpless (initially) in such cases. They have no means to combat "troughs of dirt," "torrential downpours of abuse," "showers of excrement," "crippling poison," "filthy language," "the wave of excrement," "stenches," feelings of being "drenched" with hatred, or finally, the collapse—even though all of those things come from within the men themselves.

In such situations, the soldier male temporarily turns to shit himself—soiled, stinking, and oozing away. The eruption of his own unconscious pours over him, in the form of the collapse; and his desire, in the form of excrement. To understand this, we need to remember that there is a clear connection between the man's defenselessness and the situation of a child who, after claiming to be grown up, is caught by his parents with his pants full; or whose weakness is exploited to make him the target of unjust ridicule from "superior" adults (showers of excrement, the crippling poison of the press, being drenched).

The affects connected with the collapse, with the state of being drenched and debilitated, are the strongest by far: insult and bitterness. Their discharge is delayed: its name is revenge.

Summary: Republic, Revolution, War

From the mire of the collapse and the waves of the Red flood, there rose "the republic," "the morass." The republic was no longer a struggle or a movement. It was a state of being characterized by the threat of sinking: the supreme state of heterogeneity.

> Morass, Red morass, glimmering morass, pungent morass,
> miserable morass of the present, seething morass of corruption,
> filth of profiteering, flood of mire, thick pulp, slime in government, the slippery slope down into the morass, Marxist wave of
> mire (then, with the addition of separatist activities) a wave of
> blood and excrement.

---

*The same method dogmatists use to combat themselves, their "inner beings."

**For the sake of clarity, I have made sharper distinctions among the different hybrid states than my sources sometimes do. The phrase "flood of mire" (*Schlammflut*), for instance, shows that more than one threat can appear at the same time, and in the same guise. The mixture themselves mix. When one appears, the others are not far behind.

Abb. 137. Altargruppe „Deutsche Art"   Farbiger Entwurf 1918

From an altarpiece. Fidus, "German Ways," 1918.

It is not only different sexes that are mixing together here, but secretions from different orifices of the lower body. The belief among young children described by Freud as the "cloaca theory"[1]—that women have only one pelvic orifice and that birth takes place through the anus—was preserved here in its entirety in the idea of the republic as the belly of some gigantic prostitute.[2] The "dam" that burst to produce the republic was the one separating the anus from the vagina: a stinking, Red morass, formed through the attempts of crazed, lower-class criminals to impregnate Mother Germany. All they accomplished was to turn the country into a swamp of semen, blood, and shit. The woman burst—the nation was torn apart.*

When women violently overflowed their banks, as in Delmar,[3] what horrible substance was it that poured out of them? More often than not it was excrement, rather than the juices of pleasure. Novels and biographies of soldier males do not, for obvious reasons, state this directly. Works of this kind were addressed to the public and were to function as political propaganda (among other things). On the other hand, this overflowing was by no means consigned to silence; the men find expression for it in their own language. Instead of saying "the woman voided herself during intercourse," they might refer to the "filthy floods of the November revolution." Substitutions such as this were *not* unconscious; they were made for the sake of social decency. This becomes clear for example in the collected volumes of Krauss's anthology of erotica, *Antropophyteia;* especially useful for our purposes is the 1911 volume from the collection of Drs. Hellmut and Alengo, entitled *The Erotic Quatrains of Well-educated German Townspeople* (*Der erotische Vierzeiler höher gebildeter deutscher Städter*). The book contains 334 stanzas of a song entitled "Die Wirtin an der Lahn" ("The Innkeeper's wife on the River Lahn"), collected from male drinking circles and student residences in Jena, Stettin, and Halle.[4] Stanza 97: "Frau Wirtin's** sixth aunt, everyone knows,/Went by the name of 'Pretty Rose'/She had a dam, 'twas clearly split/And when you tried to fuck her/Your prick got soaked with shit." The language of this verse is not exceptional.[5] Equally common here is the notion of the undifferentiatedness within woman (in at the front, and out at the back, or vice versa; there is no

---

*Terms like "pudenda" (from *pudere*, "to be ashamed") aren't the only ones to have been coined by an oppressive, anxiety-ridden masculine sensibility. Women have every reason to reject the term *Damm* ("dam") as a designation for the area between the anus and vagina (perineum); as well as *Dammriss* (literally, "ruptured dam"), the medical term used to denote the tearing of the perineum during childbirth. This use of "dam" arises from male fears that moist substances in the pelvic region may mix. The "dam" is the man's guarantee that he won't run into shit or fall into that huge, devouring hole. Compare the widespread fear among young males of not finding the "right hole" in the dark the "first time."

**Off-color poems and songs about "Frau Wirtin" (the innkeeper's wife) and her daughter are a German tradition, still popular today, roughly akin to "farmer's daughter" stories in the United States.—Trans.

difference). Inside is crap: "And if you want to screw her,/with a broomstick you must woo her/To push the crap back down through her."[6] And there was "overflowing": "But when she tried to take a piss/From her huge thing, as big as this,/It started to pour down/Like some old rusty waterpipe,/Enough to make you drown."[7] She surprises one of her guests, a "rotten muff-diver," with a "great fat stream."[8] In the same volume (*Antropophyteia IV*), there is a two-liner from the "Golden ABC"—which, according to Ottwald, formed part of the permanent repertoire at student fraternity drinking bouts.[9] "The cock crows on the dunghill crag,/She pisses while she fucks, the slag."[10] Given our knowledge of the constitution of the Freikorps, we can be sure that its male members knew and sang verses like this. And it should perhaps be noted that when Hellmut and Alengo use the term "well-educated German townspeople" in their title, they are being neither polemical nor ironic; they are simply practicing sound positivism.

In the civil war, the Freikorps soldier's proper sphere of activity, the whole morass is put on the fire and brought to a boil:

> Seething chaos; maelstrom of revolt; scum from boiling soup; everything simmering in a single pot, to a mindless, indiscriminate, stinking pulp; poison of conspiracy cooking away in a massive cauldron, an enormous cauldron in which thick blood and thin beer bubble up wildly together; a witch's cauldron, cooking up the soldierly Freikorps and their Spartacist opponents; atoms whirling in the boilers of the metropolis; all the molded forms . . . melted down again in a thousand blast furnaces; the seed of a new revolution cooking away in a massive cauldron; inspiration in its fearful glow; and more.

The boiling process triggered surprisingly few feelings of anxiety in soldier males. They were more likely to view this process as something positive, as a way (assuming they survived it) to avoid sinking into the morass. A good boiling, a thorough exposure to every kind of water, brought out the real soldier in the men. The boiling process in the witch's cauldron (of revolution) was the first step toward rebirth, as it had been for the alchemists of old. The men *needed* those cauldrons.

THE BODY AS DIRT

As we have seen, hybrid, fluid substances such as swamps or mire were regularly used to signify something other than themselves. They had nothing to do with geographical or meteorological phenomena or events; they always stood for something. How many of the men had ever been in danger of sinking into a real morass? How many had ever even seen one? Slime and pulp (the German words also mean "porridge," "pablum") were foods they had eaten as children; ebbs and floods are something that you first get to know as interesting natural phenomena, as a rule; and mire was something that formed on the streets when it rained, or that lay along riverbanks—not very threatening, all in all, when these things turned up in nature (as long as they were not part of some "natural catastrophe").

I've tried to show that whenever those things did turn up, they referred largely to the bodies of the men in question. You could almost say that erect, soldierly bodies were the sole reference points for those states and substances (which at times could even surface in, and exit from, the bodies). In fact, all of the anxiety-producing substances introduced in this work have something in common: they could be called upon to describe processes occurring in or upon the human body, especially its orifices. "Floods," "morasses," "mire," "slime," and "pulp"—this whole battery of terms can describe bodily secretions if you start out with a negative attitude toward them. This points to a reversal of the affects originally associated with the elimination of such substances from the body: pleasurable sensations. The pleasurable sensations have been replaced by a panic defense against the possibility of their occurrence. The emotional intensity relates to that struggle, not to the geographical existence of some morass (and only partly to the political existence of a republic).

How was that connection made? Through the process of association?[1] It's easy enough to find examples. All of the substances are defined by their ability to flow and their hybrid status. A third common property is their ability to absorb objects without changing in the process: after they spill over a man or allow him to sink into themselves, their surfaces become calm again. In other words, they are remarkably alive; they can move autonomously, fast or slow, however they wish.

Their hybrid condition (= "impurity") and their capacity for killing made them very well suited as "displaced" designations for danger and the forbidden. Their "aliveness" made them attractive for representing processes within living bodies. And the attribute of leaving no traces of their activity, of closing up again after every action, invited the presence of hidden things, things from secret realms and from the domain of the dead (corpses buried in peat bogs). Someone was already lying in every morass or swamp you sank into. And since swamps became peaceful again afterward, since you couldn't tell how dangerous they were, it was easy for them to be seen as embodiments of *deceptiveness*. A veil of mist over the wet lowlands.

In another sphere of activity—the household—women were the living entities associated with hybrid substances. They turned solids into liquids when they cooked; and when they washed clothes and dishes, or took care of babies, they worked with, and in, things that were swampy, mushy. They

German postcard (late nineteenth century).

stripped off the babies' wet pants and wiped the shit from their behinds. They cleared black muck out of stopped-up drains and cleaned toilets. They boiled the juice out of fruits and stored the extract. They wiped the floors and got their hands into liquid manure. And on and on.

The average bourgeois male of the Wilhelmine era would have let himself be shot rather than touch those substances in any context that was reminiscent of "women's work." One of the nastier ploys of the military was to condemn men to perform such female chores (and there, men had to do them). Even in the military, the hybrid and the fluid fell under the heading of dirt, punishment, women's work, or, worse still, unmanliness.

Those associations might explain the reaction of defense, but not the soldier male's intense fear of the hybrid (nor the attraction it always held for him). The explanation for this must lie closer to his body. At some point, his bodily fluids must have been negativized to such an extent that they became the physical manifestations of all that was terrifying. Included in this category were all of the hybrid substances that were produced by the body and flowed on, in, over, and out of the body: the floods and stickiness of sucking kisses; the swamps of the vagina, with their slime and mire; the pap and slime of male semen; the film of sweat that settles on the stomach, thighs, and in the anal crevice, and that turns two pelvic regions into a sub-tropical landscape; the slimy stream of menstruation; the damp spots wherever bodies touch; the warmth that dissolves physical boundaries (meaning not that it makes *one* body out of a man and woman, but that it transgresses boundaries: the infinite body; the body as flow). Also the floods of orgasm: the streams of semen, the streams of relaxation flowing through the musculature, the streams of blood from bitten lips, the sticky wetness of hair soaked with sweat. And all the flowing delights of infancy: the warm piss-stream running down naked legs; the mire and pulp of fresh shit in the infant's diapers, the fragrant warmth that lets the body expand, the milk-stream from the mother's breast, the smacking of lips on the comforter, the sweet pap that spreads over hands and face, the sucking on a never-ending thumb, the good-tasting stream of snot running from the nose into the mouth, not to mention the liberating stream of hot tears that turns a mask into a pulp and then a face again. (Lament the tears you shed/No longer, my dear souls./They also are the rain/For blooms most delicate./Would not the bush from too much fortune/Wither, verily,/Without suffering's/Cloud-bursts?)[2]

Dried-up streams. More than that: streams converted into their opposites. Death in place of pleasure. We can get an idea when and why that must have happened by reading what Margaret Mahler has to say about the function of the infant's bodily fluids: "The newborn's waking life centers around his continuous attempts to achieve homeostasis."[3] All that can be used to attain that state are "somatic defense mechanisms, i.e., overflow and discharge reactions."[4] In the course of this discharge, certain things occur:

> The effect of his mother's ministrations in reducing the pangs of need-hunger cannot be isolated, nor can it be differentiated by the young infant from tension-reducing attempts of his own, such as urinating, defecating, coughing, sneezing, spitting, regurgitating, vomiting, all the ways by which the infant tries to rid himself of unpleasurable tension.[5]

The nursing infant is depicted as a little machine that keeps itself running by flowing over occasionally.

> The effect of these expulsive phenomena as well as the gratification gained by his mother's ministrations help the infant, in time, to differentiate between a "pleasurable" and "good" quality and a "painful" and "bad" quality of experience.[6]

What if the child is unable to make that crucial distinction because it has been denied sufficient opportunity for pleasurable overflowing? What if it is subjected to the diaper-changing routine, the daily round of mopping up, from the very first day? What if the people taking care of the child react to its overflows with defensiveness, disgust, displeasure? Then, according to Margaret Mahler, the child will withdraw its psychic cathexes from its own periphery; it will be unable to break the (unpleasant) symbiotic connection to its mother; and if it is ripped violently out of that symbiosis, it will perceive itself as a thing filled with "evil" streams and will have no sense of its own boundaries.[7] Where other people have skin, this child (under certain social conditions) will grow armor.*

Wilhelmine society organized such conditions. It is too late to peer into the cradles of the children who would later become soldier males, but we can still see Wilhelmine women and how they were alienated from their own "streams" and we know that era's attitude toward "dirt."[8] One thing is certain: as part of the boys' very early training to be soldier males (and what Wilhelmine bourgeois—or, indeed, what social-democratic—education didn't have that as its goal?), harsh punishments were meted out if any of the wet substances in question turned up other than in its specifically designated place or situation. One after the other, the streams were cut off or banished to the back of beyond. A social dam and drainage system captured every stream—even beer-laden streams of vomit, which had to vanish into a particular basin in the clubhouse before any of the "old boys" caught sight of them. As far as I can see, only three streams were permissible: streams of sweat; streams of speech; and the inexhaustible streams of alcohol. Under specific conditions (toward which the entire system steered), a fourth stream was added: the stream of blood from murdered victims, or the stream of your own "raging blood."[9]

When the republic was called a "morass," it was not just a case of one word being substituted for another; the things a man felt on his body were real pap and slime. He had no choice but to perceive them in that way, because they surfaced on his body as forbidden, negativized things. And for these things to be connected with the rebels (of the Red flood), there was no need for long associative chains. The visible evidence was enough: those people don't dam themselves up as much as I (have to).

Ferenczi has described an important aspect of the way in which children's perceptions of their own bodies are negativized. With more concrete insight into the process of "identification with the aggressor" than Anna Freud,[10] he sees the sexual behavior that adults living in a guilt-laden world display toward "innocent" children as the one form of aggression children cannot escape.[11] When a vastly more powerful adult handles a child, the adult's feelings of guilt and anxiety turn that act into a violation. The child can only work the act out psychically as subjection to the adult's will. Hence, the adult's touch is tantamount to a seduction. Ferenczi calls the change effected in the child "introjection of the adult's guilt feelings."[12] Where the child once felt pleasure, it now begins to feel guilt. But it does not begin, for instance, to *think* or *know* guilt; only later will its forced receptivity to guilt feelings be filled with the (socially defined) contents of specific "transgressions," ideologies, and so on.[13]

---

*For a more thorough discussion of this, refer to the chapter "Male Bodies" in volume 2.

So-called toilet training turns out then, to be a process of drying up the child and instilling guilt feelings. Traditional psychoanalysis wrongly limits the consequences of that process to the creation of the "anal" type, the character with a compulsion for order: the pedant, the collector, the happy statistician, the bureaucrat, or the inspired positivist. "Toilet training" must have broader consequences than that. With its compulsion for mopping up, it emerges as the primary force for implementing sexual repression in the widest sense and, in combination with the installation of adult guilt feelings in children's bodies, as the essential process for producing sexual anxiety.

Profoundly rejecting all of the bodily fluids and demoting them to the status of streams of dirt—with the help of systematically enforced prohibitions and threatened punishments—has to be a far more effective means of anchoring sexual anxiety in the person than having mothers or priests tell you that God sees everything. If you're a child who wants to succumb to "temptation" anyway, banishing the god who can peer under blankets must be at least a bit easier (especially in a dark room where you're not so afraid of *eyes*) than blocking out the sensory perception of the product of the pleasure taken in your body, namely, that feeling that you've dirtied yourself when your vagina turns damp from rubbing or when semen drops onto your stomach after you masturbate. The "all-seeing" god lives inside your own skin, in your peripheral areas, in your body's orifices and musculature. He is a part of the perception of pleasure itself; he is the one who converts pleasure into anxiety. The punitive god-figure owes his effectiveness (in the culture of "mopping up") to the fear that phenomena of dissolution may occur along the borders of the body. The same fear makes the protective god-figure possible.

Unless the child really felt that fear, how could the threat, mostly expressed by fathers, that onanism will produce debility be so enormously persuasive? Something really does *escape* during orgasm—physical tension—and suddenly, what we thought were streams of pleasure are our minds running out of our diseased spinal cords.[14] Hard reality: there they are, those droplets of pulpy slime, manifestations of our wickedness and future idiocy.

When Freud says that the superego functions in the same manner as the "conscience," the description represents a further step along the road to making psychoanalytic concepts less distinct and less concrete (substituting one vague term for another).[15] The real issue has to do with a bodily sensation, not with words, thoughts, or naive prohibitions. "You mustn't do that!"—how would a ploy like that ever stop anyone from doing something forbidden? It is the body that reacts: the wincing that cramps your muscles when you hear an indecent word; the impression that you'd die of heart failure if you said something unspeakable; hard, defensive cheek muscles set in rugged faces; the hollow feeling in the stomach and the urge to pee before a test; the wave of nausea that shakes a spinster's body when she spies a pair of young lovers; and so on. That is the "superego": the installation of displeasure and anxiety in the experience of pleasure itself. The awful word "internalization" (*Verinnerlichung*), which Freud occasionally used and the Frankfurt School elaborated until it became the most common currency in the "socialization debate," completely fails to describe the process in question. Yet it has become customary, whenever a person forgoes a desired action without the direct intercession of a social prohibition, to say that the renunciation resulted from an "internalization" of the relevant prohibition. The "head" has gradually emerged as the exclusive site of the "superego." The prohibitions of the "superego" have been equated with moral precepts, ethical teachings, and so on. The entire process has been dematerialized by people (especially the Frankfurt School) focusing their interest on ideologies, rather than on what human bodies feel when they reject pleasure. Yet the real issue is those feelings and the prohibition against using our own bodies in a manner consistent with their sexual needs and potential.

That prohibition, the law that bodies cannot know themselves, has been used to recreate susceptibility to repression ever since people first began ruling other people. Every regime has employed this method of inscribing itself upon the bodies of its subjects and on the bodies of the rulers themselves (probably first on women's bodies by their exclusion from social production during menstruation.)[16]

In societies ruled by a single person, the despot was the only one who could (theoretically) use his body in any way he pleased—except in a human way, since no other was like him. For everyone else, denial of social power coincided with a denial of possibilities for sexual satisfaction. This denial was set down in laws and commandments, but it was etched into bodies by harsh punishments at the hands of educators.[17] The authority of rulers is implanted into subjects' bodies in the form of a lack in overflowing (a prohibition against using what *belongs* to you). These subjects have always experienced their lack of social power as a lack of power over specific areas of their own bodies. The body must not become familiar, "known"; it must be an object and source of fear. The biblical "fall of man" occurred when Eve "seduced" Adam into eating from the tree of knowledge. ("And they knew each other"—the biblical phrase for sexual intercourse, a form of "knowledge" that has always been strictly regulated and kept within narrow limits.) Seen in this light, the "fall of man" depicts a failed revolution from the victor's standpoint. For attempting to put into practice their slogan "Our bodies belong to us," the rebels were sentenced to a life of forced labor in the sweat of their brows. "Your bodies belong to your ruler!"—that was the response. (The "paradise" they were driven out of was the blissful state of being ruled without realizing it. Even today, being driven out of "paradise" is the penalty for trying to create a paradise.)

Paolo Ucello, "George Battling the Dragon."

Once there were unfamiliar territories—parts of the body that prohibitions rendered inaccessible—it was easy to spread rumors (elevated to the status of laws) about the deadly perils they concealed.[18] The many-headed Hydras, Medusas, and dragons that the hazy vision of oppressed men saw living in the vagina,[19] were the images of the authority of the ruler (whose head also kept growing back), who had established penalties for entering that grotto. They were, so to speak, the heraldic emblem with which he branded the bodies of his subjects. (Enter only with his seal, under his law: borrowed potency.)

Installing dark territories, sources of terror and anxiety, in and on people's own bodies and the bodies of those they desired, was evidently the prerequisite for subjugating them later with an ideological assault. The assault reaped the harvest of fear and uncertainty, of people's feeling that there were many places within themselves that no one could enter—neither they themselves, nor anyone else. Those were the territories occupied by the gods, the police, laws, Medusas, and other monsters. And by the parents, who maintained autocratic fiefdoms in the unconquered niches of their children's bodies, exacting high tolls for the privilege of crossing those areas.[20]

In the most important fiefdom lived Oedipus, King of Castration.

Without the physical manifestations of all those monsters, the church, the schools, the factories, the government, and the military would have had nowhere to anchor their ideological and practical oppression. Those monsters were the basis, within the human body, for what Elias calls the system of self-constraints.

"Wipe the stamp of the state, the meat-inspection stamp, off your neck"* (a divorce process), as opposed to the Freudian idea, "Where id was, there ego shall be."[21] It isn't our "ids" we need to get rid of, it is the domination installed in our bodies. Those dark territories and blank spots must become our own flesh, with *our own* feelings. Fenichel's corrective, "let there be ego where there was superego,"[22] represents "progress," but still clings to the superego construct. Within that scheme it is impossible to formulate the real problem. As long as domination remains, the hopeless, self-destructive task of trying to comprehend yourself as an "ego," a monad with an identity, will inevitably resemble the colonial African's determined effort to feel French. Compare Fanon's famous case of the Senegalese who was the only Frenchman trying to write like Corneille.[23] That's what happens when you attempt to become an integral "ego" (a unified nation) before eliminating the autocratic fiefdoms, the colonial masters. Certain parts of our bodies and certain bodily effluvia are colonial territories, colonized phenomena (defined by the authority of the state, our parents, the gods, the CIA of our muscular contractions). They are occupied territories that we drag around with us.

All of the lines of scientific research based purely on ideological criticism, or *ideologiekritik* (headed by the Frankfurt School), and all of the theoretical approaches that practice historical-materialist-philosophical-metapsychological manipulations in an attempt to thrust Freud and Marx (or vice versa) onto a single pedestal—and *finally* create the homunculus, the omniscient one, from a retort—ignore the same basic area: the things that happen in, and to, human bodies (psychic matter).[24] They have no category for the desiring-production of the unconscious, from which all reality, "psychic" as well as "social," derives.

Ideologiekritik-based studies of paperbacks written for "the masses" show the same tendencies. They don't give any thought to the thrills that run through the body of a woman reading a hospital romance; they merely find the errors in her thinking.[25] Yet what the masses (all of us, that is) suffer

---

*Two lines by Rolf Dieter Brinkmann, the dead, prizewinning, and therefore unknown German poet—the only recent poet writing in German who had a real way with words. (See *Westwärts 1 & 2*, p. 114, "Sequenz, Sweet Was My Rose.") Wondratschek wrote a poem about him—not as good as Brinkmann's own poetry, but Wondratschek knows about it: "Brinkmann was too much for all of you." He was also too much for Rowohlt's *The New Book* (*Das neue Buch*); he blinks from its glossy red spine in the bookcase, stuffed into the same category as the so-called poems of Theobaldy ("Easter in Esslingen, 1968": "The whole thing lasted until 4 A.M. . . . . I had brought along my raincoat"—who else's would he have taken?). He had an editor, Jürgen Manthey, who sympathized with the police state whenever the need arose (see his letter to Hellmuth Costard in *Die Republik*, nos. 1–4, edited and published by Uwe Nettelbeck of Vertrieb 2001). "When the music had ended,/The light was switched on" (he wrote, using a line of one of his American friends, Jim Morrison). . .

Title page of a book on the use of chastity belts.

most from are "false" *feelings*, feelings that are perverted, alienated from their goals, and turned into their opposites. The real problem isn't that shop-girls have incorrect views about God and doctors. The real problem is that our bodies cramp up when they try to feel pleasure; sweat breaks out where love should; our soft, erect members become unsatisfied bones; our desire to penetrate another person's body becomes a lethal act; and contact between two sets of skin, two bodies, produces tension, dirt, and death, instead of release, purification, and rebirth.

By the same token, the "family" is also an erroneous focus for re-searchers into socialization from the *Ideologiekritik* school. Granted, the family provides the pattern for sexual oppression that is necessitated or demanded by capitalist patriarchy: the model of Oedipalization, of im-prisonment within the double bind of incest prohibition-incest command-ment, which, in making parents into private and public persons, beings who are sexual but forbid sexuality, becomes the model for all of the splittings to which the child will later subject other people and itself. It is the prototype for all the ambivalent feelings and inescapable contradictions that will cause the child to lose its bearings and its potential for freedom. The process of in-jecting displeasure into physical pleasure occurs before any of this, however, and is not tied to the family. In other words, demands to abolish the family fail to take the significance of this earlier phase into account (the mother-child symbiosis is a prefamilial phase). You can begin the comprehensive drying-up process even without the family or Oedipalization. The sharp fingers of disgust a nursing infant feels along its skin aren't called "mother" yet, nor is the special treatment meted out to certain areas of the body at bathtime. When the guilt-ridden hands of unconsciously violating adults cause the child's body to react in terror, they don't have family names either. Or consider the practice (once not so uncommon and still extant) of tying the child's hands to the mattress: physical punishment as a reaction to the child's physical desires (its messy secretions). All those things predate the triangle. They don't have to be implemented by families, though they do prepare the ground for familialization. The subsequent abandonment of the anus as territory, by contrast, is already within the realm of the family. It occurs at a time when the child has already begun to see itself as part of a mother-father configuration, to react accordingly, and to take up its position within the triangle. This may explain why psychoanalysis has given such inordinate attention to the "anal" type, the product of disturbances in the process of excommunicating the anus. Although that type can be "anal-ized" (Arno Schmidt's etymization) within the Oedipal framework, the earlier conflicts cannot. This is confirmed by Margaret Mahler's remarks about "cleanliness habituation" in children whose disturbances stem from the displeasurable mother-child symbiosis. We would expect habituation to be difficult in such cases, but

> These children are, more often than not, toilet trained at the age when normal children are. This relative ease of toilet training seems, however, to stem from two factors: one of these seems to be an insufficient erotization of the body surfaces and orifices; the second is the paradoxical situation that it is precisely the lack of emotional involvement that makes toilet training an uncharged *conditioning* process for these children.[26]

Toward the end of the nineteenth century, lack of affection during infancy and insufficient erotization of the body's surface seem to have become the rule. That development marked a new phase in the "armoring" of the body (the process Elias attempted to describe in *Process of Civilization* [*Prozess der Zivilisation*]). The new body had no feel for its psychic boundaries; if it cathected its own periphery at all, it did so in a tentative, incomplete way. The body did acquire boundaries, of course, but they were drawn *from the outside,* by the disciplinary agencies of imperialist society.* We can see why fascist propaganda and social practice places such great emphasis on setting boundaries of all kinds.

Christian Enzensberger (operating at his tentative distance) has identified an important link:

---

*For a more thorough discussion of this process and the type of male body it produces, see volume 2. For now, let's just say that it is fundamentally different from the body described by the ego-id-superego model of psychoanalysis.

Early capitalism must have brought on a more restrictive phase. Every upheaval of an existing social order, including our present industrial-technological revolution, inevitably generates immense quantities of dirt. Definitions become blurred, and everything threatens to migrate permanently to peripheral areas and turn into dirt. As a result, people proceed with extreme caution, paying equally strict attention to external and internal cleanliness. With the advent of Puritanism, the skin's susceptibility to dirt must have become universal; from this point on, that is, the skin avoided every type of contact. Hygiene entered the scene as a form of piety (with the maxim, "Cleanliness is next to godliness").

Individuals and the community used strikingly similar means to avert the new threat. The new nation-state gradually shifted its attention from the capital city to the border areas; eventually, the state proudly envisioned itself as the place between Memel and the Meuse.* Individuals began to monitor their own skins just as carefully and exclusively. The boundary of defilement slowly shifted from the inside to the outside, becoming increasingly sharp and sensitive in the process.[27]

The "god within," who had supplanted the "god of heaven," eventually died himself. He was replaced in turn by a "god without," who dwelt on the skin and whose name was Cleanliness. Enzensberger is undoubtedly right in seeing the new hygiene as a form of piety.

A major supporting role in this drama must have been played by the abandonment of confession within Protestantism. That change didn't make things any easier for the faithful. The judge within (and on) them was far stricter than the old priest, especially in parceling out absolution. As long as there was confession, with its process of atonement and purification, people felt free to "sin" (an act that even felt *pleasant* on occasion). But as the minute confession was replaced by internal monitoring—and defense-systems, sin became "dirty" (stay clean *from the start*).

We can add to all this the process of the introduction of antiproduction into production itself. This reached its most pronounced form on the bodies of men living in the second half of the nineteenth century, men who were being shaped for the coming wars. It did so in the provision of a body armor that can, I think, only be described as antagonistic to what it enclosed.

Antiproduction was introduced into factories in a similar way; it arrived on the back of the new element of production, the machine. Machines produced two things: goods (with the help of workers) and workers themselves

---

*And from the Etsch to the Northern Belt. Germany: a rock in the flood. [Enzensberger's place names illustrate the extreme borders of pre-World War I Germany; Theweleit's do the same for the Federal Republic.—Trans.]

(by the manner of their construction). In capitalist production, machines turned out workers as waste products, "dirt." And if that mode of production is on its last legs now, workers have been in that predicament for a long time. The agonizing physical positions those mechanical monstrosities imposed on workers (not just because of technological backwardness, then or now) prevented proletarians from escaping their exploiter even in their own beds.[28] The second characteristic of industrial production is that from the very start, it had the capacity to create specific abundance in the midst of general scarcity: toys and baubles for the rich, fashionwear, and every other kind of garbage imaginable.

Just as guilt and fear had been injected as antiproduction directly into the bodies and erotic productions of the nonproletarian strata, now the production of wasteful goods and of the human body as waste were introduced as antiproduction into industrial production. From this point on, every act of lovemaking, every industrial process entitled a modicum of self-destruction. Working and making love became exercises in dying; only to a limited extent were they still creative, life-affirming processes. Every single commodity a worker produced was a piece of his own death. Every act of lovemaking carries the bodies deeper into a debt of guilt that accumulated toward death. (Nowadays, one learns how to die by subjecting all of one's expressions of life to a strict self-censorship. Antiproduction has begun to stifle production.)

Lovers and workers now produce "dirt" from the moment they start their activities. The citizen of a society that began "placing a cover over piano legs, as a simple precaution,"[29] set about keeping both things at a distance, factories and love (flowings as well as machines).

Is it any wonder with all that "dirt" around that the quality of water changed? The habits of washing and swimming in water, including in rivers and lakes, originated in the eighteenth century, in the context of the bourgeoisie's "moral superiority" over the absolutist nobility. We need to consider the enormously heightened significance of water, in these attempts to implement hygiene in bourgeois society in relation to the simultaneous social proscription of other wet substances (especially those of the body) and the demotion of these substances to the status of "dirt." At the same time, the phrase "hygiene as a new form of piety" describes only one aspect of the process.

Regarding another aspect, the coupling of erotic woman and water, we can finally see what kind of woman the bourgeois men with their yearning to break down boundaries, allowed to flow in the seas, fountains, surfs, and rivers of their poetic productions. It is the pure woman without boundaries. (The erotic, "dirty" woman is once again excluded.) And so water becomes an ideological as well as a practical weapon against the historical possibility of a liberating sexuality.

In the guise of the promised ocean, the "infinite vagina," water not only hides the reality of women, but flows forth against the ("dirty") sexuality of the women of oppressed classes and strata: that is, "proletarian" women. At the same time, splashing out of the sink and on to the bodies of bourgeois men, water became the new religion of Asexuality. There, it wasn't water, it was anti-dirt.[30] Water comes to be the only clean liquid. It is a means of purification, even when it is flowing on the vaginas of the women nonfascist men desire, vaginas that have been expanded to become oceans. Water guarantees that the desires of these men are clean, that their unconsciouses are pure (as clean and clear as their theories).*

In the eyes of men who fear streams (because they seem "unclean"), the bodies of erotic women, especially proletarian ones, become so much wet dirt. In Rudolf Herzog's novel *Comrades* (*Kameraden*), the hero, Volker, is clearing out some young female workers, who, by ensconcing themselves on an estate à la Sythen Castle, have come too close to Volker's beloved, Hanna Westerland:

> Shrieking loudly, the half-naked women leaped onto the back of his neck. He felt their slippery bodies pressing against him, felt their wine fumes enveloping him, felt their nails digging into his flesh. His skull was pounding: "Defilement! Defilement!" As if trying to shake off vermin, he arched his back and sprung up.
>
> Three screams shattered the surrounding space. The whores tumbled off, threw themselves onto their backs, and began bellowing like animals.
>
> There, behind his superior, stood Niklas, stroking his steel rod. "I was just combing the animals' backsides, Colonel. All I used was this soul-warmer, Sir, and now look at them tearing up the ground."
>
> Volker shook himself. He could still feel the slippery bodies and smell the wine fumes of the women. "Poor you, my Germany," he managed to cough out. "You . . . you! Oh, no . . ."
>
> He saw Hanna Westerland's tear-streaked face, saw her arms coming toward him, saw her willowy figure stretching out, seeking the comfort of his breast. "Don't touch me!" he stammered. "Don't touch me! Can't you see I've been defiled from top to bottom? No, not you! Not like this!"[31]

He has to wash himself first. Later, one of Volker's men tells him he'd have been happy to do that "dirty work" himself.[32]

*   *   *

*This is where the tributes to swimming in rivers and seas begin to merge with Brecht's youthful diatribe against "that whore Zoff . . . that cracked vase" full of filthy "discharges."

What is it that gushes out of our water pipes, then? If the desire for a flowing, sexual, yet clean woman has merged with the boundless oceans, with their (once) transparent clarity, endlessness, and indestructibility, then what we wash ourselves with every day is that same ocean in its domesticated form, tamed within our water pipes. We use that substance, that "pure mother," to cleanse ourselves of the dirt of the world, the dirt of our beds, of love, of women—the dirt that we are ourselves. In other words, tap water has become (among other things) the material incarnation of the antisexual abstraction "white woman" ("pure mother"; "white countess–nurse"). It is a substance not of this earth.*

Applying that substance to the skin made it possible for consciousness to hone in on the perception of the borders of the body as "borders of dirt." This use of water allowed the senses (the eyes) to perceive the difference between "dirt" and "non-dirt" and, with it, that between "ego" and "nonego" (= dirt). Purification became an entirely external process (Louis XIV and his contemporaries weren't at all afflicted with this dark compulsion, They felt no need yet to safeguard their borders by cleaning their penises, vaginas, and other parts in between one sexual encounter and the next. What a notion of cleansing: to wash away the traces of pleasure.)

Water was precisely the substance that possessed adequate redemptive qualities. No other substance could make people feel "reborn" after such a brief immersion. Water acquired the function of providing healthy competition for true "rebirths," those that involved real orgasms. That the intention of preventing free and equal bodies from producing pleasure together (a sanction dictated by the demands of primary accumulation) was in no sense simple to achieve, becomes clear when we consider that the most beautiful substance on earth, free-flowing water, had to be set free in order to suppress freedom once more. (Goethe and his companions used to plunge jubilantly into nocturnal lakes. There was nothing wrong with that, except that they paid too high a price for their newfound state of grace.)

What about our soldier males? What was their bathing like?

> It's wonderful to be in the swimming pool. The sun sends
> quivering coils through the glass roof onto the tile lining. I glide
> through the water with fervor. From the diving board, naked
> bodies smile at me. My comrades have arrived. (Jünger)[33]

"Fervor," "comrades." There are many similar bathing scenes in the works of these men. Most occur along rivers; during lulls in the fighting, all those powerful, naked bodies plunge right in.[34]

As a first officer, von Selchow was accorded the supreme honor of a private bathing session with his superior:

---

*We wash our hands in Innocence.

On Wednesday, February 1, 1905, my mother's birthday, Lieutenant Mörsberger and I went ashore on Mahé, the main island of the Seychelles. The equatorial sun was beating down on us with its vertical rays. After a while, we discovered a spring whose ice-cold waters emptied into a pool between the rocks. We undressed and sat down beneath this wonderful waterfall, which had carved two thronelike seats out of the rocks. The water streaming over our backs was so delightful that we forgot everything else. We had no idea how long we'd been sitting there. We finally summoned the courage—or was it cowardice?—to get up, and then we had ourselves brought back on board by canoe through the coral reef. I've done a lot of stupid things in my life, but getting up at that point was one of the stupidest.[35]*

Through the epidermal experience of bathing, water creates an imaginative link to the mother, paralleling the child's experience at her breast. In this way, water allows the child to verify its imaginative experiences in a setting that offers nearly absolute protection from persecutory and depressive anxieties.[36]

Isn't what Franco Fornari says here about the "epidermal experience" of bathing infants a pretty fair description of what Selchow felt under that waterfall? Time and place dissolved. He finally had to "summon the courage" (in German, *ermannen*, literally—and rarely if ever more appropriately—to make himself a man), to pull himself out of the blissful union that had absorbed him: the experience of a pleasurable symbiosis. It was Wednesday, February 1, 1905 (everything real and under control); and he was united with her on her birthday (perfect encoding). The free-flowing spring on the Seychelles is linked to his desire for his nondevouring mother, his desire that he himself be "clean" and unthreatening inside. The spring is a kind of natural shower for washing off the "dirt" of society. And showers like that found their way into houses. I'm a little surprised to find that I've arrived at the conjecture that plumbing had to be installed in private residences to help carry out the repression of human desires in bourgeois societies.** (That repression took the form of gender segregation and sexual repression.) In the long run, something had to be found that

---

*It is not that the lieutenant's presence wasn't significant in itself, as that of a man—but what it really signified was the absence of women. Women would immediately have embodied the threat of consuming symbioses, the very thing Selchow was trying to evade. In this case, the constellation spring-pleasure-woman cannot be expressed as it could in the case of a left-wing male. There are some bathing scenes, incidentally, that are dedicated to the beauty of the nude male body. (See Blüher, p. 271.)

**Indoor plumbing isolated women from each other as well. The public fountain was laid to rest as a meeting place. Fountains became ornamental, further monuments to the canalized female gender.

Illustration from *Have no Fear, Dear Fatherland*. The cupid of the parade ground, a wish-fulfillment dream of starting drills early on.

would be continuously on hand to dispose quickly and reliably of the "dirt" that was constantly building up and the threat of dissolution it carried.[37] Drains.[38]

For almost every human ailment, from repressed sexuality to corns, a "bathing therapy" was invented: washings, dousings, even a kind of washing machine for the insane. (The popular remedy, meanwhile, was pouring a bucket of water on the head of anyone who got too hot, anyone who was just begging for the whip or for love.)[39]

Starting from the kitchen and the bedroom, Cleanliness began its triumphal march through the house. White linens, white morals, white tablecloths: an incessant rustling of white (no longer audible, but ever present). With the drying up of the streams in the bedroom, moving through the water pipes that were the heart of any clean kitchen, the image of the Pure Mother (the propaganda about clean interiors in houses and bodies) slowly gained ascendancy within the house.* The housewife gradually came to embody whiteness, while her husband despaired or started dreaming about the sexual allure of nonhousewives (images of the ocean). Water,

---

*And within the clean state: "CIA Probes Water Poisoning" [headline of an Associated Press article of September 20, 1975, reporting alleged attempts by the U.S. Army to introduce poison into public water supplies as an experiment—Trans.] General Jack the Ripper, the man who sent out U.S. H-bomb squadrons against the Soviet Union in Stanley Kubrick's *Dr. Strangelove*, drank only whiskey and Coca Cola. He knew what the Russians were up to—they were poisoning the earth's groundwater system. Women were somehow part of that system: Jack wouldn't give them one drop of his "juices."

Ferenczi supposes an identification of the ego with the genital secretion, which is "released only in an entirely friendly environment" (*Schriften*, II, 332). The answer to the constellation groundwater-women-communism is sexual abstinence-whiskey-hydrogen bomb.

Lettow-Vorbeck tugging at the ear of his studious son for the camera.

water everywhere, but not a drop to drink. Couples in the New World had a model that was already a parody of reterritorialization: the honeymoon at Niagara Falls. Now, there was a flood to end all floods.

It was no accident that diaper-based education had its heyday in the Wilhelmine era. The incredible esteem accorded to professional soldiers (the army and, in a perverse way, even officers) didn't develop spontaneously. The victory of 1870-71 was systematically hammered into the bodies of Ger-

From the English comic strip "The Sad Adventures of Little and Big Willie" (World War I).

man boys: there would have been no Germany without that victory, that army, those soldiers; and if you didn't want to be like them, you didn't deserve to be called a German man. Succeeding generations were brought up as monuments to that victory. Once the German Empire began to show its true colors, though—a military dictatorship preparing to do battle with the other imperialist world powers for global markets and colonial territories— producing young men in that mold became a practical necessity as well. (In parallel fashion, German girls were trained to love soldiers.) Even before the two world wars, Germans were being instructed to breed "the best soldiers possible" in order to "compensate" for their patent inferiority in the concrete realms of productive capacity, access to raw materials, and so on.[40]

On one hand, then, you had men fated to become soldiers and women fated to become soldiers' wives, with the prohibition against flowing branded into the flesh of both sexes. On the other hand, you had the events touched off by the 1918 revolution: a mass of humanity that no longer hesitated to violate prohibitions, which the soldier males had been trained to keep in check. The "Red flood" that streamed forth was no real threat to the soldier males' interests; what really started swimming were the men's boundaries—the boundaries of their perception, the boundaries of their bodies.

The phenomenon behind the assault on the "Red flood" and its related hybrid forms was very much like the phenomenon behind the attacks on Red nurses. I have attempted to describe the latter as a "hallucinatory object-substitution": The men treated "Red" nurses as if these proletarian women were their own sisters, as if the men were watching their own sisters doing what they weren't supposed to be doing, turning into "whores" and therefore "deserving" to die. Similarly, the men treated the "Red flood" as if it were their own unconsciouses (the things that had to remain locked up, hidden in the dark) blithely pouring out onto the streets. The crucial point here is that for the soldier male, the flood set loose by the rebels was connected, in some frightening, intolerable way, with his own pent-up streams (which, as we've seen, he could perceive only as negativized things, threatening him with dissolution). He could hardly remain indifferent to what those people were doing out there, because the flood, if it came, would burst his boundaries. It wasn't so much his economic position he was defending as his psychic constitution—and in that sense, his very survival.

We can describe the hallucinatory nature of the soldier male's perception more precisely here than in the first chapter. His erupted unconscious "inundated" his thinking in more than just a metaphorical sense. He actually found himself in a process of disintegration, dissolution, molecularization—a process that threatened to completely cancel him out as an entity, to attack the controlled coherence of his sense perceptions and explode it into an infinite number of mutually hostile particles.[41]

He "judged" the actions of the "Reds" solely in the context of that danger, which was very real for him. More precisely, his "judgments" arose almost independently out of the reactions of his body, out of his intense struggle against wetness on/in his own body. Anything that affected his boundaries or orifices—anything that exited, entered, became moist, or flowed—was not only "forbidden," but lethal. And since those other people showed no similar fear, opening up the floodgates and becoming part of the flood themselves, they came to embody all that was forbidden (as *he* had been taught to feel it). They were a putrid amalgam of every fluid in existence, an incarnation of everything deadly.

„Helm ab" zum Gebet.

"Helmets off in prayer." German field postcard (1917).

It was a physical certainty for him: If that stream reaches me, touches me, spills over me, then I will dissolve, sink, explode with nausea, disintegrate in fear, turn horrified into slime that will gum me up, mire that will suffocate me, a pulp that will swallow me like quicksand. I'll be in a state where everything is the same, inextricably mixed together, and no one will be able to tell what it is that's flowing down there. A demented inner scream—Heeeelp! Who's going to pull me out of this? Who's going to put me back together, dry me out, and keep me dry? . . . White mother! Come over here quickly with your rough washcloths and your bony hands and rub me down! Strict father, give me your gun (if YOU can't hold back this flood any longer) and let me go hunting for all those people who are letting it run out of themselves like animals. . . . I'm about to explode!

Eventually the message pounded its way into the men—in the rhythm of their heartbeats, the pulsing of their temples, the stamping of their feet along country roads: blood, blood, blood must flow, thick as a rain of hail. What was needed for defense was deliverance, a losing and rediscovery of boundaries, which, as the central process in the acts of murder committed by these men, will occupy us in volume 2.

The flood also had its attractive qualities. We can see what an important part those qualities played in the final deliverance of the men by looking, for instance, at Dwinger's narrative. Dwinger doesn't allow his Captain Truchs to order shots fired into the crowd of women until the advance wave of that slimy stream is already upon them. Not until the spit of one of the working-class women is already dripping down his medal of honor does Donat fire into the woman's open mouth. And not until then does Donat perceive that what was once a face is now only a bloody pulp. By waiting, Dwinger has managed to reduce the rebellious Other to its concept. There is your proof: that whore lying there can finally be seen as the viscous thing she always was. Meanwhile the man, Donat, is standing dry amid the powder fumes. The slime on his medal of honor has been effaced. (Dry wines, doubles extra dry, and women on the rocks.) Or like Baron von Münchhausen, pull yourself up by your own hair, haul your prick out of the swamp, put an end to all that confusion and dissolution.

DAM AND FLOOD: THE RITUAL OF PARADING IN MASS

After seizing power, the Nazis tamed the floods and let them flow inside their rituals. Streams became dams, and much more. Consider the "parade of political leaders" (*Appell der politischen Leiter*). The participants: all party members with leadership roles. For a description, we turn to the *Niederelbischer Tageblatt* (Lower-Elbe Daily) of September 12, 1937:

> Dr. Ley announced the "Entry March of the Banners." For a moment, one could see nothing. But then they emerged from the blackness of the night, over on the south side. In seven columns, they poured into the spaces between the formations. You couldn't see the people, couldn't recognize the standard-bearers. All you saw was a broad, red, surging stream, its surface spar- kling gold and silver, advancing slowly like fiery lava. Feeling the dynamism of that slow advance, you got some small impression of what those sacred symbols meant.[1]

The flood had a name now: "Entry March of the Banners" (encoded stream). The threat of inundation had been eradicated. But even without the danger of sinking within it, the flood remained exciting, fascinating. Its ominous aspect had been removed by those formations, by transforming streams into "columns," by converting the flowing "feminine" into a rigid "masculine." Where did the excitement come from, then? What made that "broad, red, surging stream . . . sacred"?

In *Moses and Monotheism*, Freud identified the link between the sacred and prohibition:

> What is sacred is obviously something that may not be touched. A sacred prohibition has a very strong emotional tone but has in fact no rational basis.[2]

With a characteristic (irresistible) twist, he concluded that sacredness was the hallmark of the incest taboo, which existed solely because of paternal authority and solely in order to perpetuate that authority. *Sacer*, he added, meant not only "sacred" (*heilig*), but "wicked" (*verrucht*), "detestable" (*verabscheuenswert*).[3] Sacred rituals allowed "wickedness" to be represented; that was the whole purpose of such rituals.

Seen in that light, a ritual such as the "Entry March of the Banners" becomes a public staging of the forbidden—not only of incest, but also, if we strip off the Freudian encoding, of flowing desire in general. In the ritual, desiring-production is allowed to surface symbolically, as a representation of itself. Drives are given an outlet: "But then they emerged from the blackness of the night . . . poured into the spaces between the formations."

That explains the enormous attraction of fascist celebrations and their overwhelming impact on participants: "I can't believe my eyes . . . what in the world are they doing?"—and then the liberating thought, "But everybody's doing it . . . my God, they're actually *doing* it!" (in the name of the law, too). This symbolic liberation of desires, this staged affirmation of drives (in the form of a monumental ornament, a model for the repression of drives), was fascism's way of depicting the dawn of freedom, a freedom in which the fascist precisely does *not* dissolve himself. In this ritual, the Nazis symbolically suspended the primary double bind by allowing access to its normally unattainable aspect: to incest at the very least, but also to the state of noncastration, nondismemberment; to power; and to flowing that did not signify death. Deleuze and Guattari are probably right when they suggest in passing that Hitler enabled fascists to have an erection.[4] "At last, not to be castrated for once!" In a ritual that allowed the penis itself (the penis no one had) to be represented in abstract form (the seven columns), the individual, for once, was no longer castrated; he became part of the transcendantal phallus that gave meaning to everything (the emphasis on "You couldn't see the people, couldn't recognize the standard-bearers" is revealing). For the moment at least, he felt privileged to be a stream himself, one small part of an enormous, tamed flood; for that one moment, he was lifted out of every double bind. The scenario of the parade abolished the contradiction between the desiring-production of the individual and the demands of social power. In the course of the ritual, the fascist came to represent both his own liberated drives and the principle that suppressed them. This inherent contradiction never manifested itself because, during the staging of the ritual, the individual participated in power. Benjamin's assertion that fascism built its monuments "primarily [with] so-called human material" is based on this truth: the substance of those monuments was the flow of desire.[5] But even Benjamin seems to show traces of the Weimar Left's rationalist reflex when he says that the "execution" of fascist

The standards of victory. Nuremberg Rally, 1933.

mass art (he rightly includes parades in this category) put the masses "into a trance that made them see themselves as monumental, that is, incapable of deliberate, autonomous actions."[6] Revolutionary acts certainly don't need to be "deliberate"; and it is almost impossible for them to be "autonomous" in Benjamin's sense, since the type of "ego" on which that notion of "autonomy" is based rarely surfaces in oppressed classes. When the emphasis is put on the production of "trances" or incapacitation, what is left out of account is precisely the side of things that fascists have never neglected. It is far more important to stress the sense of relief, the Utopia of deliverance, which participants in such rituals find: "At last I don't have to hide anymore. . . . At last, I can see and sense that other people feel the same way I do."

That is how fascism translates internal states into massive, external monuments or ornaments as a canalization system, which large numbers of people flow into; where their desire can flow, at least within (monumentally enlarged) preordained channels; where they can discover that they are not split off and isolated, but that they are sharing the violation of prohibitions with so many others (preferably with all others). That's why these masses can't stand to see one man marching alone alongside their great blocks. Such a man isn't participating in their forbidden games. Worse yet, he is observing them. And how can you let yourself be observed when you are in the process of turning into a stream and becoming god?

Fine, except for one thing: All of that affirmation is theatrical; it never gets beyond representation, the illusion of production. Benjamin is right in saying that fascism may help the masses to express themselves, but that it certainly doesn't help them to gain their rights.[7] We need to go one step further, though, and specify *what* is being expressed. For fascism does not allow the masses to express their interests (class interests, economic interests)—communists, when they come to power, are the ones who tend to let those interests be *expressed*, though not satisfied. No, what fascism allows the masses to express are suppressed drives, imprisoned desires. Fascist masses may portray their desire for deliverance from the social double bind, for lives that are not inevitably entrapping, but not their desire for full stomachs. The success of fascism demonstrates that masses who become fascist suffer more from their internal states of being than from hunger or unemployment. Fascism teaches us that under certain circumstancs, human beings imprisoned within themselves, within body armor and social constraints, would rather break out than fill their stomachs; and that their politics may consist in organizing that escape, rather than an economic order that promises future generations full stomachs for life. The utopia of fascism is an edenic freedom from responsibility. That in itself, I think, is a source of "beauty in the most profound distortion." Meanwhile, communists and the left in general still stubbornly refuse to accept fascism's horrifying proof that the materialism they preach and practice only goes halfway. The desiring-production of the unconscious, as molecular driving-force of history, has never entered their materialism—an omission that has had (and still has) tragic consequences.

In patriarchy, where the work of domination has consisted in subjugating, damming in, and transforming the "natural energy" in society, that desiring-production of the unconscious has been encoded as the subjugated gender, or femaleness; and it has been affirmed and confirmed, over and over again, in the successive forms of female oppression. Luce Irigaray: "To an extent, the unconscious is historically censored femaleness."[8] In the course of the repression carried out against women, those two things—the unconscious and femaleness—were so closely coupled together that they came to be seen as nearly identical. It was almost inevitable, as Frieda Grafe says, that Freud "would use the pathology of hysterical women as a basis" for constructing his science (that is, as a basis for his subsequent male scientific system).[9] In its denial of this coupling, male-rationalist thinking repeatedly renews its demand for the oppression of women each time it calls for the subjugation of "nature." When Kracauer writes that "the mass ornamental display represents silent nature without anything built upon it,"[10] he fails to recognize what kind of "nature" is involved here. This allows him to conclude, in Goethian fashion, that the process of humanization can "forge ahead only if thought can curb nature and create man on rational

lines."[11] We do have to force ahead, don't we? And we already know who will get left behind. Here, Kracauer was on the right track in beginning his reflections on the mass ornamental displays with the Tillergirls,* those "indissoluble formations of young women whose movements are mathematical demonstrations";[12] and on the mass displays of "physical culture" which took place in stadiums, and whose ornamental configurations were carried far and wide by the newsreels. Thanks to Lippe and Elias, we know that the process in question here was nothing new: Ornaments made of human beings have helped the European ego adjust to new forms of the human body ever since the Renaissance. In fact, Kracauer's description of ornamental displays in stadiums closely resembles Beaujoyeulx's account of the ballet at the court of Henry III:

> They consist of angles and circles, the kind one finds in textbooks on euclidean geometry. They also make use of the fundamental shapes of physics, waves, and spirals. What they reject are the exuberance of organic forms and the emanations of spiritual life. (Kracauer)[13]

What had changed? Well, the ornamental displays were no longer carried out by the "white" women of the court, or by any other women, but by

---

*The "Tillergirls" were a precision female dancing troupe, popular in Germany in the 1920s and 1930s. The Hitler era, in particular, featured mass performances of calisthenics (and other physical exercises) in stadiums.—Trans.

"the masses." And the displays had become more elaborate in accordance with technological progress. Kracauer completely misreads the situation, though, when he says that organic and "spiritual" elements were simply "rejected." Those elements were the very *substance* of the ornamental displays. The purpose of the displays, in fact, was to transform organic "exuberance" into spirals; the purpose of the fascist mass ritual was to channel streams into a monumental system of dams. Benjamin writes:

> Under the gaze of the fascist rulers (which, as we've seen, sweeps
> across millennia), the distinctions between the slaves who built
> the pyramids out of blocks, and the proletarian masses who
> formed themselves into blocks before the Führer on exercise
> grounds and in open squares, begin to disappear.[14]

The "rulers' gaze"—the fascists weren't the first to have it, but they did see something new. Their public rituals no longer depicted the subjugation of "nature" (the desiring-production of the unconscious) directly as the subjugation of women, but instead as the subjugation of the masses, masses of men. In attempting to fend off the very real possibility of socialism, fascists found that women's bodies were no longer adequate for public stagings of the subjugation of "nature." Fascist rituals went directly inside men, taking their material from the male unconscious.

Men themselves were now split into a (female) interior and a (male) exterior—the body armor. And as we know, the interior and exterior were mortal enemies. What we see being portrayed in the rituals are the armor's separation from, and superiority over the interior: the interior was allowed to flow, but only within the masculine boundaries of the mass formations. Before any of this could happen, the body had to be split apart thoroughly enough to create an interior and exterior that could be opposed to each other as enemies. Only then could the two parts re-form "in peace" in the ritual. What fascism promised men was the reintegration of their hostile components under tolerable conditions, dominance of the hostile "female" element within themselves. This explains why the word "boundaries," in fascist parlance, refers primarily to the boundaries of the body (as we have seen).

As a matter of course, fascism excluded women from the public arena and the realms of male production. But fascism added a further oppression to the oppression of women: When a fascist male went into combat against erotic, "flowing," nonsubjugated women, he was also fighting his own unconscious, his own desiring-production. In this process, the wife of the ruler lost all function as a representative subjugated woman. This is clear from the fact that whereas in World War I, the Hohenzollern women had posed as nurses, Hitler concealed his "beloved" from the public. Not only was she useless for the rituals that maintained Hitler's rule, she would have gotten in

the way. For the Führer's "wife," in that fascist ritual, was the unconscious of the masses who were pouring into block formations.

> And now the screams of "Heil!" erupt, becoming overwhelming, like some all-fulfilling wave that rips everything along with it. Fifty thousand voices merge into a single cry of "Heil Hitler!" Fifty thousand arms shoot out in salutes. Fifty thousand hearts beat for this man who is now striding, bareheaded, through the narrow passage formed by all those thousands.[15]

This is one of the endings of the song, and the end of this first volume. In the next chapter (chapter 3, volume 2), we'll examine how the process of encoding life's contradictions and perplexities (as maleness/femaleness; dam/stream; filth/purity, heights/depths) functioned in the formation of the central concepts of fascist discourse. What did those "men" really mean when they used the words "masses," "people" (*Volk*), "nation"? Or when they conjured up the stream of the Führer's oratory, the flash of his steel-blue eyes (even if his eyes were really only steel-brown)?

Chapter 4 examines how those concepts emerged from the bodies of the soldier males, and how the men came to have those bodies. I'll have more to say, in particular, about the alleged connection between homosexuality and the White terror; and about the other questions that arose, but couldn't be answered, in the present volume.

I have largely avoided confronting recent literature on fascism in this volume, but will pay more attention to that in the next.

Notes

Notes

The notes cite editions of works used in the preparation of this book. Full publication information for English translations and original-language editions appears in the bibliography.

Citations to Freud's works are to *The Standard Edition of the Complete Psychological Works of Sigmund Freud* (referred to in the notes as *SE*), translated under the general editorship of James Strachey (London: Hogarth Press, 1953-74).

Abbreviations

The following abbreviations appear after the titles of works taken from the anthologies listed below:

HoDA	Hotzel, Curt. *Deutscher Aufstad*
JKR	Jünger, Ernst. *Der Kampf um das Reich*
RDS	Roden, Hans. *Deutsche Soldaten*
SB	Salomon, Ernst. *Das Buch vom deutschen Freikorpsd*ämpfer

Introduction

1. Robert G. L. Waite, *Vanguard of Nazism: The Free Corps Movement in Postwar Germany, 1918-1923* (New York: W. W. Norton, 1952), 42.
2. Richard F. Hamilton, *Who Voted for Hitler?* (Princeton, N.J.: Princeton University Press, 1982).

Chapter 1: Men and Women

Seven Marriages
1. Friedrich Freksa, *Kapitän Ehrhardt*, 45.

2. Ibid.
3. Ibid.
4. Ibid., 347.
5. Frau Kapitän Ehrhardt (née Princess Hohenlohe), "Moderne Geisel," in *Wir klagen an*, ed. Hartmut Plaas, 127-30. Ehrhardt's wife turns the half year in prison into a full year. For confirmation of the half year, see Gumbel, *Verschwörer*, 85.
6. Charles Bloch, *Die SA und die Krise des NS-Regimes (1934)*, 71-102, 163; Sohn-Rethel, *Ökonomie und Klassenstruktur*, 200-10.
7. Rossbach, *Mein Weg durch die Zeit*, 176.
8. Ibid., 35ff.
9. Martin Niemöller, *Vom U-Boot zur Kanzel*, 148ff.
10. Ibid., 62.
11. Ibid., 116.
12. Ibid., 116ff.
13. Ibid., 157.
14. Rudolf Höss, *Kommandant in Auschwitz*, 36ff. A lenient account of Höss's secret-tribunal murder. Höss was pardoned in 1928. For other accounts of the murder, see H. and E. Hannover, *Politische Justiz 1918-1933*, 157ff.; E. J. Gumbel, *Verschwörer*, 94ff.; Gumbel, *Verräter verfallen der Feme*, 188-97; Rossbach, *Mein Weg durch die Zeit*, 196ff.
15. Ibid., 53.
16. Ernst von Salomon, *Die Geächteten*, 216ff.
17. Ibid., 481.
18. Ibid., 480. See also Ewers, *Reiter in deutscher Nacht*, 419.
19. Paul von Lettow-Vorbeck, *Mein Leben*, 114ff.
20. Ibid., 172ff.
21. Ibid., 174.
22. Ibid., 199.
23. Ibid., 201.
24. Ibid., 266ff.
25. Ibid., 266ff.
26. Manfred von Killinger, *Der Klabautermann*, 164.
27. Ibid., 189.
28. Ibid., 252.
29. Ibid., 263.
30. Ibid., 297.
31. Ibid., 310.
32. Ibid., 317ff.
33. Regarding marriages, see also Engelhardt, *Ritt nach Riga*, 59; Stadtler, *Als Antibolshewist 1918/19*, 7, 80, 165 ("You are marvelous at waiting," he wrote to his wife, comforting her in his absence [she was pregnant] with letters full of heroic deeds.); Buschbecker, *Wie unser Gesetz es befahl*, 395ff.; Volck, *Rebellen um Ehre*, 367ff.; Henningsen, "Erkundungsvorstoss nach Radziwilischky," SB, 150.

The Historical Context and the Nature of the Material

1. See Günter Paulus, "Die soziale Struktur der Freikorps in den ersten Monaten nach der Novemberrevolution," *Zeitschrift für Geschichtswissenschaft* 3 (1955); Erwin Könnemann, *Einwohnerwehren und Zeitfreiwilligenverbände* (1971); Robert G. L. Waite, *Vanguard of Nazism*, 40ff.
2. Gumbel, *Verschwörer*, 88, 100; Waite, *Vanguard of Nazism*, 192ff.; Roegels, *Marsch auf Berlin*, 142.

3. Peter von Heydebreck, *Wir Wehrwölfe*, 123ff., 161ff.
4. Ödin von Horvath, *Sladek oder die schwarze Armee, Historie in drei Akten* (published 1928; reprinted Frankfurt, 1974).
5. Martin Niemöller, *Vom U-Boot*, 162.
6. E. J. Gumbel, *Vier Jahre politischer Mord* (1922); *Verschwörer* (1924): *Verräter verfallen der Feme* (1929).
7. They were appropriately feted. See F. W. Heinz, "Politische Attentate in Deutschland," HoDA, 202-6; Heinz, *Die Nation greift an*, 129ff. Regarding the "OC," see Salomon, *Die Geächteten*, 253ff. (underplays its importance); Roegels, *Marsch auf Berlin*, 159ff. (overplays it); Heinz, *Die Nation greift an*, 133ff.; H. and E. Hannover, *Politische Justiz*, 118, 135ff.; Gumbel, *Verschwörer*, 76ff.; Waite, *Vanguard of Nazism*, 213ff.; Ernst Posse, *Die politischen Kampfbünde Deutschlands* (Berlin, 1930), 12ff.; Maser, *Frühgeschichte der NSDAP*, 191.
8. Gabriele Krüger, *Die Brigade Ehrhardt*, 89; Krüger (vaguer), *Naziführer sehen dich an: Eine anonyme Schrift von Pariser Emigranten* (1934), 147ff.
9. See von Selchow, *Hundert Tage aus meinem Leben*, 347. Regarding "Orgesch," see Heinz, *Politische Attentate*, 197; Heinz, *Die Nation greift an*, 114ff.; Gumbel, *Verschwörer*, 141ff.; Waite, *Vanguard*, 201ff.
10. Niemöller, *Vom U-Boot*, 148.
11. Maximilian Scheer, *Blut und Ehre*, 136ff.
12. Salomon, *Die Geächteten*, 284-90.
13. Arnolt Bronne, *Rossbach*, 19; Salomon, *Die Geächteten*, 284ff.; Heinz, *Politische Attentate*, 199ff.; Heinz, *Kämpfe im Dunkeln*, 119ff.; Volck, *Rebellen um Ehre*, 50. The latter describes a snowy landscape, knowing that it will soon be blood-red.
14. Most evident in Gumbel, *Verräter verfallen der Feme*; H. and E. Hannover, *Politische Justiz*. Both accounts are vague on many details.
15. See Heinz, *Politische Attentate*, 200.
16. Waite, *Vanguard*, 254ff.
17. Franz Nord, "Der Krieg im Baltikum," JKR, 93.
18. Sohn-Rethel, *Ökonomie und Klassenstruktur*, 194.
19. According to von Hülsen (in Roden, *Deutsche Soldaten*, 113) and von Loewenfeld (ibid., 152ff.), Freikorps soldiers assumed the role of strikebreakers in Upper Silesia, August 1919, and in the Berlin railroad strike of June-July 1919. General Lüttwitz, *Im Kampf gegen die Novemberrevolution*, 103, describes the situation at the close of 1919: "My supreme command had created a kind of 'emergency technical service,' but was not strong enough to carry out life-sustaining operations throughout the city." Gumbel's *Verschwörer*, 140, contains the following excerpt from the minutes of a meeting of the Citizens' Defense Committee of the State of Bavaria (the minutes were signed by Escherich; Orgesch used the committee as a legal front): "Government representative trying to avoid mention of the 'Emergency Technical Service' in statutes." Hence there were definite areas of overlap between the "Baltic volunteers" and the "Emergency Technical Service." See also Gumbel, *Verschwörer*, 140; Roegels, *Marsch auf Berlin*, 154.
20. On the level of "meaning" or "expression," the most we can accomplish is to entangle the language of militant men in contradictions, point out its inconsistencies, its "irrationality," and proceed from there to denunciatory "valuations." A good example of this type of fruitless endeavor is Karl Prümm's dissertation on Ernst Jünger, published in 1974 under the misleading title, *Die Literatur des soldatischen Nationalismus der zwanziger Jahre 1918-1933*). Characteristically, the book is written from the standpoint of a hypothetical "critical rationality" that refers to nothing and has no purpose beyond itself. On the basis of that standpoint, Prümm constantly

reproaches Jünger, saying, for instance, that he "alternately [uses] the ideas of mysticism, neoplatonism, and magic" (p. 307). *What* mysticism, and *what* magic, does Prümm have in mind here? And even if Prümm made that clear, what would he have told us about Jünger?

Prümm's thinking is arbitrary from start to finish. He talks about the discharge of "aggressive drives" (147). What does that mean? The "libidinal connection to war" he discovers in Jünger (153) is only an empty phrase; and he talks about "psychic mechanisms" (162) without naming a single one. The irrelevance of Prümm's brand of decorative "scientific" theory is evident in his citations as well. Mentioning Freud's notion of the army as an "artificial mass" (*Massenpsychologie und Ich-Analyse*, 1923) does not stop Prümm from calling troops "the military collective" two paragraphs later (96). Is this a case of variable expressions? Prümm uses well-chosen citations to convey a picture of Jünger, but not an understanding. In the end, Prümm avenges himself on the object of his research. He says that Jünger's "pubescent hunger for stimulation remained unsatisfied even at the age of thirty-two" (361). That is the dilemma all approaches based on intellectual history and ideological criticism face whenever phenomena fall outside their frame of inquiry; that is especially true of linguistic affectivity. We can see the same failing in the following collection of essays: H. Denkler and K. Prümm, eds., *Die deutsche Literatur im Dritten Reich* (Stuttgart, 1976). Here, again, the standpint of "critical rationality" proves extremely selective in its perception of fascistic phenomena. Winckler has spelled out the limitations of "immanent" linguistic criticism, which is based primarily on the assumption that one's own level of culture is "superior"; see his commentaries on Storz, Sternberger, and Süskind, *Aus dem Wörterbuch des Unmenschen* (1945); Cornelia Berning, *Die Sprache des Nationalsozialismus* (1961); or his critiques of the related approaches of K. Korn, *Sprache in der verwalteten Welt* (1962); V. Klemperer, *Die unbewältigte Sprache* (1967). Refer to Winckler's *Studie zur gesammten Funktion faschistischer Sprache* (Frankfurt, 1971), 17ff., 111ff. See also Winckler's criticism of H. Arendt, *Elemente und Ursprünge totalitärer Herrschaft* (1955); and of E. Seidel and I. Seidel-Slotty, *Sprachwandel im Dritten Reich. Eine kritische Untersuchung faschistischer Einflüsse* (1961) is especially enlightening; the book's negative attitude toward the "affective nature of fascist language" makes it unable to resolve the contradictions of that language. "In trying to unmask the stupidity of the [fascist] seducers, [the book] is forced to accuse the seduced masses of the stupidity" (22). Winckler goes both too far and not far enough when he makes this sweeping claim for his own work: "Every conceit of fascist ideology can be logically derived from its role as an instrument of social repression, political reaction, and psychic repression" (11). Not far enough: He, too, fails to inquire into the origins of fascistic language, into how that language was used by individual speakers. He goes too far in defining the social function of fascistic language in advance (as an instrument of social repression); this bypasses the essential question of whether, aside from such pure purposiveness, fascist language might not have something to say about the less intentional, but very real existence of its users.

Jean-Pierre Faye's *Totalitäre Sprachen*, recently published in German (Frankfurt, 1977), is like the present study in taking the speech of the 1920s in Germany as its starting point. From there it takes a different turn, however. Faye's main concern is with how the collaboration and opposition among the idioms of the "nationalistic" camp—idioms that gradually diverged but remained essentially similar—structured the arena of public life in the Germany of the 1920s and early 1930s in such a way that almost all the currents arising during that era flowed into the Nazi Party. He begins with the contemporary political organizations, with their newsletters, their quarrels, and the crossovers among them, right up to when, where, and by whom things were published (i.e., not published). In doing so he provides an excellent history of the public faces of these groups, against the background of their momentary meeting places and circles. He is especially interested in crossovers between the extreme "left" of the Nazi Party and the extreme "right" of the German Communist Party (KPD), that is, in the roles of so-called nationalistic revolutionaries, nationalistic Bolshevists, and so on. In the time available to me, I was unable to test the accuracy of his historical lines of convergence; that would have required far more work. The fact that Faye's books (especially the first volume) are full of misspelled names, incorrect dates, etc., is in most cases attributable, as far as I can see, to the sloppy work of his German publisher, Ullstein.

Faye's approach is like that of the present work in the sense that he begins not with individual writers, but with a kind of political energy field in which specific idioms combine in specific ways that allow specific positions to be "assumed" linguistically. Faye's energy field corresponds to the notion of group fantasies and to the role they play in the present work.

Faye comes to similar conclusions in individual matters as well, for instance the role of antibourgeois alliances in the origins of fascistic language (566); the role of violence in Jünger's language (602, 612ff.); and the role of male societies (616ff.), which was far more important than that of political parties in the 1920s. He describes the language of male societies not as a medium of specific contents, but as a "diction," a "tempo," just as in volume 2 of the present work I have described that language as being attuned to a certain evocation of "speed." His emphasis on the specific "vascillations" of "totalitarian language" indicates that his understanding of the dilemma of fascism is very similar to the one I have tried to elaborate—using other ideas and other starting-points—in the section "Ego-Decay and Work."

Faye's books show that a precise analysis of "totalitarian idioms," as they emerge in the public political arena, can produce conclusions very similar to those of the route I have taken: inquiring into the *origins* of those idioms. This similarity is possible when ideological criticism is abandoned in favor of examining language as a *reality-structuring* force and pursuing all of its ramifications. The prerequisites for such an endeavor is tying together the network of historical ramifications tightly enough, and Faye (unlike writers such as Prümm) does that.

His work strikes me as the best to date on the idioms of right-wing groups of the 1920s. While my own work centers on the relationship of language and bodies, Faye's inquiry focuses on the relationship of language and history, language and behavioral possibilities. Hence he and I have taken entirely different routes in our investigations. I shall have to postpone my analysis of where the two routes converge and where they differ.

21. See the previous note and the (superfluous) afterword to the first edition of the present work.

22. Lutz Winckler, *Studien zur gesellschaftlichen Funktion faschistischer Sprache*, 31. Winckler refers to Werner Maser, *Hitlers Mein Kampf* (Munich, 1966), 26ff. Genesis; construction; style; emendations; sources; evaluation of sources; extracts with commentaries.

23. Scheer, *Blut und Ehre*, 88. In *Nürnberger Tagebuch*, Gilbert reports that Göring had to be undressed before he could negotiate. He was captured with two trunks full of codeine (17, 270, 345, 430). See also Speer, *Spandauer Tagebücher*, 284.

24. Waite, *Vanguard*, 279, 5ln.

25. Salomon, *Der Fragebogen* (Reinbek, 1951), 352.

26. Niemöller, *Vom U-Boot*, 180. In the appendix to his fundamental work on the Freikorps, *Vanguard of Nazism*, Robert Waite gives brief biographical sketches of the 250 men who are his subjects (Freikorps members who later became Nazis). See also Maser, *Frühgeschichte*, 41.

Unless otherwise indicated, all references in this section have been taken directly from the biographies and other contemporary works listed here.

Biographical Tradition

1. I am not about to use literature to make this point. Anyone who is interested can discuss it at length with actual women.
2. Ernst Blüher, *Die Rolle der Erotik in der männlichen Gesellschaft*, 176, 178.

Partings

1. Rudolf Mann, *Mit Ehrhardt durch Deutschland*, 20, 22.
2. Bronnen, *Rossbach*, 114. For a similar description, see Schaper, "Freikorps-geist—Annaberg," RDS, 165.
3. Tüdel Weller, *Peter Mönkemann*, 23.
4. Kurt Eggers, *Berg der Rebellen*, 134.
5. Franz Josef Freiherr von Steinaecker, *Mit der Eisernen Division im Baltenland*, 8. See the partings in Koll, "Die Männer von Tirschtiegel," SB, 231; Franz Schauwecker, *Aufbruch der Nation*, 35, 40-42; Weller, *Mönkemann*, 16; Richter, *Freiwilliger Soltau*, 51ff.; 188; Stadtler, *Als Antibolshewist 1918/19*, 7.

Brides

1. Edwin Erich Dwinger, *Auf halbem Wege*, 209.
2. Weller, *Peter Mönkemann*, 359.
3. Dwinger, *Auf halbem Wege*, 209.
4. Thor Goote, *Kamerad Berthold*, 256, 261.
5. See Thor Goote, *Die Fahne Hoch*, 291.
6. Dwinger, *Auf halbem Wege*, 530ff.
7. Ibid., 84.
8. Ibid., 419. In the Ehrhardt Brigade, Rudolf Mann found "a shocking number of married men who were either divorced or in the process of getting divorced" (*Mit Ehrhardt durch Deutschland*, 216).
9. Dwinger, *Auf halbem Wege*, 170.

De-Realization

1. Josef Goebbels, *Michael*, 16ff. Goebbels's work (1923), though not a Freikorps novel, takes place during the postwar era in Germany and has a "soldier" as its protagonist. Michael is a soldier in the battle for correct thinking. His main problem is how a nationalistic man can live in the republic. The novel is also interesting as a record of Goebbels's brand of fascism at a time when no one (including himself) had any hint about his later career.
2. Lettow-Vorbeck, *Mein Leben*, 101.
3. Salomon, "Hexenkessel Deutschland," JKR, 18.

Hands Off!

1. Mann, *Mit Ehrhardt durch Deutschland*, 79.
2. Ibid.
3. Hans Fischer, "Die Räteherrschaft in München," JKR, 161.
4. Salomon, *Die Geächteten*, 149.

5. Ernst Jünger, *Der Kampf als Inneres Erlebnis*, 67.
6. Ibid., 69.
7. Brecht, "Flüchtlingsgespräche," *Gesammelte Werke*, vol. 14, 1486.
8. Jünger, *Der Kampf als inneres Erlebnis*, 69.
9. Goote, *Kamerad Berthold*, 174ff.

Visions
1. Erich Balla, *Landsknechte wurden wir*, 108ff.
2. Ibid., 109.
3. Franz Schauwecker, *Aufbruch der Nation*, 317-22.
4. See similar visions in Ekkehard, *Sturmgeschlecht*, 188ff.; Buschbecker, *Wie unser Gesetz es befahl*, 52; Ettighoffer, *Wo bist du, Kamerad*, 335.

Erasing the Stain
1. Lettow-Vorbeck, 116.
2. Ibid., 117.
3. Freksa, *Kapitän Ehrhardt*, 42.
4. Ibid., 26ff.
5. Lettow-Vorbeck, *Mein Leben*, 180.
6. Dwinger, *Auf halbem Wege*, 353.
7. Ibid., 381ff.
8. Killinger, *Klabautermann*, 42ff.
9. Heydebreck, *Wehrwölfe*, 32.
10. Schauwecker, *Aufbruch der Nation*, 220.

Forms of Defense
1. For the same switch, see Schauwecker, *Aufbruch der Nation*, 179; Killinger, *Das waren Kerle*, 19; Gilbert, *Landsknechte*, 48; Delmer, *Französische Frauen*, 182; Eggers, *Berg der Rebellen*, 19; Jünger, *Der Kampf als inneres Erlebnis*, 34; Engelhardt, *Ritt nach Riga*, 27; Buschbecker, *Wie unser Gesetz es befahl*, 8, 14; Goote, *Wir fahren in den Tod*, 103ff.; Ewers, *Kriegslieder*, 16; Bochow, *Soldaten*, 198ff.
2. Ewers, *Reiter in deutscher Nacht*, 55. Cf., Heinz, *Sprengstoff*, 54; Goote, *Wir tragen das Leben*, 262.

A Soldier's Love
1. Dwinger, *Auf halbem Wege,* 308ff.
2. Ibid., 37.
3. Dwinger, *Die letzten Reiter*, 425.
4. Dwinger, *Auf halbem Wege*, 308ff.
5. Ibid., 41.

Excursus on "Homosexuality"
1. Wilhelm Reich, *Funktion des Orgasmus*, 168.
2. Freud, *Group Psychology and the Analysis of the Ego, SE*, vol. XVIII, 141.
3. Adorno, *Minima Moralia*, 52.
4. Brecht, *Arbeitsjournal*, 236.
5. Ibid., 279.
6. E.g., Odo Marquard, *Schwierigkeiten mit der Geschichtsphilosophie* (Frankfurt, 1973).
7. Reich emphasizes "that affects are instinctual manifestations and the unconscious is

inherently and specifically composed of drives" (*Funktion des Orgasmus*, 94). What that means in the present context is that analyzing affects is a better way to reach the "unconscious" than analyzing symbols.

A Soldier's Love (continued)

1. Höss, *Kommandant in Auschwitz*, 24.
2. Ibid., 133.
3. The dedication of Killinger's autobiography (*Klabautermann*) was less grandiose: "Dedicated to my brave wife." No matter.
4. Niemöller, *Vom U-Boot*, 200.
5. Freksa, *Kapitän Ehrhardt*, 7. For love of weapons, see also Maercker, *Vom Kaiserheer zur Reichswehr*, 170.
6. Salomon, *Die Geächteten*, 401.
7. Lettow-Vorbeck, *Mein Leben*, 274.
8. Ludwig F. Gengler, *Rudolf Berthold*, 104. Includes major portions of Berthold's diary.
9. Roden, *Deutsche Soldaten*, 146.
10. Killinger, *Kampf um Oberschlesien*, 123.
11. Ferdinand Crasemann, *Freikorps Maercker*, 9.
12. Salomon, *Die Kadetten*, 49.
13. Walter Frank, *Franz von Epp*, 48.
14. Rüdiger von der Goltz, *Meine Sendung in Finnland und im Baltikum*, 16.
15. Dwinger, *Auf halbem Wege*, 308. See Höss, *Kommandant in Auschwitz*, 69.
16. Jünger, *Kampf als inneres Erlebnis*, 12.
17. Dwinger, *Auf halbem Wege*, 538.
18. Jünger, *Kampf als inneres Erlebnis*, 12.
19. Freksa, *Kapitän Ehrhardt*, 142.
20. Mann, *Mit Ehrhardt durch Deutschland*, 11.
21. Heinz Schauwecker, "Freikorps von Epp," HoDA, 162.
22. Mahnken, "Gegenstoss im Westen 1919," RDS, 59.
23. Höss, *Kammandant in Auschwitz*, 74.
24. Gengler, *Rudolf Berthold*, 41.
25. As we shall see, certain women play a part in defending against relationships to objects.
26. Goote, *Kamerad Berthold*, 337.
27. Goote, *Wir tragen das Leben*, 57ff., 184.
28. Dwinger, *Auf halbem Wege*, 464.

Woman as Agressor

1. Jünger, *Kampf als inneres Erlebnis*, 16.
2. Waite, *Vanguard*, appendix.
3. Heinz, "Die Freikorps retten Oberschlesien," HoDA, 81.
4. Selchow, *Hundert Tage aus meinem Leben*, 35ff. In *Das Deutsche Führerlexikon 1934/35* (Berlin, 1934), Selchow is mentioned as a "philosopher of history." He had big plans. The *Führerlexikon* says this of him: "became a student in 1919; in March 1920, as leader of the Marburg Student Corps, put down the communist rebellion in Tübingen; together with an attorney, Dr. Luetgebrune, handled a two-year-long murder trial against fifteen members of his Freikorps; following his return from the Thüringen campaign, became Orgesch leader of western Germany; resolved to spend ten years in total isolation, until the end of 1933, laying down the intellectual basis for the new Germany in an ambitious work on the philosophy of history" (54).

Nothing further seems to have come of the latter project. Regarding Selchow's role in Thüringen (he exaggerates it wildly) and the trial of the murderers of fifteen workers from Thal, compare Henning Duderstadt, *Der Schrei nach dem Recht* (Marburg, 1920).

5. Salomon, *Die Geächteten*, 39ff.
6. Ibid., 180, 184ff.
7. Weller, *Peter Mönnkemann*, 125.
8. Dwinger, *Auf halbem Wege*, 432ff.
9. Ibid., 204.
10. Goote, *Kamerad Berthold*, 353.
11. Ibid., 354.
12. Hans Zöberlein, *Der Befehl des Gewissens*, 892ff.
13. Salomon, *Die Geächteten*, 51.
14. Maximilian Delmar, *Französische Frauen*, 114. Delmar's book is an exception here. He was not in the Freikorps, nor did he write about the German "postwar era." But he did write about women—a rare event for a major in the imperial army and one I did not want to pass up as a source, especially since Delmar's ideas about women are essentially the same as those of the other writers we've encountered, but are expressed more openly.
15. Similar sections in Maercker, *Vom Kaiserheer*, 119, 138, 143ff., 151; Salomon, *Putsch und Verschwörung*, 25; Salomon, "Hexenkessel Deutschland," JKR, 22ff.; Mahnken, "Kampf der Batterie Hasenclever," RDS, 138; Nord, "Krieg im Baltikum," JKR, 74; Wittman, *Erinnerungen der Eisernen Schar Berthold*, 146; Günther, "Hamburg," JKR, 45ff.; Weller, *Peter Mönkemann*, 83; Iger, *Spartakustage*, 15; Zöberlein, *Befehl des Gewissens*, 673; W. Frank, *Franz von Epp*, 68; Delmar, *Französische Frauen*, 133ff.; Heinz, *Die Nation greift an*, 32; Kohlhaas, *Der Häuptling und die Republik*, 213; Müller, *Soldat und Vaterland*, 22; Ettighoffer, *Revolver über der Stadt*, 65; Rodermund, "Rote Armee an Rhein und Ruhr," HoDA, 203ff.; Seitz, "Die Eiserne Schar Berthold in Hamburg," SB, 356ff.; see Theodore Abel, *Why Hitler Came to Power*, 98.
16. Delmar, *Französische Frauen*, 133.
17. Hartmann, "Erinnerungen aus den Kämpfen der baltischen Landeswehr," JKR, 119.
18. Delmar, *Französische Frauen*, 126.
19. Goote, *Kamerad Berthold*, 126ff.
20. Heinz, *Die Nation greift an*, 32. See Salomon, SB, 44; Günther, "Hamburg," JKR, 45.
21. Delmar, *Französische Frauen*, 153.
22. Ottwald, *Ruhe und Ordnung*, 107.
23. Zöberlein, *Befehl des Gewissens*, 171.

Rifle-Women: The Castrating Woman
1. Dwinger, *Auf halbem Wege*, 557-62.
2. Ibid., 566.
3. See Heinz Schauwecker, "Der Kampf der Gruppe Epp," SB, 115.
4. *Kölnische Zeitung*, 27 March 1920. Cited in Lucas, *Märzrevolution 1920*, vol. 2, 186ff.
5. F. W. von Oertzen, *Die deutschen Freikorps 1918-1920*, 303.
6. Some examples. Katharina Pint, shot in Pelkum by the Epp Brigade, 2 April 1920. Her husband's official pronouncement: "A woman from Pelkum says that K. P. was shot in accordance with martial law, allegedly because a revolver was found sewn into her slip. I can testify under oath that her report is false." Reported in

Volksstimme für Westfalen und Lippe, organ of the Independent Social-Democratic Party, 16 April 1920 (Hagen); in the *Bergische Arbeiterstimme*, organ of the working populace of the Solingen area, 19 April 1920; and by Gumbel, *Vier Jahre politischer Mord*, 61: ". . . shot because she had allegedly hidden a revolver in her stockings. . . . We also shot ten Red Cross nurses immediately, each one with a pistol in her possession." A member of the Epp Brigade, Sergeant Max Zeller, sent a similar report to an army reserve hospital in Dresden on 2 April 1920. The letter appeared in Erwin Brauer, *Der Ruhraufstand von 1920* (Berlin, 1920), 94; Otto Hennicke, *Die Rote Ruhrarmee* (East Berlin, 1956); and was heavily reproduced in other places as well. (See page 150 of the present work.)

On 26 March 1920, the Loewenfeld Naval Brigade had its first "enemy contact" in Raesfeld, after being transported there from Silesia. An article submitted by a military source appeared in the *Westfälischer Merkur*, 3 April 1920, under the title "Havoc in Rasefeld": "After the army troops were already on site, a car came racing by, stuffed full of gunnysacks, the insignia of the Red Cross nurses (prostitutes) on its hood, and inside, a machine-gun that immediately began to roar. The occupants were given a brief trial, of course, especially when it came to light that the 'nurses' were carrying various poisons." This is a variation of the "weapon under the dress." (Were they referring to the medicines the nurses had on them?) Later on, we shall encounter a depiction of the same event by a staff officer of the Loewenfeld Brigade, Ulrich von Bose; he does not mention any "hidden poisons."

7. Goote, *Kamerad Berthold*, 286.
8. Ibid., 297. See the nearly identical scenes in Ihno Meyer, *Das Jägerbataillon der Eisernen Division im Kampf gegen den Bolschewismus*, 40ff.; Wagener, *Von der Heimat geächtet*, 29; Dwinger, *Die letzten Reiter*, 344; Salomon, *Die Geächteten*, *130ff.;* also reprinted in JKR, 109ff.; Johannes Zobel, *Zwischen Krieg und Frieden*, 95; Volck, *Rebellen um Ehre*, 61; Bochow, *Soldaten ohne Befehl*, 63; Schricker, *Blutz, Erz und Kohle*, 56; Brandis, *Baltikumer*, 175ff.
9. Dwinger, *Die letzten Reiter*, 72.
10. A few examples. Juliette in Balla's *Landsknechte wurden wir;* Ulrica and Natascha in Gilbert's *Landsknechte*; "Princess" Ilse Cornelius in Weller's *Peter Mönkemann*; Hertha Holk in Goebbels's *Michael*; Gerte in Schauwecker's *Aufbruch der Nation*; the "Polish woman" (that is her *name*) in Buschbecker's *Wie unser Gesetz es befahl*. All of these women either evaporate, die, prove unfaithful to their former lovers, or show that they are available for other men as well. Not so the beautiful Gine-Maria in Götz Stoffregen's *Vaterland*. She proves to be both erotic (in moderation) and faithful. She holds onto her life, though at the price of having her soldier, Lieutenant Eschenhof, lose his. Soon after he gives her his promise of marriage (she is a widow), the bullet gets him.
11. Zöberlein, *Befehl des Gewissens*, 171ff.
12. E. F. Berendt, *Soldaten der Freiheit*, 89. What Goebbels had to say about this later is interesting (his diary, 1 March 1945): "We must issue orders for the second *Volkssturm* to begin, and will eventually have to set up women's batallions." 5 March: "He [the Führer] has now agreed to our plans for setting up women's batallions in Berlin. Countless women are reporting to the front nowadays, and the Führer is also of the opinion that they will fight fanatically, as long as they come forward as volunteers. We will have to place them in the second lines; this will take away the men's desire to slacken in the front lines" (Josef Goebbels, *Tagebücher 1945: Die letzten Aufzeichnungen*. Hamburg, 1977).
13. Dwinger, *Die letzten Reiter*, 129. In Schramm's *Rote Tage*, two lesbians try to poison themselves with veronal because of the unnaturalness of their lives. Other rifle

women may be found in Major Fletcher (commander of the Baltic Home Guard), "Die Eroberung Tuckums," SB, 156; Lautenbacher, *Widerstand im roten München*, 106; Balla, *Landsknechte wurden wir*, 70; Meyer, *Das Jägerbataillon der Eisernen Division*, 18; Steinaecker, *Mit der Eisernen Division im Baltenland*, 32; Erbt, *Der Narr von Kreyingen*, 229ff.; Nord, "Der Krieg im Baltikum, JKR, 74; Richter, *Freiwilliger Soltau*, 83; Engelhardt, *Der Ritt nach Riga*, 56; Brandis, *Baltikumer*, 74, 77, 174ff.; Volck, *Rebellen um Ehre*, 96; Erich Czech-Jochberg, *Im Osten Feuer*, 116; Kohlhaas, "Männer und Sicherheitskompanien 1918/19," SB, 112; Dwinger, *Die letzten Reiter*, 73, 107; Stenbock-Fermor, *Freiwilliger Stenbock*, 113, 117ff.

14. *Illustrierte Geschichte der deutschen Revolution*, 236.
15. Ekkehard, *Sturmgeschlecht*, 12, 14-19.
16. Roheim, "Aphrodite oder die Frau mit einem Penis," *Die Panik der Götter*, 228-64.
17. Elias Canetti, *Masse und Macht* (Crowds and Power), 436. See also Thomas Szasz, *Die Fabrikation des Wahnsinns* (The Manufacture of Madness), 114-96; Barbara Ehrenreich and Deirdre English, *Witches, Midwives and Nurses*, 15ff.
18. Brecht, *Arbeitsjournal*, 1938-42, 161.

The Red Nurse

1. E. Lucas, *Märzrevolution 1920*, vol. 2, 82.
2. Ibid., 83.
3. RDS, 139.
4. Troop newsletter of Army District Command IV, in *Acta: Reports of the General Command of the Seventh Army Corps*, Kölpien Office of the Munich State Archive.
5. Anonymous, "Freikorps Epp bei Pelkum," SB, 403.
6. Adolf Schulz, *Ein Freikorps im Industriegebiet*, 35.
7. Rodermund, "Rote Armee an Rhein und Ruhr," HoDA, 104.
8. Hans Schwarz van Berk, "Rote Armee an der Ruhr," JKR, 221. See von Oertzen, *Die deutschen Freikorps*, 273. For a time, van Berk was editor-in-chief of Goebbels's *Angriff*. See J.-P. Faye, *Totalitäre Sprachen* (Frankfurt, 1977), 583.
9. von Oertzen, *Die deutschen Freikorps*, 411.
10. Adolf Schmalix, *Gerechtigkeit für Kapitän Ehrhardt* (Leipzig, n.d.), 22.

On Sythen's Ground

1. van Berk, "Rote Armee an der Ruhr," JKR, 213ff.
2. Captain Schneider, "Vandalen," *Berliner Tag*. Reprinted in the *Buersche Zeitung*, 8 April 1920.
3. Steinaecker, *Mit der Eisernen Division*, 31. Cf. Eggers, *Berg der Rebellen*, 159.
4. Freud, *Interpretation of Dreams, SE*, vols. IV and V, 354; see also *Introductory Lectures on Psychoanalysis, SE*, vol. XV, 159ff., especially 163.
5. Dwinger, *Die letzten Reiter*, 72.
6. Hartmann, "Erinnerungen aus den Kämpfen der baltischen Landeswehr," JKR, 135ff. Other "Sythens" in Killinger, *Der Kampf um OS*, 60ff.; Killinger, *Die SA*, 77; Plehwe, *Im Kampf gegen die Bolschewisten*, 11; Heinz, *Sprengstoff*, 34; Herzog, *Kameraden*, 244; Steinaecker, *Mit der Eisernen Division*, 29.
7. M. Rohrwasser, *Saubere Mädel, starke Genossen*, especially 79ff.
8. The clearest illustration, in my opinion, is in A. Sohl-Rethel, *Ökonomie und Klassenstruktur des deutschen Faschismus*.
9. Just as it is imprudent to approach fascism with the "primacy" of any theory in mind. A multiplicity of approaches is not the same thing as "pluralism."
10. The role "repression" plays for "psychotics" is discussed in the final section of this chapter ("Preliminary Findings").

11. Freud, *Notes on a Case of Obsessional Neurosis, SE*, vol. X, 202.

The White Nurse—Countess of Sythen Castle

1. Dwinger, *Die letzten Reiter*, 103.
2. Captain Schneider, *Buersche Zeitung*, 8 April 1920.
3. Lucas, *Märzrevolution*, vol. 1, 284ff.
4. Rodermund, "Rote Armee an Rhein und Ruhr," HoDA, 107.
5. Dwinger, *Auf halbem Wege*, 458-60.
6. Freud, *Totem and Taboo, SE*, vol. XIII, 105: "The appearance of the totem in or about the house is often regarded as an omen of death; the totem has come to fetch his kinsman.." In a footnote Freud adds: "This therefore resembles the white woman of many noble races." See also *The Theme of Three Caskets, SE*, vol. XII, 294.
7. Dwinger, *Die letzten Reiter*, 134ff.
8. Ibid., 140.
9. Ibid., 137.
10. Ibid., 180.
11. Ibid., 248.
12. *Buersche Zeitung*, 4 May 1920.
13. T. [Heinrich Teuber], "Zwei Urteile," *Sozialistische Politik und Wirtschaft* (Berlin), 10 June 1926.
14. Dwinger, *Die letzten Reiter*, 445ff.
15. Ibid., 450.
16. Dwinger, *Auf halbem Wege*, 458.
17. See Lucas, *Märzrevolution*, vol. 1, 284ff.; Marchwitza, *Sturm auf Essen* (Berlin, 1934), 158ff.

Mothers

1. Ernst Röhm, *Die Geschichte eines Hochverräters*, 14.
2. Heydebreck, *Wehrwölfe*, 7ff.
3. Lettow-Vorbeck, *Mein Leben*, 18.
4. Höss, *Kommandant in Auschwitz*, 34.
5. Freksa, *Kapitän Ehrhardt*, 9.
6. Ibid., 25ff.
7. Killinger, *Klabautermann*, 57 and also 29. For another mother, see Goebbels, *Michael*, 12.
8. Delmar, *Französische Frauen*, 200.
9. Niemöller, *Vom U-Boot*, 144ff.
10. Lettow-Vorbeck, *Mein Leben*, 58ff.
11. von der Goltz, *Meine Sendung*, 193.
12. Ewers, *Reiter in deutscher Nacht*, 48. Mothers of iron also appear in Ettighoffer, *Wo bist du, Kamerad*, 20, 74, 325.
13. F. Schauwecker (*Aufbruch der Nation*, 17) and Ernst Jünger (*Feuer und Blut*, 109) expressly combat the notion that such mothers might be *their own*.
14. Lettow-Vorbeck, *Mein Leben*, 179ff.
15. See Ewers, *Kriegslieder*, 19ff.
16. Salomon, *Die Geächteten*, 446.
17. Dwinger, *Die letzten Reiter*, 444ff.
18. Rudolf Herzog, *Wieland der Schmied*, 49.
19. Ibid., 348ff.
20. On the theme "The kaiser should have died," see Jünger, *Kampf als inneres Erleb-*

nis, 52; Bronen, *Rossbach*, 81; Rossbach, *Mein Weg durch die Zeit*, 52ff.; Hotzel, "Offizier 18," HoDA, 24; Goote, *Kamerad Berthold*, 237-41; Crasemann, *Freikorps Maercker*, 10.

Sisters

1. Goote, *Kamerad Berthold*, 127-29.
2. Ibid., 303ff.
3. Killinger, *Klabautermann*, 109ff.
4. Ewers, *Reiter in deutscher Nacht*, 55.
5. Ibid., 187.
6. Ibid., 389-95.
7. Ibid., 286.
8. Ibid., 283ff., 290.
9. Ibid., 46ff.
10. Ibid., 176.
11. Ibid., 184-87.
12. Ibid., 176, 209.
13. Ibid., 255.
14. Ibid., 259.
15. Ibid., 301.
16. Ibid., 308.
17. Ibid., 371.
18. Ibid., 318ff.
19. Ibid., 375.
20. Ibid., 380-83.
21. Ibid., 378.
22. Ibid., 391.
23. Ibid., 420-24.
24. Ibid., 431ff.
25. Ibid., 429.
26. Ibid., 434.
27. Ibid., 444ff.
28. Ibid., 447.
29. Ibid., 464.
30. Ibid., 470.

Marriage—Sisters of Comrades

1. Heydebreck, *Wehrwölfe*, 16. Regarding "sisters of comrades," see also Ekkehard, *Sturmgeschlecht*, 34ff.; Richter, *Freiwillger Soltau*, 51ff; Gilbert, *Landsknechte*, 209 (a marriage between look-alike cousins). The other relationships in Ewers's *Reiter* operate in the same way. Lannwitz informs his comrade Scholz that he wants to marry Scholz's sister before asking the sister herself (115). Käte Scholz's original fiancé (died in battle) had befriended her older brother Paul at the front (46,115). Ewers's prewar novel *Alraune* focuses on the same constellations. (cf., especially, the sections between the chapters).
2. See also Zöberlein, *Befehl des Gewissens*, 256, 616; W. Frank, *Epp*, 69; Krumbach, *Epp*, 54; Weigand, *Rote Flut*, 427; Schauwecker, *Aufbruch der Nation*, 60; Wittman, *Erinnerungen der Eisernen Schar*, 147-50.
3. Goote, *Wir tragen das Leben*, 31. In the preceding volume (*Wir fahren den Tod*), his sister Lore had informed him by letter of Karin Brandt's death.

The Lady with the Light

1. Schauwecker, *Aufbruch der Nation*, 129.
2. Ibid., 132.
3. See, for instance, Goote, *Kamerad Berthold*, 84; or Kohlhaas, *Der Häuptling und die Republik*, 111.
4. Jünger, *In Stahlgewittern*, 247ff.
5. There are also oral reports about nurses. See the song about Nurse Esther and Doctor Versalzer on G. Kreisler's album *Purzelbäume* (Preiser Records, EMI 1975), 1C062-30234.
6. Nicely illustrated in Schauwecker, *Aufbruch der Nation*, 129.
7. Goote, *Wir tragen das Leben*, 107.
8. Ibid., 106-11, 121.
9. von der Goltz, *Meine Sendung*, 298. Other "white nurses" in Weller, *Peter Mönkemann*, 153; Eggers, *Berg der Rebellen*, 162, 165, 176ff.; Ewers, *Reiter*, 9, 228; Herzog, *Kameraden*, 354, 373; Wrangell, *Geschichte des Baltenregiments*, 73; Richter, *Freiwilliger Soltau*, 88; Engelhardt, *Ritt nach Riga*, 143; Brandis, *Baltikumer*, 132; Kohlhaas, *Der Häuptling*, 104.
10. Bischoff, *Die letzte Front*, 113.
11. Ehrenreich and English, *Witches, Midwives and Nurses*, 17-26; Thomas Szasz, "The Witch as Healer," *The Manufacture of Madness* (New York: Harper and Row, 1970).
12. Ehrenreich and English, *Witches*, 48.
13. Ibid., 44ff. See Cecil Woodham-Smith's biography, *Florence Nightingale* (McGraw Hill, 1951); Lytton Strachey's *Eminent Victorians* (1918).
14. Ehrenreich and English, *Witches*, 45.
15. Ibid., 46.
16. A few titles: Erika von Babo, *Aus dem Kriegstagebuch einer badischen Schwester* (Karlsruhe, 1918); Rosa Barth, *Aus dem Heldenleben einer Diakonisse* (Stuttgart, 1915); Marie Luise Becker, *Frau hinter der Front, Roman* (Berlin, 1934); Mary Bohny, *Nächstenliebe im Weltenbrand* (Heidelberg, 1934); Dora Brooke, *Kriegserlenisse der Kaiserswerther Diakonissen in Alexandrien* (Kaiserswerth, 1916); Enrica von Handel-Mazzetti, *Unter dem österreichischen Roten Kreuz* (Regensburg, n.d.); Anna Katterfeld, *Engel von Sibirien: Aus dem Leben Elsa Brandströms* (Wuppertal, 1940); Ulrike Garbe, "Elsa Brandström," in *Frauenschicksal* (Stuttgart, 1939); Sister Magdalene von Walsleben, *Die deutsche Schwester in Sibirien* (Berlin, 1919); and many others.
17. Höss, *Kommandant in Auschwitz*, 32ff.

An Aside on Proletarian Reality

1. Alexander Stenbock-Fermor, *Meine Erlebnisse als Bergarbeiter*, 80-83.
2. Lucas, *Zwei Formen von Radikalismus in der deutschen Arbeiterbewegung*, 73ff.
3. Ibid., 70-76.
4. Stenbock-Fermor, *Meine Erlebnisse*, 102-29.
5. Georg Werner, *Ein Kumpel*, 69. In *Deutsche Presse und Propaganda des Abstimmungskampfes in Oberschlesien* (Beuthen, 1931), R. Vogel complains about the "family-destroying boardinghouse system" in Upper Silesia (9).
6. Ibid., 69ff.
7. Ibid., 44ff., 61.
8. Li Fischer-Eckert, *Die wirtschaftliche und soziale Lage der Frauen in dem modernen Industrieort Hamborn im Rheinland*, 90.

9. Ibid., 90-92.
10. Ibid., 82. See Lucas, *Zwei Formen*, 57-70.
11. Stenbock-Fermor, *Meine Erlebnisse*, 181-86; 191-97.
12. In *Sozialistische Politik und Wirtschaft*, 4 March 1927.
13. Stenbock-Fermor, *Meine Erlebnisse*, 80.
14. The system of military bordellos was regulated and did not make many demands of the soldiers regarding their behavior toward the women. See Magnus Hirschfeld, *Sittengeschichte des Weltkriegs*, vol. 1, 305ff. References to "open" prostitution are rare, but do occur. See Gilbert, *Landsknechte*, 140; Plehwe, *Im Kampf gegen die Bolshewisten*, 28 (women in the white camp). In *Schutzhaft* (Berlin, 1919), Wieland Herzfelde reports seeing Berlin voluntary troops mixing freely with prostitutes (informers, he guesses) in March 1919, in the Hotel Eden and in the state prison; he also reports seeing numerous "soldiers' girlfriends" (3, 10). Hence some of the soldiers certainly had "access" to women. But they did not have *relationships*—a crucial distinction.
15. I examine this point in greater detail in the conclusion of volume 2 (section entitled "Peace").
16. Heinrich Teuber, *Für die Sozialisierung des Ruhrbergbaus*, 21.
17. Josef Ernst, *Kapptage im Industriegebiet*, 68.
18. Pitrof, *Gegen Spartakus in München*, 39.
19. Werner, *Ein Kumpel*, 112ff.
20. Grünberg, *Brennende Ruhr*, 119.
21. E. Lucas, *Märzrevolution*, vol. 3 (manuscript).
22. Ibid., vol. 2. This citation and those immediately following are taken from pages 82ff.
23. Also printed in RDS, 119.
24. Spektator, *Die Schreckenstage im rheinisch-westfälischen Industriebezirk*, 7.
25. This citation and those immediately following are from Lucas, *Märzrevolution*, vol. 2, 82-84.
26. Clara Zetkin, *Erinnerungen an Lenin* (Berlin, 1961), 63-97.
27. Karl Marx, *Economic and Philosophic manuscripts*, in K. Marx and F. Engels, *Collected Works*, vol. 3, 295 (New York; International Publishers, 1975).
28. Brecht, *Tagebücher 1920-1922*, entry for 30 April 1921.
29. Ibid., 9 May 1921.
30. Hugo E. Lüdecke, "Deutsche Bordellgassen," in *Antropophyteia IV*, edited by S. F. Krauss, 261ff.
31. Henriette Arendt, *Menschen, die den Pfad verloren*, 36ff.
32. Parent-Duchalet, *Die Prostitution in Paris*. Cited by Lüdecke, "Deutsche Bordellgassen," in *Antropophyteia IV*, edited by Krauss, 261. See Schidowitz, *Sittengeschichte des Proletariats*, 252; and, on the trade in innocent young proletarian women, 254ff.
33. Otto Rühle, *Illustrierte Kultur- und Sittengeschichte des Proletariats*, 444-89 (the section on prostitution). The book contains many similar pieces of information.
34. Hoffman Hays, *Mythos Frau* (Düsseldorf, 1969), 297.
35. Arendt, *Menschen, die den Pfad verloren*, 38.
36. Fischer-Eckert, *Die wirtschaftliche und soziale Lage der Frauen*, 74.
37. *Ästhetik und Kommunikation* 6 (September 1975), 46. In the same issue see Chryssoula Kambas, "Frühsozialismus und Prostitution," 34-49.
38. Ernst Bloch, *Das Prinzip Hoffnung* (Frankfurt, 1967). This citation and these immediately preceding are from pages 695-97.
39. W. Blumberg, *Karl Marx*, 117 (Rowohlt monograph number 76).

Attacks on Women

1. Freksa, *Kapitän Ehrhardt*, 102.
2. Mann, *Mit Ehrhardt durch Deutschland*, 42.
3. Killinger, *Ernstes und Heiteres aus dem Putschleben*, 14ff.
4. Herzog, *Kameraden*, 34.
5. Ottwald, *Ruhe und Ordnung*, 90.
6. Maercker, *Vom Kaiserheer zur Reichswehr*, 201ff.
7. Ulrich von Bose, "Vormarsch gegen Essen," SB, 395.
8. Zöberlein, *Befehl des Gewissens*, 193.
9. Dwinger, *Auf halbem Wege*, 296.
10. Ibid., 230.
11. Ibid., 276ff.
12. Eggers, *Berg der Rebellen*, 106. Other attacks on women: Melzer, "Die Auswirkungen des Kapp-Putsches in Leipzig," JKR, 229; Weller, *Peter Mönkemann*, 102; Weigand, *Die rote Flut*, 422ff.; Goebbels, *Michael*, 143; Zimmermann, *Vorfrühling*, 38; Salomon, *Die Geächteten*, 67; Zöberlein, *Befehl des Gewissens*, 752; Balla, *Landsknechte wurden wir*, 97ff.; Buschbecker, *Wie unser Gesetz es befahl*, 162; Siegert, *Aus Münchens schwerster Zeit*, 54; Brandis, *Baltikumer*, 174ff.; Volck, *Rebellen um Ehre*, 87; Brandt, *Schlageter*, 36ff.; Grothe/Kern, "Strassenkampf in München," SB, 124; Glombowski, "Einsatz der Selbstschutz-Sturm-Abteilung Heinz," SB, 268.

Sexual Murder

1. Balla, *Landsknechte wurden wir*, 111.
2. Ibid., 112.
3. Ibid., 184-88 (all references to "Red Marie").
4. Dwinger, *Die letzten Reiter*, 141ff.
5. Ibid., 144.
6. Ibid., 145ff.
7. Heinz, *Sprengstoff*, 36.
8. Freud, *Interpretation of Dreams, SE*, vols. IV and V, 387. "The frequency with which sexual repression makes use of transpositions from a lower to an upper part of the body. Thanks to them it becomes possible in hysteria for all kinds of sensations and intentions to be put into effect, if not where they properly belong—in relation to the genitals, at least in relation to other, unobjectionable parts of the body. One instance of a transposition of this kind is the replacement of the genitals by the face in the symbolism of unconscious thinking. Linguistic usage follows the same line in recognizing the buttocks ['*Hinterbacken*', literally 'back-cheeks'] as homologous to the cheeks, and by drawing a parallel between the '*labia*' and the lips which frame the aperture of the mouth. Comparisons between nose and penis are common, and the similarity is made more complete by the presence of hair in both places."
9. Ibid., 359. "The secretions of the human body—mucus, tears, urine, semen, etc.—can replace one another in dreams."
10. ". . . the male organ, finds symbolic substitutes in the first instance in things that resemble it in shape—things, accordingly, that are long and up-standing, such as *sticks, umbrellas, posts, trees* and so on; further, in objects which share with the thing they represent the characteristic of penetrating into the body and injuring—thus, sharp *weapons* of every kind, *knives, daggers, spears, sabres*, but also fire-arms, *rifles, pistols* and *revolvers*" (*Introductory Lectures on Psychoanalysis, SE*, vol. XV, 154). "This symbolism is not peculiar to dreams, but is characteristic of unconscious ideation, in particular among the people, and it is to be found in folklore,

and in popular myths, legends, linguistic idioms, proverbial wisdom and current jokes, to a more complete extent than in dreams." (*Interpretation of Dreams, SE*, vols. IV and V, 351). "There is scarcely one of the symbolic representations of the male genitals which does not recur in joking, vulgar or poetic usage." (*Introductory Lectures*, 163). These speech habits, incidentally, seem to belie that argument that the "symbols" in question have to do with *unconscious* representations. More about that in the next section.

11. See Freud's "wolfman," *From the History of an Infantile Neurosis, SE*, vol. XVII, 92ff.
12. Particularly evident in Thor Goote, *Die Fahne hoch*, 240ff.
13. Freud, *Interpretation of Dreams, SE*, vols. IV and V, 410.
14. Salomon, *Die Geächteten*, 167.
15. Ekkehard, *Sturmgeschlecht*, 26.
16. Freud, *Medusa's Head, SE*, vol. XVIII, 273-74.
17. For tributes to formality, see also Jünger, *In Stahlgewittern*, 30; Brandis, *Baltikumer*, 12.
18. Heinz, *Sprengstoff*, 36.
19. Dwinger, *Die letzten Reiter*, 107.
20. Ibid., 105. For sights of "bloody masses," see also Volck, *Rebellen um Ehre*, 64, 83, 95, 142; Goote, *Wir fahren den Tod*, 76, 168; Salomon, *Putsch und Verschwörung*, 16, 19, 25; Bochow, *Soldaten ohne Befehl*, 198ff.; Heinz, *Sprengstoff*, 60ff.

Preliminary Findings
1. Freud, *The Ego and the Id, SE*, vol. XIX, 56.
2. Freud, *The Dissolution of the Oedipus Complex, SE*, vol. XIX, 176-77; Laplanche and Pontalis, *The Language of Psychoanalysis* (New York: Norton, 1973), 444-45. On the concept of "identification," see Freud, *Group Psychology and the Analysis of the Ego, SE*, vol. XVIII, 105-10 (section 7, "identification").
3. Laplanche and Pontalis, *Language of Psychoanalysis*. Almost identical language in Freud, *Introductory Lectures on Psychoanalysis, SE*, vol. XV, 153.
4. Melanie Klein, *the Psycho-Analysis of Children* (London: Hogarth Press, 1975), especially chapter 8; Klein, "The Importance of Symbol-Formation in the Development of the Ego," in *Love, Guilt and Reparation and Other Works* (London: Hogarth Press, 1975); and, following her lead, Michael Balint, *Therapeutic Aspects of Regression*.
5. Balint, *Therapeutic Aspects*, 18. In this context, Melanie Klein's discovery that children's games constitute a language useful in therapy is of special significance.
6. Jean Piaget, *The Origins of Intelligence in Children* (New York: International Universities Press, 1966), tr. by Margaret Cook; René Spitz, *The First Year of Life: A Psychoanalytic Study of Normal and Deviant Development of Object-Relations* (New York: International Universities Press, 1965); Spitz, "Diacritic and Coenesthetic Organizations," *Psychoanalytic Review* 32 (1945); Franco Fornari, *Psychoanalyse des ersten Lebensjahres*; Margaret Mahler, *On Human Symbiosis*.
7. Mahler, *On Human Symbiosis*. On the meaning of symbiosis and the symbiotic phase, see pp. 8-14. Like every other psychoanalyst who writes about the analysis of children, Mahler is more heavily indebted to Melanie Klein than she admits.
8. Ibid., pp. 19-31. Fornari, *Psychoanalyse des ersten Lebensjahres*, 161-85. Volume 2 of the present work contains a thorough analysis of this process.
9. See the introduction to Fornari's *Psychoanalyse des ersten Lebensjahres*.
10. Mahler, "Prototypes of Mother-Child Interaction," chapter 5 of *On Human Symbiosis*, 145-160.

11. Balint, *Therapeutic Aspects*, 26.
12. Ibid., 40. Wilhelm Reich introduces the same distinction when he distinguishes between "compromise formations" and "defects," and when he tries to present disturbances of genital functions as "functional inhibitions," rather than as "symptoms in the dynamic sense" (*Funktion des Orgasmus*, 98ff.).
13. Freud, *The Unconscious, SE*, vol. XIV, 183-84; *Repression, SE*, vol. XIV, 147; elaborated especially by Anna Freud, *Das Ich und die Abwehrmechanismen* (1936). See also Laplanche and Pontalis, *Language of Psychoanalysis*, "Defense Mechanisms" (109).
14. Melanie Klein discovered that the conscious and unconscious are more closely linked in infants than in adults, and that infantile repression is less intensive, "The Emotional Life of the Infant," in *Envy and Gratitude and Other Works* (New York: Delta, 1975), 132; furthermore, that repression does not simply exist, but is made use of and that the capacity to use it must be developed (86). Reich noted that even incestuous desires are consciously present in cases of compulsive neuroses, though analysts claim such desires are "unconscious" because they have lost their affective contents (*Die Entdeckung des Orgons/Die Funktion des Orgasmus*, 238). Something other than "incestuous desire" is being repressed in such cases, in other words.

   Gisela Pankow's book *Gesprengte Fesseln der Psychose* is very instructive in this regard. She describes twelve successful treatments of neuroses. The notion of repression does not enter into her thinking. For her, the analyst's task is not to actualize "discarded material," but to assist the patient in achieving a sense of physical wholeness, a recognition of the borders of the body. When psychotics seem to be expressing themselves in a disconnected fashion, it is not because they are "repressing," but because every connection, especially the connection to their own bodies, has been ripped away from them.
15. Freud, *An Outline of Psychoanalysis, SE*, vol. XXIII, 163; Freud, *Moses and Monotheism, SE*, vol. XXIII, 95-96; Freud, *The Ego and the Id, SE*, vol. XIX, 17. See also Balint, *Therapeutic Aspects*, 16-18; and the entries "Working-through" (488) and "Affect" (13), in Laplanche and Pontalis, *The Language of Psychoanalysis*.
16. Balint, *Therapeutic Aspects*, 41.
17. Deleuze and Guattari, *Anti-Oedipus*, chapter 2.
18. Paul Parin, Fritz Morgenthaler, and Goldy Parin-Matthey, *Die Weissen denken zu viel: Psychoanalytische Untersuchungen in Westafrika* (Munich, n.d.), 429ff. See Reimut Reiche, "Ist der Ödipus-Komplex universell?" *Kursbuch* 2 (1972).
19. Deleuze and Guattari, *Anti-Oedipus*, passim.
20. Ibid., 58ff.
21. M. Klein, *The Emotional Life of the Infant* and *The Importance of Symbol-Formation*. Laplanche and Pontalis, "Partial object," *Language of Psychoanalysis*. Deleuze and Guattari, *Anti-Oedipus*, 421ff., 56ff.
22. Klein, *The Emotional Life of the Infant* and *Psycho-Analytic Play Technique*.
23. Deleuze and Guattari, *Anti-Oedipus*, passim, especially chapter 1, "The Desiring-Machines."
24. Ibid., 495.
25. Ibid., 498.
26. Ibid., chapter 2.
27. Ibid., passim.
28. Ibid., 147ff., 154ff.
29. Ibid., 109.
30. Freud, *The Dissolution of the Oedipus Complex, SE*, vol. XIX; Freud, *Civilization*

and Its Discontents, SE, vol. XXI. Laplanche and Pontalis, "Sublimation" (431), *The Language of Psychoanalysis.*

31. Deleuze and Guattari, *Anti-Oedipus,* 39, 383ff.
32. Ibid., passim.
33. Ibid., 114.
34. For instance, in *An Outline of Psychoanalysis, SE,* vol. XXIII, 202, where Freud ascribes "psychosis" to an "orientation . . . that separates the ego from reality, under the influence of drives." On chaos, see Freud, *New Introductory Lectures, SE,* vol. XXII, 73. Melanie Klein's experience with ego-weak children, conversely, showed that even in these children who had no relationship to reality, the id would not overwhelm the ego as long as the ego could stand up to having repression lifted with the help of analysis (*The Importance of Symbol-Formation,* 40).
35. Deleuze and Guattari, *Anti-Oedipus,* 339.
36. Ibid., 54 and passim.
37. Ibid., 339. More on this method of criticizing Freud in Ulrich Sonnemann, "Die entdämmte Vergangenheit: Freud," *Negative Anthropoligie,* 61-96.
38. Freud, *The Loss of Reality in Neurosis and Psychosis, SE,* vol. XIX, 185-87. Or again, in *The Question of Lay Analysis, SE,* vol. XX, 196: "The ego lies between reality and the id, which is what is truly mental."
39. Deleuze and Guattari, *anti-Oedipus,* 32.
40. Ibid., 26-27.
41. Ibid., 28-29.
42. Ibid., 29.
43. Introduced by Freud in *Beyond the Pleasure Principle* (1920).
44. See *The Question of Lay Analysis, SE,* vol. XX, 212; *Female Sexuality, SE,* vol. XXI, 225-43, *New Introductory Lectures, SE,* vol. XII, 112-35.
45. For instance in *Charakteranalyse,* 188-96. The same holds true for the sequence "oral-anal-genital," 235ff.
46. Ibid., 228.
47. Ibid., 236ff. See also *Die Funktion des Orgasmus,* 152ff.; *Die Entdeckung des Orgons/Die Funktion des Orgasmus,* 98ff., 119ff. The latter work (1942), an expanded reworking of *Die Funktion des Orgasmus* (1927), contains features that depart from the situation I have criticized. See 119ff., where Reich abandons his fixation on Freudian terminology. (Some say that is the older, "crazy" Reich; more about that "craziness" later.)
48. Reich pointedly criticized this setup, though he held the death-drive solely responsible for it.
49. *Die Entdeckung des Orgons/Die Funktion des Orgasmus* (1942) makes it apparent that Reich was aware of this contradiction. He simply was not confident enough yet to operate on the basis of his divergent views. Evidence of the same awareness emerges in an interview Reich gave to Dr. Eissler in 1952, under the auspices of the Freud Archive (see bibliography).
50. Reich, *Mass Psychology of Fascism,* 56.
51. Reich, *Charakteranalyse,* 57ff., 244ff.; *Die Entdeckung des Orgons,* 106ff., 129ff., 189-97.
52. Reich, *Charakteranalyse,* 36-55.
53. Reich, *Die Entdeckung des Orgons,* 128ff., 145ff., 155ff.
54. Reich, *Der Einbruch der Sexualmoral* (Berlin, 1932).
55. Deleuze and Guattari, *Anti-Oedipus,* 29.
56. Reich, *Massenpsychologie des Fascismus,* 82; Reich, *Die Entdeckung des Orgons,* 125.

57. Deleuze and Guattari, *Anti-Oedipus*, 112, 137.
58. Alain Besançon, "Vers une histoire psychanalytique," *Histoire et expérience du moi*, Flammarion, 1971, 69, 75, 76.
59. W. Benjamin, "Ein Jakobiner von heute," *Angelus Novus*, 449.
60. Ibid.

Chapter 2: Floods, Bodies, History

Aggregate States of the Bodily Interior

The Red Flood

1. Brecht, "Über die Gewalt," *GW*, vol. 9, 602.
2. W. von Oertzen, *Baltenland*, 300.
3. Hartmann, "Erinnerungen aus den Kämpfen der baltischen Landeswehr," JKR, 141.
4. Ibid., 145.
5. W. Frank, *Epp*, 76.
6. Wiemers-Borchelshof, "Freikorps-Arbeitsdienst-Siedlung," SB, 407.
7. Osten, "Der Kampf um Oberschlesien," JKR, 263.
8. Eggers, *Berg der Rebellen*, 237.
9. They had remained there since August 1919, defying the German government's order to withdraw. In other words, they were freebooters. The commander of the "Iron Division," Major Bischoff, had personally opposed the order to return to Germany. As the Iron Division and the "German Legion," his troops allied themselves with the White Russian army of Prince von Avaloff-Bermondt. See Waite, *Vanguard*, 122ff; Faye, *Totalitäre Sprachen*, 46; Bischoff, *Die letzte Front*, 189.
10. Wagener, *Von der Heimat geächtet*, 8.
11. Mann, *Mit Ehrhardt*, 11.
12. Comrade Schottenhammel is depicted in Giorgio Pellizi, *Bernie, der Milliardenflipper* (Berlin, 1974).
13. True within limits to be discussed in volume 2 ("The Militant Body in Battle").
14. Lüttwitz, *Im Kampf gegen die Novemberrevolution*, 65.
15. From the diary of H. Fiesinger, SB, 109.
16. Jünger, *Der Kampf als inneres Erlebnis*, 61. Stadtler (*Als Antibolshewist 1918/19*) felt the defeat and its consequences as a "cloudburst."
17. Salomon, *Die Geächteten*, 347.
18. Lutz Rossin, *Aus dem roten Sumpf*, 3.
19. Ibid., foreword.
20. Dwinger, "Die Armee hinter Stacheldraht," in vol. 1 of *Deutsches Schicksal* (Jena, 1929), 76. See Buschbecker, *Wie unser Gesetz es befahl*, 12.
21. Heydebreck, *Wehrwölfe*, 32.
22. Ekkehardt, *Sturmgeschlecht*, 47. See Kessel, *Handgranaten und rote Fahnen*, 157.
23. Heinz Schauwecker, "Freikorps von Epp," HoDA, 161.
24. Dwinger, *Auf halbem Wege*, 502.
25. Roden, "Hauptmann Berthold—ein Soldatenschicksal," RDS, 140. On floods, in the senses in question, see also Dwinger, *Auf halbem Wege*, 459; Schmidt-Pauli, *Die Männer um Hitler*, 69; Wittmann, *Erinnerungen der Eisernen Schar*, 123; Crasemann, *Freikorps Maercker*, 9; Schramm, *Rote Tage*, 82; Mann, *Mit Ehrhardt*, 204; Killinger, *Klabautermann*, 263; Gengler, *Berthold* (diary), 104; Stenbock-Fermor, *Als Freiwilliger*, 117; Schauroth, "Revolte in Libau," SB, 164; Salomon,

"Der Berliner Märzaufstand 1919," SB, 44ff.; Salomon, *Nahe Geschichte*, 34; Balla, *Landsknechte*, 124; Rodermund, "Rote Armee an Rhein und Ruhr," HoDA, 113; von Oertzen, *Die deutschen Freikorps*, 245; Zobbel, *Zwischen Krieg und Frieden*, 69; Bochow, *Soldaten ohne Befehl*, 33; Niemöller, *Vom U-Boot*, 141; Karl Stephan, *Der Todeskampf in der Ostmark*, 73, 78; G. Günther, *Die Bändigung des Krieges durch den Staat*, 201; Czech-Jochberg, *Im Osten Feuer*, 105; Hans zue Megede, *Hakenkreuz am Stahlhelm*, 130. Solf (*Deutschlands Auferstehung 1934*, 12) viewed the currency of the inflation as a "paper flood."

26. These lines turn up in Bronnen (*Rossbach*, 37) and Rossbach (*Mein Weg*, 50) as a cadets' song of protest against arbitrary treatment from "up above." Hanns Heinz Ewers's *Kriegslieder 1916* (34-37) contains one song that repeats the following refrain eleven times: "In blood we must stand./In blood we must walk./Up to, up to our ankles."

27. Banning this song was one of the Weimar regime's futile measures against fascism. See Bremen State Archives, *Konvolut 241*, vol. 4, 521, under the heading "Confiscated Literature—General."

28. Lucas, *Märzrevolution*, 1:290.

29. Ibid., 290-93.

30. Salomon, *Die Geächteten*, 177ff.

31. Salomon, *Nahe Geschichte*, 84.

32. Portrayed in Lucas, *Märzrevolution*, 2:150ff.

33. The legend about "Red terror" in German workers' uprisings of the postwar era may have been due in large part to the fact that the workers killed hardly any of their tormentors or their lackeys. Hence an army of survivors could become an army of "eyewitnesses" to the "terror" once the workers had been defeated. Those eyewitnesses were certain the workers would not commit acts of vengeance. From 1933 onward, the secondary school in which Berthold's men had holed up was called the "Berthold School" (SB, 357).

Street of Blood

1. Goote, *Berthold*, 126.
2. Jünger, *Kampf als inneres Erlebnis*, 30.
3. E. Lissauer, *Worte in die Zeit: Flugblätter 1914* (Göttingen, 1914).
4. Lissauer, *Luther und Thomas Münzer* (Berlin, 1929), 44.
5. Bächtold, *Deutscher Soldatenbrauch und Soldatenglaube* (Strasbourg, 1917), 3. See B. Grabinski, *Neuere Mystik, der Weltkrieg im Aberglauben und im Lichte der Prophetie* (Hildesheim, 1916), 268-72. Grabinski also shows (270) that "attacks against the cosmopolitan proletariat" were the raw material for prophecies of war.
6. Eberhard W. Möller, "Kantate auf einen grossen Mann," *Berufung der Zeit* (Berlin, 1935), 15.

Boiling

1. Salomon, "Hexenkessel Deutschland," JKR, 33.
2. Selchow, *Hundert Tage aus meinem Leben*, 342.
3. Wagener, *Von der Heimat geächtet*, 25.
4. Ibid., 8.
5. H. H. Hollenbach, *Opfergang*, 99.
6. Heinz, *Die Nation greift an*, 29.
7. Heinz, *Sprengstoff*, 8.
8. Ibid.
9. Jünger, *Kampf als inneres Erlebnis*, 1.

10. Ibid.
11. Salomon, "Hexenkessel Deutschland," JKR, 13.
12. Ibid., 13.
13. Herzog, *Kameraden*, 299.
14. See Jünger, *Kampf als inneres Erlebnis*, 28. On cooking and bubbling, see Freiwald, *Der Wag der braunen Kämpfer*, 259; Höfer, *Oberschlesien in der Aufstandszeit*, 14; Salomon, *Der verlorene Haufe*, 108.
15. Freud, *Interpretation of Dreams, SE*, vols. IV and V, 354, 359; Freud, *Introductory Lectures, SE*, vol. XV, 156, 163, 267; Freud, *The Psychopathology of Everyday Life, SE*, VI, 170-72.
16. See the chapter "Psychoanalysis and Familialism" in Deleuze and Guattari, *Anti-Oedipus*.
17. Freud, *New Introductory Lectures, SE*, vol. XXII, 73, 101-2. In *Die Intelligenz und der Krieg*, Albrecht Erich Günther demands that war "lead the nation into a new aggregate state" (87).

Exploding Earth/Lava

1. Dwinger, *Auf halbem Wege*, 509.
2. See Michael Balint, *Angstlust und Regression*.
3. Schauwecker, *Aufbruch der Nation*, 75.
4. W. Erbt, *Der Narr von Kreyingen*, 170.
5. Ibid.
6. Ibid.
7. Jünger, *Kampf als inneres Erlebnis*, 97.
8. Ibid., 72.
9. Ibid., 2.
10. Ibid. See Friedrich Georg Jünger, *Krieg und Krieger*, 59.

Warding Off the Red Floods

1. Jünger, *Kampf als inneres Erlebnis*, 33ff.
2. Osten, "Der Kampf um Oberschlesien," JKR, 263.
3. Bronnen, *Oberschlesien*, 120.
4. Hülsen, "Freikorps im Osten," RDS, 114.
5. Heydebreck, *Wehrwölfe*, 32.
6. From "Am Feuer auf dem Kreuzberg, vor der Einsegnung der Wandervogel-hunderschaft zu Rogau," SB, 245.
7. Berendt, *Soldaten der Freiheit*, 92.
8. Mahnken, "Gegenstoss im Westen 1919," RDS, 61ff.
9. Erbt, *Der Narr*, 150.
10. Gengler, *Berthold*, 130.
11. W. Reich, *Die Entdeckung des Orgons/Die Funktion des Orgasmus*, 126; Reich, *Die Funktion des Orgasmus*, 109ff.
12. On the theme of warding off floods, see also Kessel, *Handgranaten und rote Fahnen*, 130; Höfer, *Oberschlesien in der Aufstandszeit*, 30; Engelhardt, *Ritt nach Riga*, 7, 9, 27; Freiwald, *Der Weg der braunen Kämfer*, 38; Goote, *Wir fahren den Tod*, 5; Eggers, *Von der Freiheit des Kriegers*, 7; Liemann, "Felsen in roter Flut," SB, 20.
   More than anyone else, Jünger submits to the enticements of the floods: "And for us as well there is a demise, a thunderous sinking into the flood; a chain of dramatic scenes races around in a small area, and the person in question is hurled into the deepest abysses of horror and onto the highest peaks of exaltation." As we shall see, Jünger submits to the floods so thoroughly because he is certain of his resurrection (*Feuer und Blut*, 67).

There is one writer who submits fully to the enticements of the flood and lets himself sink. That writer is Friedrich Wilhelm Heinz, author of the novel *Sprengstoff* (Explosives). Heinz was one of the most important figures in the Nazi underground of the 1920s, leading sabotage campaigns in Upper Silesia (1921) and in the Ruhr region during the French occupation (1923). The only reason we do not recognize his name as that of a highly decorated Nazi is that, like so many of his comrades, he failed to survive June 1934. "Suddenly, there are a lot of Negroes, Indians, and Chinese around me. They climb up the mountains and dance around in the clear-flowing streams. The water is troubled. The streams begin to swell. I climb a tower, which is high and sublime beyond all human imagining. I feel afraid of the height and the isolation. Just then the tower begins to sway. I am terrified by a scream from my right. An even higher wave of water, green-black, is rolling toward me, inundating all the mountains. Lightning bolts shudder. Resigned, I wait for the water. It crashes over me, and I am swimming on my back, long past drowning now, in a clear, deep flood. Ships sail past me. Fish and sea plants surround me with the most luminous colors. I am happy I can drift like this to the ends of the earth" (*Sprengstoff*, 146ff.)

Happiness in dreams. (A passage like the one above could appear in a fascist novel only as a recounted dream "very dry, just the sequence of the dream.") The inventory also includes dreams about a "slutty young girl," a "witch," a unicorn, mountains of lava, explosions.

Streams

All That Flows

1. Deleuze and Guattari, *Anti-Oedipus*, 67.
2. Wilhelm Reich, *Die Funktion des Orgasmus*, 24ff.
3. Jean Starobinski, "Über die Geschichte der imaginären Ströme," *Literatur und Psychoanalyse*, 24.
4. Ibid., 27ff.
5. Ibid., 30ff.
6. Ibid., 32.
7. Ibid., 33.
8. Freud, *Studies on Hysteria*, SE, vol. II, 193-94.
9. This will have to suffice as an evocation of the long tradition of attempts to envision the internal functioning of human beings as something flowing, that is, as something mechanical. That tradition seems to be as old as European history itself. Consider that the four temperaments of the Greeks were thought of as fluid mixtures. And the fluids were external: "We enter the same streams and enter them not; they are us, and are not us" (Heraclitus, quoted in Jaspers, *Psychologie der Weltanschauungen*, 208). See Leonardo da Vinci's idea that "the sea of blood around the heart is the ocean" (Bloch, *Das Prinzip Hoffnung*, 757). Somewhat different, and closer to the writers under discussion, is Oswald Spengler, to whom life seems "an ineffable mystery made up of cosmic currents" *Der Untergang des Abendlandes* (The Decline of the West) Munich, 1920, vol. 2, 403.

    See Freud, *The Neuro-Psychoses of Defence, SE*, vol. III, 60. "I refer to the concept that in mental functions something is to be distinguished—a quota of affect or sum of excitation—which possesses all the characteristics of a quantity (though we have no means of measuring it), which is capable of increase, diminution, displacement and discharge, and which is spread over the memory-traces of ideas somewhat as an electric charge is spread over the surface of a body."
10. Reich believed that *Civilization and Its Discontents* was written as a defense against

Reich's own "blossoming work and the danger it represented" (*Die Entdeckung des Orgons*, 157).

11. Freud, *Civilization and Its Discontents*, SE, vol. XXI, 64.

12. Ibid., 64-65 (all quotes). Michael Balint also failed, later on, to remove the idea of a "primitive" process of "regression" from his term "freundliche Weiten" (friendly expanses), which was intended to generate the type he called the "philobate," in "memory" of earlier conditions in the unstructured ocean of prenatal existence. For a critique of the idea of "regression," see, in volume 2 of the present work, the section entitled "All Kinds of Things Having to Do with the Egos of the Not-Completely-Born."

13. Freud, *Civilization and Its Discontents*, 73 (all quotes).

14. *Reich Speaks of Freud*, ed. Mary Higgins and Chester M. Raphael (New York: Noonday Press, 1968). An interview held from October 18 to 20, 1952. At Reich's request (and contrary to the usual practice of the Sigmund Freud Archive, which had initiated the interview), it was published in the United States in 1954 (with unauthorized editions in West Germany, 1969 and 1976).

15. Ibid., 61.

16. This is what happens in *Ödipuskomplex und seine politischen Folgen* (Berlin, 1975). On the cover of this anonymous work, there is an emblem with the words, "Marx, Freud, Reich." The group that distributed the work in Freiburg called itself the Marxian-Reichian Initiative. They reserved special venom for *The Discovery of the Orgone*, which is very much worth reading because it contains a kind of biography on the evolution of Reich's scientific ideas, as well as a running debate with Freud and the Psychoanalytic Society, encompassing various stages of the society's growth. Reich was apparently labeled "crazy" by disciples who could not tolerate the thought that their master's opinions could change.

17. Deleuze and Guattari, *Anti-Oedipus*, 8.

18. Marx, *Capital*, vol. 1 (New York: International Publishers, 1967), 487.

19. Not so Buster Keaton, whose foibles are remarkably suited to machines. Machines begin to work *for* him, especially in *The Navigator*, but also in *The General*. Deleuze and Guattari call Keaton "one of the greatest artists of the desiring-machine" (*Anti-Oedipus*, 514). The *Navigator* also shows Buster drifting aimlessly on the ocean, yet landing exactly where he wants to (with the help of a *machina ex mare*—a submarine).

20. Freud, *New Introductory Lectures, SE*, vol. XXII, 80.

21. Ibid. The metaphor gains importance by being introduced in connection with the final idea of the lecture: the dismemberment of the psychic personality.

22. Herman Melville, *Moby Dick, or the Whale*. Berkeley: University of California Press, 1981, 3.

23. Eduard Mörike, "Mein Fluss," *Gesammelte Werke*, 10.

24. A. Césaire, "Notizen von einer Heimkehr," in *Schwarzer Orpheus*, 92.

25. Walt Whitman, "One Hour to Madness and Joy," in *Leaves of Grass*. Philadelphia: Rees Welsh Co., 1882, 91-92.

26. W. Majakowski, "150,000,000," *Frühe Gedichte*, 94.

27. Henry Miller, *Tropic of Cancer*. (New York: Grove Press, 1961) 290.

28. Saint-John Perse, "Preislieder," *Ausgewählte Gedichte*, 41, 76-146.

29. Rafael Alberti, "Arion/Einfälle über das Meer," in *Museum der modernen Poesie*, edited by H. M. Enzensberger, 112.

30. Pablo Neruda, "Der grosse Ozean," *Gedichte*, 165-67.

31. Elias Canetti, *Masse und Macht* (Crowds and Power), 89: "The ocean is the model for a humanity that is content, that contains everything, and into which all life

empties." Stadler: "O, my desire is like dark water stored up by floodgates" ("In diesen Nächten," in *Dein Leib ist mein Gedicht*, edited by Arnold, 137). Benn: "The only music you want to hear on the radio is Volga,/Distant, alien, and coming from the steppes" ("Es gibt," *Destille*, 9). Benn: "Eingeengt," *Destille*, 39: "Hemmed in by feelings and thoughts,/A massive stream lies within you,/Its melody limitless,/Unmournful and light and self-propelled." Benn: "Melodien," *Destille*, 8: "Melodies, oh yes—the question-poser pales,/No longer the counting-/and cityman./The clouds dust his camp,/The oceans strike up below." Benn: "Orpheus Tod," *Statische Gedichte*, 14: "And now the lyre downriver—/The banks resound." Rafael Alberti, "Arion/Einfälle über das Meer" (see note 29):

> I opened the door. The sea
> Came to my bed so confidently
> That my dog saw it and didn't flick an ear.
> How happy I was, ocean. I went so far as to think
> I was you, and everyone already called me
> By your name. They cried, "Rafael!"
> And I could already
> Carry ships on my back.

Friederike Kempner, "Vermutlich ja," in *Der Schlesische Schwan*, edited by H. Mostar, 92: "Little silver-blue brook, little brook in the meadow./Are you making belts there? Do you empty anywhere?" Goethe, "Buch der Sprüche 5," *Gedichte in zwei Bänden*, vol. 2, 51: "The sea flows ever,/The land holds it never." Aimé Césaire, "An Afrika," in *Schwarzer Orpheus*, edited by Jahn, 101: "Your gesture is a howling wave caught in the hollow of a beloved cliff, as though it were trying to finish giving birth to an island of rebellion." Harold Telemaque, "Wurzeln," in *Schwarzer Orpheus*, 117ff.: "Hint of cool rivers,/Fresh and sweet./The man who followed crooked coastlines/Between two seasons,/and felt the islands in his own hands,/His weight/Is the weight of dreams/From loins of fatigue." Ovidio Martins, "Salziges Gedicht," in *Afrikanische Lyrik aus zwei Kontinenten*, 9: "I was born at the edge of the shore,/And I carry within me all the oceans of the world."

32. Deleuze and Guattari, *Anti-Oedipus*, 5-6; Miller, *Tropic of Cancer*, 261.
33. Starobinski, *Über imaginäre Ströme*, 24.
34. Deleuze and Guattari, *Anti-Oedipus*, 6.
35. Ibid., 67.
36. Miller, *Tropic of Cancer*, 250.
37. Canetti, *Masse und Macht*, 429.
38. Ibid., 439.
39. Robert Louis Stevenson, *Dr. Jekyll and Mr. Hyde* (New York: Bantam Books, 1981).
40. Mary Shelly, *Frankenstein, or the New Prometheus* (1817). The novel is based, among other things, on an awareness that bourgeois society certainly did not expect the "New Human Being."
41. Deleuze and Guattari, *Anti-Oedipus*, 34ff.
42. Jules Verne, *Meister Zacharias* (*Master Zacharias*), in *Künstliche Menschen*, edited by Völker, 264ff.
43. Ambrose Bierce, *Moxons Herr und Meister* (*Moxon's Master*), ibid., 250ff.
44. Deleuze and Guattari, *Anti-Oedipus*, 34.
45. Mahler, *Symboise und Individuation*, 67.
46. Neruda, "Der machtvolle Tod," *Gedichte*, 59.

47. Gottfried Benn, "Der Ptolomäer," *Leben ist Brückenschlagen* (Wiesbaden, 1962), 164.

48. Roussan Camille, "Unser Lied," in *Schwarzer Orpheus*, edited by Jahn, 79ff.

49. Fernando Pessao, "Aus der Meeresode," in *Museum der modernen Poesie*, edited by Enzensberger, 120. "The sea, the sea no longer roars, no longer whispers. . . . And look, the sea, the sea has also died" (Giuseppe Ungaretti, "Finale," in *Museum*, 111). "On the day I die, at that very hour, I want you, ocean, to die too" (Rafael Alberti, "Arion/Einfälle," 111). "Stream, why do you carry/water, cold and mysterious,/Water that has preserved the hard dawn of the rocks/in its inaccessible cathedral,/Down to the wounded feet of my people?/Turn around, turn back to your snow-filled hollow, bitter river./Turn, turn back to your basin of immeasurable frost./Drop your silver roots into your mysterious beginnings,/Or plummet downward, scatter into a different ocean, one without tears!" (Pablo Neruda, "Winterode an den Mapochofluss," *Geidichte*, 153). "Red lions without manes, lacerated by thirst, the stench of dried-up rivers in the evening" (Aimé Césaire, "Exvoto Für einen Schiffbruch," in *Schwarzer Orpheus*, 97). "In the cinema, in the synagogue, in the coffee house, wherever one sits, two kinds of music playing—one bitter, one sweet. One sits in the middle of a river called Nostalgia. A river filled with little souvenirs gathered from the wreckage of the world. Souvenirs of the homeless, of birds of refuge building again and again with sticks and twigs. Everywhere broken nests, egg shells, fledgelings with twisted necks and dead eyes staring into space. Nostalgic river dreams under tin copings, under rusty sheds, under capsized boats. A world of mutilated hopes, of strangled aspirations, of bullet-proof starvation. A world where even the warm breath of life has to be smuggled in, where gems big as pigeons' hearts are traded for a yard of space, an ounce of freedom. All is compounded into a familiar liver paste which is swallowed on a tasteless wafer. In one gulp there is swallowed down five thousand years of bitterness, five thousand years of ashes, five thousand years of broken wings, smashed egg-shells, strangled fledgelings. . . .

   In the deep sub-cellar of the human heart the dolorous twang of the iron harp rings out" (Miller, *Sexus* [New York: Grove Press, 1965]).

50. Simone de Beauvoir, *The Coming of Age* (New York: Putnam, 1972), tr. by Patrick O'Brien.

51. Hanns Eisler, "L'automne prussien," *Lieder und Kantaten* (Leipzig, 1957), 81.

52. Deleuze and Guattari, *Anti-Oedipus*, 116.

53. We will often be talking about things not only "changing," but *being* changed, *being* implemented by momentary rulers who wish to preserve their authority. A favorite related question is exactly *how* that occurs. We would not want to concoct some vague "conspiracy theory" that makes the rulers responsible for every evil, and we certainly cannot say that they always act intentionally. (Just between you and me, rulers are not smart enough for that, though an oppressor does not need to be especially bright or *conscious* of his role; he just needs to be very good at doing what is necessary for preserving power.) It seems to me that the whole question arises because people do not like to think about such unpleasant things; or perhaps the question reflects taste that is too refined to work with legal writings and administrative ordinances. Most of the processes in question have been described by Michel Foucault, "Power and Norm: Notes" in *Power, Truth, and Strategy*, M. Morris and P. Patton, eds. (Sydney: Feral Publications, 1979).

54. Ernest Bornemann, *Das Patriarchat* (Frankfurt, 1975). A sort of main theme of the work, printed on the back cover.

55. Mörike, *Elegien und Lieder*, 341.
56. See Geza Roheim, *Aphrodite oder die Frau mit einem Penis*, 228.
57. Mörike, *Elegien und Lieder*, 341.
58. Benn, "Liebe," *Statische Gedichte*, 64.
59. H. Heine, "Die Heimkehr," *Insel Heine*, vol. 1, 49.
60. Goethe, "The Fisherman" (Der Fischer), in *The Works of J. W. von Goethe*, edited by Nathan Haskell Dole (London: Francis A. Niccolls, 1902), vol. 9, 163.
61. Brecht, "Vom Schwimmen in Seen und Flüssen," *Gesammelte Werke*, vol. 8, 210.
62. Oskar Davico, "Die Liebe," in *Museum der modernen Poesie*, edited by Enzensberger, 189.
63. Jacques Romain, "Wenn das Tam-Tam pocht," in *Schwarzer Orpheus*, 74.
64. Mörike, "Mein Fluss," *Elegien und Lieder*, 7.
65. Heine, "Der Tannhäuser," *Insel Heine*, vol. 1, 102ff.
66. Josef Czechowicsz, "Fragment eines zerrissenen Gedichts," in *Museum der modernen Poesie*, 191.
67. Brecht, "Vor Jahren in meiner verflossenen Arche," *Gesammelte Werke*, vol. 8, 102.
68. Octavio Paz, "Das Liebespaar," in *Museum*, 190.
69. F. G. Lorca, "Die untreue Frau," in *Museum*, 184.
70. Nicolás Guillén, "Glutofenstein," *Gedichte*, 191.
71. A Césaire, "An Afrika," in *Schwarzer Orpheus*, 101.
72. Miller, *Tropic of Capricorn* (New York: Grove Press, 1961), 183.
73. Guillaume Apollinaire, "Das geheime Gedicht," in *Museum*, 186.
74. Miller, *Tropic of Capricorn*, 182-83.
75. Biermann, "Von mir und meiner Dicken in den Fichten," in *Marx- und Engelszungen*, 49.
76. Miller, "Mademoiselle Claude," in *The Wisdom of the Heart* (Norfolk, Conn.: New Directions, 1941), 145-46.
77. T. Moser, *Lehrjahre auf der Couch*, 99.
78. Ovidio Martins, "Salziges Gedicht," in *Afrikanische Lyrik aus zwei Kontinenten*, edited by Klemisch, 9.
79. P. Neruda, "Der Regen," *Gedichte*, 175, 177.
80. Leopold Sedar Senghor, "Kongo," in *Schwarzer Orpheus*, 10.
81. N. Guillén, "Madrigal," *Gedichte*, 187.
82. H. Telemaque, "Adina," in *Schwarzer Orpheus*, 118.
83. N. Guillén, "Das neue Weib," *Gedichte*, 183.
84. Mörike, "An Dionysos," *Elegien und Lieder*, 310.
85. G. Benn, "Bar," *Destille*, 21.
86. A. Breton, "Freie Liebe," in *Museum*, 183.
87. W. Biermann, "Die Elbe bei Dresden," on the CBS record *Liebeslieder*.
88. W. Majakowski, "Ballade vom Zuchthaus zu Reading," *Frühe Gedichte*, 126.

> "Of the wet of woods, of the lapping of waves,
> Of the mad pushes of waves upon the land, I them chanting,
> The overture lightly sounding, the strain anticipating,
> The welcome nearness, the sight of the perfect body,
> The swimmer swimming naked in the bath, or motionless on
>   his back lying and floating,
> The female form approaching, I pensive, love-flesh tremulous
>   aching,
> The divine list for myself or you or for any one making,

The face, the limbs, the index from head to foot, and what it
  arouses,
The mystic deliria, the madness amorous, the utter
  abandonment,
(Hark close and still what I now whisper to you,
I love you, O you entirely possess me,
O that you and I escape from the rest and go utterly off, free
  and lawless,
Two hawks in the air, two fishes swimming in the sea not
  more lawless than we)"

(W. Whitman, "From Pent-Up Aching Rivers," in "Children of Adam," in *Leaves of Grass*, p. 80.)

"Her thighs slipped away from me/Like frightened fish,/Half full of fire,/Half full of frost" (Gunnar Ekelöf, "Meeresverwandlung," in *Museum*, 124). "I see her breasts they are stars on waves/her breasts in which forever and ever the invisible blue milk cries" (Lorca, "Die ungetreue Frau," in *Museum*, 185). "After the ocean and the moon, there is a ceaseless life and movement/Of slips and stockings beneath the elegant coconut palms,/The sound of silk stockings being stroked,/And of female breasts shining like eyes" (Breton, "Ein Mann und eine Frau vollkommen weiss," in *Museum*, 186). "No, the queen must not recognize your face. It is/Sweeter/This way, darling, far from all images, the weight/Of your flowing hair in my hands; Remember/That Mangareva tree whose blossoms floated down/Onto your hair? These fingers are unlike those white petals. Look at them: the roots/Are like stone plant-stems with lizards/Scurrying over them. Don't be afraid. We will wait naked until the rain falls,/The same rain that comes down over Manu Tara" (Neruda, "Einsamer Heer," *Gedichte*, 17). "I also discovered that the sea/Smelled like the despair of a waiting woman" (Alberti, "Arion/Einfälle," in *Museum*, 112). There are many more instances of the connection between women and water, an almost infinite number from the various "folk" traditions: song, fairytales, myths, etc.

I would like to briefly point out the remarkable juxtapositioning of women and cities. That connection is probably rooted in the historical fact that the entire ancient world built its great cities on rivers and coastlines, because water transport was superior then. The freer forms of commerce among cities released a certain proportion of women from the most stringent patriarchal relationships and monitoring. As early as the gospel of John, we find Babylon described as "the whore sitting beside the waters." Elias describes the situation in early medieval Europe (*Über den Prozess der Zivilisation*, vol. 2, 65): "The larger, municipal settlements were situated throughout the broad expanses of land near water routes, like tiny nerve fibers. The cities collected the energy of surrounding areas as well as the products of their labor until, with the collapse of the centralized ruling apparatus, and partly because of the active struggle of rural elements against their municipal rulers, the agrarian sector freed itself once again from the hegemony of the cities." Thus the predominance of the cities was also the predominance of the water over the land. The core of the "backward" countryside's rebellion against the cities/water continued right through the fascist era and is still far from being extinguished.

89. Georg Büchner, *Leonce und Lena*, act 1, sc. 4, *Gesammelte Werke*, 187.
90. Büchner, *Dantons Tod*, act 1, sc. 5, *Gesammelte Werke*, 89ff.
91. Ibid., 90.
92. Ibid., 101.

Very Early History: The Woman from the Water

1. Elaine Morgan, *The Descent of Woman* (New York: Stein and Day, 1972), 4-5
2. Ibid., 3.
3. Ibid., 15.
4. Ibid., 19.
5. Ibid., 7ff.
6. Ibid., 21-28 (this and the contextual quotes immediately following).
7. Ibid., 21-22. Other parallels: the slowing down of metabolic processes during diving (as evidenced in seals); the placement of our nostrils, which are no longer exposed to the odor-carrying wind, but project outward to prevent water from penetrating during swimming; the fact that only humans can lower their eyebrows externally and raise them internally; the wrinkling of the brow that eyebrow movement causes, again found only in humans (how else could they protect themselves against the blinding sunlight on the water's surface?). And why are humans the only primates who cry? Not because humans are the only ones with feelings; but because, like any animal that frequently ingests salt water or nourishment containing salt water, humans have developed ducts that secrete almost pure saline solutions. Sea birds and marine amphibians "cry." "And if you want to find the only carnivorous mammals that cry, you have to go back to the ocean and get acquainted with the crying seals and crying sea otters." The fact that the angle formed when we extend our thumbs and forefingers is barely more than ninety degrees, whereas it easily exceeds 180 degrees in apes, is due to the vestiges of webs we have there. We are the only ones who have those remnants of skin and flesh. And on and on. (Ibid., 29, 37-45.)
8. Ibid., 12.
9. Ibid., 28-32.
10. Ibid., 26.
11. Ibid., 47.
12. Ibid., 46-50.
13. Ibid., 51.
14. Ibid., 55.
15. Ibid., 180-89. See Lionel Tiger, *Warum die Männer wirklich herrschen*, 203ff., 225.
16. Morgan, *Descent*, 250.
17. Sandor Ferenczi, "Versuch einer Genitaltheorie," vol. 2, *Schriften zur Psychoanalyse*.
18. Ibid., 363ff.
19. Ibid., 366.
20. Ibid., 365. It is hard to understand why Ferenczi also talks about a tendency to regress to the womb (363ff.) and thereby recodes his ideas in the obligatory familialism of psychoanalysis. Reich appropriately criticized this trait of Ferenczi's theory, which otherwise impressed Reich (*Die Funktion des Orgasmus*, 49n).
21. This description of incest appears in Deleuze and Guattari, *Anti-Oedipus*, 206.
22. Morgan, *Descent*, 85.
23. Ibid., 70.
24. Ibid., 60-71 (in the discussion of the gesture of humiliation).
25. Ibid., 105ff. Morgan also traces the human capacity for language back to our twelve-million-year interlude in the water. For obvious reasons, the system of communicating by *scents*, which evolved on land and was adequate in that setting, and the social system of respecting the space immediately around another animal became useless in the water. It is not so easy to leave olfactory markings in the softly rolling surf or on a beach that is constantly being pummeled. Living in water demanded switching to acoustical signals; when the head is the only thing sticking

out of the water, even a system of body language is difficult to develop. Morgan leaves open the question of exactly when language arose. She suspects male hunters' need to cooperate in order to finish off larger marine animals may have been the starting point. That seems less plausible to me than her other ideas. Is it not more likely that an advance of that magnitude would have occurred in connection with some problem more serious than that of finding food, which, as she herself stresses, was plentiful near the ocean? Is it not far more likely that the male emitted the first sounds in connection with the previously discussed problem of frontal sexual intercourse? The need to explain to the female that this novel approach would not *kill* her must have been immense in itself, and crucially important for the preservation of the species. Anyway, I am a lot happier with the idea that the first human sounds occurred during a male's plea for love than with the version about cooperation during the hunt. (We may have sorely neglected the fact that the serpent of the Biblical creation myth *speaks*.)

The process just described brought about another crucial problem in the female. Elaine Morgan thinks that the female may have lost her ability to have an orgasm temporarily, or perhaps for an extended time; more precisely, the male may have lost the ability to produce an orgasm in the female. Comparing humans with many other animals, Morgan confirmed that female orgasm is vaginal, produced along the vaginal wall *facing the stomach* by brief rubbing and pressure from the penis. Morgan completely agrees with Masters and Johnson's contention that the mucous membrane of this vaginal region contains no nerve endings at all, and is therefore insensitive; but she also believes that the mucous membrane has nothing to do with the capacity for orgasm. That capacity is located in the musculature along the ventral side of the vaginal passage. Orgasms are engendered there through rapid rubbing movements, like those used to scratch an itch, rather than through the "soft stroking" Masters and Johnson employed when they discovered that the mucous membranes were insensitive.

In frontal sexual intercourse, however, the tip of the penis could only reach the dorsal side of the vaginal passage, where the woman had no sensation. That state of affairs has persisted, essentially unchanged, right through the present. Clitoral orgasm evolved as a substitute and is probably still caught up in that evolution. The characteristic posture of a woman lying under a man—thrusting her pelvis upward and slightly tilting it—becomes an attempt by the woman to expose the ventral side of her vaginal passage more fully to the movement of the tip of the penis. ("If you can't adjust the angle of the piston, I'll have to alter the angle of the cylinder.")

Woman: Territory of Desire

1. Such as H. A. and E. Frenzel, *Daten deutscher Dichtung: Chronologischer Abriss der deutschen Literaturgeschichte*, 5th ed. (Munich, 1969), vol. 1, 33. On the *Minnelieder* of Heinrich von Morungen.
2. The earliest extant legend of Mary (*Marienlegende*) in German, the "Driu liet von der maget," brings Mary closer to the noblewoman of courtly love.
3. Fuchs, "Galante Zeit," *Illustrierte Sittengeschichte der Neuzeit*, 136.
4. Deleuze and Guattari, *Anti-Oedipus*, 273. They refer to Lévi-Strauss, who says of incest-guilt (*The Raw and the Cooked*, 48): "Yet the idea that he is 'guilty' seems to exist mainly in the mind of the father, who desires his son's death and schemes to bring it about."

Origins of the Anti-Female Armor

Early Bourgeois History: The Expansion and Contraction of Bodies and the World
1. "Central perspective engenders space that is mathematically correct, but psycho-physiologically unrealistic" (Arnold Hauser, *Sozialgeschichte der Kunst und Literatur*, 357. Cited by Lippe, vol. 2, 224). From a terminological standpoint, Hauser's formulation is indefensible; it presupposes something along the lines of an actual, inherent "psycho-physiological" reality and ignores the fact that this reality is also subject to change. In the end, perspectivistic space is absolutely real for a certain "psycho-physis," but it is artificial. And there's the rub.
2. Rudolf zur Lippe, *Naturbeherrschung am Menschen*, vol. 2, 226. Cf. Elias, *Der Prozess der Zivilisation*, (The Civilizing Process) vol. 1, 280ff.
3. Elias, *Der Prozess der Zivilisation*, vol. 2, 60.
4. Ibid., vol. 2, 58-67. The chapter entitled "Ausdehnung der Gesellschaft im Innern: Bildung neuer Organe und Instrumente."
5. Ibid., vol. 1, 262ff., 278.
6. Mary Douglas, *Purity and Danger* (New York: Praeger, 1966), 106, 109ff., 160. On the same theme, see also Michel Foucault, *Discipline and Punish: The Birth of the Prison* (New York: Pantheon, 1977), tr. by Alan Sheridan. Lippe, *Naturbeherrschung*, vol. 2, 215; Deleuze, *Nietzsche und die Philosophie* (Munich, 1976), 45ff.
7. Elias, *Prozess*, vol. 2, 60ff.
8. See Leo Kofler, *Zur Geschichte der bürgerlichen Gesellschaft*, 110, 123ff.
9. Elias talks about the evolution of a "professional bourgeoisie" (*Prozess*, 59). In similar fashion, the urban ruling stratum, the patriciate, separated itself from the guilds. According to Kofler, the guilds understood how to "exclude undesirable elements by means of very high entrance fees" (*Geschichte der bürgerlichen Gesellschaft*, 112).
10. Kofler, *Geschichte*, 217-29.
11. Nicely described in Jules Michelet's *Die Hexe* (Munich, 1974), a kind of historical-fantasy novel (1862) by a French history professor.
12. I, at least, have not been able to find much evidence of such resistance in historical records.

Expansion and Contraction, A.D. 1500: The Ocean Wide and the "God Within"
1. See the chapter "Zur Soziogenese des Staates," in Elias, *Prozess*, vol. 2. Especially the "Exkurs über einige Unterschiede im Entwicklungsgang Englands, Frankreichs und Deutschlands."
2. The confession of the prince determined the confession of his subjects. That regulation cemented the existence of various principalities for a long time. Each principality developed its own centralized authority. Consolidation into a single centralized empire could no longer be expected.
3. Elias, *Prozess*, vol. 1, 278.
4. See Kofler, *Zur Geschichte der bürgerlichen Gesellschaft*, 228ff.
5. E.g., *Die Geschichte des Pfarrers von Kalengerg* (1473); Heinrich Bebel, *Bücher der scherzhaftesten Fazetien* (1508, 1521); Johannes Pauli, *Schimpf und Ernst* (1522); *Das Rollwagenbüchlein* (1555), edited by Jörg Wickram; *Die Gartengesellschaft* (1557), edited and collated by Jakob Frey; Martinus Montanus, *Das andere Teil der Gartengesellschaft* (ca. 1560); and many others besides.
6. H. A. and E. Frenzel, *Daten deutscher Dichtung*, vol. 1, 58. The authors offer further proof of the "loss of feeling for form," citing Arthur Hübner, who found

"breeding replaced by obscenity," and De Boor, who regretted "the loss of moderation (*mâze*)." These men apparently wanted to show, in their own way, that "culture" was produced by renunciation of drives.

7. The same thing happened within literature. See Elias, "Zur Soziogenese des Minnesangs und der courtoisen Umgangsformen," *Prozess*, vol. 2, esp. 105ff.
8. Lippe, *Naturbeherrschung*, vol. 1, 109.
9. See the introduction to Boccaccio's *Decameron*.
10. Elias, *Prozess*, vol. 1, 276ff.
11. A. C. Crombie, *Von Augustinus bis Galilei: Die Emanzipation der Naturwissenschaft*.
12. See Kofler, "Die lutherische Reformation," *Geschichte der bürgerlichen Gesellschaft*, 262-84.
13. One hundred years after Luther, Angelus Silesius wrote (*Geistreiche Sinn- und Schlussreime*, 1665): "Hold on! Where are you running to? Heaven is in thee;/If you seek God elsewhere,/You'll seek Him eternally."
14. On this point and the discussion that follows, see Michel Foucault, *Wahnsinn und Gesellschaft*, 77ff.
15. Ibid., 84.
16. Ibid.
17. Ibid., 65.

Monogamization

1. Michel Foucault, *Discipline and Punish*.
2. Ibid., 83.
3. Ibid., 81, 84, 87, 92ff. "When Henry IV besieged Paris, over 30,000 of the city's 100,000 inhabitants were beggars."
4. Ibid., 88ff.
5. For instance, the volume on the Renaissance in Eduard Fuchs's *Sittengeschichte der Neuzeit*, 16. The discussion there centers on L. H. Morgan's investigations into the historical origins of the family.
6. Elias, *Prozess*, vol. 1, 260. In *Discipline and Punish*, Foucault sketches the development of this process after the eighteenth century (277): "One day we will be able to show how intrafamilial relationships, particularly the parent-children cell, became 'disciplined' by adopting external models (educational, military; then medical, psychiatric, psychological) starting in classical antiquity. Adopting those models made the family the principal site for determining normal and abnormal behavior in disciplinary matters."
7. Elias, *Prozess der Zivilisation*. See especially the summary at the end of volume 2, "Entwurf zu einer Theorie der Zivilisation," 312-41.
8. Ibid., 397-408 and vol. 1, 174ff.
9. Ibid., vol. 1, 251.
10. H. A. and E. Frenzel, *Daten deutscher Dichtung*, vol. 1, 89.

Centralization and the "White Lady": The Geometricizing of Bodies

1. Balthasar de Beaujoyeulx, *Le Balet comique de la Royne, faict aux nopces de Monsieur le Duc de Joyeuse & mademoyselle de Vaudemont, sa soeur* (Paris, 1582).
2. Lippe, "Circe," *Naturbeherrschung am Menschen*, vol. 2, 426-56.
3. Ibid., 433.
4. Ibid., 452ff.
5. Ibid., 444.
6. Ibid., 445.

7. Ibid., 441.
8. Ibid.
9. Ibid., 456.
10. Ibid., "Exkurs II: Geometrisierung der Wahrnehmung des Menschen," vol. 2, 209ff.
11. Ibid., 441.

Solo with Accompaniment: Falcon and Medusa, or "Let There be Ego"

1. Mikhail Bakhtin, *Literatur und Karneval: Zur Romantheorie und Lachkultur* (Munich, 1969).
2. Michel Foucault, *Wahnsinn und Gesellschaft.*
3. Lippe, *Naturbeherrschung*, vol. 1, 104ff.
4. Ibid., 134.
5. Margaret Mahler, *On Human Symbiosis*, pp. 8ff.
6. Jacques Lacan, "The Mirror Stage as Formative of the Function of the I" in *Ecrits*, a selection (New York: Norton, 1977), tr. by Alan Sheridan.
7. René Zazzo, *Conduites et conscience* (Neuchâtel, 1962).
8. Franco Fornari, *Psychoanalyse des ersten Lebensjahres*, 182.
9. Lippe, *Naturbeherrschung*, vol. 2, 228.
10. Ibid., vol. 1, 167.
11. Ibid., vol. 1, 180.
12. Ibid., vol. 1, 168.
13. Ibid., vol. 1, 181ff.
14. Ibid., vol. 1, 192.
15. Part of the process of reterritorializing new attributes is making them functional for competition; the ego-ideal of the Renaissance man was to surpass every other man in the areas he felt most competent in. (Lippe, *Naturbeherrschung*, vol. 1, 153.)

Some of the Principal Features of the Reterritorialization: Through Women and Images of Women

1. See Kofler, the section on the Lutheran reformation, in *Geschichte der bürgerlichen Gesellschaft*, 262ff.
2. Studying historical documents on behavioral changes can easily lead to this viewpoint. Naturally, those documents were written by members of the strata closest to the rulers. The fact that the documents were also reactions to what was developing "below" is less evident.
3. Cecilia Rentmeister alludes to this point in her article "Berufsverbot für Musen," *Ästhetik und Kommunikation* 25 (September 1976). She misses much of the fate of the female body, however, when she describes it as "an empty mold of passive representation, which can be filled at will; an embodying body with no independent existence; a receptable for ideals, pure and simple." Most of all, Rentmeister stays within the history of images, never considering what happened to living bodies (a surprising omission, but one that has occurred in many recent publications by women).

The "One-and-Only" and Doubts about the Nature of Reality

1. Elias, *Die höfische Gesellschaft*, 364ff.
2. Ibid., 366. Elias simply believes that "art often provides a social enclave, a retreat for the politically vanquished."
3. Ibid., 365.
4. Ibid., 378ff.
5. Ibid., 369.

6. Ibid., 382ff.
7. Ibid., 365.
8. Ibid., 379.
9. Ibid., 378ff.
10. Ibid.
11. Ibid., 368.
12. Ibid., 382ff.
13. Ibid., 383.
14. Ibid., 363.
15. Ibid., 370ff.
16. See Elias, *Prozess*, vol. 2, 369ff. The section "Blick auf das Leben eines Ritters" (ibid., vol. 1, 283-301) provides a good insight into the lost "panoramic" view of things.
17. Elias, *Die höfische Gesellschaft*, 371.
18. Bateson et al., "Auf dem Weg zu einer Schizophrenie-Theorie," *Schizophrenie und Familie*, ("Toward a Theory of Schizophrenia" in *Steps to an Ecology of Mind*) 16ff.
19. Bateson et al. do not say whether they consider this limitation necessary. They do not dogmatize it in their work, at any rate, and the very first example they introduce (the Zen master and his disciple, 18ff.) opens up possibilities for a wider framework.
20. G. Vinnai, *Sozialpsychologie der Arbeiterklasse* (Reinbek, 1973); and Vinnai, "Identitätszerstörung im Erziehungsprozess," *Ästhetik und Kommunikation* 4 (1971). Vinnai confirmed the existence of double-bind situations in the socialization and working conditions of proletarian youth. He immediately found his critics, such as Rainer Paris, "Die Grenzen des Double-bind Konzepts," *Ästhetik und Kommunikation* 15/16 (1974). Paris's objections consist essentially in showing that the double binds introduced by Vinnai are not the same as those evinced by "pure" theory (a claim not made by Vinnai), and that they do not *necessarily* have a schizophrenic effect (family situations do not necessarily have that effect, either). Paris is evidently out to preserve a dogma other than the double bind. In the characteristic style of his argumentation, he proclaims (73) that the double bind makes history out to be "a history of illnesses!" Unfortunately, he never tells us why that might *not* be so. He ought at least to have considered the possibility, at any rate, instead of defending his own "world-view" against contrary conclusions with the help of overused exclamation points. See also G. Vinnai, "Sind die Befunde der psychiatrisehen Familienforschung generalisierbar?" *Ästhetik und Kommunikation* 15/16; Lyman C. Wynne, "Über Qual und schöpferische Leidenschaft im Banne des 'double-bind'," *Familiendynamik, interdisciplinäre Zeitschrift für Praxis und Forschung* 1 (February 1976), 24-35. Wynne also argues against interpreting the double-bind concept in an exclusively familial context.
21. Elias, *Die höfische Gesellschaft*, 380ff.
22. Ziesemer contends that the song is not by Simon Dach, who is credited with its authorship in songbooks. See Simon Dach, *Gedichte in vier Bänden*, edited by Walter Ziesemer (Halle, 1937), vol. 2. Ziesemer claims it is a traditional Low German marriage song, dating from 1636 ("Anke von Tharaw öss de my geföllt"), and that its nature was originally different from the version I have cited, especially the second half, which is full of crude sexual allusions and references to everyday married life. Herder "translated" the song as "Ännchen von Tharau" and included it in his folksongs, but used only the first ten strophes, which were originally couplets. Hence the Herder version was the one that became a popular "folksong."

Sexualization of the Bourgeois Woman
in the Seventeenth and Eighteenth Centuries

1. In the volume of E. Fuchs's *Sittengeschichte* entitled *Galante Zeit*; and in Hans Mayer, *Aussenseiter* (Frankfurt, 1975), 40, 72.
2. Elias, *Prozess*, vol. 1, 252.
3. It is this encoding that strikes many observers as evidence of new female freedom.
4. E. Fuchs, *Die Galante Zeit*, the supplemental volume of his *Sittengeschichte*. This citation and those immediately following are taken from the *Frauenzimmerlexikon*, excerpted in Fuchs's work, 22, 137.
5. Fuchs, *Galante Zeit*, 139.
6. Ibid., 129, 142.
7. Ibid., 145. On the normative physical proportions on which these comparisons are based, see ibid., 122-29 and the supplemental volume, 28-32 ("Breasts"); *Galante Zeit*, 129-31 (feet, calves, knees, thighs); ibid., 132ff. (behinds).
8. Ibid., 145.
9. Ibid., 301.
10. Ibid., 302. Women are called "minotaurs of lust" (30) and "Etnas of lasciviousness" (306). See also 137, 223, 308.
11. Fuchs's primary examples are the *Frauenzimmerlexikon* (1715); *Leibdiener der Schönheit* (1747); *Académie des Grâces* (1760); as well as *Das Frauenzimmer und dessen Schönheit* (1754), a wedding ceremony from Frankfurt. Of course, there were other types of instructional books, with bourgeois or revolutionary orientations. In Germany, they tended to be pietistic. See Theodor Gottlieb von Hippel, *Über die bürgerliche Verbesserung der Weiber* (1792); Sophie de la Roche, *Pomona für Teutschlands Töchter* (1781); and others. Emphasis is often placed on "daughters," while the sexual element is ignored.
12. Fuchs, *Galante Zeit*, 301.

13. Ibid., 141. Here the ideal of bourgeois female beauty has been assembled from the most beautiful parts of the most beautiful goddesses' bodies.
14. See Jules Michelet, *Die Hexe* (Paris, 1862), 149.
15. See Foucault, *Madness and Civilization* (New York: Vintage Books, 1973), tr. by Richard Howard.
16. Fuchs, *Galante Zeit*, 225ff.
17. Ibid., 226.
18. J. W. von Goethe, *Faust, Part 1*, trans. Philip Wayne (New York: Penguin Books, 1979), act 1, sc. 3, 42.
19. See Fuchs, *Galante Zeit*, 308ff.
20. Ibid., supplemental volume, 19.
21. Ibid., 20.
22. See ibid., 128. The opposite tendency also occurs (Rousseau and others), urging mothers to nurse their own children. Characteristically, this demand went along with campaign against feudal, absolutist life-styles; motivated primarily by political concerns, it did not proceed from the reality of "bourgeois women." Once again, women's bodies were made substitutes for something else.
23. Ibid., 234ff.
24. Frenzel, *Daten deutscher Dichtung*, vol. 1, 157.

The Reduction of Woman to the Vagina
and Her Enlargement into the Seas of Seas

1. Fuchs, *Galante Zeit*, 137ff., 223, 306ff.
2. Heinrich Anselm von Zigler und Klipphausen, *Die asiatische Banise oder das blutig-doch muthige Pegu*, cited in Fuchs, *Galante Zeit*, 139. First printing of the novel, 1689; the text of the 1707 edition was reprinted in 1965 by the Wissenschaftliche Buchgesellschaft Darmstadt. The cited passage is no isolated case; the woman-vagina-water constellation is repeated with endless variations. A further example: "Know ye meanwhile, and be certain, that at present my foster-daughter, who has already thwarted noble attempts to gain her favor, has nonetheless resolved of her own free will to drop the anchor of your devotion into the sea of her corresponding inclination. I assure you that the ship of your well-being shall henceforth be driven by winds of pure love and happiness" (35; see also 37, and, especially, 437-62). The same passage shows that it was the mother's official duty to secure union with the desired man through sexual promises. According to Frenzel (*Daten*, vol. 1, 149), the novel was a "great success," and its tenth edition (1766) was frequently imitated.
3. Fuchs, *Galante Zeit*, 144.
4. Ibid., 143.
5. Ibid., 134; see supplemental vol., 32ff.
6. Johann von Besser, "Ruhestatt der Liebe oder die Schooss der Geliebten," in *Liebeslyrik des deutschen Barock*, edited by Grützmacher, 104-10. Also reprinted in its entirety in Fuchs, *Galante Zeit* (supplemental vol.), 35-42.
7. Christian Friedrich Hunold, "Die Schooss" (1702), in Fuchs, *Galante Zeit* (supplemental vol.), 42; and in *Liebeslyrik des deutschen Barock*, 174.
8. Besser, "Ruhestatt der Liebe," in *Liebeslyrik*, 105; and in *Galante Zeit* (supplemental vol.), 36.
9. Anonymous, from the anthology *Deliciae Poeticae* (1728). Reprinted in Fuchs, *Galante Zeit* (supplemental vol.), 42; and in *Liebeslyrik*, 170. See Christian Hölmann, "Abbildungen der Schooss," in *Dein Leib ist mein Gedicht: Deutsche erotische Lyrik*, edited by Arnold, 35ff.
10. C. F. Hunold, "Die Schooss," in *Liebeslyrik*, 174; and in *Galante Zeit* (supplemental vol.), 43.

11. Gottlieb Sigmund Corvinus, "Der schlimme Traum," in *Liebeslyrik*, 154.
12. Fuchs, *Galante Zeit,* 139.
13. Ibid., 141.
14. See the attractive chapter titles in Hoffmann Hays, *Mythos Frau: Das gefährliche Geschlecht* (Düsseldorf, 1969).
15. Choderlos de Laclos, *Les Liaisons Dangereuses* (1782), cited in Fuchs, *Galante Zeit,* 226.

German Classicism: The Woman Machine and the "New Morality" as a Further Erosion of the Shores of Woman-Nature

1. See Elias, *Prozess*, vol. 1, 22, 35.
2. See "Die Weimarer Klassik und ihr Kreis" (especially the quotes from Schiller), in *Die französiche Revolution im Spiegel der deutschen Literatur*, edited by Claus Träger, 241ff.
3. Kofler, *Geschichte der bürgerlichen Gesellschaft*, 554.
4. On the social status and social origins of some of the "classical" writers, see Elias, *Prozess*, vol. 1, 21ff.
5. Goethe, *Faust, Part 2* (New York: Penguin Books, 1979), act 3, final scene, 210.
6. Ibid., act 4, sc. 1, 215.
7. Ibid.
8. Ibid., 221.
9. Ibid., act 5, sc. 5, 221.
10. Ibid., act 5, conclusion, 288.
11. The fact that these things had to be "dominated" is made clear—in appropriate imagery—in Schiller's *Räuber* as well. Franz Moor, speaking to his father about Karl Moor: "If you cease to be, he will be master of your possessions, king of his drives. The dam will be gone, and the stream of his desires will henceforth run more freely." As overt premonition of the nineteenth century's fear of drives. Schiller, *Sämtliche Werke*, edited by G. Fricke and H. G. Göpfert (Munich, 1965), vol. I, 498.
12. See Horst Kurnitzky, *Die Triebstruktur des Geldes*, especially the following passage (100): "Prohibited sexuality—that is, sexuality that has not been purchased with the sacrifice of one's own primary instinctual desires—emerges as the most serious threat to society, because it casts doubt on all of the productive relationships that are based on the dominance of nature." Kurnitzky traces the origins of money back to female sacrifice—an idea that accords well with the passage just cited. He demonstrates the subjugation of femaleness at an earlier stage of the European "cultural" process by tying that subjugation to crucial changes in the process of social reproduction in early Greek history.
13. Jean Paul, "Einfältige, aber gutgemeinte Biographie einer neuen angenehmen Frau von blossem Holze, die ich längst erfunden und geheiratet," in *Künstliche Menschen*, edited by Klaus Völker, 152.
14. Ibid., 167.
15. Ibid., 168.
16. *Vaucansons Beschreibung eines mechanischen Flötenspielers*, by Johann Nikolas Martius and Johann Christoph Wiegleb, opens with the following passage: "After Vaucanson presented his ideas on the alteration of tones in wind instruments, by means of mechanical arrangements and various movements of the parts, he success-fully *imitated* those mechanical movements in a mere machine, on the basis of the art of movements he had discovered." (My italics.) Cited in *Künstliche Menschen*, edited by Klaus Völker, 103ff. On machines in the eighteenth century, see Julien Offray de La Mettrie, "Der Mensch eine Maschine," ibid., 78ff., and the articles immediately

following it. Or consider what Walter Benjamin has to say on the subject (*Der eingetunkte Zauberstab*, 500ff.): "It is change, rather than fixed form, which offers poetry an inexhaustible supply of creatures from this source. The essence of the source is fantasy, which causes form to be transformed. This does not occur without deformation. Deforming action is the stuff of Jean Paul's writing."

17. Jean Paul, "Untertänigste Vorstellung unser, der sämtlichen Spieler und redenden Damen in Europa, entgegen und wider die Einführung der Kempelischen Spiel- und Sprachmaschinen," in *Künstliche Menschen*, ed. Klaus Völker, 137ff.

18. Jean Paul, "Einfältige, aber gutgemeinte Biographie," 167.

19. Ibid., 166.

20. Contemporary workers think the connection is commonplace and easy to describe. In an unpublished paper on his employment with Opel, Reimut Reiche tells of a group of workers who simulated lovemaking with imaginary women while waiting in a locker room for their shift to end. He was struck by that fact that the workers' coital postures corresponded precisely to the movements they were required to carry out while working at their machines. In a poem by erstwhile worker H. Lipp, the following lines occur: "My love disappeared on the assembly line. The press pulverized by beliefs and still punches the beat into that arid activity." (Lipp, "Er weidet mich," *Aufschrei aus dem Asphalt* [Berlin, n.d., circa 1919], 37)

21. Deleuze and Guattari, *Anti-Oedipus*, 38.

22. Ernst Block, *Erbschaft dieser Zeit*, 104ff.; Bloch, *Kursbuch* vol. 39, 1ff.

Into the Nineteenth Century: Crystalline Wave/ Concealed Woman—from Water to Blood

1. Heinrich Mann, *Ein Zeitalter wird besichtigt*, 18.

2. Ibid., 12-19. Mann sees Napoleon as the person who extended the French Revolution beyond France, as the most powerful enemy of traditional monarchies. According to that view, the German "wars of liberation" succeeded in expelling the liberator.

3. In *Liebe, Tod und Teufel: Die schwarze Romantik*, Mario Praz delivers up endless proofs of the manifold negativization of women in nineteenth-century literature. But like most such anthologies, his is lacking in thought. He confines himself to documenting the existence of the same specific phenomenon a thousand times: the Marquis de Sade is nailed down as the "inventor" and progenitor of evil, then condemned once again. Hoffman Hays follows a similar course in *Mythos Frau*, beginning, however, with the Greeks and "primitive peoples." For him the source of all distress is the evil manna women hold out to men. It is amazing what people come up with to avoid thinking; for instance, the notion that repression generally serves a purpose.

4. Lautréamont, *Maldoror* (New York: Schocken, 1984), tr. by Lykiard Alexis.

5. Mary Shelley, *Frankenstein, or the New Prometheus*, cited in Shelley and Förster, *Die Geschichte des Doktors Frankenstein*, 60.

6. Ibid., 61.

7. On the origins of this armor, see the section of this chapter entitled "The Body as Dirt"; and, in volume 2, the sections "Sexuality and Drilling," "Battles and Bodies," "The Ego of the Militant Man."

8. And when the connection between women and inundation was voiced *directly*, as occasionally happened, it was sealed within allusions: "Ready femininity, the lotus blossom of the asphalt, paraded there in long columns" (Jünger, *Kampf als inneres Erlebnis*, 33).

When Frank Braun, the male protagonist of Ewers's *Alraune*, hunts for women at night, he mutters the following verses to himself: "Johann von Nepomuk,/Savior from the perils of the flood,/Protect me from love!/Let others become love-crazed./Grant me peace on earth./Johann von Nepomuk./Protect me from love!" Elsewhere Johann von Nepomuk is invoked against the floods along the Rhine. (Ewers, *Alraune: Die Geschichte eines lebendigen Wesens, Phantastischer Roman* [Munich, 1911], 72.) "You know where the loveliest paradises on this earth are, don't you? At the feet of fire-spewing volcanos, where I can see the last torches of creation's wedding night flickering out. All excess and all beauty, the gardens of the world and its overflowing banks, are situated at the foot of undying danger" (from "Soireen," in Wilhelm Weigand's *Die rote Flut*, 1919). Access for everyone: "you know . . . don't you"; "wedding night"; "lava"; "overflowing banks"; "undying danger." Or consider this passage from Delmar (*Französiche Frauen*, 11): "The Loire reportedly carries 330 times more water than normal during floods. Its flood inadvertently causes terrible damage to the dams that have held the river in for a long time now." Abject fear prevents me from interpreting the meaning of that geographical insight within the framework of this chapter's purpose. We can only affirm that there are no limits to the potency of love in France.

Closing Remarks

1. Frieda Grafe, "Ein anderer Eindruck vom Begriff meines Körpers," *Filmkritik* 3 (1976), 123.
2. Friederike Pezold, *Manifest zur Befreiung des Körpers und der Frau* (1973); Pezold, "Fischgebrüll" (1974); and videos, drawings, and photos (some reprinted in *Filmkritik* 3, 1976).
3. Frieda Grafe, "Ein anderer Eindruck," 123.
4. Ibid.
5. This ought to be the topic of some dissertation.
6. For more on how "childhood" is manufactured by bourgeois society, in a way that makes us think of it as a special, "natural" time of life, see Philippe Ariès, *Geschichte der Kindheit* (Centuries of Childhood), (Munich, 1975); Shulamith Firestone, *The Dialectic of Sex: The Case for Feminist Revolution* (New York: Morrow, 1970).

Some Characteristics of an Artificial Relation: The Maintenance of Lack in Relations Between the Sexes

Preliminary Remarks

1. I agree with Paul Feyerabend (*Against Method* [New York: Schocken, 1978]) that anything goes. I also wonder what demonstrable knowledge of the connection between bodies and writing traditional literary science might claim in order to "preserve" the methods that have become dear to it.
2. Spoken by Magdelena Montezuma, in Werner Schroeter's film *Der Tod der Maria Malibran* (1971).

The Body of Woman as Object of the "New Morality"

1. See Kofler, *Geschichte der bürgerlichen Gesellschaft*, 216-29.
2. In *Das Patriarchat* (Frankfurt, 1975), Ernest Bornemann writes (384): "Christianity's tendencies toward male supremacy joined with those of the Roman patriarchy, reinforcing the latter's authoritarian aberrations." It is a mystery to me what the word "aberrations" is supposed to mean in that in that sentence, particularly because the

writer is out to expose the patriarchy, just as Marx exposed capital. Lippe found the same alliance in the rise of the bourgeois-absolute state in France (ca. 1600). He writes that "the modern elements of the bourgeois world, in union with the king, fought against Circe" (*Naturbeherrschung am Menschen*, vol. 2, 443. See also the earlier section of this chapter entitled "Centralization and the 'White Lady'").

3. This effect of the defeated parties' withdrawal into a "mimetic play-world" is ignored by Elias, who has a tendency to neglect the effects on the "lower classes" of the changes he finds among the "upper strata." This is perhaps the greatest weakness of Elias's research.

4. A fact that is constantly in the foregound of Buñuel's films.

5. See Rohrwasser, *Saubere Mädel, starke Genossen*; and, in a section of chapter 1 in the present work ("An Aside on Proletarian Reality"), Grünberg's Gisela Zenk and Mary, the proletarian girl.

6. "Adulation and demonization" were certainly not "divorced from empirical women," as Silvia Bovenschen claims. The link between the images and the actual women was always maintained, by using women, murdering them, or honoring them on festive occasions. Perhaps Bovenschen becomes blinded to that fact when she decides to turn real women into "empirical women." See Bovenschen, "Die aktuelle Hexe, die historische Hexe und der Hexenmythos: Die Hexe, Subjekt der Naturaneignung und Objekt der Naturbeherrschung," in Bovenschen et al., *Aus der Zeit der Verzweiflung* (Frankfurt, 1977), 295.

One Form of Female Sacrifice

1. Eldridge Cleaver, *Soul on Ice* (New York: McGraw-Hill, 1968).

The Incest Commandment

1. G. Kremer, "Marienverehrung und der Jungmann," *Katholisches Kirchenblatt* 18 (3 May 1931), cited in Reich, *Mass Psychology of Fascism*, 164-65.

2. Ibid., 166.

3. Ibid., 167.

4. Ibid.

5. See the earlier section "All That Flows."

6. After that date, large segments of youth managed to pry some of the power over sexual encoding away from their parents, with a big boost from rock and roll. That advance has proved to be relatively stable, even earning a special designation after the fact: "teen-age rebellion."

7. Franz Schauwecker, *Aufbruch der Nation*, 8.

8. On the difference between maternal and sororal incest, see Deleuze and Guattari, *Anti-Oedipus*, 258.

9. I use the term "strata-on-two-fronts" in a broader sense than Elias. He uses it to refer primarily to members of the upper stratum who have been defeated in a struggle for power (*Höfische Gesellschaft*, 378ff.). I believe the expanded definition is justified by the fact that similar battles for power also occurred among the lower ranks of the so-called middle strata, who were caught up in similar dilemmas; the same kinds of battles occurred between these middle strata and the proletariat, and between the proletariat and the farmers.

10. On this point, see also Luce Irigaray's wonderful essay, "Noli me tangere oder der Wert der Waren," *Waren, Körper, Sprache: Der verrückte Diskurs der Frauen*, 46-61.

The Ocean in Woman—Escape from the Double Bind—
Incest Prohibition/Incest Commandment

1. Kurt Tucholsky, "Zur soziologischen Psychologie der Löcher," vol. 9, *Gesammelte Werke* (Reinbek, 1975), 153.

Floods of Love in Workers' Poetry (Supplement)

1. Karl Bröger, "Erwachen," in *Deutsche Arbeiterdichtung 1910-1933*, edited by Günter Heintz, 316.
2. Oskar Maria Graf, "Brautsang," ibid., 317.
3. Christoph Wieprecht, untitled poem, ibid., 326.
4. Graf, "Geliebte," ibid., 317.
5. Heinrich Lersch, untitled poem, ibid., 322.
6. Ibid., 324.
7. Bröger, *Erwachen*, ibid., 316.
8. See Deleuze and Guattari, *Anti-Oedipus*, 36ff., 68-70, 163; Jacques Hochmann, *Thesen zu einer Gemeindepsychiatrie* (Frankfurt, 1973), 57ff., 279ff.
9. Höss, *Kommandant in Auschwitz*, 75-85, 101-21.
10. For example Selchow, *Hundert Tage aus meinem Leben*, 289ff.
11. Lucas, *Märzrevolution 1920*, vol. 2, 164.
12. Paul Hahn, *Der rote Hahn, eine Revolutionserscheinung*, 31; also mentioned in Max Barthel, *Der Putsch* (Berlin, 1927).
13. Printed in *Spartakus* (Essen), 26 March 1920. The article was entitled "Class Warfare" (*Klassenkampf*). The sea of humanity was also seen positively in Grünberg, *Brennende Ruhr* (Rudolfstadt, 1920), 160, 168, as well as in the union song "Brüder zur Sonne, zur Freiheit," whose second stanza includes the following line: "Watch the stream of millions/Springing endlessly out of darkness." Interesting in the same context is the wording of the excuse given to the army by those elements of the *Sturmabteilung* (SA) who were in favor of the "second revolution" in 1934: "The grey cliff has to sink into the brown floodwaters" (Charles Bloch, *Die SA*, 70).
14. From a speech delivered by Oskar Nickel on March 30, from the balcony of the Milheim city hall. Printed in the *Mühlheimer Zeitung*, 8 April 1920; cited in vol. 3 of Lucas, *Märzrevolution 1920* (manuscript).
15. Brecht, "Flüchtlingsgespräche," in vol. 14 of *Gesammelte Werke*, 1514.

Contamination of the Body's Peripheral Areas

Dirt

1. Christian Enzensberger, *Grösserer Versuch über den Schmutz*, 23ff.
2. H. Melville, "The Whiteness of the Whale," in *Moby Dick*.
3. Killinger, *Die SA in Wort und Bild*, 27ff.

The Mire

1. J. Bischoff, *Die letzte Front*, 120.
2. Zöberlein, *Befehl des Gewissens*, 671.
3. Alfred Rosenberg, in the foreword to Dietrich Eckart, *Das Vermächtnis*, 19.
4. Jünger, *Der Arbeiter*, 27.
5. Heinz, *Sprengstoff*, 35.
6. Goote, *Kamerad Berthold*, 109.
7. See Henning Duderstadt, *Der Schrei nach dem Recht: Die Tragödie von Mechterstadt*.
8. Karl Schaumlöffel, *Das Studentenkorps Marburg in Thüringen*, 13.

9. Salomon, *Die Geächteten*, 218. On mud and self-indulgence, see also Herzog, *Kameraden*, 342; Freska, *Kapitän Ehrhardt*, 141.

The Morass

1. Otto Paust, "Das Lied vom verlorenen Haufen," in F. Glombowski, *Organisation Heinz*, 6.
2. R. Mann, *Mit Ehrhardt durch Deutschland*, 133ff.
3. Wilhelm Reinhard, *1918-19: Die Wehen der Republik*, 13.
4. General Haas, *Nachlass Otto Haas 2. Denkschrift der Division Haas* (Lippstadt, 26 March 1920), folio 24. Original located in the Central State Archives (Stuttgart), Military Archives section; cited in vol. 3 (manuscript) of Lucas, *Märzrevolution 1920*.
5. Gengler, *Rudolf Berthold*, 93.
6. Ibid., 117.
7. Mann, *Mit Ehrhardt*, 133ff.
8. Ibid., 10.
9. Wilhelm Weigand, *Die rote Flut*, 499. For Krumbach (*Epp*, 76), democracy is a thing that is rotten inside.
10. Ekkehard, *Sturmgeschlecht*, 208.
11. Herzog, *Kameraden*, 230ff.
12. Salomon, *Die Geächteten*, 383 (from a letter he received in prison). More on swamps in Dwinger, *Auf halbem Wege*, 525; Schulz, *Ein Freikorps im Industriegebiet*, 24; Eggers, *Von der Freiheit des Kriegers*, 68; Stadtler, *Als Anti-Bolshewist 1918/19*, 139; Volck, *Rebellen um Ehre*, 92ff.; Freiwald, *Verratene Flotte*, 238.

Slime

1. Salomon, *Die Geächteten*, 384.
2. Heinz, *Die Nation greift an*, 105.
3. Walter Frank, *Franz Epp*, 142.
4. Bronnen, *Rossbach*, 153ff.
5. Franz Nord, "Der Krieg im Baltikum," JKR, 93.
6. Dwinger, *Auf halbem Wege*, 292.

Pulp

1. Herzog, *Mann im Sattel*, 406.
2. Jünger, *Feuer und Blut*, 64.
3. Salomon, *Die Geächteten*, 263.

"Behind"

1. Heinz, *Sprengstoff*, 14.
2. Heinz, *Die Nation greift an*, 23.
3. Berthold, *Tagebuch*, in Gengler, *Rudolf Berthold*, 108.
4. Goote, *Wir tragen das Leben*, 41.
5. Schauwecker, *Aufbruch der Nation*, 315.
6. Ibid. See also 352, 359. On shit and deserters, see also Kohlhaas, *Der Häuptling und die Republik*, 156; on shit and greed, see Eggers, *Vom mutigen Leben*, 34ff.

Shit

1. Goote, *Kamerad Berthold*, 244.
2. Heinz, *Sprengstoff*, 13.
3. Herzog, *Wieland der Schmied*, 344ff.

Through the Body

1. W. Freimüller, *Die Schreckenstage in Leipzig*, 4.
2. Heinz, *Sprengstoff*, 24.
3. Freksa, *Kapitän Ehrhardt*, 151. Manure also turns up as the stench of the soldiers' councils in Höfer, *Oberschlesien in der Aufstandszeit*, 13ff.
4. Dwinger, *Auf halbem Wege*, 525.
5. H. Schauwecker, "Freikorps von Epp: Erinnerungen eines Freikorps-Studenten," HoDA, 161.
6. Freimüller, *Schreckenstage*, 26.
7. Lanz von Liebenfels, "Rassenmystik," *Ostara* 78; cited in Manfred Nagl, *Science-fiction in Deutschland*, 176.
8. See Wilhelm Daim, *Der Mann, der Hitler die Ideen gab* (Munich, 1958).
9. Heinz, *Die Nation greift an*, 31.

Rain

1. Ihno Meyer, *Das Jägerbataillon der Eisernen Division*, 52.
2. Freska, *Kapitän Ehrhardt*, 346.
3. Zöberlein, *Befehl des Gewissens*, 3.
4. Heinz, *Sprengstoff*, 130.
5. Jünger, *Kampf als inneres Erlebnis*, 63.
6. Bronnen, *Rossbach*, 36. The common curse "Himmel, Arsch und Wolkenbruch" (Heaven, ass, and cloudburst) may spring from this context. See Schauwecker, *Aufbruch der Nation*, 191.

Defense against the Morass, Slime, Pulp

1. Quotes documented earlier will not be documented again in this section.

Summary: Republic, Revolution, War

1. Freud, *Three Essays on the Theory of Sexuality, SE*, vol. VII, 196ff. Freud, *On the Sexual Theories of Children, SE*, vol. IX, 219-20, and many other places in Freud's works.
2. In *Pornography and Obscenity*, D. H. Lawrence confirms the close relationship between sex and the elimination of excrement, adding that the two functions tend to merge in debilitated people.
3. See also Delmar, *Französische Frauen*, 18. Here he portrays the "floods of the great Germanic migrations" disappearing within the wombs of French women.
4. Hellmut and Alengo, "Der erotische Vierzeiler höher gebildeter deutscher Städter," in *Antropophyteia IV*, edited by Salomon Krauss, 210ff.
5. Ibid., stanzas 21, 47, 97, 164, 231. See the song about Bonifatius Kiesewetter cited in H. Luedecke's article "Das deutsche Herrentischlied," also in *Antropophyteia IV*, 177ff.; and elsewhere in the same work (283), Luedecke's travesty of Heine's poem "Am Meer" ("By the Sea").
6. Hellmut and Alengo, "Wirtin," stanza 284. More of the same in stanza 90. See Janine Chasseguet-Smirgel, "Die weiblichen Schuldgefühle," in *Psychoanalyse der weiblichen Sexualität*, edited by Chasseguet-Smirgel. A case study of a male patient suffering from premature ejaculation. At the age of twenty-two, the subject "had been satisfied, on three separate occasions, with touching from the outside, because he 'knew nothing' about the existence of the vagina. Though this man was otherwise intelligent, mentally alert, and animated, his fantasies and dream representations made it possible to understand his 'ignorance.' He believed that the contents of the female organ were fecal and threatening (caves full of garbage and rubble; a cow's

cloaca appearing as pancakes that were 'hard as granite'; corpses in his house; auto wrecks sitting diagonally on streets; etc.). Penetration therefore seemed dangerous. To prevent it, he had to stuff the vaginal orifice with glass splinters, fill it with cement, or use it as a chamber pot and fill it to the brim."

7. Hellmut and Alengo, *Der erotische Vierzeiler*, stanza 149.
8. Ibid., stanza 19.
9. Ottwald, *Ruhe und Ordnung*, 80ff.
10. From Wilhelm Busch's version of "The Golden ABC," known throughout Germany. Cited in H. Luedecke, "Das deutsche Herrentischlied," in *Antropophyteia IV*, ed. Krauss, 173.

The Body as Dirt

1. That is what psychoanalysts believe. "Psychoanalytic theory subsumes displacement within the economical hypothesis of a cathecting energy (*Besetzungsenergie*) capable of freeing itself from representations and gliding along the pathways of association" (Laplanche and Pontalis, *The Language of Psychoanalysis*). "Displacement" is a defense mechanism that substitutes a different word for the (discarded) desired object, condition, or process, while preserving the full affective force associated with these things.
2. Wolf Biermann, "Kleine Ermutigung," *Mit Marx- und Engelszungen*, 59.
3. Mahler, *On Human Symbiosis*, 8.
4. Ibid., 33.
5. Ibid., 8.
6. Ibid., 8.
7. Ibid., 36ff., 43ff., 70ff., 104ff. From the standpoint of Melanie Klein's theory of introjected partial objects, the prohibition (restriction of pleasurable overflowing) prevents the introjected, evil maternal breast, the focus of denial, from flowing away (Klein, *The Emotional Life of the Infant and Psycho-Analytic Play Technique*). The breast will develop into a large, evil, internal mother, the kind whose permanent state of decay Giorgio Manganelli described in *Niederfahrt* (Berlin, 1967), 52ff.
8. Here, typical of many others, is a little tale from Lieutenant Ehrhardt's childhood: "My mother had gotten me a beautiful velvet suit with a white pointed collar. I put it on one Sunday for the first time. My mother warned me not to get this holiday suit dirty. I promised not to. Then I marched proudly over to the neighbor's house to show him. The farmyard was sunny and silent. I spotted a barrel with a big fat plug, next to a rack-wagon in the middle of the yard. The barrel was full. I started playing around with the plug, and next thing I knew, the heavy wooden container banged so hard against my chest that I fell down. Out of the barrel poured a stream of liquid manure, thick as an arm. It all happened so fast, and frightened me so much, that I just lay there in spite of the powerful stream of filth. I finally pulled myself together and ran as fast as I could to my house and my mother. I dragged a long, wide trail of filth behind me, right into the Sunday parlor. When my mother saw that, she just slapped me once, as usual. She always stopped right there—but that one slap was enough. That might have been the end of it, except that the smell of the liquid manure stayed in my velvet suit after it was washed. My father would not settle for throwing the suit away. He said, 'He has to be punished. As long as there's one good threat in that suit, he's going to wear it.' The suit smelled like liquid manure for a long, long time. People wrinkled up their noses wherever I went. I found the whole thing disgusting. But as far as I was concerned, the suit never smelled unless the neighbor was joking about it. For two years, he continued to call out

behind me whenever he was with his friends: 'Hey, boy, how's it smelling?' That spoiled many a day of my childhood.'' (Freska, *Kapitän Ehrhardt*, 8ff.)

9. The "stream of blood" is considered in volume 2.

10. Anna Freud, "Identification with the Aggressor," in *The Ego and the Mechanisms of Defense* (New York: International Universities Press, 1967). In seeing this process as a defense mechanism, Anna Freud links it too closely with the psychic construct of the "ego." There is no evidence that the egos of our militant men evolved according to the topology of Sigmund Freud's second theory on the psychic apparatus, which his daughter uses as her basis. According to Sigmund Freud's theory, the process Ferenczi has in mind would not be an instance of "identification." Melanie Klein emphasized the same point: "Ferenczi holds that identification, the forerunner of symbolism, arises out of the baby's endeavor to rediscover in every object his own organs and their functioning." (M. Klein, "The Importance of Symbol-Formation in the Development of the Ego," in *Love, Guilt, and Reparation and Other Works*. Vol. I of the *Writings of M. Klein* (London: Hogarth Press, 1975), 220.

11. S. Ferenczi, "Sprachverwirrung zwischen den Erwachsenen und dem Kind," *Schriften*, vol. 2, 303-13.

12. Ibid., 309.

13. Wilhelm Reich has given us a good description of the way in which sexual feelings are transformed into religious ones. (*Massenpsychologie des Faschismus*, 158-61, 189.)

14. According to Jünger (*Kampf als inneres Erlebnis*, 92), cowards suffer from "pacifistic deterioration of the backbone." And in the view of Engelhardt (*Ritt nach Riga*, 9), the "Jewish-democratic press" was carrying out a "systematic campaign to soften the bones of the German people."

15. Freud, chapter 9 ("The Internal World") of *An Outline of Psychoanalysis, SE*, vol. XXIII, 205ff.

16. Menstruation will play a larger role in a later, extensive discussion of the dilemma of "rebirth." In contrast with initiation, where a body (or part of a body) is collectively cathected—assembled, in fact—during menstruation the vagina—or, rather, the whole woman—is not collectively cathected; that is, she is collectively repressed. Once a woman has been reduced to a bleeding vagina, she is excluded from social production. (See Deleuze and Guattari, *Anti-Oedipus*, 181.) An example of historical research on this topic: Hjalmar J. Nordin, "Die eheliche Ethik der Juden zur Zeit Jesu," in *Antropophyteia IV*, ed. Krauss, 45-50. On menstruation and prohibited sexuality, see Groddeck, *Das Buch vom Es* (Leipzig, 1923), 104-10.

17. On the way in which contact with other bodies inscribes memory traces into a human body (especially the role of hands in attempts to train and educate, and every other type of contact as well), see Serge Leclaire, *Der psychoanalytische Prozess*.

18. Using the hypothesis that masturbation is harmful as an example, Thomas Szasz has produced an excellent description of a consequent "basic tactic of medical and psychiatric imperialism" (*Die Fabrikation des Wahnsinns*, 285).

19. And the hazy vision of many women as well. See the chapter on guilt feelings in women, in Janine Chasse-Smirgel, *Psychoanalyse der Weiblichkeit*.

20. I think this is a better explanation for the resistance of many women to vaginal intercourse than the empirically unsound view that women do not feel anything there.

21. Freud, *New Introductory Lectures on Psychoanalysis, SE*, vol. XXII, 80. See the earier section of this chapter entitled "All That Flows," and footnote 21 within that section.

22. Otto Fenichel, *Psychoanalytische Neurosentheorie* (Olten, 1974), 157ff., 190.

23. See Frantz Fanon, *The Wretched of the Earth*. It is still the best explication of the ways in which colonialism has mutilated the colonized (especially in Africa).

24. This is true of M. Schneider's *Neurose und Klassenkampf* (Reinbek, 1973). Schneider's efforts are a good reflection of the photo montage on the cover of his book: a head that is half Marx, half Freud. It is even true of Peter Brückner's chapter "Marx, Freud," in vol. 2 of *Marxismus, Psychoanalyse, Sexpol* (Frankfurt, 1972), 360-95; and of all anthologies with titles like "Marxism" and "Psychoanalysis"; and, finally, of Reich's attempt to "join together" psychoanalysis and historically dialectical materialism. There is nothing to "join together" there, except for the fragments of a theoretical approach that is driven by the urge to construct philosophical totalities. The fragments, incidentally, work better by themselves than as components of forced systems.

25. I cannot think of any exceptions.

26. Mahler, *On Human Symbiosis*, 70.

27. C. Enzensberger, *Grösserer Versuch über den Schmutz*, 88.

28. From the first moment they were used in industrial mass production, machines began turning people, especially children, into pieces of scrap that were afterward good for criminal activity at best. See Marx, *Capital*, vol. 1.

29. C. Enzensberger, *Grösserer Versuch*, 90.

30. After seeing Degas's watercolors of proletarian women bathing, Joris Huysmans praised the fact that they "revealed the repulsive quality of those damp bodies, something no bath could clean off." Anti-water. Cited in Hays, *Mythos Frau* (Düsseldorf, 1969), 287.

31. R. Herzog, *Kameraden*, 246ff.

32. In his memoirs (*Mann im Sattel*, 387), Rudolf Herzog claims that Ludendorff sent him a picture with the following inscription: "To the poet of German vigor, with gratitude, Ludendorff. 27 October 1924."

33. E. Jünger, *Der Kampf als inneres Erlebnis*, 66.

34. For example, in Killinger, *Kampf um Oberschlesien*, 71, 91 (example of a water battle); other examples in Goote, *Kamerad Berthold*, 169ff., Goote, *Wir fahren den Tod*, 210ff.; Bochow, *Sie wurden Männer*, 33, 36; Buschbecker, *Wie unser Gesetz es befahl*, 57; Ettighoffer, *Wo bist du—Kamerad?*, 357ff.; Bochow, *Soldaten ohne Befehl*, 90ff.; Rossbach, *Mein Weg*, 29.

35. Selchow, *Hundert Tage*, 16ff.

36. F. Fornari, *Psychoanalyse des ersten Lebensjahres*, 126. On the meaning of water for children's games, Fornari says: "Playing with water seems to provide particularly good assurance that objects are unbreakable. Water can be manipulated and divided with extreme ease; it never breaks, since the child's divisions of the fluid element cancel themselves out, with the water returning, sooner or later, to its original state of wholeness and unity. Aside from being used for drinking, water can be collected or spilled; you can let it run, flow away, and come again at any time." Fornari sees those qualities as giving the infant crucial assurance against the fear that its mother's breast may disintegrate, and especially against the child's fear that its own advances might succeed in destroying or consuming the breast.

37. Centralized municipal water supplies were reintroduced, for the first time since ancient times, toward the close of the nineteenth century. Hamburg was the first German city to be affected, following the fire of 1848. By 1892, forty-two large and moderately sized cities in the German Empire had been supplied with water (Freiburg in 1876, at about the same time as cities in the other industrialized countries. Also Chicago, 1864). In volume 20 of Meyer's *Grosses Konversationslexikon*, 6th ed. (Leipzig, 1908), we find the following passage: "Since the time when the great significance of a rich water supply for the health and maintenance of urban residents was first recognized, many cities have installed aqueducts and instituted policies

designed to increase water use in all strata of the populace" (my italics). In wealthier neighborhoods at the turn of the century, Meyer goes on to say, water use was "more than twenty times as great, per capita, than in poorer neighborhoods." See *Die städtische Wasserversorgung im Deutschen Reich*, 2 vols. (Munich, 1898 and 1902); *Vergangenheit, Gegenwart und Zukunft der Wasserversorgung* (Hamburg Wasserwerke GmbH, 1954); *2000 Jahre zentrale Trinkwasserversorgung in Deutschland* (Deutscher Verein von Gas- und Wasserfach*männern*, 1963). My italics in the final word—*male* water experts—of the publishing organization's name.

38. The system of canals that has evolved in the territories of industrial societies is probably closer to the "model" of their inhabitants' psychic apparatuses than is the Freudian ego-id-superego construct. In *Discipline and Punish*, Foucault describes the *superimposed* disciplinary system as a prison city, and our systems of knowledge as systems of imprisonment, monitoring, judgment. He does not bother with the substructure of that city.

39. In *Angstlust und Regression*, Michael Balint says (96) that the curative powers of mineral water reside in the belief of users, their regressive fantasies, that this water is pure, that is, free of dangerous objects. Rigorous scientific analysis has failed to find any prophylactic ingredients in mineral water and has pronounced it practically free of admixtures. Once again, Balint fails to get around the notion of "regression," which partly erodes his concept of friendly expanses (see note 12, in the section of the present work entitled "All That Flows"). He runs the risk of obscuring utopias, and everything else connected with "oceanic feelings," with a reality principle he considers superior. Even in Balint, Freudian ego-psychology occasionally shines through.

40. After the fiasco of World War I, Dwinger came up with an appropriate recipe for waging the next war: "And if we should go to war again, and not shoot every shirker immediately, and not hang every profiteer in the town square right away, we'll lose again!" (*Die letzten Reiter.*)

41. Fear of contamination fits in well with the notions of "segregation of drives" and "suddenly deneutralized instinctual energies," which accompany the loss of ego control and always release aggression (Mahler, *On Human Symbiosis*, 58). Melanie Klein points out that hallucinatory satisfaction and perception involve a "denial of psychic reality"; not merely a denial of a situation and an object, but of an *object-relationship*. Consequently, the part of the ego that radiates affects onto the object is also denied and voided. Two contingent processes occur during hallucinatory satisfaction: an omnipotent evocation of the ideal object and ideal situation, and an equally omnipotent destruction of the evil, persecutory object and painful situation. The basis for those processes is the splitting off of the object from the ego. ("Notes on Some Schizoid Mechanisms," in *Envy and Gratitude and Other Works*, 7.) In volume 2, I will examine the peculiar structure of the ego, as manifested in murderous militant men (especially in the section "The Ego of the Militant Man"). The notion of "splitting" will play a smaller part there than a specific type of ego-decay.

Dam and Flood: The Ritual of Parading in Mass

1. Cited in Klaus Vondung, *Magie und Manipulation: Ideologischer Kult und politische Religion des Nationalsozialismus* (Göttingen, 1971), 190. The book is useful as an anthology of primary sources; as the title suggests, its theoretical framework is inadequate.

2. Freud, *Moses and Monotheism, SE*, XXIII, 120.

3. Ibid., 121.
4. Deleuze and Guattari *Anti-Oedipus*, 293ff. (Also 104.)
5. W. Benjamin, "Pariser Brief," *Angelus Novus*, 503ff. (Quote, 510.)
6. Ibid., 510.
7. Benjamin, "The Work of Art in the Age of Mechanical Reproduction," in *Illuminations* (New York: Schocken, 1969).
8. Luce Irigaray, cited in F. Grafe, "Ein anderer Eindruck vom Begriff meines Körpers," *Filmkritik* (March 1976), 125. See Luce Irigaray, *Waren, Körper, Sprache: Der verrückte Diskurs der Frauen*, 28ff.
9. F. Grafe, "Ein anderer Eindruck vom Begriff meines Körpers," *Filmkritik* (March 1976), 120.
10. S. Kracauer, *Das Ornament der Masse. Essays*, 63.
11. Ibid.
12. Ibid., 50.
13. Ibid., 53. See Beaujoyeulx, in the earlier section of this chapter entitled "Centralization and the 'White Lady': The Geometricizing of Bodies."
14. Benjamin, "Pariser Brief," 510.
15. Thor Goote, *Die Fahne hoch*, 413. See Freiwald, *Der Weg der braunen Kämpfer*, 284, where the shouts of *Heil!* are described as a surge.

Bibliography

Bibliography

Primary sources and other works mentioned only once in context, or contributing relatively little to the progress of arguments, have generally been omitted here. The endnotes give a more complete picture of the literature I have used.

Abbreviations

The following abbreviations appear after the titles of works taken from the anthologies listed below [section 2]:

HoDA   Hotzel, Curt. *Deutscher Aufstad*
JKR   Jünger, Ernst. *Der Kampf um das Reich*
RDS   Roden, Hans. *Deutsche Soldaten*
SB   Salomon, Ernst. *Das Buch vom deutschen Freikorpskämpfer*

Novels, Biographies, Journals

Balla, Erich. *Landsknechte wurden wir: Abenteuer aus dem Baltikum*. Berlin, 1932.
Bochow, Martin, *Soldaten ohne Befehl*. Berlin, 1933.
———. *Sie wurden Männer*. Berlin, 1935.
Brandis, Cordt von. *Baltikumer: Schicksal eines Freikorps*. Berlin, 1939.
Bronnen, Arnolt. *O.S.* Berlin, 1929. Translated under the title *O.S.* London: Secker, 1930.
———. *Rossbach*. Berlin, 1930.
Buschbecker, Karl Mathias, *Wie unser Gesetz es befahl*. Berlin, 1936.
Dwinger, Edwin Erich. *Die letzten Reiter*. Jena, 1935.
———. *Auf halbem Wege*. Jena, 1939.
Eggers, Kurt. *Der Berg der Rebellen*. Leipzig, 1937.
Ekkehard, Friedrich. *Sturmgeschlecht: Zweimal 9. November*. Munich, 1941.
Erbt, Wilhelm. *Der Narr von Kreyingen: Der Roman der deutschen Revolution*. Berlin, 1924.
Ettighoffer, Paul Coelestin. *Revolver über der Stadt: Der Kampf um Mönchengladbach 1923*. Mönchen-Gladbach, 1936.

————. *Sturm 1918.* Gütersloh, 1941.

Ewers, Hanns Heinz. *Reiter in deutscher Nacht.* Stuttgart, 1932. Translated under the title *Riders of the Night.* New York: Day, 1932.

Freksa, Friedrich. *Der Wanderer ins Nichts.* Munich, 1920.

————. *Kapitän Ehrhardt: Abenteuer und Schicksal.* Berlin, 1924.

Gengler, Ludwig F. *Rudolf Berthold: Sieger in 44 Luftschlachten, erschlagen im Bruderkampf für Deutschlands Freiheit.* Berlin, 1934.

Gilbert, Hubert E. *Landsknechte.* Hannover, 1930.

Goebbels, Josef. *Michael: Ein deutsches Schicksal in Tagebuchblättern.* Munich, 1929. See also *The Goebbels Diaries.* London: Hamilton, 1948.

Goote, Thor [Johannes M. Berg]. *Wir fahren den Tod.* Berlin, 1930.

————. *Wir tragen das Leben: Der Nachkriegsroman.* Berlin, 1932.

————. *Die Fahne hoch.* Berlin, 1933.

————. *Kamerad Berthold der "unvergleichliche Franke": Bild eines deutschen Soldaten.* Hamburg, n.d. [copyright: Braunschweig, 1937].

Grünberg, Karl. *Brennende Ruhe.* 2d ed. Berlin, 1952.

Hagener, Hermann. *Lava.* Berlin, 1921.

Heinz, Friedrich Wilhelm [Heinz Oskar Hauenstein]. *Sprengstoff.* Berlin, 1930.

Herzog, Rudolf. *Kameraden.* Rev. ed. Berlin, 1944.

————. *Wieland der Schmied.* Stuttgart, 1924.

————. *Mann im Sattel.* Berlin, 1935.

Heydebreck, Peter von. *Wir Wehrwölfe: Erinnerungen eines Freikorpsführers.* Leipzig, 1931.

Hollenbach, H. H. *Opfergang.* Hamburg, 1932.

Höss, Rudolf. *Kommandant in Auschwitz.* Munich, 1963. (Höss's own title for his memoirs was *Meine Psyche: Werden, Leben und Erleben.*)

Jünger, Ernst. *Der Kampf als inneres Erlebnis.* Berlin, 1922.

————. *In Stahlgewittern.* Berlin, 1922. Translated under the title *The Storm of Steel.* London: Chatto, 1929.

————. *Feuer und Blut.* Berlin, 1929.

Killinger, Manfred von. *Der Klabautermann: Eine Lebensgeschichte.* Munich, 1936.

Kohlhaas, Wilhelm. *Der Häuptling und die Republik: Die Geschichte eines Irrtums.* Stuttgart, 1933.

Lettow-Vorbeck, Paul von. *Mein Leben.* Biberach a. d. Riss, 1957.

Mann, Rudolf. *Mit Ehrhardt durch Deutschland.* Berlin, 1921.

Niemöller, Martin. *Vom U-Boot zur Kanzel.* Berlin, 1934. Translated under the title *From U-Boat to Pulpit.* London: Hodge, 1936.

Ottwald, Ernst. *Ruhe und Ordnung: Roman aus dem Leben der nationalgesinnten Jugend.* Berlin, 1929.

Richter, Horst. *Freiwilliger Soltau: Mit der Eisernen Division im Baltikum.* Berlin, 1933.

Röhm, Ernst. *Die Geschichte eines Hochverräters.* 4th ed. Munich, 1934.

Rossbach, Gerhard. *Mein Weg durch die Zeit: Erinnerungen und Bekenntnisse.* Weilburg/Lahn, 1950.

Salomon, Ernst. *Die Geächteten.* Berlin, 1930. Translated under the title *The Outlaws.* New York: P. Smith, 1935.

————. *Die Kadetten.* Berlin, 1933.

Schauwecker, Franz. *Im Todesrachen: Die deutsche Seele im Weltkriege.* Halle, 1919.

————. *Der Feurige Weg.* Berlin, 1928. Translated under the title *The Fiery Way.* London: Dent, 1929.

————. *Aufbruch der Nation.* Berlin, 1929.

Schramm, Wilhelm Ritter von. *Die Roten Tage.* Munich, 1933.

Selchow, Bogislav von. *Hundert Tage aus meinem Leben*. Leipzig, 1936.
Solf, Major Ferdinand. *Deutschlands Auferstehung: 1934*. Naumburg a. d. Saale, 1921.
Stadtler, Eduard. *Als Antibolshewist 1918/19*. Düsseldorf, 1935.
Stenbock-Fermor, Alexander. *Freiwilliger Stenbock*. Stuttgart, 1929.
Stoffregen, Götz Otto von. *Vaterland—Ein Zeitroman*. Bensheim, 1921.
Volck, Herbert. *Rebellen und Ehre: Mein Kampf um die nationale Erhebung*. Gütersloh, 1932.
Weigand, Wilhelm. *Die rote Flut*. Munich, 1935.
Weller, Tüdel. *Peter Mönkemann: Ein hohes des Freikorpskämpfers an der Ruhr*. Berlin, 1936.
Zöberlein, Hans. *Der Befehl des Gewissens*. Munich, 1937.

2. Battle Descriptions, Eyewitness Reports, Journal Entries, Reflections, Poems, and Songs about the Era

Arnold, Alfred. *Das Detachement Tüllmann*. Oldenburg, 1920.
Balla, Erich, "Rudolf Berthold." In *Die Unvergessenen*, edited by Ernst Jünger. Berlin, 1928.
Berendt, Erich F. *Soldaten der Freiheit: Ein Parolebuch des Nationalsozialismus 1918/25*. Berlin, 1935.
Berk, Hans Schwarz van. "Rote Armee an der Ruhr." JKR (1929).
Best, Werner, "Der Krieg und das Recht." In *Krieg und Krieger*, edited by Ernst Jünger. Berlin, 1930.
Bischoff, Josef. *Die letzte Front*. Berlin, 1919.
Bodenreuth, Friedrich *Das Ende der Eisenen Schar*. Leipzig, 1940.
Bose, Ulrich von. "Vormarsch gegen Essen." SB (1938).
Brandt, Rolf. *Albert Leo Schlageter: Leben und Sterben eines deutschen Helden*. Hamburg, 1926.
Brauweiler, Heinz. "Der Anteil des Stahlhelm." HoDA (1934).
Buchrucker, Franz. *Der Aufruhr bei Cottbus im März 1920*. Cottbus, 1920.
Cochenhausen, Lieutenant-General von. "Deutsches Soldatentum im Weltkriege." RDS (1935).
Cranz, Carl. "Der Ruhreinbruch." JKR (1929).
———. "Flieger im Baltikum: Aus einem Kriegstagebuch des Kampfgeschwaders Dachsenberg." SB (1938).
Crasemann, Ferdinand. *Freikorps Maercker: Erlebnisse und Erfahrungen eines Freikorpsoffiziers seit der Revolution*. Hamburg, 1920.
Curator, Karsten. *Putsche, Staat und wir!* Karlsruhe, 1931.
Czech-Jochberg, Erich. *Im Osten Feuer*. Leipzig, 1931.
Delmar, Maximilian. *Französische Frauen: Erlebnisse und Beobachtungen, Reflexionen, Paradoxe*. Freiburg, 1925.
Eckart, Dietrich. *Ein Vermächtnis*. Edited by Alfred Rosenberg. 2d ed. Munich, 1935.
Eggers, Kurt. *Annaberg*. Berlin, 1933.
———. *Sturmsignale: Revolutionäre Sprechchöre*. Leipzig, 1934.
———. *Vom mutigen Leben und tapferen Sterben*. Oldenburg, 1935.
———. *Von der Freiheit des Krieges*. Berlin, 1940.
Ehlers, Otto August. "Die Bahrenfelder Freiwilligen." SB (1938).
Ehrhardt, Hermann. *Deutschlands Zukunft*. Munich, 1921.
Engelhardt, Freiherr Eugen von. *Der Ritt nach Riga: Aus den Kämpfen der baltischen Landeswehr gegen die Rote Armee 1918-1920*. Berlin, 1938.
Ettighoffer, *Paul C. Wo bist du—Kammerad?* Essen, 1938.

Ewers, Hanns-Heinz. *Deutsche Kriegslieder*. Munich, 1915.

Feisinger, H. "Tag der Befreiung." SB (1938).

Fischer, Hans. "Die Räteherrschaft in München." JKR (1929).

Fletcher, Alfred. "Die Eroberung Tuckums." SB (1938).

Förste, Frigatte-Captain. "Vom Freikorps zur Kriegsmarine," RDS (1935).

Frank, Walter. *Franz Ritter von Epp: Der Weg eines deutschen Soldaten*. Hamburg, 1934.

Franke, Helmut. *Staat im Staate: Aufzeichnungen eines Militaristen*. Magdeburg, 1924.

Freimüller, Wilhelm. *Die Schreckenstage in Leipzig*. Leipzig, 1920.

Freiwald, Ludwig. *Die verratene Flotte*. Munich, 1931. Translated under the title *The Last Days of the German Fleet*. London: Constable, 1932.

———. *Der Weg der braunen Kämpfer*. Munich, 1934.

Frey, Richard. "Die Versenkung der deutschen Kriegsflotte bei Scapa Flow." JKR (1929).

Glombowski, Friedrich. *Organisation Heinz*. Berlin, 1934. Translated under the title *Frontiers of Terror*. London: Hurst, 1935.

———. "Einsatz der Selbstschutz-Sturm-Abteilung Heinz in Gogolin." SB (1938).

———. "Spezialpolizei im Einsatz." SB.

———. "Der Weg ins Ruhrgebiet." SB.

Goes, Gustav. "Aus dem Tagebuch des letzten Kommandanten von Kowel." SB (1938).

Goltz, Gount Rüdiger von der. *Meine Sendung in Finnland und im Baltikum*. Leipzig, 1920.

———. "Baltikum." RDS (1935).

Grothe, G., and G. Kern. "Strassenkampf in München." SB (1938).

Gruppe Lifl-Heller. *Das Freikorps "Landsberg": Eine Erinnerung an den Befreiungskampf von München in den ersten Maitagen 1919*. Munich, 1919.

Günther, Albrecht Erich. "Die Intelligenz und der Krieg." In *Krieg und Krieger*, edited by Ernst Jünger. Berlin, 1930.

Günther, Fritz. "Einsegnung der Wandervogelhundertschaft in Rogau." SB (1938).

Günther, Gerhard. "Hamburg." JKR (1929).

———. "Die Bändigung des Krieges durch den Staat." In *Krieg und Krieger*, edited by Ernst Jünger. Berlin, 1930.

———. *Deutsches Kriegertum im Wandel der Geschichte*. Hamburg, 1934.

Hahn, Paul. *Der rote Hahn; eine Revolutionserscheinung: Erinnerungen aus der Revolution in Württemberg*. Stuttgart, 1922.

Hartmann, Georg Heinrich. "Erinnerungen aus den Kämpfen der Baltischen Landeswehr." JKR (1929).

———. "Vormarsch nach Livland." SB (1938).

Heinz, Friedrich W. *Die Nation greift an: Geschichte und Kritik des soldatischen Nationalismus*. Berlin, 1932.

———. "Der deutsche Vorstoss in das Baltikum." HoDA (1934).

———. "Die Freikorps retten Oberschlesien." HoDA.

———. "Politische Attentate in Deutschland." HoDA.

Henningsen, Fritz. "Erkundungsvorstoss nach Ridziwilischky." SB (1938).

Hielscher, Friedrich. "Die grosse Verwandlung." In *Krieg und Krieger*, edited by Ernst Jünger. Berlin, 1930.

———. "Der Bauer steht auf." HoDA (1934).

Hoefer, Karl. *Oberschlesien in der Aufstandzeit 1918-1921: Erinnerungen und Dokumente*. Berlin, 1938.

Hoeppener-Flatow, Wilhelm. *Stosstrupp Markmann greift an: Der Kampf eines Frontsoldaten*. Berlin, 1934.

Hoffman, C. "Letzter Sturm." SB (1938).

Holtz, Friedrich Karl. *Haut ihn! Ein ernstes, lustiges, wildes und besinnliches Buch*. Berlin, 1934.

Hotzel, Curt. "Cer antibürgerliche Affekt." HoDA.

———. "Student 1918." HoDA.

———, ed. *Deutscher Aufstand: Die Revolution des Nachkriegs*. Stuttgart, 1934.

Hueg, Major (ret.). *Die Ereignisse in Harburg vor fünf Jahren vom 13. März bis zum 15. März 1920*. Harburg, 1920.

Hülsen, Lieutenant-General von. "Freikorps im Osten." RDS (1935).

Iger, Arthur. *Spartakustage: Aus Berlins Bolshewistenzeit*. Berlin, 1919.

Jünger, Ernst. *Der Arbeiter, Herrschaft und Gestalt*. Hamburg, 1932.

———, ed. *Der Kampf um das Reich*. Essen, 1929.

———, ed. *Krieg und Krieger*. Berlin, 1930.

Jünger, Friedrich Georg. "Aufmarsch des Nationalismus." In *Aufmarsch des Nationalismus*, edited by Ernst Jünger. Berlin, 1926.

———. "Krieg und Krieger." In *Krieg und Krieger*, edited by Ernst Jünger. Berlin, 1930.

Kern, Fritz. *Das Kapp'sche Abenteuer: Eindrücke und Feststellungen*. Leipzig, 1920.

Kessel, Hans von. *Handgranaten und rote Fahnen: Ein Tatsachenbericht aus dem Kampf gegen das rote Berlin 1918-1920*. Berlin, 1933.

Killinger, Manfred von. *Ernstes und Heiteres aus dem Putschleben*. Berlin, 1928.

———. *Männer und Macht: Die SA in Wort und Bild*. Leipzig, 1933.

———. *Kampf um Oberschlesien: Bisher unveröffentlichte Aufzeichnungen des Führers der Abteilung v. Killinger, genannt "Sturmkompagnie Koppe."* Leipzig, 1934.

———. *Das waren Kerle!* Berlin, 1937.

Kloppe, Fritz. "Kameraden." JKR (1929).

Kohlhaas, Wilhelm. "Männer und Sicherheitskompanien 1918/19." SB (1938).

———. "Münchener Sturmtagebuch: Die Kämpfe des Württembergischen Freiwilligen-Regiments Seutter." SB.

Koll, Kilian. "Die Männer von Tirtschtiegel." SB (1938).

Krumbach, Jos. H., ed. *Franz Ritter von Epp: Ein Leben für Deutschland*. Munich, 1939.

Lautenbacher, First Lieutenant (ret.). "Widerstand im roten München." SB. (1938).

Lettow-Vorbeck, Paul von, ed. *Die Weltkriegsspionage*. N.p. 1931.

Liemann, Rolf. "Felsen in roter Flut." SB (1938).

———. "Schwerer Kampf um Königsberg." SB.

———. "Sudetendeutschlands Märzgefallene." SB.

Loewenfeld, Wilfried von. "Das Freikorps von Loewenfeld." RDS (1935).

Lüttwitz, Walter. *Im Kampf gegen die Novemberrevolution*. Berlin, 1934.

———. "Einmarsch der Garde-Kavallerie-Schützendivision in Berlin." RDS (1935).

Lützkendorf, Dr. W. "Aus Halles 'roter Zeit,' nach amtlichen Berichten zusammengestellt." SB (1938).

Maercker, Ludwig Rudolf Georg. *Vom Kaiserheer zur Reichswehr*. Leipzig, 1921.

Mahnken, Heinrich. "Freikorps im Westen 1918/20." HoDA (1934).

———. "Aufmarsch gegen die Rote Armee 1920." RDS (1935).

———. "Gegenstoss im Westen 1919." RDS.

———. "Kampf der Batterie Hasenclever, 15. März 1920." RDS.

———. "Der erste Hammerschlag? Die Aktion des Freikorps Lichtschlag nördlich Essen 1919." SB (1938).

Maltzan, Freiheer von. "Die Spandauer stürmen Bauske." SB (1938).

Megede, Hans zur. "Hakenkreuz am Stahlhelm." In *Volk ans Gewehr!* edited by Walter Gruber. Wiesbaden, 1934.

Melzer, Gustav. "Die Auswirkungen des Kapp-Putsches in Leipzig." JKR (1929).

Meyer, Ihno. *Das Jägerbataillon der Eisernen Division im Kampf gegen den Bolshewismus*. Leipzig, 1920.

Müller, Josef. *Freikorps Haas: Soldat und Vaterland vor 15 Jahren*. Illertissen, 1934.

Nord, Franz. "Der Krieg im Baltikum." JKR (1929).

Oertzen, Friedrich W. von. *Baltenland: Eine Geschichte des deutschen Sendung im Baltikum.* Munich, 1933.

———. *Kamerad, reich mir die Hände: Freikorps und Grenzschutz im Baltikum und in der Heimat.* Berlin, 1933.

Oertzen, Wilhelm von. *Die deutschen Freikorps 1918-1923.* Munich, 1936.

"Offizier 1918." HoDA (1934).

Osten, Edmund. "Der Kampf um Oberschlesien." JKR (1929).

Pabst, W. "Spartakus." HoDA (1934).

Pikarski, Hans Albert. "Freiwilligen-Regiment Pommern." SB (1938).

Pitrof, Daniel Ritter von. *Gegen Spartakus in München und im Allgäu: Erinnerungsblätter des Freikorps Schwaben.* Munich, 1937.

Plaas, Hartmut. "Das Kapp-Unternehmen." JKR (1929).

———. "Das Kapp-Unternehmen: Aus dem Tagebuch eines Sturmsoldaten." SB (1938).

———, ed. *Wir klagen an! Nationalisten in den Kerkern der Bourgeoisie.* Berlin, 1928.

Plehwe, Karl von. *Im Kampf gegen die Bolshewisten: Die Kämpfer des 2. Garde-Reserveregiments zum Schutz der Grenze Ostpreussens.* Berlin, 1926.

———. "Von der Westfront ins Baltikum: Der Weg der 1. Garde-Reserve-Division." SB (1938).

Reetz, Walter. "Der rote Vormarsch." JKR (1929).

Reinhard, Wilhelm. *Die Wehen der Republik.* Berlin, 1932.

———. "Belagerungszustand über Moabit." RDS (1935).

———. "Sturm auf das Leipziger Volkshaus 19. März 1920." RDS.

———. "Kampf um Berlin." SB (1938).

Roden, Hans. "Die 'Bahnenfelder' kommen!" RDS (1935).

———. "Einmarsch in Mitteldeutschland—Das Landesjägerkorps des Generals Maercker" (1919). RDS.

———. "Einmarsch in Mitteldeutschland" (1920). RDS.

———. "Einmarsch in Mitteldeutschland" (1921). RDS.

———. "Einmarsch in Mitteldeutschland" (1923). RDS.

———. "Hauptmann Berthold—ein Soldatenschicksal." RDS.

———, ed. *Deutsche Soldaten.* Leipzig, 1935.

Rodermund, Eduard. "Rote Armee an Rhein und Ruhr." HoDA (1934).

———. "Separatismus." HoDA.

Roegels, Lutz. *Aus dem roten Sumpf: Korruptionsbilder aus der Revolution.* Berlin, 1924.

Rossmann and Schmidthuysen. "Der blutige Montag in Duisburg." SB (1938).

Roth, Bert, ed. *Kampf: Lebensdokumente deutscher Jugend 1914-1934.* Leipzig, 1934.

Sager, Walter. "Vom Kampf der Essener Einwohnerwehr." SB (1938).

Salomon, Ernst. "Hexenkessel in Deutschland." JKR (1929).

———. "Sturm auf Riga." JKR.

———. "Die Versprengten." JKR. (Excerpt from *Die Geächteten*.)

———. "Der verlorene Haufe." In *Krieg und Krieger*, edited by Ernst Jünger. Berlin, 1930.

———. "Die Brigade Ehrhardt." RDS (1935).

———. *Nahe Geschichte.* Berlin, 1935.

———. "Der Berliner Märzaufstand 1919." SB (1938).

———. *Putsch und Verschwörung.* Frankfurt, 1938.

———, ed. *Das Buch vom deutschen Freikorpskämpfer.* Berlin, 1938.

Schaper, Cavalry Captain (ret.). "Freikorpsgeist—Annaberg." RDS (1935).

Schaumlöffel, Karl. *Das Studentenkorps Marburg in Thüringen: Ein Kriegstagebuch im Frieden.* Marburg, 1920.

Schauroth, Colonel (ret.) von. "Revolte in Libau." SB (1938).

Schauwecker, Franz. "Der Aufbruch der Nation aus dem Kriege." HoDA (1934).

Schauwecker, Heinz. "Freikorps Epp." HoDA (1934).

Schirach, Baldur von. *Pioniere des Dritten Reiches.* Essen, 1933.

Schleisner, Sepp. "Panzerug." SB (1938).

Schmidt-Pauli, Edgar von. *Die Männer um Hitler.* Berlin, 1932.

Schramm, Wilhelm von. "Schöpferische Kritik des Kriegers." In *Krieg und Krieger,* edited by Ernst Jünger. Berlin, 1930.

Schricker, Rudolf. *Blut—Erz—Kohle: Der Kampf um Oberschlesien.* Berlin, 1930.

———. *Rotmord über München.* Berlin, 1934.

Schulz, Adolf. *Ein Freikorps im Industriegebiet.* Mülheim, 1922.

Seitz, Georg. "Die Eiserne Schar Berthold in Hamburg." SB (1938).

Siegert, Max. *Aus Münchens schwerster Zeit.* Regensburg, 1928.

Spektator [B. Wolf]. *Die Schreckenstage im rheinisch-westfälischen Industriebezirk.* Hannover, 1920

Steinaecker, Freiherr Franz Josef von. *Mit der Eisernen Division im Baltenland.* Hamburg, 1920.

Stephan, Karl. *Der Todeskampf der Ostmark 1918/19: Die Geschichte eines Grenzschutzbataillons.* Schneidemühl, 1919.

Stoffregen, Götz Otto von. *Aufstand.* Berlin, 1931.

Strasser, Otto. "Der 9. November 1923: Erlebnisse eines Mitkämpfers." JKR (1929).

———. "Der Sinn des 9. November 1923." JKR.

Wagener, Wilhelm Heinrich. *Von der Heimat geächtet: Im Auftrag der Deutschen Legion bearbeitet.* Stuttgart, 1920.

Watter, Freiherr von. "Die Bedeutung der Freikorps." RDS (1935).

Wiemers-Borchelhof, Dr. Franz. "Freikorps-Arbeitsdienst-Siedlung: Schicksal eines Vorkämpfers der Freikorpssiedler." SB (1938).

Wittman, Hans. *Erinnerungen der Eisernen Schar Berthold.* Oberviechtach, 1926.

Wrangell, Baron Wilhelm von. *Geschichte des Baltenregiments.* Reval, 1928.

Zeschau, Major von. "Streiflichter aus den Kämpfen um Litauen." SB (1938).

Zimmermann, Adolf. *Vorfrühling 1920: Aus den Tagen der Kapp'schen Wirren.* Berlin, 1920.

Zobel, Johannes. *Zwischen Krieg und Frieden: Schüler als Freiwillige im Grenzschutz und Freikorps.* Berlin, 1934.

3. Other Literature and Theory

Abel, Theodore. *Why Hitler Came into Power: An Answer Based on the Original Life Stories of Six Hundred of His Followers.* New York: AMS Press, 1938.

Abraham, Karl. "Über Einschränkungen und Umwandlungen der Schaulust bei den Psychoneurotikern nebst Bemerkungen über analoge Erscheinungen in der Völkerpsychologie." In *Psychoanalytische Studien,* vol. 1. Frankfurt, 1969.

Adorno, Theodor W. *Minima Moralia: Reflexionenen aus dem beschädigten Leben.* Frankfurt, 1970. Translated under the title *Reflections from a Damaged Life.* London: New Left Books, 1974.

———. "Engagement." *Noten zur Literatur III.* Frankfurt, 1971.

———, and Max Horkheimer. *Dialektik der Aufklärung.* Lichtenstein, 1955. Translated under the title *Dialectic of Enlightenment.* New York: Herder and Herder, 1972.

———, et al. *Der autoritäre Charakter: Studien über Autorität und Vorurteil.* 2 vols. Amsterdam, 1968. Translated under the title *The Authoritarian Personality.* New York: Harper & Row, 1950.

Améry, Jean. *Jenseits von Schuld und Sühne: Bewältigungsversuche eines Überwältigten.* Munich, 1970.

Arendt, Henriette. *Menschen, die den Pfad verloren.* Stuttgart, 1907.

Ariès, Philippe. *L'enfant et la vie familiale sous l'Ancien Régime.* Paris: Plon, 1960. Translated into English under the title *Centuries of Childhood, Social History of Family Life.* New York: Vintage Books, 1962.

Arnold, Heinz Ludwig, ed. *Dein Leib ist mein Gedicht: Deutsche erotische Lyrik aus fünf Jahrhunderten.* Frankfurt, 1973.

Balint, Michael. *The Basic Fault: Therapeutic Aspects of Regression.* London: Tavistock Publications, 1968.

―――. *Thrills and Regressions.* London: Hogarth Press, 1959.

Bateson, Gregory. "Toward a Theory of Schizophrenia" in *Steps To an Ecology of Mind.* San Francisco: Chandler, 1972.

Baumgarth, Christa. *Geschichte des Futurismus.* Reinbek, 1966.

Bebel, August, *Die Frau und der Sozialismus (Die Frau in der Vergangenheit; Gegenwart und Zukunft).* Stuttgart, 1891. Translated under the title *Woman under Socialism.* New York: Labor News, 1904.

Benjamin, Walter. "Theorien des deutschen Fascismus." *Das Argument* 6, no. 30 (1964). Reprinted in the journal *Die Gesellschaft,* edited by Rudolf Hilferding. A discussion of the anthology *Krieg und Krieger,* edited by Ernst Jünger. Berlin, 1930.

―――. "Der Autor als Produzent" and "Kommentare zu Gedichten von Brecht." *Versuche über Brecht.* Frankfurt, 1966. Also in *Understanding Brecht.* London: New Left Books, 1973.

―――. "Ein Jakobiner von Heute" and "Der eingetunkte Zauberstab." *Angelus Novus: Gesammelte Schriften.* Frankfurt, 1966.

―――. "Das Kunstwerk im Zeitalter seiner technischen Reproduzierbarkeit." *Illuminationen.* Frankfurt, 1969.

Benn, Gottfried. *Statische Gedichte.* Zurich, 1948.

―――. *Destillationen.* Wiesbaden, 1953.

Besançon, Alain. "Vers une histoire psychanalytique," *Histoire et expérience du moi,* Flammarion, 1971.

Bierce, Ambrose. "Moxon's Master." In *The Complete Short Stories.* Garden City, NY: Doubleday, 1970.

Biermann, Wolf. *Mit Marx- und Engelszungen.* Berlin, 1968.

Bloch, Charles. *Die SA und die Krise des NS-Regimes 1934.* Frankfurt, n.d.

Bloch, Ernst. *Das Prinzip Hoffnung.* Frankfurt, 1959.

―――. *Erbschaft dieser Zeit.* Frankfurt, 1962.

Blüher, Hans. *Wandervogel: Geschichte einer Jugendbewegung.* Prien, 1922.

―――. *Führer und Volk in der Jugendbewegung.* Jena, 1924.

―――. *Die Rolle der Erotik in der männlichen Gesellschaft.* Stuttgart, 1962.

Boehm, Felix. "Beiträge zur Psychologie der Homosexualität." *Internationale Zeitschrift für Psychoanalyse* 8 (1922).

Brecht, Bertolt. *Gesammelte Werke.* Vol. 8, *Gedichte 1.* Frankfurt, 1967.

―――. "Die Horst-Wessel-Legende." *Gesammelte Werke.* Vol. 20, *Schriften zur Politik und Gesellschaft.* Frankfurt, 1967.

―――. *Tagebücher 1920-1922 / Autobiographische Aufzeichnungen 1920-1954.* Frankfurt, 1975.

Büchner, Georg. *Gesammelte Werke.* Vol. 1, *Dantons Tod.* Vienna, 1947. Translated under the title *Danton's Death.* London: Faber, 1939.

Canetti, Elias, *Masse und Macht.* Hamburg, 1960. Translated by Carol Stewart, under the title *Crowds and Power.* New York: Viking Press, 1962.

Chasseguet-Smirgel, ed. *Psychoanalyse der weiblichen Sexualität*. Frankfurt, 1974. Translated under the title *Female Sexuality*. London: Virago, 1981.

Crombie, A. C. *Von Augustinus bis Galilei: Die Emanzipation der Naturwissenschaft*. Cologne, 1964.

Dannecker, Martin, and Reimut Reiche. *Der gewöhnliche Homosexuelle*. Frankfurt, 1974.

Darstellungen aus den Nachkriegskämpfen deutscher Truppen und Freikorps. Edited and published by the Forschungsanstalt für Kriegs- und Heeresgeschichte, under the auspices of the Reichskriegsministerium. 7 vols. Berlin, 1936-39.

de Beavoir, Simone. *The Coming of Age*, tr. by Patrick O'Brien. New York: Putnam, 1972.

Deleuze, Gilles, and Félix Guattari. *Anti-Oedipus: Capitalism and Schizophrenia*. Translated from the French by Robert Hurley, Mark Seem, and Helen R. Lane. Minneapolis: University of Minnesota Press, 1983.

Demeter, Karl. *Das deutsche Heer und seine Offiziere*. Berlin, 1930. Translated under the title *The German Officer-corps in Society and State*. London: Weidenfeld & Nicholson, 1965.

Douglas, Mary. *Purity and Danger: An Analysis of Concepts of Pollution and Taboo*. New York: Praeger, 1966.

Duderstadt, Henning. *Der Schrei nach dem Recht: Die Tragödie von Mechterstädt*. Marburg, [1920].

Durrell, Lawrence, ed. *The Henry Miller Reader*. New York: New Directions, 1959.

Ehrenreich, Barbara, and Deirdre English. *Witches, Midwives and Nurses: A History of Women Healers*. Old Westbury, N.Y.: Feminist Press, 1973.

Eisler, Hanns. *Lieder und Kantaten*. Leipzig, 1957.

Elias, Norbert. *Über den Prozess der Zivilisation* (1936). 2 vols. Bern, 1969. Translated by Edmund Jephcott, under the title *The Civilizing Process*. New York: Urizen Books, 1978.

Enzensberger, Christian. *Grösserer Versuch über den Schmutz*. Munich, 1968. Translated under the title *Smut: An Anatomy of Dirt*. New York: Seabury, 1974.

Enzensberger, Hans M., ed. *Museum der deutschen Poesie*. Frankfurt, 1964.

Erickson, Erick. "The Legend of Hitler's Childhood." In *Childhood and Society*, 2nd ed., revised and enlarged. New York: W. W. Norton, 1963.

Ernst, Josef. *Kapptage im Industriegebiet*. Hagen, 1921.

Ettlinger, Karl. *Die Reglementierung der Prostitution*. Leipzig, 1903.

Fanon, Franz. *Les damnés de la terre*. Paris: F. Maspero, 1961.

Ferenczi, Sandor. *Schriften zur Psychoanalyse*, vol. 1, Frankfurt, 1970.

———. "Versuch einer Genitaltheorie." In *Schriften zur Psychoanalyse*, vol. 2, Frankfurt, 1971.

Firestone, Shulamith. *The Dialectic of Sex: The Case for Feminist Revolution*. New York: Morrow, 1970.

Fischer-Eckert, Li. *Die wirtschaftliche und soziale Lage der Frauen in dem modernen Industrieort Hamborn im Rheinland*. Hagen, 1913.

Fornari, Franco. *Psychoanalyse des ersten Lebensjahres*. Frankfurt, 1970.

Foucault, M. *Folie et déraison: histoire de la folie à l'âge classique*. Paris: Plon, 1961. Translated into English under the title *Madness and Civilization: A History of Insanity in the Age of Reason*. New York: Pantheon Books, 1965.

———. "Notes on a lecture delivered by Foucault at the Collège de France, 28 March 1973"; translated as "Power and Norm" in *Power, Truth and Strategy*, Meaghan Morris and Paul Patton, eds. Sydney, Australia: Feral Publications, 1979, pp. 59-66.

———. *Surveiller et punir: naissance de la prison*. Paris: Gallimard, 1975. Translated into English under the title *Discipline and Punish: the Birth of the Prison.* New York: Pantheon Books, 1977.

————, and Gilles Deleuze. "Les intellectuels et le pouvoir," *Arc,* 49, 1972. Translated into English under the title "The Intellectuals and Power," in *Language, Counter-Memory, Practice: Selected Essays and Interviews,* ed. D. F. Bouchard. Ithaca, N.Y.: Cornell U. Press, 1977.

Frenzel, H. A., and E. Frenzel. *Daten deutscher Dichtung: Chronologischer Abriss der deutschen Literaturgeschichte.* Munich, 1975.

Freud, Anna. *Das Ich und die Abwehrmechanismen.* Munich, n.d. Translated under the title *The Ego and the Mechanisms of Defence.* London: Hogarth Press, 1937.

Freud, Sigmund. *The Standard Edition of the Complete Psychological Works of Sigmund Freud.* Translated from the German under general editorship of James Strachey, in collaboration with Anna Freud, assisted by Alix Strachey and Alan Tyson. 24 vols. London: Hogarth Press, 1953-74.

Fromm, Erich. *The Anatomy of Human Destructiveness.* New York: Holt, Rinehart and Winston, 1973.

Fuchs, Eduard. *Illustrierte Sittengeschichte vom Mittelalter bis zur Gegenwart.* 6 vols. Munich, 1909-12.

Gilbert, G. M. *Nürnberger Tagebuch.* Frankfurt, 1962. Translated under the title *Nürnberg Diary.* New York: New American Library, 1961.

Goethe, J. W. von. *Gedichte in zwei Bänden.* Frankfurt, 1974.

————. *Faust, Parts One and Two.* Translated by Philip Wayne. 2 vols. New York: Penguin Books, 1979.

Grafe, Frieda. "Ein anderer Eindruch vom Begriff meines Körpers." *Filmkritik* 20, no. 3 (1976).

Groddek, Georg. *Das Buch vom Es.* Leipzig, 1923. Translated under the title *The Book of It.* New York: Funk & Wagnalls, 1961.

Grützmacher, Kurt. *Liebeslyrik des deutschen Barock.* Munich, 1975.

Guillén, Nicolás. *Obra Poética, 1920-1972.* Havana: Editorial de Arte y Literatura, 1974.

Gumbel, Emil Julius. *Vier Jahre politischer Mord.* Berlin, 1922.

————. *Verschwörer: Beiträge zur Geschichte und Soziologie der deutschen nationalistischen Geheimbünde seit 1918.* Vienna, 1924.

————. *Verräter verfallen der Feme: Opfer, Mörder, Richter.* Berlin, 1929.

————. *Vom Fememord zur Reichskanzlei.* Heidelberg, 1962.

Hannover, Heinrich, and Elisabeth Hannover-Drück. *Politische Justiz 1918-1933.* Frankfurt, 1966.

Hauser, Arnold. *The Social History of Art.* New York: Random House, 1985.

Heger, Heinz. *Die Männer mit dem rosa Winkel.* Hamburg, 1972.

Heine, Heinrich. *Insel Heine.* Vol. 1, *Gedichte.* Frankfurt, 1968.

Heintz, Günter, ed. *Deutsche Arbeiterduchtung 1910-1933.* Stuttgart, 1974.

Hirschfeld, Magnus. *Die Homosexualität des Mannes und des Weibes: Homosexuelle Männer und Frauen als biologische Erscheinung.* Köppern i.T., 1963.

Hocquenghem, Guy. *Homosexual Desire.* Tr. by D. Dangoor. New York: Schocken, 1980.

Illustrierte Geschichte der deutschen Revolution. Berlin, 1929. Reprint. Frankfurt, 1970.

Irigaray, Luce. "Neue Körper, neue Imagination." Interview by Martine Storti in *Alternative* 19, nos. 108/109 (June-August 1976).

————. *Wesen, Körper, Sprache: Der verrückte Diskurs der Frauen.* Berlin, 1976.

Jahn, Janheinz. *Schwarzer Orpheus: Moderne Dichtung afrikanischer Völker beider Hemisphären.* N.p., n.d.

Jean Paul [Jean Paul Friedrich Richter]. "Einfältige, aber gut gemeinte Biographie einer neuen angenehmen Frau von blossem Holz, die ich längst erfunden und geheiratet." In Völker: *Künstliche Menschen*. Munich, 1971.

————. "Untertänigste Vorstellung unser, der sämtlichen Spieler und redenden Damen in Europa, entgegen und wider die Einführung der Kempelischen Spiel- und Sprachmaschinen." In Völker, *Künstliche Menschen*. Munich, 1971.

Kläber, Kurt. *Barrikaden an der Ruhr: Erzählungen*. Frankfurt, 1973.

Klein, Melanie. "The Importance of Symbol-Formation in the Development of the Ego" in *Love, Guilt and Reparation and Other Works*. London: Hogarth Press, 1975.

————. "Notes on Some Schizoid Mechanisms"; "Some Theoretical Conclusions Regarding the Emotional Life of the Infant"; "The Psycho-Analytic Play Technique: Its History and Significance" in *Envy and Gratitude and Other Works*. New York: Delta, 1975.

————. *The Psycho-analysis of Children*. London: Hogarth Press, 1975.

Klemisch, Franz Josef, ed. *Afrikanische Lyrik aus zwei Kontinenten*. Stuttgart, 1966.

Kofler, Leo. *Zur Geschichte der bürgerlichen Gesellschaft*. Vienna, 1974.

Könnemann, Erwin. *Einwohnerwehren und Zeitfreiwilligenverbände: Ihre Funktion beim Aufbau eines neuen imperialistischen Militärsystems* (1918-20). East Berlin, 1971.

————, and Krusch. *Aktionseinheit contra Kapp-Putsch: Der Kapp-Putsch im März 1920 und der Kampf der deutschen Arbeiterklasse sowie anderer Werktätiger gegen die Errichtung der Militärdiktatur und für demokratische Verhältnisse*. East Berlin, 1972.

Kracauer, Siegfried. *Das Ornament der Masse*. Frankfurt, 1963.

Krauss, Friedrich Salomon, ed. *Jahrbücher für folkloristische Erhebungen und Forschungen zur Entwicklungsgeschichte der geschlechtlichen Moral*. Vol. 4, *Beiwerke zum Studium der Antropohyteia*.

Krüger, Gabriele. *Die Brigade Ehrhardt*. Hamburg, 1971.

Kurnitzky, Horst. *Triebstruktur des Geldes: Ein Beitrag zur Theorie der Weiblichkeit*. Berlin, 1974.

Lacan, Jacques. *Écrits*. Paris: Editions du Seuil, 1966, 1970. Translated into English under the title *Écrits: A Selection*. New York: Norton, 1977.

Laplanche, Jean and J-B. Pontalis. *The Language of Psychoanalysis*. Tr. by D. Nicholson-Smith. New York: Norton, 1973.

Lautréamont (Ducasse, Isidore Lucien). *Oeuvres complètes de Lautréamont et Germain Nouveau*; edited by Pierre-Olivier Walzer. Paris: Gallimard, 1970.

Leclaire, Serge. *Psychanalyser*. Paris: Seuil, 1968.

Lipp, Herbert. *Aufschrei aus dem Asphalt*. Berlin, n.d. [ca. 1920].

Lippe, Rudolf zur. *Naturbeherrschung am Menschen*. 2 vols. Frankfurt, 1974.

Lucas, Erhard. *Märzrevolution im Ruhrgebiet*. Vol. 1, *Vom Generalstreik gegen den Militärputsch zum bewaffneten Arbeiteraufstand, März-April 1920*. Frankfurt, 1970.

————. *Märzrevolution im Ruhrgebiet*. Vol. 2, *Der bewaffnete Arbeiteraufstand im Ruhrgebiet in seiner inneren Struktur und in seinem Verhältnis zu den Klassenkämpfen in den verschiedenen Regionen des Reiches*. Frankfurt, 1973.

————. *Zwei Formen von Radikalismus in der deutschen Arbeiterbewegung*. Frankfurt, 1976.

————. Vol. 3 of *Märzrevolution in Ruhrgebiet*. Manuscript to be published in spring 1978.

Mahler, Margaret S. *Symbiose und Individuation*. Vol. 1, *Psychosen im Frühen Kindesalter*. Stuttgart, 1972. Translated under the title *The Psychological Birth of the Human Infant: Symbiosis and Individuation*. New York: Basic Books, 1975.

Majakowski, Wladimir. *Frühe Gedichte*. Frankfurt, 1965.

————. *Politische Poesie*. Frankfurt, 1966.

Mann, Heinrich. *Ein Zeitalter wird besichtigt*. Reinbek, 1976.

Mantell, David Mark. *Familie und Aggression: Zur Einübung von Gewalt und Gewaltlosigkeit; Eine empirische Untersuchung.* Frankfurt, 1972.

Marx, Karl. *Das Kapital*, vol. 1. East Berlin, 1972. Numerous English translations under the title *Capital.*

Maser, Werner. *Die Frühgeschichte der NSDAP: Hitlers Weg bis 1924.* Frankfurt, 1965.

Mason, Tim. "Zur Lage der Frauen in Deutschland 1930 bis 1940: Wohlfahrt, Arbeit, Familien." In *Gesellschaft, Beiträge zur Marxschen Theorie.* Frankfurt, 1976.

Mayer, Hans. *Aussenseiter.* Frankfurt, 1975.

Melville, Herman. *Moby Dick, or the White Whale.* New York: New American Library (Signet Classic), 1961.

Michelet, Jules. *La sorcière.* Edited by Lucien Refort. Paris: M. Didier, 1952. Translated into English under the title *Satanism and Witchcraft, a study in Medieval Superstition.* New York: Citadel Press, 1965.

Montagu, Ashley. *Touching: The Human Significance of the Skin.* New York: Columbia Univ. Press, 1971.

Morgan, Elaine. *The Descent of Woman.* New York: Stein and Day, 1972.

Mörike, Eduard. *Gesammelte Werke.* Bergen, n.d. In English, see *Poems*, selected and edited by Lionel Thomas. Oxford: Blackwell, 1960.

Moser, Tilmann. *Lehrjahre auf der Couch: Bruchstücke meine Psychoanalyse.* Frankfurt, 1974.

Mostar, Gerhart, ed. *Frederike Kempner, der schlesische Schwan.* Munich, 1965.

Nagl, Manfred. *Science-fiction in Deutschland.* Tübingen, 1972.

Naziführer sehen dich an. 33 Biographien aus dem 3. Reich. Paris, 1934.

Neruda, Pablo. *Obras completas*, 4. Edited by M. Aguirre. Bibliography by A. A. Escudero H. Loyola. Buenos Aires: Editorial Losada, 1973.

Pankow, Gisela. *Gesprengte Fesseln der Psychose.* Munich, 1974.

Perse, Saint-John. *Oeuvres complètes.* Paris: Gallimard, 1972.

Radical America Comix. Edited by Bernd Brummbär. Frankfurt, 1970.

Reich, Wilhelm. *Charakteranalyse.* Berlin, 1933. Translated by Vincent R. Carfagno, under the title *Character Analysis.* New York: Farrar, Straus, and Giroux, 1972.

―――. *The Mass Psychology of Fascism.* Translated from the German manuscript by Theodore P. Wolfe. 3d ed., rev. and enl. New York: Orgone Institute Press, 1946.

―――. *Reich Speaks of Freud.* Edited by Mary Higgins and Chester M. Raphael. With translations from the German by Therese Pol. New York: Noonday Press, 1968.

―――. *Die Entdeckung des Orgons/Die Funktion des Orgasmus.* Frankfurt, 1972. First part of the work translated by Theodore P. Wolfe, under the title *The Discovery of the Orgone.* New York: Noonday Press, 1971. Second part translated by Vincent R. Carfagno, under the title *The Function of the Orgasm.* New York: Farrar, Straus, and Giroux, 1973.

Reiche, Reimut. "Eine Entgegnung: Socarides, der versteckt Anti-Homosexuelle." *Psyche* 26 (1972).

―――. "Ist der Ödipuskomplex universell?" *Kursbuch* 29 (1972).

Reiche, Volker, *Liebe: Ein Comic.* 1974.

Richards, Donald Ray. *The German Bestseller in the Twentieth Century: A Complete Bibliography and Analysis 1915-1940.* Berne, 1968.

Roheim, Geza. "Aphrodite oder die Frau mit dem Penis." *Die Panik der Götter.* Munich, 1975.

Rohrwasser, Michael. *Saubere Mädel, starkᵒ Genossen.* Frankfurt, 1975.

Rühle, Otto. *Illustrierte Kultur- und Sittengeschichte des Proletariats.* Berlin, 1930.

Sadger, J. "Über Gesässerotik." *Internationale Zeitschrift für ärtzliche Psychoanalyse*, no. 1 (1931).

Scheer, Maximilian. *Blut und Ehre*. Paris, 1937.

Schidrowitz, Leo, ed. *Die Sittengeschichte der Kulturwelt*. Vol. 7, *Sittengeschichte des Proletariats*. Vienna, 1926.

Schilder, Paul. *Das Körperschema: Ein Beitrag zur Lehre vom Bewusstsein des eigenen Körpers*. Berlin, 1923. Translated under the title *The Image and Appearance of the Human Body: Energies of the Psyche*. International University Press, 1950.

Schmidt-Pauli, Edgar von. *Geschichte der Freikorps 1918-1924*. Stuttgart, 1936.

Schumann, Wolfgang. *Oberschlesien 1918/19, vom gemeinsamen Kampf deutscher und polnischer Arbeiter*. East Berlin, 1961.

Schwendter, Rolf. *Theorie der Subkultur*. Cologne, 1973.

Severing, Carl. *1919/20 im Wetter- und Watterwinkel: Aufzeichnungen und Erinnerungen*. Bielefeld, 1927.

Shelley, Mary. *The Annotated Frankenstein*. New York: C. N. Potter, 1977.

Sohn-Rethel, Alfred. *Ökonomie und Klassenstruktur des deutschen Faschismus*. Frankfurt, 1973. Translated by S.-R. Martin, under the title *Economy and Class Structure of German Fascism*. London, 1974.

Sonnemann, Ulrich. *Negative Anthropologie: Vorstudien zur Sabotage des Schicksals*. Reinbek, 1969.

Sontheimer, Kurt. *Antidemokratisches Denken in der Weimarer Republik: Die politischen Ideen des deutschen Nationalismus zwischen 1918 und 1933*. Munich, 1962.

Speer, Albert. *Spandauer Tagebücher*. Frankfurt, 1975. Translated under the title *Inside the Walls of Spandau: The Prison Diaries of Albert Speer*. London: Collins, 1976.

Starobinski, Jean. *Literatur und Psychoanalyse: Die Geschichte der imaginären Ströme*. Frankfurt, n.d.

Stenbock-Fermor, Count Alexander von. *Meine Erlebnisse als Bergarbeiter*. Stuttgart, 1929.

―――. *Deutschland von unten: Reise durch die proletarische Provinz*. Stuttgart, 1931.

Stierlin, Helm. "Einige Anmerkungen zu Reimut Reiches Kritik an Socarides' Buch'Der offen Homosexuelle." *Psyche* 26 (1972).

Szasz, Thomas. *The Manufacture of Madness*. New York: Harper & Row, 1977.

Teuber, Heinrich. *Für die Sozialisierung des Ruhrbergbaus*. A collection of articles from 1926. Reprint. Frankfurt, 1973.

Tiger, Lionel. *Men in Groups*. New York: Random House, 1969.

Träger, Klaus, ed. *Die Französische Revolution im Spiegel der deutschen Literatur*. Frankfurt, 1975.

Verne, Jules. *Master Zacharias Amid the Ice*. Aeonian Pr.

Völker, Klaus, ed. *Künstliche Menschen: Dichtungen und Dokumente über Golems, Homunculi, Androiden und liebende Statuen*. Munich, 1971.

Waite, Robert G. L. *Vanguard of Nazism: The Free Corps Movement in Postwar Germany 1918-1923*. Cambridge, Mass. 1952.

Wenders, Wim. "Ein Genre, das es nicht gibt." *Filmkritik* 14, no. 9 (1970).

Werner, Georg. *Ein Kumpel: Erzählung aus dem Leben eines Bergarbeiters*. Berlin, 1930.

Winckler, Lutz. *Studie zur gesellschaftlichen Funktion faschistischer Sprache*. Frankfurt, 1971.

Index

Index

292, 346-50, 354-55, 360, 380; as "one-and-only," 296, 312, 327-28, 330-31, 332, 333, 350, 378-79; "phallic," 72, 73-74, 76, 79, 107n, 144, 181-83, 197-204, 349; religion, excluded from, 309n; in Renaissance, 304; reterritorialization on, 299, 322-25, 373; sacrifice of, 343-44, 368-73; sexualization of, 296, 324, 332-46, 349, 350, 360; social construction of bodies of, 334-42, 358; as "stain," 47-48; as territory of male desire, 294-300, 323, 331, 359, 381; as threat, 46, 49-50, 63-72, 76, 152, 183, 227, 299, 362, 377; treatment of in patriarchy, 79, 221, 272, 294, 432; as undifferentiated, 407; vagina, reduced to, 346-50, 380; violence against by soldier males, 171-224; as "whores," 9, 50, 64-65, 66-68, 72, 75, 81-83, 87, 113, 115, 117, 123, 152-53, 161-62, 163-64, 171, 172-73, 195, 367, 372, 390-91, 392, 427; in working-class literature, 89, 158-59, 382-85. See also Defense mechanisms, against women; Nurse; Rifle-women; Working-class women

Working class: attitudes of toward military, 145-52; boardinghouses, 141-42; illegitimacy among, 140; love among, 144-45; marriage among, 157-58, 166; suicide among, 143-44; upward mobility of, 372; women in literature of, 89, 158-59, 382-85

Working-class women, 138-71; leftist men's attitudes toward, 79-81, 157-71, 383-85; living conditions of, 143; role of in workers' movement, 79-81, 141, 159-62; sexuality among, 139-43; as sister substitute, 152-54; social role of, 144; "soldier males'" attitudes toward, 39-41, 65-70, 76, 79, 82-84, 145-57, 215, 367, 421, 427; working-class men's attitudes toward, 79-81, 157

Writing: as outlet for aggression, 85-86; as projection, 87-88; as self-dissolution, 356

Young Man and Veneration of the Virgin Mary (Marienverehrung und der Jungmann), 373

Zazzo, René, 320
Zeller, Max, 155
Zetkin, Clara, 162-64
Ziegler, H. A., 346
Zöberlein, Hans, 387, 388, 400, 403; women in works by, 66, 69, 75-76, 90, 175-77, 192, 195, 201
Zoff, Marianne (actress), 163-64

Klaus Theweleit earned his Ph.D. in German literature at the University of Freiburg and is now a freelance writer working in West Germany.

Stephen Conway earned masters degrees in German literature at Columbia University and in comparative literature at Brandeis University. He is a freelance editor and translator and works at a public relations firm in Minneapolis. **Erica Carter** and **Chris Turner** are directors of Material Word, a translation cooperative in Birmingham, England. Carter holds degrees in French and German from the University of Birmingham, and Turner, in modern languages and French from Cambridge University and the University of Sussex.

Barbara Ehrenreich is a fellow at the New York Institute for the Humanities and the Institute for Policy Studies in Washington, D.C. Her most recent books are *The Hearts of Men: American Dreams and the Flight from Commitment* (1983) and, with Elizabeth Hess and Gloria Jacobs, *Re-Making Love: The Feminization of Sex* (1986).